YOGHURT
SCIENCE AND TECHNOLOGY

By

A. Y. Tamime

The West of Scotland Agricultural College,
Department of Dairy Technology, Auchincruive

and

R. K. Robinson

Department of Food Science,
University of Reading.

PERGAMON PRESS
OXFORD · NEW YORK · TORONTO · SYDNEY · PARIS · FRANKFURT

U.K.	Pergamon Press Ltd., Headington Hill Hall, Oxford OX3 0BW, England
U.S.A	Pergamon Press Inc., Maxwell House, Fairview Park, Elmsford, New York 10523, U.S.A.
CANADA	Pergamon Press Canada Ltd., Suite 104, 150 Consumers Rd., Willowdale, Ontario M2J 1P9, Canada
AUSTRALIA	Pergamon Press (Aust.) Pty. Ltd., P.O. Box 544, Potts Point, N.S.W. 2011, Australia
FRANCE	Pergamon Press SARL, 24 rue des Ecoles, 75240 Paris, Cedex 05, France
FEDERAL REPUBLIC OF GERMANY	Pergamon Press GmbH, Hammerweg 6, D-6242 Kronberg-Taunus, Federal Republic of Germany

First edition 1985

Library of Congress Cataloging in Publication Data

Tamime, A. Y.
Yoghurt: science and technology.
(Pergamon international library of science, technology, engineering, and social studies)
Includes index.
1. Yoghurt. I. Robinson, R. K.
II. Title. III. Series.
SF275.Y6T36 1984   637'.146   83-24940

British Library Cataloguing in Publication Data

Tamime, A. Y.
Yoghurt: science and technology.
1. Yoghurt
I. Title   II. Robinson, R. K.
637'.146   SF275.Y6

ISBN 0–08–025503–5 (Hard cover) ✓
ISBN 0–08–025502–7 (Flexicover) ✓

Printed in Great Britain by A. Wheaton and Co. Ltd., Exeter

PERGAMON INTERNATIONAL LIBRARY
of Science, Technology, Engineering and Social Studies
The 1000-volume original paperback library in aid of education,
industrial training and the enjoyment of leisure
Publisher: Robert Maxwell, M.C.

YOGHURT

SCIENCE AND TECHNOLOGY

LIBRARY

THE PERGAMON TEXTBOOK
INSPECTION COPY SERVICE

An inspection copy of any book published in the Pergamon International Library will gladly
be sent to academic staff without obligation for their consideration for course adoption or
recommendation. Copies may be retained for a period of 60 days from receipt and returned
if not suitable. When a particular title is adopted or recommended for adoption for class use
and the recommendation results in a sale of 12 or more copies, the inspection copy may be
retained with our compliments. The Publishers will be pleased to receive suggestions for
revised editions and new titles to be published in this important International Library.

This book is dedicated to our families

Foreword

It is only three decades or so ago that much of the interest in many Western countries in yoghurt was restricted to the products of simple fermentations, resulting in products mainly sold through health food shops. Production levels were limited and procedures were simple and in many cases the products were unpredictably variable in characteristics and quality. The instruction of dairy students and industry personnel was largely based on simple methods, which had evolved slowly over many centuries in the Balkans and one or two Western European countries.

The growth in the demand for fruited yoghurt and modified types has led to dramatic commercialisation of basic processes and today the student and industrialist alike require a much wider knowledge of the effects of various biological and mechanical processes on the efficiency of yoghurt production and on the quality and nutritional characteristics of the product reaching the growing number of regular consumers of this fine dairy product.

The authors have considerable experience of the needs of students in further and higher education in this subject, and also bring to their textbook an enthusiasm for the product and a background of providing commercial organisations with information and advice.

Department of Dairy Technology,   R. J. M. CRAWFORD
Auchincruive,
Ayr

Preface

Although there are numerous fermented milks produced on a local basis around the world, only yoghurt has achieved a truly international distribution. This popularity stems from a number of sources: the pleasant, aromatic flavour of natural yoghurt, its reputation as a foodstuff associated with good health, but perhaps above all from the fact that the thick, creamy consistency makes it an ideal vehicle for fruit. Thus, it was the natural compatibility with fruit that really brought yoghurt into the retail markets, and since the introduction of fruit yoghurts during the fifties sales have climbed steadily upwards.

Today millions of gallons of yoghurt are produced each year, and yet because manufacture is still, in essence, a natural biological process, success can never be taken for granted. It is this capricious nature of the fermentation that makes it so fascinating, and indeed if the system were not so prone to variation, then there would have been little motivation to produce this book at all. Some aspects of production have, of course, become fairly standard, but so many areas of potential difficulty remain that only a thorough appreciation of the nature of yoghurt can provide those associated with its production and distribution with the confidence that eliminates product failure.

It goes without saying that the best teacher is experience, but if this book can offer some preliminary guidance on the intricacies of handling yoghurt, then its compilation will have been worthwhile.

1983

A. Y. TAMIME
R. K. ROBINSON

Acknowledgements

The authors are grateful to Dr. R. J. M. Crawford of the West of Scotland Agricultural College for his advice and encouragement during the preparation of this book, and would also like to thank colleagues in various research and similar establishments for their help in the acquisition of certain technical data:

Dr. W. IJ. Aalsberberg, Nederlands Institute voor Zuivelonderzoek (NIZO), 2 Kernhemseweg, P.O. Box 20, 6710 BA Ede, The Netherlands.

Dr. J. P. Accolas, Institute National de la Recherche Agronomique, Laboratoire de Microbiologie Laitiere de Genie Alimentaire, Domaine de Vilvert, 78350 Jouy-en-Josas, France.

Dr. F. L. Davies, National Institute for Research in Dairying, Shinfield, Reading RG2 9AT, U.K.

Dr. M. Kalab, Food Research Institute, Agriculture Canada, Ottawa, Ontario K1A 0C6, Canada.

Dr. H. Spillmann, Labor fur Milchwissenschaft, Eidgenossische Technische Hochschule Zurich (ETH-Z), Eisgasse 8, CH-8004 Zurich, Switzerland.

The authors are also grateful for the enthusiastic response and assistance of the following companies in providing the extensive technical data required:

Adolf Jllig Maschinenbau GmbH & Co., Manerstrasse 100, D-7100 Heilbronn, West Germany.

Alfa-Laval Company Ltd., Great West Road, Brentford, Middlesex TW8 9BT, U.K.

Alfa-Laval A/B, Box 1008, S-221 03 Lund, Sweden.

Alpha Technical Services Ltd., Altec House, Brigade Close, Harrow, Middlesex HA2 0NW, U.K.

A.P.V. Company Ltd., P.O. Box 4, Manor Royal, Crawley, West Sussex RH10 2QB, U.K.

AS Jenogand, 121–123 Hvidsaermervej, DK-2610 Rodovre, Denmark.

Astell Hearson Ltd., 172 Brownhill Road, Catford, London SE6 2DL, U.K.

Austin 4P Ltd., Exchange House, Exchange Road, Watford WD1 7BW, U.K.

Burnett & Rolfe Ltd., Commissioners Road, Strood, Rochester, Kent ME2 4EJ, U.K.

Caleb Duckworth Ltd., Colunio Works, Phillips Lane, Colne, Lancashire BB8 9PJ, U.K.

Caleb Duckworth Ltd., Manton Lane, Bedford MK41 7PB, U.K.

Chr. Hansen's Laboratory Ltd., 476 Basingstoke Road, Reading RG2 0QL, U.K.

Cocks & Sons (London) Ltd., Windham Road, Chilton Industrial Estate, Sudbury, Suffolk CO10 6XD, U.K.

Coldstream (Engineering) Ltd., 12 Fellbrigg Road, East Dulwich, London SE22 9HH, U.K.

Crepaco International Inc., 28 Bld. St. Michel, 1040-Brussels, Belgium.

DEC International (Damrow), Kingsvel 18, DK-6000, Kolding, Denmark.

De Melkindustrie Veghel (DMV) BV, n.c.b.—laan 80, P.O. Box 80, 5460 BA, Veghel, Holland.

Diessel GmbH & Co., P.O. Box 470, D-3200 Hildesheim, West Germany.

Diessel GmbH & Co. (UK Branch), 2 Links Road, Wimslow SK9 6HQ, U.K.

Engelmann & Buckham Machinery Ltd., Willam Curtis House, Alton, Hampshire GU34 1HH, U.K.

Enolacto Ltd., 3 The Drive, Wembley Park, Middlesex HA9 9EF, U.K.

E. P. Remey & Co. Ltd., 66 Tilehurst Road, Reading RG3 2JH, U.K.

Express Dairy—UK—Ltd., Victoria Road, South Ruislip, Middlesex HA4 0HF, U.K.

F. Stamp KG GmbH & Co., P.O. Box 800880, 55 Kampchaussee, D-2050 Hamburg 80, West Germany.

Food and Agriculture Organisation of the United Nations (FAO), Via delle Terme di Caracalla, 00100 Rome, Italy.

Foss Electric (UK) Ltd., The Chantry, Bishopthorpe, York YO2 1QF, U.K.

4P Rube Gottingen GmbH, Karl—Gruneklee—Strasse 23/25, D-3400 Gottingen, West Germany.

Gasti—Verpackungsmaschmen GmbH & Co., P.O. Box 100264, D-7170 Schwabisch Hall, West Germany.

Goavec S. A., P.O. Box 205, 13 Rue Eiffel, 61006 Alencon cedex, France.

Golden Vale Engineering, Limerick Road, Charleville (Rathluric), County Cork, Ireland.

Hamba Maschinenfabrik—Hans A. Muller GmbH & Co. KG, 5600 Wuppertal—Vohwinkel, West Germany.

Hans Rychiger AG, P.O. Box 30–8625, CH-3613 Steffisburg, Switzerland.

Hansen & Fredsgaard A/S, Oesterled 20, DK-4300 Hlbaek, Denmark.

Hassia Verpakung GmbH, P.O. Box 1120, D-6479 Ranstadt, West Germany.

Holstein & Kappert GmbH, Zechenstrasse 49, D-4750 Unna-Koingsborn, West Germany.

IBEX Engineering Co. Ltd., Drury Lane, Hastings TN34 1Xr, U.K.

Ing. Herwig Burgert (Burdosa), Industriestrasse 3, D-6300 Lahn-Rodgen, West Germany.

International Flavours and Fragrances (IFF) (G.B.) Ltd., Duddery Hill, Haverhill, Suffolk.

International Paper Company, International Paper Plaza, 77 West 45th Street, New York 10036, U.S.A.

ITT Jabsco Ltd., Bingley Road, Hoddesdon, Hertfordshire, U.K.

J. Sainsbury Ltd., Stamford Street, London SE1 9LL, U.K.

Joshua Greaves & Sons Ltd., P.O. Box 2, Atlas Engineering Works, Ramsbottom, Bury, Lancashire BL0 9BA, U.K.

Karl Engelhardt, 28 Bremen 15, Waller Heerstrasse 31 a, West Germany.

Ladish Company, Tri-Clover Division, Kenosha, Wisconsin 53141, U.S.A.

Liquid Packaging Ltd., Caxton Way, Stevenage, Hertfordshire SG1 2DH, U.K.

Medcalfe & Co. (1950) Ltd., 55 Farring Road, London EC1M 3LP, U.K.

Metal Box Ltd., Cowlairs Industrial Estate, Springburn, Glasgow G21 1EQ, U.K.

Milk Marketing Board, Thames Ditton, Surrey KT7 0EL, U.K.

Milk Marketing Board for Northern Ireland, 456 Antrim Road, Belfast BT15 5GD, U.K.

Mono Pumps Ltd., Arnfield Works, Martin Street, Andenshaw, Manchester M34 5JA, U.K.

Mortimer Plastics Machinery Ltd., Coronation Road, Park Royal, London NW10 7PT, U.K.

N.V. Machinenfabriek Terlet, Oostzeesstraat 6, 7202 CM Zutfen, Holland.

Newmac A/S, 16 Raadhuspladsen, DK-1550 Copenhagen V., Denmark.

Nouva Frau SPA, 36010 Carre (Vicenza), Italy.

Pasilac A/S, DK-8600 Silkeborg, Denmark.

Peter Holland Food Machinery Ltd., St. Peter's Hill, Stamford, Lincolnshire PE9 2PE, U.K.

PHB Weserhutte AG, P.O. Box 100940, Mindener Str. 18–24, D-4970 Bad Oeynhausen, West Germany.

Primodan Dairy Equipment A/S, DK-4440 Mørkøv, Denmark.

Rannie A/S, Roholmsvej 8, DK-2620 Albertslund, Denmark.

Rowenta (UK) Ltd., 9 The Street, Ashtead, Surrey, U.K.

Rudolf Dinkelberg KG., Zepelinstasse 11, D-7910 Neu-Ulm/Schwaighofen, West Germany.

Rutherford Research U.K. Branch, 27/29 Tonge Bridgeway, Tonge Bridgeway Industrial Estate, Bolton BL2 6AD, U.K.

Schleuter Company, P.O. Box 548, Janesville, Wisconsin, 53545, U.S.A.

Silkeborg Ltd., 415 Walton Summit, Bamber Bridge, Preston PR5 8AT, U.K.

Silverson Machines Ltd., Waterside, Chesham, Buckinghamshire HP5 1 PQ, U.K.

Specialist Dairy Ingredients, Giggs Hill Road, Thames Ditton KT7 0EL, U.K.

SSP Pump Ltd., Birch Road, Lottbridge Grove, Eastbourne, East Sussex BN23 6PQ, U.K.

Stork Amsterdam International Ltd., Stork House, 4 Hercies Road, Hillingdon, Middlesex UB10 9NA, U.K.

Sussex & Berkshire Machinery Company Ltd., Chown Industrial Estate, Newman Lane, Alton, Hampshire GU34 2QR, U.K.

T. Giusti & Son Ltd., Belle Islle Works, 202/214 York Way, Kings Cross, London N7 9AW, U.K.

Tetra Pak Ltd., Orchard Road, Lower Richmond Road, Surrey TW9 4NU, U.K.

Textima AG, P.O. Box 80–17497, CH-8335 Hittnau ZH, Switzerland.

Trano Marketing International Ltd., 21A Finkle Street, Selby, North Yorkshire YO8 0DT, U.K.

Van den Bergh & Partners Ltd., 7 Fairacres, Dedworth Road, Windsor SL4 4LE, U.K.

Watson-Marlow Ltd., Falmouth, Cornwall TR11 4RU, U.K.

Waukesha Division, Abex Corporation, 1300 Lincoln Avenue, Waukesha, Wisconsin, 53186, U.S.A.

Weserhutte Aktiengesellschaft, P.O. Box 100940, D-4970 Bad Oeynhausen, West Germany.

Westfalia Separator Ltd., Habig House, Old Wolverton, Milton Keynes MK12 5PY, U.K.

Wincanton Engineering Ltd., South Street, Sterbourne, Dorset DT9 3ND, U.K.

Some technical data have been reproduced in this book with the approval of the following publishers:

Applied Science Publishers Ltd., The Royal Institution, 19 Albemarble Street, London W1X 4BS, U.K.

British Standards Institution, 101 Pentonville Road, London N1 9ND, U.K.

Dairy Industries International, United Trade Press Ltd., 33/35 Bowling Green Lane, London EC1R 0DA, U.K.

Ecology of Food and Nutrition, Gordon and Breach Ltd., 41/42 William IV Street, London WC2, U.K.

Her Majesty's Stationery Office, St. Crispins Road, Duke Street, Norwich NR3 1PD, U.K.

International Dairy Federation (IDF), Square Vergote 41, Brussels, Belgium.

Journal of Dairy Research, Cambridge University Press, The Edinburgh Building, Shaftesbury Road, Cambridge, CB2 2RU, U.K.

Journal of Dairy Science, 309 West Clark Street, Champaign, Illinois 61820, U.S.A.

Journal of Food Protection, IAMFES Inc., P.O. Box 701, Ames, Iowa 50010, U.S.A.

Journal of the Society of Dairy Technology, 72 Ermine Street, Huntingdon PE18 6EZ, U.K.

Michwissenshaft, Wissenschaftliche Redaktion, Hermann Weigmann—Str. 1, D-2300 Kiel, West Germany.

Nordeuropaeisk Mejeri-Tidsskrift, Post box 1648, Jyllingevej 39, DK-2720 Vanløse, Denmark.

Scanning Electron Microscopy Inc., P.O. Box 66507, AMF O'Hare, Illinois 60666, U.S.A.

During the preparation of this book some of the photographs and figures have been provided by colleagues, and the authors acknowledge, with appreciation, the assistance of:

Mr. P. Archer (Bangor Dairies MMB for Northern Ireland), Shaftesbury Road, Bangor, Co. Down, U.K.

Mr. P. Evers (Campina Yoghurt Production Unit), Rijkevoort, Holland.

Mr. J. Lewis (Dairy Cultures Ltd.), C5 Haviland Road, Ferndown Industrial Estate, Wimborne Street, Dorset, U.K.

Mr. T. Parker (Bridge Farm Dairies Ltd.), Mildenhall, Bury St. Edmunds, Suffolk IP28 7DU, U.K.

Mr. G. W. Spinks (G. R. Spinks) & Co., North Road, Okehampton, Devon EX20 1BQ, U.K.

We are also grateful to Mr. S. Crawford (The West of Scotland Agricultural College) and Mr. D. Cooney (Hannah Research Institute) for their skill in taking the necessary photographs, and to Mrs. J. Craig and Miss C. Rodger for their patience in typing the manuscript.

Contents

CHAPTER 1

Introduction

Although there are no records available regarding the origin of yoghurt, the belief in its beneficial influence on human health and nutrition has existed in many civilisations for a long time. According to Persian tradition, Abraham owed his fecundity and longevity to yoghurt, and in more recent times Emperor Francis I of France was said to have been cured of a debilitating illness by consuming yoghurt made out of goat's milk (Rosell, 1932).

It is likely, however, that the origin of yoghurt was the Middle East, and the evolution of this fermented product through the ages can be attributed to the culinary skills of the nomadic people living in that part of the world.

Thus, the production of milk in the Middle East has always been seasonal, being restricted usually to no more than a few months of the year. The main reason for this limited availability of milk is that intensive animal production has never really existed, so that, as in early history, farming is in the hands of nomadic peoples who move from one area to another following the pastures. This type of existence forces the nomads to be in the wilderness for months at a time, and far away from populated cities and villages where they could sell their animal produce. Another major factor is that the Middle East area has a subtropical climate, and summer temperatures can reach as high as 40°C. In such a climate, milk turns sour and coagulates within a short time after milking, particularly as the milk is produced under primitive conditions. Thus, the animals are hand-milked, no cooling of the milk is possible, and the risk of contamination by micro-organisms from the air, the animal, the feeding stuff, or the hands of the milker is extremely high. Under these conditions the possibility of transporting or even keeping milk for any length of time is non-existent. As a result the bulk of the population consume milk only rarely, and even the nomadic people have to utilise the milk virtually as it is produced.

However, it may well have been evident even at an early stage that the souring of milk was by no means a uniform process. Thus, the fermentation brought about by the non-lactic acid bacteria gives rise to a product which is insipid and stale, and, furthermore, the coagulum is irregular, filled with gas holes and shows extreme whey syneresis. The lactic acid bacteria, however, act on the milk to produce a fermented product which is pleasant to eat or drink; this latter product was usually referred to as "sour milk".

The animals that are raised by the nomadic people in the Middle East are cows, goats, sheep and camels, and gradually the nomadic tribes devised a fermentation process which brought under control the souring of these various milks. The main feature of this standardisation involved heating the milk over an open fire, and the effect of this procedure would have been:

(i) to concentrate the milk slightly, so that the final coagulum would have acquired an attractive viscosity;

1

(ii) to modify the properties of the casein, again a change which would have improved the quality of the end-product;

(iii) to ensure a gradual selection of lactic acid bacteria capable of tolerating high levels of lactic acid, and of giving the product its distinctive flavour;

(iv) to eradicate any pathogenic micro-organisms present in the milk;

(v) to encourage the fermentation of the milk to take place at a slightly higher temperature, i.e. during cooling, so enabling the thermophilic strains of lactic acid bacteria to become predominant.

Although the evolution of the process was strictly intuitive, the production of "sour milk" soon became the established pattern of preservation. Gradually other communities learnt of this simple preservative treatment for milk, and one such product became known as "yoghurt" from the Turkish word "Jugurt"; numerous variants of this word have appeared over the years, and a selection of alternatives is shown in Table 1.1.

TABLE 1.1. *A selection of yoghurt and yoghurt-like products that have been identified in the Middle East and elsewhere*

Traditional name	Capacity
Jugurt/Eyran/Ayran	Turkey
Busa	Turkestan
Kissel Mleka	Balkans
Urgotnic	Balkan Mountains
Leban/Laban	Lebanon and some Arab countries
Zabady	Egypt and Sudan
Mast/Dough	Iran and Afghanistan
Roba	Iraq
Dahi/Dadhi/Dahee	India
Mazun/Matzoon/Matsun/Matsoni	Armenia
Katyk	Transcaucasia
Tiaourti	Greece
Cieddu	Italy
Mezzoradu	Sicily
Gioddu	Sardinia
Tarho	Hungary
Fiili	Finland
Filmjolk/Fillbunke/Filbunk/Surmelk/Taettemjolk/Tettemelk	Scandinavia
Iogurte	Brazil and Portugal
Skyr	Iceland
Gruzovina	Yugoslavia
Donskaya/Varenetes/Kurunga/Ryzhenka/Guslyanka	Russia
Tarag	Mongolia
Shosim/Sho/Thara	Nepal
Yoghurt/Yogurt/Yaort/Yourt/Yaourti/Yahourth/ Yogur/Yaghourt	Rest of the world ("Y" is replaced by "J" in some cases)

After: Tamime and Deeth (1980); Accolas, Deffontaines and Aubin (1978); Tokita *et al.* (1982).

However, although yoghurt has many desirable properties, it is still prone to deterioration, especially at ambient temperature, within a matter of days, and one discernible trend in the Middle East has been the search for simple techniques to extend the keeping quality even further.

The first step in this process turned out to be relatively simple, because the containers traditionally used by the nomads for the production of yoghurt were made from animal skins. In normal use the yoghurt would have been consumed fairly rapidly, but if left hanging in the skin for any length of time, the nature of the product altered dramatically. Thus, as the whey seeped through the skin and evaporated, so the total solids content of the yoghurt rose and with it the acidity, and the end result was a condensed or concentrated yoghurt with an acidity of >2.0 %; lactic acid and a total solids in the region of 25 %; the original yoghurt might have had a solids content of 12–13 % and an acidity of around 1.5 % lactic acid. To the nomadic people, whose main sources of wealth and nourishment are the animals that can be raised and the milk that they produce, the relative resistance of the condensed yoghurt to spoilage must have appeared attractive.

Evidence of this trend can be found in Armenia where the "mazun" (Armenian yoghurt) is usually pressed to yield a product called "tan" or "than". Similarly, Yaygin (1971) reports how the surplus of milk production in remote villages in Turkey is turned into concentrated yoghurt by the daily addition of milk to the yoghurt hanging in goat's or sheep's skins. Another method of concentration of yoghurt is reported by Morcos, Hegazi and Al-Damhougy (1973) where the yoghurt is placed in an earthenware vessel; the Egyptians call this product "leben zeer".

Nevertheless, even condensed yoghurt becomes unpalatable within a week or two, and it was for this reason that salted yoghurt rapidly became popular. Salting is an old method used by man to preserve his food, but the incorporation of salt into concentrated yoghurt acts also as a neutralising agent to reduce the acid taste of the product. Thus, Yonez (1965) reports that different types of concentrated yoghurt are made in Turkey by the addition of various quantities of salt. Another typical way to prolong the keeping quality of concentrated yoghurt is employed in the Lebanon, where the salted product is made into small balls about 2 cm in diameter, and placed in the sun to dry. Afterwards the "yoghurt balls" (which are partially dried) are placed in either glazed earthenware pots or glass jars and covered with olive oil. The product is then referred to as winter yoghurt, i.e. it is available when natural yoghurt is out of season, and furthermore the product is spread easily on bread and consumed.

An alternative preservation process involved the heating of yoghurt for a few hours over low fires of a special type of wood; the end product is referred to as "smoked yoghurt". This type of yoghurt is also preserved over the winter months by placing it in jars and covering it with either olive oil or tallow.

In some countries, e.g. Turkey, Lebanon, Syria, Iraq and Iran, the concentrated yoghurt is processed even further to produce a totally different product with almost indefinite keeping quality. This is the dried form of yoghurt; milk is processed into yoghurt in a traditional manner, and then wheat flour, semolina or parboiled wheat, known locally as "bourghol" (Garnier, 1957), is rubbed into it. The yoghurt–wheat mixture is shaped into small rolls, and placed in the sun to dry. This product is called "kishk" and it is sold either as rolls or in a ground-up form as flour. "Kishk" (as a dish) is prepared by reconstituting the yoghurt–wheat mixture with water, and then simmering the mix gently over a fire. The consistency of this product, which is normally consumed with bread, is rather similar to porridge.

The yoghurt–wheat mixture can be also processed into a different product called "chanklich". Here the product is partially dried, but is heavily mixed with spices and herbs (presumably to assist in preservation). The mixture is then formed into balls, placed into glass jars and finally covered with olive oil; the relationship between these various products is discussed further in Chapter 5.

However, as refrigeration became widespread, so interest in these traditional products declined, except among certain communities in the Middle East, and in their place a new generation of yoghurts emerged, with production typically centred on a large, modern creamery, and success in the market place depending on the existence of a network of retail outlets with storage facilities at <7°C. Initially, production was confined to natural yoghurt, and the market was limited, in large

TABLE 1.2. Per capita annual consumption of yoghurt (kg/head)

Country	1966	1967	1968	1969	1970	1971	1972	1973	1974	1975	1976	1977	1978	1979	1980	1981
Australia	2.7*	–	–	–	–	–	–	–	–	1.0	1.0	1.4	1.6	1.7	1.8	1.9
Austria	1.9	2.9*	2.6*	3.0*	1.8	2.2	2.4	2.9	3.2	3.4	3.7	4.1	4.6	5.3	5.8	6.2
Belgium	–	2.1	2.4	2.9	3.5	4.0	4.7	3.9	4.7	5.1	5.0	4.2	4.4	4.8	4.9	4.8
Brazil	–	–	–	–	–	–	0.01	0.07	0.02	0.6	0.6	0.6	0.6	0.5	0.6	–
Bulgaria	–	–	–	–	–	–	27.0	–	–	31.5	–	–	–	–	–	–
Canada	0.1	0.1	0.2	0.3	0.3	0.4	0.5	0.6	0.6	0.7	0.9	1.2	1.8	1.7	1.7	1.8
Chile	–	–	–	–	–	–	–	–	–	–	–	–	–	1.0	1.4	1.8
Czechoslovakia	–	–	–	–	–	–	1.0	1.1	1.2	1.3	1.4	1.6	1.7	1.6	1.7	1.8
Denmark	2.8*	3.6*	4.9*	6.6*	1.7	2.3	2.8	3.5	5.1	5.9	6.6	7.6	8.2	9.2	9.1	8.8
Federal Germany	3.4*	3.8*	2.3	3.2	3.8	4.5	4.5	4.7	4.3	4.5	5.2	5.3	6.4	6.6	6.7	6.9
Finland	12.0*	21.6*	23.4*	26.0*	2.7	5.2	6.9	7.8	6.5	6.3	6.4	6.7	7.0	8.0	8.4	8.1
France*	4.2	4.6	5.0	6.0	6.1	6.5	6.7	7.2	7.3	7.8	7.9	7.9	8.0	8.8	9.3	10.2
Iceland	–	–	–	–	–	–	–	1.4	1.6	1.7	1.9	1.7	2.0	5.4	5.7	5.7
India	–	–	–	–	–	–	–	–	–	–	–	–	–	3.5	3.7	3.8
Ireland	4.2*	5.4*	5.9*	5.1*	6.9*	7.4*	7.7*	1.0	0.8	1.0	1.3	1.5	1.7	1.8	2.0	2.5
Israel	8.0*	8.1*	8.6*	9.2*	0.9	1.3	2.0	3.0	2.6	3.4	4.6	4.6	4.8	5.8	4.7	6.0
Italy	–	–	–	–	–	–	1.1	1.1	–	1.0	1.3	1.1	1.1	1.2	1.3	1.3
Japan	–	–	–	–	0.3	–	–	–	–	–	–	–	–	–	–	–
Luxemburg	1.9*	2.3*	1.8*	2.0*	2.3	2.2	2.3	2.5	3.2	3.3	3.9	4.4	5.1	5.1	5.1	5.2
Malta	–	–	–	0.1	0.1	0.1	0.2	0.2	0.2	0.2	0.2	0.2	–	–	–	–
Netherland	12.9	13.3	13.3	13.8	13.7	13.4	13.5	13.4	13.2	14.2	14.9	15.5	15.6	16.2	17.8	16.9
New Zealand	–	–	–	–	–	–	–	–	–	–	1.5	–	–	–	–	–
Norway	10.3*	10.6*	10.9*	11.5*	0.2	0.4	0.6	0.9	1.2	1.2	1.4	1.2	2.0	2.0	2.2	2.7
Poland*	–	1.6	1.8	2.0	2.0	2.6	2.8	3.2	3.2	3.2	2.9	2.7	2.7	2.5	2.0	2.1
Spain*	1.2	1.2	1.2	1.5	2.4	3.0	2.9	3.2	3.2	3.4	3.4	4.3	4.7	5.6	6.0	6.1
Sweden	11.9*	12.5*	13.3*	14.4*	0.1	1.2	1.7	1.7	1.7	2.3	2.5	2.9	3.3	3.9	4.2	4.2
Switzerland	5.5	6.1	6.3	7.0	7.5	8.1	7.8	9.8	10.4	10.9	12.0	12.6	13.2	13.5	13.8	14.1
UK	0.4	0.5	0.6	0.6	0.7	0.8	1.0	0.7	1.5	1.6	1.7	1.8	1.9	2.5	2.8	2.9
USA	0.04	0.05	0.07	0.1	0.1	0.5	0.6	0.7	0.7	0.9	1.1	1.2	1.2	1.2	1.2	1.2
USSR*	–	–	5.6	6.2	6.3	6.6	6.7	6.7	7.0	7.2	6.8	6.8	6.8	6.5	6.2	6.1

– Data not available.

* Data of yoghurt represents other fermented dairy products.

Data compiled from IDF (1975, 1977, 1982 and 1983)

measure, to those who believed that yoghurt was beneficial to health. Gradually, however, attitudes towards yoghurt changed, and the advent of fruit yoghurts during the fifties gave the product an entirely fresh image. Instead of being a speciality item for the health food market, it became a popular and inexpensive snack-food or dessert, and production figures reflect the expanding market. In the U.K., for example, the value of yoghurt sold per annum in 1982 ran to around £120 million pounds (sterling) and such figures are now commonplace around the world. Indeed total production is still rising, a trend confirmed by the data shown in Table 1.2.

Nevertheless, the method of production of yoghurt has, in essence, changed little over the years, and although there have been some refinements, especially in relation to the lactic acid bacteria that bring about fermentation, the essential steps in the process are still the same, namely:

1. Raising the level of total solids in the process milk to around 14–16%.
2. Heating the milk, ideally by some method that allows the milk to be held at high temperature for a period of 10–30 minutes; the precise time will depend on the temperature selected.
3. Inoculating the milk with a bacterial culture in which *Lactobacillus bulgaricus* and *Streptococcus thermophilus* are the dominant organisms.
4. Incubating the inoculated milk, in bulk or retail units, under conditions that promote the formation of a smooth viscous coagulum and the desired aromatic flavour/aroma.
5. Cooling and, if desired, further processing, e.g. the admixture of fruit and other ingredients, pasteurisation or concentration (see Chapter 5).
6. Packaging for distribution to the consumer under chilled conditions.

The fact that all commercial processes share this common "core" has lead to the word "yoghurt" being applied to the whole range of products, e.g. Dried Yoghurt, Frozen Yoghurt and even Pasteurised Yoghurt. The inclusion of these varieties under the banner of yoghurt offends some people, because yoghurt *per se* must, by virtue of the process, contain an abundance of viable bacteria originating from the starter culture. However, popular usage appears to have determined that so long as a carton is clearly labelled as to the nature of the finishing process, e.g. Pasteurised Yoghurt, then the integrity of the basic product has not been compromised, and commonsense would suggest that this view will prevail.

This approach implies also that yoghurt manufacture must always include a fermentation stage, i.e. a coagulum produced by the direct addition of lactic acid should never be designated as a "yoghurt" or even "yoghurt-like"—and yet it is this very stage that can, in commercial practice, prove temperamental in the extreme. Variations in milk composition, irregular behaviour of the starter organisms, faulty regulation of the incubation temperature, along with a number of other process variables, can all give rise to an end-product that is deficient in respect of overall quality, and only a thorough understanding of the fermentation can provide an operative with the foresight to reduce the risk of product failure. It is with this background in mind that the relevant issues have been isolated for discussion, for although the different steps in production are interrelated, it is convenient to discuss them within the confines of an individual compartment, and the following chapters are a reflection of this view.

REFERENCES

ACCOLAS, J. P., DEFFONTAINES, J. P. and AUBIN, F. (1978) *Le Lait,* **58,** 278.
GARNIER, M. (1957) In *Les Produits Laitiers du Liban et de la Syrie—Etude Biologique et Vitaminologique,* Vigot Freres Editeurs, Paris, France.

IDF (1975) In *Consumption Statistics for Milk and Milk Products/1972–1973*, IDF Doc. No. 84, Brussels, Belgium.
IDF (1977) *Ibid*. Doc. No. 93.
IDF (1982) *Ibid*. Doc. No. 144.
IDF (1983) *Ibid*. Doc. No. 160.
MORCOS, S. R., HEGAZI, S. M. and EL-DAMHOUGY, S. T. (1973) *Journal of the Science of Food and Agriculture*, **24,** 1153.
ROSELL, J. M. (1932) *Canadian Medical Association Journal*, **26,** 341.
TAMIME, A. Y. and DEETH, H. C. (1980) *Journal of Food Protection*, **43,** 939.
TOKITA, F., HOSONO, A., TAKAHASHI, F., ISHIDA, T. and OTANI, H. (1982) *Dairy Science Abstracts*, **44,** 728.
YAYGIN, H. (1971) *Dairy Science Abstracts*, **33,** 686.
YONEZ, A. (1965) In *Year Book Faculty of Agriculture, University of Ankara*, **5, 4.**

CHAPTER 2

Background to Manufacturing Practice

The process of yoghurt making is an ancient craft which dates back thousands of years, and possibly even to the domestication of the cow, sheep or goat, but it is safe to assume that prior to the nineteenth century the various stages involved in the production of yoghurt were little understood. The survival of the process through the ages can be attributed, therefore, to the fact that the scale of manufacture was relatively small, and hence the craft was handed down from parents to children. However, over the last few decades the process has become more rational, mainly due to various discoveries and/or improvements in such disciplines as:

(a) microbiology and enzymology;
(b) physics and engineering;
(c) chemistry and biochemistry;

and yet by today's standards of industrial technology the process of yoghurt making is still a complex process which combines both "Art" and "Science" together.

The micro-organisms and their enzymes, i.e. the yoghurt starter cultures, play an important role during the production of yoghurt, e.g. the development of acid and flavour, and their classification, behaviour and characteristics are discussed in detail in Chapter 7. However, in order to understand the principles of yoghurt making it will be useful to describe separately the various stages of manufacture and their consequent effects on the quality of yoghurt. The technology of the process, i.e. the equipment required for small- and large-scale production, will be discussed in Chapter 3.

The traditional and the "improved" methods for the manufacture of yoghurt are illustrated in Fig. 2.1, and it can be observed that the former process has several drawbacks, such as:

(a) successive inoculations of the starter culture tend to upset the ratio between *Streptococcus thermophilus* and *Lactobacillus bulgaricus*, or may lead to mutation beyond the 15–20th subculturing;
(b) the low incubation temperature, e.g. ambient, results in slow acidification of the milk (18 hours or more), as compared with the optimum conditions of 40–45°C for $2\frac{1}{2}$–3 hours;
(c) the slow rate of acid development may promote undesirable side effects, e.g. whey syneresis, which can adversely affect the quality of yoghurt;
(d) the traditional process provides no control over the level of lactic acid produced during the fermentation stage.

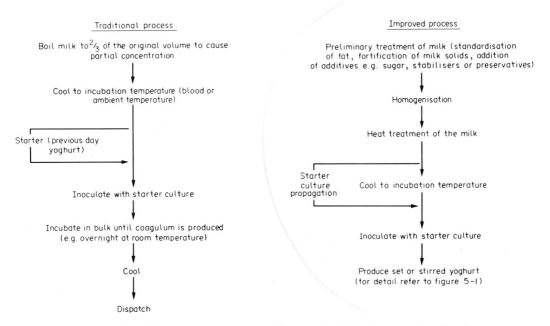

Fig. 2.1. Generalised scheme illustrating the different methods for the production of yoghurt

Nevertheless, despite these drawbacks it is obvious that the traditional process has laid the basic foundation for the production of yoghurt as practised in the industry at the present time (see Fig. 2.1), and the basic changes depend, in reality, on the following:

(a) the purity of the yoghurt starter cultures which can be obtained from commercial starter manufacturers, starter banks or research establishments;
(b) the ability of dairies to propagate these cultures in sterile milk under aseptic conditions, so giving rise to active reliable starters;
(c) the temperature of incubation can be accurately controlled, so that the rate of acid development and the processing time is known in advance;
(d) the cooling of the yoghurt can be carried out quickly at the desired level of acidity, and the quality of yoghurt is more uniform;
(e) the development of easy methods for measuring the rate of acid development in milk (using pH meters and/or acidimeters) enables even a semi-skilled operator to control the process adequately.

PRELIMINARY TREATMENT OF THE BASIC MIX

A. Milk as a Raw Material

Milks of different species of mammals have been used for the production of yoghurt, and Table 2.1 illustrates the major differences in the chemical composition of these milks. As a result, variations in the quality of yoghurt do occur, depending on the type of milk used. For example, milk

TABLE 2.1. *Chemical composition (%) of milk of different species of mammal*

Species	Water	Fat	Protein	Lactose	Ash
Ass	89.0	2.5	2.0	6.0	0.5
Buffalo	82.1	8.0	4.2	4.9	0.8
Camel	87.1	4.2	3.7	4.1	0.9
Cow	87.6	3.8	3.3	4.7	0.6
Goat	87.0	4.5	3.3	4.6	0.6
Mare	89.0	1.5	2.6	6.2	0.7
Reindeer	63.3	22.5	10.3	2.5	1.4
Sheep	81.6	7.5	5.6	4.4	0.9

Adapted from Johnson (1974), Anon. (1975), Paul and Southgate (1978).

containing a high percentage of fat (sheep, buffalo and reindeer) produces a "rich" and "creamy" yoghurt with an excellent "mouth-feel" as compared with yoghurt manufactured from milk containing a low level of fat, or milk deprived of its fat content, e.g. skim milk. The lactose in milk provides the energy source for the yoghurt starter organisms, but the protein plays an important role in the formation of the coagulum, and hence the consistency/viscosity of the product is directly proportional to the level of protein present; yoghurt produced from unfortified mare's and ass's milk would be less viscous than yoghurt made from sheep's or reindeer's milk.

Although the flavour of yoghurt is mainly the result of complex biochemical reactions initiated by microbial activity, the flavour of the basic milk varies from species to species, and this characteristic is reflected in the end-product.

However, since cow's milk is widely available in most countries around the world, the emphasis will be on the use of this type of milk for the manufacture of yoghurt, but even when considering cow's milk there are quite large differences in composition (Table 2.2). The major constituents of milk are: water, fat, protein, lactose and minerals (ash), and a detailed breakdown of these components is shown in Fig. 2.2.

TABLE 2.2. *Commercial (average expected) composition of cow's milk (%)*

Breed	Fat	Protein	Lactose	Ash
Ayrshire	3.85	3.35	4.95	0.69
Friesian	3.40	3.15	4.60	0.73
Guernsey	4.90	3.85	4.95	0.75
Jersey	5.14	3.80	5.00	0.75
Shorthorn	3.65	3.30	4.80	0.69

After Scott (1981).
Reproduced by permission of Applied Science Publishers Ltd.

Inevitably the composition of fresh milk varies from day to day within any particular breed depending on such factors as: breeding policy, stage of lactation and age of the animal, health or infection of the udder, feeding management of the herd, climatic conditions and season of the year, and even the intervals between milking; Table 2.3 illustrates the national monthly average of butterfat and protein contents of milk from different breeds in England and Wales, while Fig. 2.3 shows the monthly variations in the major constituents of Friesian milk from the Crichton Royal Farm of the West of Scotland Agricultural College (W.S.A.C.).

In order to overcome these inherent variations in composition, fresh liquid milk has to be standardised and/or fortified:

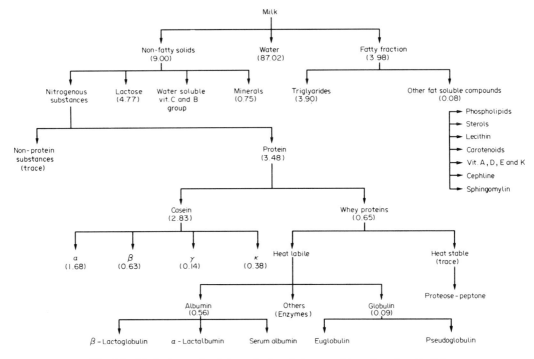

Fig. 2.2. Typical example of the main chemical composition of cow's milk (%)

The milk also contains dissolved gases (O_2, CO_2 and N_2), enzymes (lipases, reductases, proteases, phosphatases, lactoperoxidases, catalases, oxidases etc.), cellular matter (epithelial cells, leucocytes), micro-organisms (bacteria, yeasts and moulds) and contaminants due to carelessness during milking (straw, leaves, soil, disinfectant etc.).

Adapted from Kon and Cowie (1961), Scott (*loc. cit.*), Ferns (1981), and Jenness (1974).

(a) to comply with existing or proposed legal standards for yoghurt, i.e. the % of fat and/or solids-not-fat (see Table 10.5).

(b) to standardise the quality of yoghurt, e.g. acidity, sweetness and consistency/viscosity of the coagulum to meet the demands of the consumer; the former two factors can be controlled during the production stages, but the consistency/viscosity of yoghurt is affected by the level of protein present in the milk, and hence fortification of the milk solids-not-fat fraction is of primary importance.

B. Separation of Cellular Matter and Other Contaminants Present in the Milk

Liquid milk may contain cellular material, e.g. epithelial cells and leucocytes, which originates from the udder of the cow, and in some instances, due to carelessness during milk production, the milk is prone to further contamination with straw, leaves, hair, seeds, soil, etc. The primary objective of a milk processor is to remove such contaminants from the milk in order to ensure a better quality end-product, and while different methods are employed in dairies, the most universal system is the cloth filter. However, this method of filtration does have its limitations, one of which is that it can only remove the large debris present in the milk.

TABLE 2.3. *National average of butterfat and protein (%) in milk by breed in England and Wales*

1980/81 Month	Butterfat							Protein						
	Ayrshire	Friesian	Guernsey	Jersey	Shorthorn	Others	Average	Ayrshire	Friesian	Guernsey	Jersey	Shorthorn	Others	Average
October	4.14	4.04	4.92	5.57	3.83	3.96	4.10	3.65	3.52	3.88	4.19	3.57	3.47	3.55
November	4.22	4.07	5.00	5.64	3.91	4.01	4.13	3.55	3.41	3.78	4.11	3.50	3.37	3.44
December	4.19	4.06	4.97	5.66	3.91	4.02	4.12	3.44	3.32	3.69	4.01	3.40	3.29	3.35
January	4.09	3.98	4.87	5.53	3.81	3.94	4.04	3.36	3.24	3.62	3.90	3.29	3.22	3.27
February	4.03	3.92	4.78	5.39	3.77	3.88	3.98	3.33	3.21	3.58	3.84	3.27	3.18	3.23
March	4.03	3.93	4.75	5.37	3.75	3.88	3.98	3.30	3.18	3.54	3.78	3.23	3.16	3.21
April	3.97	3.90	4.64	5.21	3.68	3.85	3.95	3.30	3.19	3.55	3.74	3.24	3.16	3.21
May	3.80	3.71	4.54	5.03	3.49	3.69	3.76	3.47	3.37	3.74	3.89	3.42	3.32	3.39
June	3.84	3.77	4.63	5.09	3.53	3.74	3.82	3.50	3.39	3.73	3.93	3.41	3.34	3.41
July	3.81	3.80	4.61	5.11	3.54	3.74	3.84	3.52	3.42	3.77	3.97	3.43	3.36	3.44
August	3.91	3.87	4.70	5.20	3.64	3.81	3.92	3.56	3.46	3.78	3.97	3.44	3.40	3.48
September	3.97	3.94	4.78	5.32	3.67	3.85	3.99	3.64	3.54	3.86	4.08	3.52	3.40	3.56

After Nicholls (1981).

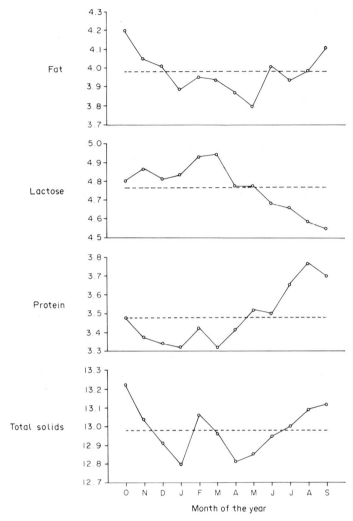

Fig. 2.3. Monthly variation (%) of Freisian milk obtained from the Crichton Royal farm of the W.S.A.C.

(a) Each monthly average is the mean of weekly values, i.e. either 4 or 5.
(b) Since the ash content in bulk milk varies little, a figure of 0.75 is taken as a constant.
(c) The data obtained is between October 1980 and September 1981.
(d) – – – – – – yearly average.

After Ferns (*loc. cit.*).

During the manufacture of some varieties of cheese, the presence of spore-forming organisms and/or cellular matter can affect the quality of the product and, since the level of heat treatment of the cheese milk is limited to 72°C for 15 seconds, survival of the spores can lead to product loss.

Centrifugal clarification has been employed, with limited success, to remove spores, but unfortunately the treatment tends to break the bacterial clumps and the milk sours more quickly. However, the principle of centrifugation has been exploited in a high-speed separator known as a bactofuge, and this type of separator can remove many undesirable micro-organisms from milk plus a very small amount of the milk constituents; in practice, the separated fraction (bactofugate) amounts to around 2–3% of the total throughput of milk. The bactofugate is then subjected to a sterilisation treatment by live steam injection at 130–140°C for 3–4 seconds, and after cooling is added back into the pasteurised cheese milk. The application of this high heat treatment to only a small portion of the milk does overcome the problems associated with the presence of spore-forming organisms, and at the same time does not affect the quality of the cheese.

However, the use of bactofuge separators on a yoghurt processing line is not really necessary, since the heat treatment of the basic mix (refer later) is high enough to eliminate, or at least reduce drastically, the level of spore-forming organisms in the yoghurt milk and, in any case, organisms of this type do not cause any major problems in the yoghurt industry. Thus, the use of cloth filters is more than adequate for raw milk, although, in some instances, an in-line metal sieve has to be installed when dried milk products are used to fortify the total solids in the milk; the metal sieves serve to separate any scorched or undissolved milk powder particles.

C. Standardisation of Fat Content in Milk

The fat content of yoghurt manufactured in different parts of the world can vary from as low as 0.1% to as high as 10% (see Table 10.5) and in order to meet existing or proposed compositional standards for yoghurt it is necessary to standardise the milk. For example, in the United Kingdom the average butterfat content in milk ranges from 3.7 to 4.2% (Table 2.3 and Fig. 2.3), but the fat content of commercial yoghurt averages around 1.5% (medium-fat yoghurt) or 0.5% (low-fat yoghurt). The methods employed for standardisation are as follows:

(i) removal of part of the fat content from milk;
(ii) mixing full cream milk with skim milk;
(iii) addition of cream to full fat milk or skim milk;
(iv) a process which combines methods (i) and (iii), i.e. the use of standardising centrifuges.

The components required to achieve a standard milk, using one of the above methods, can be easily calculated using the Pearsons Square method.

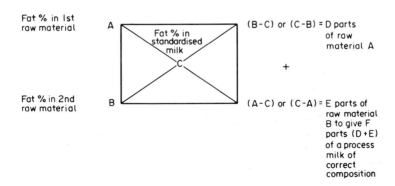

Alternatively, to calculate the amount of each type of raw material required, for example, per batch of a 1000 litres of standardised milk:

$$A = \frac{(B-C) \text{ or } (C-B) \times 1000}{F}$$

$$B = \frac{(A-C) \text{ or } (C-A) \times 1000}{F}$$

1st Example

How many litres of full cream milk (4% fat) and skim milk (0.1% fat) are required to produce 1000 litres of yoghurt milk at 1.5% fat?

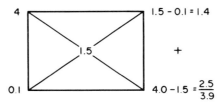

The amount of full cream milk required $= \dfrac{1.4 \times 1000}{3.9} = 359$ litres.

The amount of skim milk required $= \dfrac{2.5 \times 1000}{3.9} = 641$ litres.

$$\text{Total} \quad \underline{\underline{1000 \text{ litres}}}$$

2nd Example

How many litres of cream (50% fat) and skim milk (0.1% fat) are required to produce 1000 litres of yoghurt milk at 1.5% fat?

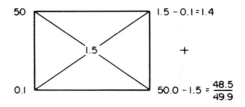

The amount of cream required $= \dfrac{1.4 \times 1000}{49.9} = 28.1$ litres.

The amount of skim milk required $= \dfrac{48.5 \times 1000}{49.9} = \underline{971.9 \text{ litres.}}$

$$\text{Total} \quad 1000.0 \text{ litres}$$

3rd Example

How many litres of cream (50% fat) and full cream milk (4% fat) are required to produce 1000 litres of yoghurt milk at 10% fat?

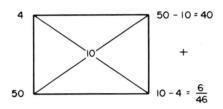

The amount of full cream milk required $= \dfrac{40 \times 1000}{46} = 869.6$ litres.

The amount of cream required $= \dfrac{6 \times 1000}{46} = \underline{130.4 \text{ litres.}}$

$$\text{Total} \quad 1000.0 \text{ litres}$$

D. Standardisation of the Solids-not-fat Content in Milk

The percentage of solids-not-fat (mainly the lactose, protein and mineral matter) in milk for the manufacture of yoghurt is governed either directly by legal standards of the country concerned or indirectly by the manufacturer seeking to produce an end-product with certain physical properties and flavour.

In the case of existing legal standards, the required solids-not-fat content in yoghurt ranges from 8.2 to 8.6% (see Table 10.5), and this minimum percentage seeks merely to protect the consumer; i.e. the SNF level is roughly comparable to the level present in liquid milk. From the manufacturer's point of view, the physical properties of yoghurt, e.g. viscosity/consistency of the coagulum, are of great importance, and in general the higher the level of solids in the yoghurt mix the greater the viscosity/consistency of the end-product. The relationship between the level of solids in the milk and the consistency of yoghurt was studied by Tamime (1977), and he observed that this property

15

was greatly improved as the milk solids increased from 12 to 20%. Fig. 2.4 shows this improvement in consistency as measured by the penetrometer (see Fig. 10.3), and it must be emphasised that the greater the depth of penetration, the softer the coagulum and vice versa. However, the change in consistency between 16 and 20% tends to be less pronounced, and hence there may be little value, in terms of product quality, in using a solids level above 16%.

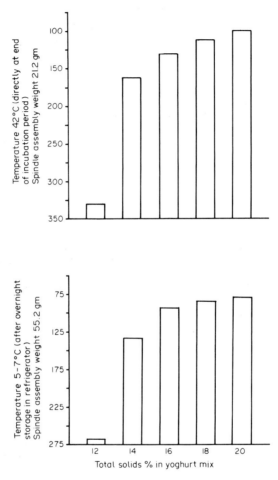

Fig. 2.4.   Consistency measurement of yoghurt (12–20% total solids) after $3\frac{1}{2}$ hours of incubation at 42°C

After Tamime (*loc. cit.*).

According to the reviews by Humphreys and Plunkett (1969), Robinson and Tamime (1975) and Tamime and Deeth (1980), the level of solids in milk (including the fat content) for the manufacture of yoghurt ranges from as low as 9% in low-fat yoghurt to as high as 30% in other types of yoghurt. The best yoghurt is probably made from milk containing 15–16% total solids, and it is of note that the composition of most commercial yoghurts falls within the range of 14–15%. Although 30% total solids has been suggested for the production of "Super Yoghurt", the end-product could well resemble "Concentrated Yoghurt" in its consistency rather than normal yoghurt (see Fig. 5.6).

Furthermore, if the total solids level in the yoghurt mix is in excess of 25%, it can adversely affect the availability of moisture to the starter culture, and this in turn can hinder their activity (Pulay and Krasz, 1974).

As a result of increasing the level of solids-not-fat in the mix, the titratable acidity of the milk is raised due to the buffering action of the additional proteins, phosphates, citrates, lactates and other miscellaneous milk constituents (Jenness and Patton, 1959), and this function can lead to a reduced coagulation time (see Table 2.4). A similar view is held by Davis (1973), who reported that doubling the solids-not-fat content in milk resulted in a doubling of its titratable acidity.

The fortification of the total solids in the yoghurt mix can be achieved by a number of different methods, such as:

TABLE 2.4. *The effect of total solids in the mix in relation to natural acidity (NA), titratable acidity (TA) and developed acidity (DA) after incubation at 42°C*

Total solids % in yoghurt milk	Time of incubation in hours	% lactic acid		
		NA	TA	DA
12	$3\frac{1}{2}$	0.15	0.80	0.65
14	$3\frac{1}{2}$	0.19	0.84	0.65
16	3	0.21	0.83	0.62
18	$2\frac{1}{2}$	0.24	0.88	0.64
20	3	0.29	0.93	0.64

(a) Full cream spray dried milk powder was reconstituted to different levels of total solids in the mix.
(b) Starter culture was CH-1 obtained from Chr. Hansen's Laboratorium A/S, Copenhagen, Denmark.

Adapted from Tamime (*loc. cit.*)

1. Traditional process

The application of heat to milk has long been practised traditionally, i.e. boiling to reduce the volume of the milk to 2/3 of its original value, and although the objective was to increase the concentration of total solids in the milk, the application of heat caused many physicochemical changes (refer to section on Heat Treatment). The degree of concentration achieved by the "boiling" process is rarely calculated with any accuracy, but if, for example, the total solids level in the milk is 13%, the result of boiling the milk to reduce its volume to 2/3 will be to raise the total solids content to around 19–20%. This method of fortification is still used in rural communities where the scale of yoghurt manufacture is very small.

2. Addition of milk powder

Milk powder (full cream or skim) is widely used in the industry to fortify liquid milk for the manufacture of a thick smooth yoghurt. Since the majority of the commercial yoghurt produced in the United Kingdom is of the low-fat type, it is probable that skim milk powder is the more popular ingredient. The rate of addition to the basic mix may range from as little as 1% to as high as 6 %, but the recommended level is 3–4 %, since the addition of higher levels of milk powder may lead to a "powdery" taste in the yoghurt.

3. Addition of buttermilk powder

This material is a by-product of sweet cream butter manufacture, but an acid type can also be obtained from the churning of cultured cream. The value of this low fat powder to the food and dairy industry is that, due to the presence of high levels of phospholipids, it has considerable emulsifying properties, and a method of manufacturing yoghurt from recombined dairy ingredients has been reported by Gilles and Lawrence (1979, 1982); the suggested formula is as follows:

25 kg anhydrous milk fat, 125 kg skim milk powder, 10 kg buttermilk powder, and 840 kg water.

4. Addition of whey powder

This product originates in the cheese industry, and its utilisation in the food and the dairy industry has been recently reviewed by Robinson and Tamime (1978). There are many different types of whey powder available on the market, and the characteristics of each are related to the processing technique applied before the drying stages, e.g. demineralisation, lactose removal, protein concentration or straightforward drying. According to Jelen and Horbal (1974), Hartman (1975), Nielsen (1976) and Spurgeon (1976), the recommended level of addition of any whey powder to the yoghurt mix is around 1–2 %, since higher levels can impart an undesirable "whey" flavour.

5. Addition of casein powder

Different types of casein powder are manufactured from skim milk, and their properties vary according to the technique used to precipitate the original casein, e.g. acid casein (hydrochloric, lactic or sulphuric acid precipitation), co-precipitated casein and rennet casein.

Casein powder, as the name indicates, consists mainly of casein, and its addition to the yoghurt mix increases both the level of protein in the product and its viscosity; the level of addition, as compared with skim milk powder, is comparatively low (see Fig. 2.6).

6. Concentration by evaporation

This method of concentrating the total solids in the basic mix is widely used in the industry (Fig. 3.27). The basic requirement is a single effect plate evaporator which can be easily incorporated into a yoghurt processing line, and the evaporation and/or concentration process is carried out on the milk before the final heat treatment. In practice, the yoghurt milk must first be standardised, e.g.

the fat content, since the evaporation concentrates all the milk constituents with the exception of minor losses of volatile compounds in the condensate. The amount of water removed from the milk ranges from 10 to 25 %, and this is equivalent to an increase in the total solids of 2–4 %. Some other advantages claimed for the evaporation process are: *firstly*, the removal of water from the milk takes place under vacuum which, in turn, aids in the removal of the entrapped air, and hence improves the stability of the coagulum and reduces syneresis during storage (Gradhage and Thurell, 1978). *Secondly*, during the manufacture of goat's milk yoghurt the evaporation process improves the consistency of, and reduces the "goaty" flavour of, the end-product (Hadland and Hoffmann, 1974).

7. Concentration by membrane filtration

Membrane filtration is a process which was developed to concentrate and/or separate solids from an aqueous mixture, and the usual membrane processes are reverse osmosis (RO—sometimes known as hyperfiltration) and ultrafiltration (UF).

The applications of RO and UF in the dairy industry have been recently reviewed by Glover *et al.* (1978), and the major functional differences between RO and UF are as follows:

(a) The RO process *separates* low molecular weight solutes, i.e. < 500, and only water molecules are allowed to pass through the membrane. Thus, the membranes are basically impermeable (or slightly permeable) to organic compounds or inorganic ions, and consequently the osmotic pressure becomes an important feature in the process. The RO system is operated at high pressures, i.e. 27–100 kg/cm^2 (2.7–10.4 Mega-pascals (MPa)).

(b) The UF process merely *sieves* or *filters* the milk, and the membranes can only retain high molecular weight fractions, i.e. > 1000. The operating pressures are, therefore, much lower than with the RO process, e.g. 1–10 kg/cm^2 (0.1–1 MPa).

The material that passes through the membrane is referred to as the permeate, and during the processing of milk (whole or skim) and/or whey the major difference between the permeates is that while the RO permeate consist only of water, the UF permeate contains, besides water, lactose, ash and vitamins. A comparison of the chemical compositions of whole milk, skim milk and whey concentrated by RO and UF (and their permeates) is illustrated in Table 2.5.

The industrial-scale production of yoghurt from milk concentrated by RO or UF has been reported by Jepsen (1977, 1979), and according to the data compiled by Tamime and Deeth (*loc. cit.*) the qualities of yoghurt produced from RO and UF concentrated milks are as follows:

(a) Whole milk, concentrated by UF to 18–20% total solids, produced a smooth, creamy yoghurt with a typical acid flavour; homogenisation was not required during subsequent treatment of the milk.

(b) A process similar to (a), but with the lactose content adjusted to 2%, resulted in a yoghurt rated as "superior" to ordinary commercial brands.

(c) Skim milk concentrated by UF to 13% total solids was also suitable for yoghurt making.

(d) The manufacture of yoghurt from skim milk concentrated by RO to 15% total solids resulted in a yoghurt of similar quality (viscosity, acid and flavour) to yoghurt produced from skim milk fortified to 15% total solids with skim milk powder.

TABLE 2.5. *Chemical analysis of the permeate and retentate of whole milk, skim milk and whey after concentration by ultrafiltration or reverse osmosis (all figures as % except as indicated)*

Process	Concentration factor	Product	Total solids	Fat	Nitrogen (a)	Lactose	Ash	Vitamin C	Pantothenic acid	Nicotinic acid	Riboflavin	Biotin	Vitamin B_{12}	Thiamin	Vitamin B_6	Folic acid
UF	X 2.0	Whole milk	11.80	2.9	0.55	4.9	0.70	(176)	(219)	(122)	(376)	(244)	(1357)	(301)	(170)	(441)
		Permeate	5.40	nil	0.05	4.6	0.50	13	68	58	61	63	98	62	64	95
		Retentate (b)	78.40	100.0	94.60	57.0	68.40	—								
	X 1.6	Skim milk	9.40	—	0.58	4.7	0.80									
		Permeate	3.30	—	0.03	3.1	0.30	—	74	69	79	84	100	77	80	100
		Retentate (b)	87.30	—	96.40	76.1	85.70									
	X 2.9	Whey	6.60	—	0.16	4.5	0.60									
		Permeate	5.30	—	0.08	4.2	0.50	—	38	31	50	40	100	33	38	99
		Retentate (b)	31.10	—	67.10	38.1	69.10									
RO	X 2.0	Whole milk	11.70	3.2	0.48	4.3	0.70									
		Permeate	0.08	nil	nil	nil	0.03									
		Retentate (b)	96.60	100.0	100.00	100.0	97.80	—	100	92.1	100	100	100	100	96.6	100
	X 2.2	Skim milk	8.80	—	0.49	4.7	0.70									
		Permeate	0.33	—	nil	nil	0.20									
		Retentate (b)	98.80	—	100.00	100.0	84.60			100			100	100		
	X 2.7	Whey	6.80	—	0.13	4.4	0.60									
		Permeate	0.11	—	nil	nil	0.09									
		Retentate (b)	99.00	—	100.00	100.0	90.30									

(a) Nitrogen from protein and non-protein nitrogenous compounds.

(b) Retentate (i.e. membrane retention) stated as amount in concentrate expressed as % of the component in the original sample.

(c) Figures in brackets represents molecular weight.

Adapted from Glover (1971).

It can be observed, therefore, that there are many methods of fortification/standardisation of the fat and/or solids-not-fat content of the basic mix, and a comparison of the chemical composition of these potential ingredients is given in Table 2.6. The choice of any one particular method of fortification is, in a given situation, governed primarily by the following factors:

TABLE 2.6. *Comparison of the composition of raw materials used for the manufacture of yoghurt*

Product	Component (%)				
	Moisture	Protein	Fat	Lactose	Ash
I Liquid					
Whole milk	87.4	3.5	3.5	4.8	0.70
Skim milk	90.5	3.6	0.1	5.1	0.70
Whey (Cheddar)	93.5	0.8	0.4	4.9	0.56
Whey (Cottage)	94.8	0.6	–	4.3	0.46
Cream (Single)	74.5	2.8	18.0	4.1	0.60
Cream (Double)	47.2	1.8	48.0	2.6	0.40
II Dried					
Whole milk	2.0	26.4	27.5	38.2	5.9
Skim milk	3.0	35.9	0.9	52.2	8.0
Whey — Commercial	3.0	13.5	1.0	74.0	8.5
Whey — Demineralised	3.0	14.5	1.0	80.5	1.0
Whey — Low lactose	4.0	32.0	2.0	53.0	8.0
Whey — Protein	5.0	61.0	5.0	22.0	7.0
Casein — Sodium	5.0	89.0	1.2	0.3	4.5
Casein — Calcium	5.0	88.6	1.2	0.2	5.0
Casein — Potassium	5.0	88.7	1.2	0.3	4.8
Casein — Ca-coprecipitate	4.0	83.0	1.5	1.0	10.5
Casein — Acid	9.0	88.0	1.3	0.2	1.5
Buttermilk	3.0	34.0	5.0	48.0	7.9
Cream	0.8	13.4	65.0	18.0	2.9
III Miscellaneous					
Anhydrous milk fat	0.1	–	99.9	–	–
Evaporated milk	73.8	7.0	7.9	9.7	1.6
Evaporated skim	73.0	10.0	0.3	14.7	2.3

Adapted from: Hargrove and Alford (1974), Harper and Seiberling (1976), ADMI (1971), Gennip (1973, 1980, 1981a, b), Hamilton (1981).

(a) cost and availability of the raw materials;
(b) scale of production;
(c) capital investment in the processing equipment;

but it is important to note that the degree of supplementation of each of the different milk constituents does vary with the method used; a summary of possible increases or decreases in the level of protein, lactose, and fat is illustrated in Table 2.7. However, other considerations may be equally relevant, and, for example, the addition of milk powder (whole or skim) beyond a certain level may result in a "powdery" flavour in the yoghurt and, due to the high level of lactose present in the mix, can also lead to excessive acid production during cold storage. Nevertheless, the viscosity/consistency of the coagulum is of primary importance during the manufacture of yoghurt, and this feature is wholly dependent on the level of protein in the basic mix; Fig. 2.5

TABLE 2.7. *Some suggested methods of fortification/standardisation of the basic mix applicable for the manufacture of yoghurt*

Raw materials		Process	Principal effect on process milk	
			Increase	Decrease
I. Liquid				
Whole milk		Evaporation	All constituents	–
		Reverse osmosis	,, ,,	–
		Ultrafiltration	Protein, fat	Lactose
	Partial fat separation	Evaporation	Solids-not-fat	Fat
		Reverse osmosis	,, ,, ,,	Fat
		Ultrafiltration	Protein	Lactose, Fat
	Addition of skim milk	Evaporation	Solids-not-fat	Fat
		Reverse osmosis	,, ,, ,,	Fat
		Ultrafiltration	Protein	Lactose, Fat
Skim milk		Evaporation	Solids-not-fat	–
		Reverse osmosis	,, ,, ,,	–
		Ultrafiltration	Protein	Lactose
II. Liquid + Powder				
Whole milk		Whole milk	All constituents	–
		Skim milk	Solids-not-fat	Fat
		Buttermilk	All constituents	–
	Addition of dried powder	Caseinate	Casein	Lactose, Fat
		Whey	Lactose, Whey proteins	Fat
Skim milk		Skim milk	Solids-not-fat	–
		Buttermilk	All constituents	–
		Caseinate	Casein	Lactose
		Whey	Lactose, Whey proteins	–
III. Liquid + concentrated milk				
Whole milk		Evaporated milk	All constituents	–
		Reverse osmosis milk (Whole milk)	,, ,,	–
		Ultrafiltrated milk	Protein, Fat	Lactose
	Addition of concentrated	Evaporated milk	Solids-not-fat	Fat
		Reverse osmosis milk (Skim milk)	,, ,, ,,	Fat
		Ultrafiltrated milk	Protein	Lactose, Fat
Skim milk		Evaporated milk	Solids-not-fat	–
		Reverse osmosis (Skim milk)	,, ,, ,,	–
		Ultrafiltrated milk	Protein	Lactose

illustrates this relationship in respect to the variations in protein content of milk throughout the year. Commercially, of course, a high protein content in the yoghurt milk can be achieved by the addition of caseinate powder, concentrating the milk by the UF method, or, to a lesser degree, by the addition of a high protein whey powder and/or buttermilk powder (see Table 2.6).

Although, in broad terms, the overall level of protein in the mix affects the characteristics of the coagulum, the formation of the gel is entirely dependent on the functional properties of the casein fraction. Thus, the lactic acid produced by the starter culture destabilises the casein micelles, and at pH 4.6–4.7 in the presence of divalent ions (calcium and magnesium) the casein forms a three-dimensional network entrapping all the milk constituents including the aqueous phase. It is not surprising, therefore, that according to Gennip (1981b) fortification of the milk base with casein or caseinate offers the following advantages:

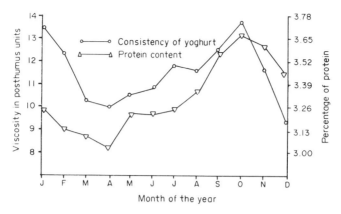

Fig. 2.5. Relationship between the protein content of milk and the consistency of yoghurt during the year

After Gennip (1973, 1981a, b).

(a) concentration of the milk, in order to increase the protein content, is not required;
(b) the natural flavour and texture of the yoghurt is maintained;
(c) it enhances the hydrophilic properties of the existing protein, and so acts as a stabiliser;
(d) it improves the viscosity of yoghurt, and decreases the problem of syneresis during cold storage;
(e) the recommended level of fortification, as compared with skim milk powder, is in the proportion of 1 to 3 respectively, and the efficacy of caseinate *vis-à-vis* skim milk powder in enchancing the consistency of yoghurt is shown in Fig. 2.6.

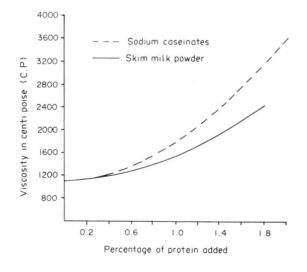

Fig. 2.6. Effect of an increase of protein content on viscosity of yoghurt

After Gennip (1973, 1981a, b).

23

It is clearly feasible, therefore, to manufacture yoghurt from either concentrated or fortified milk, and in an effort to isolate one particular method Abrahamsen and Holmen, (1980) compared the quality of yoghurt manufactured from a number of processed milks, i.e. reverse osmosis milk (RO), ultrafiltered milk (UF), vacuum evaporated milk (VE), with a product made from milk with added milk powder (MP). The chemical composition of the basic mixes is illustrated in Table 2.8, and their conclusions can be summarised as follows:

(a) UF yoghurt gave the highest reading for viscosity and firmness of the coagulum.
(b) The favourable instrumental assessment of UF yoghurt was not supported by the organoleptic appraisal, and, as shown below, yoghurt prepared from vacuum evaporated milk proved the most popular.

TABLE 2.8. *Chemical composition (%) of yoghurt milks concentrated/fortified by different methods*

Treatment	Total solids	Fat	Protein	Lactose*	Ash	Lactic acid in yoghurt One day	14 days
Control	11.84	3.43	3.12	4.45	0.84	1.01	1.16
Vacuum evaporated	14.57	3.49	4.12	6.03	0.93	1.33	1.39
Ultrafiltration	14.13	3.60	4.97	4.63	0.93	1.37	1.53
Reverse osmosis	14.54	3.52	4.03	6.07	0.92	1.32	1.44
Addition of milk powder	14.32	3.32	4.14	5.93	0.93	1.35	1.45

* Figures for lactose were obtained by difference.

Adapted from Abrahamsen and Holmen (1980).

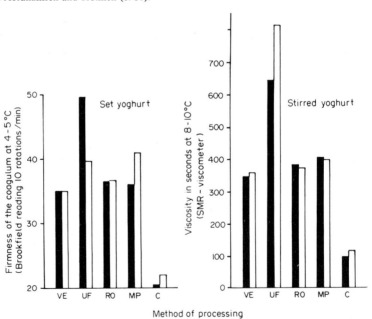

Fig. 2.7. Rheological properties of yoghurts manufactured from milk concentrated/fortified by different methods

VE—vacuum evaporation; UF—ultrafiltration; RO—reverse osmosis; MP—milk powder addition; C—control (liquid milk)

■ One day old at 4°C   □ After 14 days storage at 4°C

Adapted from Abrahamsen and Holmen (1980).

Property	Age/Type of yoghurt	RO	Treatment of milk UF	VE	MP
Body/ Consistency	Stirred (1 day)	4.6	4.8	4.8	4.7
	(14 day)	4.6	4.4	4.6	4.6
	Set (1 day)	4.6	3.9	4.8	4.4
	(14 day)	4.0	4.0	4.4	4.1
Flavour/	(1 day)	4.35	3.7	4.7	4.25
Aroma	(14 day)	3.9	3.5	3.9	3.9

(all scores out of 5)

It is noticeable, however, that, with the exception of UF yoghurt, the scores are remarkably similar, and hence the selection of a procedure for fortification can, in fact, be based principally on practical or economic considerations.

During the preparation of the basic mix it is probable that a number of different dairy ingredients will be used, and it is essential that the level of solids-not-fat and fat are calculated properly in order to achieve a balanced yoghurt milk. Two approaches can be considered: *firstly*, an approximate formulation can be worked out by the Pearsons Square formula, or, *secondly*, an Algebraic method can be used to calculate exactly the quantities of fat and solids-not-fat that will be obtained from the various raw materials. The former method of calculation is most satisfactory for small-scale yoghurt producers, but the Algebraic method is usually recommended for large-scale manufacture, especially when considering the economics of the operation. Hypothetical examples of the above two methods of calculation are shown in Appendix 9.

E. Addition of Stabilisers/Emulsifiers

Stabilisers and/or emulsifiers are used during the manufacture of some dairy products, including yoghurt, and their application in most countries is governed by legislative regulation. At the international level, the FAO/WHO (1976) have drafted a list of compounds (with permitted concentrations) which can be used in the production of yoghurt, and a similar approach has been adopted in the United Kingdom.

The classification of these food-grade stabilisers/emulsifiers has always proved something of a problem, and a number of different schemes have been suggested, such as:

(a) all compounds to be referred to as polysaccharide materials;
(b) the name to include the botanical origin;
(c) their general origin, i.e. plant, animal or synthetic;
(d) chemical grouping.

However, the latter approach has been recently modified by Glicksman (1969, 1979), and his proposed classification includes a reference to the processing technique, e.g.

(a) natural gums (those found in nature);

(b) modified natural or semi-synthetic gums (i.e. chemical modifications of natural gums or gum-like materials);

(c) synthetic gums (those prepared by chemical synthesis).

Some stabilisers permitted by FAO/WHO (1976) and the Food and Drugs Act (1975, 1980) are illustrated in Table 2.9, and, for convenience, Glicksman's method of classification has been used for the arrangement of the various product-groups.

TABLE 2.9. *Classification and functions of gums which could be used during the manufacture of yoghurt*

Natural gums	Modified gums	Synthetic gums
Plant	Cellulose derivatives (1)	Polymers*
Exudates	Carboxymethylcellulose	Polyvinyl derivatives
Arabic (1, 3)	Methylcellulose	Polyethylene derivative
Tragacanth (1)	Hydroxyethylcellulose	
Karaya	Hydroxypropylcellulose	
Extracts	Hydroxypropylmethylcellulose	
Pectins (2, 3)	Microcrystallinecellulose	
Seed Flour		
Locust (Carob) (1)	Microbial fermentation	
Guar (1)		
	Dextran	
	Xanthan (1, β)	
Seaweed		
Extracts	Miscellaneous derivatives	
Agar (2, 3)		
Alginates (1, 2, 3)	Low-methoxy pectin	
Carrageenan (2, 3)	Propylene glycole alginate	
Furcellaran (1, 2, 3)	Pre-gelatinised starches	
	Modified starches	
Cereal starches (1, 2, 3)	Carboxymethyl starch	
Wheat	Hydroxyethyl starch	
Corn	Hydroxypropyl starch	
Animal		
Gelatin		
Casein		
Vegetable		
Soy protein		

* Limited in its application in yoghurt, since it is not listed in the Food and Drugs Act (1975, 1980) or FAO/WHO (1976).
The permitted level of these stabilising compounds in yoghurt is 5000 mg/kg with the exception of pectins, gelatin and starches, i.e. 10 g/kg.
Figures in parentheses indicate the function of the hydrocolloid, i.e. (1) thickener, (2) gelling agent and (3) stabiliser.

After: Powell (1969), Glicksman (1969; 1979), Pedersen (1979).

The primary aim of adding stabilisers to the basic mix is to enhance and maintain the desirable characteristics in yoghurt, e.g. body and texture, viscosity/consistency, appearance and mouth-feel. Thus the yoghurt coagulum is often subjected to mechanical treatment during manufacture, e.g.:

(a) stirring of the coagulum in the fermentation tank at the end of the incubation period, e.g. in-tank cooling;

(b) pumping of the coagulum to a plate/tubular cooler;

(c) mixing to incorporate the fruit/flavours into the coagulum, followed by pumping to the filling/packaging machine;

(d) subsequent post-fermentation heat treatment of the coagulum for the manufacture of "Pasteurised, UHT or Long-life Yoghurt", and, as a result, the yoghurt may become less viscous or, in extreme cases, may show whey separation; the addition of stabilisers can overcome these defects.

Stabilisers are sometimes referred to as hydrocolloids, and their mode of action in yoghurt includes two basic functions: firstly, the binding of water, and secondly, promotion of an increase in viscosity (Boyle, 1972). Thus, the molecules of stabiliser are capable of forming a network of linkages between the milk constituent(s) and themselves due to the presence of a negatively charged group, e.g. hydrogen or carboxyle radicals, or to the presence of a salt possessing the power to sequester calcium ions. These negative groups are concentrated at the interfacial areas, and according to Boyle (*loc. cit.*), Ingenpass (1980) and Dexter (1976) the binding of water into the basic mix is achieved by the stabiliser as follows:

(a) it binds the water as water of hydration;

(b) it reacts with the milk constituents (mainly the proteins) to increase their level of water hydration;

(c) stabilises the protein molecule to form a network that retards the free movement of water (see Figs. 2.8 and 2.9).

Therefore, the functions of hydrocolloids in yoghurt are as:

(a) gelling or thickening agents; and

(b) stabilising agents.

As can be seen from Table 2.9, there is a wide range of compounds which can be added to milk for the production of a viscous yoghurt, and these stabilisers can be added as single compounds or as a blend. The latter approach is more widely used, since most commercial preparations are a mixture of stabilising compounds (unless it is declared otherwise).

The object of blending these compounds together is to achieve a specific function or, in the majority of cases, to overcome one of the limiting properties associated with a specific compound. For example, a single stabilising compound (X) may be suitable for the manufacture of a fruit/flavoured yoghurt, but it may not be suitable, on its own, for the production of frozen, dried or pasteurised yoghurt, and hence the choice of a particular type of "stabiliser" is dependent on a multitude of factors, including:

1. Functional properties, effect and/or mode of action of the selected compound.

2. Optimum concentration to be used.

The level of stabiliser(s) in yoghurt is sometimes governed by legislation (FAO/WHO, 1976; UK Food Standards, 1975) and/or side effects, i.e. appearance or undesirable mouth-feel, which could

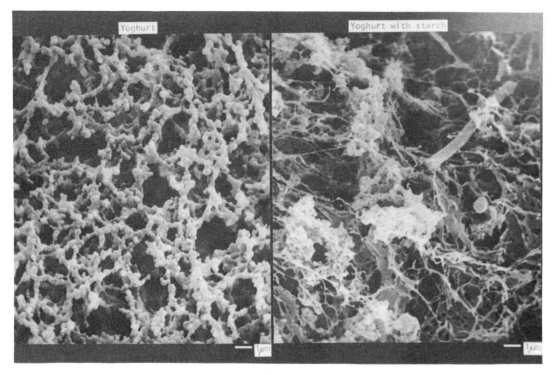

Fig. 2.8. Microstructure of yoghurt with or without added starch as shown by scanning electron microscopy

Magnification 6000×.
Bars represent 1 μm (9.3 mm).
m chain of casein micelles
(1) *L. bulgaricus.*
(2) *S. thermophilus.*
f short fibres
n sheets

After Kalab (1982a).

Fig. 2.9. Differences in the microstructure of yoghurt in the presence of different stabilising agents

Micrographs (left-hand side) scanning electron microscopy
(right-hand side) transmission electron microscopy

(A) yoghurt supplemented with 0.4% carrageenan, and (B) supplemented with 2% pre-gelatinised waxy maize starch.

The addition of carrageenan resulted in the formation of a fibrillar microstructure which connected large clusters of casein micelles. It can be observed that the fibres had no free terminations, but were thin and long.

The presence of starch gave rise to short fibres and sheets, and the fibres frequently had free terminations where some of them were connected with small clusters of casein micelles.

Transmission electron microscopy showed no differences between the microstructure of yoghurt with starch or carregeenan stabilisers; however, the scanning method could be used to detect different additives in yoghurt.

Bars represent 1 μm (9.3 mm), (g) fat globules, (f) flat fibres, (h) sheets, (m) casein micelles, magnification 6000 × .

After Kalab, Emmons and Sargant (1975).
Reproduced by permission of *Journal of Dairy Research.*

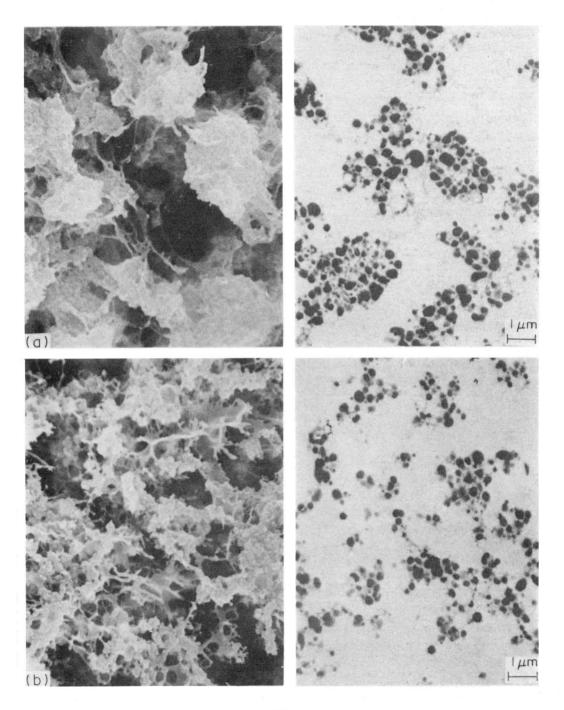

Fig. 2.9

be caused by the addition of too large a quantity. Some recommended levels of stabiliser for the manufacture of yoghurt are:

(i) 0.02–0.2% of pectins or some modified starches (Winterton and Meiklejohn, 1978; Zmarlicki, Pijanowski and Molska, 1977);

(ii) 0.2–0.5% of agar-agar, locust (carob) gum, guar gum, alginate, gelatin or carrageenan (Volker, 1972; Schrieber, 1973; Ledder and Thomasow, 1975; Steinitz, 1975);

(iii) 1–2% of some starch preparations (Thomasow and Hoffmann, 1978).

Another factor which determines the level of stabiliser added to the yoghurt milk is the percentage of milk solids present, and according to Hall (1975) the optimum concentrations for a gelatin/plant gum mixture were 0.5, 0.45, 0.4, 0.3 and 0.25% to yoghurt milks containing 12.5, 14.5, 16.5, 19.0 and 22.0% milk solids respectively.

3. Toxic or inhibitory effects

Although tragacanth and locust (carob) gum are still awaiting toxicological clearance for use in foodstuffs (FAO/WHO, 1976), in general, stabilising compounds do not, at the rates normally employed, inhibit the yoghurt organisms.

4. Legal aspect

The statutory regulations differ with the country concerned, and not all stabilising compounds are permitted for the production of yoghurt.

5. Solubility and dissolution

Some starch preparations and Na-carrageenan are soluble at a low temperature, and hence they can be added to cold milk during the preparation of the basic mix. The majority of the stabilising compounds are, however, only soluble at higher temperatures, e.g. 50–85°C (with the exception of agar-agar at 90–95°C), so that in practice these stabilisers are added to warm milk before pasteurisation, or alternatively to hot milk after the heat treatment. In some instances complete dissolution of a particular stabiliser blend, e.g. one which contains some starch preparation, may necessitate a holding time at high temperature in order for the mixture to become active as a "stabiliser".

In view of the different properties of these compounds, it is difficult to recommend one method for incorporation into the basic mix, but the following points may help to overcome any problems:

(i) follow the instructions provided by the manufacturer; or in the absence of any information

(ii) mix the stabiliser with the milk powder and add to the water or milk with high-speed stirrer at the temperature recommended for the milk powder;

(iii) alternatively, mix the stabiliser with the sugar and add to the basic mix under high-speed agitation at the temperature recommended for the sugar;

(iv) hydrate the stabiliser (e.g. gelatin powder) in water or milk, and then add to the basic mix with high-speed stirring.

6. Effect on the casein

The addition of some hydrocolloids (Na-carboxymethyl-cellulose, guar gum and locust gum) at levels as low as 0.05 % to sweet milk can destabilise the casein micelle (Powell, *loc. cit.*), and although the destabilised casein micelles will eventually coagulate, the matrix has a rather limited ability to retain water, and as a result syneresis becomes evident. Furthermore, such destabilised casein can give rise to a course coagulum with an open texture. The problem can be minimised, however, by blending the above compounds with carrageenan or alginates (see also Dexter, *loc. cit.*).

7. Processing conditions

As can be seen from Chapter 5, various yoghurt-based products have been developed, and the quality of these is dependent on the addition of stabilisers. For example:

(i) "Pasteurised, UHT or Long-life" yoghurt—it is recommended that a gelling agent is added consisting of a blend of locust gum and agar-agar and/or xanthan (Anon., 1980a); the presence of starch derivatives (diamylopectin glycerol ether or diamylopectin phosphate) can improve the appearance of heat-treated yoghurt (Vanderpoorten and Martens, 1976).

(ii) "Frozen" yoghurt—an unspecified mixture of stabilisers/emulsifiers is recommended by Gautneb, Steinsholt and Abrahamsen (1979), but the addition of modified starch proved unsatisfactory (Winterston and Meiklejohn, *loc. cit.*).

(iii) "Stirred" yoghurt—a blend of 1 % Na-proteinate (possibly Na-caseinate), 0.1 % Frimulsion J5, 0.1 % Genu Gum CH 200, 0.3 % Genu carrageenan with Malto-Dextrin or 0.16 % Frimulsion JQ improved the viscosity of the product (Luczynska *et al.*, 1978).

(iv) "Drinking" yoghurt—an agar-agar based stabiliser is added at a rate of 0.25 %, and this helps to maintain the suspension of fruit in the product (Morley, 1978).

(v) 'Freeze-dried Dahi'—the quality of the product was improved by the addition of corn starch and lecithin or glycerol monostearate to the fermented milk prior to drying (Baisya and Bose, 1975).

Since casein precipitation may occur in "sweet milk" or during the development of acid, some of the stabilisers may be added to the yoghurt after the formation of the coagulum. In this case it is recommended that the stabilising compound (e.g. liquified agar-agar and/or "pre-swollen" gelatin) is mixed with the sugar and then incorporated into the coagulum.

8. Solidification characteristics

The majority of stabilisers used in the production of yoghurt will solidify at ordinary refrigeration temperature, with the exception of gelatin and agar-agar which solidify at 25°C and 42–45°C respectively. These latter stabilising compounds can, therefore, cause problems during the cooling stage, i.e. difficulty in pumping and/or packaging, and in addition the use of gelatin may give the coagulum a "rough texture". This latter fault can be reduced or eliminated by passing the coagulum through a fine mesh screen/sieve.

9. Hygienic standards

The temperature used during the processing of the yoghurt milk (85°C for 30 minutes or 90–95°C for 5–10 minutes) is high enough to destroy the majority of micro-organisms which could be present in the stabiliser; however, stabilisers added to the coagulum after the incubation period must be of excellent microbiological quality, otherwise the shelf-life of the product could be reduced.

F. Addition of Sweetening Agents

Sweetening compounds are normally added during the manufacture of fruit/flavoured yoghurt, and in some instances for the production of "sweet" natural yoghurt; the latter product is of limited demand.

The main object of the adding sweetening agents to yoghurt is to tone down the acidity of the product and the level of incorporation is dependent on:

(i) the type of sweetening compound used;
(ii) consumer preference;
(iii) the type of fruit used;
(iv) possible inhibitory effects on the yoghurt starter organisms;
(v) legal aspects;
(vi) economic considerations.

On average, fruit/flavoured yoghurts may contain as high as 20% carbohydrates, and these are derived from:

(a) residual milk sugars (lactose, galactose, and glucose—the level varies in relation to the level of solids in the basic mix and the method of fortification);
(b) natural sugars present in the fruit (sucrose, fructose, glucose and maltose);
(c) sugars added by the yoghurt manufacturer and/or the fruit processor.

Fruit may contain different levels and types of natural carbohydrate, and the total content ranges from as low at 1.6% in lemon to as high as 65% in raisins (Paul and Southgate, *loc. cit.*; Shallenberger and Birch, 1975), and the fruits, which are in regular demand, have the following natural carbohydrate content:

Apricot	7.5	
Black-cherry	12.0	
Blackcurrant	6.6	
Mandarine	14.2	%
Peaches	9.0	
Pineapple	11.6	
Raspberry	5.6	
Strawberry	6.2	

The main carbohydrates present in fruits are glucose, fructose, sucrose and maltose, and hence the perceived sweetness of each type of fruit is dependent on the level and type of carbohydrate present. The comparative sweetness of various carbohydrates, including milk sugars, is illustrated in Table 2.10; sucrose is given a nominal rating of 1.

TABLE 2.10. *List of various sweetening compounds*

Sweetening compound	Relative sweetness : Sucrose = 1
Lactose	0.4
Dulcitol	0.4
Maltose	0.4
Sorbitol	0.5
Mannose	0.6
Galactose	0.6
Glucose	0.7
Xylose	0.7
Mannitol	0.7
Glycine	0.7
Invert sugar	0.7–0.9
Glycerol	0.8
Sucrose	1.0
Fructose	1.1–1.5
Cyclamate	30–80
Saccharin	240–350

After: Beck (1974), Crosby and Wingard (1979), Shallenberger and Birch (*loc. cit.*), Meade and Chen (1977).

The fruit preparations, which are utilised by the yoghurt industry, may be divided into two main categories: firstly, fruit preserves which do not contain any added sweetening agent, and, secondly, fruits with added sweeteners. The latter type is more popular, and according to Spinks (1982) the level of added sweeteners in processed fruits for yoghurt manufacture ranges from 25 to 65%, with the most popular level being 30–35%.

It is now almost universal practice to add preserves and similar materials to the finished yoghurt, for the presence of carbohydrates in the basic mix can inhibit the growth of the yoghurt organisms. Thus, Tramer (1973) reported a reduction in the rate of acid development by *S. thermophilus* and *L. bulgaricus* in concentrated milk (16.5% TS) as the sugar level was increased from 6 to 12% (Table 2.11), and a microscopic examination of these different types of yoghurt showed firstly that *S. thermophilus* was more tolerant of high sugar concentrations than *L. bulgaricus* (Table 2.12) (a view which was confirmed by Steinsholt and Abrahamsen, 1978; Marshall and Mabbitt, 1980), and secondly that morphological changes occurred, i.e. the cells were distorted, elongated and "unhealthy looking". It was evident, however, that the sugar tolerance of the starter cultures was strain dependent, and it was recommended that the strains of starter culture to be employed in presweetened milks should be carefully screened.

The inhibition of the yoghurt starter cultures grown in milk (14–16% TS) plus added sugar (10–12%) is due mainly to the adverse osmotic effect of the solutes in the milk, but low "water activity" (Labuza, 1980; Shallenberger and Birch, *loc. cit.*) may also be involved. The "water activity" (A_w) of a food is described as

$$A_w = \frac{P_f}{P_0} = \frac{\text{ERH}}{100}$$

TABLE 2.11. *The effect of various sugar concentrations on the rate of acid development by a mixed strain yoghurt culture*

(%) Added sugar	(%) Lactic acid after 4 hours incubation at 42°C
0	1.60
6	1.25
9	0.75
12	0.40

The level of milk solids in the mix was 16.5%.

Adapted from Tramer (*loc. cit.*).

TABLE 2.12. *The effect of different sugar concentrations on the activity and ratio of cocci to rods of yoghurt starter cultures*

Sugar concentration (%) in milk	Strain of the yoghurt cultures	Results
5.5	1731 & 1732	Active growth; rods became slightly predominant over the cocci
	SY	Active growth; balanced ratio
7.8	1731 & 1732	Active growth; balance ratio.
	SY	Inhibition of growth; cocci dominante over rods.
9.0	1731 & 1732	Some growth inhibition.
	SY	Severe growth inhibition.
11.0	1731 & 1732	Severe growth inhibition; cocci showed morphological distortion; few rods present

Adapted from Tramer (*loc. cit.*).

where A_w = water activity,
   P_f = vapour pressure of water in food,
   P_0 = vapour pressure of pure water at the same temperature,
   ERH = equilibrium relative humidity.

This latter concept, i.e. A_w, is important from a quality control point of view, since both microbial growth and enzyme activity in food are related to the A_w (Acker, 1969), and hence it is possible to suggest that both osmotic pressure and A_w may be associated with the inhibitory effect on the yoghurt starter organisms. However, starter cultures propagated in milks with high total solids, e.g. 30% TS, can also show reduced activity (Zmarlicki *et al.*, 1974), a condition which could be entirely related to the A_w of the growth medium. This observation was also reported by Tramer (*loc. cit.*), who observed the inhibition of yoghurt starter cultures propagated milk (21% TS) plus 3% added sugar; the inhibitory effect was attributed to A_w since it was considered unlikely that 3% sugar in solution could create enough osmotic pressure to retard the growth of the organisms.

In view of the above data, the normal methods used for the addition of sweetening agents are as follows:

(a) the yoghurt manufacturer adds up to 5% sweetener (sugar) to the basic mix; and
(b) the sweetness desired in the final product is attained by the addition of a sweetened fruit preparation.

It is worthwhile pointing out at this stage that the sugar content of frozen yoghurt is much higher than in ordinary fruit/flavoured yoghurt, and it is recommended that the quantity of sugar (sucrose) added to the basic mix must not exceed 10%; the balance is added to the cold yoghurt prior to freezing. Different types of carbohydrates may be used during the manufacture of sweetened fruit/flavoured yoghurt, and some examples of these are as follows.

1. Sucrose (Saccharose)

This carbohydrate is abundant in the plant kingdom, and it is normally referred to as "sugar". Sucrose has the empirical formula $C_{12}H_{22}O_{11}$ and the refined carbohydrate is obtained commercially from sugar cane or sugar beet. It is widely used in the food industry as a sweetening agent, and it can be obtained in a granulated or syrup form. The former type requires strong agitation/stirring for complete dissolution when added to liquid milk, and in practice it is added with the rest of the dry ingredients at around 40°C. The syrup type, which contains 65–67% sugar (saturated at 20°C), is easily mixed with the aqueous phase of the basic mix, but since it contains 33–35% moisture it dilutes the level of solids in the yoghurt milk, and this added water must be allowed for when calculating a "balanced mix".

The addition of sugar before the heat treatment of the milk is highly desirable, since it ensures the destruction of any vegetative contaminants, e.g. osmophilic yeast and moulds, and possibly some spores as well. However, if the sugar has to be added after the formation of the coagulum, steps must be taken to avoid firstly uneven distribution of the sugar, and secondly excessive reduction in the consistency of the product.

2. Invert sugar

This type of carbohydrate results from the "inversion" of a sugar with dextrorotatory optical activity to one that is levorotatory or vice versa. The different types of invert sugar depend on the raw material.

(a) Invert sucrose syrup. This syrup is formed when sucrose undergoes acid hydrolysis in the presence of heat, and the degree of inversion can range from 10 to 90%.

$$C_{12}H_{22}O_{11} + \quad H_2O \quad \xrightarrow[\text{and heat}]{\text{Acid}} \quad C_6H_{12}O_6 + \quad C_6H_{12}O_6$$

			D-Glucose	D-Fructose
Sucrose	Water		(Dextrose)	(Levulose)

Invert sugar

One advantage of this conversion is that a product (50% inversion) contains 23% moisture (Junk and Pancoast, 1973), and yet can be handled at this high sugar concentration without crystallisation.

(b) Invert corn syrup. The hydrolysis of corn starch results in the production of D-glucose (Dextrose), and the degree of conversion is measured in terms of dextrose equivalent (DE), i.e.

Types I (20–37 DE), II (38–57 DE), III (58–72 DE) and IV (>73 DE) (Junk and Pancoast, *loc. cit.*). The process of hydrolysis is normally achieved by one of these methods:

total acid hydrolysis,
acid liquefaction/enzyme saccharification,
total enzyme hydrolysis,

although in recent years starch syrups have also been processed into other types of sugars, e.g. syrups high in maltose or fructose. The latter syrup has many potential applications in the food industry, and according to Martin (1979) high-fructose (corn) syrups are commercially produced in the United States containing 42, 55 or 95 % fructose; the corresponding sucrose equivalent, in terms of sweetness (sucrose = 1), is 1, 1.1–1.2 and 1.5 respectively (see also Dordovic *et al.*, 1981).

3. Fructose (Levulose)

Fructose or fruit sugar has the same empirical formula as glucose, i.e. $C_6H_{12}O_6$, and as can be seen from Table 2.10 is sweeter than both sucrose and glucose. Commercially, fructose is derived mainly from the conversion of starch.

4. Glucose (Dextrose)

Glucose has the same empirical formula as fructose, i.e. $C_6H_{12}O_6$, and is commercially produced from the hydrolysis of corn starch.

5. Glucose/Galactose syrup

This type of syrup is produced from whey, a by-product from the cheese and casein industry, and to a lesser degree from the permeate of UF concentrated milk. The amount of lactose in whey is usually in the region of 5 %, but as illustrated in Table 2.10 the relative sweetness of lactose is only 0.4 compared with sucrose; hence the lactose has to be converted to its monomer constituents—glucose and galactose—before it can impart any real sweetness (see Table 2.10). The process of hydrolysis of lactose can be achieved using either acid or enzymes, and Fig. 2.10 illustrates schematically some details of these processes; Table 2.13 shows the chemical composition of the different syrups.

6. Miscellaneous sweeteners

Sorbitol is an alcohol produced commercially from glucose by a hydrogenation process, i.e. the aldehyde group (CHO) in the glucose molecule is converted to an alcohol group (CH_2OH). Although sorbitol has only half the sweetness of sucrose (see Table 2.10), its possible application in fruit/flavoured yoghurts would be for patients suffering from diabetes.

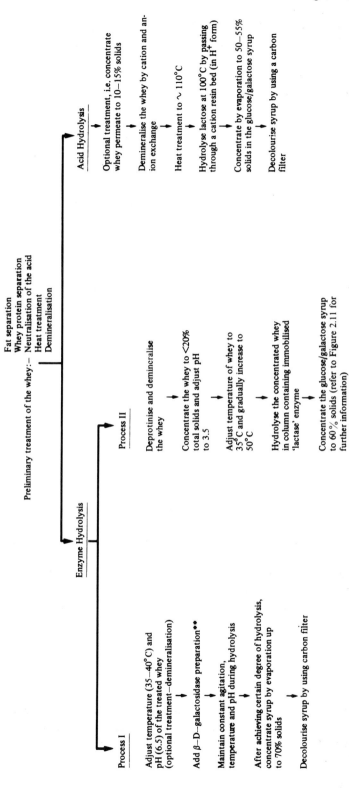

Preliminary treatment of the whey:–
Fat separation
Whey protein separation
Neutralisation of the acid
Heat treatment
Demineralisation

Enzyme Hydrolysis

Process I

Adjust temperature (35—40°C) and pH (6.5) of the treated whey (optional treatment—demineralisation)

Add β–D–galactosidase preparation**

Maintain constant agitation, temperature and pH during hydrolysis

After achieving certain degree of hydrolysis, concentrate syrup by evaporation up to 70% solids

Decolourise syrup by using carbon filter

Process II

Deprotinise and demineralise the whey

Concentrate the whey to <20% total solids and adjust pH to 3.5

Adjust temperature of whey to 35°C and gradually increase to 50°C

Hydrolyse the concentrated whey in column containing immobilised 'lactase' enzyme

Concentrate the glucose/galactose syrup to 60% solids (refer to Figure 2.11 for further information)

Acid Hydrolysis

Optional treatment, i.e. concentrate whey permeate to 10—15% solids

Demineralise the whey by cation and anion exchange

Heat treatment to ~ 110°C

Hydrolyse lactose at 100°C by passing through a cation resin bed (in H⁺ form)

Concentrate by evaporation to 50—55% solids in the glucose/galactose syrup

Decolourise syrup by using a carbon filter

Fig. 2.10. Some of different processes for the manufacture of glucose/galactose syrup from whey*

– * An alternative source of whey is the permeate from UF concentrated skim milk.
– ** β-D-galactosidase preparations are commercially obtained from *Kluyveromyces lactis*, *Aspergillus niger* or *Aspergillus oryzae*.

– Refer to Table 2.13 for comparative chemical analysis of these different types of glucose/galactose syrups.

After: Woychik and Holsinger (1977), Davies (1982), Johansson (1982), Anon. (1976, 1982a, b).

TABLE 2.13. *Chemical composition (%) of glucose/galactose syrups from hydrolysed whey*

Process	Water	Lactose	Glucose	Galactose	Di-Tri-saccharides	Proteins	Ash	Fat	References
I. Enzymatic hydrolysis by *K. lactis*									
A. Hydrolysed whey (80%)	30	6	21	20	3	11	6	3	
B. Hydrolysed (80%) & demineralised whey (50%)	30	7	22	21	3	11	3	3	Anon. (1978)
C. Hydrolysed lactose 80%	30	10	26	25	3	(−)	2	4	
II. Enzymatic hydrolysis by immobilised *A. niger*									
A. Hydrolysed whey (90%)		6–8	34–37	34–37	less than 2% of total sugars	11–13	8–10	1	
B. Hydrolysed (90%) demineralised whey (50%)		7–9	36–38	36–38		11–13	4–5	1	Elsey (1982)
C. Hydrolysed (90%) & demineralised whey (90%)		8–10	37–38	37–38		11–13	1	1	
III. Acid hydrolysis	45–48	1	25	25	(NA)	(NA)	0.1–0.2	(NA)	Davies (*loc. cit.*)

Figures are expressed as % of dry solids basis

− Not present.
NA Not tested.

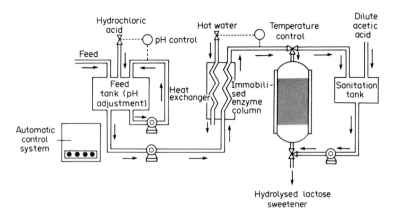

Fig. 2.11.   Flow diagram of the immobilised enzyme process (Corning Glass Works) for lactose hydrolysis

After Dicker (1982), Anon. (1982a), Coton (1980).
Reprinted with permission of Specialist Dairy Ingredients, Surrey, UK.

Thus, the rate of absorption of sorbitol in the gut is slower than that of glucose, and hence it has little effect on the level of sugar in the blood. No recommended daily intake is given since large intakes cause diarrhoea (Davidson *et al.*, 1979).

Saccharin and cyclamate are artificial sweeteners, and their sweetness compared with sucrose is 240–350 and 30–80 respectively (Table 2.10). However, due to possible toxic effects, cyclamate has been banned in many countries as an additive, and although saccharin is still permitted, its use is closely observed by food and drug administrators world wide. The use of these such sweeteners in the food industry is, therefore, restricted, and in the present context it should be noted that little information is available regarding the effect of the above sweetening agents on the activity of yoghurt starter cultures. However, Gautneb, Steinsholt and Abrahamsen (*loc. cit.*) reported an inhibition of acid production by *S. thermophilus* and *L. bulgaricus* when the yoghurt milk was fortified with a sweetening agent composed of 99.9 % sorbitol and 0.1 % saccharin, and hence as safeguard these types of sweetener should be added after the fermentation of the milk (see also Hyvonen and Slotte, 1983).

Any of these different types of sweetening agents could be employed for the manufacture of fruit/flavoured yoghurts, and the choice of any one particular "sugar" is determined by one or more of the following factors:

(a) Availability and cost of the sweetening compound; for these reasons it is probable that sucrose is the most widely used.
(b) Legal aspects; whether a certain "sugar" is permitted as a food additive, although since most sweetening agents are derived from natural products, with the exception of the artificial sweeteners, prohibition is unlikely.
(c) Storage facilities; granulated products are stored in multi-layer bags or large silos, and humidity control in the storage area is essential to prevent "caking"; details of bulk storage

39

requirements are discussed by Junk and Pancoast (*loc. cit.*) and Meade and Chen (*loc. cit.*); syrups are mainly stored in large metal containers or silos.

(d) Nutritional aspects—fructose is a very sweet sugar, and a sucrose/fructose syrup mixture, used at a low level, can provide both sweetness and a reduced calorie intake; in addition, fructose, like sorbitol, is absorbed only slowly into the bloodstream, and its use in "diabetic yoghurt" production is a clear possibility.

G. Addition of Miscellaneous Compounds

During the preparation of the basic mix, some yoghurt manufacturers add compounds to the milk with the aim of achieving certain rather specific objectives, and some examples of such additives are as follow.

1. Penicillinase

The intra-mammary injection of antibiotics is widely used for the treatment of mastitis in the dairy cow, and residues of these compounds in milk can inhibit the growth of *S. thermophilus* and *L. bulgaricus* (see Table 6.3). Although statutory regulations have been introduced in different countries to limit the level of these inhibitory compounds in milk, even the permitted values can reduce the activity of the yoghurt starter culture. As a result, methods have been sought to inactivate the different antibiotics, and notable success has been achieved in the case on penicillin. The inactivation of penicillin is carried out enzymatically using penicillinase (β-lactamase, EC 3.5.2.6), which is contained in the filtrate from different cultures of *Bacillus* species, and one such preparation is commercially available under the name Bacto-Penase (Anon., 1971). The β-lactamase is specific in hydrolysing cyclic amides, i.e. β-lactam in penicillin, thus producing an antibiotically ineffective compound; the structure of penicillin and the neutralising action of β-lactamase is illustrated in Fig. 2.12.

The activity of penicillinase preparations can be assayed by chemical or microbiological methods. Results from the former technique are expressed in Levy Units (LU) or Kersey Kinetic Units (KKU), while the microbiological method measures the "units" of penicillin being inactivated. For example, 1 ml of "Bacto-Penase" has a potency of 2000 LU, 200,000 KKU, or can inactivate 1,000,000 "units" of penicillin G; the "Bacto-Penase-Concentrate" is ten times more active than the standard penicillinase preparation.

In commercial practice, penicillinase is added to the milk with the rest of the dry ingredients; and it is recommended that it should be added at ambient temperature; high temperatures, e.g. as employed for the heat treatment of yoghurt milk, can inactivate it. However, it is important to note that penicillinase is only effective against penicillin, and that it should only be added to milk known to be contaminated with penicillin—a situation which is difficult to determine. Thus, routine addition to the yoghurt milk may prove uneconomical in the long run, especially as 60% of the antibiotics used in the United Kingdom for mastitis therapy are not penicillin(s).

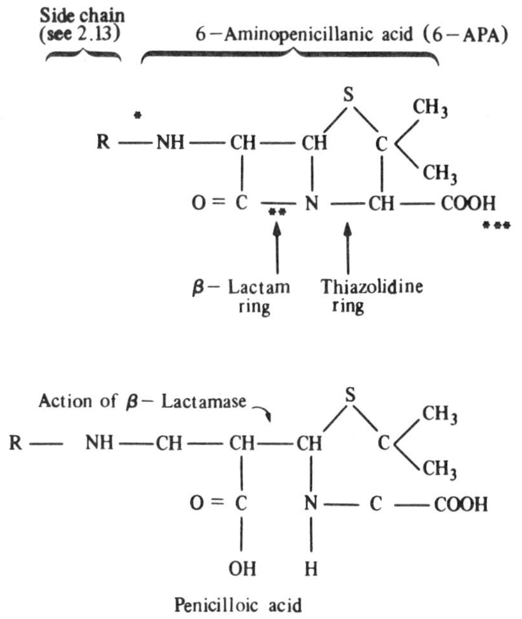

Fig. 2.12.   Basic structure of penicillin and the mode of action of β-lactamase

* Site of action of amidase
** Site of action of β-lactamase
*** Site of salt formation

The β-lactam ring of the 6-APA is split by the action of β-lactamase to produce a bacteriologically inert penicilloic acid; however, the specific action is reduced or increased by the nature of the side chain.

Adapted from Ball, Gray and Murdoch (1978), Edwards (1980).

2. Preservatives

Different types of preservative are used in the food industry, including the processing of fruits, where they are effective growth inhibitors against yeast and moulds. The addition of such fruits to yoghurt results in the carry-over of some of these compounds, and hence, in the United Kingdom for example (Food and Drugs Act, 1979—amended 1980), the following preservatives are permitted in fruit yoghurt, but not in natural yoghurt:

	sulphur dioxide	60	
	benzoic acid	120	
	methyl 4-hydroxybenzoate	120	
or			ppm or mg/kg
	ethyl 4-hydroxybenzoate	120	
	propyl 4-hydroxybenzoate	120	
	sorbic acid	300	

41

Side chain of 6–APA structure	Generic Name	Approximate amount of bacto–penase (s) LU/ml required to inactivate 30 and 300 mg of penicillins respectively*		Properties
	Ampicillin (D - α - aminobenzyl penicillin)	400	4,000	B,D & E
	Anicillin (2–biphenyl penicillin)	8,000	80,000	A,D & F
	Methicillin (2,6–dimethoxyphenyl penicillin)	4,000	40,000	A,C & F
	Nafcillin (2–ethoxy–1–naphthyl penicillin)	8,000	80,000	B,C & F
	Oxacillin (3–phenyl–5 methyl–4 isoxazolyl penicillin)	4,000	40,000	A,D & F
	Penicillin G (benzyl penicillin)	400	4,000	A,C & E
	Penicillin V (phenoxymethyl penicillin)	400	4,000	A,D & E
	Phenethicillin (DL –α–phenoxybenzyl penicillin)	400	4,000	A,D & E
	Cephalothin** (illustrating the tull structure)	8,000	80,000	B,C & F

$R_1 =$

$R_2 = -O - \overset{O}{\overset{\|}{C}} - CH_3$

In view of the fact that preservatives are allowed in fruit yoghurt, some manufacturers are inclined to fortify the basic mix with one of the above-mentioned preservatives in the hope of prolonging the keeping quality of the product. This approach is not, however, one to recommend, partly because the end-products may not comply with statutory regulations of an intended market, and partly because the presence of such compound(s) in the milk may affect the growth of the starter culture. One preservative which might be an exception to this rule, and which is widely used in the dairy industry (cheese and cheese products), is sorbic acid.

This compound is commercially available as a powder in the acid form ($CH_3.CH-CH.CH-CH.COOH$) or as the potassium or sodium salt ($CH_3.CH-CH.CH-CH.COOK$ or Na), i.e. potassium or sodium sorbate. These salts are used more commonly than the acid, and their antimycotic activity is released at low pH, i.e. < 6.5, where the salt is ionised to produce the free acid (Anon., 1974, 1981b). It should also be noted that K- or Na-sorbates yield only 75% of the inhibitory strength shown by sorbic acid.

For example:

$$0.13\% \text{ K or Na-sorbate} \cong 0.1\% \text{ sorbic acid} \cong 1000 \text{ ppm.}$$

Sorbic acid is a mycostatic agent in that it does not reduce the actual number of yeasts and moulds in the product, but merely inhibits their activity, perhaps by interfering with their dehydrogenase systems.

The effect of potassium on the activity of yoghurt starter cultures has been studied by Hamdan, Deane and Kunsman (1971), and they reported a reduction in growth, acid development and acetaldehyde production. The dose rate of potassium sorbate was 0.05 and 0.1 % by weight, which would be equivalent to 375 and 750 ppm of free sorbic acid respectively. The rate of acid production by three different commercial starter cultures is illustrated in Table 2.14, and it can be observed that at the lower concentration the inhibition delayed the processing time by 1 hour; the higher dose rate is, in any case, above the level permitted in the United Kingdom.

Since this type of preservative is obtained in a powder form, it is added to the yoghurt milk with the rest of the dry ingredients; the heat treatment of the milk does not affect the stability of sorbic acid or sorbates. However, in order to obtain maximum benefit from the preservative the yoghurt must be of good quality, and hence it is arguable whether its use is ever really justified.

HOMOGENISATION

Homogenisation means, quite literally, the provision of a homogeneous emulsion between two immiscible liquids, e.g. oil/fat and water. The types of emulsion that may exist in dairy products are divided into two categories:

Fig. 2.13. The structure of side chains of different types of penicillins and the amount of bacto-penase preparation(s) required to inactivate them

* 30 mg is treated with "Bacto-Penase", and 300 mg treated by 'Bacto-Penase-Concentrate'.

** Cephalothin is similar to the penicillins in so far it contains the β-lactam ring.

A) Narrow spectrum ⎫
B) Broad spectrum ⎬ in terms of its activity against bacterial species
C) Acid labile ⎭
D) Acid stable
E) None penicillinase resistant
F) Penicillinase resistant

Data compiled from Ball, Gray and Murdoch (*loc. cit.*), Edwards (*loc. cit.*), Anon. (1971), Rolinson and Sutherland (1973).

TABLE 2.14. *The effect of potassium sorbate $(C_3H_7O_2K)$ on pH values developed by three commercial yoghurt starter cultures (3% inoculation rate) incubated at 45°C*

Time of incubation in hours	Starter culture R$_1$			Starter culture 403			Starter culture 405		
	A	B	C	A	B	C	A	B	C
					pH				
2	4.75	5.00	5.10	4.75	4.90	5.15	4.85	5.05	5.25
3	4.35	4.60	4.70	4.40	4.50	4.60	4.45	4.65	4.75
4	4.10	4.40	4.50	4.20	4.30	4.40	4.20	4.40	4.50

(A) Control, no $C_6H_7O_2K$ added.
(B) Milk contains 0.05% by weight $C_6H_7O_2K$.
(C) Milk contains 0.1% by weight $C_6H_7O_2K$.

Adapted from Hamdan, Deane and Kunsman (*loc. cit.*).

TABLE 2.15. *Physical–chemical changes caused by homogenisation of milk used for yoghurt manufacture*

Effect of homogenisation	Changes related to yoghurt
Increase	
Viscosity	Reduction in fat globule size and increased adsorption on to the casein micelle which increases the effective total volume of "suspended" matter.
Xanthin oxidase activity	Due to the disruption of the fat globule membrane which contains about half of the enzyme present in milk.
Colour (Whiter)	Increase in number of fat globules which effects light reflectance and scattering.
Lipolysis	Increase in total fat surface area available to lipases. Destruction of fat globule membrane which may enhance lypolysis by the starter culture.
Proper mixing	Especially if milk is fortified with dried milk powder.
Phospholipids in skim milk	As result of the physical action, more fat globule membrane material is transferred to skim milk.
Foaming	As result of increased phospholipids in the skim milk phase, pumping of yoghurt milk can cause foaming in the incubation tanks.
Decrease	
Fat globule size	Prevents "cream line" formation in yoghurt, especially during incubation.
Oxidised flavour	Due to the migration of phospholipids to skim milk phase and formation of sulphydryl compounds which act as antioxidants; possibly through denaturation of whey proteins causing exposure of hidden SH groups.
Protein stability	Changes in protein–protein interaction as a result of some denaturation and shift in salt balance.
Agglutination and effective buoyancy	Decrease in fat clustering due to adsorption of casein micelles and sub-micelles to fat globules.
Casein in skim phase	Partial transfer to casein from skim milk to form a new membrane around newly formed small fat globules (see Fig. 2.14).
Syneresis	Increase in hydrophilicity and water binding capacity due to casein fat globule membrane interaction and other protein–protein interactions.

Adapted from Brunner (1974), Mulder and Walstra (1974), Harper (1976).
After Tamime and Deeth (*loc. cit.*).
Reprinted with permission of *Journal of Food Protection*.

(a) *Oil-in-water* emulsion where the oil droplets are dispersed in the aqueous phase—the majority of homogenised dairy products fall into this category.

(b) *Water-in-oil* emulsion where the water droplets are dispersed in the oil phase—a typical example is butter.

Yoghurt milk is a typical oil-in-water emulsion, and as a result the fat has a tendency to separate upon standing (especially in the fermentation tanks during the incubation period). In order to prevent this, the basic mix is subjected to high-speed mixing or homogenisation, i.e. forcing the milk under high pressure through a small orifice or annulus, and the overall relevance of this process to the manufacture of yoghurt is illustrated in Table 2.15.

However, these general effects are a reflection of the impact of homogenisation on specific milk constituents, and in particular as follow.

A. Effects on Milk Fat

The diameter of the fat globules in milk ranges from 1 to 10 μ, with an average around 3.5 μ. This variation in globule size is directly dependent on the same factors that influence the chemical composition of milk, i.e.

—breed of the cow,
—stage of lactation,
—age and health of the cow,
—type of feed, etc.

But the effect of homogenisation is to:

(i) reduce the average diameter of the fat globules to $< 2\mu$ (see Fig. 2.14);
(ii) prevent cluster formation and the tendency of the fat to rise to the surface;
(iii) decrease agglutination and effective bouyancy, due to the adsorption of casein micelles and submicelles.

B. Effects on Milk Proteins

The proteins in milk (casein and whey/serum protein) may undergo one or more of the following changes:

(a) denaturation of some serum protein may occur;
(b) casein/whey protein interactions may take place as result of denaturation of the latter type of protein and/or a shift in the salt balance;
(c) production of sulphydryl compounds from denatured whey proteins may be observed.

C. Effects on Miscellaneous Milk Constituents

These effects and/or changes are documented in Table 2.15.

45

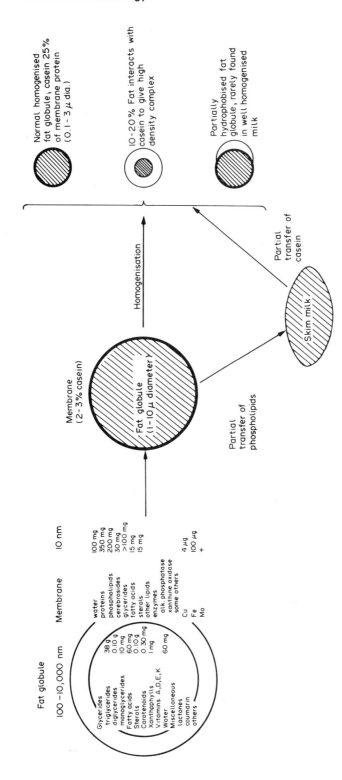

Fig. 2.14. Fat globule structure, composition and schematic representation of the effect of homogenisation on size

1 mm = 10^3 μm = 10^6 nm = 10^7 Å.

Adapted from Harper (*loc. cit.*), Mulder and Walstra (*loc. cit.*).

These desirable effects of homogenisation can only be achieved if certain processing conditions are observed, namely:

   (i) correct level of fat content in the process mix;
   (ii) correct homogenisation pressure;
   (iii) correct temperature of homogenisation.

The use of single- or double-stage homogenisation is only critical in products containing high levels of fat, e.g. cream, and since the fat in cream has a tendency to recluster, double-stage homogenisation is recommended. However, yoghurt milk is usually processed through a single-stage homogeniser at around 50–70°C, and at pressures ranging between 100–200 kg/cm². Pressures up to 300 kg/cm² have been reported, but in practice they are not widely used.

In some instances homogenisation of the yoghurt milk takes place after heat treatment of the basic mix, but this approach carries with it the risk of contamination unless high standards of hygiene are observed. The improved viscosity of yoghurt that is reported to follow homogenisation of the milk is due primarily to:

   (a) the change in water-holding capacity of the milk proteins which tends to reduce syneresis (Grigorov, 1966a);

   (b) the increased amount of milk fat globule membrane material, i.e. phospholipids and proteins, in the skim phase may also improve the water-holding capacity of the coagulum (Samuelsson and Christiansen, 1978);

but the processing conditions (temperature and pressure) employed during the homogenisation of the basic mix can affect the extent of any changes. Thus, Storgards (1964) produced an increase in the viscosity of sour milk by progressively increasing the pressure of homogenisation without heating the milk; a similar trend was also reported for milk subjected to heat treatment (Fig. 2.15); this effect was previously reported by Galesloot (1958), and a summary of his results is presented in Table 2.16. More recently Abrahamsen and Holmen (1981) studied the quality of goat's milk yoghurt manufactured from homogenised and non-homogenised milks concentrated by different methods, and they concluded that:

   (i) homogenisation of goat's milk was essential for yoghurt production (Fig. 2.16);

   (ii) a reduction in the consistency of set yoghurt was reported after 14 days' storage, and the best results were obtained when the goat's milk was concentrated using ultrafiltration;

   (iii) goat's milk yoghurt had a lower viscosity than yoghurt made with cow's milk, due to the low protein content of the former milk (Abrahamsen and Holmen, 1980, 1981).

HEAT TREATMENT

Although the application of heat, i.e. the boiling of milk, has long been practised during the manufacture of yoghurt as a method to increase the concentration of milk solids in the basic mix,

47

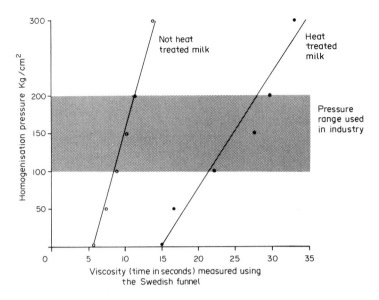

Fig. 2.15.   Effect of homogenisation pressure on the viscosity of sour milk

Data compiled from Storgards (*loc. cit.*).

TABLE 2.16.   *The effect of homogenisation and heat treatment on the consistency/viscosity of yoghurt*

Measurement of consistency/viscosity of yoghurt	Heat treatment of milk for 30 minutes at							
	70°C		78°C		86°C		95°C	
	A	B	A	B	A	B	A	B
Falling sphere (depth in cm)	3.0	> 15.0	1.5	10.5	1.2	6.0	1.2	2.7
Posthumus funnel (time in seconds)	9.0	5.0	14.0	7.5	17.0	8.5	18.7	9.0

"Falling Sphere"—The deeper the sphere sinks into the yoghurt, the thinner is the product.
"Posthumus Funnel"—The longer the time required for the yoghurt to pass through the funnel, the more viscous is the product.
A—Homogenised milk.
B—Non-homogenised milk.

Data compiled from Galesloot (*loc. cit.*).

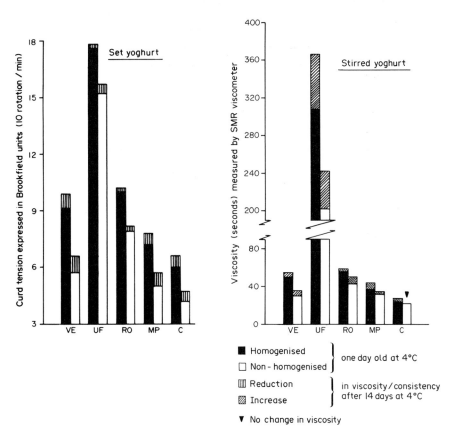

Fig. 2.16.   Viscosity/consistency of goat's milk yoghurt (homogenised and non-homogenised) concentrated in different methods and stored for 1 to 14 days at 4°C

VE—Vacuum Evaporation
UF—Ultrafiltration
RO—Reverse Osmosis
MP—Milk Powder Addition
  C—Control

Data compiled from Abrahamsen and Holmen (1981).

TABLE 2.17. *Some time–temperature combinations used during the processing of liquid milk and the yoghurt basic mix*

Time	Temperature (°C)		Process	Comments
30 minutes	65	Pasteurisation	Low temperature long time (Holder method)	Destruction of about 99 % of vegetative cells of micro-organisms
15 seconds	72		High temperature short time (HTST)	
*30 minutes	85		High temperature long time (HTLT)	Kills all vegetative cells and possibly some spores
*5 minutes	90–95		Very high temperature short time (VHTST)	
20 minutes (+)	110–115		Conventional sterilisation (in-bottle)	As above, but may kill nearly all spores
*3 seconds	115	Ultra-High Temperature	Low temperature UHT (GEA Ahlborn Gmbh)	Kills all organisms including all spores with the exception of low temperature UHT
*16 seconds	135		Long time UHT (Stork-Amsterdam)	
1–2 seconds	140		UHT	
0.8 seconds	150		UHT French process (ATAD)	

* Heat treatments which are widely used in the yoghurt industry.
(+) Indicates longer holding time.

Adapted from Davis (1968), Ged and Alias (1976), Lyster (1979).

in this present context the effects of heat treatment can be broadly summarised as:

(a) destruction and/or elimination of pathogens and other undesirable micro-organisms;

(b) production of factors stimulatory/inhibitory to the yoghurt starter cultures;

(c) changes in the physicochemical properties of the milk constituents.

In commercial practice, milk for the manufacture of yoghurt is heated at different temperatures, and the reported treatments, including the processing of "liquid milk", are illustrated in Table 2.17. The choice of any one particular time–temperature combination is based on a number of factors, but assuming that there are no limitations imposed by the plant itself, those mentioned above tend to be the dominant considerations.

A. The Destruction of Pathogens

The heat treatment of the yoghurt milk (Table 2.17) is sufficient enough to kill the majority, if not all, of the vegetative cells of micro-organisms associated with raw milk (Gilmour and Rowe, 1981), but spore-formers and some heat-stable enzymes will remain. This reduced competition ensures that the heated milk will provide a good growth medium for the yoghurt starter culture, but nevertheless, the bacteriological quality of the raw milk and any dry ingredients used in the basic mix is of great importance.

Thus, a high level of psychotrophic bacteria can break down both the casein (β and α_{s1}- DeBeukellar *et al.*, 1977) and the fat constituents in milk, and while the degradation of casein can lead to the formation of a weak coagulum and subsequent whey separation, hydrolytic rancidity can give rise to serious off-flavours (Cousin, 1977; Cousin and Marth, 1977a, b). It is also important that the enzymes (peptide hydrolases and lipases) of some *Pseudomonas* spp. are heat stable, and extremely high heat treatments are required to inactivate them, i.e. 150°C (Mayerhofer *et al.*, 1973; Adams, Barach and Speck, 1975; Barach, Adams and Speck, 1976; Kishonti, 1975; Hedlung, 1976; Adams and Brawley, 1981). Fortunately, the survival of these enzymes has not been identified as a significant problem in the yoghurt industry (Cogan, 1977).

B. Production of Stimulatory/Inhibitory Factors

The heating of milk can result in the release of certain factors that can either stimulate or inhibit the activity of lactic starter cultures, and the work of Greene and Jezeski (1957a, b, c) summarises the overall events as:

(1) stimulation of the starter culture in milk heated between 62°C for 30 minutes and 72°C for 40 minutes;

(2) inhibition of the starter culture in milk heated between 72°C for 45 minutes and 82°C for 10–120 minutes or 90°C for 1–45 minutes;

(3) stimulation of the starter culture in milk heated between 90°C for 60–180 minutes and autoclaving at 120°C for 15–30 minutes;

(4) inhibition of the starter culture in milk heated by autoclaving (120°C) for more than 30 minutes.

The apparent stimulation/inhibition/stimulation/inhibition cycle was due to changes in the serum or whey proteins, and the above cycle could be simulated by the addition of denatured whey proteins or cysteine hydrochloride. The transition from one cycle to another, in response to the different heat treatments, could well reflect the release of the denatured nitrogenous compound(s), e.g. at concentrations of 0.15–0.20 mg/ml, or from 10 to 20 γ/ml of cysteine, for when cysteine was added artificially it augmented the sulphydryl groups made available by heating; cysteine became stimulatory in raw and low heat milks, but in highly heated milks the same concentration became inhibitory. Taking this idea further, the same worker offered the following explanation for the stimulation/inhibition cycle:

(i) the initial stimulation was attributed to the multitude of factors listed in Table 2.19;

(ii) the addition of cysteine, glutathione or thioglycolate and the expulsion of oxygen resulted in the stimulatory effect;

(iii) the inhibition was due to an excess concentration of cysteine in the milk, accompanied by an increase in toxic volatile sulphides;

(iv) the second cycle of stimulation was due to a reduction in the level of toxic sulphides as a result of further heating, or perhaps the formation of formic acid.

Dutta, Kuila and Ranganathan (1973) investigated the effect of different heat treatments on acid and flavour production by various single strains of lactic acid bacteria, including *S. thermophilus* and *L. bulgaricus*, and a summary of their work is given in Table 2.18.

Overall the degree of heating had a rather variable effect on the activity of the yoghurt starter cultures, and the reasons for this behaviour were not discussed.

TABLE 2.18. *Effect of heat treatment of milk on the activity of yoghurt starter cultures*

Value	S. thermophilus			L. bulgaricus		
	63°C/ 30 min	85°C/ 30 min	Steaming/ 30 min	63°C/ 30 min	85°C/ 30 min	Steaming/ 30 min
Titratable acidity (% lactic acid)	1.00	0.85	0.66	1.60	1.70	1.62
Volatile acidity (ml of 0.01 N NaOH/50 g of curd)	9.00	9.00	7.00	40.00	34.50	31.00
Diacetyl (ppm)*	13.00	12.00	6.00	12.00	13.00	0.00
Proteolytic activity (mg of tyrosine liberated/g of curd)	0.34	0.25	0.18	0.25	0.18	0.09

* Level of diacetyl is abnormally high (see Chapter 7).
After Dutta, Kuila and Ranganathan (*loc. cit.*).
Reprinted with permission of *Milchwissenschaft*.

TABLE 2.19. *Chemical and physical effects of heat treatment of milk and their relevance in yoghurt manufacture*

Milk constituent	Heat-induced changes	Relevance in yoghurt manufacture	Consequences for yoghurt
Nitrogenous Whey proteins	Denaturation and aggregation, inactivation of immunoglobulins	Almost complete	Destruction of lactenins, reduction in creaming ability
	Active SH group production	Maximum at 90°C/10 min	Cooked flavour, lowering of Eh, formation of antioxidant properties
	α-La–β-Lg interaction	Occurs before interaction with κ-casein	Contributes to gel stability
	β-Lg–κ-casein interaction	Very significant	Minimises syneresis, increases micelle size, stabilises gel
Casein	Partial hydrolysis, release of glycopeptide from κ-casein	Of limited significance	Slight increase in free amino acids and peptides
	Dephosphorylation	Very little	Slight redistribution of phosphorus
	Aggregation, disaggregation, interchain cross-linking, e.g. by isopeptide bonding	Occurs especially with smaller micelles	Increase in micelle size and formation of protein network
Enzymes	Inactivation	Destruction of lipases and proteases from milk and from bacteria	Minimises rancid and bitter off-flavours
Other	Decomposition of amino acids to flavour compounds	Significant effect	Contributes to flavour
	Amino acid–lactose interaction, Maillard reaction, Schiff's base formation, reduction in available lysine	Occurs to only small degree, e.g. lysine loss c. 0.3%	Slight decrease in nutritive value, significant where yoghurt fortified with high-heat powders and concentrates
	Amino acid–amino acid interaction, e.g. formation of lysino-alanine	Occurs to a limited degree	Minimal
Carbohydrates Lactose	Decomposition to form organic acids, furfural and hydroxymethylfurfural	Occurs to small extent	Reduces pH and Eh, produces formic acid and affects growth of starter cultures, contributes to yoghurt flavour
Other	Reaction with amino acids (see above) Decrease in sialic acid and hexosamines, increase in hexoses	Occurs at 85°C/10 min	Unknown
Miscellaneous Fat	Formation of lactones, methyl ketones and other volatile ketones	Occurs to small degree	Contributes to flavour
	Hydrolysis	Insignificant	Insignificant
Vitamins	Destruction of some water-soluble vitamins	C, B_1, B_6, B_{12}, folic acid, reduced	Reduction in nutritive value
Minerals	Redistribution of Ca, P, Mg between soluble and colloid forms	Significant effect, modifies surface structure of casein micelle	Reduces pH, affects curd particles, decreases coagulation time
Micro-organisms	Destruction	Elimination of pathogens and organisms which may affect quality of yoghurt	Ensures public safety and minimises quality defects
Gases	Reduction in level of dissolved oxygen, nitrogen and carbon dioxide	Produces micro-aerophilic environment for starter culture	

Compiled from Tamime and Deeth (*loc. cit.*).
Reprinted with permission of *Journal of Food Protection*.

C. Changes in the Physicochemical Properties of Milk

Fresh liquid milk is composed of around 87% water and 13% total solids (Fig. 2.2), and the composition of yoghurt milk (after being standardised and/or fortified) is slightly altered to 84–86% water and 14–16% total solids. It may appear from such data that milk is simple in its composition, but on the contrary, milk has a very complex structure (see Fig. 2.2), even though its constituents are mainly water, carbohydrates, fat, proteins and minerals. These different components appear to be dispersed between two colloidal systems, i.e. the fat globules and their membranes (Fig. 2.14), and the casein micelle complexes. In general, both colloidal systems are heat stable, but the effects of heat treatment on them, and the relevance of these to yoghurt manufacture, are summarised in Table 2.19. It is apparent from this data that the yoghurt milk undergoes several changes during the heat treatment.

1. Effect on the proteins

Detailed studies of the proteins in cow's milk have been reported by Cheeseman (1975), Whitney *et al.* (1976) and Banks, Dalgleish and Rook (1981), and the various constituents that go to make up the total protein content of milk are:

Casein		76–88% of total protein
α_{s1}-	45–55	
β-	25–35	% of fraction indicated
κ-	8–15	
γ-	3–7	
Whey proteins		15–22% of total protein
Serum albumin	0.7–1.3	
β-lactoglobulin	7–12	% of fraction indicated
α-lactalbumin	2–5	
Immunoglobulin	1.9–3.3	
Proteose/peptones		2–6% of total protein

The casein in milk constitutes the major group of bovine proteins, and they play an important role during the manufacture of certain dairy products, e.g. yoghurt and cheese. The structure of these proteins is not well established, although some models have been proposed, but in general the caseins exist as micelles or aggregates of "sub-micelles" which are basically formed of α_s- and β-casein, stabilised by κ-casein in association with calcium and calcium phosphates (Banks, Dalgleish and Rook, *loc. cit.*).

The other types of proteins, i.e. serum or whey proteins, appear to be in solution, and they have a more defined, compact, globular shape than the caseins. This structure is due to the formation of disulphide bonds (as a result of the cysteinyl residues present), the lack of phosphate groups, and the fact that they do not react with calcium or aggregate together in the native state (Banks, Dalgleish and Rook, *loc. cit.*). The function of properties of the whey proteins become more apparent after heating of the milk, for at temperatures above 80°C they are denatured, and react/bind with κ-casein to form a more stable micelle.

A good example of this effect is observed when milk is heated to 90°C (forewarmed) for a period of time that ensures complete reaction between the different types of proteins, for it can then be heated to 120–140°C to give a stable end-product, e.g. UHT milk. Comparative data of the effect of heat on the milk proteins (including caseins) of different species is illustrated in Table 2.20.

TABLE 2.20. *Changes (%) in nitrogenous fractions of milk from different species after heating*

Nitrogen fraction	Cow			Goat			Sheep		
	63°C/ 30 min	80°C/ 10 min	120°/ 15 min	63°C/ 30 min	80°C/ 10 min	120°C/ 15 min	63°C/ 30 min	80°C/ 10 min	120°C/ 15 min
Casein	+ 0.60	+ 14.95	+ 18.77	0	+ 24.43	+ 25.31	+ 3.98	+ 26.35	+ 2.35
Non-casein	− 1.61	− 45.63	− 57.77	0	− 35.90	− 41.81	− 10.50	− 68.06	− 76.05
Soluble protein	− 2.23	− 62.40	− 89.48	0	− 58.08	− 70.58	− 15.07	− 79.39	− 93.96
β-Lactoglobulin	− 1.80	− 59.56	− 94.30	0	–	− 100.00	− 34.65	− 74.25	− 100.00
Non-protein	0	0	+ 25.00	0	+ 4.76	+ 4.76	+ 11.36	+ 15.00	+ 15.00

Adapted from Ramos (1978).

The formation of gels during the manufacture of certain dairy products is basically due to the destabilisation of the casein complex. These gels are irreversible, and are classified into three different groups: firstly, *enzymic gels*, which are formed as the result of rennet action which destabilises the κ-casein allowing aggregation of the casein, in the presence of calcium ions; secondly, *heat-induced gels*, which can arise as a fault where gelation occurs in UHT milk or evaporated milk if the protein fraction is not well stabilised; and thirdly, *acid gels* formed by the acid fermentation of milk, e.g. yoghurt.

It is likely that the stability of the yoghurt coagulum is primarily dependent on the formation of an acid gel, and to a lesser degree to the type of "heat" gel reported by Banks, Dalgleish and Rook (*loc. cit.*), and confirmation of this view can be gleaned from the following:

(a) The optimum hydrophilic properties of the proteins, and hence coagulation of the yoghurt mix, are obtained when the milk is heated to 85°C for 30 minutes (Grigorov, 1966b, c), and the effect of different heat treatments on the coagulation of cow's milk is shown in Table 2.21. The observed improvements in the rate of gel formation are possibly due to interactions between the β-lactoglobulin (β-Lg) and the casein, since heating milk at 80°C for 30 minutes denatures more than 90% of the β-Lg as compared with only 60% of the α-lactalbumin (α-La) (Larson and Rolleri, 1955). Maximal hydration of the protein, according to Grigorov (1966c), occurs when milk is heated at 85°C, and decreases gradually as the temperature rises; this view is shared by many researchers, including Prodanski (1967) and Iyengar, Nambudripad and Dudani (1967). This decrease in the hydrophilic properties of the casein/β-Lg complex can adversely affect the quality of the yoghurt, possibly increasing the tendency to syneresis, and hence, ignoring other

TABLE 2.21. *Effect of heat treatment on the coagulation process during the manufacture of yoghurt*

Item	Heat treatment of milk					
	85°C	85°C/ 30 min	90°C	90°C/ 30 min	95°C	95°C/ 30 min
Coagulation time (hr)	2.43	2.01	2.34	2.04	2.29	2.04
Acidity at coagulation (% lactic acid)	0.63	0.49	0.63	0.50	0.63	0.50
pH at coagulation	4.70	5.16	4.78	5.12	4.80	5.08

Adapted from Grigorov (1966b).

considerations, the heat treatment of milk intended for the production of yoghurt should not exceed 85°C.

(b) The effect of heat on the proteins, according to Parry (1974), is a two-stage process: firstly, the structure is altered, causing denaturation, and secondly, aggregation takes place followed by coagulation, depending on the level and duration of heating; β-Lg undergoes such a process where —SH groups are reactivated as a result of heating (Jenness and Patton, *loc. cit.*). The aggregates are of two sizes, depending upon which reactive groups are involved, i.e small aggregates of β-Lg (3.7 S) with interlinking —SH groups, and larger aggregates of β-Lg (29 S) in which the formation of disulphide (—SS) bonds may be important (Sawyer, 1969; Lyster, *loc. cit.*; McKenzie, 1971).

Information published on the heat denaturation of β-Lg has long recognised the interaction between β-Lg and κ-casein, but recent reports by Elfagm and Wheelock (1977, 1978a, b) suggest α-La is also involved. In brief the interaction is as follows:

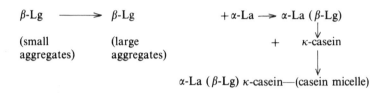

(c) Scanning electron microscope (SEM) studies on the structure of gels derived from heated and unheated milks revealed some distinctive characteristics of the casein micelles. In heated milks the gel is formed as the casein micelles gradually increase in size and form a *chain matrix*. This behaviour results in an even distribution of the protein throughout the yoghurt, and the aqueous phase is immobilised within the network; the resultant coagulum is firm and less susceptible to syneresis. On the other hand, the casein micelles in the unheated milk form *aggregates or clusters* in which the protein is unevenly distributed, and this heterogeneity impairs the immobilisation of the water; the coagulum is much weaker, i.e. by 50 % compared with the previous coagulum (Kalab and Harwalker, 1973, 1974; Kalab, Emmons and Sargant, 1976; Kalab, 1979a, b; Harwalker and Kalab, 1980). The contrast is well illustrated in Fig. 2.17.

(d) An investigation of milks subjected to heat (95°C for 10 minutes) revealed filamentous appendages composed of β-Lg/κ-casein, and the interaction appears to involve —SS linkages, and possibly the involvement of various salts, e.g. calcium phosphate and citrates (Davies *et al.*, 1978; Harwalker and Kalab, 1981). These appendages tend to become "diffuse" after fermentation, but their presence in the coagulum of heated milks inhibited micellar coalescence, so giving rise to firmer curds with reduced tendencies to syneresis.

(e) SEM studies by Kalab (1979a) showed that *S. thermophilus* and *L. bulgaricus* form "pockets" in the protein matrix of the yoghurt coagulum. These "pockets" were regarded by some workers in this field as artifacts caused by freeze-drying of the sample, but both transmission electron microscopy (TEM) and the freeze-fracturing of yoghurts, i.e. sectioning while the aqueous phase is still present, confirmed the presence of the "pockets" (Kaleb, 1982a); Fig. 2.18 shows some lactic acid bacteria in a "void space". Furthermore, SEM micrographs (Kalab, 1979b) also revealed the filaments of polysaccharide produced by "slime" or "ropy" strains of yoghurt starter cultures, and Fig. 2.18 illustrates how such filaments are attached to the protein matrix (see also Brooker, 1979).

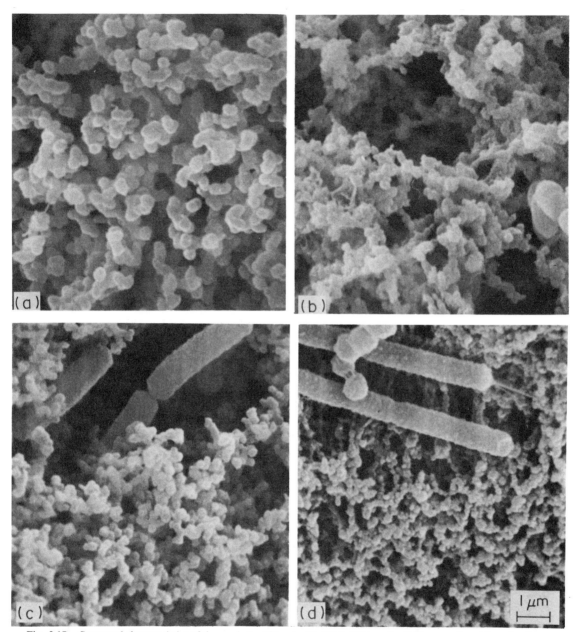

Fig. 2.17.   Structural characteristics of the casein in different milk (10 & 20% total solids) reconstituted from low heat skim milk powder and heated to 90°C, or unheated for 10 minutes

(a)   Unheated milk (10% TS)
(b)   Heated milk (10% TS)
(c)   Unheated milk (20% TS)
(d)   Heated milk (20% TS)
   Notice the differences in the structure of the coagulum in unheated and heated milks (a and b or c and d), and the size of the casein micelle as the level of solids increases in the milk (b and d).

After Kalab (1979a, 1982a).

(f) Dimensions of the casein particles in yoghurt milk are affected by the level of the total solids in the basic mix, and Kalab (1979b, 1982b) observed that the size of the casein particles decreased with increasing levels of solids in the milk (see Fig. 2.17a, b, c, d); the reason for this behaviour is not well established.

(g) Normal creaming in cold milk is influenced by the action of the globulins, which assist in the formation of clusters among the rising fat globules (Mulder and Walstra, *loc. cit.*). Therefore, the denaturation of the globulin fractions in milk, as a result of heat treatment, causes a reduction in the cream layer (Jenness and Patton, *loc. cit.*). This action could work in favour of the small yoghurt producers whose production lines do not include a homogeniser. Furthermore, milk becomes whiter in colour on heat treatment, before the appearance of browning, and according to Burton (1954) this could be due to:

(i) flocculation of the whey proteins;
(ii) changes in the casein aggregates;
(iii) calcium being converted from the soluble state to a colloidal or insoluble form.

2. Effects on other milk constituents

It is evident that the component(s) in milk which are most dramatically modified by heat treatment, at the temperatures practised in the yoghurt industry, are the whey proteins, but other heat-induced changes that can occur in milk, and are of some significance, include:

(a) The increased surface area of the fat globule, as a result of homogenisation at 60°C or above, is occupied partly by the membrane material and partly by surface-active components such as casein or denatured whey proteins. Lyster (*loc. cit.*) suggested that it is more likely to be the whey proteins, since at these low temperatures only slight modification/denaturation of the whey proteins will have taken place.

(b) The heating of milk can affect the state of the milk salts, particularly calcium, phosphate, citrate and magnesium. Thus these salts may exist in milk as soluble ions, or in the colloidal phase as part of the casein micelle complex, and heating milk to 85°C for 30 minutes can change up to 16% of the soluble calcium into the colloidal phase (Kannan and Jenness, 1961).

(c) Miscellaneous changes

(i) Undesirable flavours in milk are removed by ordinary heat treatments, but severe heating can induce off-flavours, e.g. the caramel flavour that results from the Maillard reaction between lactose and the amino groups of the proteins.
(ii) The viscosity of the milk is improved, and according to Labropoulos, Lopez and Palmer (1981) UHT milk (149°C for 3.3. seconds) had an apparent viscosity of 2.7 centipoises (cP) and HTLT (82°C for 30 minutes) was 2.3 cP; however, the apparent viscosity of yoghurt prepared from UHT and HTLT treated milks were 0.8 and 3.8 cP after 14 minutes' shear (shear rate $\gamma = 29.4$ sec^{-1}). It is evident that heating the yoghurt milk at 82°C produced a more viscous yoghurt.

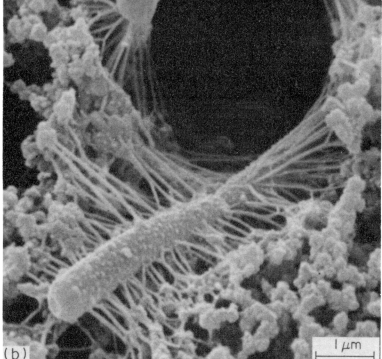

Fig. 2.18.   Filaments anchoring lactic starter cultures in the protein matrix of the yoghurt

(a)   After Kalab (1979b).
(b)   After Tamime, Kalab and Davies (1984).

Reprinted with permission of *Scanning Electron Microscopy*

(iii) The vitamins in milk are subdivided into two main groups, the so-called *fat-soluble vitamins* (e.g. A, D, E and K) associated with the fat component of milk, and the *water-soluble vitamins* (e.g. B group and C). The former vitamins are fairly heat stable, while vitamins B_6, B_{12} and C are heat labile, and Table 2.22 illustrates the percentage losses of the heat-sensitive vitamins in milk during different heat treatments. The relatively high heat treatments used in yoghurt manufacture may, therefore, cause significant decreases in some vitamins; the presence of dissolved oxygen greatly enhances the sensitivity of the heat-labile vitamins (Hartman and Dryden, 1974).

TABLE 2.22. *Typical values of vitamin losses (%) from milk during different heat treatments or processes*

Vitamins	Pasteurisation				UHT	Evaporated	Dried	
	HTST		Holder	In-bottle sterilisation*			Roller	Spray
Thiamine (B_1)	<10		10	20–35	10	20–60	20–30	10–15
Riboflavin (B_2)		(N)		<10	10	0	10–15	<10
Folic acid	0		0	40–50	15	(–)	(–)	(–)
Biotin		<10		<10	<10	10–15	10–15	10–5
Pantothenic acid		(N)		<10	<10	<10	<10	<10
B_6	0		10	60–90	<10	90	20	35
B_{12}	10		20	40–50	10	60	30	20

* Heat treatments used – 110°C for 15 minutes and 115°C for 30 minutes; higher losses resulted in latter treatment.
(–) Data not available.
(N) Negligible.
  Vitamins not listed (A, D, E, K, Niacin and B_6) are not affected.
After: Chapman *et al.* (1957), Porter and Thompson (1972), Kon (1972).

It should be noted, however, that most of this technical data is collated from studies carried out on whole or skim milk, and although the various ultimate physicochemical changes will occur in the yoghurt milk, the extent may be dependent on the composition of the basic mix.

FERMENTATION PROCESS

During the manufacture of yoghurt, the heat-treated milk is cooled to the incubation temperature of the starter culture (*S. thermophilus* and *L. bulgaricus*), and in general the milk is fermented at 40–45°C, i.e. the optimum growth condition for the mixed culture—the *short incubation method*. In some cases the incubation period can be as short as $2\frac{1}{2}$ hours, assuming that the starter culture (3%) is an active one and the ratio between the rods and the cocci is well balanced. However, the *longer incubation method*, i.e. overnight, can be used, and the incubation conditions are 30°C for around 18 hours, or until the desired acidity is reached (refer to Chapter 6 for further details).

While the cooled milk is being pumped to the fermentation tanks, the starter culture is normally metered directly into the milk, or alternatively, if a multi-purpose tank is being used, the starter culture is added either manually or, if the volume of the tank is large, the desired quantity of starter is pumped to the tank. As can be seen later, the actual fermentation stage can take place either in the retail container for the production of *set yoghurt*, or the milk is incubated in bulk for the manufacture of *stirred yoghurt*. However, no matter what type of yoghurt is being produced, the biochemical reactions responsible for the formation of the gel/coagulum are exactly the same, and the intricacies of the fermentation processes are discussed in detail in Chapter 7. Thus, the only real difference between set and stirred yoghurt is the rheological property of the coagulum, for in the former type the milk is left undisturbed during the incubation period, and the resultant gel is in the form of continuous semi-solid mass, while stirred yoghurts are, by contrast, the result of breaking the gel structure at the end of the incubation period prior to cooling and further processing (refer to Chapter 5 for further details).

Briefly, the formation of the yoghurt gel is the result of the following biological and physical actions on milk:

(a) The yoghurt starter culture utilises the lactose in milk for its energy requirements, and as a result the production of lactic acid and other relevant compounds becomes inevitable.
(b) The gradual development of lactic acid starts to destabilise the casein micelle/denatured whey protein complex by solubilisation of the calcium phosphate/citrates.
(c) Aggregates of casein micelles and/or the individual micelles group together and partially coalesce as the pH approaches the isoelectric point, i.e. pH 4.6–4.7.
(d) It is most likely that the α-La/β-Lg interaction with the κ-casein (linked by —SH and —SS bridges) partially protects the micelles against complete destabilisation or disruption, and as a result the gel network or matrix consists of a regular structure which entraps within it all the other constituents of the basic mix, including the water phase.

COOLING

Yoghurt production is a biological process, and cooling is one of the popular methods used to control the metabolic activity of the starter culture and its enzymes. Cooling of the coagulum commences directly after the product reaches the desired acidity, e.g. around pH 4.6 or 0.9 % lactic acid depending on the type of yoghurt produced, the method of cooling used and/or the efficiency of heat transfer.

Since the yoghurt organisms show limited growth activity around 10°C, the primary objective of cooling is to drop the temperature of the coagulum from 30–45°C to < 10°C (best at around 5°C) as quickly as possible so as to control the final acidity of the product.

The process of cooling yoghurt may be carried out using one of the following approaches.

A. One-phase Cooling

In this process the coagulum is cooled directly from the incubation temperature to <10°C prior to the addition of flavouring material(s) and packaging. This approach is based on the fact that a cold coagulum is more stable than one >20°C, and hence less damage will occur during the subsequent stages, e.g. mechanical handling while introducing the fruit/flavours, and filling the retail cartons.

B. Two-phase Cooling

The first phase of the cooling stage reduces the temperature of the coagulum from 30–45°C to 15–20°C prior to addition of the flavouring material(s) and filling. The *second* phase of cooling takes place in the cold store where the "coolish" yoghurt is cooled to < 10°C. The final cooling of yoghurt takes place, therefore, in the retail container, and as the coagulum is left undisturbed the viscosity of the yoghurt improves after 1–2 days' storage.

These two approaches to cooling are widely used in the industry for the production of acceptable, viscous yoghurts, and it is difficult to favour any one particular method. However, the influence of cooling rate on the physical characteristics of stirred yoghurt was recently evaluated at the Danish Dairy Research Institute (Anon., 1977), and they concluded their Report with the following recommendations:

(i) The quality of stirred yoghurt may be greatly improved by packaging yoghurt at 24°C, followed by final cooling of the product in the container.

(ii) To achieve the maximum effect on yoghurt quality, the second stage of cooling must be carried out as slowly as possible over a 12-hour period.

(iii) Concentration of the yoghurt milk, i.e. by evaporation and removal of approximately 10% water, was identified as the factor that most improved the quality of yoghurt.

(iv) The recommended procedure was as follows:

(1) before cooling commences, stir the yoghurt in the incubation tank until mixture is homogenous;

(2) cool the yoghurt (primary cooling) to 24°C and package;

(3) cool the packed yoghurt (secondary cooling) in a cold store controlled by a two-step temperature regulator, i.e. the first 5–6 hours at an air temperature of 7–10°C, and then at an air temperature of 1–2°C for the remainder of the cooling period;

(4) forced air circulation in the cold store is highly recommended to obtain uniform cooling of the packaged yoghurt;

(5) the design and construction of the crate and the material(s) used for packaging can affect the cooling rate of the packed yoghurt.

It should be noted, however, that the cooling of yoghurt starts at a relatively "high" pH value, and hence the rate of cooling (slow or fast) determines the final acidity in the product.

ADDITION OF FLAVOURING/COLOURING INGREDIENTS

The increase in the *per capita* annual consumption of yoghurt in the majority of the countries (see Table 1.2) has been attributed to both the ever-increasing availability of fruit and/or flavoured yoghurts, and to the diversity of presentations of the product. Thus, in the United Kingdom, for example, the yoghurt market in 1981 was valued at £103 million (i.e. £93 million for fruit yoghurts and £10 million for natural yoghurt), and these figures represent growth of 10 and 7% over the previous year's sales for each type of yoghurt respectively (Anon., 1982c).

A variety of different flavouring ingredients (fruits, natural flavours and/or synthetic flavours) are currently added to yoghurt, and Table 2.23 indicates the range of available additives. It can be observed that the flavours, which are in regular demand, are surprisingly few in number, and the rest are introduced by the yoghurt manufacturers merely to encourage a wider popularity for the product. The types of flavouring material used in the yoghurt industry are as follows.

A. Fruits

Fresh fruits can be used to flavour yoghurt, but due to the seasonal availability of such materials and their variable quality, their use in the industry is very limited. Processed fruits are, therefore, more widely employed, particularly as the desired fruit mixture can be standardised by the fruit processor to meet the specifications required by the customer, and these types of fruits are classified as follows.

1. Fruit preserves

In this case the fruit is processed in a small quantity of sugar syrup to give an end-product consisting of 70% fruit, 30% water, and this product may be referred to as "pure" or "natural", since no colouring matter or preservatives are added. Depending on the processing technique, the product may become highly aromatic, but the natural colours of any fruit become dull due to the effect of heat treatment. It is also relevant that such products are expensive, so that overall demand from the yoghurt industry is limited.

2. Canned fruit

This type of fruit is similar to the product mentioned above, except that canned fruits are permitted to contain certain additives, such as:

(a) colouring ingredients which help to mask the loss of the natural colours of the fruit;
(b) stabilisers which assist in protecting the structure of the processed fruit, and improve the viscosity of the fruit product;
(c) flavouring agents which help to enhance the consumer appeal of the finished yoghurt.

Canned fruit is packaged in special lacquered tin cans, plastic drums with polyliners or stainless steel tanks (Fig. 2.19). The level of sugar is maintained at 30–35% and the pH is adjusted to <3, and although this latter factor helps to protect the product against spoilage, it may lead to minor problems of whey separation. Different time/temperature conditions are used for the heat treatment of the various fruits, and the microbiological specifications of such products can either be "sterile" or to standards proposed by the fruit processors (see Table 10.3).

Although the processing of fruit is sometimes carried out by large dairy organisations, the majority of yoghurt manufacturers rely on the specialist fruit processors. Thus, fruit processing is a rather specialised procedure, and a brief description of what might take place is illustrated in Fig. 2.20.

TABLE 2.23. *Fruits and fruit flavours currently used in production of yoghurt*

	Regular demand	Average demand	Poor demand
I. Single	Apricot	Banana	Apple
	Black cherry	Bilberry	Cranberry
	Blackcurrant	Blackberry	Damson
	Mandarine	Gooseberry	Elderberry
	Peach	Grapefruit	Grape
	Pineapple	Lemon	Guanabana
	Raspberry	Melon	Guava
	Strawberry	Orange	Kiwi
		Plum	Lime
		Prune	Loganberry
		Rhubarb	Mango
		Tangerine	Passion fruit
			Pear
			Pina Colada
			Quince
			Redcurrant
			Wortleberry
II. Mixed	Fruit cocktail	Apple/Raisin	Cherry/Elderberry
	Peach/Raspberry	Apple/Orange	Kiwi/Gooseberry
	Raspberry/Redcurrant	Cherry/Orange	Peach/Passion fruit
		Cherry/Pineapple	Grape/Figs
		Mixed Citrus	Strawberry/Kiwi
		Pear/Banana	
		Strawberry/Blackberry	
III. Miscellaneous flavours	Buchwheat Honey	Moccaa	
	Butterscotch	Muesli	
	Champagne	Tomato	
	Chocolate	Vanilla	
	Coconut	Walnut	
	Coffee	Wine	
	Cucumber	Mirabella/Vanilla	
	Hazel nuts	Paprika/Celery	
	Honey	Pear/Vanilla	
	Maple syrup	Raspberry/Vanilla	
	Mint		

The classification of the above fruit/flavoured yoghurt is only applicable to the U.K. market as suggested by Tamime and Hamilton (1982) (unpublished data).

Data compiled from Robinson and Tamime (*loc. cit.*), Chase (1981), Anon. (1981a, b), Lang (1981a, b), Muller (1977).

Fig. 2.19. Different types of containers currently used for packaging of processed fruit for the yoghurt industry

(a) On-site filling lines using metal cans (2 or 5 kg capacity) and polypropylene buckets or drums fitted with polyliners which can be heat sealed or clipped with a plastic band. The covers are secured using metal lid-clips.
(b) Stainless steel tanks at washing and sterilisation bay used for $\frac{1}{2}$ tonne bulk containers for transport of processed fruit.

Reproduced by courtesy of G R Spinks & Co. Ltd., Devon UK; International Flavours & Fragrances (GB) Ltd., Suffolk, UK.

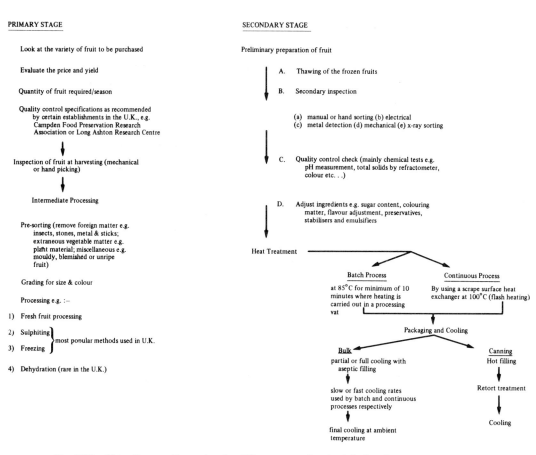

PRIMARY STAGE

Look at the variety of fruit to be purchased

Evaluate the price and yield

Quantity of fruit required/season

Quality control specifications as recommended
by certain establishments in the U.K., e.g.
Campden Food Preservation Research
Association or Long Ashton Research Centre

Inspection of fruit at harvesting (mechanical
or hand picking)

Intermediate Processing

Pre-sorting (remove foreign matter e.g.
insects, stones, metal & sticks;
extraneous vegetable matter e.g.
plant material; miscellaneous e.g.
mouldy, blemished or unripe
fruit)

Grading for size & colour

Processing e.g. :—

1) Fresh fruit processing

2) Sulphiting } most popular methods used in U.K.

3) Freezing

4) Dehydration (rare in the U.K.)

SECONDARY STAGE

Preliminary preparation of fruit

A.   Thawing of the frozen fruits

B.   Secondary inspection

(a) manual or hand sorting (b) electrical
(c) metal detection (d) mechanical (e) x-ray sorting

C.   Quality control check (mainly chemical tests e.g.
pH measurement, total solids by refractometer,
colour etc. . .)

D.   Adjust ingredients e.g. sugar content, colouring
matter, flavour adjustment, preservatives,
stabilisers and emulsifiers

Heat Treatment

Batch Process
at 85°C for minimum of 10
minutes where heating is
carried out in a processing
vat

Continuous Process
By using a scrape surface heat
exchanger at 100°C (flash heating)

Packaging and Cooling

Bulk
partial or full cooling with
aseptic filling

slow or fast cooling rates
used by batch and continuous
processes respectively

final cooling at ambient
temperature

Canning
Hot filling

Retort treatment

Cooling

Fig. 2.20.   Flow diagram illustrating the different stages involved during the processing of fruits

After Spinks (*loc. cit.*).

3. *Frozen fruits*

Some fruits can be frozen at around $-20°C$ for use whenever required. The product is then thawed, sweetened and finally heat-treated, and depending on the acidity of the fruit, the temperature of the heat treatment can vary from as low as $60°C$ to as high as $95°C$. Since the freezing process can damage the structure of the fruit, care must be exercised to minimise the injury, i.e. by harvesting the fruit at a certain degree of ripeness, quick freezing, and/or the addition of stabilisers during the heating stage. Colouring matter is sometimes added during processing to offset the "browning" reactions (enzymatic or oxidative) that can occur during thawing/subsequent heating. The final processing of frozen fruit can be carried out at the dairy, an approach which may be attractive to large-scale creameries.

4. Miscellaneous fruit products

(a) Fruit puree—the fruit is homogenised to give an end-product in the form of a paste. The shape of the fruit is lost altogether, and the fibrous material may also be removed.

(b) Fruit syrup—this is a clear product devoid of solid contents but with a sweetening agent added to it. It is used during the manufacture of flavoured set yoghurt or drinking yoghurt. In the former type, the syrup is added to the inoculated milk before the packaging and the incubation stages, but for drinking yoghurt the syrup could be added to the cold natural yoghurt.

(c) Jam—jam is only used during the manufacture of certain types of set yoghurt, or in the absence of other processed fruit sources. It is not advisable to add jam to stirred yoghurt since the high viscosity of jam may make it difficult to mix properly with the natural yoghurt, while prolonged mixing can result in whey separation or a reduction in the viscosity of yoghurt. If jam is used to flavour set yoghurt, a special metering device must be installed on the filling machine so that the required amount of jam is deposited in the carton before it is filled with the inoculated milk.

B. Flavouring Agents

Heat treatment of fruit preparations can result in a reduction in their flavour intensity, and hence it is the practice to add flavouring agents to compensate for such losses. Flavouring agents are divided into three categories depending on their source.

(i) natural flavours and flavouring substances   }
(ii) nature-identical flavouring substances   }   botanical origin
(iii) artificial/synthetic substances (chemical origin).

Although the above classification may seem simple, in actual fact the list of possible agents can run into thousands. Flavouring compounds of chemical/synthetic origin are sometimes used due to their provision of a flavour similar to that of a natural ingredient (see Table 2.24), but the list of permitted compounds varies from one country and another. In the United Kingdom the Food Standards Committee (1965, 1976) have proposed a list of flavouring agents which could be added to food, but it has not become a statutory instrument (see also FAO/WHO, 1979); these compounds are also used during the manufacture of "flavoured" (set or stirred), drinking, frozen and, possibly, dried yoghurt.

C. Miscellaneous Flavouring Ingredients

Different food products, including alcoholic drinks, have been used to flavour yoghurt (see Table 2.23), and some examples of these are:

TABLE 2.24. *Some popular varieties of yoghurt, and an indication of the additives (nature-identical and synthetic) that can enhance the flavour of a fruit base*[1]

Retail flavour	Compounds naturally present		Important synthetic compounds
	Character-impact compound[2]	Important contributory flavour compounds	
Apricot		γ-Decalactone γ-Octalactone Linalool 3-Methylbutryic acid	γ-Undecalactone
Banana	3-Methylbutyl acetate	Pentyl acetate Pentyl propionate Eugenol	
Bilberry		Ethyl 2- and 3-methylbutyrate trans-2-Hexenal	
Blackcurrant			trans- and cis-ρ-Methane-8-thiol-3-one
Grape, Concord	Methyl anthranilate		
Grapefruit	Nootkatone	Limonene Octanal Decanal	
Lemon	Citral	Limonene	
Orange		Limonene Linalool Octanal Ethyl butyrate Geranial β-Sinensal	
Melon	cis-6-Nonenal		
Peach		γ- and δ-Decalactone γ-Dodecalactone	γ-Undecalactone
Pear	Methyl and ethyl trans-2, cis-4-decadienoate		
Plum		Ethyl acetate Butyl acetate Hexyl acetate γ-Octalactone γ-Decalactone Benzaldehyde Linalool 2-Phenethanol Methyl cinnamate	
Raspberry	1-ρ-Hydroxyphenyl-3-butanone	cis-3-Hexenol Damascenone α- and β-Ionone	
Strawberry		Methyl and ethyl hexanoate Methyl and ethyl butyrate Ethyl 2-methylbutyrate cis-3-Hexenal	Ethyl 3-methyl-3-phenylglycidate
Tangerine		Methyl N-methylanthranilate Thymol Limonene	

1. Concentration is an important variable. Flavour houses are very skilled in providing concentrates of approved components in the appropriate proportions in an appropriate base. Whether and which compounds may be added differs by country, and is usually legally controlled.
2. A character-impact compound is one the odour of which by itself is already strongly characteristic of the named food. Data compiled from Nursten (1977), Buttery (1981).

 (i) sweet products (honey, maple syrup, butterscotch),
 (ii) nuts (coconut, hazel, brazil, walnut),
(iii) cereals (muesli),
(iv) vegetables (cucumber, tomato, celery),
 (v) miscellaneous (coffee, mocca, spices, paprika, vanilla).

D. Colouring Matter

The addition of colour to fruit and flavoured yoghurts is aimed at making the products more attractive, and the active agents may be of natural origin or synthetic organic dyes. The list of colours which may be used as food additives in the United Kingdom comes to around 39 in number, and their inclusion is covered by the Food and Drugs Act (1973) (amended 1975, 1976, 1978). Other countries have similar lists, but it should be noted that the colouring agents permitted in one country may not be identical to those allowed in another. However, the FAO/WHO (1976) have offered some guidance as to which colour compounds should be permitted and at what concentrations in yoghurt, assuming that the agents come entirely from the fruit/flavouring ingredients (see Table 2.25).

TABLE 2.25. *Permitted food colouring which comes exclusively from the flavouring ingredients*

Name of colouring matter	Colour index (1971) number	Maximum level (mg/kg)
Tartrazine	19140	18
Sunset Yellow FCP or Orange Yellow S	15985	12
Cochineal or Carminic acid*	75470	20
Carmoisine or Azorubine	14720	57
Ponceau 4R or Cochineal Red A	16255	48
Erythrosine BS	45430	27
Indigo Carmine or Indigotine	73015	6
Green S or Acid Brilliant Green BS or Lissamine Green*	44090	2
Caramel Colours 3	–	150
Black PN or Brilliant Black BN	28440	12
Beetreet Red or Betanin	–	250
Chocolate Brown FB*	–	30
Red 2 G	18050	30
F.D. and C. Blue No. 1 (Brilliant Blue FCF)	42090	–
Other colouring ingredients extracted from natural fruit and vegetable sources*	–	–

* Not yet cleared toxicologically.

After FAO/WHO (1976).

PACKAGING

Packaging is an important step during the production of yoghurt, and Paine (1967) has defined the objective of packaging food as follows:

"Packaging is a means of ensuring the safe delivery of product to the ultimate consumer in sound condition at minimum overall cost."

It is obvious, therefore, that if yoghurt is to reach the consumer in a sound condition, then the packaging material will play an important role, and that the retail package should be designed to meet the following aims.

1. Provide protection

Yoghurt is a highly perishable product, and the purpose of the container is to protect it against the environment, i.e.

—dirt or other foreign bodies;
—micro-organisms (bacteria, yeast and moulds) which can affect the keeping quality of yoghurt;
—gases, e.g. oxygen, which can help the yeasts and moulds to grow and spoil the product;
—light which may cause discolouration of fruit/flavoured yoghurts or possibly oxidation of the fat.

Product protection also seeks to avoid spillage, pilferage or loss by evaporation. The latter aspect is doubly important, since loss of moisture can affect not only the chemical composition of the product, but may also lead to deviations from the declared weight on the package and possible problems with the Weights and Measures Authorities. In addition, the package must prevent the loss of flavour volatiles or the absorption of undesirable odours.

2. Ease of handling

Yoghurt and yoghurt-based products usually exist in the form of viscous liquids, and hence the retail container must provide a convenient means of handling the product in the factory, during storage and transport, and throughout the sale period in supermarkets and shops.

3. Provide a message

The printing and other graphic work on the exterior of the package will serve to:

—provide the product with a "brand image" and/or display a message to persuade a potential buyer to purchase;
—contain the information proposed in the guidelines for food labelling, i.e.
(a) identity of the product;
(b) name and address of the manufacturer;
(c) approximate chemical composition of the product, or the ingredients listed in descending order by weight;
(d) expiry date;
(e) possible suggestions of recipes or other instructions for use.

4. Miscellaneous functions

In general a packaging material which is in direct contact with a foodstuff must be non-toxic, and no chemical reactions should take place between the material and the food product (refer to Crosby, 1981; Jensen, 1972). For these reasons plastics are widely used in the dairy industry, and due to the acidic nature of yoghurt, aluminium foil for lids, unless plastic "push-on" lids are more suitable.

It is against this general background that the following approaches to marketing yoghurt have evolved.

A. Types of Packaging Materials

Packaging materials for yoghurt are basically divided into two main categories:

1. The unit container—the vessel which comes into actual contact with the yoghurt, and the specifications mentioned above regarding the "ideal package" are applicable to such containers.
2. The outer or shipping container—does not come into contact with the yoghurt, but is used to facilitate handling and dispensing of the unit containers along the retail chain.

Different types of unit container are available on the market, and these packs may be classified into three main types depending on the physical strength of the container.

1. Rigid unit containers

(a) Glass bottles. Glass containers are still used in some countries to package yoghurt, e.g. France, Eastern Europe, and some parts of the Middle East (Fluckiger, 1980), and although glass is an excellent packaging material, its use is limited basically by the high cost of manufacture, and the current market trend in favour of "single-trip containers". Nevertheless, a few decades ago the glass bottle was very popular and even today wide-mouth glass bottles (see Fig. 2.21) are a most attractive form of packaging for flavoured drinking yoghurts; the closure is of the metal "pull-ring" type. However, the development of a closure system to heat-seal glass bottles using aluminium foil laminates could make the merits of the glass bottle as a packaging container worth considering anew.

Fig. 2.21.   A wide mouth glass bottle used in the United Kingdom for the packaging of drinking yoghurt

The glass bottle is manufactured by Rockware Glass Ltd., and it is sealed by using a metal closure, i.e. aluminium "pull ring" type.

Reproduced by courtesy of Bridge Farm Dairies Ltd., Suffolk, UK.

(b) Earthenware vessels. These types of pots are produced from clay, and that part of the container which comes in contact with the yoghurt is normally glazed. They are returnable, and are used in the Middle East and India to package set yoghurt and Dahi respectively. During the incubation period the pots are left uncovered so that a crust is formed on the surface, and before the cooling stage the pots are covered with parchment held firmly in position using a rubber band. These containers are not widely used due to the problems of achieving a high standard of hygiene and the cost of manufacture. Thus, Singh (1978) evaluated the microflora of earthenware pots used for Dahi, and he reported that high total counts, as well as coliforms, *Staphylococcus* spp. and yeast and moulds were normally present. Improvements in the microbiological standards of these pots could be achieved if the pots were immersed in boiling water for at least 2 minutes or water containing 250–500 ppm chlorine.

(c) Miscellaneous. For the packaging of some types of yoghurt-based products e.g. dried yoghurt, the use of metal cans is recommended, and the keeping quality of the product is improved by gas flushing (nitrogen or carbon dioxide)—the former gas is more widely used; these metal containers are similar to those used for packaging of whole milk powder. Rigid, semi-rigid or flexible plastic containers could also be used (see later), as could composite containers coated internally with a layer of plastics.

2. Semi-rigid unit containers

These types of container are normally manufactured from plastics, and some technical properties of the different types of plastic material that can be used for the manufacture of containers for yoghurt are shown in Table 2.26. The actual plastic materials, i.e. the polymers, are relatively inert, but the chemicals and monomers used during the fabrication stages can end up in the finished material. Although such compounds may be harmless *per se*, they can react with the food and give rise to off-flavours, and hence great care has to be exercised to ensure that such compounds are absent.

In the case of yoghurt, the container must be acid-resistant, prevent the loss of flavour volatiles and be impermeable to oxygen, since the presence of the latter can encourage yeast and moulds to grow.

Examples of materials which could be used for the manufacture of the yoghurt containers are: polyethylene (PE), polypropylene (PP), polystyrene (PS), polyvinyl chloride (PVC), polyvinylidene chloride (PVDC). In the United Kingdom the majority of the containers are manufactured from PS, although the use of PP is becoming popular. However, irrespective of the material, the containers can be either rigid, semi-rigid or flexible, and while the former categories are normally used to package set and stirred yoghurt, concentrated yoghurt and/or frozen yoghurt, the flexible type (i.e. film—see later) can only be used to package dry yoghurt-based products.

The finished containers are referred to as cartons, tubs or cups, and they can be manufactured in any shape or design that appears to possess "consumer appeal"; some typical examples are

TABLE 2.26. *Properties of some plastics film*

	Density range (g/ml at 20°C)	Water vapour (g/m² 24h at) (38°C & 90% RH)	Permeability* (ml/m² 24 h atmosphere at 23°C)			Basic structure of monomer	Molecular weight
			Oxygen	Carbon dioxide	Nitrogen		
Polyethylene (PE)						$CH_2 = CH_2$	28.05
Low density (LDPE)	0.915–0.925	12–20	6400–9600				
Medium density (MDPE)	0.926–0.940	12–20	6400–9600				
High density (HDPE)	0.941–0.965	5–8	2400–4000				
Ethylene vinyl acetate copolymer (EVA)		30–240	8000–13000				
Ionomers		800–1000	8000–11000				
Cross-linked oriented		10	7000–8000				
Polypropylene (PP)	0.52					$CH_2 = CH.CH_3$	42.06
Cast		10–14	2500				
Biaxially oriented		6–8	900–1800				
Biaxially oriented PVDC coated		4–6	0.2–1.0				
Polyvinyl chloride (PVC)	0.98				**(40–100)	$CH_2 = CH.Cl$	62.5
Rigid		14–80	** {75–450	** {300–1500			
Extruded flexible		80–400	{450–30000	{1500–90000			
Calendered flexible		60–400					
Polystyrene (PS)		60–70	3000–5000			$CH_2 = CH.\bigcirc$	104.14
Polyvinylidene chloride (PVDC)	1.22					$CH_2 = CCl_2$	96.95

* Film thickness 25 μm.
** Film thickness 100 μm.

Data adapted from: Crosby (*loc. cit.*), Briston (1980), BSI (1976).

illustrated in Fig. 2.22. Basically, there are two different techniques that can be used for the manufacture of "plastic" cups. Firstly, the Injection Moulding Process in which the material is softened in a heated cylinder prior to injection under high pressure into a cooler/mould where it hardens. After the cup is formed, it is ejected from the mould, and this type of container is characterised by having a relatively thick wall, i.e. it is a rigid cup. These preformed cups (see Fig. 2.22) are then delivered to the dairy "nested" in rows inside a thin PE bag, i.e. of 25 μm thickness. Usually the bags are sealed to prevent the ingress of dust or other contaminants, and are overwrapped with a fibre-board box to ensure safe transit and prevent crushing. At the dairy the rows of cups are fitted onto the filler, and the process of packaging is then referred to as a "fill/seal" operation. Secondly, the Thermoforming Process, in which the "plastic" material is delivered to the dairy in the form of a continuous roll, one end of which is then fed into the first section of the yoghurt filling/packaging machine. The sheet of "plastic" is heat-softened, and formed into or around a mould, so that the unit container is formed immediately prior to filling with the yoghurt. This system of packaging is referred to as a "form/fill/seal" operation. In the thermoforming process (Fig. 2.23) the yoghurt cups have a relatively lower wall thickness than those produced by the injection moulding system, and the containers could, therefore, be classified as "semi-rigid".

Fig. 2.22. Illustrations of some containers for the packaging of yoghurt.

(a) Cylindrical shape with a false bottom.
(b) Goblet shape and wide mouth Goblet shape which is used in some European countries.
(c) Cylindrical shape (most popular type used in the United Kingdom).
(d) Conical shape (used to be popular but not any more).
(e) Family size tubs suitable for 'push-on' plastic lids.

Fig. 2.23. Examples of thermoformed plastic containers.

(a) Clear plastic container;
(b) Opaque plastic containers (cylindrical or square in shape);
(c) Opaque wide mouth plastic container;
(d) Translucent 'glass cup shape' container;

a, b & c are supplied by Hassia machinery, and it can be observed that while the labelling is restricted mainly to the lids, the flat sided containers (a & c) provides an extra surface for promotion; container (d) is supplied by Sweetheart International Ltd., Hampshire, UK.

Reproduced by courtesy of Hassia Verpackung GmbH, Ranstadt, West Germany; Sussex & Berkshire Machinery, Hampshire, UK; Bridge Farm Dairies Ltd., Suffolk, UK.

Incidentally, the reels must be delivered to the dairy well overwrapped so that they do not get damaged in transit or storage.

Irrespective of what type of cups are used, closure of the container is usually achieved using aluminium foil (i.e. capping/crimping or heat sealing) or "plastic" press-on lids. Heat-sealed caps are more popular, since the cups are then watertight, and subsequent contamination and seepage are prevented. Aluminium foil is used because its permeability to gases and odours is negligible, and, in addition, it is greaseproof, opaque, "brilliant" in appearance and can be easily decorated. Because of the acidic nature of yoghurt, it is recommended that the foil should be lacquered to prevent corrosion, and to provide the cohesion during heat sealing the foil should be coated with PE, ethylene acetate copolymer (EVA), PS or PVC (see later for further details). Heat-sealed plastic lids are sometimes used, and the Bach Process (see Chapter 5) which was developed primarily for all plastic containers is illustrated schematically in Fig. 2.24.

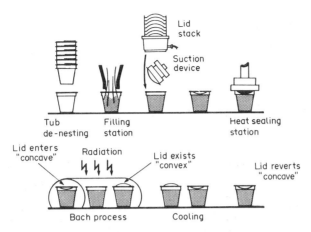

Fig. 2.24. Schematic illustration of how thermoformed plastic lids are applied to microwave processed yoghurt (Bach process).

Reproduced by courtesy of 4P Rube Göttingen GmbH, Göttingen, West Germany and Austin 4P Ltd., Watford, U.K.

Plastic packaging materials are also used in the yoghurt industry to provide so-called "fresh crunch" products for the consumer. An example of one such innovation was reported by Colangelo (1980) in which the yoghurt was packaged in what was referred to as a "piggy-back" configuration. In this system the flavoured yoghurt is filled and sealed into a plastic cup using a Flex-E-Fill machine supplied by the Sweetheart Division of the Maryland Cup Company. Either on the same machine, or on a different unit, the nuts, raisins and carob chips (known as granola) are filled into another transparent cup which is also heat-sealed. Then the yoghurt tub and the cup containing the granola slot together so that the latter container completely covers the yoghurt tub prior to the two packages being heat-sealed together. In theory, the freshness of the fruit/nut mixture is retained until the consumer mixes the two components together just before consumption, but there is little evidence to date that the additional labour is really justified.

3. Flexible unit containers

Flexible unit container(s) are either in the form of plastic sachets or paper cartons. The former type is made from laminates, e.g. PE/aluminium foil/PE or PE/paper/aluminium foil/PE, and they are only used to package dehydrated yoghurt. The most popular method of filling is the "form/fill/seal" approach, and fundamentally the container must be impermeable to gases and water vapour; a similar pack is illustrated in Fig. 8.4/J for the packaging of concentrated freeze-dried starter cultures.

Paper board cartons became a popular container for dairy products in the 1950s with the introduction of the waxed cartons. These containers were used in the past for the packaging of yoghurt, but their popularity has diminished in favour of "plastic" cups and/or laminated paper cartons. One disadvantage associated with the waxed carton is its tendency to leak, and despite improvements in manufacture, i.e. the application of a multi-layer coat of wax and EVA copolymer, their use as yoghurt containers in the United Kingdom has remained limited.

However, the use of cartons to package liquid milk is widely practised in North America, Europe and to a lesser degree in the United Kingdom, and such containers could be easily used to package yoghurt (Fig. 2.25). Two types of carton are normally available, and they are: firstly, a simple type where ordinary paper board is coated on both sides with a plastic material, e.g. PE, and secondly, the multi-layer type which consists of the following layers: PE/paper board/aluminium foil/PE. The latter type of carton is normally used for the packaging of UHT milk, since the aluminium foil layer not only renders the carton impermeable, but also helps to improve the rigidity of the container.

Fig. 2.25.   Examples of laminated paper board cartons used for the packaging of different yoghurt products

(a)   Natural yoghurt packaged in 1 litre Pure Pak carton.
(b)   Drinking yoghurt packaged in a 500 g Pure Pak carton—"Flat Top".
(c)   Drinking yoghurt produced in the Republic of Ireland and packaged in a Tetra Rex "Flat Top".
(d)   Drinking yoghurt packaged using the Tetra Brik system.

Reproduced by courtesy of Tetra Pak Ltd., Surrey, UK; Liquid Packaging Ltd., Hertfordshire, UK; J. Sainsbury Ltd., London, UK.

Depending on the exact system employed, the paper board cartons are delivered to the dairy either as collapsed, preformed cartons, e.g. the Pure Pak, Combibloc or Tetra Rex methods, or in the form of a reel (Tetra Brik). The sequence of packaging followed with preformed cartons is:

—a bank of collapsed cartons is fed into a special sleeve of the filling machine;
—a single carton is automatically removed from the sleeve, opened and the bottom is sealed;
—the carton is then filled with yoghurt and the top sealed;
—the packaged product is ready for dispatch (see Fig. 2.26).

Alternatively, the cartons can be formed from a reel using the technique of form/fill/seal, and Fig. 2.27 illustrates the sequences involved in the formation of one such container, a Tetra Brik carton prior to filling it with yoghurt.

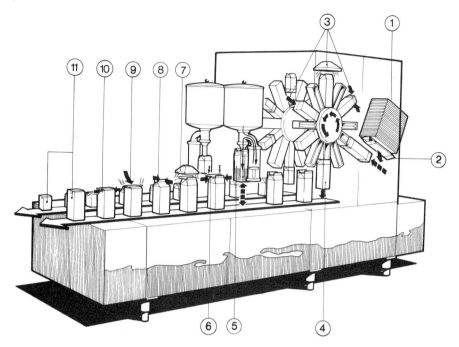

Fig. 2.26.   Schematic illustration showing the packaging of yoghurt in a Tetra Rex (type RC6) flat top machine

1) The machine has two lines, each of which is independently adjustable. The implication is that two carton sizes containing different yoghurt flavours can be produced at the same time. The carton blanks are placed in the two magazines at the back of the machine. The lines are synchronized and what occurs on each line is as follows:

2) The blanks are fed out from the bottom of the magazine and passed onto mandrels which are mounted on a wheel. These are two sizes of mandrels, one for 1-litre cartons and one for others.

3) The carton bases are formed and sealed on the mandrels. This is done in three stages: firstly, the bottom flaps are folded inwards and after this they are turned up before being pressed together and sealed.

4) The cartons, the bases of which are now sealed, are withdrawn from the mandrels and placed in compartments on the conveyer.

5) The cartons are filled in accordance with the Tetra Pak patented method, which is fitted with a special filling nozzle.

6) At this station, the small flaps, which are subsequently to be sealed to the sides of the carton, are folded out.

7) The top flaps are heated.

8) The top flaps are pressed together and sealed.

9) The top seal is folded downwards and at the same time the small protruding flaps are heated.

10) The flaps are sealed to the carton.

11) The finished carton is discharged from the machine and passed on for packing in transport packaging.

Reproduced by courtesy of Tetra Pak Ltd., Surrey, UK.

One common feature of these packaging systems, e.g. Pure Pak, Tetra Rex (premier design) or Combibloc, is that the carton has a gable-end. In some instances this gable structure may prove to be useful for pouring the product, but one disadvantage is the large storage area required as compared with yoghurt packed in flat-top cartons. However, the recent development of a "Flat Top" Tetra Rex and Pure Pak cartons, which are relatively square in shape, combines the desirable features of a gable, i.e. excellent pouring characteristics, with efficient utilisation of the space in refrigerated cabinets.

One last type of container is the laminated paper cup, and this is used in the United States of America where the cups are preformed and delivered to the dairy nested in cardboard boxes. These cups are sealed using press-on lids, or possibly foil lids heat-sealed.

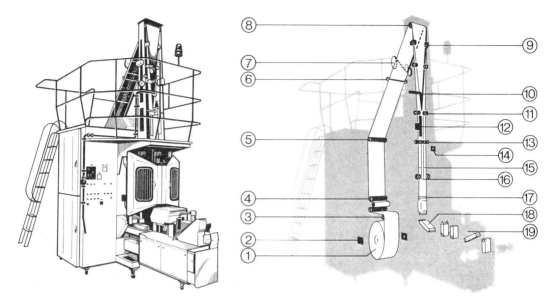

Fig. 2.27.   Description of the form/fill/seal technique of yoghurt packaging using the Tetra Brik system.

1) The roll of packaging material is placed in a magazine at the rear of the machine.
2) The diameter of the roll is sensed by a photocell, which gives a signal when it is time to change a new roll.
3) The packaging material is fed round this breaker roller to the creasing rollers.
4) The creasing rollers prepare folds in the packaging material so as to make the final forming of the cartons easier.
5) Breaker roller.
6) Rollers to guide the packaging material through the seam strengthener.
7) In the seam strengthener, one edge of the packaging material is warmed with hot air and fitted with a plastic strip, which subsequently forms part of longitudinal seam.
8) Upper breaker roller.
9) Forming yoke, which starts forming the packaging material into a tube.
10) The filling pipe enters the paper tube at this point; the mouth of the pipe (16) is situated below the level of the liquid (15).
11) Forming ring.
12) The element of the longitudinal seam, heats one edge of the packaging material.
13) In this forming ring the two edges of the packaging material are pressed together and the plastic strip which was applied earlier is sealed along the inside of the seam.
14) The cartons have registered printing and consequently the machine has an automatic design-holding system. This is controlled by a photocell that is triggered by the design mark printed on the packaging material.
15) Level of the liquid in the tube.
16) The mouth of the filling pipe is below the level of the liquid, which prevents frothing.
17) The tube, filled with liquid, then arrives at two pairs of jaws which operate continuously, sealing the cross seams on the cartons and separating these from the tube.
18) The cartons drop into the final folder, where the top and bottom flaps are folded in and sealed, giving the carton its final shape.
19) A spine strengthener, if required, is fitted here, after which the finished cartons are fed out of the machine.

Reproduced by courtesy of the Tetra Pak Ltd., Surrey, UK.

The size of the above containers is divided into two main groups: firstly, the "single serve" cartons where the yoghurt content ranges between 150 and 200 ml, or in some cases it may be less, and secondly, the "family size" where the capacity of the container ranges from 250 to 1000 ml. In the latter sizes, press-on lids are mainly used because:

(i) it is rather difficult to heat-seal a wide mouth, plastic tub;

(ii) since not all the yoghurt may be consumed at the same time, it is necessary to provide, for reasons of hygiene, a lid which can be reclosed (Fig. 2.22e).

Incidentally, a type of intermediate container which is becoming very popular is the special purpose multi-pack (see Fig. 2.28), where four or six yoghurt cartons are packaged together (Lang, 1972). These multi-packs are sometimes used when launching a new fruit yoghurt on the market, or alternatively they are used as a "family pack". A similar type of family pack is now widely produced on form-fill-seal machines (i.e. thermoformed), where four yoghurt cartons (each pair is a different flavour) are formed as one composite unit (see Fig. 2.28).

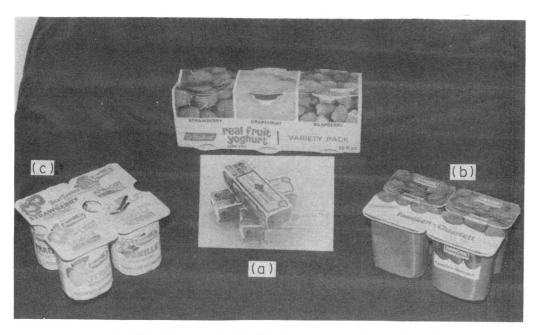

Fig. 2.28. Few examples of multi-pack systems of yoghurt containers

(a) Illustrates Jak—et—Pak packaging system in the USA; the cup is made out of waxed paper cups.
(b) Thermoformed multi-flavour yoghurt pack and the containers diagonally opposite each other are of the same flavour.
(c) Thermoformed multi-flavour yoghurt pack and each container is of different flavour.

Reproduced by courtesy of Metal Box Ltd., Reading, UK.
Hassia Verpacking GmbH, Ranstadt, West Germany.
Sussex & Berkshire Machinery, Hampshire, UK.

B. Aluminium Foil Lids

Aluminium foil is widely used to seal yoghurt containers, e.g. plastic cups, and due to the acidic nature of yoghurt, and the necessity of heat-sealing, the aluminium foil is normally coated with a layer of "plastic". If the preformed type of plastic cups are used, the aluminium foil lids are usually precut, and around 2500–3000 lids are packed into a special magazine to minimise mechanical damage. The diameter of these lids is < 100 mm, and they usually have a pull-tab for easy opening.

The gauge of the foil is around 40 μ, and each lid is normally embossed. The embossing pattern can be varied to suit the customer's requirements, and the impression can be up to 100 μ in depth. The embossing is essential to facilitate easy "pick-up" of single lids from the magazine assembly prior to placing over the filled cup and heat-sealing.

For yoghurt packaged using the form-fill-seal technique, the aluminium foil is delivered to the dairy as a reel, with the width of the reel being varied in relation to the number of filling heads (abreast) on the packaging machine. The aluminium foil gauge (around 40 μ) is similar to that of the precut type, but the embossing process is omitted since it would serve no function.

As can be observed from packaged yoghurt on the market, both types of lid (precut or from a reel) can be printed with different information and attractive designs. The technique of printing used could be the flexograph or the gravure. The latter method is normally used where more than five different printing colours are required. However, the reverse side of the lids is mainly coated with heat-sealable material, and the thickness of the laminate ranges between 6–10 g/m². The variation in the thickness of the lacquer is directly dependent on the type of heat-sealing material used, and for example 6–8 g/m² of EVA is applied on foil intended for heat-sealing to polystyrene or polypropylene. For the latter type of plastic cup a modified version of EVA is used, i.e. has a stronger solvent intended for higher temperature sealing purposes. On the printed side of the aluminium foil the EVA lacquer is coated with a layer of high heat varnish in order to protect the graphic design during the heat-sealing stage of the yoghurt plastic container at the dairy (Englehart, 1982).

C. Outer or Shipping Container

These types of packaging material do not come in contact with the yoghurt, but their importance in the industry is to facilitate easy handling and stacking of the cups during storage, transport and display in supermarkets (Fig. 2. 29).

Different types of containers can be used, and they are divided into two groups:

(i) returnable,
(ii) single-trip.

The returnable containers (or crates) are made of metal or rigid plastic, but since the crates require to be collected, they are not widely used. However, the metal crates are popular where set yoghurt is produced in glass bottles, and the fermentation process takes place in a water bath.

Single-trip containers are more widely used than the returnable type, and some of the different types available on the market, are:

(a) semi-rigid plastic crates,
(b) nest trays (flexible plastic or any similar material—see Anon., 1980b),
(c) cardboard trays.

The latter two types of tray can be overwrapped with a heat-shrink material (Fig. 2.29), or alternatively the nested trays can be piled on top of each other (4–6 trays high) inside a cardboard box.

The choice of any one particular system and/or type of outer container is governed primarily by such factors as:

Fig. 2.29. An example of yoghurt outer shipping containers

Illustration of a metal trolly stacked with yoghurt cups which are nested in trays and over-wrapped with heat shrink material

Reproduced by courtesy of Express Dairy UK Ltd., Middlesex, UK.

—cost,
—degree of mechanisation,
—ease of dispensing and marketing,
—stackability and ease of cold air circulation in the refrigerated store.

This latter aspect is important if the yoghurt is filled at 20°C and final cooling takes place in the cold store

In large organisations the trays (overwrapped with heat-shrink material) or cardboard boxes of packaged yoghurt are usually stacked on a wooden pallet which is later shifted using forklift trucks, i.e. from production area–cold store–transport vehicle.

Alternatively, metal trollies could be used, for example the Tetra-tainer type produced by the Tetra group. The packaged yoghurt in its single-trip shipping container is stacked onto these trollies, and the advantage of the system is the ease of movement of the product:

—from cold store to transport vehicle,
—from transport vehicle to supermarket and place in a refrigerated cabinet,

so that the retail cartons are not handled at all from the time that they leave the dairy until they are picked up by the consumer.

REFRIGERATED COLD STORAGE, TRANSPORT AND DISTRIBUTION

Cooling the yoghurt to $<10°C$, and maintaining this low temperature until it reaches the consumer, helps to "slow down" the biological and biochemical reaction(s) that are taking place in the yoghurt. The former reactions result from the metabolic activity of the yoghurt starter culture, and possibly any microbial contaminants that resisted the heat treatment and survived the fermentation process, or were introduced as post-production contaminants, e.g. yeast and moulds, while the possible biochemical reactions are:

—fat oxidation in the presence of oxygen;
—hydration of the protein constituent in yoghurt;
—due to acidic condition of the product, changes in the colour of the fruit additive can take place, e.g. becomes dull and pale;
—slight dehydration may take place, and the exposed surface of the yoghurt may change its physical appearance;
—presence of added hydrocolloids (stabilisers) and/or pectins from the fruit improve the viscosity/consistency of yoghurt during storage.

In order to minimise some of these reactions, the refrigeration of yoghurt is essential, and with this proviso the keeping quality of the product could well be up to 3 weeks from the date of production. However, during the first 24–48 hours of cold storage an improvement in the physical characteristics of the coagulum is observed, mainly due to the hydration and/or stabilisation of the casein micelles (refer to Fig. 3.63), and hence it may be desirable to delay the sale/distribution of the yoghurt accordingly.

Since the quality of yoghurt is dependent on a multitude of factors after production, the following recommendations may help to ensure that the product reaches the consumer in a satisfactory condition.

1. The cold store

—Reduce, as far as possible, rough mechanical handling of the packaged yoghurt.
—Maintain the storage temperature as low as possible, i.e. $<5°C$, and avoid any fluctuation.
—Provide good cold air circulation in the store, especially if the yoghurt is filled at $20°C$ and final cooling takes place in the cold store.
—Avoid losses of cold air through the use of a poorly designed insulated store.
—If the yoghurt is packaged in a transparent container, protect the product using special lighting to reduce decolorisation or oxidation.
—Always retain the packaged yoghurt for at least 48 hours before dispatch, so that the final stability of the coagulum is achieved.

2. During Transport

—Refrigerated transport is required during the summer months in the temperate zones of the northern or southern hemispheres; during the winter months insulated lorries could be used.

—In tropical and sub-tropical areas refrigeration of the transport vehicle is necessary.

—During transport, shaking of the yoghurt can lead to a reduction in viscosity and whey syneresis; it is difficult to overcome this effect, especially during long road journeys.

3. The retail shop and the consumer

—The yoghurt must be displayed in refrigerated cabinets until it is purchased.

—Yoghurt should be consumed directly, or otherwise stored in a domestic refrigerator until required.

—Yoghurt should be consumed around 10°C, as below this temperature the flavour profile is not appreciated due to the coldness, and above 10°C the product loses its freshness and may undergo a reduction in viscosity.

REFERENCES

ABRAHAMSEN, R. K. and HOLMEN, T. B. (1980) *Milchwissenschaft*, **35,** 399.

ABRAHAMSEN, R. K. and HOLMEN, T. B. (1981) *Journal of Dairy Research*, **48,** 457.

ACKER, L. (1969) *Food Technology*, **23,** 1257.

ADAMS, D. M. and BRAWLEY, T. G. (1981) *Journal of Dairy Science*, **64,** 1951.

ADAMS, D. M., BARACH, J. T. and SPECK, M. L. (1975) *Journal of Dairy Science*, **58,** 828.

ADMI (1973) In *Standards for Grades of Dry Milks—Including Methods of Analysis*, American Dry Milk Institute Inc., Chicago, U.S.A.

ANON. (1971) Difco Technical Information Bulletin No. 0272, UK Division of Difco Laboratory Ltd., Surrey, U.K.

ANON. (1974) Pfizer Technical Bulletin Sorbistat-K, Pfizer Ltd., Kent, U.K.

ANON. (1975) In *Geigy Scientific Tables*, 7th Edition, Ed. by Diem, K. and Lentner, C. Published by Geigy Pharmaceuticals, Macclesfield, U.K.

ANON. (1976) Maxilact Technical Data Sheet—HN/CdH 10–76, Gist Brocades NV, Delft, Holland.

ANON. (1977) In *The Influence of the Cooling Rate in the Quality of Stirred Yoghurt*, Publication No. 225, Danish Dairy Research Institute, Hillerød, Denmark.

ANON. (1978) Maxilact Technical Data Sheet—Mil 01–01/78.05, En. 03, Gist Brocades NV, Delft, Holland.

ANON. (1980a) British Patent 1 565 006.

ANON. (1980b) *American Dairy Review*, **42**(8), 26.

ANON. (1981a) *Dairy Record*, **82**(11), 40.

ANON. (1981b) In *Food Preservatives—Sorbistat, Sorbistat-K and Sodium Benzoate*, Pfizer (Chemical Division) Technical Data, Pfizer Ltd., Kent, U.K.

ANON. (1982a) In *Whey: A Problem Becomes Opportunity*, Corning Technical Bulletin No. IBS-10, Corning Glass Works, Avon, France.

ANON. (1982b) In *Lactose Hydrolysis System*, Corning Technical Bulletin No. IBS-10B, *Ibid.*

ANON. (1982c) In *A Report on the Dairy Industry in 1981*, Dairy Trade Federation, London, U.K.

ANON. (1982d) *Dairy Industries International*, **47**(3), 23.

BAISYA, R. K. and BOSE, A. N. (1975) *Journal of Food Science and Technology India*, **12,** 306.

BALL, A. P., GRAY, J. A. and MURDOCH, J. McC. (1978) In *Antibacterial Drugs Today*, 2nd Edition, University Park Press, Maryland, U.S.A.

BANKS, W., DALGLEISH, D. G. and ROOK, J. A. F. (1981) In *Dairy Microbiology*, Vol. 1, Ed. by Robinson, R. K. Applied Science Publishers Ltd., London, U.K.

BARACH, J. T., ADAMS, D. M. and SPECK, M. L. (1976) *Journal of Dairy Scinece*, **59,** 391.

BECK, K. M. (1974) In *Symposium on Sweeteners*, Ed. by Inglett, G. E. AVI Publishing Co. Inc., Connecticut, U.S.A.

BOYLE, J. L. (1972) In *The Stabilisation of Cultured Milk Products by Alginates*. Paper Presented at the Symposium on New Technical Developments in the Milk Industry, held in October 1972 at Vratney Doline, Czechoslovakia.

BRISTON, J. H. (1980) In *Developments in Food Packaging—1*, Ed. by Palling, S. J. Applied Science Publishers Ltd., London, U.K.

BSI (1976) BS 1133—Section 21, British Standards Institution, London, U.K.

BROOKER, B. E. (1979) In *Food Microscopy*, Ed. by Vaughan, J. G. Academic Press Inc. (London) Ltd., London, U.K.

BRUNNER, J. R. (1974) In *Fundamentals of Dairy Chemistry*, 2nd Edition, Ed. by Webb, B. H., Johnson, A. H. and Alford, J. A. AVI Publishing Co. Inc., Connecticut, U.S.A.

BURTON, H. (1954) *Journal of Dairy Research*, **21**, 194.

BUTTERY, R. G. (1981) In *Flavour Research: Recent Advances*, Food Science Series, Vol. 7, Ed. by Teranishi, R., Flath, R. A. and Sugisawa, H. Dekker, New York, USA.

CHAPMAN, H. R., FORD, J. E., KON, S. K., THOMPSON, S. Y., ROWLAND, S. J., CROSSLEY, E. L. and ROTHWELL, J. (1957) *Journal of Dairy Research*, **24**, 191.

CHASE, D. (1981) *Milk Industry*, **83**(5), 29.

CHEESEMAN, G. C. (1975) *Journal of the Society of Dairy Technology*, **28**, 181.

COGAN, T. M. (1977) *Irish Journal of Food Science & Technology*, **1**, 95.

COLANGELO, M. (1980) *Dairy Field*, **163**(10) 95.

COTON, S. G. (1980) *Journal of the Society of Dairy Technology*, **33**, 89.

COUSIN, M. A. (1977) *Dissertation Abstracts International B*, **37**, 4966.

COUSIN, M. A. and MARTH, E. H. (1977a) *Journal of Food Protection*, **40**, 475.

COUSIN, M. A. and MARTH, E. H. (1977b) *Cultured Dairy Products Journal*, **12** (2), 15.

CROSBY, N. T. (1981) In *Food Packaging Materials—Aspects of Analysis and Migration of Contaminants*, Applied Science Publishers Ltd., London, U.K.

CROSBY, G. A. and WINGARD Jr., R. E. (1979) In *Developments in Sweeteners-1*, Ed. by Hough, E. A. M., Parker, K. J. and Vlitos, A. J. Applied Science Publishers Ltd., London, U.K.

DAVIDSON, S., PASSMORE, R., BROCK, J. F. and TRUSWELL, A. S. (1979) In *Human Nutrition and Dietetics*, 7th Edition, Churchill Livingstone, Edinburgh, U.K.

Davies, G. (1982) Personal communication.

DAVIES, F. L., SHANKAR, P. A., BROOKER, B. E. and HOBBS, D. G. (1978) *Journal of Dairy Research*, **45**, 53.

DAVIS, J. G. (1968) In *Quality Control in the Food Industry*, Vol. 2, Ed. by Herscdoerfer, S. M. Academic Press Inc. (London) Ltd., London, U.K.

DAVIS, J. G. (1973) *Food Manufacture*, **48**(6), 23.

DEBEUKELAR, N. J., COUSIN, M. A., BRADLEY, R. L. Jr. and MARTH, E. H. (1977) *Journal of Dairy Science*, **60**, 857.

DEXTER, C. (1976) *Food Manufacture*, **51**(2), 17.

DICKER, R. (1982) *Dairy Industries International*, **47**(4), 19.

DORDOVIC, J., MACEJ, O., MISIC, D. and ASANIN, S. (1981) *Dairy Science Abstracts*, **43**, 254.

DUTTA, S. M., KUILA, R. K. and RANGANATHAN, B. (1973) *Milchwissenschaft*, **28**, 231.

EDWARDS, D. I. (1980) In *Antimicrobial Drug Action*, Macmillan Press Ltd., London, U.K.

ELFAGM, A. A. and WHEELOCK, J. V. (1977) *Journal of Dairy Research*, **44**, 367.

ELFAGM, A. A. and WHEELOCK, J. V. (1978a) *Journal of Dairy Science*, **61**, 28.

ELFAGM, A. A. and WHEELOCK, J. V. (1978b) *Journal of Dairy Science*, **61**, 159.

ELSEY, W. F. (1982) Personal communication.

ENGLEHART, J. R. (1982) Personal communication.

FAO/WHO (1976) In *Joint FAO/WHO Committee of Government Experts on the Code of Principles Concerning Milk and Milk Products*. Report of the 18th Session, No. C × 5/70, FAO, Rome, Italy.

FAO/WHO (1979) In *Joint FAO/WHO Food Standards Programme Codex Alimentarius Commission–Guide to the Safe Use of Additives*, Second Series, CAC/FAL 5, FAO, Rome, Italy.

FERNS, H. (1981) Personal communication.

FLÜCKIGER, E. (1980) In *Dairy Packaging—Newsletter*, No. 5, IDF, Brussels, Belgium.

FOOD and DRUGS ACT (1973) In *Composition and Labelling—The Colouring Matter in Food Regulations*, No. 1340, Statutory Instruments, HMSO, London, U.K. Amended in (1975) No. 1488, *Ibid.*; (1976) No. 2086, *Ibid.*; (1978) No. 1787, *Ibid.*

FOOD and DRUGS ACT (1975) In *Composition and Labelling—The Emulsifiers and Stabilisers in Food Regulations*, No. 1486, Statutory Instruments, HMSO, London, U.K.

FOOD and DRUGS ACT (1979) In *Composition and Labelling—The Preservatives in Food Regulations*, No. 752, Statutory Instruments, HMSO, London, U.K. Amended in (1980) No. 931, *Ibid.*

FOOD and DRUGS ACT (1980) In *Composition and Labelling—The Emulsifiers and Stabilisers in Food Regulations*, No. 1833, Statutory Instruments, HMSO, London, U.K.

GALESLOOT, Th. E. (1958) *Netherland Milk and Dairy Journal*, **12**, 130.

GAUTNEB, T., STEINSHOLT, K. and ABRAHAMSEN, R. K. (1979) *Dairy Science Abstracts*, **41**, 478.

GED, J. and ALAIS, C. (1976) *Le Lait*, **56**, 407.

GENNIP, A. J. M. van (1973) In *Milk Proteins and Their Use in Practical Emulsions*. Lecture Presented at International Symposium on Emulsions and Foams in Food Technology, Ebeltoft, Denmark.

GENNIP, A. H. M. van (1980) In *Modern Milk Products for the Confectionary and Chocolate Industry*. Lecture presented at Rohstoffkunde und Training Seminar fur Einkaufer der Susswarenindustrie, Solingen.

GENNIP, A. H. M. van (1981a) In *Whey—A Valuable Raw Material for Food in the Eighties*. Lecture presented at the Agricultural College of Athens, Greece.

GENNIP, A. H. M. van (1981b) In *Milk Proteins in Some Practical Applications.* Lecture presented at the Agricultural College of Athens, Greece.

GILMOUR, A. and ROWE, M. T. (1981) In *Dairy Microbiology,* Vol. 1, Ed. by Robinson, R. K. Applied Science Publishers Ltd., London, U.K.

GILLES, J. and LAWRENCE, R. C. (1979) In *Monograph on Recombination of Milk and Milk Products—Technology and Engineering Aspects,* IDF Doc. 116, Brussels, Belgium.

GILLES, J. and LAWRENCE, R. C. (1982) In *Proceedings of IDF Seminar on Recombination of Milk and Milk Products,* IDF Doc. 142, Brussels, Belgium.

GLICKSMAN, M. (1969) In *Gum Technology in the Food Industry,* Food Science and Technology, A Series of Monographs, Academic Press Inc. (London) Ltd., London, U.K.

GLICKSMAN, M. (1979) In *Polysaccharides in Food,* Ed. by Blanchard, J. M. V. and Mitchell, J. R. Butterworth, London, U.K.

GLOVER, F. A. (1971) *Journal of Dairy Research,* **38,** 373.

GLOVER, F. A., SKUDDER, P. J., STOTHART, P. H. and EVANS, E. W. (1978) *Journal of Dairy Research,* **45,** 291.

GRADHAGE, L. and THURELL, K. E. (1978) *XXth International Dairy Congress,* **E,** 1019.

GREENE, V. W. and JEZESKI, J. J. (1957a) *Journal of Dairy Science,* **40,** 1046.

GREENE, V. W. and JEZESKI, J. J. (1957b) *Journal of Dairy Science,* **40,** 1053.

GREENE, V. W. and JEZESKI, J. J. (1957c) *Journal of Dairy Science,* **40,** 1062.

GRIGOROV, H. (1966a) *XVIIth International Dairy Congress,* **F:5,** 655.

GRIGOROV, H. (1966b) *XVIIth International Dairy Congress,* **F:5,** 643.

GRIGOROV, H. (1966c) *XVIIth International Dairy Congress,* **F:5,** 649.

HADLAND, G. and HOFFMANN, T. (1974) *XIXth International Dairy Congress,* **IE,** 740.

HALL, T. A. (1975) *Cultured Dairy Products Journal,* **10**(3), 12.

HAMDAN, I. Y., DEANE, D. D. and KUNSMAN J. E. Jr. (1971) *Journal of Milk and Food Technology,* **34,** 307.

HAMILTON, M. (1981) Personal communication.

HARGROVE, R. E. and ALFORD, J. A. (1974) In *Fundamentals of Dairy Chemistry,* 2nd Edition, Ed. by Webb, B. H., Johnson, A. and Alford, J. A. AVI Publishing Co. Inc., Connecticut, U.S.A.

HARPER, W. J. (1976) In *Dairy Technology and Engineering,* Ed. by Harper, W. J. and Hall, C. W. AVI Publishing Co. Inc., Connecticut, U.S.A.

HARPER, W. J. and SEIBERLING, D. A. (1976) In *Dairy Technology and Engineering,* Ed. by Harper, W. J. and Hall, C. W. AVI Publishing Co. Inc., Connecticut, U.S.A.

HARTMAN, G. H. (1975) *Cultured Dairy Products Journal,* **10**(2), 6.

HARTMAN, A. M. and DRYDEN, L. P. (1974) In *Fundamentals of Dairy Chemistry,* 2nd Edition, Ed. by Webb, B. H., Johnson, A. H. and Alford, J. A. AVI Publishing Co. Inc., Connecticut, U.S.A.

HARWALKER, V. R. and KALAB, M. (1980) *Journal of Texture Studies,* **III,** 35.

HARWALKER, V. R. and KALAB, M. (1981) *Scanning Electron Microscopy,* **III,** 503.

HEDLUNG, B. (1976) *Nordeuropaeisk Mejeri—Tidsskrift,* **42,** 224.

HUMPHREYS, C. L. and PLUNKETT, M. (1969) *Dairy Science Abstracts* (Review Article No. 154), **31,** 607.

HYDE, K. A. and ROTHWELL, J. (1973) In *Ice Cream,* Churchill Livingstone Ltd., London, U.K.

HYVONEN, L. and SLOTTE, M. (1983) *Journal of Food Technology,* **18,** 97.

INGENPASS, P. (1980) *Food, Flavouring, Packaging and Processing Journal,* **2**(1), 16.

IYENGAR, M. K., NAMBUDRIPAD, V. K. N. and DUDANI, A. T. (1967) *Indian Journal of Dairy Science,* **20,** 8.

JELEN, P. and HORBAL, H. (1974) *Journal of Dairy Science,* **57,** 584.

JENNESS, R. (1974) In *Lactation,* Vol. III, Ed. by Larson, B. L. and Smith, V. R. Academic Press Inc., New York, U.S.A.

JENNESS, R. and PATTON, S. (1959) In *Principles of Dairy Chemistry,* Chapman & Hall Ltd., London, U.K.

JENSEN, F. (1972) *Annali Del Instituto Superiore Di Sanita,* **8,** 443.

JEPSEN, S. (1977) *American Dairy Review,* **39**(1), 29.

JEPSEN, S. (1979) *Cultured Dairy Products Journal,* **14**(1), 5.

JOHANSSON, G. (1982) *Dairy Science Abstracts,* **44,** 97.

JOHNSON, A. H. (1974) In *Fundamentals of Dairy Chemistry,* 2nd Edition, Ed. by Webb, B. H., Johnson, A. H. and Alford, J. A. AVI Publishing Co. Inc., Connecticut, U.S.A.

JUNK, W. R. and PANCOAST, H. M. (1973) In *Handbook of Sugars,* AVI Publishing Co. Inc., Connecticut, U.S.A.

KALAB, M. (1979a) *Journal of Dairy Science,* **62,** 1352.

KALAB, M. (1979b) *Scanning Electron Microscopy,* **III,** 261.

KALAB, M. (1982a) Personal communication.

KALAB, M. (1982b) Personal communication—in press.

KALAB, M. and HARWALKER, V. R. (1973) *Journal of Dairy Science,* **56,** 835.

KALAB, M. and HARWALKER, V. R. (1974) *Journal of Dairy Research,* **41,** 131.

KALAB, M., EMMONS, D. B. and SARGANT, A. G. (1975) *Journal of Dairy Research,* **42,** 453.

KALAB, M., EMMONS, D. B. and SARGANT, A. G. (1976) *Milchwissenschaft,* **31,** 402.

KANNAN, A. and JENNESS, R. (1961) *Journal of Dairy Science,* **44,** 808.

KISHONTI, E. (1975) In *Proceedings of the Lipolysis Symposium*, IDF Annual Bulletin, Doc. 86, IDF, Brussels, Belgium.

KON, S. K. (1972) In *Milk and Milk Products in Human Nutrition*, FAO Nutritional Studies Publication No. 27, 2nd Edition, FAO, Rome, Italy.

KON, S. K. and COWIE, A. T. (1961) In *Milk: The Mammary Gland and its Secretion*, Academic Press Inc. (London) Ltd., London, U.K.

LABROPOULOS, A. E., LOPEZ, A. and PALMER, J. K. (1981) *Journal of Food Protection*, **44**, 874.

LABUZA, T. P. (1980) *Food Technology*, **34**(4), 36.

LANG, A. (1972) *Journal of Food Technology in Australia*, **24**, 350.

LANG, F. (1981a) *Milk Industry*, **83**(2), 42.

LANG, F. (1981b) *Milk Industry*, **83**(3), 25.

LARSON, B. L. and ROLLERI, G. D. (1955) *Journal of Dairy Science*, **38**, 351.

LEDDER, K. H. and THOMASOW, J. (1975) *Dairy Science Abstracts*, **37**, 520.

LUCZYNSKA, A., BIJOK, F., WAJNERT, T., KAZIMIERCZAK, W., LIPINSKA, E., KOSIKOWSKA, M. and JAKUBCZYK, E. (1978) *XXth International Dairy Congress*, **IE**, 836.

LYSTER, R. L. J. (1979) In *Effect of Heating on Foodstuffs*, Ed. by Priestley, R. J. Applied Science Publishers Ltd., London, U.K.

MARSHALL, V. M. E. and MABBITT, L. A. (1980) *Journal of the Society of Dairy Technology*, **33**, 129.

MARTIN, R. L. (1979) *Dairy & Ice Cream Field*, **162**(4), 64.

MAYERHOFER, M. J., MARSHALL, R. T., WHITE, C. H. and LEE, M. (1973) *Applied Microbiology*, **25**, 44.

McKENZIE, H. A. (1971) In *Milk Proteins*, Vol. II. Ed. by McKenzie, H. A. Academic Press Inc. (London) Ltd., London, U.K.

MEADE, G. P. and CHEN, J. C. P. (1977) In *Cane Sugar Handbook*, 10th Edition, John Wiley and Sons Inc., London, U.K.

MORLEY, R. G. (1978) *American Dairy Review*, **40**(5), 28.

MULDER, H. and WALSTRA, P. (1974) In *The Milk Fat Globule—Emulsion Science Applied to Milk Products and Comparable Foods*, Commonwealth Agricultural Bureau, Farnham Royal, U.K.

MULLER, H. P. (1977) *Acta Horticulurae*, No. 61, 343.

NICHOLLS, G. J. (1981) Personal communication.

NIELSEN, V. H. (1976) *Cultured Dairy Products Journal*, **11**(1), 12.

NURSTEN, H. E. (1977) In *Sensory Properties of Foods*, Ed. by Birch, G. G., Brennan, J. G. and Parker, K. J. Applied Science Publishers Ltd., London, U.K.

PAINE, F. A. (1967) In *Fundamentals of Packaging*, Ed. by Paine, F. A. Blackie & Son Ltd., London, U.K.

PARRY, R. M. (1974) In *Fundamentals of Dairy Chemistry*, 2nd Edition, Ed. by Webb, B. H., Johnson, A. H. and Alford, J. A. AVI Publishing Co. Inc., Connecticut, U.S.A.

PAUL, A. A. and SOUTHGATE, D. A. T. (1978) In McCance and Widdowson's *The Composition of Foods*, 4th Revised Edition, HMSO, London, U.K.

PEDERSEN, J. K. (1979) In *Polysaccharides in Food*, Ed. by Blanshard, J. M. V. and Mitchell, J. R. Butterworth, London, U.K.

PORTER, J. W. G. and THOMPSON, S. Y. (1972) In *Monograph on UHT Milk*, IDF Annual Bulletin, Part V, Doc. No. 68, IDF, Brussels, Belgium.

POWELL, M. E. (1969) *Cultured Dairy Products Journal*, **4**(3), 3.

PRODANSKI, P. (1967) *Milchwissenschaft*, **22**, 167.

PULAY, G. and KRASZ, A. (1974) *XIXth International Dairy Congress*, **IE**, 413.

RAMOS, M. (1978) *XXth International Dairy Congress*, **IE**, 613.

ROBINSON, R. K. and TAMIME, A. Y. (1975) *Journal of the Society of Dairy Technology*, **28**, 149.

ROBINSON, R. K. and TAMIME, A. Y. (1978) *Dairy Industries International*, **43**(3), 14.

ROLINSON, G. N. and SUTHERLAND, R. (1973) In *Advances in Pharmacology and Chemotherapy*, Vol. II, Academic Press Inc., New York, U.S.A.

SAMUELSSON, E. G. and CHRISTIANSEN, P. (1978) *XXth International Dairy Congress*, **IE**, 838.

SAWYER, W. H. (1969) *Journal of Dairy Science*, **52**, 1347.

SCHRIEBER, R. (1973) *Deutsche Milchwirtschalf*, **24**, 358.

SCOTT, R. (1981) In *Cheesemaking Practice*, Applied Science Publishers, Ltd., London, U.K.

SHALLENBERGER, R. S. and BIRCH, G. G. (1975) In *Sugar Chemistry*, AVI Publishing Co. Inc., Connecticut, U.S.A.

SINGH, R. S. (1978) *Indian Journal of Dairy Science*, **31**, 73.

SPINKS, J. G. (1982) Personal communication.

SPURGEON, K. R. (1976) *Cultured Dairy Products Journal*, **11**(4) 8.

STEINITZ, W. S. (1975) *Dairy & Ice Cream Field*, **158**, 46.

STEINSHOLT, K. and ABRAHAMSEN, R. K. (1978) *Meldinger fra Norges Landbrukshogkok*, **57**, 24.

STOGARDS, T. (1964) In *Fermented Milks*, IDF Annual Bulletin, Part III, IDF, Brussels, Belgium.

TAMIME, A. Y. (1977) In *Some Aspects of the Production of Yoghurt and Condensed Yoghurt*. PhD Thesis, University of Reading, Berkshire, U.K.

TAMIME, A. Y. and DEETH, H. C. (1980) *Journal of Food Protection*, **43**, 939.

TAMIME, A. Y. and HAMILTON, M. (1982) Unpublished data.

88

TAMIME, A. Y., KALAB, M. and DAVIES, G. (1984) *Food Microstructure*, **3**, 83.

THOMASOW, J. and HOFFMANN, W. (1978) *Dairy Science Abstracts*, **40**, 367.

TRAMER, J. (1973) *Journal of the Society of Dairy Technology*, **26**, 16.

UK Food Standards (1965) In *Food Standards Committee Report on Flavouring Agents*, Ref. FSC/FAC/REP 5, HMSO, London, U.K.

UK Food Standards (1975) In *Food Standards Committee Report on Yoghurt*, Ref. FSC/REP/64, HMSO, London, U.K.

UK Food Standards (1976) In *Food Additives and Contaminants Committee—Report on the Review of Flavourings in Food*, Ref. FAC/REP 22, HMSO, London, U.K.

VANDERPOORTEN, R. and MARTENS, R. (1976) *Revue de L'Agriculture*, **29**, 1509.

VOLKER, H. H. (1972) *Dairy Science Abstracts*, **34**, 677.

WHITNEY, R. McL., BRUNNER, J. R., EBNER, K. E., FARRELL Jr., H. M., JOSEPHSON, R. V., MORR, C. V. and SWAISGOOD, H. E. (1976) *Journal of Dairy Science*, **59**, 795.

WINTERTON, D. and MEIKLEJOHN, P. G. (1978) *Australian Journal of Dairy Technology*, **33**, 55.

WOYCHIK, J. H. and HOLSINGER, V. H. (1977) In *Enzymes in Food Beverage Processing*, American Chemical Society Symposium Series No. 47, Ed. by Ory, R. L. and St. Angelo, A. J. Published by American Chemical Society, U.S.A.

ZMARLICKI, S., GAWEL, J., PIJANOWSKI, E. and MOLSKA, I. (1974) *XIXth International Dairy Congress*, **IE**, 771.

ZMARLICKI, S., PIJANOWSKI, E. and MOLSKA, I. (1977) *Dairy Science Abstracts*, **39**, 566.

CHAPTER 3

Processing Plants and Equipment

The process of yoghurt production has evolved through the ages from a simple preparation carried out by the housewife on a very small scale to medium- and large-scale production centres handling many thousands of litres per day. The utensils and equipment required vary in relation to the type of yoghurt produced, scale of production and the level of technology adopted. Hence, it would seem logical to review the available equipment and plant against a scale of yoghurt produced per day:

   (i) home or small-scale production;
  (ii) medium-scale or manufacture by a small producer/retailer;
 (iii) large-scale production.

HOME OR SMALL-SCALE PRODUCTION

Traditionally, yoghurt is prepared by the housewife, and ordinary kitchen utensils are used. The milk is heated in a cooking pot, and the production of the coagulum takes place in the same container; Fig. 2.1 described briefly the overall process. However, one factor, which is critical during the incubation period, is the maintenance of a uniform temperature, and this is achieved by wrapping the pot in a woollen blanket and placing it in a warm place, e.g. near a cooker. Although the traditional process could still be recommended to housewives producing their own yoghurt, a simplified recipe is illustrated in Fig. 3.1.

Furthermore, the linen airing cupboard, i.e. area beside the hot water cylinder in a modern house, is sometimes used during the fermentation period, but recently yoghurt "makers" (Fig. 3.2) have become available for yoghurt enthusiasts to produce yoghurt under controlled conditions. Alternatively, the warm milk, inoculated with the starter culture (or natural yoghurt), is placed in a thermos and left undisturbed, allowing the milk to ferment and coagulate. Cooling is carried out directly after coagulation has taken place, and fruit and/or sugar are normally added to the cold yoghurt.

MEDIUM-SCALE PRODUCTION

The volume of yoghurt production in this category is rather low, perhaps in the region of a few hundred litres per day, and such small producer/retailers aim to market their yoghurt within a limited area. The different types of equipment which could be used at this level are as follows.

Place ½ – 1 litre of whole milk in a saucepan and heat to near boiling (for the production of thick viscous yoghurt add 20–40 g of skim milk powder, ≙ to 2.5 – 5 tablespoons); the addition of sugar is optional.

↓

Cool to 45° C (or just above blood temperature) and add 1 level tablespoon of plain unsweetened yoghurt.

↓

Pour into the containers of a yoghurt "maker" and seal with snap-on lids; alternatively, wrap the pot with a blanket, or pour the inoculated milk into clean, wide mouth thermos flask.

↓

Depending on the activity of the yoghurt organisms and/or temperature of incubation, the milk should coagulate in 3–18 hours.

↓

Cool the yoghurt as quickly as possible—preferably overnight in the refrigerator.

↓

Blend in fruit and sugar (fresh fruit, puree or jam) in accordance with personal preference and stir gently.

↓

Maintain product under refrigeration until consumed.

Fig. 3.1. Production of yoghurt at home

One pot of the natural yoghurt produced could be used as a starter culture to inoculate the following batch.

Excessive sub-culturing can lead to a prolonged incubation period, and hence it is recommended that a "fresh yoghurt" should be introduced weekly.

Short incubation periods are obtained using fresh, active starter cultures, an approach which is highly recommended.

A. Hand Operated, Multi-purpose Vat

The different steps involved during the production of yoghurt can be summarised as follows:

1. Sterilise the equipment directly before use, using chemical sterilising agents, drain and rinse with clean water.
2. Pour the milk into the vat (see Fig. 3.3), add the required amount of dried ingredients (milk powder), and mix with the aid of a stainless steel wire whisk.
3. Start the heating cycle using an electric element to heat the insulated water jacket, and hand agitate the milk.
4. After reaching the desired temperature, the heating element is switched off, and the milk is held for 10–30 minutes (depending on temperature), prior to cooling.
5. During cooling the water in the jacket is replaced by circulating mains water. At 40–45°C the milk is inoculated with starter culture and left undisturbed during the fermentation period.
6. After a few hours, or at the desired acidity, mains water is circulated through the jacket to cool the coagulum, a process that may be assisted by gentle agitation.
7. At around 15–20°C a known volume of yoghurt is drained out, mixed with fruit/flavouring additives and hand-filled into plastic cups.

91

Fig. 3.2. Example of yoghurt "Maker"

A yoghurt "maker" where glass jars (200 ml capacity) with screw-on plastic caps are used.

Reproduced by courtesy of Rowenta (UK) Ltd., Surrey, U.K.

B. Multi-purpose Vat

This type of vat is really a batch pasteuriser which is slightly modified to meet the requirements of yoghurt manufacture, and it is widely used for the production of viscous yoghurt (Fig. 3.4). These vats are usually made of stainless steel and insulated with a water jacket, and the capacity may be in the region of 1000 litres. Another type of vessel, which could be used for the same purpose, is an ordinary bulk starter vat (see Fig. 8.6), but irrespective of the type of vat used, the processing stages of stirred yoghurt production usually follow two alternative patterns. In the first approach the vat is utilised for all the different steps necessary for the *preparation* and *production* of yoghurt (Fig. 3.5, Process A). However, in the second approach the vat is merely used for the *preparation* of milk, i.e. mixing the dried ingredients with milk, heat treatment and cooling to incubation temperature (Fig. 3.5, Process B).

Fig. 3.3. Illustration of the processing vat

The working capacity is 30 litres. and it is fitted with a 3 kW heating element and automatic temperature controller; note also the insulated water jacket, hand-operated agitator, visual thermometer and manual setting for temperature control.

Reproduced by courtesy of Cockx & Sons (London) Ltd., Suffolk, UK.

Processes A and B described in Fig. 3.5 illustrate clearly the steps necessary for the production of stirred yoghurt, but for the manufacture of set yoghurt, Process C (Fig. 3.5) should be followed. It can be observed that Processes B and C are similar except that in the former method the milk is fermented in bulk, while in Process C the milk is incubated in the retail container. The major differences between set and stirred yoghurt are illustrated in Figs. 2.1 and 5.1.

The multi-purpose vat can be heated using different sources of energy, e.g. electrical, steam or gas, and this versatility makes this type of processing equipment very popular with the small producer. During the cooling stages mains water can be used or a closed-circuit cooling system circulating chilled water. Fig. 3.6 shows a typical example of the temperature profile observed during the manufacture of yoghurt using the Cockx multi-purpose vat which is electrically heated;

Fig. 3.4. A modified batch pasteuriser which is used as multi-purpose vat for the production of yoghurt

Giusti—electrically heated 'Pastolux' fitted with a high speed emulsifier which is used during the preparation and heat treatment of the basic mix; the slow speed stirrer replaces the high speed mixer during the cooling of the coagulum—mains water may be used for cooling the yoghurt from 40–45°C to 20°C.

Reproduced by courtesy of T. Giusti & Son Ltd., London, U.K.

the coolant agent is mains water. However, if Process A (Fig. 3.5) is chosen as the method of manufacture, the batch pasteuriser must have the following modifications:

(i) The agitator must be fitted with a two-speed motor; the "fast" speed (e.g. >35–40 revolutions per minute—rpm) is used during the blending of the milk with the dried ingredients

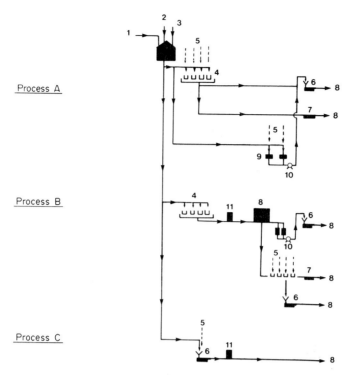

Fig. 3.5. The small-scale production of yoghurt using a multi-purpose vat

1. Inlet for liquid milk
2. Dried ingredients (milk powder and sugar) added manually
3. Starter culture added manually
4. Stainless steel cans or churns (they contain cold yoghurt—Process A or heated/cooled milk inoculated with starter culture—Process B)
5. Fruit added manually
6. Small-scale filling machine (Fig. 3.7).
7. Hand-filling machine
8. Cold store
9. Two small tanks (in parallel) used for the addition of fruit-filling can be continuous.
10. Positive pump
11. Incubation cabinet

and during the heating stage; the slow speed (e.g. 17–20 rpm) is operated to mix the coagulum gently during the cooling stage, so inflicting the minimum reduction in viscosity to the product.

(ii) The diameter of the outlet valve must be ≥5 cm in order to facilitate ease of drainage of the yoghurt. On such a small scale of production the stages of fruit mixing and filling can be carried out manually, but great care must be taken to minimise post-production contamination of the yoghurt. Figure 3.5(B) illustrates this approach, and the fruit is added to each can/churn and gently mixed with the yoghurt by means of a milk/cream plunger.

Although hand filling has been adopted by many small dairies, the use of a proper filling machine does offer some advantages. A wide range of fillers is available on the market, and Fig. 3.7 illustrates an example of one currently in use. These filling machines are equipped with a diversity

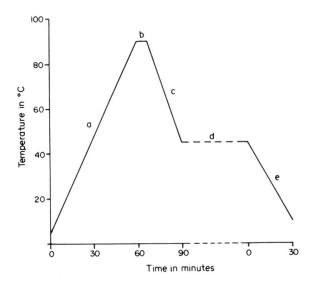

Fig. 3.6. Temperature profile observed during the manufacture of yoghurt using a Cockx type multi-purpose vat (500l capacity)

(a) Preparation and heating of yoghurt mix, e.g. 1 hour
(b) Holding time e.g. 5 minutes
(c) Cooling stage 20–30 minutes
(d) Incubation period (possibly 3 hours)
(e) Cooling of the coagulum 20–30 minutes

The vat is electrically operated to heat the insulated water jacket; mains water is used during stages (c and e); the total processing time is around 5 hours (excluding filling).

After Cockx (1982).

of sealing mechanisms, for example heat sealing of foil lids, crimping of foil lids or the use of snap-on plastic lids, and the ultimate selection of a particular type is largely a matter of personal preference. Alternatively paper board cartons (e.g. Pure-Pak) could be used for the packaging of yoghurt using a hand-operated cartoning/filling machine. The unit is basically designed for filling liquid milk, but by slightly modifying the filling head it becomes feasible to fill a viscous product such as yoghurt, (see Fig. 3.8).

(b)

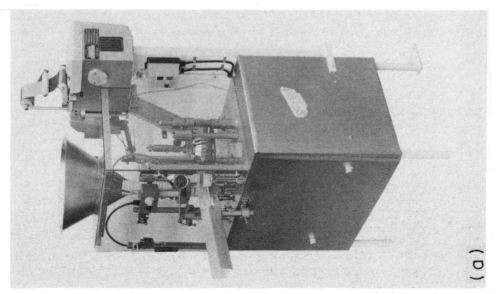

(a)

Fig. 3.7 (a) and (b)

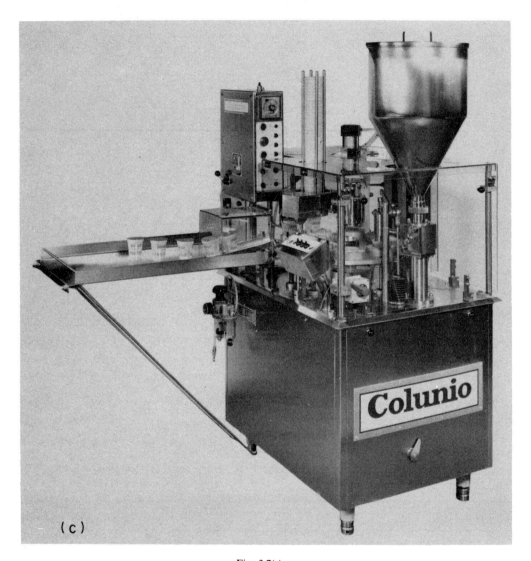

(c)

Fig. 3.7(c)

Fig. 3.7.   Illustrations of yoghurt filling machines recommended for small/medium scale producers

(a) The Cockx rotary cup filler and sealer:
   1. the alternative sealing mechanisms are: crimp sealer for foil lids, snap-on 'lidder' for plastic lids, or heat sealing.
   2. Specifications:

	Model R750	R1000
Capacity	85–600 ml	85–285 ml
Speed (cups/hour)	750	1000 +

   Reproduced by courtesy of Cockx & Sons (London) Ltd., Suffolk, U.K.

(b) Hans Rychiger filling and heat sealing machine 1693
   —Front and back view of the filler
   —Output per hour is 3000 cups
   —Notice aluminium lids are provided from a reel
   —Sealing pressure is 500 kg/cm²
   —Some machines are equipped to seal product under vacuum
   Reproduced by courtesy of Hans Rychiger AG, Steffisburg, Switzerland.

(c) Colunio 2000 H
   —Filling capacity maximum 300 ml
   —Maximum output, depending on container size, is up to 2000 per hour.
   —The heat sealing head is controlled by a thyristor temperature controller.
   Reproduced by courtesy of Caleb Duckworth Ltd., Bedford, U.K.

(d) Hittpac ALH—12
   —On-site view of Hittpack machine filling yoghurt into square containers.
   Reproduced by courtesy of Textima AG, Hittnau, Switzerland.

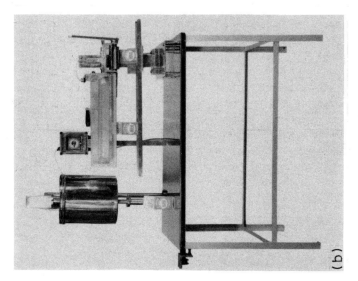

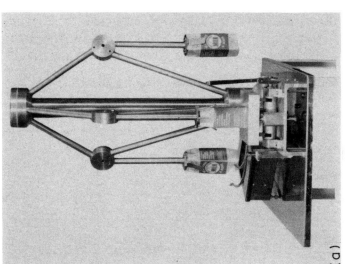

Fig. 3.8. Hand-operated packaging equipment (Barnes) for filling yoghurt into cartons (Pure-Pak)

(a) Carton Maker/Sealer—The unit is manually operated, and crimps, heats, folds and bottom seals all sizes of Pure-Pak carton;

(b) Hand Filler/Sealer—Manual filling and sealing of the cartons (the filling head must be slightly modified to accommodate yoghurt).

Reproduced by courtesy of Cockx & Sons (London) Ltd., Suffolk, U.K.

C. Miscellaneous System(s)

The equipment required and the processing steps involved in the manufacture of set or stirred yoghurt by this simple procedure are:

(i) the basic mix is prepared in cans/churns;

(ii) a water bath is required for the heat treatment of the milk, and the cans are immersed in the water; the heat source could be steam or electrical; at the cooling stage the hot water is replaced by cold water from the mains;

(iii) at 45°C the milk is inoculated with starter culture and incubated in bulk (stirred yoghurt), or for set yoghurt the milk is dispensed into cups prior to incubation; special cabinets can be used for the fermentation, or alternatively the temperature in the water bath can be maintained at 45°C to ferment the milk in bulk;

(iv) at the desired acidity the cans/churns are removed from the incubator unit(s) and stored overnight in the cold store;

(v) fruit is added separately to each can/churn and mixed gently using a milk/cream plunger;

(vi) filling and packaging is carried out using hand-operated units.

D. Mini Dairy

The "Mini Dairy" is a small compact processing plant which was developed in the late 1970s by Alfa-Laval A/B, Lund in Sweden—a project sponsored by the Swedish government for the establishment of small-scale milk processing units in the developing countries. The plant is capable of handling up to 1000 litres per batch of yoghurt per 10–12-hour day. All the necessary equipment is assembled on a metal platform by the manufacturer, and it is basically designed for the processing of market milk, some soft cheese varieties and/or yoghurt. The energy required for heating and cooling is provided by mains electricity or a diesel-powered electric generator, and hot water is generated by an oil- or wood-fired furnace. Figure 3.9 illustrates the unit as prepared for the manufacture of yoghurt; an optional unit (not shown) is the yoghurt filling machine.

Fig. 3.9.   A general view of the base unit of the "mini dairy" processing plant

(1) Reception tank fitted with a sieve
(2) Processing tanks
(3) Milk pasteuriser

Reproduced by courtesy of Alfa-Laval Co. Ltd., Middlesex, UK.

LARGE-SCALE PRODUCTION

In this section the equipment employed for the manufacture of yoghurt is specially designed to handle thousands of litres per day, and during the past few decades a highly sophisticated technology has evolved which offers a dairy both improved mechanisation and automation. The diversity of these technologies can be discussed most easily in relation to:

(i) type of yoghurt produced, e.g. set or stirred;
(ii) the effect of mechanisation on the quality of yoghurt.

There are, of course, several approaches that can be employed for the production of yoghurt, and as each yoghurt manufacturer has his own specific requirements each plant is supplied, in effect, "tailor made".

Figure 3.10 illustrates the general features of a plant suitable for the production of set yoghurt, and a combined processing plant (set and/or stirred yoghurt) is shown in Figs. 3.11 and 3.12. Some of the stages are similar for both processes, for example milk reception and handling, preparation of the basic mix, homogenisation of the yoghurt milk, and heat treatment, and hence it is appropriate to review the relevant equipment in relation to the different stages of manufacture; more specialised units are discussed separately.

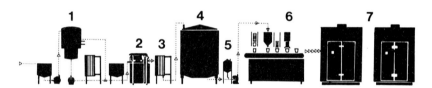

Fig. 3.10. Flow diagram of the production of set-yoghurt

The outline of the process is as follows:−

Standardised milk is concentrated in a plate evaporator (1) to the desired solids.
Pre-heated milk at 55–60°C is homogenised at 200 kg/cm² (2).
Heat treatment of milk to 85–95°C for 5–10 minutes or 135°C for 16 seconds takes place in a plate heat exchanger (3).
The heated milk is cooled to 45°C and stored in tank (4).
The starter culture (5) is metered into the milk before it is cartoned in the filler (6).
The cups of yoghurt are incubated for 2½–3 hours at 45°C in incubating chamber (7); followed by cooling to 2–5°C prior to distribution.

Reproduced by courtesy of Stork-Amsterdam Int., Middlesex, U.K.

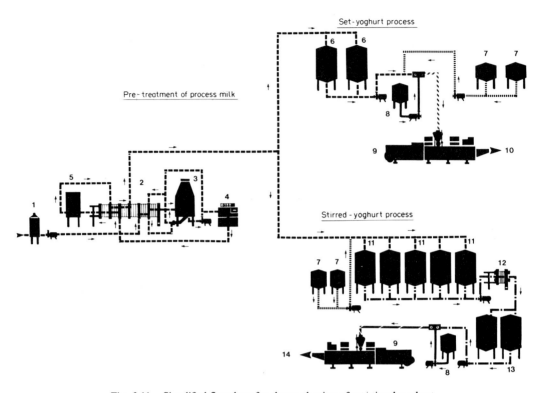

Fig. 3.11. Simplified flowchart for the production of set/stirred yoghurt

Standardised and/or clarified milk is pumped from storage tank to balance tank (1)
Pre-heat the milk to 90°C in plate heat exchanger (2), and concentrate under vacuum in an evaporator (3) by removing 15–20% water in order to increase milk solids by 2–4%. (If the alternative method, i.e. addition of skim milk powder, is used instead of evaporation, the powder is mixed as illustrated in Figs. 3.18 and 3.19.)

The condensate from the evaporator is used for "regeneration", i.e. to pre-heat the incoming milk.
In the evaporator (3) the temperature of milk drops to 70°C before it is homogenised at 200 kg/cm² (4).
The homogenised milk is fed back to the plate heat exchanger (2) where it is heated to 90–95°C with holding for 3–5 minutes in a holding tube (5)
The heated milk is then cooled to 43–44°C for the production of

Set Yoghurt	*Stirred Yoghurt*
The milk is fed into an intermediate tank (6), inoculated with starter culture (7) and/or flavours (8) before it is packed in the filling machine (9).	The milk is delivered to insulated tanks (11) where it is inoculated with 2–3% starter culture (7).
Incubate for 3 hours in special chambers (10); at the end of fermentation period the yoghurt cups are cooled to 15–20°C before transport to the cold store.	After incubation the coagulum is passed through a "structuriser" (see Fig. 3.62), and cooled quickly to 15–20°C in a plate cooler (12).
	Cool yoghurt is kept in intermediate tanks (13) before it is mixed with fruit (8) and finally packaged in the filling machine (9).
	Packed yoghurt is kept under refrigeration in cold store (14).

------- Process milk   ·············· Bulk Starter culture   ·—·—·— Yoghurt   ,,,,,,, Flavoured yoghurt milk
———— Flavouring materials   ·—·——·— Flavoured yoghurt

Adapted from Anon. (1976a).
Reproduced by courtesy of Alfa-Laval A/B, Lund, Sweden.

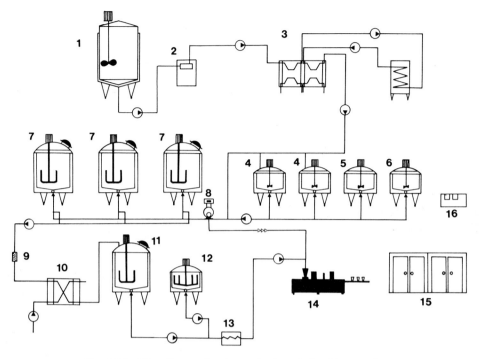

Fig. 3.12. Flow diagram for the production of stirred/set—yoghurt

1. Mixing vat (for dry ingredients)
2. Homogeniser
3. Plate heat exchanger
4. Bulk starter culture vats
5. Sugar syrup tanks
6. Gelatin tanks
7. Incubation/fermentation vats
8. Metering pump
9. Double strainer (to break up white specks or nodules in the coagulum)
10. Plate cooler
11. Yoghurt storage tanks
12. Fruit storage tanks
13. Static or in-line mixer
14. Packaging machine
15. Incubation rooms
16. Unit for the production of mother starter culture

▷▷▷ Production of set-yoghurt

Reproduced by courtesy of Diessel GmbH & Co. (UK Branch), Wilmslow, UK.

A. Milk Reception, Handling and Storage

At present milk collection from farms in the United Kingdom is carried out in bulk, using a road tanker, although rail tankers or churns could be used. The facilities provided at a typical dairy for reception of this bulk milk are illustrated in Fig. 3.13, and in the case of road or rail tanker deliveries the milk intake can either be metered or weighed, e.g. at a weighbridge. After taking a sample of milk for chemical and microbiological analysis, the general practice is to cool the milk

<5°C using plate coolers, prior to storing the milk in a silo. An optional treatment of the milk at this stage is the installation of a separator in the reception line for clarifying the milk before cooling. The reception of milk in churns is also illustrated in Fig. 3.13. Normally the churns are unloaded in the reception area, and the lids removed. The freshness of the product is quickly determined by "sniffing" at the churns, and if any unusual smells are noted the milk is rejected; a composite sample of milk from each farm is further analysed chemically and for bacteriological quality.

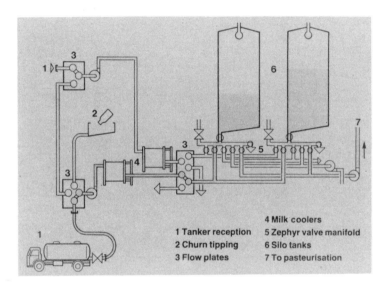

1 Tanker reception   4 Milk coolers
2 Churn tipping   5 Zephyr valve manifold
3 Flow plates   6 Silo tanks
                    7 To pasteurisation

Fig. 3.13.   Milk reception, handling and storage

Reproduced by courtesy of APV Co. Ltd., West Sussex, UK.

B. Preliminary Treatment of the Basic Mix

As already discussed elsewhere (see Chapter 2), the milk is subjected to a number of treatments before it becomes yoghurt, and one of these processes is the standardisation of the milk constituents in the basic mix.

1. Milk standardisation

The fat content of milk can vary according to source and season, but in yoghurt the level is prescribed by consumer taste or the statutory instruments of the countries concerned, so that standardisation becomes essential.

The theoretical approach to milk standardisation can best be visualised as follows:

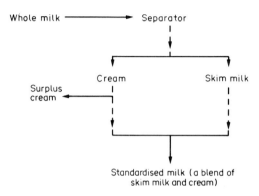

and the accuracy of the process is dependent on such factors as:

(i) type of equipment used, and the efficiency of fat separation obtained;
(ii) control system used.

The skimming efficiency of the available plant has greatly improved over the years, so that the residual fat in skim milk usually falls between 0.05–0.07%; the skimming efficiency of the separators is thus referred to as 0.05–0.07 respectively. The control system employed in milk standardisation lines can be either manual or automatic, and while the former may be recommended for small/medium size producers, the automatic system is essential for dairies handling large volumes of milk per day.

A number of different systems can be used for milk standardisation (Figs. 3.14, 3.15, 3.16 and 3.17), and the efficacy of any one particular system depends on its ability to ensure that:

(i) the pressure of the skim milk at outlet pipe is lower than the pressure in the tank where the skim milk and cream are remixed;
(ii) the fat content in the cream remains constant; the proportion of cream remixing with skim milk (if (i) and (ii) are constant) can be stabilised, i.e. proportional mixing controls the final fat content of the process milk.

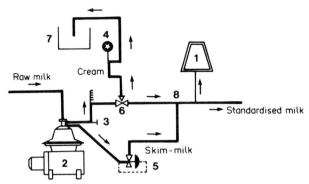

Fig. 3.14. On line milk standardisation using a butter fat monitoring (BMS) system

1. Milko-Tester Control unit
2. Separator
3. Cream screw
4. Adjustment
5. Constant pressure valve
6. 3-way valve
7. Excess cream
8. Mixing point

Reproduced by courtesy of Foss Electric (UK) Ltd., York, U.K.

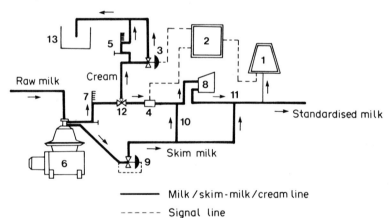

——— Milk / skim-milk / cream line

------ Signal line

Fig. 3.15. Principle of the Milko-tester control (MTC) system at Borup Andelsmejeri/Denmark

1. MTC with sample-taker
2. Control Unit (MTC Controller)
3. Control valve (automatic)
4. Flowmeter with transmitter
5. By-pass valve (manual)
6. Separator, 12,500 l/h
7. Cream screw
8. Homogenizer, 5,000 l/h
9. Constant pressure valve
10. Shunt line
11. Mixing point
12. 3-way valve
13. Balance tank for cream

(1–5 are necessary parts of the standardization system)

Reproduced by courtesy of Foss Electric (UK) Ltd., York, U.K.

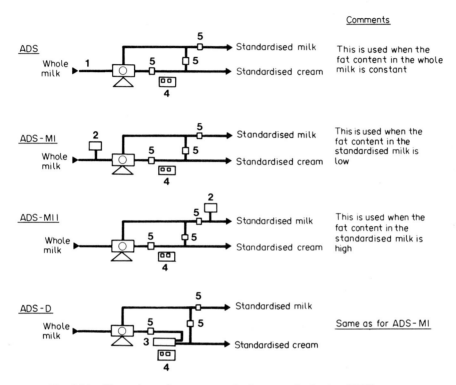

Comments

ADS — This is used when the fat content in the whole milk is constant

ADS-MI — This is used when the fat content in the standardised milk is low

ADS-MII — This is used when the fat content in the standardised milk is high

ADS-D — Same as for ADS-MI

Fig. 3.16. Illustrations of some automatic direct standardisation (ADS) systems

1. Manual or Milko-Tester fat content analysis
2. Milko-Tester Control (MTC)
3. Density meter
4. Panel with micro computer and recorder
5. Flow meter

All the above ADS systems use a flow control regulator based on a micro computer.

Reproduced by courtesy of Alfa-Laval A/B, Lund, Sweden.

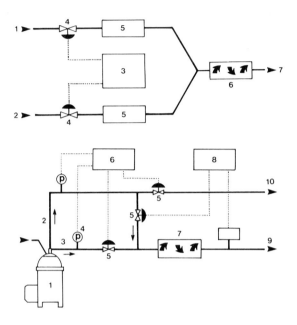

Fig. 3.17. Milk standardisation systems

Process I (Ratio Controller Method)

This system involves blending two stream of milk products, e.g. skim milk/cream or skim milk/whole milk, and the principal features are:–

a) control of the total flow rate;
b) the components must have a constant fat content;
c) no on-line measurement
1) Skim milk
2) Cream or whole milk
3) Flow ratio controllers
4) Zephyr valves
5) Flow meters
6) In-line mixer
7) Standardised milk

Process II (Automatic Operation of Milk Separator)

The process employs continuous, on-line control of a centrifugal milk separator.

The back pressure controllers maintain a steady degree of separation producing cream and skim streams of constant quality.

A proportion of the cream is blended into the skim-milk, and the quantity is controlled automatically by monitoring the fat content in the final product.
1) Separator
2) Cream
3) Skim milk
4) Pressure gauges
5) Zephyr valves
6) Separator back-pressure controller
7) In-line mixer
8) Fat content monitoring unit
9) Standardised milk
10) Surplus cream

Reproduced by courtesy of APV Co. Ltd., West Sussex, U.K.

The application of these systems to the manufacture of yoghurt could be considered under the following conditions:

(a) If the solids content of the milk is fortified using an evaporator (Figs. 3.10 and 3.11), then it is necessary to standardise the fat content in the milk before the concentration process commences.
(b) Skim milk could be concentrated by evaporation, and then before further treatments (i.e. homogenisation and heat treatment) the concentrated skim could be standardised with cream.
(c) Concentrated skim milk may be standardised with cream.
(d) Membrane filtration (UF or RO) is sometimes used to concentrate the yoghurt milk. Normally the fat is separated from whole milk, and the skim milk is concentrated to the desired level of solids; the concentrated skim is then standardised with the cream (see Fig. 3.30).

In general, therefore, the yoghurt milk is standardised for fat content before evaporation commences, but if the skim milk is concentrated in a UF plant the addition of cream takes place later. The reason for adding the fat to the concentrated skim in the latter method is that the high pressure used during the concentration process could damage some of the physical properties of the fat, which in turn may affect the quality of yoghurt, e.g. oiling-off or a "churning effect".

2. Fortification of milk solids

The level of milk solids in the basic mix can be raised by one or more of the following methods.

(a) Traditional process. Boiling the milk can be carried out in a tank similar to a batch pasteuriser, and the aim of this approach is the evaporation of 1/3 of the milk volume under atmospheric pressure. However, this method of concentration of the milk solids is not used under industrial conditions, mainly due to the high cost involved, but the generation of too much steam in the processing area can also be unacceptable to personnel.

(b) Addition of milk powder. Different types of milk powder can be used to fortify the yoghurt milk, but skim milk powder is used most widely. The dried ingredients are incorporated into the aqueous phase which could be whole milk, skim milk or water, and the available equipment is designed to provide the following features:

—complete dispersion of the dried ingredients into the aqueous phase;
—complete hydration of the dried particles with no residual lumps;
—minimise the incorporation of air in order to reduce the problems of foaming;
—the unit must be capable of easy cleaning and sanitisation.

The powder-handling equipment found in a dairy is dependent on the daily throughput, and the method of bulk delivery. Basically, milk powder is packed into either small capacity units (25–50 kg multi-layer paper sacks with polythene liners), medium capacity units (up to a tonne in metal or plastic containers), or in road tankers for bulk storage in metal silos. The machinery available for emptying the powder also varies, so that while the sacks (small quantities) may be emptied directly into reconstitution units, larger volumes are emptied into a sifter for delivery into the mixing unit. The powder stored in metal/plastic bins or silos is transferred using either a screw-feed (of variable speed) or a blower; dust filters must be used to recover any fine particles, especially in plants handling large capacities. Some examples of milk powder mixing units are as follows.

(i) Mixing funnel/hopper. Reconstitution of the powder is carried out in batches, and a "closed circuit" consisting of a tank, pipe connection, centrifugal pump and the funnel/hopper assembly is required. The tank is normally filled with the aqueous phase at around 40–50°C and

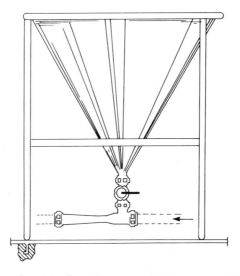

Fig. 3.18.   Illustration of a mixing funnel/hopper used for the reconstitution of milk powders

The sack of milk powder is placed on the table, and then emptied into the funnel. The force of the circulating liquid causes the powder to be aspirated downward and mixed with the water. Circulation is continued until the powder is dissolved. Notice that the funnel has a valve connection, which has a slight constriction/restriction in the pipe to provide a venturi effect. Reproduced by courtesy of Pasilac/Silkeborg Ltd., Preston, UK.

the circulation started. The positioning of the hopper in relation to the centrifugal pump is important and two options are available (see Fig. 3.18).

Firstly, if the hopper is assembled on the suction side of the centrifugal pump it offers the advantage of rapid dispersal and adequate dissolution of the powder due to the action of the pump; the disadvantage is that frequent blockages may occur in the hopper.

Secondly, by placing the hopper on the outlet side of the centrifugal pump directly after a specially designed venturi unit, the problem of blockage is overcome, but full dispersal of powder may be a little slower, for the venturi unit creates a vacuum within the pipe causing the powder to be sucked into the recirculating solution (Newstead, Goldmann and Zadow, 1979; Sanderson, 1982). The two circuits are illustrated in Fig. 3.19, and it is noticeable that in the latter approach any suction of air is returned to the tank rather than the suction side of the pump, because if air is introduced into the system, the action of the pump's impeller can increase the amount of air incorporated into the product. Furthermore, a reduction in aeration and/or frothing can be achieved by installing a special valve on the mixing hopper, and ensuring that the return line in the mixing tank is below the level of the liquid. If additional mixing of the added powder is required, one of the following units could be employed:

—in-line static mixer;
—high-speed agitator in the mixing tank;
—high-velocity liquid jet.

(ii) In-line mixers. An alternative method to the funnel/hopper instalation is the "in-line" mixer, and some examples of such units are as follows:

(1) Tri-blender. This mixing unit is supplied by the Ladish Company (Tri-Clover Division) of Wisconsin (USA). The principle of this mixing unit is that the venturi jet mixer is replaced by a high-speed blender; the powder is fed into the hopper of the mixer, and dispersed into the liquid stream inside the mixer itself. This mixing/blending device is sometimes known as a "tube-in-tube" diffuser, and the efficiency of the blending is due to the fact that, at the bottom of the mixer where the blender is situated, there is a screen which reduces lump formation and foaming, and so ensures an homogenous dispersion. Model F3218MD (Fig. 3.20) is fitted with a butterfly valve that is prevented from opening before the blender motor is operating, and provision for automatic feeding of the powder to the Tri-Blender is also available.

(2) Silverson mixers. These types of mixer operate at very high speed, and exert an homogenising effect during the recombining of dried ingredients. The models, which could be used for the reconstitution of milk powder, are known as the "In-Line" and the "Flashmix", and a unit combining both mixers together is also available (see Fig. 3.21). These machines are designed for continuous operation at high speeds, and each has incorporated a high-shear rotor/stator processing workhead; the "In-Line" mixer has one such head, and the "Flashmix" has two. The operating characteristics of these workheads are briefly described by the manufacturer as follows:

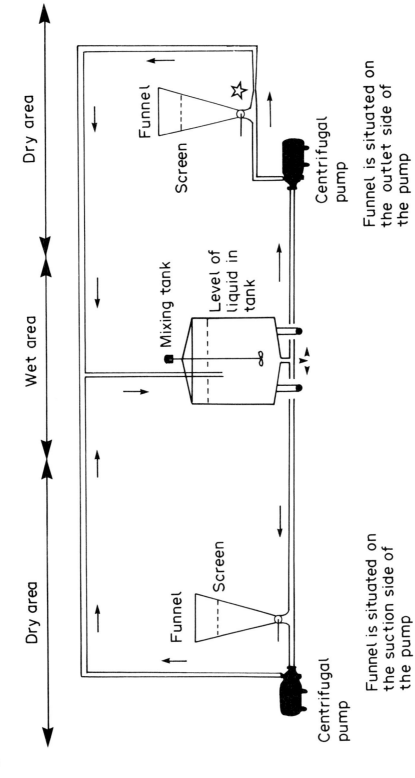

Funnel is situated on
the outlet side of
the pump

Funnel is situated on
the suction side of
the pump

Fig. 3.19. A schematic illustration showing the two possible installations of the funnel/hopper unit for the reconstitution of milk powder

☆ The venturi assembly where the velocity of the circulating liquid is increased, the pressure reduced, and funnel blockage is minimised.

Fig. 3.20. Illustration to the Tri-blender which is patented as a 'tube-in-tube' diffuser

Model F3218MD

Reproduced by courtesy of Ladish Co., (Tri-Clover Division), Wisconsin, USA.

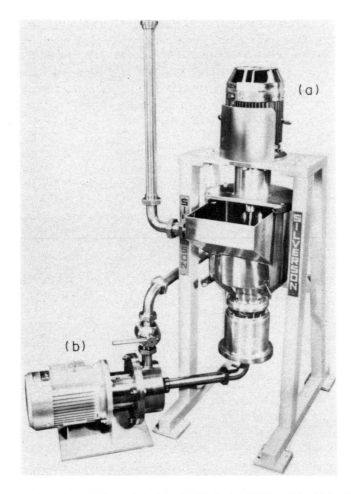

Fig. 3.21. A combination mixer which consists of the (a) 'Flashmix' (EFF) and the (b) 'In-line' mixer (450L)

Reproduced by courtesy of Silverson Machines Ltd., Buckinghamshire, U.K.

Materials inside the head are subjected to intense hydraulic shear by the high-speed rotation of
the rotor inside the confined space of the stator chamber.

Centrifugal force generated by the rotor drives the contents of the head towards the periphery of
the head where solid and liquid ingredients are milled in the fine precision clearance between
the rotor blade ends and the inner stator wall.

Further centrifugal force expels materials from the head, imparting mechanical shear between
the rotor tips and the edges of the stator perforations.

Finally the contents of the head are driven by the same centrifugal force through the machine
outlet and along the pipeline; at the same time fresh materials are drawn in at the inlet to keep
the head continuously charged.

The use of an "In-Line" mixer alone has its limitations, because the delivery of milk powder through a funnel in a recirculating circuit inevitably leads to "arching". However, the use of a "Flashmix" mixer overcomes this difficulty, due to the fact that the liquid and solid ingredients are fed simultaneously into a specially designed hopper and before being sucked immediately into the upper rotor/stator. This workhead converts the milk powder/liquid phase into a slurry which is then dispersed as the result of the high-speed shearing effect of the bottom or second workhead. It is obvious that each mixer is designed for a particular purpose, and a combination of these two types of mixer in the recombining process brings the advantages of both units, i.e. the mixing process involves three workheads rather than one or two, so ensuring complete dissolution of the powder with minimum incorporation of air. Some degree of homogenisation of the mix can be obtained by using different types of stator head or screen on the high-speed mixer, so that, for example, a disintegrating effect is achieved using large circular holes or slots, a fine screen produces an emulsification/homogenisation effect, and a screen with square holes imparts a high shearing effect.

(iii) In-tank mixing unit. Efficient mixing of powder in a tank relies entirely on the agitation system provided, and the familiar flow pattern which occurs during liquid mixing is illustrated in Fig. 3.22. These patterns are largely influenced by:

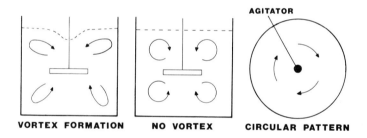

Fig. 3.22. Liquid mixing flow patterns

The paddles are perpendicular, top-entering and centrally mounted.

After Tamime and Greig (1979).

Reprinted with permission of Dairy Industries International.

—shape and size of the agitator system (e.g. paddle, turbine, propeller, scraped surface, anchor, etc.);

—position of the agitator, i.e. top or bottom entering, perpendicular or sloped, and/or centrally mounted or not;

117

—speed of rotation of the agitator;
—shape of the processing vessel, while more specifically the efficiency of mixing is related to:
—speed of rotation of the agitator;
—velocity difference between the bulk fluid and the agitator;
—the creation of a vortex;
—incorporation of air into the bulk fluid;
—any shearing effects.

All these factors are relevant to the dispersal of powder into the bulk fluid, and hence an equipment manufacturer has various options in terms of design.

(1) Multi-purpose processing tank. This type of tank (i.e. the batch pasteuriser) can be utilised during all stages of yoghurt making (see Fig. 3.4), for the agitation system consists of:

—a high-speed motor which is operated during the preparation and processing of the milk;
—a slow-speed motor for mixing in the starter, and later for cooling of the starter, and later for cooling of the coagulum;
—the drive shaft of the slow-speed motor can be fitted with a one- or two-propellor agitator, and is usually top entering and sloped.

(2) Simple mixing tank. Different types of high-speed mixers (Silverson, Greaves and Ystral) which could be used in simple tanks that resemble a batch pasteuriser, but do not have a properly mounted agitation system. Thus in a yoghurt production two of these tanks will be installed in parallel for preparation of the basic mix, so that while one tank is being emptied, the other tank is normally being filled up; a continuous flow of yoghurt milk to the incubation tanks can be achieved in this way. In practice, a tank is filled with water or milk warmed to around 40–50°C, and the milk powder is emptied from the sacks. Recombination is achieved using a high-shear mixer/homogeniser, and the mixers can be mounted permanently in each tank, or alternatively can be removed from one tank to the other with the aid of an hydraulic lift (see Fig. 3.23).

An alternative type of a high-speed, in-tank mixer is the Ystral mixer (Dalhuisen, 1972), and Fig. 3.24 illustrates the overall assembly. The powder mixing procedure is as follows:

—the powder is emptied into the special chute;
—the high-speed action of the mixing head creates a vacuum at the tip of the powder delivery pipe, thus transferring the powder down the pipe from the chute;
—the powder/liquid mixing takes place in the absence of air, and there is little risk of the powder forming clumps.

(3) Crepaco "Blender/Incorporator". This is a specially designed tank that provides rapid and complete dispersion of the dried ingredients into the liquid slurry (see Fig. 3.25). The tank has a 15° cone bottom which facilitates easy and rapid unloading, and it is fitted with a high-speed motor (400 rpm) which drives a special centrifugal agitator. This unique agitator incorporates a 'squirrel cage' design which results in a dual blending action combining an overal swirl with a deep-

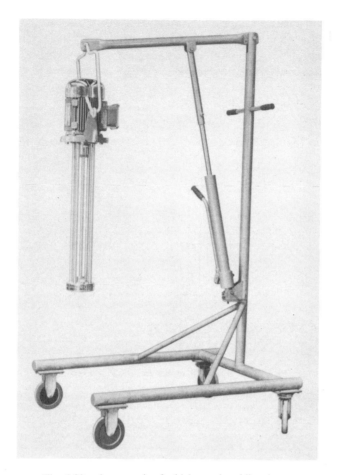

Fig. 3.23. An example of a high-speed mobile mixer

Silverson—Typical medium range immersion mixer (model BX) which is mounted on a mobile, hydraulic floor stand. Reproduced by courtesy of Silverson Machines Ltd., Buckinghamshire, UK.

draw vortex that quickly and effectively disperses the milk powder into the aqueous phase with a minimum of foam. Although the tank is specifically designed to emulsify two or more immiscible products, the blending action is especially effective in dispersing any fatty constituents in the yoghurt milk. Furthermore, the tank can also be fitted with a cleaning-in-place system.

(4) Crepaco "Liquiverter". This high-speed blender/disperser is capable of both dispersing the dry ingredients and of incorporating fat into the liquid phase. The impeller/agitator is centrally mounted from the bottom of the square tank, and the action of the "LiquiVerter" pulls the added milk powder through the liquid vortex at the centre, and forces the mixture up the walls into continuous circulation.

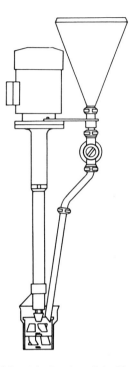

Fig. 3.24.   Schematic drawing of the Ystral type mixer

Reproduced by courtesy of Stork-Amsterdam, Int., Middlesex, U.K.

(iv) Primodan continuous recombiner. The incorporation of air during the reconstitution of milk powder is unavoidable by the methods described above, and as the presence of air can affect the efficiency of the pasteuriser and/or homogeniser, deaeration of the reconstituted milk is necessary before further treatment. The method of deaeration may involve a simple physical separation, i.e. where the milk is left undisturbed for a period of time in a mixing or buffer tank, or separation under vacuum could be considered. Alternatively, if the powder is mixed in under vacuum, the deaeration step can be avoided, and the Primodan Recombiner is a typical example. This method of recombination can be used for powder mixing in a yoghurt processing line. Anon. (1981a) describes the Primodan system as follows:

(a) the recombining section consists of a dosing unit, special pump and a combined balance/recirculation tank;
(b) the powder is conveyed to the dosing unit pneumatically or mechanically;
(c) the unit automatically adds the powder to the recirculating liquid as a result of the pump action creating a vacuum under the dosing unit; the level of vacuum generated can be adjusted by a butterfly valve;
(d) the dosing device consists of a flexible rubber pipe fitted with two sets of pressure roller; these rollers operate alternatively, so that where the bottom rollers are in the closed position

Fig. 3.25.   A general view of the Crepaco "blender/incorporator" tank

Reproduced by courtesy of Crepaco International Inc., Brussels, Belgium

Fig. 3.26. A close-up view of the Primodan powder dosing device

(1) General view of the dosing unit
(2) Dosing device—notice the upper and the bottom sets of rollers
(3) The rubber pipe—the dosing unit can deliver 300 g at each dosing operation.

Reproduced by courtesy of Primodan Dairy Equipment A/S, Mørkøv, Denmark.

for the delivery of the powder to the dosing unit, the top rollers are in the open position and vice versa (see Fig. 3.26);

(e) the powder is sucked into the recirculating liquid under vacuum;

(f) a vacuum is also maintained outside the rubber pipe in the dosing unit in order to prevent the pipe collapsing;

(g) the balance/recirculation tank is designed to liberate any air which is incorporated accidentally or was originally present in the powder; this tank is also fitted with sensors to regulate the incoming (water or milk) and the outgoing (reconstituted/standardised milk) liquid.

When dealing with the recombination of milk powder(s), two conditions in the reconstituted milk have to be monitored:

Firstly, not all the particles of milk may dissolve during the recombining process, perhaps through the use of poor quality powder(s), inefficient mixing equipment and/or the presence of scorched particles, and any undissolved particles must be removed as follows:

—in-line stainless steel mesh, or a stainless steel mesh and nylon filter called the Duplex;
—centrifugal clarifiers.

Clarifiers are excellent for the removal of any fine or undissolved particles and any extraneous matter, but for convenience filters are more commonly used. Normally two interchangeable filters are installed in a milk reconstituted line, especially in large dairies, so that in the case of clogging the flow of milk can be easily diverted while one of the filters is being cleaned. The removal of such particles is essential, since their presence in the milk can damage the orifices in an homogeniser and/or increase soiling in heat exchangers.

Secondly, reconstituted powder(s) requires up to 15 minute's duration to achieve complete hydration, otherwise sedimentation becomes evident. The hydration effect may not be important during the manufacture of yoghurt, since the time required between recombining and the end of heat treatment of the milk can be as long as 15 minutes.

(c) Evaporation of milk. Concentration of the standardised yoghurt milk can be achieved by the use of an evaporator, in which the average amount of water removed is 10–25% and the total solids is increased by 2–4%, corresponding to the recommended fortification with milk powder. In order to remove the desired amount of water, and avoid damage of the milk constituents at high temperatures, the process of evaporation is normally carried out under vacuum.

Single-effect evaporators can be used directly in a yoghurt processing line. The yoghurt milk is pumped from the balance tank to the condensor where it is preheated, and then enters the plate section of the evaporator for further heating. After reaching the preset temperature, the milk flows to the "separator" section and water vapour is removed from the milk; the cycle is repeated until the desired concentration of total solids in the basic mix has been reached. Heat recovery during the evaporation process is very efficient, and it is achieved using a thermocompressor, i.e. factory steam is mixed with the vapour produced from the evaporator (see Fig. 3.27).

Fig. 3.27. On-site view of a single-effect plate evaporator for the concentration of yoghurt milk

Reproduced by courtesy of Stork-Amsterdam Int., Middlesex, UK.

Another type of single-effect evaporator which could be used to concentrate the yoghurt milk is supplied by Alfa-Laval A/B, and the sequence of operations is as follows:

—the standardised yoghurt milk is preheated to 60°C in the regeneration section of the plate heat exchanger using the condensate from the evaporator (see Fig. 3.11);
—subsequently the milk is heated to 85–90°C in the heating section of the plate heat exchanger;
—the hot milk enters the vacuum chamber where the inlet is shaped as an expansion tube to prevent burning of the milk;
—the milk is recirculated until the desired concentration is achieved; the recirculation cycle is controlled by the capacity of the vacuum chamber, evacuation pump, and the float controller; during each recycle approximately 3–4% of water is removed; therefore, to obtain 20% evaporation the recirculated flow must be 5–6 times the capacity of the plant, i.e. plate heat exchanger (see Fig. 3.11); the capacity of such evaporators is up to 8000 litres per hour, but for larger plants different types of evaporators are installed;
—during the evaporation of the basic mix, the temperature drops to 70°C.

In general these evaporators offer the following advantages:

—minimum requirement for space;
—efficient heat recovery;
—immediacy of use.

Furthermore, yoghurt made from milk concentrated in this way exhibits an excellent organoleptic quality.

(d) Membrane concentration of milk. An alternative method of fortification of the basic mix is by concentration of the milk (whole and/or skim) by membrane filtration, i.e. UF and RO. The basic differences between the UF and the RO systems are that firstly the operational pressures are much higher in the case of RO, and secondly, the RO membrane is less permeable than the UF membrane; the pore size for RO is <4 Å and for UF is >20 Å (1 mm = 10^7 Å).

The milk constituents that pass through a membrane are referred to as the permeate, and the material that does not pass through the membrane, i.e. concentrated fraction, is known as the retentate. The different components present in milk can be divided into three main groups based on the molecular weight, i.e. large molecules (proteins and fats), medium (lactose and salts) and small (water). The RO membrane allows only the small molecules (water) to pass through the membrane, and the retentate consists of a concentrate of all the milk constituents, while the UF membrane permits small and medium-size molecular weight solutes (e.g. water, lactose and salts) to pass through; the retentate is a concentration of the macro-molecules of proteins and fats. The differences in the composition of the permeate and the retentate of the RO and UF processes are illustrated in Fig. 3.28.

The application of membrane filtration in the yoghurt industry is most likely to involve the use of UF, since it has the advantage of giving an increased concentration of proteins, but a reduced level of lactose in the basic mix; Fig. 3.29 shows a UF plant in a dairy in Denmark being employed during production of yoghurt, and Fig. 3.30 illustrates the production of yoghurt, ymer and/or ylette using a "conventional" process or a UF plant.

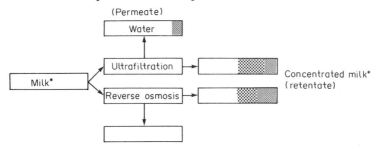

Fig. 3.28.   Illustration of the major differences in composition of the retentate and permeate during membrane filtration

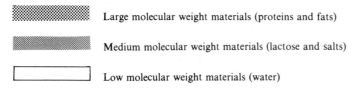

Large molecular weight materials (proteins and fats)

Medium molecular weight materials (lactose and salts)

Low molecular weight materials (water)

Refer to Table 2.5 (Chapter 2) for the milk constituent losses in the permeate
*Whole or skim milk
Drawing is not to scale, i.e. constituent lost in permeate or retained in retentate.

Fig. 3.29. A view of an ultrafiltration plant at Nordjysk Mejeriselskab in Denmark employed for the production of yoghurt and ymer

Reproduced by courtesy of Pasilac/Silkeborg Ltd., Preston, UK.

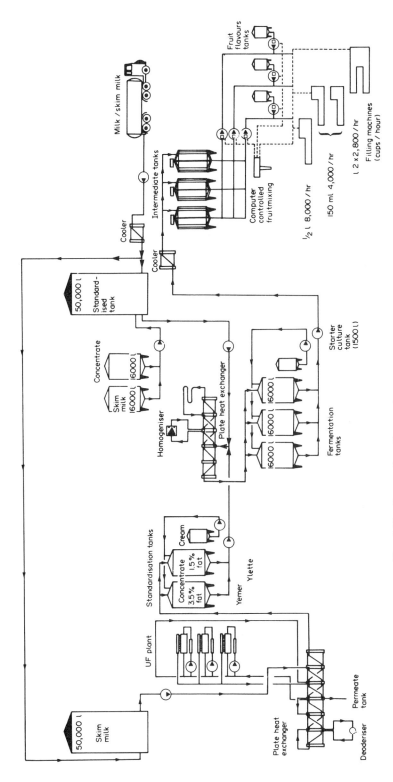

Fig. 3.30. Process flow diagram for yoghurt, ymer and ylette production

Chemical composition (%) of raw materials and different fermented dairy products

	Whole milk	Skim milk	Yoghurt	Ymer	Ylette
Fat	4.8	–	3.5	3.5	1.5
Protein	3.6	3.6	3.8	6.0	6.0

The UF treatment of skim milk, e.g. 180 kg will produce 100 kg of concentrate and 80 kg of permeate.

Adapted from Anon. (1981b, c).

Reproduced by courtesy of Pasilac/Silkeborg Ltd., Preston, U.K.

C. Homogenisation

Homogenisers are used mainly for the purpose of providing stable fat-in-water emulsions so that the fat in the yoghurt milk does not separate, but homogenisation also brings about some desirable physical changes in the basic mix which contribute towards the production of a viscous yoghurt. The process is accomplished by forcing the milk through a narrow orifice under high pressure, and hence an homogeniser is simply a unit consisting of:

(i) a high-pressure pump,
(ii) an homogeniser head or valve.

The high-pressure pump usually consists of three or five pistons which are driven by a heavy duty electric motor. The motor drives an eccentric crankshaft connected to a transmission rod, and the latter converts the rotary motion of the electric motor into the reciprocating action of the pistons. Each piston is run through a bore in a high-pressure cylinder block upon which is mounted the homogeniser head or valve. The cylinder of each piston has two valves, the suction valve normally situated at the bottom of the cylinder and the discharge valve at the top. The suction and the discharge valves have independent passages (bottom or upper respectively) connecting all the cylinders.

The homogenisation pressure, which is normally indicated on a gauge, is adjusted manually with a pressure-setting lever, and the flow of product through the homogeniser is as follows:

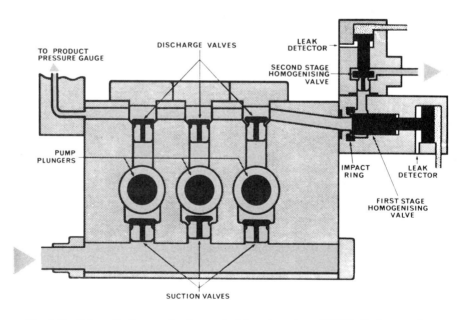

Fig. 3.31.   Schematic diagram showing product flow through an APV/Gaulin homogeniser

Reproduced by courtesy of APV Co. Ltd., West Sussex, UK.

—on the backward/suction stroke of the piston the milk enters the cylinder through the suction valve of the bottom passage while the discharge valves remains closed;

—on the forward stroke of the piston the suction valve is closed and the milk is forced through the discharge valve into the upper passage towards the homogeniser head or valve;

—the milk is then forced under pressure through the restricting flow area of the homogeniser head or valve;

—a single-stage homogenisation or followed by another valve in a two-stage homogeniser (see Fig. 3.31).

In addition, the pistons are normally fitted with special rings to prevent any contamination of the product by oil, and the pistons are cooled with water. In aseptic homogenisers the water is replaced with steam and condensate to eliminate contamination of sterile products, e.g. UHT milk.

The effectiveness of the homogenisation process is governed mainly by the design of the homogeniser head and the pressure applied during operation, and Harper, Seiberling and Blaisdell (1976) have illustrated some of the possible designs. In principle, the cross-section of any homogeniser head consists of the following:

(i) valve seat or outer ring;

(ii) impact ring or homogeniser ring;

(iii) valve or core;

(iv) apparature for passage of the product (Anon., 1979a), and the passage of milk through the homogeniser head can be envisaged as follows:

—the milk is fed at high pressure into the homogeniser, and the first impact forces open the preloaded adjustable valve, i.e. forming the space between (i) and (ii) above;

—the resultant pressure drop produces a shearing action together with cavitation bubbles, so that the fat globules are slightly reduced in size;

—the milk is still travelling at high velocity (in the region of 12,000–18,000 metres per minute), and hitting the impact or homogeniser ring (ii) results in change of direction of the milk flow causing where further shearing or shattering to take place by impact and implosion of the bubbles;

—the aperature is around 300 microns;

—the homogenisation effect can be enhanced by passing the product through a second homogeniser head (see Fig. 3.31) and the pressure exerted at the second stage is lower than at the first stage;

—the back pressure generated from the second homogenisation stage can be adjusted to produce the desired degree of homogenisation (Anon., 1980).

HEAT TREATMENT

The purpose of the heat treatment of yoghurt milk has been discussed in detail elsewhere, and hence in this section only the important technical aspects will be reviewed.

A. The Fundamental Principles of Heat Transfer

Heating of the yoghurt milk and the cooling of the coagulum both involve one fundamental aspect of thermodynamics, i.e. heat transfer (Hall, 1976; Loncin and Merson, 1979; Kessler, 1981). In general, the flow of heat takes place from a warmer medium to a cooler, and the greater the temperature differential between the two media the greater and/or more rapid the heat flow. This transfer of heat can be either by conduction, convection or radiation (see Table 3.1), but in the dairy industry the former two processes are more important. The actual application of heat may be carried out in a "direct" or "indirect" manner, but for practical reasons the latter is most widely used in the yoghurt industry. Thus instead of steam (food grade) being injected into the milk during the heating stage, the heating medium and the milk never come into contact with each other; and the chemical composition of the yoghurt milk remains unaltered during the heat treatment. Similarly, the "indirect" method of heat transfer is used for cooling the coagulum.

TABLE 3.1. *Brief definition of types of heat transfer and factors affecting their thermal conductivity*

Types of heat transfer	Factors influencing thermal conductivity
Conduction: is the transfer of thermal energy from one molecule to another, and this may take place through solid bodies or through layers of liquid at rest in which no physical flow or mixing takes place in the direction of heat transfer.	(a) Area (b) Thickness or length of heat transfer path (c) Temperature difference
Convection: is the transfer of thermal energy due to the movement of mass, and this occurs when particles at high temperatures are mixed with particles at a lower temperature.	(i) Ibid (ii) Movement of fluid (iii) Fluid characteristics (thickness, viscosity, turbulence, velocity and temperature of fluid)
Radiation: is the emission of thermal energy by radiation (hot or cold) across an absolute vacuum in which the electromagnetic radiation of a body causes molecules vibrate and emit radiant energy.	(a) Surface property of the body ⎫ e.g. a black body shows (b) Temperature of the body ⎬ good absorbance and ⎭ emission of heat

The types of equipment that can be employed for the heat treatment of milk include:

(i) The batch process (batch pasteurisers or multipurpose tanks) in which the milk can be heated by "direct" steam injection into the milk, or "indirectly" by one of the following methods:
—steam injection into the jacket (this system allows excellent heat transfer, but may lead to severe denaturation of the milk due to localised heating).
—steam injection into the water jacket (this system of heating is widely used); alternatively, the water can be heated by gas or electricity, and such processing tanks are very popular with the small-scale producers (see Fig. 3.4).
(ii) The continuous process (plate, tubular or scraped surface heat exchangers) in which the milk is heated by the "indirect" method using either direct steam (under reduced pressure) in the heating section of the heat exchanger, or alternatively hot water.

B. Types of Equipment Used for Heating the Yoghurt Milk

1. Batch or the multipurpose tanks

These tanks resemble batch pasteurisers, and they are normally water-jacketed. Steam is injected into the water during the heating stage of the yoghurt milk, and chilled water is circulated during the cooling of the coagulum. The capacity of these tanks is several thousand litres, and according to Kessler (*loc. cit.*) the time required for heating the yoghurt milk with *vigorous stirring* can be calculated from the following equation:

$$\text{Time of heating (seconds)} = \frac{\text{Volume (m}^3) \times \text{Density (kg/m}^3) \times \text{Specific heat (J/kg K)}}{\text{Effective heat exchange area (m}^2) \times \text{Heat transfer coefficient (W/m}^2\text{ K)}} \ln \frac{\text{Temperature of heated medium} - \text{Starting temperature of yoghurt milk}}{\text{Temperature of heated medium} - \text{Desired temperature required to heat the yoghurt milk}}$$

ln = natural logarithm

In a large processing plant a series of these tanks could be used at regular intervals for the production of yoghurt on a semi-continuous basis, and typical processing cycle using a multipurpose tanks could involve the following stages:

(i) filling the tank with fortified and homogenised milk at 60°C;
(ii) heating the milk to 85–90°C for 15–30 minutes;
(iii) cooling the milk to the incubation temperature, i.e. 40–45°C (short set) or to 30°C (long set);
(iv) incubating the milk to the desired acidity;
(v) cooling the coagulum to 20°C or <10°C.

An example of such a tank is illustrated in Fig. 3.32 and according to Jay (1979) the time required for the manufacture of yoghurt (5000 litres) starting from *cold* milk and cooling the coagulum to 5°C was 9 hours and 15 minutes. Similar types of tanks are manufactured by Crepaco Incorporated in the United States of America (see Fig. 3.33), and the models which are suitable for the manufacture of yoghurt are types "PC" and "B". The general specifications of these tanks are:

—Both tanks have a direct steam or hot water as the heat exchange medium, and for cooling glycol is circulated in the jacket.
—Both tanks are fitted with total sweep, scraper blades and/or for heavy products a special scraper blade/agitator (the features of this agitation system will be discussed later).
—The only difference between these models is in the bottom construction of the tank; the "PC" type is made from a 35° cone, while the "B" model has a 15° cone; the cone-shaped tank is an advantage for discharging the coagulum.
—The capacities of these tanks range from 570 to 7570 litres for model "B", and 760 to 7570 litres for model "PC".

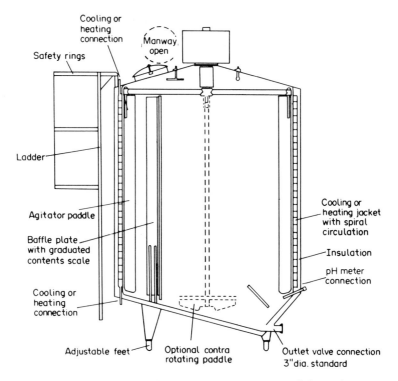

Fig. 3.32. Illustration of a multi-purpose processing tank for yoghurt

Capacities range from 2500 to 20,000 litres, and the maximum working pressure in the jacket is 1.05 kg/cm² (15 psi). Reproduced by courtesy of Wincanton Engineering Ltd., Dorset, U.K.

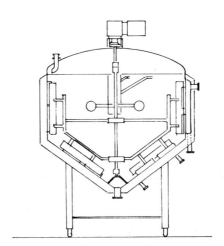

Fig. 3.33. A schematic drawing of a Crepaco type "PC" tank

The tank is fitted with "scraped surface" agitator and has a 35° cone base.

Reproduced by courtesy of Crepaco International Inc., Brussels, Belgium.

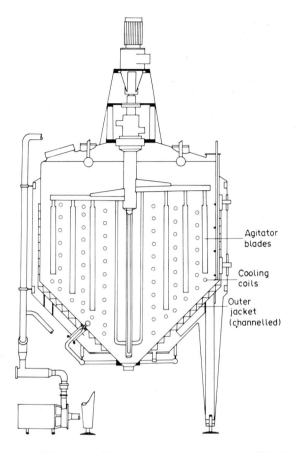

Fig. 3.34.   Illustration of Goavec yoghurt processing tank (5000 litres)

The total surface area for cooling is 40 m².

Reproduced by courtesy of Goavec S.A., Alençon Cedex, France and Engelmann & Buckham Machinery Ltd., Hampshire, U.K.

Another type of multipurpose tank has been recently launched on the market by Goavec S.A. of Alençon Cedex in France. The general structure of the tank is illustrated in Fig. 3.34, and it is of note that the heating surface is both around the body and the conical base of the tank. The increased surface area is also beneficial during the cooling stages, but in order to improve the efficiency of the tank, the cooling area is increased by fitting stationary coils; the agitators are also cooled internally (see Fig. 3.35). Thus, the system of yoghurt manufacture is roughly similar to any batch process, and a typical time–temperature profile for heating the yoghurt milk, the incubation period and cooling the coagulum is illustrated in Fig. 3.36. It can be observed that the Goavec tank exhibits excellent heat transfer characteristics during the heating and the cooling stages.

133

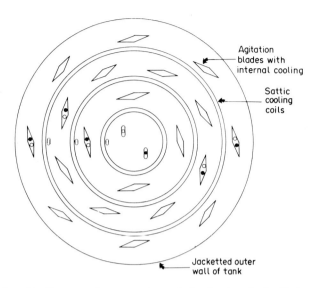

Fig. 3.35. A cross section of the Goavec yoghurt processing tank showing the agitation blades and the static cooling coils

Reproduced by courtesy of Goavec S.A., Alençon Cedex, France and Engelmann & Buckham Machinery Ltd., Hampshire, UK.

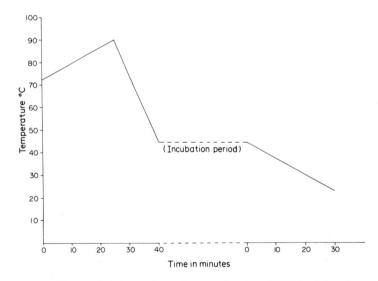

Fig. 3.36. Temperature profile recorded during the production of yoghurt (5000 litres) in a Goavec processing tank

After Hale (1982).

2. Continuous process

The types of heat exchangers most commonly used in the dairy industry are:

134

—plate heat exchanger,
—tubular heat exchanger,
—scraped/swept surface heat exchanger.

The former two types are widely installed in yoghurt plants for the heat treatment of the milk, but the swept surface heat exchanger is used for the heat treatment of fruit preparations. These heat exchangers can be visualised as "two-channel" units in which the heating medium (hot water) flows in one channel, and is separated by a partition from the yoghurt milk flowing in the other.

The milk is processed, therefore, on a continuous basis, and when compared with the batch process heat exchangers offer the following advantages:

(i) a small floor area is required;
(ii) less energy is required due to the improved efficiency of heat transfer and heat recovery;
(iii) productivity can be increased by utilising the fermentation tanks more than once per day;
(iv) the system is more versatile, e.g. the processed milk could be removed from the plant at a certain temperature to be homogenised.

A plate heat exchanger is a unit which consists of a series of corrugated stainless steel plates held together in a frame, and along the boundary of the plate a rubber gasket is fitted to prevent leakage between the milk and water passages. The corrugation of the plate helps to increase the turbulence of the liquid flow and/or the surface area, and hence improve the efficiency of heat transfer. The thickness of the gasket does, of course, alter space between the plates, for while a narrow gap is desirable for the heat treatment of milk, a larger gap is recommended for cooling of coagulum. In the former instance the milk flows in a thin film across the width of the plate, so that heat transfer is rapid, but the large gap is necessary during the cooling of the yoghurt in order to avoid too great a drop in viscosity.

In practice, a plate heat exchanger consists of several sections in which different treatments of the milk may take place, e.g. preheating/regeneration, final heating, holding and/or cooling sections. The heating medium is normally hot water, but if the milk is to be heated to temperatures above 100°C, steam (under reduced pressure) may be used. The cooling medium can be cold water, chilled water or brine, and the type of coolant circulated in a plate heat exchanger is dependent on the desired outlet temperature of the product.

The flow of both milk and heating/cooling medium in a plate heat exchanger can run alternatively, i.e. "single-channel" operation, but the efficiency of heat transfer is difficult to maintain. To overcome this disadvantage the flow of fluids in a plate heat exchanger may be arranged into special patterns, and one Alfa-Laval type plate heat exchanger has, for example, a combination of a $4 \times 2/2 \times 4$ (Anon., 1980). Such a combination means that the heating medium is in four parallel channels and changes its direction twice, and the flow of milk is in two parallel channels and changes direction four times.

The tubular heat exchanger is, as the name indicates, constructed out of tubes or pipes, and may be in the form of a single-tube heat exchanger, or may consist of a bundle of tubes. In a single-tube type the heat exchanger consists of a tube inside a tube (coaxial double tube), but if a larger surface area is required, the tubes can be arranged spirally within an upright cylindrical tank. This latter type of a heat exchanger is manufactured by Stork-Amsterdam. The flow of liquids in this unit can be either parallel or counter current, and the latter is usually recommended for the heat treatment of yoghurt milk. More recently, Stork-Amsterdam have developed a tubular heat exchanger in which

135

three tubes are fitted inside each other; the heating medium flows in the inner and outer spaces of the tube, and the milk flows through the middle.

In the other type of tubular heat exchanger, bundles of tubes are enclosed within an outer shell, and while the milk flows through the pipes the heating/cooling medium circulates inside the shell. For the heat treatment of viscous products the scraped/swept surface heat type is used, and the unit consists of a jacketed cylinder fitted with a scraper blade. The blades, which rotate at a high speed, remove the continuously processed product from the heated surface and as a result the effective surface area is large; heat transfer is normally rapid, depending on the speed of rotation of the blades. These heat exchangers can be mounted vertically or horizontally.

In principle, irrespective what type of heat exchanger is used, it is safe to assume that heat transfer through a partition wall resembles the profile illustrated by Anon. (1980). The flow of fluids, i.e. hot water and milk, in a heat exchanger can be either in the same direction (parallel flow) or in the opposite direction (counter-current flow), and in each situation the profile of temperature changes during the heat treatment of milk is different (see Fig. 3.37). In counter-current flow the milk and the heating medium enter the heat exchanger from opposite ends, i.e. the cold milk meets the "cooled"

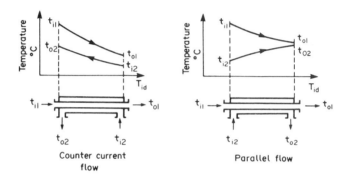

Fig. 3.37. Differences in the temperature profiles for heat transfer in a heat exchanger either with parallel or counter current flow

t_{i1} inlet temperature of hot water
t_{o1} outlet temperature of hot water
t_{i2} inlet temperature of milk
t_{o2} outlet temperature of milk
T_{id} temperature change/drop of heated surface

After Anon. (1976b, 1980).

Reproduced by courtesy of Alfa-Laval Co. Ltd., Middlesex, U.K.

heating medium, and the temperature is progressively raised as it passes through the heat exchanger. The overall temperature of the heated milk is always a few degrees below the temperature of the heating medium at the corresponding point (see Fig. 3.37). However, in parallel flow both the milk and the heating medium enter the heat exchanger from the same end, and as a result the increase in temperature of the product is never higher than if the milk and the hot water were mixed together (see Fig. 3.37). Different efficiencies of heat transfer are, therefore, obtained from the contrasted types of flow, and Kessler (*loc. cit.*) reported a 50% maximum efficiency for parallel flow; the efficiency was much higher with the counter-current system.

Anon. (1980) summarised the factors that can affect the efficiency of heat transfer in a plate heat exchanger as follows:

(i) by appropriate design, a good flow rate of the product and heating medium is maintained;
(ii) having a large surface area, i.e. thin gap between the plates and suitable corrugation, improves the rate of heat transfer between the milk and the heating medium;
(iii) providing a wide, mean differential temperature between the fluids is advantageous, but the difference is governed by the heat sensitivity of the product;
(iv) avoiding a pressure drop across a plate heat exchanger, e.g. by installing a pump, improves the heat transfer characteristics of the plant.

As mentioned earlier, the equipment for continuous heat processing is made up of different sections, and in a plant designed for the heat treatment of yoghurt milk these sections are:

—regeneration section,
—heating/cooling section,
—holding unit.

It is also important that the plant is installed with a balance tank in order to maintain a continuous flow of milk, and balance tanks are normally situated in the area where the milk is being fortified and/or standardised. Different types of balance tanks are available on the market, and they are fitted either with a special float or with level sensors that ensure that milk is always available.

(a) Regeneration section

In this section the incoming cold yoghurt milk is prewarmed by the heated milk and vice versa, and hence the aim is to utilise energy more efficiently and economically. For example, if the temperature of the yoghurt milk is raised from 5° to 90°C (hot water) and then cooled to 40–45°C (cold water) the energy demand is high; energy is required to heat the hot water and also to cool the cold water. However, if the heat energy can be utilised in the regeneration sections of the plant, the result is energy conservation, and the efficiency of regeneration is sometimes expressed as a percentage. Fearn (1982) has provided the following energy data relating to two different types of Alfa-Laval yoghurt processing plants.

First Example. The capacity of this plant was 4000 litres per hour, and the yoghurt milk was fortified by the addition of milk powder. The temperature progression using a plate heat exchanger fitted with a regeneration section was as follows:

—the temperature of the yoghurt milk was raised from 5° to 45°C by *regeneration*, i.e. utilising the heat from the already heated milk, and the temperature change was 40°C;
—the prewarmed milk was heated from 45° to 90°C by hot water (incidentally, at around 60–70°C the milk left the heat exchanger to be homogenised before returning to the plant for final heating);
—the heated milk was cooled from 90° to 50°C by *regeneration*, i.e. transferring the energy to the incoming cold milk, and the temperature change was 40°C;
—the partially cooled milk at 50°C was further cooled to 40–45°C (incubation temperature) by water.

137

It can be observed that the yoghurt milk was heated from 5° to 90°C (a temperature increase of 85°C), and that the increase in the regeneration section was 40°C. Therefore, the percentage of regeneration was equal to:

$$\frac{40}{85} \times 100 = 47\%.$$

Although this figure is relatively low compared with HTST or UHT plants which may be above 90%, this is due to the fact that the product outlet temperature in the case of HTST and UHT milks is around 5°C and 20°C respectively, as compared with yoghurt milk at 40–45°C. Thus, the energy requirements of such 4000 litres per hour plant are: 325 kg/hour of steam and 4000 litres/hour of water.

Second Example. The same capacity plant (4000 litres/hour) was used for the heat treatment of the yoghurt milk, but the plant was installed with a single-effect evaporator to concentrate the milk to the desired level of solids (see Fig. 3.11). The temperature progression was as follows:

—the incoming cold milk was prewarmed from 5° to 60°C by *regeneration*, i.e. utilising the energy available in the condensate from the evaporator;
—the partially heated milk at 60°C was then heated by hot water to 90°C before entering the evaporator (in order to achieve the correct concentration of solids in the basic mix, the milk was circulated within the evaporator and the heating section of heat exchanger at a flow rate of 19,000 litres/hour);
—the concentrated milk left the evaporator at 70°C and was homogenised; later it was heated to 82°C by *regeneration*, i.e. utilising the energy available from already heated milk;
—then the concentrated milk at 82°C was heated to 90°C with hot water;
—the yoghurt milk was cooled from 90° to 78°C by *regeneration*, i.e. a transfer of energy to the concentrated milk at 70°C;
—the yoghurt milk was then cooled from 78°C to 40–45°C (e.g. the incubation temperature) by cold water.

To calculate the percentage regeneration of such a system is more complicated than with the first example, and the simplest approach is to divide the overall thermal load by the amount of heat obtained from regeneration which × 100 is equal to the percentage regeneration. If the specific heat and the density of the yoghurt milk are assumed to be the same as water, i.e. 1, the calculations are as follows:

(i) 5–60°C (regeneration)—heat obtained is 55 × 4,700 = 258,500 kcal/hour
(ii) 60–90°C (hot water)—thermal load is 30 × 19,700 = 591,000 kcal/hour
(iii) 70–82°C (regeneration)—heat obtained is 12 × 4,000 = 48,000 kcal/hour
(iv) 82–90°C (hot water)—thermal load is 8 × 4,000 = 32,000 kcal/hour

Therefore the overall thermal load is:

258,500 + 591,000 + 48,000 + 32,000 = 929,500 kcal/hour.

The heat obtained by regeneration is:

258,500 + 48,000 = 306,500 kcal/hour.

The percentage of regeneration is:

$$\frac{306,500 \times 100}{929,500} = 33\% \text{ (approximately)}.$$

Thus, the energy requirements of such a plant are 840 kg/hour of steam and 9200 litres/hour of water.

Although the percentage regeneration in the second example is slightly lower than with the former case, two factors must not be overlooked: firstly, the cost of the skim milk powder, and secondly, the quality of yoghurt produced from concentrated milk. The latter aspect has already been illustrated in Fig. 2.16.

(b) Heating section

In this part of the heat exchanger the yoghurt milk is heated to the desired temperature, and under commercial practice the final temperature may range from 85° to 115°C.

(c) Holding section

The holding section of a heat exchanger is that part of the plant in which the heated milk can be maintained at temperature for a specified period of time. The objective is to provide for those time–temperature relationships that comply with existing legislations, for example pasteurised milk (HTST) must be heated to 72°C and held at that temperature for 15 seconds. There are, of course, no regulations regarding the heat treatment of yoghurt milk, so in practice the time–temperature combination is chosen both to ensure the destruction of pathogens and to bring about the desirable physicochemical changes in the milk.

In the holding section no heating or cooling of the milk takes place, and depending on the holding time desired, the unit can be built either as part of the heat exchanger or as a separate unit on its own.

Different time–temperature relationships have been employed for the heat treatment of yoghurt milk, and some examples of these combinations are:

—30 minutes at 85°C (long holding time),
—5 minutes at 90–95°C (medium holding time),
—3 seconds at 115°C (short holding time).

It is evident, however, that the holding section of a yoghurt processing plant will, in most cases, have to be built as an external unit of the heat exchanger, and the equipment available for holding milk for the specified times includes as follows.

Fig. 3.38. A view of yoghurt milk processing equipment used for "long time" holding

Two cone base, insulated tanks (4545 litre capacity) are used as holding tanks for the heated milk to be held for 30 minutes or more prior to cooling and fermentation.

Reproduced by courtesy of Express Dairy—UK Ltd., Middlesex, U.K.

(i) Holding for "long time". In order to provide a 30-minute holding time in a continuous processing plant, a well-insulated or water-jacketed tank can be used instead of the usual holding unit (see Fig. 3.38).

(ii) Holding for "medium time". Spiral or zigzag arrangements of pipework are often used as holding units for up to 5–6 minutes, and two typical examples are: the Alfa-Laval holding tube (Fig. 3.39) which is constructed of two spirals of stainless steel pipe enclosed in an insulated, upright cylindrical tank, and a modified version in which a 6-minute holding time can be achieved by having the large capacity zigzag piping (Fig. 3.40).

140

Fig. 3.39. A schematic illustration of Alfa-Laval holding tube/cell

The approximate holding time in the "cell" is around 3 minutes, but the overall holding time, i.e. including associated pipework, is 5 minutes.

Reproduced by courtesy of Alfa-Laval A/B, Lund, Sweden.

Fig. 3.40. A view of a large holding tube in the zig-zag arrangement

During the cleaning cycle, the side plates are removed and the tubes are "elbow greased" before the detergent wash in order to maintain high standards of sanitation of the plant; incidentally, the holding time of such a tube is 6 minutes.

Reproduced by courtesy of Northern Ireland Milk Marketing Board, Belfast, UK.

141

(iii) Holding for "short time". In this case the holding section can be incorporated within the heat exchanger, but if a larger capacity of holding unit is required, then the pipe can be installed outside the plant.

Heat processing plants, e.g. for HTST and UHT milks, are fitted with a temperature-sensor safety device known as flow diversion valve (FDV). At the start of the processing operation the milk is normally diverted back to the balance tank until the right temperature is achieved and maintained, and only then does the milk flow through the rest of the plant to complete the processing cycle. However, the milk is always diverted back to the balance tank at any time that the temperature drops, so making sure that all the processed milk is heat treated to the specified temperature. The FDV unit is not, however, normally installed in a yoghurt plant, for if the temperature of the heated milk starts to drop, manual diversion of the milk back to the balance tank via a special piping arrangement is quite acceptable.

Normally, at the start of the heat treatment process, water is circulated through the plant to both sanitise the pipework and warm the plant to the desired processing temperatures; the latter avoids prolonged circulation of the initial milk intake.

FERMENTATION/INCUBATION EQUIPMENT

At this stage of yoghurt manufacture the processed milk (i.e. standardised/fortified, homogenised and heated milk) is cooled to the incubation temperature, which would be in the range of $40-45°C$ (short fermentation—$2\frac{1}{2}$ to 3 hours) or $30°C$ (long fermentation—overnight), and there are many different types of fermentation vessels which can be used. Basically the equipment is designed to provide and maintain the necessary processing condition(s), especially temperature, and the form of the equipment depends on the type of yoghurt produced, i.e. set yoghurt or stirred yoghurt.

A. Equipment for the Production of Set Yoghurt

The fermentation/coagulation of the milk takes place in the retail container and, in brief, the process may involve the following stages:

—cool the processed yoghurt milk to $40-45°C$ or $30°C$;
—add the following ingredients to the milk: starter culture, and, if desired, flavouring materials and/or colouring matter; incidentally, for the production of fruit set yoghurt (sundae style), the fruit is delivered into the retail container followed by the inoculated milk;
—seal the retail containers, incubate, cool and dispatch.

The conditions for fermentation are then provided employing one of the following approaches.

1. Water baths or tanks

In this system the yoghurt containers, which are often glass bottles in this case, are placed in metal trays immersed in shallow tanks of warm water; details of this method were reported by

Crawford (1962). The water level is maintained just below the tops of the bottles to avoid contamination of the product, and after the coagulation period the warm water is replaced by circulating cold water that cools the coagulum very quickly. When the yoghurt is partially cooled, the trays are removed and transferred to the refrigerated store for final chilling. Since this method necessitates the use of glass bottles, the use of water baths/tanks is of limited popularity.

2. Cabinets

In the cabinet system incubation takes place in small insulated chambers with average capacities ranging from 250 to 750 litres, while forced hot air is circulated during the fermentation stage; it is later replaced by chilled air. In order to improve the heat transfer characteristics of these units the cabinet manufactured by Stork-Amsterdam N.V. has the facility to moisten the hot air; if the retail container is moisture-sensitive, then hot dry air is recommended.

Fig. 3.41.   An illustration of an incubator/cooler cabinet for the production of set yoghurt

The cabinet is made out of stainless steel and is divided into three chambers.

Reproduced by courtesy of A/S Jenogand, Rødovre, Denmark.

143

Rapid cooling at the end of the fermentation stage is achieved by circulating chilled air, and the yoghurt is then left until dispatched, or when the temperature is low enough moved to the main cold store. All units of this type are electrically operated, and an illustration of a typical incubator/cooler cabinet is shown in Fig. 3.41.

Some incubator/cooler cabinets are fitted with a pH controller so that the fermentation/cooling cycle can be automated, but in many cases the processing cycle is worked on a time basis; nevertheless, the production of a uniform yoghurt does necessitate attention to the following points:

—the cabinets must be relatively small in size, so that the pallets can be stacked very quickly; the time lag between the first and the last yoghurt containers being placed in the cabinet should be very short;

—the air must circulate uniformly to all parts of the cabinet;

—there must be provision for accurate and reliable temperature control in the cabinet.

In some instances the cabinets are used only as incubators, and the yoghurt is cooled in a refrigerated cold store. The disadvantage of this approach is that the coagulum is in motion while it is still warm, and hence may suffer some structural damage and/or whey separation. However, the system may be less expensive to install in the first instance.

3. Tunnel

Large quantities of set yoghurt could be produced in batteries of individual cabinets, but the process can be mechanised for "continuous" production by adopting a tunnel system. The pallets containing the yoghurt pots are placed on smooth rollers/conveyor belt which travel through a tunnel consisting of two sections. Warm air is circulated in the incubation part of the tunnel, and the speed of the pallet is governed by the speed of the conveyor belt, which in turn is regulated by the rate of lactic acid production in the milk. At the end of the fermentation period, which is equivalent to pH 4.5, the pallets pass through the cooling section, and the hot air is replaced by a blast of chilled air. The yoghurt is partially cooled in this section, and final cooling takes place in the cold store. Since the yoghurt is in motion during the incubation/cooling periods, extreme care must be exercised to avoid damage to the coagulum.

However, a combined system for the production of set yoghurt consisting of incubation rooms and a cooling tunnel is used at the S.V. Inza Co-operative in Belgium (Cottenie, 1978). The advantage of this approach may be that while the yoghurt cups are not in motion during the incubation period, the cooling rate of yoghurt containers in a tunnel is much faster than can be achieved with other methods. Thus, in practice the milk is acidified to pH 4.5 in the incubation room(s), and there transported to the cooling tunnel where the temperature of the yoghurt reaches $10°C$ in around $1\frac{1}{2}$ hours. Incidentally, the cooling tunnel is connected directly to the cold store so that the palletised cups of yoghurt can be transferred easily using a forklift truck.

The different systems used for the manufacture of set yoghurt have been evaluated by Cottenie (loc. cit.), and a summary of their main features is shown in Table 3.2. The conclusion emerges that while the water bath system was at one time popular in Europe for the production of set yoghurt, the present trend is to use cabinets for medium-size production runs and the tunnel system for more extensive batches.

TABLE 3.2. *Different systems of incubators/coolers used for the manufacture of set yoghurt*

	Water bath tanks	Cabinet	Tunnel
Incubation/cooling in the same compartment	Yes	Yes/alternatively cabinets may be used only as incubators and then pallets removed and cooled in cold store	The first part of the tunnel is the incubator and the final section is used as a blast cooler
Heating and cooling agent	Water	Air	Air
System of production	Batch*	Batch*	Continuous
Packaging material	Glass	Glass, cartons or plastics	Glass, cartons or plastics
Variation in the quality of yoghurt	Yes**	Yes**	Slightly
Energy consumption	High	High	Low
Processing floor area	Large	Medium	Small

* Semicontinuous production line can be achieved if water tanks or cabinets are in series.
** If filling time of pallets exceeds 15 minutes.

After Tamime and Greig (*loc. cit.*).
Reprinted with permission of Dairy Industries International.

B. Equipment for the Production of Stirred Yoghurt

By contrast, the coagulum of stirred yoghurt is produced in bulk, and the gel structure is broken before or during the cooling and packaging stages. The types of fermentation tanks used in the industry for the production of stirred yoghurt could be classified as follows.

1. Multipurpose tank

This type of tank has been discussed elsewhere, and is designed as a multiple duty unit, i.e. (i) milk processing (heating) and fermentation; (ii) same as (i) but also used for cooling the coagulum; (iii) fermentation and cooling only.

These tanks are water-jacketed so that steam can be used during the heating stage, and circulating cold water is used to cool the milk to $40-45°C$; the temperature is maintained at $42°C$ during the fermentation period; and finally, chilled water is circulated to cool the coagulum (see Fig. 3.42).

2. Fermentation tank only

These tanks are merely insulated in order to maintain an even temperature during the incubation period. The agitation system in the Alfa-Laval tank is optional, since the cone-shaped base facilitates easy removal of the coagulum (see Fig. 3.43).

145

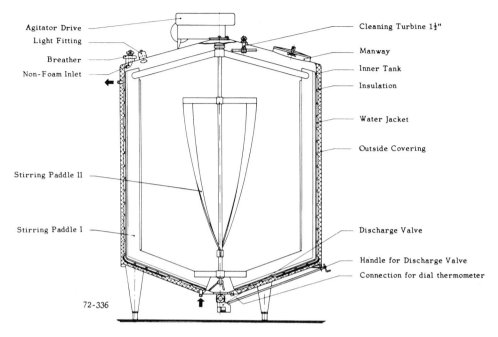

Fig. 3.42. An illustration of a multi-purpose tank suitable for the in-tank cooling of yoghurt

The tank has an effective double paddle agitator for gently breaking the coagulum during the cooling stage; see also Fig. 3.46 which illustrates the paddle design.

Reproduced by courtesy of Pasilac/Silkeborg Ltd., Preston, U.K.

3. Fermentation/cooling tank

This type of tank is water-jacketed, and warm water at 40–45°C is circulated during the incubation period, followed by cold or chilled water for cooling the coagulum (see Fig. 3.44).

4. Aseptic fermentation tank

This type of tank is a modified version of the standard fermentation unit, and the tank is used for the production of yoghurt under aseptic conditions. The overall specifications are:

—the tank is insulated;
—it is fitted with two pH electrodes and a resistance thermometer;
—the air entering or leaving the tank is filtered;
—the agitator has a double-shaft seal with steam barrier to minimise contamination.

It is also important to note that all the tanks mentioned have a foam-reducing inlet fitting that reduces the problem of froth formation in the tank.

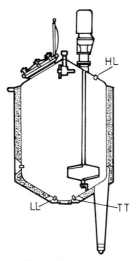

Fig. 3.43. A schematic illustration of an insulated fermentation tank

HL = High level pH electrode, LL = Low level pH electrode, TT = Resistance thermometer, Propeller agitator—optional

Reproduced by courtesy of Alfa-Laval Co. Ltd., Middlesex, UK.

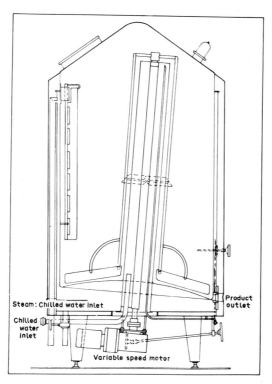

Fig. 3.44. A fermentation/cooling tank fitted with an inner cylinder for cooling

Reproduced by courtesy of N.V. Machinenfabriek, Terlet, Zutphen, Holland.

COOLING

At the desired level of acidification cooling of the coagulum commences, so that the temperature is reduced from 40–45°C to 20°C or in some cases <10°C (Anon., 1977a). The basic objective is, of course, to slow down the metabolic activity of the yoghurt starter culture, i.e. *S. thermophilus* and *L. bulgaricus*, and if the cooling process is delayed the yoghurt may become unpalatable due to the presence of too high a level of acidity. Depending on the type of equipment used for cooling the yoghurt and the duration of the cooling period, it is recommended that cooling should start at around 0.8–1.0% lactic acid, so that the acidity of the cool yoghurt will be between 1.2–1.4% lactic acid.

The systems available for cooling the yoghurt are as follow.

A. Chilled Air

This method of cooling is widely employed in two areas in the yoghurt industry: *firstly*, chilled air is circulated in cabinets and tunnels for cooling set yoghurt at the end of fermentation period, and *secondly*, in the cold store, transport vehicles and retail stores. The recommended temperature for yoghurt during storage is <10°C, otherwise the keeping quality of the product will be severely impaired.

B. In-tank Cooling

The system by which yoghurt is cooled in the fermentation or multipurpose tank is known as in-tank cooling, and chilled water is usually circulated in the jacket during the cooling period. The rate of cooling the coagulum from 40–45°C to 20°C or <10°C is governed by:

(i) area of the contact surface;
(ii) speed of agitation;
(iii) temperature differential between the cooling medium and the product;
(iv) mass flow rate of the cooling agent;
(v) contact time between the product and the cooling surface,

and hence a fast rate of cooling can be achieved by providing:

—as large as possible cooling surface;
—a rapid flow rate of the cooling agent by forced circulation;
—a steep temperature gradient between the yoghurt (40–45°C) and the cooling agent, i.e. chilled brine at −3.8 to −4.0°C;
—adjustment of the contact time between product and cooling surface, i.e. by continually replacing the "cooled" yoghurt with "warm" yoghurt.

These factors are, of course, interrelated, but for convenience their effect on the efficiency of in-tank yoghurt coolers can be assessed separately.

1. Surface area

The surface area available for cooling yoghurt may vary considerably from one tank to another, and Fig. 3.45 shows how this area could be maximised. An example of tank (4) is illustrated in Fig. 3.34, and the 5000-litre tank has a total surface area of 40 m²; the yoghurt can be cooled from 45°C to 20°C in ½ hour (see Fig. 3.36); where the cooling agent can be circulated in the inner cylinder (see Fig. 3.44), the drop in temperature takes a little longer. A tank with the cooling surfaces on the side and base is supplied by Wincanton Engineering Ltd. (see Fig. 3.32), Pasilac/Silkeborg Ltd. (Fig. 3.42) or the Crepaco Incorporation (see Fig. 3.33), and according to Jay (*loc. cit.*), a tank of the Wincanton type requires 4 hours to cool 5000 litres of yoghurt from the incubation temperature to 5°C.

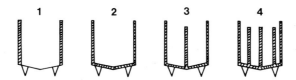

Fig. 3.45. Diagram of the surface areas of some in-tank yoghurt coolers

Shaded area is the cooled region.

1. Side of a tank
2. Side & bottom of a tank
3. Side, bottom and inner cylinder
4. Same as (3) plus in-tank cooling coils

2. Agitation system

The different flow patterns which occur during liquid mixing are discussed elsewhere (see Fig. 3.22), and the factors that affect the performance of an in-tank yoghurt cooler are basically:

—the shape of the tank;
—the shape of the agitator system (paddle, propeller, scrape surface or anchor);
—the size and position of the agitator;
—the speed of rotation;
—the velocity difference between the bulk fluid and the agitator.

The creation of a vortex and/or incorporation of air into the bulk of the yoghurt are not desirable, and similarly, stirring of the warm coagulum may cause shearing; these effects can be minimised by controlling the speed of rotation and adjusting the shape of the agitator. The shearing effect is also influenced by the difference in velocity between the bulk yoghurt and the agitator tip, and a reduction in velocity differential will minimise the rate of shear and a typical example where more than one type of agitation system is provided in a yoghurt tank. The design of the agitation

149

system seeks, therefore, to minimise structural damage to the coagulum, and some examples of suitable systems are:

— the "scraped surface" agitator plus a centrally mounted helical paddle (Pasilac/Silkeborg type tank—see Fig. 3.46);
— the contrarotating paddle (Wincanton Engineering type tank—see Fig. 3.32);
— the "scraped surface" agitator only (Fig. 3.33); the 35° cone base assists in turning the yoghurt gel with minimum structural damage; furthermore, the scraping action of the agitator

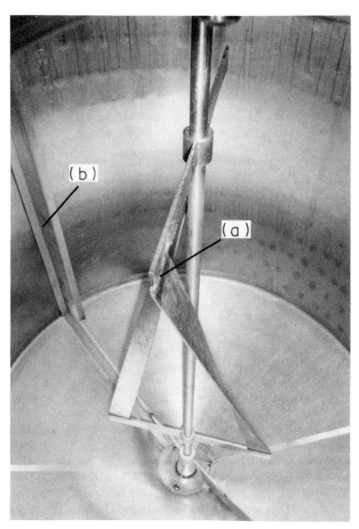

Fig. 3.46. Two different types of agitator system

The helical paddle (a) rotates at 15 rpm and the surface scraper (b) at 7 rpm.
Reproduced by courtsey of Pasilac/Silkeborg Ltd., Preston U.K.

150

continually replaces the "cool" yoghurt with "warm" yoghurt, thus improving the rate of cooling.

—the paddle agitator plus fixed baffles along the side of the tank (see Fig. 3.44).

3. Speed of rotation

The agitator speed is reduced as much as possible to give "effective" mixing of the coagulum but minimum "shearing", and some commercially available tanks reflect this aim:

—Pasilac/Silkeborg—7 rpm for the scraped surface agitator, and 15 rpm for the helical paddle;
—Terlet/Zutphen—the velocity of the agitator ranges from 32 to 48 rpm;
—Goavec S.A.—the agitator speed is 8 rpm maximum (clock- and anticlockwise).

The in-tank cooling of yoghurt requires a long time, and according to Kessler (*loc. cit.*) the formula used to measure the heat transfer in a tank during the heating of milk can be used to calculate the time required to cool the yoghurt. He illustrated this point with the following example:

$$\text{Time of cooling (seconds)} = \frac{\text{Volume (m}^3) \times \text{Density of yoghurt (kg/m}^3) \times \text{Specific heat (J/kg K)}}{\text{Effective heat/cool exchange area (m}^2) \times \text{Heat transfer coefficient (W/m}^2\text{ K)}} \; \ln \frac{\text{Temperature of warm yoghurt} - \text{Temperature of cooling medium}}{\text{Temperature of cool yoghurt} - \text{Temperature of cooling medium}}$$

$$= \frac{3 \times 1040 \times 3800}{9.55 \times 150} \; \ln \frac{40 - 15}{20 - 15}$$

$$= \frac{3 \times 1040 \times 3800}{9.55 \times 150} \times 1.61$$

$$= 13{,}325 \text{ seconds} = 222 \text{ minutes} = 3.7 \text{ hours.}$$

$\ln$ = natural logarithm

$$\ln \frac{40 - 15}{20 - 15} = 1.61$$

High-speed agitation was used during cooling.

It is clear that chilled water rather than mains water should be used in order to maximise the temperature differential between the warm yoghurt and the cooling agent, and if the surface area can be increased, as with the Goavec S.A. tank, the cooling time will also be reduced.

An alternative technique for the in-tank cooling of yoghurt would be the insertion of a heat exchanger (plate or coil) into the coagulum at the end of the fermentation stage (Ehrmann, 1972). However, this type of apparatus restricts the use of agitators in the tank, and since these coolers are inserted into the coagulum after the incubation period, may pose problems of contamination.

151

C. Continuous Coolers

In contrast with the slow heat transfer of in-tank or batch coolers, more rapid cooling of yoghurt can be achieved using either plate or tubular heat exchangers. The flow pattern of yoghurt through a heat exchanger is illustrated in Fig. 3.47, and it is normally accepted that the throughput/unit time of plate or tubular cooler should be roughly double the capacity of the processing plant; i.e. if the plant capacity ranges from 3500 to 4000 litres/hour, then the capacity of the cooler(s) should be in the region of 8000 litres/hour.

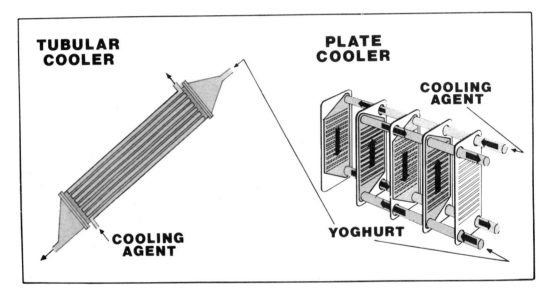

Fig. 3.47. The flow of yoghurt through different types of cooler

Notice that the streams of yoghurt and cooling agent run counter-current.
After Tamime & Greig (*loc. cit.*)

Reprinted with permission of Dairy Industries International.

The plate cooler is similar in design to the conventional plate heat exchanger described earlier, except that the gap between the plates is much larger, so minimising the risk of structural damage to the coagulum. In addition, because of the tendency of back pressure to build up in a plate cooler, either the passage of yoghurt has to be restricted, or alternatively, the gap between the plates is increased progressively across the unit. It is further recommended that the throughput of a plant should be increased by installing a number of small units in parallel rather than by increasing the number of plates on a large unit. The cooling agent in a plate cooler is usually chilled water, and an approximate water consumption of 40,000 litres/hour can be anticipated for a plate heat exchanger cooling 8000 litres of yoghurt per hour.

The tubular cooler is constructed of a bundle of tubes enclosed in a shell, and as the product passes through the tubes a counter-current flow of cooling agent passes around them; Fig. 3.48 shows this type of cooler in operation in a yoghurt factory. Some technical specifications of the Terlet/Zutphen tubular cooler are:

—sizes range from 1000 to 10,000 litres/hour, and it is recommended that capacity should be the same as the filling machine;
—chilled water flows counter-current to the yoghurt, and the consumption of water is roughly 5 times product volume;
—the time required to cool yoghurt from the incubation temperature (40–45°C) to 8°C is 1 hour, and the velocity of the yoghurt through the tubes is 0.65 cm/second;
—any reduction in viscosity is minimised by transferring the yoghurt from the Terlet fermentation tank to the cooler by air pressure (0.5 kg/cm^2) rather than using a pump;
—plant design is simplified by the fact that these coolers can be placed in various positions, i.e. vertically or horizontally.

Fig. 3.48. An on-site view of a tubular cooler

Reproduced by courtesy of N.V. Machinenfabriek Terlet, Zutphen, Holland.

153

It is inevitable that some structural damage to the coagulum will occur during the passage of yoghurt through either plate or tubular coolers, but Steenbergen (1971a) and Piersma and Steenbergen (1973) concluded that least loss of viscosity occurred in a tubular cooler.

FRUIT MIXING AND PACKAGING MACHINES

The cool (e.g. at 20°C) or cold (e.g. at 10°C) yoghurt is delivered to an intermediate storage tank prior to further processing, i.e. fruit mixing and packaging. The yoghurt will be retained in this tank for a short period of time or, alternatively, stored overnight, and the primary purpose of these tanks is:

(i) the tanks are insulated, and hence the temperature of yoghurt can be maintained at any desired level;

(ii) in the event of breakdown in another section of the yoghurt factory the tanks can act as a buffer vessel;

(iii) overnight storage of yoghurt in the intermediate tanks can provide sufficient reserves for packaging to start first thing in the morning, rather than the machines remaining idle until the freshly produced yoghurt is available.

In this section of the processing line, equipment is required for handling the fruit, mixing the fruit with the yoghurt and finally packaging it; some selected units are as follows:

A. Equipment for Fruit Handling

As mentioned elsewhere (see Chapter 2), the processed fruit used in the yoghurt industry is usually packaged in one of the following containers:

—metal cans;
—polypropylene containers (drums or buckets);
—stainless steel tanks.

The packaging of fruit in metal cans is very popular, and these cans are widely used by small- and medium-scale yoghurt manufacturers. However, large-scale producers only obtain fruit in metal cans if the demand is low, and the popular flavours are either processed in the dairy or obtained in bulk in stainless steel tanks. If metal cans are used, a number of different types of can openers can be used, i.e. hand-operated, semi-automatic or fully automated. The hand-operated openers employ either an electric motor or compressed air to cut the metal and remove the lid. A semi-automatic type opener can be automated to give a throughput of 1500 cans/hour (see Fig. 3.49).

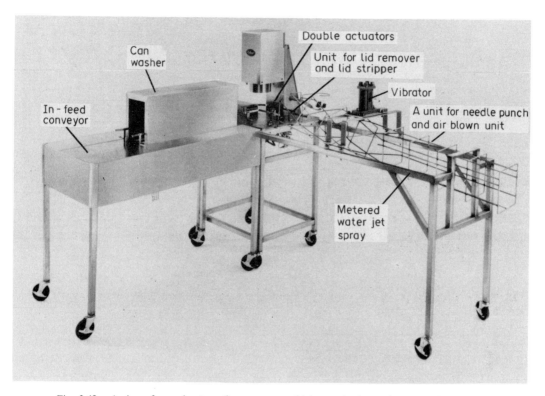

Fig. 3.49. A view of a semi-automatic can opener which can also be used on a continuous line

* Model 825—this is a heavy duty, semi-automatic can opener—opening is by the 'crown punch' method.
Reproduced by courtesy of Peter Holland Food Machinery Ltd., Lincolnshire, UK.

Fruits in plastic containers have to be handled manually, but if the ingredients are received in stainless steel tanks, the normal approach is to meter them directly into the yoghurt immediately prior to packaging.

In some yoghurt processing lines the fruit is emptied onto an inclined stainless steel table and the fruit is inspected for any residual plant matter, i.e. stems and/or leaves, before mixing it with the yoghurt; as a further precautionary measure; the fruit may also be subjected to screening by metal detectors.

B. Equipment for Fruit/Yoghurt Blending

1. Manual blending

This method of fruit/yoghurt mixing is illustrated in Fig. 3.5. Two tanks are used in parallel, and in each tank the required amount of fruit is added to a given volume of yoghurt, mixed gently with a plunger, and the finished blend is pumped to the packaging machines. While the first tank is being emptied, the second one is being prepared, so that the process can, in practice, become continuous.

2. Batch blending

In principle, the approach is similar to that described above, except that the volume of the mix is larger, and hence the fruit and yoghurt are metered into a tank, mixed and then pumped to the packaging machine. Again the process becomes, in effect, continuous through the installation of two tanks in parallel.

3. Continuous blending

A continuous fruit/yoghurt mixer consists of three different units: firstly, a metering device for dosing the correct amount of fruit into the yoghurt line, secondly, a metering device for measuring the required volume of yoghurt; and thirdly, a mixing chamber that ensures uniform distribution of the fruit into the yoghurt. Different types of continuous mixer are available into the market, and the primary requirements are:

—proper mixing of the fruit and yoghurt;
—minimum structural damage to the coagulum;
—the fruit metering unit must be accurate to allow different fruits to be mixed with the yoghurt in the desired proportions;
—easily dismantled for cleaning, or suitable for cleaning-in-place;
—all contact surfaces to be of good quality stainless steel, and some continuous fruit/yoghurt blenders that meet these requirements are as follows.

(i) Static-in-line mixer. This type of a mixer is supplied by Alfa-Laval A/B of Sweden, and consists of a stainless steel pipe into which a number of helical blades are welded. In practice, the static mixer is, if possible, mounted vertically with a T-piece at the bottom through which the fruit and yoghurt are metered from their respective tanks:

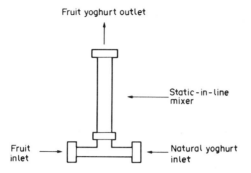

The flow of yoghurt/fruit through the twisted blades in the mixer ensures uniform distribution of the fruit throughout the coagulum, and the specifications of such mixers are:

—flow rates from 500 to 10,000 litres/hour;
—pipe diameters up to 6.35 cm;
—lengths of the mixer ranges from 750 to 1150 mm;
—number of blades is 10.

Although such units can be cleaned using a CIP system, it is usually recommended that the mixers should be dismantled and rinsed before starting the CIP programme.

(ii) The Gasti-mixing and feeding pump. This system consists of two suction units that draw the yoghurt and fruit from their respective storage tanks, and while the yoghurt pump delivers a constant volume of 50 litres per minute, the fruit pump operates at an infinitely variable ratio between 1:5 and 1:20. The mixing of the two ingredients takes place in a common pressure pipe, and the unequal flows of yoghurt and fruit are converted into a uniform flow inside an air pressure vessel; the fruit yoghurt is then delivered directly to the hopper of the filling machine. The operation of the Gasti (D 125–25 M) mixing and feeding pump is actuated by level control probes (maximum/minimum) in the hopper of the packaging unit.

The more recent Gasti DOGAmix 60 is rather different, in that: *firstly*, two plunger-type pumps draw the yoghurt and fruit from their respective storage tanks in preset proportions, and transfer them to a mixing compartment fitted with a dynamic agitator with a continuously variable drive. The yoghurt/fruit are delivered to the mixing section through a common discharge pipe, and fluctuations in product flow caused by the plunger pumps are eliminated by the dynamic agitator. The yoghurt/fruit mixture is then delivered to the hopper of the filling machine. Bacterial contamination of the product during the mixing stages is avoided by isolating the "moving" parts of the DOGAmix, i.e. the rods of the plunger pumps and the mixer drive of the dynamic agitator, from the surrounding atmosphere by sterile air chambers (see Fig. 3.50).

The feed rate of the Gasti DOGAmix 60 is up to 75 litres per minute and the mixing ratios can vary from 1:5 to 1:20 with an accuracy of $\pm 0.5\%$ for homogeneous products. The unit is capable of being cleaned by CIP (e.g. 1–2% caustic at 80°C or 1–2% nitric acid at 80°C) and sterilised using steam at 140°C.

157

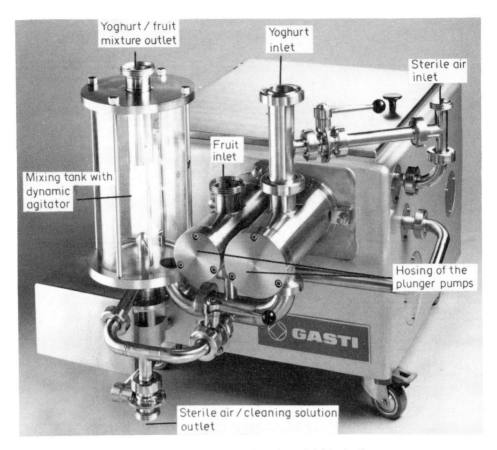

Fig. 3.50. A front view of the Gasti DOGAmix 60

Reproduced by courtesy of Engelmann & Buckham Machinery Ltd., Hampshire, UK; Gasti Verpackungsmaschinen GmbH & Co., Schwabisch Hall, West Germany.

(iii) The Burdosa-fruit blender. This pump uses one motor to drive a duplex metering pump, one head of which move the fruit base, the other the natural yoghurt. The pump heads are hydraulically actuated using sterile glycerine of pharmaceutical standard, and are hermetically sealed. Precise metering of the fruit base is achieved by externally actuated suction and discharge valves of special design, and maximum injection rate for the fruit is 250 cm³/litre of yoghurt; the flow rate of the yoghurt is constant (see Fig. 3.51).

Some specifications of the Burdosa duplex blender are:

—the blending capacity of standard models ranges from 715 to 4510 litres/hr;
—adjustments to the fruit dosage rate can be carried out manually or automatically;
—the on/off control of the pump is controlled by level sensors in the hopper of the filling machine;
—the installation of a further in-line mixer is only required if the retention/discharge time to the filler is short;
—if the fruit base is handled in bulk, it must be held under pressure (e.g. $\frac{1}{2}$ kg/cm² of CO_2 or N_2) to minimise viscosity and cavitation problems at low temperature.

158

Fig. 3.51. A view of the Burdosa fruit/yoghurt blender model M 4500 A

Capacity is 4510 l/hr; it is capable of being sterilised by steam at 140°C, or by CIP up to 110°C.

Reproduced by courtesy of Alpha Technical Services Ltd., Middlesex, UK; Ing. Herwig Burgert (Burdosa), Lahn-Rodgen, West Germany.

C. Equipment for Yoghurt Packaging

A multitude of high-speed yoghurt filling machines are available on the market, and although capital cost could be one of the major factors in choosing a certain piece of equipment, from a technical point of view certain important specifications must not be overlooked. For example:

159

—proposed method of filling and sealing;
—type of unit container being used;
—desirability of filling under a controlled atmosphere;
—degree of automation being sought;
—need for a high standard of hygiene (e.g. all contact surfaces must be stainless steel, and accessible for sterilisation/sanitisation).
—time required to change from one flavour to another, or from one volume of carton to another;
—versatility and reliability of the machine;
—accuracy of filling, and the elimination of 'drip' between individual 'fills';
—power and labour requirements of the machine;
—other specifications such as:—
—availability of date marking;
—method of dispensing the cups;
—safety measures (e.g. no cup/no fill).

It would be impractical, of course, to discuss all the different types of yoghurt filling machines in detail, but it is safe to assume that the use of the positive displacer or piston pump is almost universal, and that the measures are volumetric. In addition, most filling machines are equipped with marking attachments (e.g. sell-by date) and/or label application units (e.g. for large containers with snap-on lids), and some examples of these yoghurt filling machines are as follow.

1. Machines for filling yoghurt into preformed plastic containers

(a) Colunio (8,000 cups per hour). The specifications of the machine are:

—The cup dispenser has four rotating scrolls to separate the plastic cups before dropping them into the cup holders.
—The filling head supplied is suitable for packaging fruit yoghurt, and the capacities range from 85 to 285 ml.
—The machine is equipped with four filling lanes, and it is possible to fill four different capacities simultaneously.
—Heat seal and/or snap-on-lids can be used.
—The filled/sealed cups are ejected from the cup holders in the conveyor in a precise formation.

(b) Weserhutte multi-track filling machine. This type of filling machine is capable of packaging up to 48,000 cups/hour, and Fig. 3.52 shows the automatic dispenser of the pre-formed plastic cups, the filling head and the heat sealing unit. The cups are crated automatically into special trays, and then stacked ready for transfer to cold store.

(c) DOGAtherm 81 & 81 S. This machine is manufactured by Gasti in West Germany, and are two versions of this filler. The common specifications of these models are:

—automatic cup loader;
—two lane filling conveyor with 8 filling heads;
—closure of the cups by heat sealing;
—maximum output of 15,000 cups/hour;
—the machine cleaned using a CIP system.

The difference between the two models is that the DOGAtherm 81 S is fitted with a clean air cabinet over the machine so that filling takes place in a controlled atmosphere, and the shelf-life of the product is extended. Furthermore, this model is also suitable for filling multi-layer desserts into plastic cups.

Fig. 3.52.   An illustration of the automatic cup dispenser and magazine of an eight track Weserhutte filling machine

Reproduced by courtesy of Weserhutte Aktiengesellscaft, Bad Oeynhausen, West Germany.

(d) EP Remy Type 54.   This machine is capable of packaging yoghurt into 500 g plastic containers with snap-on-lids. The plastic cups are dispensed from an enclosed magazine holder, and the filling and capping stations are in a sterile, laminar air flow cabinet that reduces contamination of the yoghurt. The capacity of this machine, depending on the number of filling heads, ranges from 3,000 to 24,000 containers per hour; the packaging machine is also fitted with an automatic tray packer.

(e) EP Remy Type 50. This 'carrousel' filling machine is equipped to handle waxed paper pots, and the output can reach 12,000 pots per hour. After the cartons have been filled with yoghurt, they are transferred to the first 'sealing' carrousel where the aluminium foil cap is crimped, and then onto a second 'carrousel' for the lid to be heat-sealed.

(f) DOGAseptic 42. This is an aseptic filling machine in which the plastic container (before filling) and the aluminium foil lid (before heat sealing) are sterilised with hydrogen peroxide (H_2O_2). The sterilised packaging material is then exposed to hot air so that the sterilant is vaporised and exhausted into the atmosphere; filling of the containers takes place in a pressurised, sterile air compartment. This unit has four filling lanes; the DOGAseptic 62 is similar in design, but has six filling lanes. The maximum output of the DOGAseptic 42 is only 9,000 cups per hour, but this machine is capable of handling single and/or multi-layer products, and hence is suitable for long-life cream, yoghurt and/or desserts with cream topping. The entire filling machine is cleaned by CIP, and the filling head can be steam sterilised at 143°C.

(g) Aseptic EP Remy Type 54. This yoghurt machine which is equipped to offer a high standard of hygiene, and in particular:

—an automatic cup loader and dispensing unit;
—the cups are sprayed with H_2O_2 and dried-off with sterile hot air prior to filling;
—the filling of the yoghurt takes place in a sterile, laminar air flow;
—the aluminium foil diaphragms are sterilised by UV-C lamps;
—the lids are heat sealed;
—the filled cups are fed to an automatic tray packer;
—the capacity of the machine is 24,000 cups per hour;
—the filling unit is cleaned by CIP, and sterilisation is achieved using steam under pressure at $0.5 \times 10^5 N/m^2$ (0.5 bar).

(h) Hamba BK 10010/10. The capacity of the Hamba BK 10010/10 yoghurt filling machine is 36,000 cups per hour, and all the packaging materials, e.g. plastic cups and aluminium foil lids, are sterilised using UV-C lamps. The filling/closure operations take place in a cabinet which is kept free of contaminants by a stream of sterile air at 30–40°C; this air temperature is recommended to prevent condensation. The components of the filling machine are cleaned and sterilised using CIP.

The development of UV-C lamps for Hamba machines has been well documented by Möller (1981) in a paper presented at a lecture in the Department of Milk and Dairy Industry at Hanover University in West Germany (see also Möller, 1982). The intensity of the UV-C lamp is in the range of 100–200 mW/cm², and the distance between the UV-C lamp and the packaging material is adjusted in such a way that the cups are at a distance of 10.5 cm; the total exposure time is around 7.5 seconds, and three emitters are used to sterilise the entire inner surface of the cup. The aluminium foil lids are exposed for two seconds at a distance of 4 cm. The efficiency of UV-C lamps against different bacterial species is illustrated in Fig. 3.53, and according to Möller (1982), the shelf life of fruit yoghurt packaged in containers sterilised by UV-C lamps was extended to 42 days at 5–7° C.

2. Machines for filling 'form-fill-seal' plastic containers

The packaging material is delivered to the dairy in large reels of plastic sheet, and the process of thermoforming transforms the sheet into the shapes and sizes of container required. The finished cartons are then filled with yoghurt and later heat sealed. Some examples of this type of filling machine are as follow.

(a) Hassia THM 17/48. The thermoplastic material, e.g. PVC, is fed from a reel to the heating section of the filling machine, and the warm sheet is stretched over the moulds; the cup shape is obtained by forcing the plastic material into a cool mould with compressed air. The following stage transfers the containers to the filling head of the machine to be filled with yoghurt, and heat sealed.

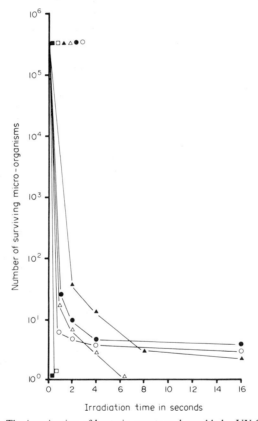

Fig. 3.53. The inactivation of bacteria, yeasts and moulds by UV-C radiation

Total microbial load—5×10^5
Test area—36 cm^2

Bacillus stearothermophilus
Bacillus subtilis
Aspergillus niger
Penicillium frequentans
Saccharomyces cerevisiae
Rhodotorula graminis

After Möller (1981).

Fig. 3.54 illustrates such a filler, and the specifications of the Hassia THM 17/48 are:

—the output is 30 cartons per minute for medium-size capacity units.
—lid material is lacquered or coated aluminium, or PVC film.

(b) Illig FS 32. This filler also forms the thermoplastic material into coherent containers, and the formed containers are then filled, sealed and finally punched. However, this filler makes use of a sterile atmosphere in different sections of the operation, for example the forming unit and the filling section. UV-C radiation is used to sterilise the unformed 'plastic'.

Fig. 3.54. A general view of Hassia thermoform filling machine type 17/48

1. Bottom material reel
2. Web pre-draw-off
3. Contact heating
4. Compressed air forming station
5. Fill area
6. Heatsealing station
7. Lidding material reel
8. Punching station
9. Waste cut-off device with take-off conveyor
10. Take-off conveyor

Reproduced by courtesy of Sussex & Berkshire Machinery Ltd., Hampshire, UK; Hassia Verpacking GmbH, Ranstadt, West Germany.

The maximum capacity of the Illig FS 32 filler is 30 cycles per minute. The filler is fitted with a special unit called the 'KODOS' filler which is a volumetric filling head allowing a wide range of settings.

Type	Metering range (cm³)	Maximum number of filling points	Hopper capacity (litres)
I	10–55	26	
II	50–280	12	80–150
III	100–550	18	

3. Machines for filling yoghurt into cartons/paper containers

Cartons coated with a layer of polyethlene are widely used in the dairy industry for packaging liquid milk, and they can also be used for packaging yoghurt; a slight modification of the filling head is necessary to avoid reducing the viscosity of the yoghurt. As mentioned in Chapter 2, the containers are either formed from a reel (form-fill-seal) or from collapsed/folded preformed cartons; the output may reach 10,000 cartons per hour. "Sterile" yoghurt can be packaged using similar machines, but the filler must be of the aseptic type.

4. Machines for filling hot/cold slurries

This versatile filling machine known as the "Akra-Pak" can handle cold slurries (e.g. margarine or yoghurt) or hot slurries (e.g. processed cheese), and is manufactured by Rutherford Research Inc. in the United States of America. The filler utilises pre-formed plastic containers of any shape, and the closures can be press-on lids or heat-sealed, aluminium foil lids. The filling head is made out of polypropylene and uses a pneumatically operated ball valve designed to give a pre-set fill (by volume) with a clean, drip-free cut-off. The unit can handle solids in suspension up to 1.9 cm³, and hence is ideal for filling yoghurt containing large fruit particles. The capacity of the machine is 300 containers per minute depending on the volume of fill, and fill volumes are available from 50 cm³ to 25 litres (see Fig. 3.55).

5. Machines for filling yoghurt under controlled environment

Some packaging machines are equipped for, or have the facility for, gas flushing of the containers of fruit yoghurt before sealing. The objective is to replace the oxygen in the head space of the carton with carbon dioxide or nitrogen, and so restrict the growth of yeasts and moulds. Such an approach may indeed extend the shelf-life of the product, but it is important not to overlook the facts that: *firstly*, the packaging materials must be impermeable to these gases, and *secondly*, the process of gas flushing is only effective against obligate aerobes.

PUMPS USED IN THE YOGHURT INDUSTRY

A variety of different pumps are used in the dairy industry, depending on their intended function, and for simplicity the production line can be divided into the following sections:

—liquid milk handling and processing;
—coagulum production and handling;
—fruit/yoghurt blending and packaging.

165

Fig. 3.55. Akra-Pak filling machine

(1) Scroll feed tub dispenser
(2) Socketed belt conveyor
(3) Conveyor/filling head/discharge flight bar speed controller
(4) Stainless steel product hopper with a lid; also available with probe level controls.
(5) Rotary ball filling head
(6) Filling head speed controls
(7) Volume of fill adjustment
(8) Spinning ball lid dispenser
(9) Tamper unit (removes creases in deep punted lids caused during application)
(10) Discharge assembly

Reproduced by courtesy of Rutherford Research Inc. Uk Branch Office, Bolton, UK.

The physical characteristics/consistency of the materials differs in each section, and it is vital that the type of pump chosen is suitable for its duty. This is especially true after the formation of the coagulum, since any harsh mechanical treatment(s) can ultimately affect the viscosity of the product.

A. Centrifugal Pump

Basically, this pump consists of an electric motor (to supply the energy), a rotating impeller enclosed in a casing, and a delivery chamber. The fluid enters the impeller chamber, and is accelerated centrifugally until it is forced outward along the tip of the impeller. As a result, the fluid is discharged into the delivery chamber and out through a port of the exterior of the pump. The pressure generated is always equivalent to the flow resistance of the process line, and according to Anon. (1980) the efficiency of the pump, i.e. the transmission of energy from the motor to the liquid via the impeller, is equal to:

$$\text{Efficiency of centrifugal pump} = \frac{\text{Kinetic energy} + \text{Pressure energy imparted to the liquid at the discharge}}{\text{Energy delivered by motor to the impeller}}$$

(Note: energy loss in the form of heat is ignored.)

All centrifugal pumps are the same in principle, but the design of the impeller can vary, and also certain other factors have to be considered, namely:

—the discharge pressure at the pump;
—the flow rate or velocity of the liquid;
—degree of cavitation (this is the result of liquid being transferred from one side of the pump to the other, thus creating a vacuum; the "new" liquid enters the pump by suction);
—the viscosity of the product can affect pressure loss in the pump, and losses are higher when viscous products are being moved due to an increase in frictional losses;
—if pressure losses occur in the processing line, the velocity of the fluid is controlled either by installing regulating valves or by using a speed control, or by changing the diameter of the impeller.

The centrifugal action of these pumps is capable of producing high shear forces in the liquid being pumped, and hence their application in yoghurt processing is restricted to liquid milk handling and the pumping of water (hot or cold) through the heat exchangers.

B. Piston Pump

This type of pump is used to achieve high pressures during the processing of milk, and a typical example is an homogeniser (see Chapter 2).

C. Positive Displacement Pumps

The positive displacement pumps are classified into three different groups:

(i) pumps with reciprocating displacers;
(ii) pumps with rotating displacers;
(iii) miscellaneous.

A pump in the former category is, in effect, a low-pressure piston pump, and although not used for direct movement of the yoghurt coagulum, the majority of the filling machines incorporate the basic design. Thus, although this type of pump may exert a slight shearing effect, damage to the coagulum is minimised due to:

(i) the short contact time between the pump and the yoghurt;

(ii) the low temperature of filling, i.e. 10–15°C or less;

(iii) the absence of back pressure.

The rotating displacement pump is the most popular type for yoghurt, for the product moves through a rotating cavity between two rotors, or a stationary wall and one rotor. An example of a positive rotating pump is illustrated in Fig. 3.56. The two bladed rotors are suitable for pumping yoghurt containing delicate solids, e.g. large fruit pieces.

The flow pattern of yoghurt through these different pumps is illustrated in Fig. 3.57. The fluid enters the pump by gravity or by differential pressure, and due to the rotational action of the lobes a portion of yoghurt is trapped between the lobe and the pump casing, and gently transferred to the other side of the pump.

According to Tamime and Greig (*loc. cit.*) the advantages of these positive displacement pumps, as compared with reciprocating pumps, are:

—cheaper drive train;

—can operate at a higher speed (these pumps are cheaper and smaller than piston pumps with comparable delivery rates; however, since the speed of pumping affects the viscosity of yoghurt, the application of high speed is not recommended);

—negligible surges of flow;

—the pumps are self-priming;

—suitable for applications where large heads are involved;

—high delivery rates;

—suitable for pumping viscous products (e.g. yoghurt), or mixtures of solids and liquids (the suspended solids should not be sharp or abrasive);

—volumetric efficiency hardly diminishes with increasing counter-pressure.

One criticism of the rotary displacement pumps is that the seals are prone to leakage, and Harper, Seiberling and Blaisdell (*loc. cit.*) have pointed out that the seals between the pressure and suction sides are not as efficient as in reciprocating pumps; the seals between the rotary gears and the face plate are also prone to leakage. Regular inspection of the seals can reduce these problems to a minimum.

Another type of positive displacement pump is the screw pump, and this is widely used for pumping fruit yoghurt. It consists of a single helical rotor turning within a resilient stator (Anon., 1977b) and the fruit/yoghurt travels along a continuous spiral path without changing volume; in this way the yoghurt coagulum is treated gently, and the fruit particles remain intact (see Fig. 3.58).

Positive displacement of yoghurt can also be achieved using a rotary, flexible vane pump, e.g. the Jabsco pump (see Fig. 3.59). This pump works on the principle that as the impeller blade leaves the offset plate it creates a vacuum drawing in yoghurt, which is then carried through the pump from the inlet side to the outlet port. As the flexible vanes come into contact with the offset plate again they bend and, as a result, the "squeezing" action forces the product to be discharged continuously. The impeller can be manufactured from various types of inert material, e.g. neoprene, nitrile and viton, but the former is widely employed in the dairy industry for operating temperatures between 4° and 80°C.

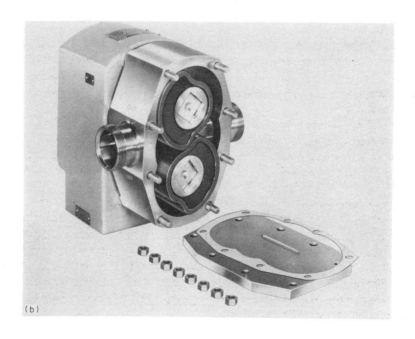

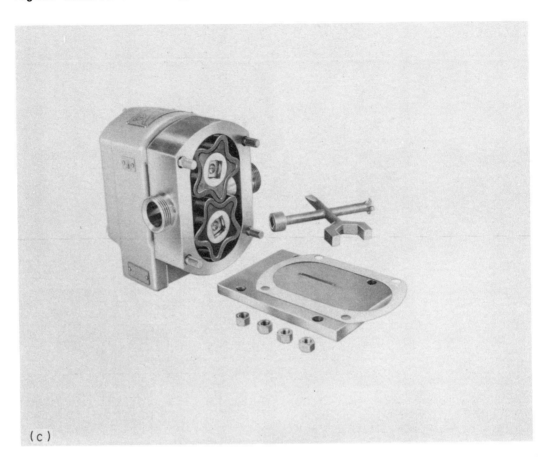

(c)

(d)

(e)

Fig. 3.56.   Illustration of the different types of lobe used in rotary positive displacement pumps

(a) Twin wing—this type of pump (from the Waukesha Universal Series) is capable of delivering 5, 22.7, 60.6, 94.6 or 189.3 litres of product at 100 rpm.

Reproduced by courtesy of Waukesha Foundry Division (ABEX Corporation), Wisconsin, USA.

(b) Single lobe—this type of rotor is suitable for pumping products containing pieces up to $1.9\,cm^2$.

Reproduced by courtesy of Crepaco International Inc. Brussels, Belgium.

(c) Five lobes—the arrangement of the rotors resembles a gear pump, and it is available in five sizes.

Reproduced by courtesy of Crepaco International Inc., Brussels, Belgium.

(d) Three lobes—this is a Jabsco lobe pump, and the capacity ranges from 10.4–161 1/100 revolutions.

Reproduced by courtesy of ITT Jabsco Ltd., Hertfordshire, UK.

(e) Twin bladed rotor for delicate solids—this is a MOG IBEX pump which is suitable to handle yoghurt containing large fruit pieces.

Reproduced by courtesy of Ibex Engineering Co. Ltd., Hastings, UK.

D. Miscellaneous Types of Pump

Different types of pump are sometimes installed in a processing line for a special purpose, e.g.:

—"in-line" addition of the starter culture into the yoghurt milk during the production of set and/or stirred yoghurt;

171

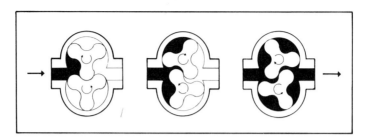

Fig. 3.57.   Flow of yoghurt through a positive displacement pump

After Tamime & Greig (*loc. cit.*).

Reprinted with permission of Dairy Industries International.

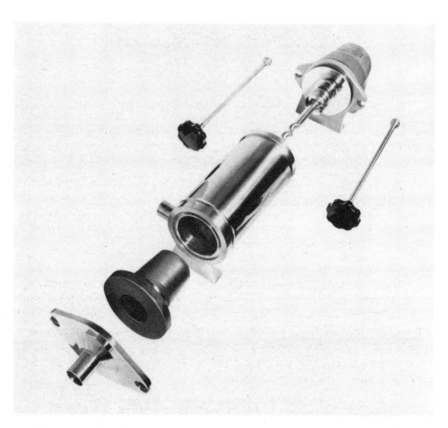

Fig. 3.58.   The mono pump—"J" range

The capacity of the "J" range Mono pumps at 1.0×10^5 N/m² (1 bar) pressure ranges from 136.4 to 2527.6 litres of water at 100 rpm; notice that the pump has a vertical outlet.

Reproduced by courtesy of Mono pumps Ltd., Manchester, UK.

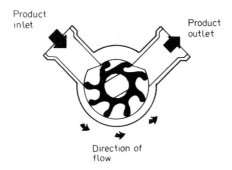

Fig. 3.59.   Diagram to show the operation of a flexible vane positive displacement pump

—the addition of colouring matter and/or liquid (flavour) essences (natural or synthetic) into the milk during the production of set yoghurt.

Some examples of pumps which could be employed are as follow.

1. Peristaltic pump

This type of pump consists of three parts: firstly, a flexible plastic pipe, secondly, a curved track which houses the plastic pipe, and thirdly, a motor that drives a series of rollers which, in turn, occlude the tube and thus push the fluid along. The action of the roller also creates a powerful suction in the tube, and as a result fluid is drawn in to replace that being driven forward; the flow rate is governed by the speed of the roller and the internal diameter of the flexible plastic pipe.

2. Diaphragm metering pump

This type of pump is normally mounted on the tank containing the solution to be metered and is suitable for metering colouring matter and flavours into the yoghurt milk or coagulum, and/or dosing chlorine solution into the water system. The dose rate is controlled either by altering the stroke length, i.e. the delivered volume, or by adjusting the frequency of the stroking action.

It can be observed that different types of pump are used in a yoghurt processing line, and in choosing the right pump for the right job a number of interrelated factors must be taken into account. Some practical considerations may include:

(1) length and diameter of the piping used on the suction and the discharge sides of the pump;
(2) number and types of fitting installed, i.e. elbows, T-pieces and type of valve;
(3) types of metering/mixing device used;
(4) manufacturer's specifications provided on the plate/tubular coolers intended for cooling the coagulum;
(5) restrictions in the processing line, e.g. static in-line mixers, strainers or "structurisers";

(6) product variables, which may include:
—level of solids in the milk/yoghurt;
—effect of shear on the product;
—final viscosity of the yoghurt;
—ability of the product to withstand high-pressure pumping;
—product type, e.g. level of pH, presence of particulate solids (fruit pieces);
—type of fluid flow in the sytem, e.g. for yoghurt it is a laminar flow-R <2000.
(7) total pressure losses in the system.

Few data are available regarding the damage that may result from pumping the yoghurt coagulum from one point to another, but Steenbergen (1971b) has studied the effect of pumping on the viscosity of yoghurt (see Fig. 3.60) and concluded that the important aspects were:

—speed of the pump;
—shape and type of the impeller;
—counter-pressure in the processing line.

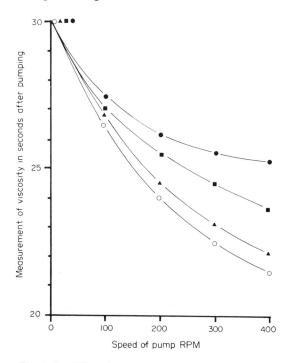

Fig. 3.60.   Effect of pumping on the viscosity of yoghurt

● Fristam FK 15—stroke volume 18.4 ⎫
■ Moineau LBF 6/R46—stroke volume 93 ⎬ cm³
▲ Mono SH 22/R8—stroke volume 8.5 ⎪
○ Waukesha 25DO—stroke volume 224 ⎭

—Viscosity measurement was carried out using the Posthumus funnel
—Counter/back pressure is 0 bar
—1 Bar is equivalent to 1×10^5 N/m²

Adapted from Steenbergen (1971 b).

It can be observed from Fig. 3.60 that minimal reductions in viscosity occurred when the speed of the pump was maintained at 100 rpm; the loss in viscosity varied from 8.3 to 11.7% depending on the type of pump used. However, as the speed of the pump was gradually increased from 100 to 400 rpm, structural damage to the coagulum did occur, and if an increase in throughput is required, it is advisable to choose a pump with a larger stroke volume, rather than increase the speed of the pump.

The development of counter-pressure in any type of yoghurt plant is the result of a multitude of factors, e.g. the type and number of fittings, arrangement of pipework and/or heat exchangers, and the greater the counter-pressure in the system the lower the viscosity of the yoghurt after pumping; Table 3.3 illustrates this effect. However, a high fluid flow is desirable in the plant during the CIP stage, and hence the pumps used between the fermentation tanks and the filling machines must be of variable speed.

Alternatively, the positive pumps can be by-passed by lines including centrifugal pumps, so that the latter pumps can be brought into operation during cleaning. In the latter case, cleaning of the

TABLE 3.3. *Reduction in the viscosity of yoghurt as affected by counter/back pressure*

| Pressure (bar) | Pump speed (rpm) | Viscosity | | Reduction (%) |
		Initial (seconds)	Observed (seconds)	
0	100	60	51.0	15.0
1	100	60	47.5	20.8
2	100	60	45.0	25.0

Type of pump—Waukesha 25 DO.
Viscosity measurement by Posthumus funnel (see Galesloot, 1958).
1 bar is equivalent to $1 \times 10^5 \, N/m^2$.

Adapted from Steenbergen (1971b).

positive pumps is usually carried out manually, followed by sterilisation, with the rest of the plant, with circulating hot or chlorinated water.

Whatever precautions are taken, however, mechanical handling of the coagulum does ultimately reduce its viscosity, and some recommended precautionary measures include:

—fortification of the yoghurt milk to a higher total solids;
—the addition of stabilisers (this may be prohibited in some countries);
—the use of "viscous" starter cultures;
—agitation of the coagulum is avoided in some types of fermentation tank, e.g. the tank supplied by Alfa-Laval A/B in Sweden;
—the use of pumps between the fermentation tank and the filling machine is not required with the Terlet-type tank. The transfer of the coagulum is achieved by air pressure in the fermentation tank (e.g. $0.5 \times 10^5 \, N/m^2 \doteq$ to 0.5 atmosphere), which forces the coagulum from the tank to the tubular cooler, and finally to the intermediate tank.

175

MISCELLANEOUS FITTINGS IN A YOGHURT PROCESSING LINE

The different items of equipment in a yoghurt processing line are linked together with a series of pipes, fittings (elbows, T-pieces, pipe couplings, etc.), valves, and sometimes strainers, and the passage of the yoghurt through these miscellaneous parts of the plant can cause some structural damage of the coagulum. This damage may arise from the following.

A. Pipes

As the yoghurt coagulum is pumped at a low rpm, and it is safe to assume that the flow pattern through the pipes is laminar. However, other factors can affect this flow pattern, namely:

—the length and diameter of the pipe;
—the number of fittings;
—the internal "roughness" of the pipe surface;
—fluctuations in fluid velocity.

Steenbergen (1971b, c) studied the effect of pipe length and diameter on the viscosity of yoghurt, and some of his results are shown in Table 3.4. From this data it can be concluded that:

TABLE 3.4. *The effect of transport through pipes on yoghurt viscosity*

	Yoghurt I (initial viscosity)* 30 seconds			Yoghurt II (initial viscosity) 40 seconds		
Length of pipe (m)	10	20	30	10	20	30
		Reduction in viscosity (seconds)				
Diameter of pipe (cm)						
3.81	10	14	17	17	22	24
5.08	6	9	12	11	16	20
6.35	3	5	8	6	10	14
7.62	1	4	6	2	8	11

The flow rate is 3600 litres/hour.
* For definition—see text.

After Steenbergen (1971c).

(i) If the *velocity* and *diameter* of pipe are kept constant, reduction in the viscosity of yoghurt is proportional to the *length* of the pipe.
(ii) If the *velocity* and *length* of pipe are kept constant, the larger the *diameter* of the pipe, the least structural damage occurs to the coagulum.

It is recommended, therefore, that large diameter pipes should be installed between the fermentation tanks and the filling machines, and that, at the same time, the connections should be as short as possible.

B. Fittings

Fittings, valves and other restrictions in a processing line can interfere with the flow pattern of the yoghurt, and as a result affect the viscosity of the product. Steenbergen (1971c, 1973) evaluated the effect of these different fittings, and observed that the viscosity of yoghurt was reduced by between 0.2 and 20 seconds (the initial viscosity of the product was 30 seconds as measured by the Posthumus funnel), which is equivalent to lowering the consistency of the yoghurt by 0.7 and 67 % respectively. The most severe structural damage to the coagulum took place where fittings reduced the diameter of the piping, and if such fittings could be avoided, the reduction in viscosity was minimised.

C. Screens or Strainers

One fault, which sometimes occurs during the manufacture of stirred yoghurt, is the appearance of non-dispersable particles referred to as "nodules", "lumpiness", "granules" or "graininess" (see Fig. 3.61), and the nature and/or origin(s) of nodule formation is not well established (see Robinson, 1981). Although the fault can be avoided by fermenting the milk at precisely 42°C (short set) and not disturbing the gel during the coagulation period, an alternative approach is to disperse the nodules by pumping the coagulum through a stainless steel mesh. This restriction in the pipe line does affect the viscosity of yoghurt, but the advantage is that it produces a smooth textured coagulum free from nodules, a feature confirmed by Nielson (1972); unfortunately no figure was given in relation to loss in viscosity.

One such unit sometimes known as a 'structuriser' is shown in Fig. 3.62 (a & b), and in commercial practice, the warm coagulum is pumped through the strainer in order to break up the nodules; pumping cold yoghurt through the strainer would severely damage the viscosity of the product, since high pressures would be required to achieve the necessary flow.

MECHANISATION OF YOGHURT PRODUCTION AND PLANT DESIGN

As the scale of yoghurt production increases, the use of mechanisation to handle the milk and the coagulum becomes inevitable. A wide range of equipment is available, but the final choice is governed primarily by the method of processing adopted, and Table 3.5 lists those items of equipment that might be required for the production of yoghurt from milk fortified with skim-milk powder, or alternatively from standardised milk concentrated by evaporation. It can be observed from Table 3.5 that while different equipment is required for the handling and processing of the milk, the process for the production and handling of the coagulum is broadly similar, and it is relevant that this mechanical handling can lead to structural damage to the coagulum. An illustration of the effect of handling the coagulum on the viscosity of the final yoghurt is shown in Fig. 3.63 (Norling, 1979), and it is of note that if the coagulum is handled carefully, the viscosity of the yoghurt recovers rapidly in cold storage, but the power to recuperate is lost when the coagulum is handled roughly.

Another important feature is, of course, the overall plant design, but the permutations available, particularly within existing buildings, means that each plant layout has to be considered in its own

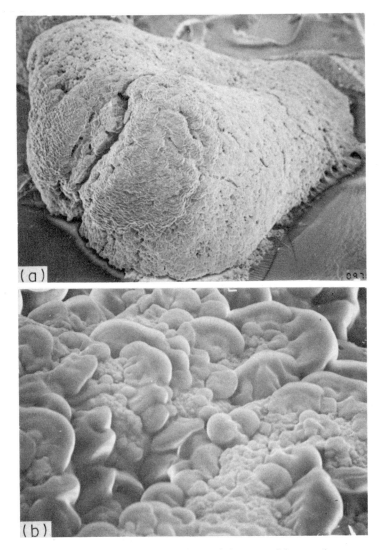

Fig. 3.61. A typical "granule" or nodule extracted from yoghurt

(a) Notice the compact nature of the structure is clearly evident (× 35).
(b) Surface view of a nodule that emphasises the lack of connection between the particles and the suspending coagulum (× 750); this extreme compaction may not, however, be typical.

After Robinson (*loc. cit.*).

Reprinted with permission of Dairy Industries International.

right. For example, Fig. 3.64 shows the different equipment used for the production of yoghurt in a dairy in Belgium, and the close proximity between the fermentation tanks, the cooler and the intermediate yoghurt storage tank(s) is clearly visible. In some instances the equipment has to be installed in an already existing building (which could be a limiting factor), but considering the recommendations mentioned earlier, the reduction in viscosity of the yoghurt could still be minimised. In an ideal situation, i.e. factory construction and plant installation carried out

Fig. 3.62. On-site illustration of an Alfa-Laval 'structuriser' on a yoghurt processing plant

(a) The 'structuriser' is installed between the yoghurt fermentation tanks and the plate cooler.
(b) An exploded view of a dismantled 'structuriser'.

Reproduced with permission of Northern Ireland Milk Marketing Board, Belfast, UK.

TABLE 3.5. *Plant specification of a yoghurt production line—capacity 2 000 l/hr*

	Number required	Plant I	Number required	Plant II
Method of fortification		Addition of skim milk powder		Concentration by evaporation
Preliminary treatment of milk	1	Centrifugal pump for circulating the milk through the powder mixing funnel and storage tanks.		
	1	Powder mixing funnel.		
	2	Vertical storage tanks for holding standardised/fortified milk.		
	1	Centrifugal pump for pumping the stored milk to the balance tank.	1	*Ibid.*
	1	Balance tank for intake of yoghurt milk to the plant.	1	*Ibid.*
	1	Centrifugal for pumping fortified/standardised milk to the plate heat exchanger.	1	*Ibid.*
Processing of milk	1	Plate heat exchanger capacity 2000 l/hr for heat treatment of milk and cooling it to the incubation temperature.	1	*Ibid.*
	1	Holding tube for holding the milk at the heat treatment temperature for 3 minutes.	1	*Ibid.*
	1	Homogeniser (capacity 2000 l/hr) for homogenising the milk at 60°C.	1	*Ibid.*
	1	Hot water unit for providing the thermal energy required to heat the milk.	1	*Ibid.* (for heating the milk before entering the evaporator).
			1	Vacuum chamber for concentration of the standardised milk.
			1	Centrifugal pump for pumping milk from the evaporator to the homogeniser, and recirculation of milk to the plate heat exchanger until the desired concentration is achieved.
			1	Vacuum pump for pumping the condensate from the evaporator to the regeneration section of the plate heat exchanger.
			1	Vacuum pump for pumping concentrated milk through the plate heat exchanger.
Starter preparation/Yoghurt production	1	Viscuabator for the preparation of mother and intermediate/feeder starter culture.		
	2	Starter vat for the production of the bulk starter culture.		
	1	Positive displacement pump for pumping the bulk starter to the yoghurt incubation tank.		
	1	Positive metering pump for continuous "in-line" inoculation of milk with the bulk starter culture either for the production of stirred or set yoghurt.		
	4–5	Vertical incubation tanks each has the capacity of 2000 litres; and/or incubation cabinets/tunnel for production of set yoghurt where the number is dependent on method adopted.		
	1	Positive displacement pump for pumping the yoghurt coagulum to the plate cooler.		
	1	Plate heat exchanger (capacity 4000 l/hr) for cooling the yoghurt.		
	1	"Cold" water unit for cooling the yoghurt.		
	1	Centrifugal pump used as a by-pass for pumping recirculated water on the cold water side.		
Fruit Blending/Packaging	2	Vertical intermediate storage tanks each has capacity of 3000 litres depending on production schedule.		
	2	Positive displacement pumps (metering type) for pumping yoghurt and fruit flavours to the blending unit.		
	1	Fruit/yoghurt blending unit.		
	1–2	Yoghurt filling machine(s) of total throughput 2,000 l/hr.		
CIP System	1	Control panel.		
	3	Tanks for detergent solutions.		
	4	Liquid ring pumps used as return pumps for cleaning.		
	1	Plate heat exchanger for heating the detergent solutions.		
	1	Centrifugal pump used as feed pump for detergent solution.		
	1	Filter for removal of large soil particles from the CIP system.		
	1	Steam controller.		
Miscellaneous	1	Main control panel.		
	–	Number of valves, fittings and pipes required in each of the sections mentioned above.		

Data compiled from Alfa-Laval A/B technical specification of yoghurt plants.

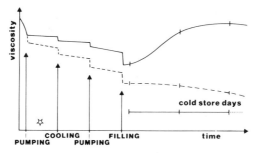

Fig. 3.63. Viscosity curve in relation to mechanical treatment (shearing stress)

(—) Viscosity curve of yoghurt in an Alfa-Laval processing plant (the coagulum is extracted by means of a positive displacement pump without agitation in the fermentation tank).

(–––) Viscosity curve of yoghurt as a result of severe mechanical treatment.

*Before the cooler, the yoghurt passes through an in-line 'Structurising Strainer'.

After Norling (*loc. cit.*)

Fig. 3.64. A view of a plant for the production of set and/or stirred yoghurt at the Inza dairy in Belgium

Notice the equipment from right to left:—holding tube, evaporator, homogeniser; incubation tanks, plate cooler and intermediate storage tank.

Reproduced by courtesy of Alfa-Laval A/B, Lund, Sweden.

simultaneously, the layout of a yoghurt plant might take the form illustrated in Fig. 3.65. Notice that the flow of yoghurt from the incubation tanks to the cooler and storage tanks is virtually in a straight line, and that the distance is as short as possible. The situation is similar for the transfer of yoghurt from the storage tanks to the filling machines.

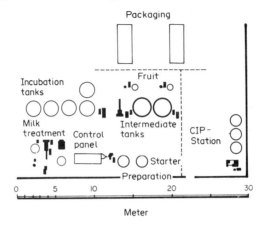

Fig. 3.65.   Layout of a yoghurt plant to handle 3000–4000 litres per hour

The space requirements for some Alfa-Laval yoghurt plants based on the layout above; excluding the areas required for the CIP unit and the packaging machinery are:

Plant Capacity (l/h)	Floor Area (m²)
1000	16 × 10 = 160
2000	18 × 11 = 198 (200)
3000	20 × 12 = 240
6000	25 × 12 = 300
10000	26 × 13 = 338 (340)

Reproduced by courtesy of Alfa-Laval A/B, Lund, Sweden.

AUTOMATION/PROCESS CONTROL

A few decades ago practically all the operations involved in the manufacture of yoghurt, including the cleaning stages, were carried out manually, so that the process was very labour-intensive, and the quality of yoghurt dependent on the efficiency and reliability of the dairy operator(s). The consequence was low productivity and high cost of production. However, yoghurt processing does necessitate a "certain logic" on the part of the operator, and hence the introduction of computer control was an obvious step to:

—check that all the required raw materials are available;
—check that the plant is clean and sanitised, and that the different parts of the plant are properly connected and in the right sequence;
—when everything is ready, start the processing operation;
—maintain proper vigilance during the processing period, in order to terminate a given function or initiate a new one;
—check that the right amount of starter culture is added to the yoghurt milk;
—monitor the development of acidity and, at the right level, start the cooling stage;
—when the fermentation tank is empty, start the cleaning cycle so that the tank is ready to be re-used;

182

—check that the correct amount of fruit is blended with the coagulum prior to packaging;
—finally, shut down the plant and clean any remaining equipment.

Trained personnel could, of course, easily carry out the above functions, but humans are prone, due to fatigue or negligence, to make mistakes, whereas an automated system, programmed with the correct sequences of instructions, should be able to perform the same duties without error. The degree of automation in a yoghurt plant is governed by many factors, such as type of equipment and method of operation, and its introduction has to take into account the possible need to:

(a) supplement existing human endeavour;
(b) improve/increase productivity;
(c) improve/increase plant efficiency;
(d) improve safety (Anon., 1980a, b).

The degree of automation in a yoghurt plant is primarily dependent on capacity (Anon., 1979b, 1981d, e; IDF, 1973), but in the absence of any constraint the present-day approach is to divide a processing plant into different areas/departments interlinked via a central data processing unit. Thus, in order to achieve a high degree of automation in a yoghurt plant it may be divided into the following sections.

Area/Department 1

In this area reception and storage of the milk takes place, together with preparation of the basic mix, and automation covers handling of the liquid milk, controlling the flow of milk from the storage tanks, cleaning the tanks, and the automatic selection of the dry ingredients (milk powder and sugar).

Area/Department 2

Milk standardisation, homogenisation and heat treatment takes place in this section, and the operating sequence of the heat exchanger unit can be easily programmed to both heat the milk and cool it to 40–45°C.

Area/Department 3

In this department fermentation of the milk takes place, and automation covers the control of temperature during the incubation period, monitoring the level of acidity and, if possible, initiation of the cooling stage.

Area/Department 4

In this section the following functions could be automated: fruit blending and mixing with the coagulum and packaging.

Area/Department 5

The preparation of the starter culture is carried out here, and automatic control systems are available to provide the necessary growth conditions, and, furthermore, monitor the direct in-line inoculation of the yoghurt milk.

183

Area/Department 6

Cleaning-in-place station (refer to Chapter 4 for further details).

Numerous types of automated systems are available on the market, and these can either be "custom built" or obtained as modular units. However, whatever system is chosen, the fact is that trained personnel are still required to operate and look after the plant, and hence the real attraction of automation is improved efficiency under, perhaps, more congenial conditions for the operator.

REFERENCES

ANON. (1976a) In *Cultured Milk Products,* Alfa-Laval Technical Bulletin PB 60852 E, Alfa-Laval A/B, Lund, Sweden.

ANON. (1976b) In *An Introduction to Heat Exchange,* Alfa-Laval Technical Bulletin VM 60412 E, Alfa-Laval A/B, Lund, Sweden.

ANON. (1977a) In *The Influence of the Cooling Rate on the Quality of Stirred Yoghurt,* Publication No. 225, Danish Research Institute, Hillerød, Denmark.

ANON. (1977b) In *Mono-Clean J Range Pumps,* Technical Bulletin No. 1082, Mono Pumps Ltd., Manchester, UK.

ANON. (1979a) In *APV Gaulin Homogenisers and High Pressure Pumps,* Technical Bulletin A 297 n, APV Co. Ltd., West Sussex, UK.

ANON. (1979b) In *Automatic CIP Equipment for Food Plants,* Alfa-Laval Technical Bulletin Pb 60220 E, Alfa-Laval A/B, Lund Sweden.

ANON. (1980) In *Dairy Handbook,* Alfa-Laval A/B, Lund, Sweden.

ANON. (1981a) *Nordeuropaeisk Mejeri-Tidsskrift,* **47**(3), 58.

ANON. (1981b) Pasilac Technical Flow Sheet No. 33 59 77, Pasilac/Silkeborg Ltd., Preston, UK.

ANON. (1981c) Pasilac Technical Flow Sheet No. 33 59 70, Pasilac/Silkeborg Ltd., Preston, UK.

ANON. (1981d) In *Accos 2—APV Microprocessor System for Process Plant Control,* Technical Bulletin A 500c, APV Co. Ltd., West Sussex, UK.

ANON. (1981e) In *APV—Automation,* Technical Bulletin A 388 f, APV Co. Ltd., West Sussex, UK.

COCKX, N. (1982) Personal communication.

COTTENIE, J. (1978) *Cultured Dairy Products Journal,* **13**(4), 6.

CRAWFORD, R. J. M. (1962) *Journal of Dairy Engineering,* **79**(1), 4.

DALHUISEN, J. J. (1972) In *Yoghurt Production—Technical and Technological Information,* Technical Bulletin 0772 801/00/0080, Stork-Amsterdam, Amstelveen, The Netherlands.

EHRMANN, A. (1972) *Dairy Science Abstracts,* **34,** 602.

FEARN, J. (1982) Personal communication.

GALESLOOT, Th. E. (1958) *Netherland Milk & Dairy Journal,* **12,** 130.

HALE, D. (1982) Personal communication.

HALL, C. W. (1976) In *Dairy Technology and Engineering,* Ed. by Harper, W. J. & Hall, C. W. AVI Publishing Co. Inc., Connecticut, USA.

HARPER, W. J., SEIBERLING, D. A. and BLAISDEL, J. K. (1976) In *Dairy Technology and Engineering,* Ed. by Harper, W. J. & Hall, C. W. AVI Publishing Co. Inc., Connecticut, USA.

IDF (1973) In *Automation in the Dairy Industry,* IDF Doc. No. 72, Brussels, Belgium.

KESSLER, H. G. (1981) In *Food Engineering and Dairy Technology,* Translated by Wotzilka, M. Publishing House Verlag A. Kessler, Preising, West Germany.

LONCIN, M. and MERSON, R. L. (1979) In *Food Engineering—Principles and Selected Applications,* Academic Press Inc., New York, USA.

MÖLLER, E. (1981) Personal communication.

MÖLLER, E. (1982) *Dairy Science Abstracts,* **44,** 25.

NEWSTEAD, D. F., GOLDMANN, A. and ZADOW, J. G. (1979) In *Monograph on Recombination of Milk and Milk Products— Technology and Engineering Aspects,* IDF Doc. 116, Brussels, Belgium.

NIELSEN, V. H. (1972) *American Dairy Review,* **34**(2), 26.

NORLING, H. (1979) Personal communication.

PIERSMA, H. and STEENBERGEN, A. E. (1973) *Official Orgaan FNZ,* **65,** 94.

ROBINSON, R. K. (1981) *Dairy Industries International,* **46**(3), 31.

SANDERSON, W. B. (1982) In *Proceedings of IDF Seminar on Recombination of Milk and Milk Products,* IDF Doc. 142, Brussels, Belgium.

STEENBERGEN, A. E. (1971a) *Official Orgaan FNZ,* **63,** 996.

STEENBERGEN, A. E. (1971b) *Official Orgaan FNZ,* **63,** 729.

STEENBERGEN, A. E. (1971c) *Official Orgaan FNZ,* **63,** 164.

STEENBERGEN, A. E. (1973) In *Over Yoghurt,* NIZO—Mededelingen No. 7, Nederlands Institute Voor Zuivelonderzoek, Ede, Holland.

TAMIME, A. Y. and GREIG, R. I. W. (1979) *Dairy Industries International,* **44**(9), 8.

CHAPTER 4

Plant Cleaning, Hygiene and Effluent Treatment

PRIMARY OBJECTIVES

The keeping quality of yoghurt is governed by a multiplicity of interrelated factors such as:

(a) the hygienic quality of the product which, in turn, is dependent on the effective heat treatment of the basic mix, the purity of the starter culture, the microbiological quality of added fruit/flavours and other ingredients, and the care which is exercised during storage, handling and distribution of the yoghurt (see Chapter 10);
(b) the cleanliness of surfaces coming into contact with the yoghurt, e.g. processing equipment, filling machines and packaging materials;
(c) miscellaneous, i.e. the attitudes of the dairy personnel, and the hygienic condition of the buildings/building site (refer to IDF, 1980).

Factors related to the former and latter aspects (a and c) are discussed elsewhere, so that to achieve the primary objective, i.e. an excellent yoghurt with good keeping quality, the remaining essential is the provision of hygienic processing equipment and packaging materials. The nature of contaminants from surfaces coming into contact with any food product, including yoghurt, could be physical, chemical or biological and contamination from these sources can be minimised by the following approach (Swartling, 1959; Dunsmore *et al.*, 1981):

(a) removal of residues (milk, yoghurt and other additives) which can provide nutrients for micro-organisms remaining on the surfaces of equipment;
(b) cleaning and sanitisation/sterilisation of equipment by removal and destruction of micro-organisms which survived function (a);
(c) storage of equipment under conditions that limit microbial growth/survival when the equipment is not in use;
(d) removal of residual cleaning compounds which may contaminate the yoghurt.

The efficiency of plant hygiene/sanitation is, therefore, dependent on the performance of the following operations:

(a) Cleaning, and
(b) Sterilisation.

In the commercial situation, "cleaning" is the removal of yoghurt "soil" (Table 4.1) from the surface of the processing equipment, and this is followed by "sterilisation", i.e. the destruction of most of the residual micro-organisms; these aspects will be discussed in relation to the type of equipment used in the production of yoghurt, and the degree of automation.

ASPECTS OF CLEANING

A. Principals of the Cleaning Process

The processing of milk during the manufacture of yoghurt forms different types of soiling matter on the surfaces of equipment (Table 4.1), and this "soil" consists of organic compounds (e.g. protein, fat, lactose and other non-dairy ingredients) and inorganic salts. The degree of deposition of the "soil" on the processing surfaces is governed by many factors, but is directly proportional to the amount of heat applied, which results in "more" denaturation of the milk proteins and "more" precipitation of the organic salts (from milk and water). Hence, soil resulting from the heating of milk is more difficult to remove than soiling matter from unheated milk.

The cleaning process necessitates the use of certain compounds referred to as detergents, which are available in liquid or powder forms, and the basic functions of the detergents are:

(a) establishing an intimate contact with the soiling matter through their wetting and/or penetrating properties;
(b) displacement of the soil, for example:
    (i) by melting/emulsifying the fat;
    (ii) by wetting, soaking, penetrating and peptising the proteins;
    (iii) by dissolving the mineral salts;
(c) dispersion or displacement of the undissolved "soil" by defloculation and/or emulsification;
(d) preventing redeposition of the "soil" by maintaining the properties of (c) and by ensuring good rinsing;
(e) miscellaneous, i.e. non-corrosive, no odour nor taste, non-toxic and non-irritable to skin.

In order that the above properties/functions of a detergent can be achieved, different formulations are used, and Table 4.2 illustrates some of the compounds and their properties that can be employed to manufacture a proprietary detergent.

B. Factors Involved in the Selection and Performance of a Detergent

There are many different types of detergent available on the market, and most of them have been developed for a specialised cleaning purpose.

1. Type/range of detergents used in the yoghurt industry

Different types of processing equipment are used during manufacture, and the type of detergent is chosen in relation to its cleaning function, such as:

TABLE 4.1. *Soil characteristics of a yoghurt plant*

Soil component on the surface to be cleaned	Solubility in Water	Ease of removal during cleaning			Effect of alteration by heat**	Comments
		Alkaline	Acids	Without alteration by heat*		
I. Dairy						
Lactose	G	–	–	Good	*Caramelisation/Browning* more difficult to clean	Unlikely to take place during heat treatment of the yoghurt milk
Fat	P (in solutions without surface active agents)	P	P	Good with surface active solutions	*Polymerisation* more difficult to clean	*Ibid.*; since most types of yoghurt produced in the UK are low-fat varieties; this condition may not arise
Protein	P	G	Av.	Pour with water; better with alkaline solutions	*Denaturation* difficult to clean	This effect is most likely to take place during prolonged heating of milk, e.g. HTLT (see Table 2.17) or preparation of starter culture milk
Mineral salts	G-P	–	G	Reasonably good	*Precipitation* difficult to clean	*Ibid.*
II. Dairy additives						
Sweetening agent	G	–	–	Good	*Caramelistion/Browning* more difficult to clean	Condition may arise in the case of lactose hydrolysed milk heated at 85–90°C for >45 minutes, or the high percent of sugar is added to the basic mix before heat treatment
Fruit	G-P	–	–	Good	*Ibid.*	This effect takes place in dairies that pasteurise their own fruit base before addition to yoghurt
Colouring or flavouring matter	G	–	–	Good	NA	
Stabilisers	(a)			(a)	NA	

(G) good; (Av) average; (P) poor; (NA) not applicable; (a) refer to text in Chapter 2.

* Possible places of identification are: milk reception area, preparation of basic mix, yoghurt incubation tanks and/or, yoghurt filling section.

** Possible places of identification are: heat treatment section, multi-purpose tanks, fruit processing equipment and/or bulk starter tanks.

Adapted from IDF (1979), Tamplin (1980).

TABLE 4.2. *Functional properties and characteristics of the detergent constituents*

Type	Detergent components(s)	Organic dissolving	Wetting	Dispensing suspending	Rinsing	Sequestering	Chelating	Bacteriocidal	General comments
Inorganic alkalis	1. Sodium hydroxide	E	P	P	P			E	—These compounds can affect degree of alkalinity, buffering action and rinsing power of a detergent.
	2. Sodium orthosilicate	G	F	F	P			G	—For high alkalinity preparations use alkalis (1) and (2) which can cause skin irritation; therefore, handle them with care.
	3. Sodium metasilicate	G	G-P	VG	G			F	—For removing heavy soil, alkalis (2), (3) and (4) are very effective.
	4. Trisodium phosphate	F	F-P	VG	G			F	—For low alkalinity, i.e. mild or hand detergents, use alkalis (5) and (6).
	5. Sodium carbonate	F	P	P	P			P	
	6. Sodium bicarbonate	G	P	G	F			F	
Acids	Inorganic { Nitric acid, Phosphoric acid, Sulphamic acid }								—Acids are normally used for the removal of tenacious soil, e.g. in UHT plants.
	Organic { Hydroxy acetic acid, Gluconic acid, Citric acid }	G			G				—These materials are corrosive, and can cause severe skin burns; therefore handle them with care, and if incorporated in a detergent formulation they may have to be used with corrosion inhibitors.
Surface-active agents	Anionic { Sodium alkyl aryl sulphonate, Sodium primary alkyl sulphate, Sodium alkyl ether sulphate }		E	E	E				—The classification is dependent upon how these compounds dissociate in aqueous solution, e.g. surface-active anions, cations, etc.
	Non-ionic Polyethenory compounds		E	E	E				—Some of these compounds are also used as emulsifying agents
	Cationic Quaternary ammonium compounds	(see sterilising agents below)							—Non-ionic agents do not ionise in solution.
	Amphoteric Alkylamino carboxylic acids								—Surfactants tend to reduce surface tension of the aqueous medium, and promote good liquid/soil/surface interfaces.
Sequestering and chelating agents	Sodium polyphosphates	F	P	G	F	G			—They prevent water hardness precipitation, are heat stable, and are used for formulation of combined detergent/steriliser compounds.
	Ethylenediamine tetra acetic acid (EDTA) and its salts			VG	E	E	E	G	—Their inclusion in formulations is to "hold" calcium ions in alkali solution and prevents reprecipitation.
	Gluconic acid and its salts					E	E		—The bacteriostatic property of EDTA is achieved by withdrawing trace metals from bacterial cellular membranes.
									—Gluconic acid is a stronger chelating agent than EDTA in alkali solutions (2–5% strength).

Sterilising agents

Group	Compound	Rating	Notes
Chlorine	Chlorinated trisodium ortho-phosphate	E	—Their inclusion provides a balanced product for cleaning (i.e. detergent) and sterilisation (e.g. hypo-chlorus acid, QAC, iodine or peroxide).
	Dichlorodimethyl hydrantion		—Consult list of brands approved by the authorities concerned that can be used as detergent/sterilisers as an alternative to steam or boiling water for the sterilisation of dairy equipment.
	Sodium dichloro-isoyanurate		
	Sodium hypochlorite		
QAC	Cetyl trimethyl ammonium bromide	E	
	Benzalkonium chloride		
Iodine	Iodophors	VG VG VG	
Peroxide	Per acetic acid	G	
	Hydrogen peroxide	G	

Miscellaneous compounds

Group	Compound	Rating	Notes
(a) Inhibitors	Sodium sulphite	E	—These inhibitors minimise corrosive attacks by acids and alkalis on metal. The sulphites protect tinned surfaces, and silicates protect aluminium and its alloys from attack by alkalis.
	Sodium silicate		
(b) Anti-foaming agents		G	—Anti-foaming agents are sometimes incorporated in a detergent formulation to prevent foam formation which could be generated by pumping/jetting action during detergent recirculation.
			—Fats and alkalis may form of soaps by saponification, and these anti-foaming agents prevent foam formation.
(c) Suspending Agents			—Sodium carboxymethyl cellulose or starch assist in maintaining undissolved soiling matter in suspension, thus referred to as suspending agents.
(d) Phosphates	Orthophosphatates	G	—Some of the polyphosphate compounds hydrolyse to orthophosphates in aqueous solution at high temperature, but presence of alkalis reduce the rate of hydrolysis.
	Polyphosphates	G G	
(e) Water softening			—Precipitation of calcium and magnesium ions from hard water in order to avoid water-scale deposition on surfaces of equipment especially for the last rinsing step after cleaning.

(E) Excellent, (VG) Very good, (G) Good, (F) Fair, (P) Poor.
Data compiled from IDF (1979), Tamplin (1980), BSI (1970 and Amendment, 1974).

(a) Mild detergent. This type of detergent is employed for manual washing operations.

(b) Combined mild detergent/steriliser. This is similar to the detergent mentioned above but with improved properties of sanitation.

(c) Detergents for cleaning-in-place (CIP). The range of such detergents is extensive and they are divided into two basic categories: *firstly*, for milk processing equipment where no heating is applied, e.g.:

—milk reception area,
—storage tanks and silos,
—equipment used for preparation of the basic yoghurt mix,
—incubation tanks,
—plate/tubular coolers,
—intermediate yoghurt tanks,
—filling machines,
—UF or RO plants.

Secondly, for cleaning equipment involved in the heat treatment of milk, for example:

—heat exchangers,
—evaporators,
—bulk starter culture tanks,
—equipment for processing fruit.

(d) Bulk liquid detergents. These detergents are similar to those mentioned above (c), and are normally used by large dairies using automatically controlled CIP systems. They are in liquid form, since it is easier to dispense into the cleaning cycle and control the concentration of the detergent.

(e) Detergents for bottle washers. The use and application of these detergents is very limited, since most yoghurt is packaged in single-trip containers.

(f) Detergents for churn washers. These types of detergent are used to protect certain metals, e.g. aluminium, in that they tend to reduce the problem of corrosion and/or oxidation, i.e. dark or black discolouration of the aluminium surface.

Hence the choice of a detergent for a specific cleaning purpose and/or particular item of yoghurt processing equipment is directly related to its functional properties, and some suggested formulations are shown in Table 4.3.

2. Type of soiling matter

The soiling matter produced during the manufacture of yoghurt (Table 4.1) may be of two types: firstly, the "soil" which is easy to remove (for example milk and yoghurt), and secondly, a more difficult type of "soil" (for example, heated milk and/or fruit). It is obvious that the choice of certain compounds to be incorporated into a detergent must take heed of the nature of these differing residues.

TABLE 4.3. *Some examples of suggested detergent formulations (composition %)*

Cleaning duty	Sodium bicarbonate	Sodium carbonate	Sodium chloride	Sodium hydroxide	Sodium gluconate	Sodium metasilicate	Sodium sulphate	Sodium tripolyphosphate	Tetra sodium pyrosphate	Tri sodium phosphate	Metasilicate (crystals)	Dodecylbenzene sodium sulphonate (LAS) 50% acidic	Phosphoric acid	Surfactant	Water
Bottle soak		14				6			8	4					
Bottle washer				95											
Dairy equipment cleaner (manual)						10						10		4*	
Milk can washing (machine)		20				12	26	40						2	
Milk can washing						10	51	25				10		4	
Pipeline cleaner		30				10	32	25						3	
Heavy duty CIP				95	5										
Dairy cleaner		7.2				8		15.4		45.5				5.5	
Vat cleaner	6	6	18.4					20		30	38				
Acid descaler													30	0.3	68.7
Acid cleaner												2	26		72
Acid cleaner (milkstone remover)													50	10	40

* Non-ionic.

Data compiled from Neiditch (1972), Tamplin (1980), IDF (1979).

3. Water hardness and quality

Water is used during all the cleaning cycles in a processing plant, and it is essential that two factors are considered: firstly, it is essential that good quality potable water is used (Table 4.4 illustrates some suggested standards for chemical specification and bacteriological quality), and secondly, the degree of hardness. This latter aspect is important, since detergents are formulated in relation to the degree of water hardness, and the presence of excess inorganic salts, mainly calcium and magnesium, can reduce their effectiveness. In addition, these salts can leave deposits on the surfaces of equipment which are difficult to remove.

TABLE 4.4. *Some suggested chemical and bacteriological standards for water used in food processing plants*

Chemical specifications		Bacteriological standards
Total hardness (as $CaCo_3$)	$\leqslant 50$ ppm	(1) Throughout any year 95 % of samples should not contain any coliform organisms or *Escherchia coli* in 100 ml.
Chloride (as NaCl)	$\leqslant 50$ ppm	(2) No sample should contain more than 10 coliform organisms per 100 ml.
Chloride (elementary)	$\leqslant 1$ ppm	(3) No sample should contain more than 2 *E. coli* per 100 ml.
pH	6.5–7.5	(4) No sample should contain 1 or 2 *E. coli* per 100 ml in conjunction with a total coliform of 3 or more per 100 ml.
Iron (as Fe)	1 ppm	(5) Coliform organisms should not be detectable in 100 ml of any two consecutive samples.
Manganese (as Mn)	0.5 ppm	
Suspended solids	Substantially free	

After Anon. (1969), IDF (1979).

Reprinted with permission of: International Dairy Federation, Brussels, Belgium; HMSO Publication, London U.K.

Water hardness may be of two types:

(a) Temporary or carbonate hardness. This is due to the carbonates and bicarbonates of calcium and magnesium, and these salts are easily precipitated or removed by heating; a typical example is scale formation on the inside of a kettle. In a yoghurt plant the same situation may arise in the evaporator and heat exchangers, since these sections are normally sterilised by circulating hot water, e.g. 85°C for 30–45 minutes. Deposits of calcium and magnesium salts on the surfaces of such equipment not only reduce the overall heat transfer efficiency of the plant, but can also provide a nucleus for other "soil" depositions to take place.

(b) Permanent or non-carbonate hardness. This type of water hardness is due to formation of other types of calcium and magnesium salts, e.g. sulphates and chlorides. Their conversion into insoluble deposits is due to the presence of certain alkalis, and for this reason specific constituents are incorporated into a detergent to minimise the precipitation.

The degree of water hardness is a measure of the mass of dissolved calcium and magnesium salts in the water, and according to Anon. (1967) and IDF (1979), the United States Geological survey classified water supplies as soft, moderately hard, hard and very hard if the total hardness (expressed as calcium carbonate) was 0–60, 60–120, 120–180 and over 180 respectively. However, water hardness is sometimes expressed in different terms/units/degrees in different countries, and Table 4.5 gives a comparison of the units used in Germany, the United Kingdom, France and the United States.

TABLE 4.5. *Units for hardness of water and equivalents in degrees of hardness*

Units	Earth alkali ions m val/l	Equipment in degrees of hardness			
		German°	English°	French°	US°
1 m val/litre of alkali earth ions	1.000	2.800	3.51	5.00	50.00
German 1° = 10 mg CaO/l or 7.19 mg MgO/l	0.375	1.000	1.25	1.79	17.85
English 1° = 10 mg $CaCO_3$/0.7 l	0.268	0.800	1.00	1.43	14.30
French 1° = 10 mg $CaCO_3$/l	0.200	0.560	0.70	1.00	10.00
US 1° = 1 mg $CaCO_3$/kg	0.020	0.056	0.07	0.10	1.00

The expression "val/litre (gram equivalent/litre)" is an alternative for "equivalent weight/litre", so that "m val/litre" $\cong$ m EW litre e.g. if the EW/litre of $CaCO_3$ = 50 g/litre, an m val/litre = 0.05 g/litre.

After IDF (1979c).
Reprinted with permission of International Dairy Federation, Brussels, Belgium.

4. Miscellaneous factors

The formulation of a dairy detergent is also influenced by such factors as:

(a) method of cleaning adopted;
(b) the materials used for the construction of the equipment, plant and other utensils; this factor is discussed elsewhere.

C. Cleaning Methods

The cleaning of any part of a yoghurt processing plant may involve one of the following methods:

(a) manual cleaning;
(b) cleaning-in-place (CIP);
(c) miscellaneous cleaning methods, but the basic steps involved in any of the above methods are somewhat similar. In principle they consist of the following operations.

(a) Preliminary rinse. The processing plant, including starter culture equipment, filling machines, and churns are rinsed with water to remove the bulk of the milk residues, yoghurt and/or fruit from the equipment. For conservation purposes, the final rinse (item "g"—see below) is recovered, especially in large plants, and used as preliminary rinse.

(b) Detergent wash. Alkali compounds are usually used (refer to Tables 4.2 and 4.3 for specific applications), and during this stage the aim is to remove any adhering soil.

193

(c) Intermediate rinse. To remove any detergent residues from the equipment prior to the following operation.

(d) Acid wash. This cleaning operation is optional, and it may be performed only once a week to clean the heat processing equipment. It is important to point out that acids are harmful to the skin, and hence an acid wash is normally used in CIP.

Inorganic (nitric and phosphoric) and/or organic (acetic, gluconic, oxyacetic) acids may be used, since they have the ability to dissolve milkstone and remove hard water scale, and although phosphoric is only a medium-strong acid, both mineral acids are corrosive against certain metals, e.g. tinned. However, the organic acids do not pose the same problem, even at high concentrations. Nitric acid also has good sanitising properties (Zall, 1981).

(e) Intermediate rinse. To remove any acid residues from the equipment prior to the sterilisation/sanitation treatment.

(f) Sterilisation/sanitation treatment. The plant and processing utensils have to be sterilised before commencing production, and this aim is achieved using one of the following methods:

—nitric acid;
—chemical compounds (QAC, chlorine, chloramine, etc.);
—heat (live steam is limited in its application, but hot water circulation at 85–90°C for 15–30 minutes is a valuable procedure; the temperature must be maintained on the return side of the plant and at the product outlet points);
—miscellaneous (refer to section on sterilisation).

(g) Final rinse. Good quality potable water is used as a final rinse to remove the sterilant residues from the processing plant. If hot water circulation is used at step (f), this stage is obviously omitted, but the plant must be properly drained before production commences.

1. Manual cleaning

Some parts of a processing plant, e.g. utensils and filling machines, can only be cleaned by hand, while others, such as homogenisers and separators, if not designed to be cleaned-in-place, have to be dismantled and cleaned-out-of-place (COP) as indicated by Custer (1982).

The sequence of hand cleaning is as follows:

—disconnect and dismantle the equipment;
—prerinse with potable tepid water at around 20–30°C;
—prepare the mild/hand detergent solution at the appropriate concentration in water at 40–50°C;
—brush/wash the various parts;
—intermediate rinse with tap water;
—sterilise using chemical agent;
—final rinse with water.

The factors which may influence the results of hand cleaning are:

(i) the human element which may manifest itself in the form of low detergent concentrations, or inefficient scrubbing action;
(ii) the upper temperature limit of the detergent solution may not be high enough;
(iii) since chemical sterilisation is dependent on concentration *and* contact time, operators may overlook one or other of these facets.

However, proper management, supervision and personnel training can all help to achieve the desired aims, and discussions with the detergent manufacturer can also ensure that correct cleaning procedures are introduced.

Manual cleaning can also be improved by providing a COP tank (Fig. 4.1), so that the cleaning operations are:

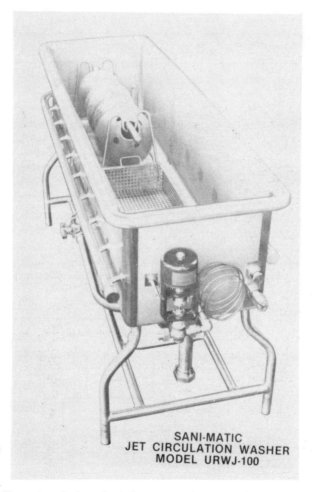

Fig. 4.1.   Illustration of a jet recirculation unit suitable for cleaning-out-of-place (COP)

Reproduced by courtesy of The Schlueter Co., Wisconsin, U.S.A.

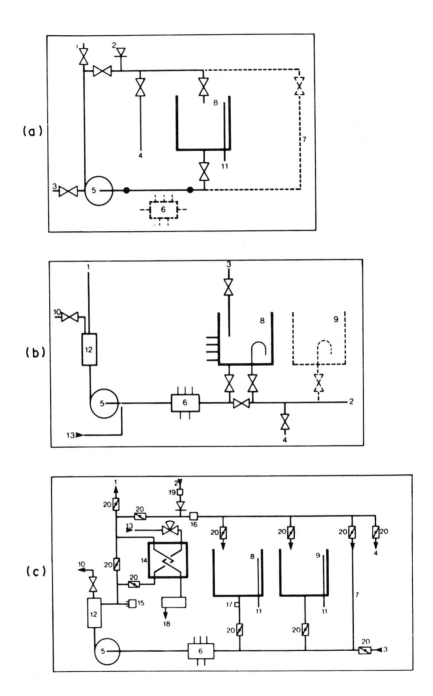

—place the dismantled and pre-rinsed parts in the tank;

—fill the tank with hot water;

—add the correct amount of detergent, and circulate the hot detergent solution for up to 30 minutes;

—drain detergent to waste or collect for other cleaning purposes;

—rinse parts with continuous circulation of mains water;

—drain and sterilise by submerging all parts in hot water or chemical sterilant.

The COP method could also be used for cleaning pipe lines in a small dairy, or in those parts of a factory where it may be difficult to provide a proper CIP system.

2. Cleaning-in-place (CIP)

This system of cleaning is engineered to clean processing equipment without dismantling and reassembling the different units, and in addition to minimising manual operations the CIP system has proved beneficial in respect of:

—improved hygiene, possibly through a combination of the chemical action of the detergent and the physical action of the circulating solution(s);

—better plant utilisation;

—increased savings (of detergent, steam and sterilising agents);

—greater safety.

In order to make use of a CIP system, it is essential to have a closed circuit through which the cleaning solution(s) can be circulated, and a typical basic unit is illustrated in Fig. 4.2(a). The design of any CIP system is tailor-made for a specific cleaning objective, but the principal methods of CIP cleaning are classified into three basic systems: the single-use system, the re-use system, and a combination of the two systems known as the multi-use system.

Fig. 4.2.   Schematic illustrations of CIP systems

APV Paraclean CIP units

(a) Basic model

(b) 1. Single-use system
    2. Single-use system with limited recovery.

(c) Multi-use system

1. CIP feed; 2. CIP return; 3. Water inlet; 4. Drain; 5. Puma pump; 6 Injection sleeve; 7. Recirculating loop; 8. Detergent tank; 9. Water recovery; 10. Sample cock; 11. Overflow; 12. Filter; 13. Steam in; 14. Paraflow heat exchanger; 15. Temperature probe; 16. Soluvisor; 17. Conductivity probe; 18. Condensate; 19. No-flow probe; 20. Butterfly valve.

After Anon. (1979a)

Reproduced by courtesy of APV Co. Ltd., West Sussex, U.K.

(a) Single-use CIP system. The unit is basically small, and it is normally situated as close as possible to the equipment being cleaned. In a single-use cleaning system the detergent is only used once, and the washing solution is run to waste; this system is ideal for small plants.

The disposal of the detergent solution could be a disadvantage, especially if the strength and the functional properties of the solution are still available; however, after cleaning heavily soiled equipment in a large plant it is then the normal practice to discard the detergent solution after use because it has lost its strength. Such a system could be employed in a yoghurt plant, for example, for the cleaning of the bulk starter vats and/or multi-purpose yoghurt tanks.

Figure 4.2(b) illustrates the basic components and the overall principle of the single-use system. However, these units can be supplied for automatic or manual operation, and can be further modified, i.e. with the addition of a recovery tank (e.g. dotted tank in Fig. 4.2b), so that the wash solution and water rinse are recovered for the next preliminary water rinse; it is then known as the single-use system with limited recovery option.

(b) Re-use system. In this system the detergent and/or acid solutions are recovered and re-used as many times as possible, especially in parts of the yoghurt plant where the equipment is not heavily soiled, for example in the milk reception area, the fortification/standardisation tanks, and/or the yoghurt fermentation tanks. Thus, the preliminary rinse of such equipment removes a high percentage of the "soil", and therefore the detergent solution circulated during the wash cycle is not heavily polluted, and can be re-used many times.

The re-use CIP system can be described as having these essential components, i.e. the detergent (Lye) tank(s), acid tank, water tank, water recovery tank and heating system, all interconnected with a system of pipework fitted with CIP feeds and return pumps. The concentration of the acid and lye solutions is regulated via feeds from tanks containing these corresponding compounds in a concentrated form, and the unit is also fitted with neutralisation tanks in which the lye and/or acid solutions are neutralised prior to their disposal into the effluent system. Furthermore, Tamplin (1980) pointed out that water consumption of a re-use system could be optimised by providing a recirculation facility for the hot water and the use of a return water tank. The on-site application of this system may be modified so that a low concentration of lye solution (0.5–1.0 % caustic) is used for cleaning cold milk handling equipment, yoghurt fermentation tanks and the interconnected pipelines, while another lye tank contains up to 2 % caustic for circulation during the cleaning of the milk processing plant.

Tamplin (1980) also pointed out that in a dairy operating 15–20 individual cleaning circuits per day this CIP system becomes more efficient if another CIP feed pump is incorporated, so that two circuits can be cleaned simultaneously. However, any extension of the re-use CIP system is limited, since the tank capacity is defined in advance by the circuit volume, temperature requirements and desired cleaning programmes; the latter aspect is, in most processing plants, fully automated, and the cleaning circuits are operated from a remote control panel.

(c) Multi-use system. This system of CIP cleaning attempts to combine all the most desirable features of the single and re-use systems. The system is illustrated in Fig. 4.2(c), and is described as having the following features:

—automatically controlled programmes for maximum flexibility;
—not all cleaning liquids and/or solutions need be included in every cleaning programme, i.e. modular adaptability;
—economic features are low running cost, low water consumption and minimum effluent discharge.

It can be observed that any of the above three CIP systems could be used for the cleaning of the yoghurt processing equipment (see Figs. 4.3 and 4.4), but the final selection of any one CIP system is governed primarily by factors such as:

—capital available for investment,
—desired degree of automation,
—estimated volume of yoghurt to be produced, etc., and hence the final design may well be something of a compromise.

3. Miscellaneous cleaning methods

Alternative cleaning methods can be applied to suit special purposes, and some examples of these have been reported by Haverland (1981).

(a) Soaking. Processing equipment and/or fittings are immersed in a cleaning solution at high temperature, and after a soaking period of 15–20 minutes the equipment is cleaned manually or mechanically. Unfortunately, no information was given regarding the composition of the soaking agent, but it is possible that effective cleaning relies heavily on a "digestion" of the "soil" followed by a scrubbing action.

(b) Ultrasonic treatment. This method of cleaning is a recent development of the soaking method discussed above. The equipment, utensils and fittings are immersed in a cleaning solution, and any "soil" is lifted from the surfaces by the scrubbing action of microscopic bubbles generated by the high-frequency vibrations.

(c) Spray method. This method of cleaning is widely used in the industry, and involves spraying hot water or steam onto equipment surfaces *in situ*. The cleaning solution is sprayed from special units (portable or fixed), and its function is to remove as much heavily "soiled" matter from processing equipment surfaces as possible, before they are cleaned using one of the conventional methods.

D. Factors Influencing the Efficiency of Cleaning

The result of cleaning any type of processing equipment is dependent on a multiplicity of factors, such as the following.

1. Type of soil

Residues from milk that has been heat-treated are more difficult to remove than those left behind by cold milk, and similarly residues from heat-treated fruits can adhere tenaciously to metal surfaces.

199

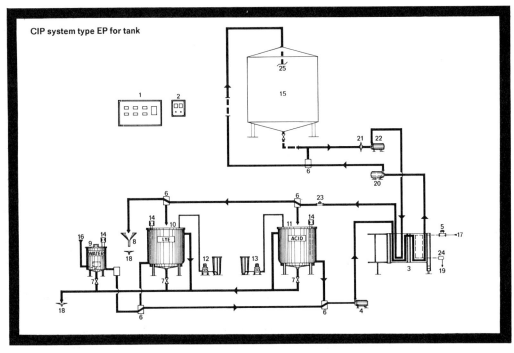

CIP system type EP for tank

1. Master panel
2. Remote control panel
3. Plate heat exchanger
4. Pressure pump
5. Steam regulating valve
6. Pneumatically operated valve
7. Straight-through plug cock
8. Discharge funnel
9. Water tank
10. Lye tank
11. Acid tank
12. Proportioning pump for concentrated lye
13. Proportioning pump for concentrated acid
14. Level electrode
15. Equipment to be cleaned
16. Water inlet
17. Steam inlet
18. Drain
19. Condensate
20. Pressure booster pump
21. Filter
22. Suction pump
23. Electrode
24. Steam trap
25. Spray turbine

Fig. 4.3. Illustration of a CIP system for tanks and pipelines

Stage	Programme	Time (min)	Temperature (°C)
1. Pre-rinse with water. Outgoing water to drain		3	ambient
2. Lye wash—1 % caustic soda solution with wetting agent and phosphates additives. Return to tank after use.		6	65
3. Hot water sterilisation, water displaces lye and goes to drain after regenerative cooling.		6	90–95
4. Gradual cooling with water by regenerative heat exchanger. Time according to desired temperature.		5	ambient

After Anon. (1979b)
Reproduced by courtesy of Alfa-Laval Co. Ltd., Middlesex, U.K.

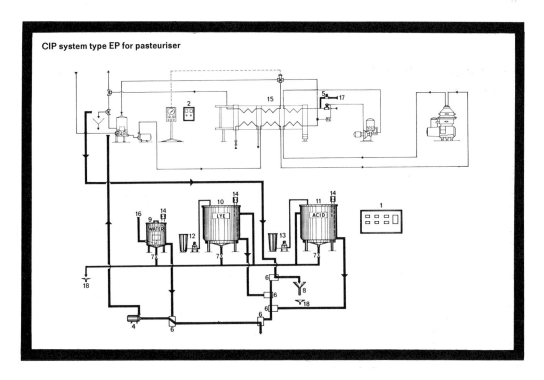

CIP system type EP for pasteuriser

1. Master panel	7. Straight-through plug cock	13. Proportioning pump for	19. Condensate
2. Remote control panel	8. Discharge funnel	concentrated acid	20. Pressure booster pump
3. Plate heat exchanger	9. Water tank	14. Level electrode	21. Filter
4. Pressure pump	10. Lye tank	15. Equipment to be cleaned	22. Suction pump
5. Steam regulating valve	11. Acid tank	16. Water inlet	23. Electrode
6. Pneumatically operated	12. Proportioning pump for	17. Steam inlet	24. Steam trap
valve	concentrated lye	18. Drain	25. Spray turbine

Fig. 4.4. Illustration of a CIP system for pasteuriser

Stage	Programme	Time (min)	Temperature (°C)
1. Pre-rinse with water		4	ambient
2. Lye-wash—1% caustic soda solution with wetting agent and phosphate additives. Returned to tank after use.		25	65
3. Intermediate rinse—water displaces detergent and goes to drain after regenerative cooling.		6	65
4. Acid wash—0.8% nitric acid solution. Returned to tank after use.		15	65
5. Hot water sterilisation—water displaces acid and goes to drain after regenerative cooling.		10	90–95
6. Cooling with cold water. The regenerative section of the heat exchanger can be bypassed for faster cooling. Outgoing water to drain.		5	ambient

After Anon (1979b).

Reproduced by courtesy of Alfa-Laval Co. Ltd., Middlesex, U.K.

2. Method of cleaning adopted

Certain factors can be controlled much more effectively under the CIP system, e.g. concentration of detergent, temperature, etc., and hence the CIP system is more reliable and efficient—on condition that the system is well maintained.

3. Contact time

Effective cleaning is time dependent, i.e. the longer the contact time between the detergent and the "soil" matter, the cleaner the equipment will be after the cleaning cycle. However, the type of "soil" must not be overlooked. For example, according to Anon. (1979b) 6 minutes is long enough for a solution of 1 % caustic soda at 65°C to clean tanks and pipelines, i.e. the "soil" is milk, but the time has to be increased to 25 minutes when cleaning an ordinary milk pasteuriser, i.e. the "soil" of heated milk (see Figs. 4.3 and 4.4).

Thus, contact time is important, since the functional properties of a detergent, e.g. wetting, penetration, dissolving, suspending, etc., have a longer time to act.

4. Concentration of the detergent solution

The concentration of the detergent solution used for manual cleaning is limited, since at high concentrations it may cause skin irritation, but in a CIP system effective cleaning is improved with high detergent concentrations, although the law of diminishing returns comes into effect above a certain level. This "ceiling" concentration, as applied to cleaning yoghurt processing equipment, would be in the region of 2–3 % for, as been reported elsewhere, a caustic soda solution <1 % is sufficient for cleaning storage tanks, pipelines and yoghurt fermentation tanks; 1–<2 % is recommended for cleaning multi-purpose tanks and plate heat exchangers, and 2–3 % for cleaning UHT plants.

It is important to monitor the strength of the detergent solution, especially in a re-use or multi-use system, but high detergent concentrations, i.e. above 2–3 %, are not economic in a yoghurt processing plant; up to 5 % may be necessary to clean a conventional evaporator if this approach is used to raise the total solids in the mix.

Acid solutions are normally used in the region of <1 %, since at higher concentrations corrosion of metal surfaces may occur.

5. Temperature

In general, the higher the temperature of the detergent solution, the more effective its cleaning action, so that while manual cleaning has to be carried out at around 45–50°C, the major sections of a yoghurt plant will be cleaned at 85–90°C using CIP; higher temperatures, e.g. 100–105°C, are used during the alkaline wash of a UHT plant. Acid treatments are usually carried out at around 60–70°C.

6. Flow rate or velocity

The flow characteristics of a liquid in a pipe can be either *laminar* or *turbulent*, and these configurations are influenced by such factors as: pipe diameter, fluid momentum and fluid viscosity. A numerical presentation of the degree of turbulence in the fluid is referred to as its Reynolds number (e.g. *Re* 2000 = laminar, Re 2000–4000 = transitional and *Re* >4000 = turbulent), i.e. the higher the number, the more disturbed the flow. Thus, the physical scrubbing action in a CIP system is greatly influenced by the flow rate of the fluid, and effectiveness of the cleaning operation is greatly improved by increasing the velocity of the solution. Although the presence of any obstruction affects the flow rate of liquid through a plant, the mean velocity can still be calculated, and Timperly and Lawson (1980) have substantiated that the residual bacteria on a surface are reduced to a minimum if the mean flow rate is maintained at 1.5 metres/second, or as Kesseler (1981) suggested $Re > 10^4$.

Silos and large storage tanks are cleaned using a CIP system, and such equipment can be fitted with either sprayballs (see Fig. 4.5) or rotating jets which help in distributing the CIP fluids. Tamplin (1980) compared these two basic types, and flow rates tend to be higher using sprayballs rather than rotating jets; this aspect could be important for achieving good results in cleaning.

Fig. 4.5.   Some different types of spray balls

Reproduced by courtesy of APV Co. Ltd., West Sussex, UK.

7. Acid wash

Effective cleaning can also be dependent on the constituents of the detergent (see Table 4.2), and the acid wash is a supplementary cleaning process for the removal of milk stone and other types of "soils". Whether or not the latter wash is conducted regularly on a daily basis or once a week is subject to plant quality control, and the final decision is based on microbiological tests.

8. Plant design

Any type of food processing plant, including yoghurt plant, is constructed from a variety of vessels, pipelines, elbows, pipecouplings, valves and pumps, and these components cannot always be relied upon as a safeguard against bacterial infection, and hence the efficiency of a cleaning programme may be dependent on plant design. Numerous factors are involved, and according to the recent reviews of Leliveld (1976), Milledge (1981), Timperley (1981) and Timperley and Lawson (loc. cit.), the relevant aspects could be summarised as follows:

—corrosiveness of the stainless steel;
—surface finish and surface grain, e.g. 80 μm average diameter grit had the effect of harbouring bacteria;
—pipe couplings—the Ring Joint Type (RJT) is unsuitable for CIP and the International Sanitary Standard (ISS) type can result in a crevices that are difficult to clean;
—good orbital welding is normally used for CIP circuits, but does not facilitate proper inspection;
—dead pockets must be avoided, but if "T" pieces cannot be ruled out, the length must be kept short;
—pumps are difficult to clean, especially reciprocating and positive displacement types;
—valves are of three types—plug cock, plug and stem, and membrane; the latter two can be cleaned easily and sterilised by CIP, but not the plug cock type;
—plant layout.

Microbial attachment to milk contact surfaces has also been studied by Zoltay, Zottola and McKay (1981) using scanning electron microscopy, and they confirmed that adhesion is influenced by such factors as metal roughness, surface treatments, welded seams, and the nature of any rubber/plastic joints, and each can affect the efficiency of cleaning and the sanitation of the processing plant.

9. Chemical composition of a detergent

It is often difficult to obtain the exact chemical composition of a given detergent, but some general data is given in Tables 4.2 and 4.3; however, according to Tamplin (1982), some typical commercial detergents have the following chemical composition.

(a) Detergent for cleaning silos and milk storage tanks

EDTA	25.0	
Sequestering agents	2.5	
Emulsifiers	1.0	% (W/W)
Anti-foam agent	0.5	
Soaps	5.0	
Water	66.0%	

The solution is used at a level of $0.2-0.5\%$ (v/v) along with a level of $1-2.5\%$ (w/v) caustic soda at $60-90°$C. Alternatively, if a blended product is used the composition is as follows:

Caustic soda	44	
Sequestering agents	1	% (W/W)
Water	55	

and depending on the level of soiling, the concentration used would be $0.7-4\%$ (v/v) circulated at $65-90°$C.

(b) Detergent for cleaning plate heat exchangers

(i) *Powder detergent*
  $30-50\%$ NaOH.
  $8-15\%$ EDTA.
  $15-25\%$ trisodium phosphate.
  Plus bulking agent (soda ash) and alkalinity booster (silicates).
  The wetting agents are generally produced *in situ* by saponification, but if required, a low foaming, non-ionic agent can be added; the recommended strength is $1-2\%$ (w/w).

(ii) *Liquid detergent*
  $40-60\%$ NaOH ($100°$ Tw. solution).
  $20-30\%$ liquid EDTA (30% concentration).
  $5-15\%$ liquid silicates.
  Plus other minor ingredients.
  It is used at a strength of $1.5-3\%$ (v/v), and due to the limited solubility of EDTA in NaOH (e.g. above 50% NaOH), it is recommended that sodium gluconate be added as an organic sequesterant.
  Formulations (i) and (ii) are used in single-stage cleaning cycles, but for two-stage cleaning (detergent/acid) the following might be more suitable.

(iii) *Powder detergent*
  $60-80\%$ NaOH.
  $2-10\%$ EDTA.
  $2-10\%$ phosphates.
  Filler (soda ash) or liquid alkali
  $85-95\%$ NaOH ($100°$ Tw. solution).
  $5-15\%$ sodium gluconate.
  The acid wash could be 1% phosphoric acid.

(c) Combined detergent/sanitiser. This type of product might include:
Sodium tripolyphosphates or calgon.
Sodium isocyanurate.
Chlorinated trisodium phosphate.
Silicate or soda ash for bulking (70 %).
Chlorate tracer and a typical formulation for use at 0.5 % would be:
15 % phosphates.
5 % silicates.
25–30 % soda ash to give 250 ppm available chlorine; maximum operating temperature is 50°C.

(d) High caustic EDTA blend. This formulation is similar to the detergent in section (*a*), but the chosen causticity and operating temperature is dependant upon water hardness (e.g. for a hard water condition, the phosphate concentration would be increased to 10–15 %). Such a detergent would be used at a rate of 0.5–1 %, and the microbiological "kill" is achieved by the combined action of causticity and temperature.

(e) Non-caustic alkaline detergent followed by a sanitiser
50–70 % soda ash.
30 % silicate.
5–12 % phosphate (variable).
5–10 % EDTA (variable).
Plus a low foam wetter.
This non-caustic detergent treatment is normally followed by sanitisation with sodium hypochlorite at ambient temperature and a concentration of about 100–150 ppm available chlorine.

(f) Acid detergent
20–50 % phosphoric acid (81 %).
3–8 % non-ionic wetter.
Formulations (*c*), (*d*), (*e*) and (*f*) could be used for cleaning yoghurt incubation tanks and/or silos or milk storage tanks, and the recommended detergent is the "high caustic with EDTA" blend.

E. Specific Cleaning and Sterilisation Operations of Yoghurt Processing Equipment and Utensils

A comprehensive account of the cleaning and sterilisation of dairy plant and equipment has been published by BSI (1970) (amendment, 1974) and BSI (1977), and the relevant data, which are applicable to a yoghurt Processing line, are illustrated in Table 4.6. Certain processing equipment, for example different heat exchangers, are used for the heat treatment of milk, and the procedures of cleaning and sterilising such plants, as compared with ordinary HSTS and UHT units, are shown in Table 4.7. However, membrane filtration plants, i.e. UF and RO, necessitate a different approach to cleaning and Table 4.8 illustrates the cleaning and sanitation procedures for those plants that are used in the dairy industry.

TABLE 4.6. *Recommended methods for cleaning and sterilisation of yoghurt processing equipment*

Equipment/Utensils	Cleaning method	Sterilisation method
1. Milk cans/churns	*Manual wash* (a) Combined detergent/steriliser Rinse can with tepid water. Add 5 litres detergent/steriliser solution at 40–50°C. Scrub thoroughly inside/outside surfaces of the can including the neck and lid. Place the can on its side and role for ½ minute. Allow at least 2 minutes contact time. Empty, rinse with clean water and invert to drain on a rack. Wash detachable can lids separately in a trough. (b) Detergent only Use same steps mentioned above	(a) Chemical sterilisation Follow recommendations of detergent's manufacturer. (b) Steam (i) Steam chest = 96°C for 30 minutes. (ii) Steam jet – not less than 2 minutes.
	Machine wash (rotary or tunnel) Drainage stage for liquid milk residues. Pre-rinse with water (cold or at 40–50°C). Drainage stage(s). External wash with water at 40–50°C. Drainage stage. Jetting with solution of detergent at 70–80°C. Drainage stage(s). Rinse with water at 85°C (minimum). Live steam injection. Hot air drying at 95–115°C.	No sterilisation required.
2. Weigh bowls and receiving tanks	Hose the weigh bowls and receiving tanks with cold water, and then with water at 50–60°C. Close outlet and add a suitable volume of solution of general purpose detergent. Brush the internal and external surfaces, covers and strainers with a suitable brush and, as the solution is drained from the tank, scrub the outlet valves and fittings. Hose the tank and fittings with clean water, reassemble, the equipment is then ready for sterilisation.	(a) Combined detergent/steriliser The equipment is ready to be used immediately after the final rinsing stage, or if this is not possible re-sterilise immediately before use. (b) Chemical sterilisation —Prepare a solution of sterilising agent. —Partially fill the weigh bowl and receiving tanks with the solution of sterilising agent. —Brush in the same manner as indicated during the "Cleaning Method" by using a brush reserved for this purpose. —Rinse residues of the sterilising agent from equipment by hosing with cold water, and use equipment immediately; if this is not possible re-sterilise immediately prior to use.

TABLE 4.6 (*Contd.*)

Equipment/Utensils	Cleaning method	Sterilisation method
3. Pumps and pipelines	CIP system (refer to Table 4.7)	*For CIP use* (a) Hot water circulation for a period of not less than 15 minutes measured from the time that all the parts of the circuit reach a temperature not less than 85°C. (b) Chemical sterilising agent – circulate the solution, for example sodium hypochlorite, i.e. 50–100 mg/l of available chlorine at 20–40°C for contact period of 10–20 minutes; discharge and rinse with clean water and use immediately, if this is not suitable, re-sterilise prior to use. *For Manual use*: – (a) Form pipe-work into a closed circulation circuit, and sterilise by one of the methods mentioned above (hot water or chemical sterilising agent). (b) Sterilise dismantled pipelines and fittings using steam for a period of 15 minutes. (c) Soak dismantled parts in solution of sterilising agent, rinse with cold water, reassemble immediately taking precautions to avoid recontamination; if equipment is not used immediately, re-sterilise immediately before use.
	Manual wash Rinse with cold water. Dismantle and wash parts in a trough filled with detergent solution. Brush all surfaces coming in contact with milk, and for pipes use long handle brush; brush pipe from both ends.	
4. Milk/Yoghurt processing plants	*HTST and UHT plants* (Refer to Table 4.7)	Refer to Table 4.7
	Batch type holding plants or (Milk is heated up to 95°C and held) *Yoghurt multi-purpose tank* —Remove as much product as possible from the vessel. —Fill with a solution of sodium hydroxide-based detergent which may contain sequestring agent. —Heat the solution to 75–85°C by passing steam through the jacket, start the stirring mechanism and maintain the temperature for 30 minutes. —Drain the cleaning solution from the vessel. —Rinse well with cold clean water. —Sterilise. Note:—should milkstone have accumulated in the vessel, treatment with a suitable acid (phosphoric acid of B.P. quality—100 ml in 5 litres of water at 40–50°C after the detergent wash has been rinsed) may become necessary.	Sterilise by using one of the following methods: – (a) *Steam* Connect a low pressure steam supply to the outlet pipe of the vessel by means of screw couplings as a safeguard against accidents; methods using trailing hoses are dangerous and should not be used. Steam for a period of not less than 10 minutes after the condensate temperature has reached a temperature, of 85°C (b) *Alkaline solution* By means of a CIP equipment, use a 1% caustic solution at a temperature of not less than 75°C for a minimum contact of 10 minutes. Rinse with cold clean water. (c) *Chemical sterilising agent* Use a solution of sterilising agent as mentioned above.

	Part of the processing plant (Refer to item "4" above)	(Refer to item "4" above)
5. Homogenisers	*Separate unit* Form all associated pipework including the homogeniser into a closed circuit. Reduce the pressure from the homogenising valve. Start up the homogeniser, and rinse out the circuit with water to remove loose milk residues. Allow the rinse water to go to waste. The pressure gauges, suction valves and inlet and outlet manifolds should be removed, cleaned rinsed manually, and reassembled for sterilisation. Add sufficient detergent of the type used on the main plant, or any specialised product for cleaning homogenisers, to approximately 90 litres of water. Introduce the detergent solution to the homogeniser and circulate for approximately 30 minutes at 70–80°C. Apply a pressure of about 5.61 kg/cm² (550 KN/m²). Leave all by-passes slightly open to allow passages of rinse water and detergent solution. Rinse with clean cold water to waste. Note: In pre-rinsing and final rinsing the time of circulation should be kept to a minimum owing to the poor lubrication properties of water on the piston rods and hoses. No special precautions other than those mentioned are necessary when alkaline detergents are used, as these provide adequate lubrication.	Release the pressure from the homogenising valves and introduce hot clean water. Continue circulation for a period of not less than 15 minutes after the return water has reached a temperature of 85°C. Note: – (a) Ensure that all drain valves, pressure gauge line, etc., are raised to temperatures of 85°C for not less a period of 15 minutes by bleeding the lines throughout the sterilising period. (b) The large mass of metal in the homogeniser blocks necessitates a long heating up period.
6. Filling machines	*Manual wash* At the end of the filling period rinse through with cold water, and wash away any product which has been rinsed on to the tracks. Dismantle removable parts. Rinse component thoroughly with cold water or at temperature 40–50°C. Clean all components manually with a solution of a suitable detergent at 40–50°C. Rinse all components thoroughly with cold water until free from detergents. Reassemble the machine, which is now ready for sterilisation.	(a) Combined detergent/steriliser (b) Chemical sterilisation agent, e.g. sodium hypochlorite 50–100 mg/l of available chlorine at ambient temperature for a contact period of not less than 10 minutes. (c) Hot water circulation for a period of not less than 15 minutes measured from the time the effluent water reaches a temperature of 85°C. (d) Steam (not widely practised). Items (c & d) may not be applicable to all machines, therefore, before using any of these methods consult the machine manufacturer.
	CIP wash If applicable, then consult the machine manufacturer for a recommended wash cycle.	*Ibid*, follow the recommendations of the machine manufacturer.

TABLE 4.6 (*Contd.*)

Equipment/Utensils	Cleaning method	Sterilisation method

7. Starter culture tanks	*Manual wash*
	(a) Small size utensils of starter culture equipment, wash by hand as described in item (1).
	(b) Vessels not equipped for CIP
	  —Dismantle all removable parts and wash separately.
	  —Hose out the residual starter with cold water as soon as the vessel is empty.
	  —Scrub the surfaces with a solution of mild alkaline detergent or detergent/steriliser at 40–50°C.
	  —Rinse with cold clean water and reassemble, the vessel is then ready for sterilisation.
	
	CIP wash
	  —Start the cleaning operation as soon as the vessel is empty, i.e. before the starter dries on to the surfaces
	  —Carry out CIP using a suitable alkaline detergent or detergent/steriliser solution; pay particular attention to the outlet valve.
	  —Rinse with clean water in accordance with the starter vessel manufacturer's instructions.
	  —The vessel is then ready for sterilisation.
		Use one of the methods mentioned in item (4).
		
		Ibid

8. Vessels for bulking fruit	These may be used in large scale yoghurt production, and the cleaning cycle may comprise: –
	  —Rinse thoroughly with water at 40–45°C.
	  —Scrub with mild detergent.
	  —Rinse with cold clean water.
	  —The vessel is ready for sterilisation.
		Ibid

9. Miscellaneous	(a) Glass bottles and crates Follow the recommendations provided for washing/sterilisation of returnable glass milk bottles. (b) Membrane (UF & RO) machines Refer to Table 4.8 for further detail. (c) Single effect evaporator Follow the instructions of the equipment manufacturer, and if such unit is used as illustrated in Figs. 3.10 and 3.11 (Chapter Three) the evaporator is cleaned with the rest of the processing equipment (see Table 4.7).	 See Table 4.8 See Table 4.7

Adapted from BSI (1970, 1974, 1977).

Reprinted with permission of British Standards Institution, London, U.K.

TABLE 4.7. *Cleaning and sterilisation method of milk and yoghurt processing plants**

| Type of processing plants | CIP Programme | |
	Detergent wash	Sterilisation
HTST**	Rinse with cold water for 15 minutes. Circulate detergent solution at 70–80°C for 20 minutes. Rinse with cold water. Note:—Change flow from "forward" to "diversion" during the detergent wash. —Plates may be opened, brushed and hosed with water. —An occasional acid wash is carried out after the alkali wash, since a straightforward acid wash may cause corrosive damage to stainless steel.	(a) Hot water circulation (Not less than 15 minutes from the time that all the sections of the plant reach a temperature of not less than 85°C – operate flow diversion valve frequently during the circulation period). (b) Chemical sterilising agent. (Refer to Table 4.10).
UHT**	Rinse with cold water for 15 minutes *Alkali wash* —Primary stage Circulate 3% solution of mixed alkali for 30 minutes at 100–105°C; change flow from "forward" to "diversion" at intervals; flush out alkali solution and rinse with water. —Secondary stage Circulate 2% solution of alkali containing a high proportion of a calcium sequestering agent, for 30 minutes at 100–105°C; flush alkali solution and rinse with water. —Alternative method Circulate higher strength of detergent solution containing high proportion of calcium sequestering agent. *Acid wash* Circulation of a 0.5% acid solution for 30 minutes at 75–80°C. Rinse with clean cold water. Plates may be opened, brushed down and hosed with cold water.	UHT plants are frequently sterilised automatically. Alternatively, circulate pressurised hot water at a temperature of not less than 140°C and not more than 150°C for a period of not less than 15 minutes and use the plant immediately. Note:—Ensure that all sections of the plant are within temperature range from 140–150°C; —A temperature greater than 150°C may cause rapid deterioration of rubber joints; —Chemical sterilisation agents are not suitable.
Yoghurt/VHTST	*First Example* (Time/Temperature relationship is 85°C for 6–10 minutes). Rinse with cold water for 20 minutes; open the holding tube (for example see Fig. 3.40) and scrub by hand, and finally rinse with water for 5 minutes. Detergent wash (2% caustic for 30 minutes at 85–90°C). Flush out the detergent and rinse with cold clean water for 20 minutes; open holding tubes for visual inspection. Once a week carry out acid wash (1% phosphoric acid) following the detergent wash at 85–90°C for 30 minutes; also once a week open the plates and check.	Hot water circulation for 30 minutes at 85–90°C.

TABLE 4.7 (*Contd.*)

Type of processing plants	CIP Programme	
	Detergent wash	Sterilisation
	Second Example (Time/Temperature relationship is 90°C for 2–5 minutes)	Hot water circulation for 20 minutes at 90–95°C.
	Preliminary cold water rinse for 3–5 minutes.	
	Detergent wash (1% concentration for 6 minutes at 65–75°C).	
	Final cold water rinse for 6 minutes.	
	Note:—Perhaps once a week use an acid rinse (1% concentration) for 6 minutes carried out after flushing out the detergent and rinsing with cold water; also carry out water rinse after the acid wash	
Yoghurt/LTUHT	(Time/temperature relationship is 115°C for 3 seconds)	Hot water circulation for 20 minutes at 85°C.
	Preliminary cold water rinse for 5 minutes.	
	Detergent solution (2% caustic) with circulation for 45 minutes at 85°C.	
	Intermediate water rinse for 5 minutes.	
	Acid solution ($1\frac{1}{2}$–2% phosphoric acid) circulation for 45 minutes at 70°C.	
	Final rinsing with cold water for 5 minutes.	

* These are plate heat exchanger plants; batch processing plant is discussed in Table 4.6.
** Data compiled from BSI (1970, 1974, 1977), Tamime (1982).
Reprinted with permission of British Standards Institution, London, U.K.

In general, the CIP system is used to clean the major sections of a yoghurt processing line, and CIP programmes can be either manually operated or fully automated. Automatic control has been achieved during the past few decades using computers and microprocessors, and as a result the process has become more efficient with better detergent recovery, a reduction in energy consumption and a reduction in the scope for human error. Many different types of computer are available on the market, but a review of these systems is unnecessary, since the layout, design and programme of a CIP system is basically "tailor made" to suit individual yoghurt plants. However, details of the different CIP control systems from the following suppliers have been reported by Anon. (1980a, b, c, d, e, f, g, 1981a, b, c):

—Wyandotte (Diversey Corporation, USA),
—Klenzade MP-1800 (Economics Laboratories Inc., USA),
—Z-746 (Industrial Control Systems, USA),
—Modicon 484 plus protable types P145 and P180 (Gould Inc., USA),
—ALSTEP plus CIPAL (Alfa-Laval A/B, Sweden),
—4K PROM, 2K EAROM and 2K RAM (Ladish Co. USA),
—CIP/Controller system (Darlington Dairy Supply Co. Inc., USA),
—PSC 763 (Tenor Co. Inc., USA),
—5Tl (A & B Contracting Inc., USA),
—ACCOS 2S (APV Co. Ltd., UK).

TABLE 4.8. *Recommended procedure for the cleaning and disinfection of UF and RO plants*

Equipment	Cleaning and disinfection programme
I. *UF plant* fitted with RG-membranes used for the processing of milk (Pasilac/Silkeborg Ltd.).	1. Rinse/flush the plant with water (5–15 minutes) until all the product has been removed; adjust pressure while recirculating water in modules e.g. inlet 3.1 kg/cm² (3 bar) and outlet 1.24 kg/cm² (1.2 bar).
	2. Detergent wash by recirculating a solution of: 0.5% P3-ultrasil 10 (Henkel), 0.25% sodium hydroxide and 0.5% EDTA-Na₄ at 70–75°C for 30 minutes.
	3. Rinse/flush the plant with water (5–15 minutes) until detergent has been removed.
	4. Acid clean by recirculating 0.3% nitric acid solution at 50–55°C for 20 minutes.
	5. Rinse/flush the plant with water (5–15 minutes) until the acid has been removed.
	6. Detergent cleaning in which a solution of 0.25% caustic soda and 0.25% EDTA-Na₄ at 70–75°C is circulated for up to 30 minutes.
	7. Rinse/flush the plant with water (5–15 minutes) until the detergent has been removed.
	8. Disinfection by circulating a solution of 1000 ppm hydrogen peroxide at 50–55°C for 15 minutes.
	9. Stop the plant.
	10. Rinse/flush the plant with water (5–15 minutes) before next production.
II. RO plant, tubular membrane system and membrane specification-ZF 99 (Paterson Candy International Ltd./PCI).	(a) Rinse the plant with water until product has been removed.
	(b) Recommended cleaning material is dependent upon the application, and the following, or suitable combinations of them, can be used:
	(i) ⎧ nitric or phosphoric acid;
	(ii) 0.1–0.5% (w/w) ⎨ sodium hydroxide;
	(iii) ⎩ alkaline detergent (e.g. Henkel, P3-ultrasil 10).
	DO NOT USE cationic surfactants
	(c) Sterilisation is achieved by recirculating one of the following:
	(i) water at 60–70°C
	(ii) 1500 ppm of hydrogen peroxide;
	(iii) 0.5% formaldehyde
	DO NOT USE sodium hypochlorite or any other material containing free chlorine at more than 0.5 ppm.
	(d) A solution of sodium metabisulphite (1000 ppm) can be used for storage of membranes.
	(e) Note, the plant is rinsed with water at every subsequent stage.

After Bloomer (1982), Tilley (1982).

Each of the above CIP control systems offers certain advantages, and the overall choice is governed by the level of capital expenditure and the degree of automation required. The programme of CIP system may include up to thirty different functions for cleaning a tank or any other processing unit, and the same programmes may also allow a prolonged cleaning operation to be introduced at certain times. Another feature which is common to these CIP control systems is the safeguard against power failure, and this precautionary factor is important, especially to accommodate a power failure taking place in the middle of a cleaning programme for otherwise the programmed function would be terminated.

Although the flexibility of any CIP controller system is assessed prior to passing the final decision as to which unit to install, some general points might be considered.

Firstly, the safety aspect to prevent the risk of the product becoming contaminated with the detergent and/or sterilant solutions. This safeguard can be achieved using one of the following systems:

(i) flow selector plate,
(ii) manual "key pieces" or "security flow pipes",
(iii) the use of special valves.

The former two types are suitable for small plant operations, and as a further precautionary measure interlock switches are often incorporated. The use of "key pieces" also offers a high degree of security, in that, for example, if installed at two places in a tank installation (bottom fed), the first will be positioned at the bottom when the product is being handled, while the second will be positioned at the top, i.e. above spray ball(s), during the operation of the CIP programme. Alternatively, different types of valve could be used, for example the three-way valve, a single valve which is arranged in such a way that in the closed position one part is open to the atmosphere and any leakage of the CIP solutions system will fall outside the vessel; thus contamination of the product is prevented. However, a double-valve system with electric interlocks has been developed (see Figs. 4.6 and 4.7) which ensures total isolation of the circuit being cleaned from the adjacent section where product could be flowing.

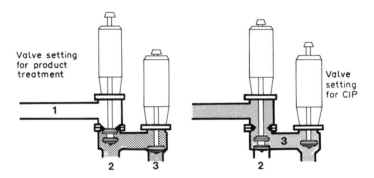

Fig. 4.6. Interlocked valve arrangement to prevent inter-leakage between product and detergent flow

(1) Product; (2) Drainage; (3) Detergent.

Reproduced by courtesy of Alfa-Laval Co. Ltd., Middlesex, U.K.

Secondly, a good drainage system so that the product and/or cleaning solutions can be quickly removed from the plant to prevent intermixing. Therefore, sound design of a plant is essential, and the piping layout must have the following features:

(i) self-drainage capability,
(ii) no parallel flow, i.e. the detergent flows in the opposite direction of the product,
(iii) no dead ends.

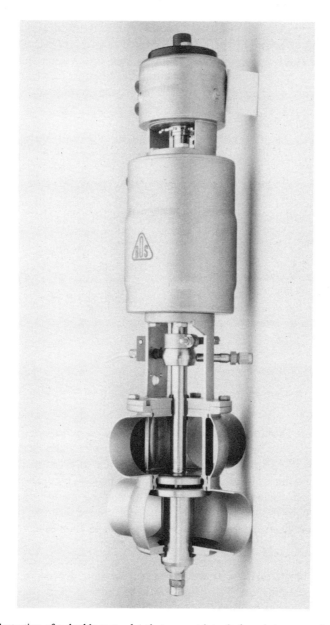

Fig. 4.7. An illustration of a double seat valve that prevent inter-leakage between product and detergent

The safety features of such a valve are:—firstly, any leakage runs automatically through a special vent or channel in the middle of the shaft and drains out; secondly, fluctuations in pressure maintain the valve either closed or open and hence leakage is prevented.

Reproduced by courtesy of Holstein & Kappert GmbH, Unna-Königsborn, West Germany.

215

Thirdly, improved cleaning efficiency using an air purging system. A blast of oil-free compressed air is forced into tanks and pipelines as a convenient method of evacuating residual product, e.g. milk or yoghurt, from the plant; the volume of air delivered and the duration of purge is calculated to empty the pipelines effectively. The result is improved product recovery, minimum soiling matter to be removed and less rinsing water required, and better utilisation of detergent in that effective concentrations can be maintained for a number of runs. Incidentally, although the air purging system is mainly operated before the cleaning cycle commences, and it is also used for evacuating residual rinsing water during and/or after cleaning, e.g. the preliminary rinse at the beginning of the cleaning cycle.

Fourthly, decentralisation of the CIP system, i.e. the use of a number of substations, is one way in which the efficiency of the cleaning system can be improved, in that only relevant sections of the plant need be cleaned.

Fifthly, in large plants the CIP system itself will need to be cleaned occasionally, and the usual approach is to install a separate CIP system for cleaning the main installation. The main problem arises from the precipitation of milk protein in the detergent tanks.

Sixthly, specific data regarding the CIP of yoghurt filling machines is not available, but Langeveld, Koning and Cuperus (1982) evaluated the efficiency of a CIP system for removing secondary contamination from a Hamba—2000 filling machine; they concluded that the CIP programme was satisfactory. This particular CIP programme included of prerinsing with water, circulation of an alkaline solution at 70°C for 20 minutes and finally rinsing with water containing 1 mg free chlorine/litre.

STERILISATION ASPECTS

A. Fundamentals of the Sterilisation Process

Milk and/or yoghurt "soiling" matter on the surfaces of processing equipment is usually contaminated with micro-organisms, and as indicated elsewhere the cleaning stage should (in theory) remove all "soil". Thus, any residual matter is an excellent medium in which micro-organisms can grow and multiply, and sterilisation of the process equipment becomes a necessity in order to destroy such organisms, for otherwise the keeping quality of yoghurt produced on subsequent days could be reduced. The effectiveness of the sterilisation process (using heat or chemical agents) is mainly dependent on the efficiency of the cleaning cycle. For example, any residual "soil" can become "baked" onto the contact surface to the extent that it becomes difficult to penetrate the soil in order to destroy the micro-organisms, especially the heat-resistant spores. Furthermore, the residual "soil" effects the subsequent cleaning process in that: firstly, the active concentration of the chemical sterilising agent will be reduced, and sterilisation becomes less effective, and secondly, it is possible that large numbers of micro-organisms may survive the heat and/or chemical sterilisation and multiply in the "soil"; in such cases, infrequently used equipment may become heavily contaminated.

Effective sterilisation of processing plant is therefore directly governed by observation of the following points:

(a) Maintain the correct cleaning cycle prior to the sterilisation stage.
(b) Follow the recommendations layed down for the sterilisation method adopted, e.g. strength of the chemical solution, correct contact time and temperature.

(c) Usually the processing equipment is sterilised directly before use, and hence after the cleaning stage the equipment must be properly drained or purged with air, for otherwise the moist condition, in the presence of any residual "soil", can encourage micro-organisms to multiply; if sterilised equipment is not used within a few hours, it is recommended that it should be resterilised before use.

(d) Any yoghurt plant has joints, valves, dead ends and rubber gaskets into which traces of "soil" and micro-organisms can penetrate, and hence frequent dismantling of these components is essential; furthermore, heat sterilisation is more effective than chemical sterilisation for reaching "blind" areas where micro-organisms could have penetrated.

(e) The hygienic condition of any yoghurt plant is governed by the rigour of the cleaning and/or sterilisation stages. For example, in a UHT plant the aim is to render the equipment sterile before use, but for other types of plant a "good sanitary" condition is acceptable by health authorities in many parts of the world.

In fact, Zall (*loc. cit.*) differentiated between sanitation and sterilisation as follows: both treatments are aimed towards the destruction of micro-organisms, and the former aspect is more easily achieved as compared with sterilisation, which is more a rigorous and difficult procedure.

(f) The use of chemical sterilising agent(s) and/or compound(s) is subject to approval by the legal authorities concerned, and in the United Kingdom a cumulative list is provided periodically by the Ministry of Agriculture, Fisheries and Food.

B. Methods of Sterilisation and/or Sanitisation

The method which can be employed to achieve either sterilisation or sanitisation include the following.

1. Heat

Heat is normally applied as dry heat or moist heat, and an example of the former is where a hot oven is used for the sterilisation of laboratory glassware at a temperature above 150°C for not less than 2 hours.

For practical reasons, dry heat is not used to sanitise yoghurt processing equipment, but by contrast moist heat is widely used, e.g.

   (i) autoclaving (steam under pressure),
   (ii) steaming or tyndalisation,
   (iii) hot water,
   (iv) steam (free flowing).

Methods (i) and (ii) are used for sterilising microbiological growth media and/or the medium for propagation of the starter cultures, e.g. mother or feeder stage. The principles of these two methods are discussed in detail by Meynell and Meynell (1970). In an autoclave, steam under pressure is used, and the recommended working condition is 121°C for 10–15 minutes (under a pressure of 0.7–1.0 kg/cm² (10–15 psi)). However, the steaming method, which was introduced by Tyndall in the 1870s, consists of heating liquids up to 100°C for a few minutes so that all the vegetative microbial cells are destroyed. The liquid is cooled to ambient or 30°C to induce the spores to germinate, and after a few hours the steaming/cooling cycle is repeated again. Further repetition of the heat treatment ensures destruction of all the viable spores in the liquid.

The steaming of milk is also practiced in laboratories for the propagation of feeder starter cultures in flasks up to 3 litres capacity, but in this case only one heating operation is required.

Processing plant can be sterilised or sanitised using hot water or steam, and the efficiency of the process is primarily dependent on the following factors:

Firstly, the time-temperature combination (i.e. the temperature reached and the time for which the temperature is maintained).

Secondly, humidity, and thirdly, pressure. The on-site applications of hot water circulation or steam (free flowing) for sanitising yoghurt equipment are illustrated in Table 4.9, and as can be observed hot water circulation is more widely used. The limited application for free flowing steam is due to:

—heat stresses that can cause pipelines to buckle or crack;

TABLE 4.9. *The effectiveness of sterilising/sanitising yoghurt equipment using different heating methods*

Type of heating	Working application	Comments
I. *Dry heat*		
Hot air in a dry oven	>150°C for at least 2 hours	Inactivates bacterial spores and it is normally used to sterilise glassware.
II. *Moist heat*		
1. Pasteurisation	72°C for 15 seconds	Inactivates mesophilic micro-organisms including pathogens, psychotophic bacteria yeast and moulds (some mould spores are heat resistant). This method is not practiced for the sanitisation of processing equipment.
2. Hot water	85°C for 15–20 minutes	Inactivates all vegetative cells (including thermoduric bacteria) with the exception of spores and bacteriophages, and this method is recommended for sanitising processing plants.
3. Boiling water	100°C	*Ibid.* Limited in its application but it is used for disinfection purposes; bacteriophages are inactivated.
4. Steaming	100°C for 10 minutes (2–3 cycles)	*Ibid.* The efficiency is dependent on spore germination; it is not used for plant disinfection.
5. Steam (free flowing)	100°C	Not more effective than boiling water, and bacterial spores are not inactivated. It is used to sterilise milk churns for 1–2 minutes or storage vessels until the condensate reaches 85°C 10 minute treatment.
6. Steam under pressure	121°C for 10–15 minutes (15–20 psi)	Achieves proper sterilisation, but this method can only be used to sterilise growth medium, e.g. starter culture milk or agar.

Data compiled from BSI (1977), Meynell & Meynell (*loc. cit.*), Zall (*loc. cit*).

—the intense heat generated could result in cracks in welding seams and can damage rubber gaskets;

—since steam cannot be recirculated, its generation is a waste of energy;

—the process is very noisy;

—the use of steam may pose a hazard to working personnel.

However, a mixture of hot air and steam (*ca.* approximately at 250°C) can be injected to sterilise yoghurt containers before filling, and the process is patented in the German Federal Republic No. 2839 543 (1980)—Ammann (1981). Such a process would, of course, be limited to certain materials due to the high temperature used, but unfortunately no specific type of container has been mentioned.

2. Chemical agents

Many chemical preparations could be used as sterilising agents, and such compounds are used either alone, i.e. as sterilant, or combined with other chemicals, e.g. detergent/sterilisers. The former type is more widely used in the yoghurt industry and the efficiency of these chemical agents is influenced by the following factors:

  (i) concentration of the chemical compound(s) in the sterilising solution;
 (ii) contact time between the chemical solution and the surfaces of the processing equipment;
 (iii) temperature and pH of the chemical disinfectant;
 (iv) amount of residual "soiling" matter in the processing equipment;
  (v) type(s) of micro-organisms being inactivated;
 (vi) hardness of the water;
(vii) inactivation by combination with residual detergent.

According to BSI (1977), the chemical disinfectants which are commonly used in the dairy industry are as follows.

(a) Chlorine. The most common source of chlorine is hypochlorite (sodium or calcium). These chemical compounds may be obtained in liquid or powder form, and their bacteriocidal effect is due to the release of chlorine, which is normally in the range of 50–250 mg/litre (ppm) depending on the application.

Chlorine compounds in the undiluted form are corrosive to equipment and can be hazardous to health, and should always be handled with care and at the correct concentrations.

The following aspects may also be considered:

 (i) Rinse the equipment thoroughly after the detergent wash, i.e. before circulating the hypochlorite solution.
(ii) If an acid wash is incorporated into the cleaning cycle, the programme will be:
   —rinse with water properly;
   —rinse/wash with alkaline solution to remove all residues of acid;
   —rinse with water;
   —sanitise with hypochlorite solution.

(iii) Due to the corrosive nature of chlorine, the sterilisation of utensils and equipment is often carried out immediately before use.

(iv) The recommended working concentration is 200–250 mg/litre (ppm) at 40°C for 10 minutes or for 15 minutes at ambient; at higher temperatures the chlorine volatilises and loses its bacteriocidal effect.

(v) The concentration of a sterilising solution of hypochlorite must be always checked to maintain its bacteriocidal power.

Although not normally used in the dairy industry, other forms of chlorine which could be used for sterilising purposes are elemental chlorine (available in a gas cylinder) and chloramine-T; the latter compound has a slow-acting bacteriocidal effect compared with the inorganic sterilising agents. The combined detergent/sterilisers contain chlorine in the form of dichlorodimethyl hydantoin and/or sodium dichloroisocyanurate, and the upper working temperatures could be around 70°C.

(b) Quaternary ammonium compounds (QACs). These compounds are basically cationic, surface-active bacteriocidal agents, and an example of such a compound is alkyldimethylbenzyl ammonium chloride (benzalkonium chloride). QACs are sometimes used as detergent/sterilisers, but as the formulation is dictated by the needs of the manufacturer rather than the user, it should be noted that certain alkaline compounds (anionic wetting agents) can reduce the bacteriocidal action of QACs. It should also be noted, regarding QACs that:

—They are stable in concentrated form and have a long shelf-life.
—In concentrated form they are much safer to handle than hypochlorite solutions, and they are relatively non-corrosive to metals.
—Due to their high surface activity, excessive foam can be produced during circulation through the plant, and hence QACs are sometimes difficult to rinse away.
—Factors that can impair their bacteriocidal effectiveness are:
   (i) the presence of organic matter;
   (ii) water hardness can reduce their activity;
   (iii) the type of organism, i.e. gram-negative bacteria, e.g. coliforms and psychotrophic organisms may be less unaffected especially at low concentrations, e.g. at < 50 mg/litre of QAC at 10°C, than gram-positive bacteria, e.g. staphylococci and streptococci, and a build-up of organisms resistant to QACs may develop in the plant.
—Recommended concentrations vary from 150–250 mg/litre of QAC at >40°C for not less than 2 minutes contact time.

(c) Iodophores. The bacteriocidal compound is iodine, and this has been combined with a suitable non-ionic surfactant to provide a usable product; the iodine complex is acidified with, for example, phosphoric acid for better stability and improved bacteriocidal effect. Iodophores are often considered as detergent/sterilisers due to the presence of the surface-active agents and the acid, in general:

—The recommended level in solutions is 50–70 mg/litre of free iodine in water of moderate hardness, and the pH of solution should be around 3; hard water can neutralise the acid in the iodophore.
—Iodophores have a good shelf life at ambient temperatures, but some iodine may vaporise; however, excessive loss occurs at temperatures above 50°C.

—Some "plastic" materials, e.g. gaskets, can react with iodine, and the product can acquire an "iodine" taint.

—Iodine stains any residual "soiling" matter on the surfaces of equipment, and visual inspection of the plant can indicate the standard of hygiene.

—Milk residues can inactivate the iodine, and an early indication of this loss is the fading of the amber colour; therefore, always check the strength of the iodophore, especially if the solution is recirculated.

(d) Miscellaneous sterilising agents

(i) Amphoteric (ampholytic) surface-active agents

These compounds are known to have good detergent/steriliser properties, but due to their high foaming characteristics they are not recommended for CIP. However, they are used for manual cleaning, since they are non-corrosive and non-irritant to skin.

(ii) Acidic sterilising agents

These acid formulations consist mainly of inorganic acids (e.g. phosphoric acid) and an anionic surfactant, and they are used as combined detergent/sterilisers, or as sterilising agents *per se*. The latter type has a strong bacteriocidal action, albeit generally slower than hypochlorite, and the sterilising effect is due to the highly acidic conditions produced at normal concentration, e.g. pH 2. However, this low pH may be corrosive to metals, for it is equivalent to the acid wash employed for the removal and prevention of milkstone.

(iii) Sodium hydroxide (caustic soda)

The bacteriocidal effect is due to the high alkalinity, and concentrations of 15–20 g/litre at 45°C for 2 minutes are sufficient to inactivate non-spore forming organisms. An improved sterilising action is achieved at higher temperature, e.g. > 70°C, as may be used for washing glass bottles.

(iv) Mixed halogens

A sterilising compound containing chlorine and bromine can be employed, and due to the synergestic effect of these halogens at lower concentrations than the individual elements.

(v) Formaldehyde

This agent is used for sterilising membrane plants, e.g. RO; for the recommended usage refer to Table 4.8.

(vi) Hydrogen peroxide (H_2O_2)

The chemical sterilisation of milk is practised in different parts of the world, and one such treatment involves the use of hydrogen peroxide. Although a large number of vegetative bacterial cells are destroyed, spore-formers (aerobic and anaerobic types) survive. However, in the present context hydrogen peroxide can be used for the sterilisation of packaging material, e.g. aseptic types of Tetra Pak, Gasti and Pure Pak, and either the packaging material is passed through a bath of H_2O_2 solution (e.g. Tetra Pak) or the finished carton is "fogged" with a mist of H_2O_2, e.g. Pure Pak. The solution contains a 15 % concentration of H_2O_2, and the carton is then heated (i.e. hot air 80–90°C) to remove any remaining H_2O_2; however, concentrations up to 30 % have been reported by Hahn (1981) for sterilising "plastic" yoghurt cups, and up to 1500 ppm is recommended for sterilising RO plants (see Table 4.8). Since H_2O_2 is a strong oxidising agent and potentially explosive, it is advisable to handle it with extreme care.

(vii) Non-acceptable types of sterilising agents

Certain compounds are used for general disinfection and/or sterilisation purposes, but are not normally used in the dairy industry; their inclusion in this section is for information only. Examples of these compounds are:

—lysol and other phenolic compounds;

—heavy metals, e.g. mercury, zinc, silver, lead and copper;

—volatile disinfectants, e.g. liquid ethylene oxide, β-propiolactone or chloroform (ethylene oxide boils at 10.7°C and is used to sterilise milk according to Meynell and Meynell (*loc. cit.*));

—alcohols are of limited application, i.e. for sterilising laboratory utensils.

3. Filtration

The sterilisation of liquids can be achieved by filtration, but it is the treatment of air which is of significance in the yoghurt industry. These air filters are normally fitted in a starter culture laboratory, so that the air is cleaned of any dust particles and airborne bacteriophages. The sterility of the culture propagation room is maintained by having the pressure of the filtered air slightly above atmospheric, so that on opening the starter room the pressurised air passes outward, so preventing unfiltered air from entering the sterile area.

4. Irradiation

Irradiation can be used in the laboratory and the processing area to maintain a clean atmosphere, and ultraviolet (UV) radiation, in particular, has been used with success. The wavelength of UV has to be less than 400 nm and more than 180 nm, e.g. *ca.* 260 nm, to be effective, and the latter figure (180 nm) is critical, since below 180 nm the radiation is absorbed by atmospheric oxygen. The effect of UV radiation on micro-organisms is either:

(i) inactivation or destruction;
(ii) mutation; or
(iii) the induction of phage growth in lysogenic bacteria.

Some practical applications in the dairy industry are: firstly, sterilising the air entering a laboratory, starter culture room and/or processing area, and secondly, the sterilisation of packaging materials before filling (Anon., 1979c). It must be emphasised that protection of the eyes from UV radiation is important, because the effective wavelengths can cause damage.

5. Spraying, fogging or fumigation

Solutions containing active chlorine or formaldehyde can be sprayed/fogged into the atmosphere of an enclosed room with the objective of destroying any aerial contamination in the form of bacteriophage particles and/or mould spores. However, excessive use of chlorine-based chemicals may result in severe rusting of exposed metal objects (e.g. window frames or steel beams), and fumigation with formalin may be hazardous, especially when used in mixtures with potassium permanganate (BSI, 1977); as a precaution, always add formalin after a permanganate treatment and not before. It must also be stressed that the inhalation of low levels of active chlorine or other "fumigants" over a long period of time could lead to pulmonary damage in susceptible individuals, and hence application of the technique must be carefully monitored.

There are, therefore, many different methods which could be employed for the sterilisation/sanitisation of yoghurt processing equipment, but by far the most popular methods are:

(i) sodium hydroxide or hypochlorite to sanitise milk storage tanks and yoghurt incubation/fermentation tanks;
(ii) hot water circulation to sanitise the milk processing equipment and, possibly, the bulk starter tanks;
(iii) chemical solutions to sanitise yoghurt filling machines;
(iv) H_2O_2 or UV radiation to sanitise packaging materials;
(v) autoclaving to sterilise laboratory utensils and bacteriological media; glassware may be treated in a hot oven.

The ultimate choice of any method of sterilisation/sanitisation is governed mainly by the recommendations of the equipment manufacturer supported by the degree of hygiene required by the quality controller manager. Obviously variations exist between one yoghurt plant and another in respect of procedures for cleaning and/or sterilisation, but a summary of some recommended methods for sterilisation is illustrated in Table 4.10.

C. Kinetics and Mechanisms of Microbial Destruction

The growth of micro-organisms is governed by such factors as:

—moisture content of the growth medium,
—availability of nutrients including trace elements,
—presence or absence of oxygen,
—pH,
—temperature,

and manipulation of these factors is used by dairy scientists and/or processors to control microbial growth in the manufactured product, and achieve their destruction/inactivation during sterilisation processes, i.e. the product or equipment.

The temperature range over which micro-organisms can survive runs from as low as $-250°C$ to as high as $150°C$ or above, but in practice the limits are less extreme. The thermal death point varies from one bacterial species to another, and the spore-forming bacteria are the most heat-resistant; their destruction relies not only on the level of heat applied, but also on various intrinsic and extrinsic factors, such as the age and thermal resistance of the organisms, as well as the water activity, pH and type of substrate. The protective action of a substrate is especially important, and it is for this reason that processing equipment must be free from any soiling matter in order to achieve an effective sterilisation.

The criterion of "death" of a micro-organism is usually equated with the loss of its ability to reproduce, including the inactivation of spores. Thus, as the temperature is gradually increased above the optimum growth condition of the organism, cell injury or stress starts to occur, and these

223

TABLE 4.10. *Guide to procedures recommended for sterilising yoghurt plant and equipment*

Yoghurt equipment to be sterilized	When sterilising is carried out separately following cleaning						When cleaning and sterilisation are carried out as a combined operation using a detergent/steriliser								
	Heat		Chemical agents				Chlorine-based products				QACs		Iodophors	
							Alkaline		Neutral					
	Steam	Hot/boiling water	Sodium hypochlorite	Iodophors	QACs	Amphoterics	Low foam	Average foam	Low foam	Average foam	Low foam	Average foam	Low foam	Average foam
Milk storage vessels	a	c	a	a	a	b	a	b	a	b	a	b	b	b
Heat exchangers	c	a	b	c	c	c	b	c	c	c	c	c	c	c
Homogenisers	c	a	c	c	c	c	c	b	c	c	c	c	c	c
Culture, fermenting and fruiting vessels	a	c	a	a	a	b	a	b	a	b	a	b	a	b
Cans and lids	a	c	c	c	c	c	a	a	a	a	a	a	b	b
Pipelines and pumps	b	a	a	a	a	b	a	a	a	a	a	a	b	b
Yoghurt bottle and carton filling and capping machines	b	b	a	a	a	b	a	a	a	a	a	a	a	a

(a) Suitable.
(b) May be suitable. Investigate thoroughly before using.
(c) Not suitable or not normally used.

After BSI (1977).

Reprinted with permission of British Standards Institution, London, U.K.

changes can ultimately lead to death. It is important, however, that although some injured cells may be unable to reproduce, they can become viable again once the damage has been repaired. This type of unpredictable behaviour highlights the complexity of thermoprocessing, and although a few general points are discussed below, it is advisable that the field should be explored further (for example, Pflug and Schmidt, 1968; Brown and Melling, 1971; Nickerson and Sinskey, 1972; Stumbo, 1973).

In pure culture and under ideal conditions the death rate of micro-organisms is considered to be logarithmic, and if the number of viable cells is plotted against time of exposure at a given temperature, a *straight line* will be obtained (see Fig. 4.8). From such a "survivor curve" the decimal reduction time D value can be calculated, and according to Stumbo (*loc. cit.*) it is defined as follows:

"D value is the time required at any temperature to destroy 90% of the spores or vegetative cells of a given organism, numerically, equal to the number of minutes required for the survivor curve to traverse one log cycle; mathematically, equal to the reciprocal of the slope of the survivor curve."

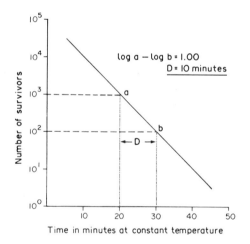

Fig. 4.8. Hypothetical illustration of a "survivor" curve

Refer to text for detailed discussion.

It is important when D values are quoted that the temperature should be stated also. For example, if the temperature of exposure is $90°C$ then the D value is expressed as $D_{90} = 10$ minutes (see Fig. 4.8). According to Olson and Nottingham (1980), the straight line of Fig. 4.8 extends, in theory, below the base line, i.e. into the area of negative logarithms, but in practice, of course, the number of organisms is rarely reduced to zero, and hence there is always the probability of survivor(s). Thus a heat treatment (e.g. during the processing of food or the cleaning/sterilisation of equipment) is predetermined in order to obtain an acceptable level of microbial destruction.

Thermal death times are a measure of relative resistance of micro-organisms to different lethal temperatures, and Fig. 4.9 illustrates a hypothetical example. The slope of the curve is referred to as the Z value, and it is defined by Stumbo (*loc. cit.*) as follows:

225

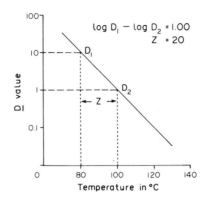

Fig. 4.9.   Hypothetical illustration of a thermal death time curve

Refer to text for detailed discussion.

"Number of degrees Celsius or Fahrenheit required for the thermal destruction curve to traverse one log cycle. Mathematically, equal to the reciprocal of the slope of thermal death curve."

Hence, both D and Z values can be used during the calculation of a heat process, and the "sterilisation" effect is expressed as the F value which is defined as follows:

"The equivalent in minutes at some given reference temperature of all heat considered, with respect to its capacity to destroy spores and vegetative cells of a particular organism" (Stumbo, *loc. cit.*).

An illustrated example of F value is the time in minutes required to destroy a specified number of spores at $121.1°C$ when $Z = 10$.

Another value, which is sometimes considered in heat processing, is the Q_{10}, and the kinetic relationship between Q_{10} and Z is discussed in detail by Stumbo (*loc. cit.*).

The mechanism(s) involved in the inactivation of micro-organisms by heat are considered to be chemical in nature, and Rahn (1945) considered the logarithmic order of death of micro-organisms to be due to a loss of reproductive power. Since moist heat is more effective than dry heat, it is suggested that the heat energy results in extensive molecular disorganisation in the microbial cell, denaturation of the protein constituents and, in particular, the deoxyribonucleic acid (DNA) units responsible for cell reproduction. By contrast, mechanisms of the inactivation by dry heat are not well established, but as reported by Meynell and Meynell (*loc. cit.*), it could be due to a mutagenic action which gives rise to multiple lesions in the DNA.

The biocidal mechanism(s) of each chemical sterilising agent is rather different, and some relevant information is illustrated in Table 4.11.

D. Means of Assessing the Sanitary Condition of a Processing Plant

Inspection of a yoghurt processing plant is a routine exercise which must be carried out in order to ensure that the cleaning and sterilisation operations are properly conducted. Different methods

TABLE 4.11. *The mode of action of chemical sterilising agents against micro-organisms*

Type of compound	Mode of action
Alcohol group	Possible actions are: (a) denaturation of proteins, or (b) interference with cell metabolism, or (c) lytic action
Phenol	Cause physical damage to the cell wall of organisms
Chlorine	Possible mechanism(s) is: *firstly*, hypochlorous acid combines with the protein in cell membranes to produce certain compounds which interfere with cell metabolism, or *secondly*, chlorine inhibits certain enzymatic reactions
Iodine	*Ibid.*

Bacteriocidal effect of chemical sterilisers is also affected by other parameters, e.g. pH, solvent composition and the presence of electrolytes.

Data compiled from Zall (*loc. cit.*).

and/or techniques have been devised by quality controllers to monitor the sanitary condition of the plant, thus maintaining a good keeping quality of the manufactured yoghurt, and at the same time meeting the requirements of the health authorities. The available methods of inspection are divided into the following categories.

1. Physical examination

This technique may involve the use of sight, feel or smell. The former two approaches can be useful to confirm the presence or absence of "soil", for the absence of "soil" indicates that the plant has been adequately cleaned. However, the use of certain chemicals, a build-up of milkstone on plant surfaces, or merely wear and tear can effect the original shine of stainless steel. An acid clean can remove the layer of milkstone and leave a bright shiny surface, but not in the other cases. Although iodophores are not widely used, they offer one advantage in that any residual "soil" on plant surfaces becomes an amber colour, and can then be detected by sight.

By contrast, "unclean" odours are indicative of inadequate cleaning, and yoghurt incubation tanks that have not properly sanitised can often be detected by smell alone.

An UV light, i.e. "black lamp", can be useful to detect "soil" on clean plant surfaces, in that where the rays are absorbed by inorganic and organic substances (e.g. calcium salts and casein) light is given off (Zall, *loc. cit.*); the use of a "black lamp" should be complementary to other types of test performed by quality controllers.

2. Chemical examination

If detergent and sterilising agents are used for cleaning and sanitising purposes it is imperative that chemical tests of rinsing water are carried out to detect residues of these compounds. Thus, the presence of detergent and/or sterilant compounds could be directly related to a faulty CIP programme, in that the final rinsing stage is either too short or not performed properly. Alternatively, it could reflect some fault in plant design, so that the cleaning and sanitising compounds are not being drained completely. The nature of the test(s) depends on the type of detergent and/or sterilising agent used, and an example of one such test is the use of Bromo Thymol Blue indicator on both the rinsing/drainage water and normal plant water (i.e. control). A colour change to yellow of the sample water indicates the presence of acid, and a blue colour is due to alkali compounds. It is debatable whether or not pH measurement is reliable enough to detect traces of acid or alkali, but rinses containing high concentrations of these compounds can be detected easily using a pH meter.

3. Bacteriological examination

Microbial counts of plant surfaces, processing equipment and packaging materials are direct evidence of the hygienic quality of the plant. Different methods have been described for bacteriological examination of equipment, and examples of these can be found in BSI (1968) and APHA (1978).

Enumeration of total counts of bacteria, coliforms and yeast and moulds are the most popular microbiological examinations carried out, and the types of micro-organisms present reflect, to some extent, the standard of plant hygiene. The examination of processing equipment, packaging containers and other utensils for microbiological purposes can involve the swab technique, the rinsing method (or a combination of both) and/or agar impression plates (Lück, 1981).

Swabs can be prepared either in the laboratory or purchased ready made (for example, the Hygicult/Uricult supplied by Orion Diagnostica Culture Media, or The Swab Test Kit supplied by Millipore); alternatively, agar contact slides could be used. In the rinsing method, a processing tank, glass bottle, milk churn or yoghurt container is rinsed with sterile water or Ringer's solution, and the sample is analysed for total bacterial numbers or the presence of different types of organism.

In cases where the volume of "rinse" is large or the microbial load is low, it is advisable to filter sterilise the sample; the filter is then incubated prior to counting the micro-organisms.

Finally, two areas which must not be overlooked are (a) the air and (b) the general state of building, e.g. walls, drains, etc. Exposing agar plates to the atmosphere can prove helpful, especially during the summer months when the aerial mould spore level is high, and can act as a possible source of contamination of the yoghurt; the risks of infection by aerial spores can be reduced by preventing drafts in processing area. In addition, the general condition of the walls and floors in the processing and packaging areas provides an insight into the overall standard of hygiene.

EFFLUENT TREATMENT

Water is used in the dairy industry for processing (e.g. heating, cooling, recombining powders) and cleaning purposes (e.g. equipment and dairy premises), and it is safe to assume that any waste water from processing will not contain as high a percentage of polluting materials as the water used for cleaning. This latter waste water or effluent has to be treated before it is disposed of, either into the public sewer, or into a river or water way, and from a yoghurt plant the effluent will consist of:

(i) dilute yoghurt,
(ii) dilute fruit,
(iii) dilute stabilising compounds,
(iv) detergent and/or sterilising agents.

The volume of effluent arising in a dairy plant is dependent on two main factors: firstly, the type of dairy product being processed, and secondly, the degree of water management being exercised and the amount of water being conserved. For example, cheese, milk powder and evaporating plants generate larger volumes of effluent than a dairy pasteurising milk, and ratios have been worked out in the dairy industry indicating the volume of water required to process a certain volume of milk. Unfortunately data concerning yoghurt production are not widely available, although the IDF (1981) reported the following water to milk ratios for the production of yoghurt in France:

(a) food grade water was 0.5–1.0 litres per litre of milk;
(b) boiler water was 0.2–0.35 litres per litre of milk;
(c) cooling water was 2–4 litres per litre of milk.

In view of the limited technical data available on yoghurt effluent it is recommended that the reader consults the following International Dairy Federation documents (IDF, 1974, 1978) for general information regarding dairy effluent treatment.

A. The Nature of Pollution

A yoghurt effluent can contain organic and inorganic matter which is then subject to biological decomposition by micro-organisms. Oxygen is required for this biological process, and if highly polluted water is discharged directly into rivers or other water ways, the dissolved oxygen in the water will be utilised. The result is that, in extreme cases, life in the water reaches a standstill, i.e. stagnant water. The amount of oxygen required to decompose the total solids in an effluent is used, therefore, by the major water authorities all over the world to assess whether waste water should be treated before discharge into rivers.

The parameters used to assess the level of pollution in dairy effluents are as follows.

1. Biological oxygen demand (BOD)

BOD is the amount or quantity of oxygen required by aerobic micro-organisms to decompose/stabilise the organic matter in effluent held at 20°C for 5–7 days. The sample is presedimented or filtered before conducting the test.

2. Chemical oxygen demand (COD)

COD is the amount or quantity of oxygen required for chemical oxidation. The effluent sample is filtered and/or sedimented, boiled in the presence of acid dichromate with silver sulphate as a catalyst and finally titrated. The organic matter reduces part of the dichromate, and the balance is determined by titration. Hence, COD is a measure of the amount of oxygen absorbed by the dichromate.

3. Permanganate value (PV)

The PV test is a quick test to determine the chemically oxidisable organic matter in a sample. The effluent sample (sedimented and/or filtered) is boiled in acid or alkaline permanganate and the balance of unoxidised permanganate is determined by iodine titration. The presence of ferrous ions or nitrite in the sample can interfere with the accuracy of the PV test, and hence this test is normally carried out before the BOD test as a preliminary indication of the magnitude of the oxygen demand.

4. Total organic carbon (TOC)

The TOC test involves the complete oxidation of all organic carbon constituents in the effluent sample to carbon dioxide.

5. Total organic solids (TOS)

The TOS content of the effluent sample is the difference between the total solids and the ash. The former is determined by drying at $> 100°C$, and ashing takes place on heating the sample to $> 550°C$.

6. Miscellaneous tests

These may comprise the determination of fat, lactose and protein in dairy effluent, and the level of surface-active agents (from detergent compounds). In the latter test, the sample is treated with methylene blue and due to the presence of anionic surfactants insoluble blue salts are formed. The salt is extracted with chloroform and measured photometrically.

Other tests, which could be of some value in assessing the inorganic pollution likely from the yoghurt effluent, are pH, ammonia nitrogen, nitrate and nitrite, and phosphorus.

B. Methods of Effluent Treatment

A dairy effluent can be treated mechanically, chemically, biologically or by a combination of these methods. The mechanical treatment simply removes the insoluble matter from the effluent with the aid of filters, screens or sedimentation. Another mechanical system is flotation, in which air bubbles are passed through the effluent, and as they rise to the surface small particles of solid matter become attached; the resultant "scum" can then be scraped off the surface.

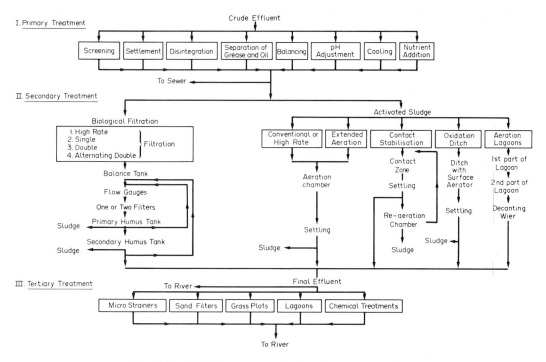

Fig. 4.10. Possible treatments of effluent from yoghurt plants

Adapted from: Cooper (1974); Zabierzewski and Thom (1978); Synnott, Kelley and Moloney (1978); Odlum and McCartney (1978).

TABLE 4.12. *Some data regarding the treatment of effluent from a yoghurt factory*

Treatment and/or process	Capacity
Daily throughput	546,000 litres
Balancing capacity	273,000 litres
Roughing treatment	Two-stage flocor tower
	590,000 litres
Polishing treatment	Two filter beds, e.g. alternating double filtration (ADF)
	271,000 litres

	BOD load
Raw effluent	$\begin{cases} 1\,000–1,500 \text{ ppm} \\ 2\,400 \text{ ppm (highest level)} \end{cases}$
To the plant	654 kg BOD/day
To biofilter	1.39 kg BOD/m³/day
% BOD reduction in roughing state	75–85
To percolating ADF	0.28 kg BOD/m³/day
Final effluent	15–25 ppm

Adapted from Gaster (*loc. cit.*).

231

The use of certain chemical compounds, e.g. iron sulphate or chloride, or aluminium sulphate, can precipitate the dissolved constituents in the effluent, and the precipitated matter is then removed by mechanical separation. However, the chemical treatment cannot remove the lactose or other dissolved sugars.

The biological treatment of dairy effluents is widely practised, and purification of any waste water is accomplished either by the decomposition of the organic substance(s) by oxidation due to the aerobic activity of micro-organisms, or as the result of anaerobic fermentation. In the oxidative approach, the oxygen is supplied artificially by means of special aeration inlets, but a septic tank is required for the anaerobic process.

The treatment of any type of dairy effluent, including that from a yoghurt plant, is usually carried out using the combined processes of mechanical separation and biological purification, and the overall process is divided into three main treatments:

(a) primary (effluent roughing),
(b) secondary,
(c) tertiary (effluent polishing).

Figure 4.10 illustrates the different types of process employed for the treatment of effluents from yoghurt plants.

Data regarding the treatment of dairy effluents are not widely published, but a study carried out by Gaster (1972) on a plant producing fruit yoghurt is summarised in Table 4.12. Two biofilters were used, and the effluent plant was capable of handling 550,000 litres/day. Settlement of the effluent was carried out prior to the roughing stage, and because of the nature of yoghurt, i.e. low pH, large volumes of sludge were removed. The reduction in BOD was about 75%, and the filter beds were relatively small, compared with other creameries, since the greater part of the effluent load was being removed by the high rate biofilters.

REFERENCES

AMMANN, S. (1981) *Dairy Science Abstracts,* **43,** 88.

ANON. (1967) In *Manual for Milk Plant Operators,* 3rd Edition, Milk Industry Foundation, Washington, U.S.A.

ANON. (1969) In *The Bacteriological Examination of Water,* 4th Edition, Reports on Public Health and Medical Subjects No. 71. Reprinted in 1970, HMSO, London, U.K.

ANON. (1979a) In *APV Paraclean—Modular CIP System,* Publication A483a, APV Co. Ltd., West Sussex, U.K.

ANON. (1979b) In *Automatic CIP Equipment for Food Plants,* Alfa-Laval Technical Bulletin PB 60 220E, Alfa-Laval A/B, Lund, Sweden.

ANON. (1979c) *Nordeuropaeisk Mejeri-Tidsskrift,* **45,** 177.

ANON. (1980a) *American Dairy Review,* **42**(6), 30.

ANON. (1980b) *Ibid.* **42**(7), 30D.

ANON. (1980c) *Ibid.* **42**(8), 28

ANON. (1980d) *Ibid.* **42**(9), 40.

ANON. (1980e) *Ibid.* **42**(10), 12.

ANON. (1980f) *Ibid.* **42**(11), 52.

ANON. (1980g) *Ibid.* **42**(12), 34 L.

ANON. (1981a) *Ibid.* **43**(1), 22.

ANON. (1981b) *Ibid.* **43**(2), 48.

ANON. (1981c) *Ibid.* **43**(3), 36.

APHA (1978) In *Standard Methods for Examination of Diary Products,* Ed. by Marth, E.H. American Public Health Association, Washington, U.S.A.

BLOOMER, P. J. (1982) Personal communication.

BSI (1968) In *BS-4285 Methods of Microbiological Examination for Dairy Purpose*, British Standards Institution, London, U.K.

BSI (1970) In *BS-2756 Recommendations for the Use of Detergents in the Dairy Industry*, British Standards Institution, London, U.K. Amended in (1974). *Ibid.*

BSI (1977) In *BS-5305 Recommendations for Sterilisation of Plant and Equipment Used in the Dairy Industry*, British Standards Institution, London, U.K.

BROWN, M. R. W. and MELLING, J. (1971) In *Inhibition and Destruction of the Microbial Cell*, Ed. by Hugo, W. B. Academic Press Inc. (London) Ltd., London, U.K.

COOPER, J. S. (1974) In *Dairy Effluent Treatment*, IDF Doc. No. 77, IDF, Brussels, Belgium.

CUSTER, E. W. (1982) *Dairy Record*, **83**(2), 95.

DUNSMORE, D. G., TWOMEY, A., WHITTLESTONE, W. G. and MORGAN, H. W. (1981) *Journal of Food Protection*, **44**, 220.

GASTER, A. J. (1972) *Journal of the Society of Dairy Technology*, **25**, 26.

HAHN, G. (1981) *Dairy Science Abstracts*, **43**, 879.

HAVERLAND, H. (1981) *Journal of Dairy and Food Sanitation*, **1**, 331.

IDF. (1974) In *Dairy Effluent Treatment*, IDF Doc. No. 77, IDF, Brussels, Belgium.

IDF. (1978) In *Proceedings of the IDF Seminar on Dairy Effluents*, IDF Doc. No. 104, IDF, Brussels, Belgium.

IDF. (1979) In *Design and Use of CIP Systems in the Dairy Industry*, IDF Bulletin—Doc. No. 117, IDF, Brussels, Belgium.

IDF (1980) In *General Code of Hygiene Practice for the Dairy Industry*, IDF Doc. No. 123, Brussels, Belgium.

IDF (1981) In *Dairy Effluents*, IDF Doc. No. 138, IDF, Brussels, Belgium.

KESSLER, H. G. (1981) In *Food Engineering and Dairy Technology*, Translated by Wotzilka, M., Publishing House Verlag A. Kessler, Freising, West Germany.

LANGEVELD, L. P. M., KONING, J. and CUPERUS, F. (1982) *Dairy Science Abstracts*, **44**, 193.

LELIEVELD, H. L. M. (1976) *Biotechnology and Bioengineering*, **18**, 1807.

LÜCK, H. (1981) In *Dairy Microbiology*, Volume 2, Ed. by Robinson, R.K. Applied Science Publishers Ltd. London, U.K.

MEYNELL, G. G. and MEYNELL, E. (1970) In *Theory and Practice in Experimental Bacteriology*, 2nd Edition, Cambridge University Press, London, U.K.

MILLEDGE, (1981) *Proc. Institute of Food Science and Technology* (IFST) **14**, 74.

NEIDITCH, O. W. (1972) In *Detergency—Theory and Test Methods/Part 1*, Vol. 5, Ed. by Cutler, W. G. and Davis, R. C. Marcel Dekker Inc., New York, U.S.A.

NICKERSON, J. T. and SINSKEY, A. J. (1972) In *Microbiology of Foods and Food Processing*, Elfabier North Holland Publishing Co., New York, U.S.A.

ODLUM, C. A. and MCCARTHY, J. (1978) In *Procedings of the IDF Seminar on Dairy Effluents*, IDF Doc. No. 104, IDF, Brussels, Belgium.

OLSON, J. C. and NOTTINGHAM, P. M. (1980) In *Microbial Ecology of Foods—Vol. 1—Factors Affecting Life and Death of Micro-organisms*, by the International Commission on Microbiological Specifications of Foods, Ed. Committee Silliker, J. H., Elliot, R. P., Baird-Parker, A. C., Bryan, F. L., Christian, J. H. B., Clark, D. S., Olson, J. C. Jr. and Roberts, T. A. Academic Press Inc. (London) Ltd., London, U.K.

PFLUG, I. J. and SCHMIDT, C. F. (1968) In *Disinfection, Sterilisation and Preservation*, Ed. by Lawrence, C. A and Block, S. S. Lea and Febiger, Pennsylvania, U.S.A.

RHAN, O. (1945) In *Injury and Death of Bacteria*, Biodynamica Monograph No. 3.

STUMBO, C. R. (1973) In *Thermobacteriology in Food Processing*, 2nd Edition, Academic Press Inc. (London) Ltd., London, U.K.

SWARTLING, P. (1959) *Dairy Science Abstracts* (Review Article No. 75), **21**, 1.

SYNNOTT, E. C.; KELLY, B. F. and MOLONEY, A. M. (1978) In *Proceedings of the IDF Seminar on Dairy Effluents*, IDF Doc. No. 104, IDF Brussels, Belgium.

TAMIME, A. Y. (1982) Unpublished data.

TAMPLIN, T. C. (1980) In *Hygienic Design and Operation of Food Plant*, Ed. by Jowitt, R., Ellis Horwood Ltd., West Sussex, U.K.

TAMPLIN, T. C. (1982) Personal communication.

TILLEY, C. H. (1982) Personal communication.

TIMPERLEY, D. A. (1981) *Journal of the Society of Dairy Technology*, **34**, 6.

TIMPERLAY, D. A. and LAWSON, G. B. (1980) In *Hygienic Design of Operation of Food Plant*, Ed. by Jowitt, R. Ellis Horwood Ltd., Chichester, U.K.

ZABIERZEWSKI, C. and THOM, R. (1978) In *Proceedings of the IDF Seminar on Dairy Effluents*, IDF Doc. No. 104, IDF, Brussels, Belgium.

ZALL, R. R. (1981) In *Dairy Microbiology*, Vol. 1, Ed. by Robinson, R. K. Applied Science Publishers Ltd., London, U.K.

ZOLTAY, P. T., ZOTTOLA, E. A. and MCKAY, L. L. (1981) *Journal of Food Protection*, **44**, 204.

233

CHAPTER 5

Traditional and Recent Developments in Yoghurt Production

The accepted homeland of yoghurt is the Balkans peninsula and the Middle East region, and to the communities living in that part of the world this type of fermented milk product is identified and known as natural/plain unsweetened yoghurt. The *per capita* annual consumption is high, and in Bulgaria, in particular, is 31.5 kg/head/year (IDF, 1977). It is evident, therefore, that yoghurt plays an important role in the diets of these communities. Furthermore, it is customary for that yoghurt to be consumed not only as a refreshing drink, but also as a main ingredient during the preparation of a wide variety of dishes including salads and soups; such food habits/consumer attitudes may well be a contributory factor to the high annual consumption. Incidentally, recipes for yoghurt dishes are increasingly being included in cookery books, e.g. Nilson (1973) and Orga (1975).

Prior to 1950, the acceptability of yoghurt by communities in other parts of the world, i.e. Western Europe and North America, was limited to very small minorities, and to some ethnic groups descended from the Balkans or the Middle East. The reason for this lack of popularity has been attributed to the fact that:

(a) natural yoghurt has a distinctive acidic, sharp flavour which can limit consumer acceptability;
(b) yoghurt does not play an important role in the diets of such communities;
(c) the type of food prepared does not require yoghurt as a raw material;
(d) the preference for other fermented dairy products, e.g. cheese.

Despite the proximity of Europe to the Middle East, the popularity of yoghurt did not spread, and it was not until 1960 in Switzerland that a major development in the yoghurt industry took place, namely the introduction of fruit flavoured and sweetened yoghurt. Since that time the popularity of yoghurt had spread to other parts of the world, and consumption has increased significantly (see Table 1.2). It could be argued that the increased acceptability of yoghurt is the result of the fact that:

(a) good marketing and advertising campaigns have been used to improve the image of the product, and hence increase sales to the consumer;
(b) the production of low fat yoghurts has been used to encourage the diet conscious consumer to include it as part of his/her slimming programme;

234

(c) communities in Western Europe and North America have a preference for sweet products, and hence the sweetened yoghurt was readily accepted;

(d) yoghurt is consumed as an "off-the-shelf" dessert and not for the preparation of yoghurt dishes;

(e) some of the yoghurt advertisements have been geared towards the younger generation, and their response to the message has been enthusiastic;

(f) continuous research and development is taking place in order to innovate yoghurt-based products which may lead to wider acceptability by the consumer.

It is the latter aspect which is of great importance in the present context, for although many recent developments have their origin in the traditional processes, pressures from industry have elicited some interesting products. Some of these yoghurt-based products have been developed by industrial organisations, and the available technical data is, as a consequence, somewhat limited. It was decided, therefore, to present the processing techniques in the form of schematic flow diagrams, for in this way the outlines of the process are more easily discerned; relevant scientific publications are referred to where possible.

STANDARD COMMERCIAL YOGHURT

Commercial yoghurts are divided into three main categories, i.e. plain/natural, fruit and flavoured, and these different types of yoghurt are manufactured in either the set or stirred form. The latter type is more popular, and the different stages of manufacture are illustrated in Fig. 5.1.

PASTEURISED/UHT/LONG-LIFE YOGHURT

Depending on the standards of hygiene observed during the manufacture of yoghurt, and the microbiological quality of the ingredients and packaging materials, the shelf-life of yoghurt is around 3 weeks under refrigerated conditions. Various techniques have been used in order to improve the keeping quality of yoghurt, such as:

(a) freezing and drying
(b) gas flushing
(c) addition of preservatives   (These are discussed under
(d) use of aseptic equipment   separate headings elsewhere)
(e) application of multiple-frequency
     "microwaves"
(f) sterilisation by heat

and each of these approaches has its adherents.

A post-production heat treatment helps to prolong the shelf-life of the product, in that the application of heat inactivates the starter culture bacteria and their enzymes, as well as other contaminants, e.g. yeasts and moulds. Traditionally yoghurt was heated for a few hours over low fires of a special type of wood. The end product was referred to as "Smoked Yoghurt", and it was preserved over the winter months by placing it in jars and covering it with either olive oil or tallow. However, in a mechanised plant the time–temperature relationships, which are used to achieve the

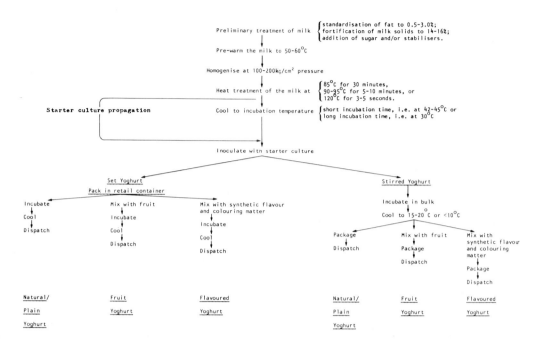

Preliminary treatment of milk — standardisation of fat to 0.5-3.0%; fortification of milk solids to 14-16%; addition of sugar and/or stabilisers.

Pre-warm the milk to 50-60°C

Homogenise at 100-200kg/cm² pressure

Heat treatment of the milk at — 85°C for 30 minutes, 90-95°C for 5-10 minutes, or 120°C for 3-5 seconds.

Starter culture propagation

Cool to incubation temperature — short incubation time, i.e. at 42-45°C or long incubation time, i.e. at 30°C

Inoculate with starter culture

Set Yoghurt — Stirred Yoghurt

Pack in retail container — Incubate in bulk — Cool to 15-20°C or <10°C

Incubate / Mix with fruit / Mix with synthetic flavour and colouring matter

Cool / Incubate / Incubate

Dispatch / Cool / Cool

Dispatch / Dispatch

Package / Mix with fruit / Mix with synthetic flavour and colouring matter

Dispatch / Package / Package

Dispatch / Dispatch

Natural/ Plain Yoghurt | Fruit Yoghurt | Flavoured Yoghurt | Natural/ Plain Yoghurt | Fruit Yoghurt | Flavoured Yoghurt

Fig. 5.1. Flavoured yoghurts

desired effect of pasteurisation, are similar to those used for liquid milk processing, although in general a lower energy input is required for yoghurt since the level of acidity is much higher than with milk (Gavin, 1966; Puhan, 1979); Table 5.1 illustrates the heat treatments that can be applied to produce yoghurt with longer keeping quality.

Two main problems have been associated with the manufacture of pasteurised yoghurt; firstly, a reduction in viscosity and whey syneresis may occur, and secondly, there may be loss of flavour (this is only significant in plain/natural yoghurt). To overcome the former problem, especially when yoghurt is heated to temperatures above 70°C, the following precautionary measures are recommended:

(a) cool the yoghurt first to 20°C, and then proceed with the heat treatment; Fig. 5.3 represents a typical example of the temperature profile observed during the manufacture of "Long-Life" yoghurt using the Nouva Frau "LL" system;

(b) hot filling of yoghurt after pasteurisation is widely practised, and final cooling takes place in the retail container (see Table 5.1 for illustrated examples);

(c) the addition of special stabilisers is sometimes recommended, but, on average, < 1 % is added depending on the type used.

It is evident, therefore, that it is technically feasible to prolong the shelf-life of yoghurt by the application of heat, although, some controversy may exist regarding its definition as "yoghurt";

TABLE 5.1. *Reported processing conditions for the manufacture of pasteurised/UHT yoghurt*

Method	References
Heat the yoghurt to 75°C for few seconds (5–10 minutes for set yoghurt); cool to 20 or 10–15°C; add the fruit under aseptic conditions; fill the product into a sterile retail container; keeping quality 4–6 weeks at 20°C. (This procedure is based on the Alfa-Laval Aseptjomatic process—see Fig. 5.2 and Fig. 5.4.)	Bake (1971), Anon. (1977a)
Cool the yoghurt to 20–25°C; mix in the sugar, fruit and other additives; pasteurise at 75°C for 40 seconds; cool to 5°C and fill in retail containers.	Schulz (1969)
Pasteurising the yoghurt at 50–55°C for 30 minutes increased the shelf-life to 3 weeks at 15°C.	Rakshy (1966)
This process is referred to as "Thermisation"; the yoghurt is pasteurised at 60–65°C, cooled and packaged; shelf-life of 6–8 weeks at 12°C.	Neirinckx (1972)
Flash pasteurise yoghurt at 65–70°C; fill the product into retail containers while hot; cool and dispatch.	Klupsch (1972)
Hot packaging of the yoghurt extended the shelf-life to 1 month at ambient temperature.	Mulcahy (1972)
Pasteurise yoghurt in container at 85–87.7°C for 10–15 minutes; shelf-life of 1 year without refrigeration.	Anon. (1977b)
Heat the yoghurt at 64°C for 5 minutes; hot package and cool to 5°C during overnight cold storage; acidity of the product did not increase after 3 weeks at 20°C.	Vanderpoorten and Martens (1976)
Heating yoghurt in a scraped-surface heat exchanger at 85°C extended the shelf-life >4 weeks at room temperature.	Holdt (1978)
Batch pasteurise yoghurt at 65°C for 20 minutes; fill containers while still hot; shelf-life of 7 days at 27°C.	Lück and Mostert (1971)
"Thermisation" of yoghurt at 57–70°C for 15–40 seconds increased the storage life by reducing the total counts and yeast and moulds.	Sebela (1979)
Heat treatment of yoghurt (in retail container) at 58°C for 5 minutes or (continuous flow) at 65°C for 30 seconds; slight drop in viscosity occurred in the latter method.	Loo (1980)
Cool yoghurt to 20–25°C; pasteurise at 70°C for 30–40 seconds; package aseptically at 55–60°C; final cooling takes place in retail container.	Dellaglio (1977, 1979), Anon. (1979a)
Pasteurisation of yoghurt at 60 or 70°C for 1 minute; survival rate of starter culture was 0.12 and 0.02% respectively; at the higher temperature the lactobacilli survived better.	Prekoppova and Slottova (1979)
Heat treatment of yoghurt in the container at around 80°C for 35 minutes.	Pavey and Mone (1976)
Sterilise yoghurt in the container in an autoclave between 60–85°C for up to 50 minutes and pressures of up to 2 atmospheres; cool to 10–15°C under pressure.	Egli and Egli (1976a, b, 1977, 1980)
Blend natural yoghurt with xanthan—guar gum mixture at a ratio of 2:1, disodium phosphate, potassium sorbate and granulated sucrose; pasteurise the mix at 87.7°C for 27 seconds, cool to 65.5°C, homogenise at 51 kg/cm², cool to 7°C, add flavour(s) and package.	Hermann (1980)

most existing standards stipulate that "yoghurt" must contain an abundant and viable population of *Streptococcus thermophilus* and *Lactobacillus bulgaricus*. Tamime and Deeth (1980) suggested that it would be reasonable to reserve the term "yoghurt" for the traditional product, and to designate the heat treated product as "Pasteurised", "UHT" or "Long-Life" yoghurt. Such an approach could help to ease the existing controversy, for essentially the only difference between pasteurised yoghurt and a traditional yoghurt is the low viable count of starter organisms in the former; this difference may, however, be relevant in relation to the nutritional and therapeutic aspects of the product (see Deeth and Tamime, 1981, and Chapter 9).

The other constituents of yoghurt that may be most affected by heat are the vitamins and the enzymes, and Felip, Croci and Gizzarelli (1979), comparing heated yoghurt (HY) and unheated yoghurt (UY), reported the following observations:

(a) the thiamin content in both types of yoghurts was not affected by heat or cold storage;
(b) vitamin B_6 losses appeared to be greater during the storage of (HY) than with (UY), i.e. 85 % as against 50 %;
(c) folic acid decreased to a trace concentrations in (HY) after 15 days, but in (UY), a similar reduction took 30 days;
(d) pantothenic acid was initially reduced by 70 % in (HY);
(e) the heat treatment reduced the activities of the enzymes protease, cellulase, amylase and β-D-galactosidase by 60 %, 25 %, 50 % and 100 % respectively.

(a)

Fig. 5.2.

Fig. 5.2. Some illustrations of plants for the production of long-life yoghurt

(a) A section of the Alfa-Laval Aseptjomatic processing plant for the production of "Long-Life" stirred yoghurt at Sösdala Dairy in Sweden

(Reproduced by courtesy of Alfa-Laval A/B, Lund, Sweden)

(b) A section of the Frau "LL" processing plant for the production of 'Medium or Long-Life' stirred yoghurt

(Reproduced by courtesy of Wincanton Engineering Co. Ltd., Sherborne, UK.)

The inactivation of the latter enzyme, i.e. β-D-galactosidase, was also reported by Speck (1977), Speck and Geoffrion (1980) and Lusiani and Bianchi-Salvadori (1978); however, the presence of this enzyme in yoghurt is highly desirable, particularly for consumers deficient in lactase. Gallgher, Molleson and Caldwell (1974) have shown that yoghurt does not have the same adverse effects as milk on lactose intolerant patients, and this benefit is most probably due to the presence of active β-D-galactosidase.

An alternative method, which could be used to pasteurise yoghurt, is the application of the multiple-frequency or microwave technique, i.e. the Bach system. The principle of this method is well documented by Bach (1978), and in brief it consists of a two-stage, rapid dielectric heating of yoghurt in plastic cups.

The first stage is applied horizontally (low-frequency microwaves with high penetration), while the second stage is applied vertically (high-frequency microwaves with low penetration). The actual "pasteurisation" is at a lower temperature than required for a conventional process, and the treatment takes place during the passage of the yoghurt cups through a water bath. The two stages are complementary to each other, and are needed to achieve adequate pasteurisation. According

239

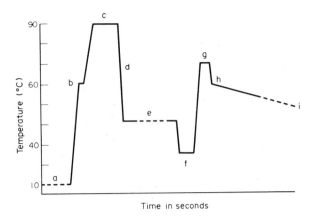

Fig. 5.3. Time-temperature profile observed during the manufacture of "long-life" yoghurt using the Nouva Frau 'LL' system

        (a) Raw milk
        (b) Homogenisation
        (c) Heat treatment of the milk
        (d) Cooling to incubation temperature
        (e) Fermentation
        (f) Partial cooling of the yoghurt
        (g) Bacterial and enzymatic inactivation
        (h) Partial cooling and aseptic packaging
        (i) Final cooling and gelling off the yoghurt
— — — — — — — — — — Represents time in hours

After: Anon (1976)

to Bach (1977), this system results in the destruction of yeasts and moulds, but has no adverse effect on the milk proteins or the starter bacteria; the keeping quality of yoghurt is extended to 4–6 weeks at room temperature. In addition, the use of this technique does not require the addition of special stabilisers to the yoghurt. According to Reuter (1978), the additional processing cost of using the Bach method is 0.01 Deutschmarks per cup of yoghurt; this increase in the cost of production is marginal when set against the improved shelf-life of the yoghurt.

LACTOSE HYDROLYSED YOGHURT (LHY)

During the manufacture of yoghurt, only part of the available lactose is utilised by the starter culture bacteria as an energy source with the production of lactic acid, and this excess lactose could be utilised to sweeten the yoghurt without increasing its calorific value. This effect could be achieved by hydrolysing the lactose using β-D-galactosidase (in powder or liquid form), which splits the lactose into glucose and galactose; the relative sweetness of lactose and these monosaccharides is, compared to a degree of sweetness for sucrose $= 1$, as follows: lactose 0.4, galactose 0.6 and glucose 0.7. However, Engel (1973) observed that only a 50 % hydrolysis of the lactose was necessary to produce, in terms of sweetness, an acceptable yoghurt, and that the process of hydrolysis could be carried out either during the cold storage of the milk or at around 35°C on the day of manufacture, i.e. prior to the heat treatment of the milk (see Fig. 5.5).

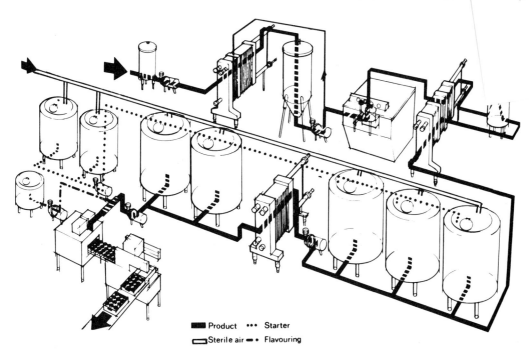

Product ■■■ ••• Starter
Sterile air ■■ • Flavouring

Fig. 5.4. Flow diagram showing the Aseptjomatic process line for the manufacture "long-life" stirred yoghurt

Reproduced by courtesy of Alfa-Laval A/B, Lund, Sweden

Hydrolysis is only desirable, of course, during the manufacture of fruit/flavoured yoghurt, since plain/natural yoghurts are not sweetened at all; nevertheless, a reduction in the level of lactose in natural yoghurt does improve its therapeutic value (Gallagher, Molleson and Caldwell, *loc. cit.*). Some proposed schemes for the industrial manufacture of LHY are illustrated in Fig. 5.5, and preliminary work in this field has associated the enhanced activity of *S. thermophilus* and *L. bulgaricus* in lactose hydrolysed milk with the presence of glucose and/or galactose in the milk.

More recently, Hemme, Vassal and Auclair (1978), Hemme *et al.* (1979) and Marschke and Dulley (1978) detected some proteolytic activity in commercial samples of β-D-galactosidase (possibly due to contamination during its preparation), and the improved activity of the yoghurt starter culture may be associated with the liberation of essential amino acids rather than with the presence of glucose and/or galactose.

It is clear, therefore, that yoghurt can be produced from lactose hydrolysed milk, but the incentive for commercial production is limited because the process is still not economic in comparison with the addition of normal sweetening agents. The use of immobilised enzymes might offer one possible solution, but the economics of the process will be the decisive factor.

DRINKING YOGHURT

Drinking yoghurt is categorised as stirred yoghurt of low viscosity, and this product is consumed as a refreshing drink. The low viscosity in drinking yoghurt can be achieved in different ways, such as:

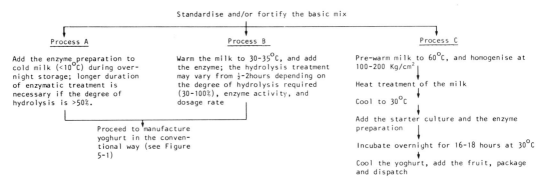

Fig. 5.5. Lactose hydrolysed yoghurt

(1) The process is referred to as
   A Low temperature hydrolysis/High incubation temperature
   B High   ,,   ,,   / ,,   ,,   ,,
   C Low   ,,   ,,   / ,,   ,,   ,,
(2) In process A & B it is essential to agitate the milk, and to adjust pH to 6.5–6.7
(3) The inactivation of the enzyme is achieved by heat treatment (Process A & B) or by the slow rate of acid development (Process C) which gradually reduces its activity; total inactivation may occur below pH 5.

After: Anon (1980, 1979b), Ismail and El-Nimr (1980), Benesova (1980), Tamime (1977, 1978), O'Leary and Woychik (1976a, b), Rossi and Terrence-Jemmet (1978), Antila, Lehto and Antila (1978), Thompson and Gyuricsek (1974), Thompson and Brower (1976), Holsinger and Guy (1974), Gyuricsek and Thompson (1976), Thomasow and Klostermeyer (1977), Woychick, Thompson and Gyuricsek (1974), Woychick and Holsinger (1977), Hilgendorf (1981).

(a) The traditional process involves the production of yoghurt from whole milk without the addition of sugar. After the incubation period, the yoghurt is stirred, cooled, and finally diluted with an equal volume of water (see Fig. 5.6). In the Middle East it is the custom to flavour this product with salt, and sometimes with flavouring extracts, e.g. mint. The product is normally bottled, and one distinctive feature of this type of drinking yoghurt is the separation of the milk solids phase from the serum or whey phase. It is customary to shake the bottle before consumption. In Turkey this product is called "Ayran".

(b) The manufacture of drinking yoghurt from a base mix of low milk solids is possible in most types of yoghurt plant. Under normal production practice the yoghurt coagulum is handled very carefully, but when drinking yoghurt is manufactured the positive pumps are replaced with centrifugal pumps to transfer the yoghurt from the incubation tanks to the coolers. Alternatively, higher speeds of agitation are used to break the coagulum after fermentation, or sometimes the cold yoghurt is passed through a homogeniser without the application of pressure. To overcome the problem of whey separation, it is necessary to incorporate a stabiliser into the basic mix, and a typical chemical composition of a drinking yoghurt might be as follows:

Fat	1–2	
Milk, solids-not-fat	9.25	
Sugar	5.5	%
Stabiliser	0.27	
Fruit syrup contains 14 % solids	5.5	

This product is sometimes heat treated, i.e. pasteurised, in order to prolong its keeping quality.

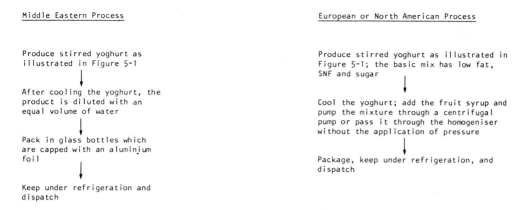

Middle Eastern Process

Produce stirred yoghurt as
illustrated in Figure 5-1

↓

After cooling the yoghurt, the
product is diluted with an
equal volume of water

↓

Pack in glass bottles which
are capped with an aluminium
foil

↓

Keep under refrigeration and
dispatch

European or North American Process

Produce stirred yoghurt as illustrated in
Figure 5-1; the basic mix has low fat,
SNF and sugar

↓

Cool the yoghurt; add the fruit syrup and
pump the mixture through a centrifugal
pump or pass it through the homogeniser
without the application of pressure

↓

Package, keep under refrigeration, and
dispatch

Fig. 5.6.   Drinking yoghurt

After: Morley (1978, 1979a, b), Lang (1980), Rousseau (1974), Rhodes (1978), Hylmar *et al.* (1979), Anon. (1979c, 1980b, 1981), Ross (1980), Klupsch (1981), Hendricus and Evers (1980), Pedersen and Poulsen (1971), Grozdova (1971), Lavrenova, Inozemtseva and Pyatnitsyna (1981), Yaygin (1980).

CONDENSED/CONCENTRATED YOGHURT

Traditionally the containers used by the nomads in the Middle East for the production of yoghurt were made from animal skin, and the yoghurt was left in these skins until it was consumed. While the yoghurt was hanging in the animal skin some of the liquid phase would have been absorbed into the skin, while some of the whey that had seeped through the skin would have been lost by evaporation. In this way concentration of the product took place, and the new product was referred to as condensed/concentrated yoghurt. This latter product would have had a better keeping quality than normal yoghurt, mainly as a result of the higher concentration of lactic acid.

Evidence of the production of condensed yoghurt can be found in Armenia where the product is called "Tan" or "Than", in Egypt "Leben Zeer", in Turkey "Torba", "Kurut" and/or "Tulum", whilst in the majority of the Arab world it is called "Labneh" or "Lebneh". For hygienic reasons the use of cloth bags rather than animal skins is now widely practised, and a typical flow sheet for the production of condensed yoghurt is illustrated in Fig. 5.7. In some countries an attempt has been made to introduce standards, e.g. Lebanon (Anon., 1965) and Jordan (Anon., 1980c), where it is stipulated that "Labneh" shall have a specific chemical composition based on fat, total solids and salt. The latter compound is basically added as a flavouring agent or in the form of and preservative, or possibly, to neutralise the "acidic" taste of the product.

According to Tamime (1977, 1978), the chemical composition of "Labneh" may vary within the following range:

Fat	9.0–10.3	
Carbohydrates	3.77–3.96	
Protein	8.8–9.0	%
Total Solids	22–26	
Lactic acid	1.6–2.5	
Salt	1	

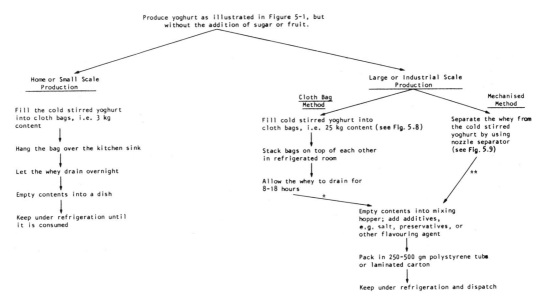

Fig. 5.7. Condensed/concentrated yoghurt

* To produce a homogenous condensed yoghurt, pass the product through a curd homogeniser.
** If no flavouring agents are added, the product is packaged directly.

After: Tamime and Robinson (1978), Yonez (1965), Robinson (1977), Zmarlicki *et al.* (1974a, b).

The large-scale manufacture of condensed yoghurt is possible either through the use of nozzle separators or alternatively in large cloth bags, i.e. containing 25 kg of yoghurt, which are piled on top of each other to assist in the removal of whey.

"Labneh" is normally consumed with bread as part of a main meal, but the possibility of promoting this product in Europe and North America has not seriously been considered. For example, the production of a dairy spread, where "Labneh" is mixed with chives, or alternatively a dairy dessert made by mixing fruit/flavours with the condensed product, could prove popular. A rather similar traditional Indian dish is called "Shirkhand", and where nutmeg and safron extract are used as flavouring agents (Ganguly, 1972).

CONCENTRATED YOGHURT-RELATED PRODUCTS

The condensed/concentrated yoghurt, i.e. "Labneh", is sometimes used as a raw material for the manufacture of some traditional dairy products popular in the Middle East. The process mainly involves extraction of more whey from the concentrated yoghurt and, in some extreme cases, the final product is dried. These traditional foods are produced from surplus milk during the spring and the summer months of the year, and are used during the winter. Examples of such products are as follow.

244

A. "Labneh Anbaris"

This type of concentrated yoghurt has a total solids content between 30–40 %, and in some instances even higher (see also Rosenthal *et al.*, 1980). The traditional process (see Fig. 5.10) starts with "Labneh" (24 % total solids), and the end-product is shaped into balls and partially sun-dried. The dried material is then placed in earthenware vessels or glass jars, and further preserved with a layer of olive oil (see Fig. 5.11). In areas where goat's and/or sheep's milk replaces cow's milk, the end-product is much stronger in flavour.

The consistency of this product resembles "Lactic Curd" cheese or "Pates Fraiches", and Davis (1971) reported a similar product called "Yoghurt Cheese"; the manufacturing process for "Yoghurt Cheese" is outlined in Fig. 5.12. In Poland, preconcentrated milk, e.g. 30–40 % total solids, is used to manufacture a product called "Super Yoghurt", and this approach could help to overcome the hygienic problems associated with the use of the cloth bags. Tamime (1981) (unpublished data) achieved a high concentration of solids in a yoghurt-type product using the cloth bag method, and in this instance ordinary yoghurt, i.e. made from whole milk fortified with

(a)

Fig. 5. 8.

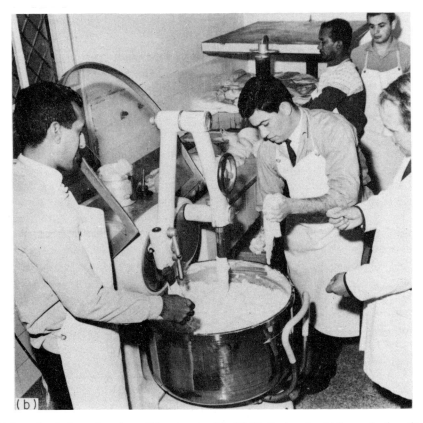

Fig. 5.8.   Dairy technologist students from different parts of the Middle East are taught the production of concentrated yoghurt 'labneh' at the FAO/UNDP dairy training center in Lebanon

(a) Special units are used for the separation of whey from natural yoghurt.
(b) The cloth bags are emptied into a special mixer in order to obtain uniform texture; notice in the right hand corner, a vertical press could be used to speed up the whey sepeartion process.
Reproduced by courtesy of UN/FAO, Rome. Italy.

skimmed-milk powder, was pressed overnight at 15 psi. The chemical composition of this product was as follows:

Total solids	31.94	
Protein	13.88	
Ash	0.92	%
Fat	12.72	
Lactose (by difference)	4.42	
pH	3.82	

B. "Chanklich"

The procedure for the manufacture of "Chanklich" is somewhat similar to that of "Labneh Anbaris" (see Fig. 5.10), and it differs only in the addition of herbs and/or spices to the highly concentrated yoghurt, i.e. 30–40 % total solids. "Chanklich" and "Labneh Anbaris" are normally consumed with bread and olive oil as appetisers, and the possibility of developing such products for markets in Europe and North America, perhaps as basic ingredients for the preparation of "cocktail dips", clearly exists.

C. "Kishk"

This product is a dry form of yoghurt–cereal mixture. It can be processed from either yoghurt or concentrated yoghurt, and in either case paraboiled wheat, known locally in Lebanon, Syria and Iraq as "Bourghoul" (Garnier, 1957; Morcos, Hagazi and El-Damhougy, 1973), is rubbed into it.

The yoghurt–wheat mixture is then shaped into rolls and placed in the sun to dry (see Fig. 5.10). The dried product is called "Kishk", and it is sold either as rolls or as a coarsely ground flour. "Kishk" (as a dish) is prepared by reconstituting the dried product with water, and then simmering the mix gently over a fire. The consistency of this product is rather similar to porridge, and it is normally consumed with bread. In some instances, flavouring agents such as chopped onion and/or chopped coriander are added to the reconstituted mix.

More recently Robinson (1978), Robinson and Cadena (1978) and Cadena and Robinson (1979) have investigated in detail the potential value of a "Kishk"-type product (see Fig. 5.13) for preserving milk protein from spoilage, and concluded that the method could prove valuable. The amino acid spectrum of the end-product was close to the FAO/WHO (1973) standard, and only

Fig. 5.9.

(b)

Fig. 5.9. Illustrations of nozzle separators used for concentration of fermented milk products

(a) Nozzle separator type MRPX 417 SGV which is installed on a Quarg processing line, and could be used to concentrate yoghurt
(Reproduced by courtesy of Alfa-Laval A/B, Lund, Sweden)

(b) A Quarg concentrator type KMA 3-06-076 which can be used for the production of concentrated yoghurt
(Reproduced by courtesy of Westfalia Separator Ltd., Milton Keynes, UK)

lysine and threonine were of limiting values. The overall chemical composition of a traditional "Kishk" (Morcos, Hegazi and El-Damhougy, *loc. cit.*) and the "Kishk"-type product (Cadena and Robinson, *loc. cit.*) is illustrated in Table 5.2.

The unusual flavour and nature of "Kishk" is widely enjoyed among the rural communities in the Middle East, but the introduction of such a mixture to other societies may be rather restricted in terms of appeal and acceptability. However, Cadena and Robinson (*loc. cit.*) conducted an experimental trial in Mexico in which a gruel-type food called "Atole" was replaced by a yoghurt–cereal product, and the yoghurt-based equivalent was readily accepted by children and mothers, especially when the product was flavoured with strawberry and vanilla extracts.

248

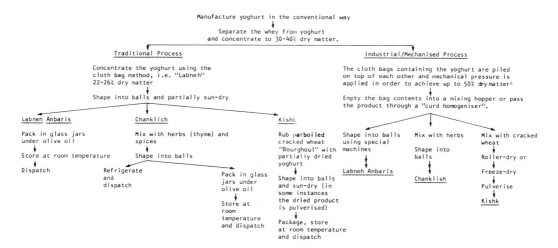

Fig. 5.10.   Concentrated (Middle Eastern) yoghurt and related products

* An alternative pre-concentration method of yoghurt is by using a nozzle separator, but the concentrated product is then filled in cloth bags for further whey separation to achieve up to 50% dry matter.

After: Morcos, Hegazi and El-Damhougy (1973), Robinson (1978), Robinson and Cadena (1978), Cadena and Robinson (1979), Anon. (1978c).

Fig. 5.11.   An illustration of the preservation of 'highly' concentrated yoghurt in olive oil

The left hand jar represents a 'highly' concentrated yoghurt manufactured from goat's milk in south of Lebanon, and the right hand jar was manufactured from cow's milk in Scotland.

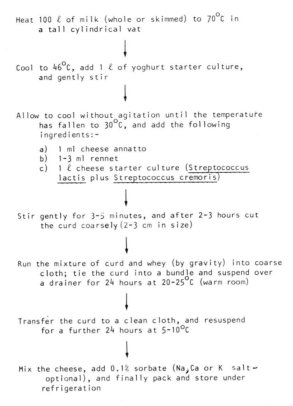

Heat 100 ℓ of milk (whole or skimmed) to 70°C in
a tall cylindrical vat

↓

Cool to 46°C, add 1 ℓ of yoghurt starter culture,
and gently stir

↓

Allow to cool without agitation until the temperature
has fallen to 30°C, and add the following
ingredients:-

a) 1 ml cheese annatto
b) 1-3 ml rennet
c) 1 ℓ cheese starter culture (Streptococcus
   lactis plus Streptococcus cremoris)

↓

Stir gently for 3-5 minutes, and after 2-3 hours cut
the curd coarsely (2-3 cm in size)

↓

Run the mixture of curd and whey (by gravity) into coarse
cloth; tie the curd into a bundle and suspend over
a drainer for 24 hours at 20-25°C (warm room)

↓

Transfer the curd to a clean cloth, and resuspend
for a further 24 hours at 5-10°C

↓

Mix the cheese, add 0.1% sorbate (Na, Ca or K salt –
optional), and finally pack and store under
refrigeration

Fig. 5.12.   Flow diagram of the production of "yoghurt cheese"

Adapted from Davis (*loc. cit.*).

It is safe to assume, therefore, that a "Flavoured Kishk" could prove to have wide acceptability among communities accustomed to gruel-type foods.

The feasibility of manufacturing the above products on an industrial scale is illustrated in Fig. 5.10, and the further development of these products for new markets will be dependent on the addition of flavours and/or the fortification of existing foods with these fermented products (see also Kosikowski, 1978).

FROZEN YOGHURT

Frozen yoghurt is classified into three main categories, soft, hard or mousse. These products resemble ice-cream in their physical state, and they are characterised simply as having the sharp, acidic taste of yoghurt combined with the coldness of ice-cream. In addition these products contain high levels of sugar and stabilisers/emulsifiers as compared with yoghurt, since these compounds are required, during the freezing process, to maintain the air-bubble structure.

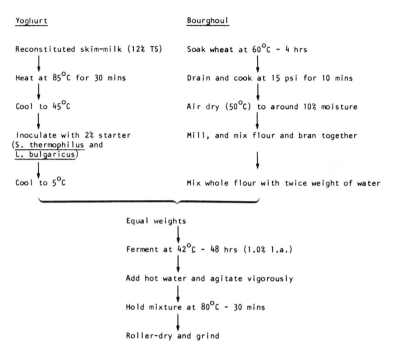

Fig. 5.13. Flow diagram of a laboratory-scale method for the manufacture a "kishk"-like product

After Robinson and Cadena (*loc. cit.*).

Reprinted with permission of *Journal of Ecology of Food and Nutrition.*

TABLE 5.2. *Comparative analysis of a traditional and an experimental "Kishk"*

| Composition | Figures expressed (%w/w) | |
	'Kishk'	'Kishk'-type
Moisture	7.8	6.0
Protein	23.5	17.1
Fat	6.9	1.7
Carbohydrate	59.0	70.6
Fibre	2.5	2.2
Ash	8.1	2.5

Adapted from Morcos, Hegazi and El-Damhougy (*loc. cit.*), Cadena and Robinson (*loc. cit.*).

The historical background of, and technical data on, frozen yoghurt has been discussed in detail by Kosikowski (1977), and Mann (1977, 1979) has compiled several international digests on frozen yoghurt; Lang (1979) has also recently reviewed the latest developments in this field. In general terms, the various stages involved in the manufacture of the different types of frozen yoghurt are similar (see Fig. 5.14), and Fig. 5.15 shows an Alfa-Laval/Hoyer flow chart of the equipment required for production. Basically, the process consists of mixing cold, natural stirred yoghurt with the cold fruit syrup base, stabilisers/emulsifiers and sugar (the latter ingredients are added hot for the manufacture of mousse yoghurt—see Fig. 5.14), then freezing the mix in a conventional ice-cream freezer. The chemical composition of the yoghurt/fruit mix and the temperature during storage can ultimately affect the physical characteristics of these frozen yoghurt products, and Table 5.3 illustrates some suggested formulae for their manufacture; the recommended percentages of yoghurt and fruit range from 65–80 to 20–35% respectively (see Fig. 5.14).

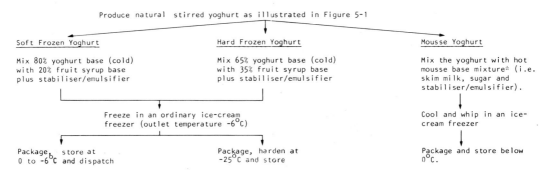

Fig. 5.14.   Frozen yoghurt

* The mousse base mixture must be well blended, heated and properly homogenised.

After: Anon. (1977d, 1978b, 1979d), Chandan (1977), Redfern and Rizk (1979), Kankare and Antila (1980), Hulsbusch (1980), Igoe (1979a), Rhodes (*loc. cit.*), Bray (1981), Kurmann (1969), Crisp and John (1969), Ziemba (1971), Gautneb, Steinsholt and Abrahamsen (1979), Hekmati and Bradley (1979), Kosikowski (1981), Bradley and Hekmati (1981), Miles and Leeder (1981).

Although the procedures for manufacture are well established, the following recommendations may help to eliminate defects in frozen yoghurt:

(a) Ensure that the fruit syrup base is pasteurised and, except in the case of mousse yoghurt, cold prior to its addition to the yoghurt.

(b) Gentle mixing of the yoghurt and fruit syrup base should be observed, since vigorous agitation can lead to loss of the refreshing taste in the frozen yoghurt.

(c) A longer shelf-life for frozen yoghurt can be achieved if the air at the whipping/freezing stage is replaced by nitrogen (Jochumsen, 1978; Anon., 1977c).

(d) The normal sweetening agent, e.g. sugar and/or corn syrup, of the fruit base can be replaced by lactose hydrolysed whey (Aries, 1977, 1978).

(e) Mousse yoghurt without sugar cannot be stored at $<0°$ C, since whey syneresis can occur upon thawing and a partial collapse of the foam.

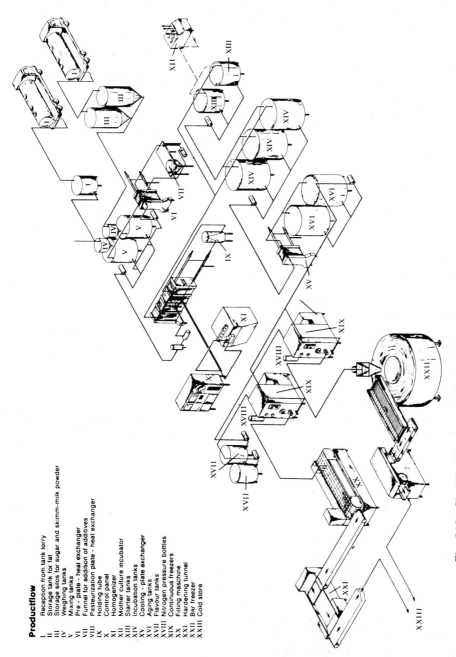

Productflow

I	Reception from tank lorry
II	Storage tank for fat
III	Storage silos for sugar and skimm-milk powder
IV	Weighing tanks
V	Mixing tanks
VI	Pre - plate - heat exchanger
VII	Funnel for addition of additives
VIII	Pasteurization plate - heat exchanger
IX	Holding tube
X	Control panel
XI	Homogenizer
XII	Mother culture incubator
XIII	Starter tanks
XIV	Incubation tanks
XV	Cooling - plate exchanger
XVI	Aging tanks
XVII	Flavour tanks
XVIII	Nitrogen pressure bottles
XIX	Continuous freezers
XX	Filling maschine
XXI	Hardening tunnel
XXII	Bar freezer
XXIII	Cold store

Fig. 5.15. Simplified flowchart of Alfa-Laval/Hoyer system for the production of frozen yoghurt

Reproduced by courtesy of Alfa-Laval A/B, Lund, Sweden

TABLE 5.3. *Suggested chemical composition (%) of yoghurt/fruit mix for the manufacture of frozen yoghurt*

Ingredients	Soft frozen yoghurt	Hard frozen yoghurt	Mousse yoghurt
Fat	2–6	2–6	3
Milk solids-not-fat	5–10	5–14	12
Sugar	8–20	8–16	8
Stabilisers/emulsifier	0.2–1.0	0.2–1.0	2.4
% Over-run	50–60	70–80	90

Adapted from: Anon. (1977c, e), Mitten (1977), Collins (1977), Bradley and Winder (1977), Anon. (1978a).

These frozen products are normally consumed while they are still frozen, but attempts have been made to freeze the normal flavoured stirred yoghurt for the freezer market; i.e. the intention is that the product shall be first thawed and then consumed.

Whey syneresis and/or the separation of the two phases of milk may occur, but the addition of stabilisers/emulsifiers can help to reduce this fault to some extent.

CARBONATED YOGHURT

Carbonated soft drinks are extremely popular worldwide, and according to Duitschaever and Ketcheson (1974) carbonation of a yoghurt beverage (flavoured with natural orange, lemon, cherry or apple flavour) has the following effects:

(a) it improves the thirst quenching quality and refreshing taste of ordinary yoghurt; and
(b) it causes a nice tingling sensation on the tongue.

Carbonated yoghurt can be manufactured either in a liquid or in a dry form. The former type is, in effect, a carbonated, flavoured drinking yoghurt, while the dry mix gradually releases the carbon dioxide (CO_2) when the powder is reconstituted with water. The differences in the manufacturing stages between the liquid and the dry type of carbonated yoghurt are illustrated in Fig. 5.16, and Schenk (1980) has reported the following advantages when using certain carbonates:

(a) the presence of metal carbonates in the mix tends to neutralise the acid in the yoghurt, so that carbonated yoghurt is less acidic and has a pH around 7;
(b) although different types of metal carbonates could be used, the addition of calcium carbonate rather than sodium carbonate is more advantageous; the former compound tends to dissolve at a slower rate in water, and so releases gradually the CO_2 into the reconstituted product—otherwise, the carbonated yoghurt tends to go flat within a very short period of time;
(c) the addition of various types of calcium compound(s) to the dried mix improves the opacity of the carbonated yoghurt, since the calcium reacts with various acids to form insoluble salts.

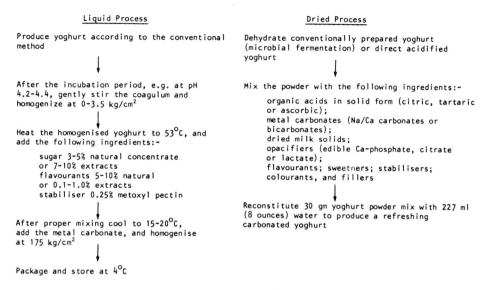

Liquid Process

Produce yoghurt according to the conventional method

↓

After the incubation period, e.g. at pH 4.2-4.4, gently stir the coagulum and homogenize at 0-3.5 kg/cm²

↓

Heat the homogenised yoghurt to 53°C, and add the following ingredients:-

    sugar 3-5% natural concentrate
    or 7-10% extracts
    flavourants 5-10% natural
    or 0.1-1.0% extracts
    stabiliser 0.25% metoxyl pectin

↓

After proper mixing cool to 15-20°C, add the metal carbonate, and homogenise at 175 kg/cm²

↓

Package and store at 4°C

Dried Process

Dehydrate conventionally prepared yoghurt (microbial fermentation) or direct acidified yoghurt

↓

Mix the powder with the following ingredients:-

    organic acids in solid form (citric, tartaric or ascorbic);
    metal carbonates (Na/Ca carbonates or bicarbonates);
    dried milk solids;
    opacifiers (edible Ca-phosphate, citrate or lactate);
    flavourants; sweetners; stabilisers; colourants, and fillers

↓

Reconstitute 30 gm yoghurt powder mix with 227 ml (8 ounces) water to produce a refreshing carbonated yoghurt

Fig. 5.16. Carbonated yoghurt

After: Schenk (*loc. cit.*), Duitschaever and Ketcheson (*loc. cit.*).

YOGHURT BEVERAGES

The fermentation of milk by lactic acid bacteria and yeasts is widely used in East Europe and Russia for the manufacture of Kefir and Koumiss, and this type of fermentation releases lactic acid, alcohol, carbon dioxide and aromatic flavouring compounds into the product. More recently a process has been developed for the Japanese market in which a yeast, e.g. genus *Kloeckera*, is precultured in the milk before the production of yoghurt. The milk is then sterilised, cooled to incubation temperature, and finally inoculated with a mixed culture of *S. thermophilus* and *L. bulgaricus*. Details of the process are illustrated in Fig. 5.17, and the yoghurt beverage has the following characteristics:

(a) It contains aromatic flavouring compounds produced by the yeast, but no alcohol or gas.
(b) It contains a higher viable cell count of *S. thermophilus* and *L. bulgaricus* than conventional yoghurt, since the yeast metabolites enhance the activity of the starter culture.
(c) The beverage does not suffer from whey separation.

A rather different Bulgarian beverage, which is specially formulated for the market in Russia, consists of 35–54 % yoghurt, 20–40 % natural fruit or vegetable puree, 28–30 % syrup plus apple

Pre-culture milk (skim or full cream) plus
2-3% sucrose with yeast (genus *Kloeckera*) at
25-30°C for 15-20 hours

↓

Sterilise the milk at 100°C for 30 minutes

↓

Cool to 35°C and inoculate with yoghurt starter
culture; incubate at the same temperature until
the acidity reaches 0.8-1.0% lactic acid

↓

Cool the coagulum, add green tea syrup*,
and mix gently

↓

Homogenise the mixture at 100 kg/cm^2

↓

Package and store under refrigeration

Fig. 5.17. Yoghurt beverage

* The syrup consists of sugar, green tea powder and water in the ratio of 27:1:12 respectively

After Kuwabara (1970).

pectin and 0.1–0.2 % citric acid. The mixture is homogenised, sterilised at 120–130°C for 50–70 seconds, cooled and packaged (Arolski *et al.*, 1979), but the popularity of the product, particularly against a wider market, has not been tested.

DRIED/INSTANT YOGHURT

The primary objective of manufacturing yoghurt in a powder form is to store milk in a stable and readily utilisable form. The first attempts to produce dried yoghurt were aimed towards the do-it-yourself consumer market, but the reconstituted yoghurt lacked a high viable cell count of starter culture organisms, as well as the pleasant taste, firm body/texture, and attractive appearance of ordinary yoghurt. Over the past two decades, however, there has been a considerable effort made to improve the quality of dried yoghurt, and in general the powder forms are now divided into two different types. In the first type, the reconstituted yoghurt is incubated for a few hours to allow the coagulation process to take place, while in the second type the gel is formed within a very short period of time—the so-called "Instant Yoghurt".

Basically there are two methods of drying that could be employed for the manufacture of dried yoghurt, e.g. spray-drying or freeze-drying, and although the latter method of drying would seem the more attractive—the temperature of drying (20–35°C) is much lower than with spray drying (55–60°C) so ultimately causing the least damage to the milk constituents, and/or loss of flavour— it is far too expensive to be considered on a commercial scale. However, a selection of methods for the production of dried yoghurt are illustrated in Table 5.4. It is evident, of course, that the

TABLE 5.4. *A selection of methods employed for the manufacture of dried "instant" yoghurt*

Method	Additional information	References

Mix the following ingredients ($\%$ w/w):
 	
9–50 vacuum dried yoghurt starter culture
20–50 instant skim milk powder
10–25 cooked and dried starch
10–25 dextrose
    5 Na-alginate
    2 Ca-acetate
up to 2.5 citric acid
    19 vegetable oil
0.5 tetra-sodium hypophosphate
	Instant thick yoghurt is obtained by mixing 66 g powder with 285 ml of water; flavouring extracts could also be incorporated into the dry mix.	Ferguson (1963)

Concentrate milk to 45–48$\%$ total solids, and homogenise at 100–150 kg/cm²; cool to 45°C, add 10–15$\%$ active yoghurt starter culture, stir vigorously and spray dry at 55–60°C (in the drying zone); cool and package in 250 g composite containers.	This is a factory-scale process, and the product is supplied to the extreme northern areas of Russia and Central Asia.	Mazaleva and Gugin (1966)
Stir yoghurt to a homogeneous consistency, freeze at minus 20–40°C within 15–30 minutes and dry for 2–4 hours; cool and package the product in glass and/or polythene containers in an atmosphere of nitrogen.	The creamery powder is dispersed easily in cold water; the acetaldehyde level is reduced by 75$\%$ during the processing.	Vitez (1968)
Freeze 100 ml of yoghurt in 500 ml bottle by rolling in a bath of acetone and dry ice; dry at 30°C for 12 hours, and to final moisture content of 1$\%$.	Rehydrate the natural plain yoghurt at 30°C; the product is improved by incubation at 42°C for 3–6 hours; fruit flavoured yoghurt is virtually the same as original product (with slight reduction in viscosity) when assessed organoleptically.	Gavin (1969)
Freeze yoghurt at minus 20–25°C; dry under vacuum at 30–35°C; cool and package the white powder in 20 g sachets.	Reconstitute sachet contents in 200 ml water or milk to produce "yoghurt".	Chamay (1967)
Freeze stirred yoghurt by spraying into a freezing chamber; the frozen droplets of yoghurt are carried to a drying chamber by conveyor belt; drying time approx. 1 minute.	Comparative costing against freeze-drying and spray drying is illustrated.	Charon (1968)
Propagate yoghurt starter culture in sterile milk at 37°C for 6 hours, and then inoculate a nutrient medium which is aerated, shaken for 15 hours and continuously neutralised and maintained at pH 5 with Na-acetate; the bulk is halved and each portion is centrifuged aseptically.	"Yoghurt" is obtained by mixing the final powder with water.	Simon and Devallerie (1968)

257

TABLE 5.4 (Contd.)

Method	Additional information	References
Portion A *Portion B* 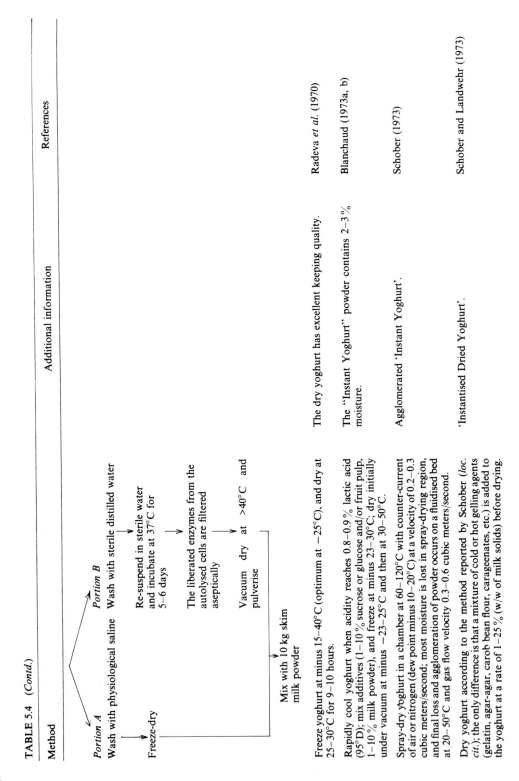 Wash with physiological saline Wash with sterile distilled water Freeze-dry Re-suspend in sterile water and incubate at 37°C for 5–6 days The liberated enzymes from the autolysed cells are filtered aseptically Vacuum dry at >40°C and pulverise Mix with 10 kg skim milk powder		
Freeze yoghurt at minus 15–40°C (optimum at −25°C), and dry at 25–30°C for 9–10 hours.	The dry yoghurt has excellent keeping quality.	Radeva *et al.* (1970)
Rapidly cool yoghurt when acidity reaches 0.8–0.9% lactic acid (95°D); mix additives (1–10% sucrose or glucose and/or fruit pulp, 1–10% milk powder), and freeze at minus 23–30°C; dry initially under vacuum at minus −23–25°C and then at 30–50°C.	The "Instant Yoghurt" powder contains 2–3% moisture.	Blanchaud (1973a, b)
Spray-dry yoghurt in a chamber at 60–120°C with counter-current of air or nitrogen (dew point minus 10–20°C) at a velocity of 0.2–0.3 cubic meters/second; most moisture is lost in spray-drying region, and final loss and agglomeration of powder occurs on a fluidised bed at 20–50°C and gas flow velocity 0.3–0.6 cubic meters/second.	Agglomerated 'Instant Yoghurt'.	Schober (1973)
Dry yoghurt according to the method reported by Schober (*loc. cit.*); the only difference is that a mixture of cold or hot gelling agents (gelatin, agar-agar, carob bean flour, carageenates, etc.) is added to the yoghurt at a rate of 1–25% (w/w of milk solids) before drying.	'Instantised Dried Yoghurt'.	Schober and Landwehr (1973)

TABLE 5.4 (*Contd.*)

Method	Additional information	References
Freeze-dry Bulgarian yoghurt which contains a special strain of *L. bulgaricus* 236 and *S. thermophilus*; the survival rate after drying is 40% and 73.4% respectively.	The dry product has good keeping quality and dietetic value; its composition is as follows:— Dry matter 95.40 Protein 29.80 Lactose 33.9 % Fat 15.1 Mineral 6.6 Lactic acid 6.0	Vitanov, Nikolov and Boydasheva (1973)
Concentrate pasteurised/homogenised milk (skim and/or standardised) to 35–45% dry matter. *Portion A* (70–80%) *Portion B* (20–30%) Add sugar and dry by conventional method Dilute the concentrated milk to 21% dry matter with sterile water or pasteurised milk Inoculate with yoghurt starter culture and incubate at 42°C; at pH 4.4, homogenise the mix and cool to 10–15°C Dry the yoghurt by conventional method Mix the two powders together; add an acid compound which is coated with an edible fat, emulsifier, colour and aroma.	Reconstitute 13.5 g powder with 86.5 ml water at 10–40°C, and in 10 minutes—2 hours, the re-hydrated yohurt regains its natural consistency.	Bohrn (1974). Anon. (1973a, b)
Mix the following ingredients (% w/w):— 11.5 yoghurt, 11.5 skim milk powder, 0.1% lactobacilli culture (dried), 5.2 Na-alginate, 1.6 sequestring agent, 69.2 dispersing agent (sugar), 0.5% flavouring agent and 0.1% colouring agent.	Instant Yoghurt an reconstitution with water.	Schur (1978)

(Continued)

TABLE 5.4 (*Contd.*)

Method	Additional information	References
Mix the following ingredients (g):	Dissolve the mix (41.75 g) in 200 ml milk (2.8 % fat) for 4 minutes, and allow to stand at room temperature for 45 minutes to produce a "Yoghurt-like" product.	Trop (1980)
25 sugar		
10 glucone delta lactone		
2 calcium phosphate		
{ precooked starch Redisol 88		
1 { freeze dried natural yoghurt		
{ Tween 60 coated on sugar		
{ monosodium citrate		
0.5 { sodium alginate (Kelton)		
{ fruit flavour		
0.15 yoghurt flavour		
0.1 colour		
Blend the following ingredients (dry weight basis):	Mix in a blender 28 g of the blended ingredients with 8 fluid ounces (US) of cold milk (1–1.5 % fat) to produce instant yoghurt drink.	Cajigas (1981a, b)
0.03 freeze dried yoghurt starter culture		
25.69 dried yoghurt		
20.16 acid whey		
0.83 citric acid		
25.19 fructose		
1.52 locust bean gum		
0.51 tricalcium phosphate		
1.01 lecithin		
20.16 sucrose		
1.25 carboxymethyl cellulose		
2.93 dried fruit		
0.63 flavours		

"instant" formation of the yoghurt gel, after rehydration of some powders, relies entirely on the presence of starch and/or other hydrocolloidal compounds rather than on the acid destabilising the casein to form the coagulum.

Such types of "yoghurt" have a different mouth-feel due to the excessive presence of stabilising compounds, and this difference could prove a limiting factor in terms of acceptability. However, alternative outlets for dried yoghurt may include:

(a) Reconstitution of the powder to 24% total solids for the production of concentrated yoghurt, e.g. "Labneh".
(b) Hill (1974) reported the addition of yoghurt (in liquid form) to dough in the manufacture of baked goods, and it could be advantageous to the bakers to use the dried form since they are more familiar with handling dry ingredients (see also Flückiger, 1973).
(c) The results of field trials on poultry feeding with dried yoghurt as compared with skim milk powder favoured the former product, due either to an increased availability of nutrients, i.e. metabolisable energy (ME) and gross protein value (GPV), or to a reduction in the amount of lactose (Simhaee and Keshavarz, 1974).
(d) Products, such as yoghurt flavoured wafers and chocolates with "yoghurt flavour inners", have appeared on the market in Europe and North America, and the manufacturers of such products may prefer to use dried yoghurt in their process.
(e) Dried yoghurt can also be used for the manufacture of "Yoghurt Flavoured Candy" (Peterson, 1979).

DIETETIC/THERAPEUTIC YOGHURT

The overall nutritive value of yoghurt is well established (see Chapter 9), but special types of yoghurts are often manufactured for dietetic and/or therapeutic purposes. The fact that most strains of *L. bulgaricus* and *S. thermophilus* do not survive in the intestinal tract may be a limiting factor if yoghurt is used for antibiotic therapy and/or any other medicinal purpose. However, although the incorporation of *L. acidophilus* and *Bifidobacterium bifidum* into the yoghurt starter culture may contravene some existing definitions of yoghurt, the resultant milk product is reported to be "of excellent therapeutic value". Mann (1978) has recently reviewed some of these products, and Table 5.5 illustrates the wide range of yoghurts that have been developed for medicine. For example, the low lactose yoghurt is beneficial for lactose-intolerant patients; the addition of different vitamins to yoghurt improves its nutritive value (see also Primatesta, 1981); the low calorie yoghurt is attractive to diet conscious consumers; cholesterol-free yoghurt could also be beneficial for certain coronary conditions; the "Yoghurt Tablet" is a specially developed, sugarless confectionary product for patients who suffer from diabetes.

It is evident, however, that the potential value of yoghurt in medicinal therapy is limited at the present time, and furthermore, that the financial rewards to industry will be dependent on the response and back-up of the medical profession.

DIRECT ACIDIFICATION OF MILK

The addition of organic acids (ascorbic, acetic, fumaric, malic, lactic, tartaric, citric, succinic, oxalic and phosphoric) to milk can result in the formation of a coagulum at pH <4.6. The end-

TABLE 5.5. *A selection of different types of dietetic/therapeutic yoghurts manufactured for medicinal purposes*

Method	Additional information	References
The milk fat in the basic mix is replaced with unsaturated oil (corn, cotton seed, coconut or soybean) at a rate of 1.5–6.4%; produce yoghurt as illustrated in Fig. 5.1.	"Cholesterol-free Yoghurt"	Metzger (1962b)
Produce yoghurt by the conventional method; before the addition of the starter culture, mix orange extract with the milk; the extract contains a high level of vitamin C in the form of Na-ascorbate, and it is claimed that in a 227 g pot of yoghurt the vitamin C content is not less than 30 mg.	"Vitamin C Enriched Yoghurt" "Vitana Yoghurt" contains 9 vitamins, and 1 cup of yoghurt covers the daily requirements of one person	Metzger (1962a) Anon. (1977f)
Manufacture yoghurt from milk, i.e. 9% solids-not-fat, 1% fat, 0.5–1.0% stabiliser (caragenan and gelatin at a ratio of 1:1); the calorific value of such natural/plain yoghurt is 170 kJ/100 g as compared with traditional yoghurt 250–335 kg/100 g (about 420 kg/100 g in fruit flavoured yoghurt).	"Low Calorie Yoghurt"	Grabs (1979)
Dilute yoghurt (low fat) with an additive which contains vegetable infusion containing vinegar, lactic acid and condiments.	*Ibid*	Munk (1980)
Add 15% wheat bran to milk before incubation with yoghurt starter culture; this yoghurt contains 200–395 mg glucose/100 ml due to the hydrolysis of the lactose by β-D-galactosidase which is present in the wheat bran; the presence of bran affected the growth of *L. bulgaricus*, but this type of yoghurt is beneficial because of its fibre content.	"Wheat Bran Yoghurt"	Costamagna and Rossi (1980)
Prepare yoghurt as illustrated in Fig. 5.1, but with the starter culture composed of the following organisms: *L. acidophilus, B. bifidium, L. bulgaricus* and *S. thermophilus*; in some instances the former two organisms are of "intestinal strains", and *B. bifidium* causes an increase in free amino acids due to its proteolytic activity.	"Antibiotic Therapy Yoghurt" or "Biograde" or "Bioghurt"	Kiza, Zbikowski and Kolenda (1974), Anon. (1974), Anon. (1977g), Rossi, Costamagna and Ingi (1978)
Concentrate standardised milk (1.6% fat) to 22–25% total solids; produce yoghurt, and at acidity 0.85–0.95% lactic acid (95–105°T) spray-dry with an inlet air temperature of 210–220°C to 3–4% moisture; the dried product contains 14–15% fat, 31–32% protein, 39–40 lactose, 6.5–7.0% minerals and 3.7–4% lactic acid.	"Biolacton" is reconstituted at a rate of 11 g/100 ml and acidity 0.4–0.45% lactic acid (45–50°T) for infant feeding.	Ivanov *et al.* (1973)
Concentrate by ultrafiltration the protein in skim-milk to 20%; dilute with water to 3.3–4.6% and standardise with cream to 1.3–2.6% fat; yoghurt produced from such milk had a lactose content of 0.3–0.6%; bitterness occurred after one week in storage; an alternative method is to hydrolyse the lactose in the milk before processing.	"Low Lactose Yoghurt"	Kosikowski (1979)

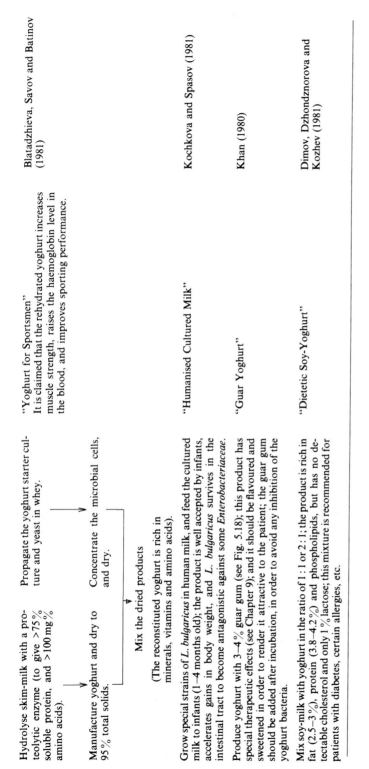

Hydrolyse skim-milk with a proteolytic enzyme (to give >75% soluble protein, and >100 mg% amino acids).

Propagate the yoghurt starter culture and yeast in whey.

Manufacture yoghurt and dry to 95% total solids.

Concentrate the microbial cells, and dry.

Mix the dried products

(The reconstituted yoghurt is rich in minerals, vitamins and amino acids).

"Yoghurt for Sportsmen"
It is claimed that the rehydrated yoghurt increases muscle strength, raises the haemoglobin level in the blood, and improves sporting performance.

Blatadzhieva, Savov and Batinov (1981)

Grow special strains of *L. bulgaricus* in human milk, and feed the cultured milk to infants (1–4 months old); the product is well accepted by infants, accelerates gains in body weight, and *L. bulgaricus* survives in the intestinal tract to become antagonistic against some *Enterobacteriaceae.*

"Humanised Cultured Milk"

Kochkova and Spasov (1981)

Produce yoghurt with 3–4% guar gum (see Fig. 5.18); this product has special therapeutic effects (see Chapter 9); and it should be flavoured and sweetened in order to render it attractive to the patient; the guar gum should be added after incubation, in order to avoid any inhibition of the yoghurt bacteria.

"Guar Yoghurt"

Khan (1980)

Mix soy-milk with yoghurt in the ratio of 1:1 or 2:1; the product is rich in fat (2.5–3%), protein (3.8–4.2%) and phospholipids, but has no detectable cholesterol and only 1% lactose; this mixture is recommended for patients with diabetes, certain allergies, etc.

"Dietetic Soy-Yoghurt"

Dimov, Dzhondznorova and Kozhev (1981)

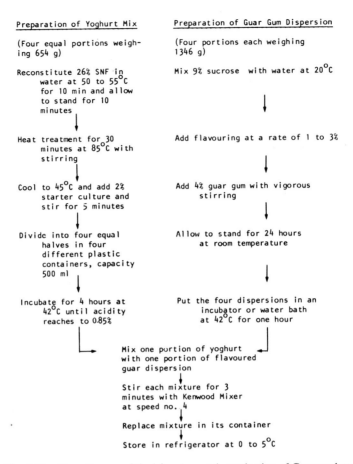

Preparation of Yoghurt Mix

(Four equal portions weighing 654 g)

Reconstitute 26% SNF in water at 50 to 55°C for 10 min and allow to stand for 10 minutes

↓

Heat treatment for 30 minutes at 85°C with stirring

↓

Cool to 45°C and add 2% starter culture and stir for 5 minutes

↓

Divide into four equal halves in four different plastic containers, capacity 500 ml

↓

Incubate for 4 hours at 42°C until acidity reaches to 0.85%

Preparation of Guar Gum Dispersion

(Four portions each weighing 1346 g)

Mix 9% sucrose with water at 20°C

↓

Add flavouring at a rate of 1 to 3%

↓

Add 4% guar gum with vigorous stirring

↓

Allow to stand for 24 hours at room temperature

↓

Put the four dispersions in an incubator or water bath at 42°C for one hour

Mix one portion of yoghurt with one portion of flavoured guar dispersion

↓

Stir each mixture for 3 minutes with Kenwood Mixer at speed no. 4

↓

Replace mixture in its container

↓

Store in refrigerator at 0 to 5°C

Fig. 5.18. Flow diagram of the laboratory-scale production of Guar yoghurt

The end product (each 250 gm serving containing 10 gm of guar gum) could be deep-frozen with no noticeable effect on quality, and hence it provided a convenient vehicle for introducing this particular non-absorbable carbohydrate into a diet

After: Khan (*loc. cit.*).

product is referred to as "Direct Acidified Yoghurt", and while it resembles yoghurt in its appearance, delicate gel, body and texture, it lacks the typical aroma, flavour and the therapeutic qualities of "cultured" yoghurt. The procedure for the manufacture of "Direct Acidified Yoghurt" is illustrated in Fig. 5.19, and it is included in this section merely for comparison. The principles of this technique are discussed in a patent (Edwards, 1969).

SOY-MILK YOGHURT

Due to the current world-wide shortage of food, attempts have been made to find alternative sources of protein, particularly for the developing countries where malnutrition exists. Since the

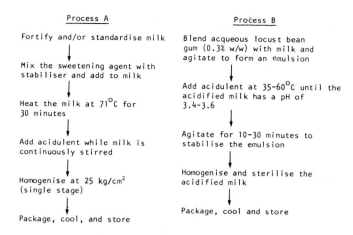

Fig. 5.19. Direct acidified yoghurt

1) Suggested formula (%w/w): milk 80–98, sweetner 0–18, acidulent 0.5–1.2, and stabiliser 1.8–4.5.
2) Examples of sweetness are:— sucrose, fructose, lactose, maltose, invert sugar, glucose and/or corn syrup.
3) The stabiliser blend could be a mixture of:— waxy maize, tapioca, Na-carboxymethylcellulose (CMC), xanthan gum and locust bean gum.

Adapted from: Igoe (1979b), Takahata (1980), Morgan, Andersen & Mook (1970).

soybean is plentiful, relatively inexpensive, and rich in protein (see Table 5.6), some effort has been devoted to exploiting it for the manufacture of more acceptable and palatable food products. Thus the main objections to soybean products by the consumer are associated with the beany flavour, and the phenomenon of flatulence (i.e. production of carbon dioxide, hydrogen and methane by the intestinal flora during the breakdown and/or metabolism of oligosaccharides present in the soybean). It is possible these problems can, of course, be overcome by various processing techniques and/or fermentations, and two current approaches to the production of fermented food(s) are: firstly, the use of soy-milk for the manufacture of a yoghurt-like product, and secondly, the extension of mammalian milk with soy extracts for the manufacture of yoghurt.

Table 5.6. *Comparative chemical analysis (%) of soy-milk and cow's milk*

Component	Soy-milk	Cow's milk*
Protein	3.58	3.48
Fat	1.90	3.98
Carbohydrate	2.84	4.77
Ash	0.43	0.75
Water	91.25	87.02

* Annual average composition (October 1980 – September 1981) of 146 Friesian Cows at the Crichton Royal Farm of the West of Scotland Agricultural College

After: Angeles and Marth (1971), Ferns (1981).

The production of yoghurt from soy-milk has been recently evaluated by Pinthong, Macrae and Rothwell (1980a, b) and Pinthong, Macrae and Dick (1980) (see also Fig. 5.20), and they concluded that:

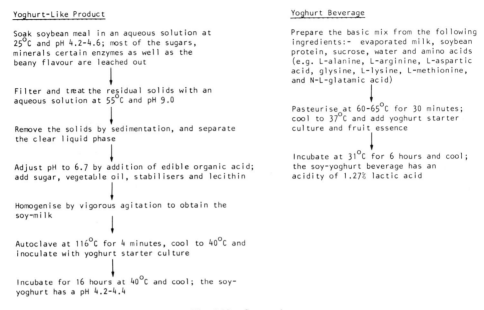

Yoghurt-Like Product

Soak soybean meal in an aqueous solution at 25°C and pH 4.2–4.6; most of the sugars, minerals certain enzymes as well as the beany flavour are leached out

↓

Filter and treat the residual solids with an aqueous solution at 55°C and pH 9.0

↓

Remove the solids by sedimentation, and separate the clear liquid phase

↓

Adjust pH to 6.7 by addition of edible organic acid; add sugar, vegetable oil, stabilisers and lecithin

↓

Homogenise by vigorous agitation to obtain the soy-milk

↓

Autoclave at 116°C for 4 minutes, cool to 40°C and inoculate with yoghurt starter culture

↓

Incubate for 16 hours at 40°C and cool; the soy-yoghurt has a pH 4.2–4.4

Yoghurt Beverage

Prepare the basic mix from the following ingredients:- evaporated milk, soybean protein, sucrose, water and amino acids (e.g. L-alanine, L-arginine, L-aspartic acid, glysine, L-lysine, L-methionine, and N-L-glatamic acid)

↓

Pasteurise at 60–65°C for 30 minutes; cool to 37°C and add yoghurt starter culture and fruit essence

↓

Incubate at 31°C for 6 hours and cool; the soy-yoghurt beverage has an acidity of 1.27% lactic acid

Fig. 5.20.   Soy-yoghurt

Adapted from: Fridman (1976), Yamanaka *et al.* (1969).

(a) using *L. bulgaricus* alone, an acceptable yoghurt-like product can be manufactured from soy-milk;

(b) optimum quality of the fermented product was observed at around 1.15% lactic acid, which resulted in the formation of a homogeneous, firm curd without whey separation, and an improved flavour as compared with soy-milk;

(c) the flavour of fermented soy-milk was directly related to the levels of n-pentanal and n-hexanal; *S. thermophilus* produces the former compound, while n-hexanal is naturally present in soy-milk;

(d) the reduction in the level of oligosaccharides was insignificant.

An example of the alternative approach is the fortification of cow's or buffalo's milk with soy extract (basically protein) for the manufacture of Zabadi (this is an Egyptian-type yoghurt). This introduction of soy-protein into the basic mix was aimed at alleviating the existing shortage of mammalian milk in Egypt, and when Abou-Donia, El-Soda and Mashaly (1980) evaluated the quality of this Zabadi they concluded that:

(a) the level of acidity, total nitrogen and volatile acids increased gradually, in both cow's and buffalo's milk, as the level of soy extract was raised from 10–50% (w/v);

(b) in general, the organoleptic assessment of these "soy" yoghurts was, in terms of body and texture, appearance and acidity, similar to the controls, but the major difference was in the flavour; a score of only 25 points out of 45 was recorded for Zabadi with 10 % soy extract, as against 40 for the control (no soy extract added);

(c) the use of soy extract concentrations above 10 % imparted a beany flavour which was not accepted by the taste panel;

(d) the method used for the preparation of the soy extract in this study could not be recommended, since other methods can eliminate the beany flavour altogether.

The fortification of cow's milk with oilseed proteins (peanut flour, soy protein isolate and cotton seed flour) for the manufacture of yoghurt and Zabadi has been evaluated recently by Schmidt *et al.* (1980) and El-Soda *et al.* (1979). They observed that the texture of the yoghurt coagulum was improved by heating the fortified milk to 90°C as compared to $\geqslant 85°$C for cow's milk fortified with skim-milk powder, and the addition of stabilisers was recommended, in particular, for milk with added peanut flour. However, the addition of high levels of cotton seed flour produced a yoghurt with a salty flavour, weak texture, yellow discoloration and slow acid production by the yoghurt organisms, and it is clear that the preparation of these oilseed proteins will have to be improved to overcome some of these drawbacks.

CONTINUOUS YOGHURT PRODUCTION

In practice, the expression the "continuous" production of set and/or stirred yoghurt is taken literally to mean the continuous flow of coagulated milk, and this can be achieved by employing a high degree of mechanisation and an appropriate plant design. For example, if a series of incubation chambers and/or fermentation tanks are used at regular intervals, the result is, in effect, a continuous production of set and/or stirred yoghurt. However, this constant flow of yoghurt should not really be termed "Continuous Yoghurt Production", since the product is still manufactured in synchronised batches, and there is almost always some variability in the quality of the end-product.

In theory, therefore, "Continuous Yoghurt Production" should only refer to a process in which the raw material (milk) is steadily and continuously transformed into a coagulum (yoghurt). One of the earliest processes reported for the continuous production of set yoghurt was the method designed by Ueno *et al.* (1966). In this system the inoculated milk is filled into glass bottles, and the stacked crates, which hold the bottles, are placed on a cradle suspended from an overhead conveyor system. The distance between successive cradles is 60 cm, and the rate of production per hour is dependent on the speed of the conveyor, e.g. 14,000 or 18,500 (app.) bottles of yoghurt at speeds of 1.2 or 1.54 metres per minute respectively. These cradles pass through the incubation chamber in a zig-zag manner up to five layers high and after a certain duration (depending on the rate of acid development and the incubation temperature) the cradles pass through a chilling room (air temperature at minus 5°C) which cools the yoghurt to 20°C; and final cooling takes place in the cold store. Hansen (1977) described a similar process used in Belgium where special trolleys (each holding 153 trays of cups filled with inoculated milk) are driven by a conveyor belt through the incubation tunnel. At pH 4.5, the yoghurt is passed to an adjacent tunnel which cools the yoghurt from 38°C to 15°C; final cooling takes place in the cold store. Incidentally, the cooling tunnel is divided into four sections, and the temperature of the cold air in circulation is successively decreased, i.e. starting at 8–10°C and finishing at 4–5°C. Other continuous systems have been reviewed by Rasic (1975).

A continuous process for the manufacture of stirred yoghurt is rather more complex than the systems mentioned above, but in 1965 Girginov developed a semi-continuous process for the production of set yoghurt in batches, and the basic principle of his technique—a two-stage fermentation—was later developed for a completely continuous process for the production of stirred yoghurt. The original Girginov method consisted of the following steps:

(a) prepare the yoghurt milk, i.e. fortify, heat-treat and cool;
(b) at 46–48°C, inoculate the milk with uncooled yoghurt starter culture (42°C);
(c) incubate the bulk until acidity reaches 0.23–0.27% lactic acid (10–12°SH);
(d) maintain a continuous prefermentation process by the constant addition of pasteurised milk at 46–48°C, and by simultaneously discharging an equal volume; thus the volume of milk and the acidity (0.23–0.27% lactic acid always remains constant;
(e) cool the prefermented milk to 32–33°C, fill into containers and incubate to the desired acidity;
(f) cool the yoghurt to 5–6°C, store and dispatch.

During the early seventies, a research team at the Netherland Institute for Dairy Research (NIZO) developed a continuous yoghurt making process based on the same two-stage fermentation, i.e. the prefermentation (pH-stat) stage followed by the coagulum formation (plug-flow fermentor) stage. A flow diagram of this process is illustrated in Fig. 5.21, and the recommended conditions for a laboratory and a pilot-scale plant operation have been well documented by Driessen, Ubbels and Stadhouders (1977a, b). A summary of their observations and recommendations are given below:

(a) The yoghurt starter culture (RR) is a "slime" producer that yields a viscous yoghurt; the ratio of cocci to rods in the starter culture is 1:4.
(b) The incubation temperature in the prefermentation tank is 45°C. This provides the optimum growth conditions for the yoghurt organisms, and the pH of the milk is reduced to 5.7 within 15–20 minutes. At this pH, the ratio of cocci to rods is around 19:1, but this changes to 1:4 in the final product. This ratio of 19:1 is essential to provide a pH-stat, because the prefermented milk is constantly diluted, and if the specific growth rates altered, the quality of the yoghurt would be affected.
(c) The phenomenon of syneresis, i.e. whey separation from the yoghurt coagulum, is directly related to the degree of physical disturbance, to which the network of the protein micelles is subjected, but it can also be brought about by careless processing of the milk, e.g. poor pH and temperature control during the incubation period. Disturbance of the protein micelles in a continuous process can take place at the following stages:
  (i) during the prefermentation, i.e. before the final network of the protein has formed, any disturbance of the coagulum below pH 5.7 could cause some damage;
  (ii) during the coagulum formation period the net work of the protein is *being formed*, and syneresis can occur if the gel is disturbed;
  (iii) after formation of the *stable network*, the yoghurt coagulum is stirred above pH 4.6 and wheying-off can occur.

Syneresis could therefore take place during the second stage of the NIZO process, as stirring of the coagulum is inevitable in a continuous process, and hence the avoidance of problems is

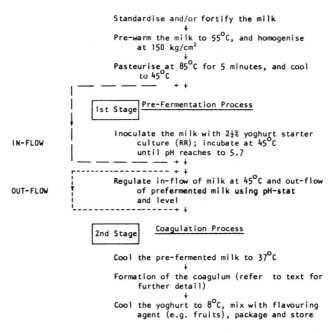

Fig. 5.21. Flow diagram of the continuous manufacture of stirred yoghurt

Adapted from Anon. (1975c), Driessen, Ubbels and Stadhouders (1977b).

dependent on the temperature of incubation and the level of acidity. For example, if a temperature of 45°C is used throughout the process, then the coagulum cannot be disturbed between pH 5.6 and 4.6 (i.e. the critical zone), while at a slightly reduced temperature of incubation, e.g. 37°C, the critical zone is between pH 5.6 and 4.8. It is for this reason that the prefermented milk is cooled to 37°C before it is transferred to the plug-flow fermentor, for at the higher pH level the coagulum can be disturbed without causing any syneresis.

(d) The dilution rate (e.g. the rate of addition of the yoghurt milk to the prefermentation tank) increases at increasing pH values, and this observation is based on the existence of the linear relationship between the concentration of lactic acid and the specific growth rate of the yoghurt organisms under controlled conditions. Thus, it is recommended that fresh milk is added to the prefermenter at a rate that maintains the pH at 5.7, so ensuring the desired balance between *S. thermophilus* and *L. bulgaricus* and the absence of syneresis (see also Lewis, 1967; Meyer, Tsuchiya and Fredrickson, 1975; MacBean, 1976; Lelieveld, 1976; MacBean, Linklater and Hall, 1978; MacBean, Hall and Linklater, 1979).

(e) The "plug-flow" fermenter unit is designed to:

(i) avoid disturbance of the coagulated milk in the fermentor during the transfer of the prefermented milk, and hence the fermentor is fitted with a special centrifugal distributor (Anon., 1975b);

(ii) prevent the coagulated milk adhering to the sides of the fermentor, and to this end the tank is coated with polytetrafluroethylene (PTFE) or lecithin;

269

Fig. 5.22.   Illustration of the first installation for the continuous manufacture of stirred yoghurt at NIZO in Holland—plant capacity is 4000 litres/hour

The continuous yoghurt line showing the pre-fermentation tank (1), the coagulation tank (2) and the tubular cooler (3).

Reproduced by courtesy of Stork-Amsterdam Int., UK.

> (iii) avoid damaging the coagulum during the stirring and removal of the coagulated milk, and hence the plug-flow fermentor is fitted with a specially designed stirring plate (Anon., 1975c).
>
> (f) The residence time of the prefermented milk in the coagulum formation unit is $2\frac{1}{2}$ hours at 37°C.
>
> (g) The development of this process was carried out in equipment capable of producing 250 litres/hour, but the recommended throughput for a large-scale plant is around 4000 litres/hour (see also Loo, 1981; Fig. 5.22 and Fig. 5.23).
>
> (h) The alleged advantages of continuous yoghurt making are: space saving, reduction in size of equipment, reduction of yoghurt losses in fermentation tanks and pipe lines, reduction in capacity of cooling and filling sections, greater flexibility in relation to total amount

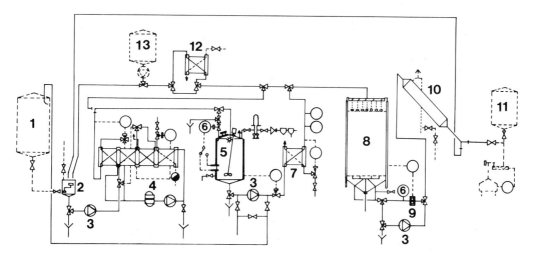

Fig. 5.23. Flow diagram showing the Stork-Amsterdam continuous process line for the production of stirred yoghurt

1. Milk storage tank. 2. Balance tank. 3. Centrifugal pump. 4. Pasteuriser. 5. Continuous fermentation tank (pH stat-fermentor). 6. pH controller. 7. Cooler. 8. Coagulation tank (pH plug-fermentor). 9. Positive displacement pump. 10. Cooler. 11. Buffer tank. 12. Emergency cooler. 13. Emergency buffer tank.

(Reproduced by courtesy of Stork-Amsterdam International, U.K.)

produced, no need for all the milk to be in stock at the start of production, uniformity of product quality and characteristics, better control over acid development and less pressure on the cooling and packaging operations.

REFERENCES

Abou-Donia, S., El-Soda, M. and Mashaly, R. (1980) *Journal of Dairy Research*, **47**, 151.
Angeles, A. G. and Marth, E. H. (1971) *Journal of Milk and Food Technology*, **34**, 30.
Anon. (1965) In *Lebanese Standards LS: 24 Milk and Milk Products*, Lebanese Standards Institution, P.O. Box 2806, Beirut, Lebanon.
Anon. (1973a) British Patent 1 330 793.
Anon. (1973b) British Patent 1 330 794.
Anon. (1974) *The Milk Industry*, **74**(5), 19.
Anon. (1975a) British Patent 1 398 799.
Anon. (1975b) Netherland Patent 7 509 155.
Anon. (1975c) Netherland Patent 7 508 982.
Anon. (1976) In *Yoghurt Plant Frau "LL" System*, Technical Bulletin Pds 2/76, Nouva Frau S.p.A., Vicenza, Italy.
Anon. (1977a) In *Fermented Milk Process Guide*, Alfa-Laval Technical Bulletin W M 60779E Alfa-laval A/B, Lund, Sweden.
Anon. (1977b) *Food Engineering International*, **2**(9), 31.
Anon. (1977c) In *Frozen Yoghurt*, Alfa-Laval Technical Bulletin PB 60 904E, Alfa-Laval A/B, Lund, Sweden.
Anon. (1977d) *The Milk Industry*, **79**(8), 21.
Anon. (1977e) *Food Engineering International*, **2**(1), 24.
Anon. (1977f) *Dairy Science Abstracts*, **39**, 262.
Anon. (1977g) French Patent 2 335 157.
Anon. (1978a) In *Yoghurt Ice-Cream*, Grindsted Products Technical Memorandum TM 10-2e & 43-1e, Grindsteadvaerket A/S, Brabrand, Denmark.
Anon. (1978b) *Food Engineering International*, **3**(2), 24.
Anon. (1978c) *Dairy Science Abstracts*, **40**, 45.

ANON. (1979a) *Dairy Science Abstracts*, **41**, 200.
ANON. (1979b) French Patent 2 409 010.
ANON. (1979c) *Milk Producer*, **26**, 9.
ANON. (1979d) French Patent 2 423 163.
ANON. (1980a) *Gist Brocades NV Technical Bulletin*, Delft, Holland.
ANON. (1980b) *Packaging*, **51**, 17.
ANON. (1980c) *Dairy Science Abstracts*, **42**, 841.
ANON. (1981) *Dairy Science Abstracts*, **43**, 173.
ANTILA, P., LEHTO, M. and ANTILA, V. (1978) *XXth International Dairy Congress*, **E**, 498.
ARIES, R. (1977) *Nordeuropaeisk Mejeri-Tiddsskrift*, **43**, 257.
ARIES, R. (1978) *Confectionery Manufacture and Marketing*, **15**, 7.
AROLSKI, A. T., USHEVA, V. B., GRUEV, P. V., RICHEV, G. T. and DONCHEVA, TS. S. (1979) *Dairy Science Abstracts*, **41**, 76.
BACH, J. (1977) *Deutsche Milchwirtschaft*, **28**, 1376.
BACH, J. (1978) British Patent, 1 507 069.
BAKE, K. (1979) *Milchwissenschaft*, **26**, 536.
BALTADZHIEVA, M., SAVOV, S. and BATINOV, K. (1981) *Dairy Science Abstracts*, **43**, 328.
BENESOVA, L. (1980) *Dairy Science Abstracts*, **42**, 386.
BLANCHAUD, M. (1973a) *Dairy Science Abstracts*, **35**, 32.
BLANCHAUD, M. (1973b) *Dairy Science Abstracts*, **35**, 165.
BOHREN, H. U. (1974) U.S. Patent 3 793 465.
BRADLEY, R. L. Jr. and HEKMATI, M. (1981) U.S. Patent 4 293 573.
BRADLEY, R. L. Jr. and WINDER, W. C. (1977) *American Dairy Review*, **39**(6), 30B.
BRAY, F. (1981) *Dairy Science Abstracts*, **43**, 502.
CADENA, M. A. and ROBINSON, R. K. (1979) *Ecology of Food and Nutrition*, **8**, 169.
CAJIGAS, S. D. (1981a) U.S. Patent 4 289 788.
CAJIGAS, S. D. (1981b) U.S. Patent 4 289 789.
CHAMAY, C. J. (1967) Swiss Patent 420 815.
CHANDAN, R. C. (1977) *Food Products Development*, **11**(9), 118.
CHARON, M. A. (1968) *Dairy Science Abstracts*, **30**, 475.
COLLINS, W. F. (1977) *American Dairy Review*, **39**(6), 30F.
COSTAMAGNA, L. and ROSSI, L. (1980) *Dairy Science Abstracts*, **42**, 127.
CRISP, D. E. and JOHN, M. G. (1969) British Patent 1 141 950.
DAVIS, J. G. (1971) *The Milk Industry*, **64**(4), 8.
DEETH, H. C. and TAMIME, A. Y. (1981) *Journal of Food Protection*, **44**, 78.
DELLAGLIO, F. (1977) In *The Production of Long-life Yoghurt by Frau 'LL' System*, Report No FD/1/77, Nouva Frau S.p.A., Vicenza, Italy.
DELLAGLIO, F. (1979) *Dairy Science Abstracts*, **41**, 478.
DIMOV, N., DZHONDZHOROVA, O. and KOZHEV, A. (1981) *Dairy Science Abstracts*, **43**, 329.
DRIESSEN, F. M., UBBELS, J. and STADHOUDERS, J. (1979a) *Journal of Biotechnology and Bioengineering*, **19**, 821.
DRIESSEN, F. M., UBBELS, J. and STADHOUDERS, J. (1977b) *Journal of Biotechnology and Bioengineering*, **19**, 841.
DUITSCHAEVER, C. L. and KETCHESON, G. (1974) *Dairy & Ice-Cream Field*, **157**(9), 66H.
EDWARDS, J. R. (1976) U.S. Patent 3 432 306.
EGLI, F. and EGLI, F. (1976a) Swiss Patent 580 920.
EGLI, F. and EGLI, F. (1976b) U.S. Patent 3 932 680.
EGLI, F. and EGLI, F. (1977) British Patent 1 467 670.
EGLI, F. and EGLI, F. (1980) U.S. Patent 4 235 934.
EL-SODA, M. A., EL-SAYED, K. M., BARY, A. A., ABOU-DOMIA, S. and MASHALY, R. (1979) *Journal of Dairy Science* (supplement 1), **62**, 61.
ENGEL, W. G. (1973) *Cultured Dairy Products Journal*, **8**(3), 6.
FAO/WHO, (1973) Cited by Cadena and Robinson (1979).
FELIP, D. DE, CROCI, L. and GIZZARELLI, S. (1979) *Dairy Science Abstracts*, **41**, 613.
FERGUSON, E. A. JR. (1963) U.S. Patent 3 080 236.
FERNS, H. (1981) Personal communication.
FLÜCKIGER, R. (1973) *Dairy Science Abstracts*, **35**, 217.
FRIDMAN, E. (1976) U.S. Patent 3 950 544.
GANGULY, A. S. (1972) British Patent, 1 282 356.
GALLAGHER, C. R., MOLLESON, A. L. and CALDWELL, J. H. (1974) *Journal of American Dietetic Association*, **65**, 418.
GARNIER, M. (1957) In *Les Produits Laitiers du Liban et de La Syrie-Etude Biologique et Vitaminologique*, Vigot Frères Editeurs, Paris, France,
GAUTNEB, T., STEINSHOLT, K. and ABRAHAMSEN, R. K. (1979) *Dairy Science Abstracts*, **41**, 478.
GAVIN, M. (1966) *XVIIth International Dairy Congress*, **E/F**, 663.

GAVIN, M. (1969) *Dairy Science Abstracts*, **31**, 8.

GIRGINOV, T. (1965) Cited by Driessen, Ubbels and Stadhouders (1977).

GRABS, G. R. (1979) Cited by Tamime and Deeth (1980).

GROZDOVA, G. N. (1971) *Dairy Science Abstracts*, **33**, 435.

GYURICSEK, D. M. and THOMPSON, M. P. (1976) *Cultured Dairy Products Journal*, **11**(3), 12.

HANSEN, R. (1977) *Nordeuropaeisk Mejeri-Tidsskrift*, **43**, 274.

HEKMATI, M. and BRADLEY, R. L. Jr. (1979) *Cultured Dairy Products Journal*, **14**(2), 6.

HEMME, D., VASSAL, L. and AUCLAIR, J. (1978) *XXth International Dairy Congress*, **E**, 513.

HEMME, D., VASSAL, L., FOYEN, H. and AUCLAIR, J. (1979) *Le Lait*, **59**, 597.

HENDRICUS, P. and EVERS, J. M. (1980) British Patent 2 044 068.

HERMANN, L. F. (1980) U.S. Patent 4 216 243.

HILGENDORF, M. J. (1981) *Cultured Dairy Products Journal*, **16**(1), 5.

HILL, L. G. (1974) U.S. Patent 3 846 561.

HOLDT, P. VON (1978) *Deutsche Milchwirtschaft*, **29**, 301.

HOLSINGER, V. H and GUY, E. J. (1974) In *Proceedings Whey Products Conference*, 18–19 September, Chicago, Illinois, USA.

HULSBUSCH, J. (1980) *Dairy Science Abstracts*, **42**, 573.

HYLMAR, B., PECH, Z., KOLAR, J. and STRAKA, M. (1979) Czechoslovak Patent 179 334.

IDF, (1977) In *Consumption Statistics for Milk and Milk Products*, Doc. No 93, IDF, Brussels, Belgium.

IGOE, R. S. (1979a) U.S. Patent, 4, 178 390.

IGOE, R. S. (1979b) U.S. Patent, 4, 169 854.

ISMAIL, A. A. and EL-NIMR, A. A. (1980) *Journal of Food Protection*, **43**, 566.

IVANOV, I. G., VELEV, S., OBERTENOVA, S. and TOSHEVA, I. (1973) *Dairy Science Abstracts*, **35**, 336.

JOCHUMSEN, A. (1978) *Cultured Dairy Products Journal*, **13**(1), 26.

KANKARE, V. and ANTILAR, V. (1980) *Dairy Science Abstracts*, **42**, 391.

KHAN, P. (1980) In *Some Aspects of the Behaviour of Guar Gum in Food and Human Nutrition*, PhD Thesis, University of Reading, Berkshire, UK.

KISZA, J., ZBIKOWSKI, Z. and KOLENDA, H. (1978) *XXth International Dairy Congress*, **E**, 545.

KLUPSCH, H. J. (1977) In *Symposium on New Technology of Fermented Milk Products and Milk Specialities*, 24–26 October Vratna Dolina, Czechoslovakia.

KLUPSCH, H. J. (1981) *Dairy Science Abstracts*, **43**, 83.

KOCHKOVA, Z. and SPASOV, S. (1981) *Dairy Science Abstracts*, **43**, 329.

KOSIKOWSKI, F. V. (1977) *Dairy & Ice-Cream Field*, **160**(8), 84.

KOSIKOWSKI, F. V. (1978) *Cultured Dairy Products Journal*, **13**(3), 5.

KOSIKOWSKI, F. V. (1979) *Journal of Dairy Science*, **62**, 41.

KOSIKOWSKI, F. V. (1981) *Journal of Food Protection*, **44**, 853.

KURMANN, J. A. (1969) *Dairy Science Abstracts*, **31**, 500.

KUWABARA, S. (1970) British Patent 1 197 257.

LANG, F. (1979) *The Milk Industry*, **81**(5), 7.

LANG, F. (1980) *The Milk Industry*, **82**(3), 44.

LAVRENOVA, G. S., INOZEMTSEVA, V. F. and PYATNITSYNA, I. N. (1981) *Dairy Science Abstracts*, **43**, 174.

LELIEVELD, H. L. N. (1976) *Journal of Process Biochemistry*, **11**, 39.

LEWIS, P. M. (1969) *Journal of Applied Bacteriology*, **30**, 406.

LOO, L. G. W. VAN DER (1980) *Dairy Science Abstracts*, **42**, 492.

LOO, L. G. W. VAN DER (1981) *Dairy Scinece Abstracts*, **43**, 25.

LÜCK, H. and MOSTERT, J. F. (1971) *South African Journal of Dairy Technology*, **3**, 75.

LUSIANI, G. and BIANCHI-SALVADORI, B. (1978) *XXth International Dairy Congress*, **E**, 351.

MACBEAN, R. D. (1976) *Dissertation Abstracts International B*, **36**, 4601.

MACBEAN, R. D., HALL, R. J. and LINKLATER, P. M. (1979) *Journal of Biotechnology and Bioengineering*, **21**, 1517.

MACBEAN, R. D., LINKLATER, P. M. and HALL, R. J. (1978) *XXth International Dairy Congress*, **E**, 827.

MANN, E. J. (1977) *Dairy Industries International*, **42**(11), 21.

MANN, E. J. (1978) *Dairy Industries International*, **43**(9), 49.

MANN, E. J. (1979) *Dairy Industries International*, **44**(4), 35.

MARSCHKE, R. J. and DULLEY, J. R. (1978) *Australian Journal of Dairy Technology*, **33**, 139.

MAZALEVA, K. and GLGIN, A. (1966) *Dairy Science Abstracts*, **28**, 71.

METZGER, J. (1962a) U.S. Patent 3 025 164.

METZGER, J. (1962b) U.S. Patent 3 025 165.

MEYER, J. S., TSUCHIYA, H. M. and FREDERICKSON (1975) *Journal of Biotechnology and Bioengineering*, **17**, 1065.

MILES, J. J. and LEEDER, J. G. (1981) *Cultured Dairy Products Journal*, **16**(3), 12.

MITTEN, H. L. (1977) *American Dairy Review*, **39**(6), 23.

MORCOS, S. R., HEGAZI, S. M. and EL-DAMHOUGY, S. T. (1973) *Journal of the Science of Food and Agriculture*, **24**, 1153.

MORGAN, D. R., ANDERSEN, D. L. and MOOK, D. E. (1970) U.S. Patent 3 539 363.

273

MORLEY, R. G. (1978) *American Dairy Review*, **40**(5), 28.

MORLEY, R. G. (1979a) *Cultured Dairy Products Journal*, **14**(1), 30.

MORLEY, R. G. (1979b) *Cultured Dairy Products Journal*, **14**(4), 30.

MULCAHY, M. J. (1972) In *Some Practical Research Findings From Moorepark*, Moorepark Research Center, County Cork, Ireland.

MUNK, W. G. (1980) *Dairy Science Abstracts*, **42**, 497.

NEIRINCKX, J. (1972) *Revue Lait Française*, **299**, 465.

NILSON, B. (1973) In *Cooking with Yoghurt, Cultured Cream and Soft Cheese*, Pelham Books Ltd., London, UK.

O'LEARY, V. S. and WOYCHIK, J. K. (1976a) *Journal of Applied and Environmental Microbiology*, **32**, 89.

O'LEARY, V. S. and WOYCHIK, J. H. (1976b) *Journal of Food Science*, **41**, 791.

ORGA, I. (1975) In *Cooking with Yoghurt*, 2nd edition, Andrew Deustch Ltd., London, UK.

PAVEY, R. L. and MONE, P. E. (1976) U.S. Patent 3 969 534.

PEDERSEN, A. H. and POULSEN, P. R. (1971) *Dairy Science Abstracts*, **33**, 686.

PETERSON, M. A. (1979) U.S. Patent 4 150 163.

PINTHONG, R., MACRAE, R. and DICK, J. (1980) *Journal of Food Technology*, **15**, 661.

PINTHONG, R., MACRAE, R. and ROTHWELL, J. (1980a) *Journal of Food Technology*, **15**, 647.

PINTHONG, R., MACRAE, R. and ROTHWELL, J. (1980b) *Journal of Food Technology*, **15**, 653.

PREKOPPOVA, J. and SLOTTAVA, A. (1979) *Dairy Science Abstracts*, **41**, 369.

PRIMATESTA, G. (1981) *Dairy Science Abstracts*, **43**, 377.

PUHAN, Z. (1979) *Journal of Food Protection*, **42**, 890.

RADAEVA, I. A., KOCHERGA, S. I., SHULKINA, S. P. and EFRON, B. G. (1970) *XVIIIth International Dairy Congress*, **1E**, 408.

RAKSHY, S. E. (1966) *Milchwissenschaft*, **21**, 81.

RASIC, J. (1975) *Nordeuropaeisk Mejeri—Tidsskrift*, **41**, 262.

REDFERN, R. B. and RIZK, S. F. (1979) U.S. Patent 4 163 802.

REUTER, H. (1978) *Dairy Science Abstracts*, **40**, 320.

RHODES, K. H. (1978) U.S. Patent 4 110 476.

ROBINSON, R. K. (1977) *South African Journal of Dairy Technology*, **9**, 2.

ROBINSON, R. K. (1978) *South African Journal of Dairy Technology*, **10**, 139.

ROBINSON, R. K. and CADENA, M. A. (1978) *Ecology of Food and Nutrition*, **7**, 131.

ROSENTHAL, I., JUVEN, B. J., GORDIN, S. and JUBRAN, N. (1980) *Journal of Dairy Science*, **63**, 1826.

ROSSI, J. and TERENCE-JEMMET, M. (1978) *Dairy Science Abstracts*, **40**, 176.

ROSSI, J., COSTAMAGNA, L. and INGI, M. (1978) *Le Lait*, **58**, 155.

ROSS, A. (1980) *Food Manufacture*, **55**(5), 49.

ROUSSEAU, M. J. (1974) *Dairy Science Abstracts*, **36**, 570.

SCHENK, R. U. (1980) U.S. Patent 4 206 244.

SCHMIDT, R. H., SISTRUNK, C. P., RICHTER, R. L. and CORNELL, J. A. (1980) *Journal of Food Science*, **45**, 471.

SCHOBER, G. (1973) *Dairy Science Abstracts*, **35**, 448.

SCHOBER, G. and LANDWEHR, W. O. (1973) *Dairy Science Abstracts*, **35**, 448.

SCHULZ, M. E. VON (1969) *Dairy Science Abstracts*, **31**, 429.

SCHUR, S. (1978) U.S. Patent 4 066 794.

SEBELA, F. (1979) *Dairy Science Abstracts*, **41**, 326.

SIMON, P. and DEVALLERIE, R. J. L. (1968) French Patent 1 529 590.

SIMHAEE, E. and KESHAVARZ, K. (1974) *Journal of Poultry Science*, **53**, 184.

SLAWAYTYCKI, A. (1972) *Journal of Confectionary Products*, **38**, 194.

SPECK, M. L. (1977) *Journal of Food Protection*, **40**, 863.

SPECK, M. L. and GEOFFRION, J. W. (1980) *Journal of Food Protection*, **43**, 26.

TAKAHATA, J. (1980) U.S. Patent 4 212 893.

TAMIME, A. Y. (1977a) In *Some Aspects of the Production of Yoghurt and Condensed Yoghurt*, PhD Thesis, University of Reading, Berkshire, UK.

TAMIME, A. Y. (1977b) *Dairy Industries International*, **42**(8), 7.

TAMIME, A. Y. (1978a) *Cultured Dairy Products Journal*, **13**(3), 16.

TAMIME, A. Y. (1978b) *The Milk Industry*, **80**(3), 4.

TAMIME, A. Y. (1981) Unpublished data.

TAMIME, A. Y. and DEETH, H. C. (1980) *Journal of Food Protection*, **43**, 939.

TAMIME, A. Y. and ROBINSON, R. K. (1978) *Milchwissenschaft*, **33**, 209.

THOMASOW, J. and KLOSTERMEYER, H. (1977) *Deutsche Milchwirtschaft*, **28**, 1316.

THOMPSON, M. P. and GYURICSEK, D. M. (1974) *Journal of Dairy Science*, **57**, 584.

THOMPSON, M. P. and BROWER, D. P. (1976) *Cultured Dairy Products Journal*, **11**(1), 22.

TROP, M. (1980) U.K. Patent 2 048 047A.

UENO, J., HANABUSA, R., NAKAI, M., MUSASHI, K., KANEKO, S. and KANBE, M. (1966) *XVIIth International Dairy Congress*, **F5**, 617.

VANDERPOORTEN, R. and MARTENS, R. (1976) *Revue de l'Agriculture,* **29,** 1509.

VITANOV, T., NIKOLOV, N. and BOYDASHEVA, L. (1973) In *Proceedings of XIIIth International Congress of Refrigeration,* Ed. Pentzer, W. T. AVI Publishing Co. Inc., Connecticut, USA.

VITEZ, L. (1968) *Dairy Science Abstracts,* **30,** 417.

WOYCHICK, J. H. and HOLSINGER, V. H. (1977) In *Enzymes in Food Beverage Proceeding,* Ed. Ory, R. L. and St. Angelo, A. J. American Chemical Society Symposium Series No. 47.

WOYCHICK, J. H., THOMPSON, M. P. and GYURICSEK, D. M. (1974) *IVth International Congress of Food Science and Technology,* Madrid, Spain.

YAMANAK, Y., OKUMURA, S., MITSUGI, K. and HASAGAWA, Y. (1969) British Patent, 1 154 139.

YAYGIN, H. (1980) *Dairy Science Abstracts,* **42,** 797.

YONEZ, A. (1965) In *Year Book Faculty of Agriculture,* University of Ankara, **5,** 4.

ZIEMBA, J. V. (1971) *Food Engineering,* **43**(4), 50.

ZMARLICKI, S., GAWEL, J., PIJANOWSKI, E. and MOLSKA, I. (1974a) *XIXth International Dairy Congress,* **1E,** 771.

ZMARLICKI, S., GAWEL, J., PIJANOWSKI, E. and MOLSKA, I. (1974b) *Dairy Science Abstracts,* **36,** 504.

CHAPTER 6

Microbiology of Yoghurt Starter Cultures

HISTORICAL BACKGROUND AND CLASSIFICATION

The first bacteriological study of yoghurt was made by Grigoroff (1905), and he observed three different micro-organisms present, namely a diplostreptococcus, a rod/coccal-shaped *Lactobacillus* and a rod-shaped *Lactobacillus*. The same observation was also reported by Lüerssen and Kühn (1908). However, the popularity of yoghurt could be attributed to Metchnikoff (1910), who postulated the theory that a prolongation of life would follow ingestion of a lactic acid bacterium named as *Bulgarian bacillus*. The presence of this organism in yoghurt was supposed to inhibit the growth of putrefactive organisms in the intestine.

The *Bulgarian bacillus* is, in fact, *Thermobacterium bulgaricum* (Orla-Jensen, 1931), and later designated as *Lactobacillus bulgaricus*. However, Rettger and Cheplin (1921) and Rettger *et al.* (1935) found that *Th. acidophilin* (*L. acidophillus*) is the lactic acid bacterium that can establish itself in the intestine, and furthermore, that the main therapeutic value of yoghurt is observed when *L. acidophilus* is one of the bacteria present in the starter culture.

The classification of the lactic acid bacteria by Orla-Jensen (*loc. cit.*) is still recognised as the standard method for distinguishing these organisms, i.e. the sphere shape was *Streptococcus* and the rod forms were *Thermobacterium*, *Streptobacterium* and *Betabacterium*. According to Orla-Jensen (*loc. cit.*), the yoghurt starter organisms were thermophilic lactic acid bacteria capable of growing at 40–45°C. These organisms were designated as: *Th. bulgaricum* (*L. bulgaricus*), *Th. jugurt* (*L. jugurti*) and *S. thermophilus*. According to the 7th edition of Bergey's Manual (1957), all the lactic acid bacteria were grouped into one family, the Lactobacillacceae, which was subdivided into the Streptococceae (ovoid or spherical in shape) and the Lactobacilleae (rod-shaped). But this classification was reorganised in the 8th edition of Bergey's Manual (1974) to give two separate families, the Streptococcaceae and the Lactobacillaceae.

S. thermophilus, which does not cause any controversy in respect of the remaining bacteria in its genera, is easily distinguished from other *Streptococcus* spp. by its growth at 45°C and failure to grow at 10°C. *S. thermophilus* lacks a group antigen for serological identification, and the main physiological characteristics of the species are summarised in Table 6.1. However, the situation is different when *Lactobacillus bulgaricus* is considered, for there are some doubts regarding *Thermobacterium jugurt* (*L. jugurti*), *L. lactis* and *L. helveticus*. Modern test methods, such as the guanine plus cytosine (G + C) content of the deoxyribonucleic acid (DNA), DNA-DNA hybridization and enzyme homology studies, can easily distinguish species which are closely

276

related. The work of Simonds, Hansen and Lakshmanan (1971) showed that *L. jugurti* is a bio
of *L. helveticus*, and that there is no reassociation between *L. bulgaricus* and *L. jugurti* as a res
DNA-DNA hybridization. The DNA homology between *L. jugurti* and *L. helveticus* is around 84–
100%, and the former is considered as maltose-negative variant of *L. helveticus* (London, 1976).
However, DNA homology does exist up to 86% between *L. bulgaricus* and *L. lactis* (Simonds,
Hansen and Lakshmanan, *loc. cit.*), and hence these two organisms are closely related;
L. bulgaricus ferments fewer sugars than *L. lactis*. Table 6.1 illustrates the overall differences
between these various lactobacilli.

THE THEORIES OF SYMBIOSIS AND STIMULATORY FACTORS

The growth association between the two organisms (*S. thermophilus* and *L. bulgaricus*) of the
yoghurt starter culture is termed a symbiosis, and this relationship has been reported by many
workers; the earliest record dates back to the work of Orla-Jensen. Pette and Lolkema (1950a)
observed that the rate of acid development was greater when mixed yoghurt cultures of
S. thermophilus and *L. bulgaricus* were used as compared with the single strains (see Fig. 6.1).
Furthermore, they also observed that the numbers of *S. thermophilus*, as recorded by the breed
smear method, were much higher in mixed cultures than when the organism was grown alone,
although no such differences in numbers of *L. bulgaricus* were noted. This observation was not true
with respect to *L. bulgaricus* as reported by Tamime (1977b). The findings of Pette and Lolkema
(1950b) led them to postulate that the interaction between these two organisms was mainly
dependent on the production of valine by *L. bulgaricus*. However, due to variations in the chemical
composition of milk during the year, other amino acids may also be deficient, and hence Pette and

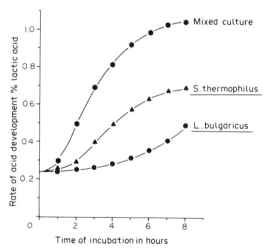

Fig. 6.1. The behaviour of single and mixed strain yoghurt cultures propagated at 40°C in autoclaved skim milk
(10% TS) and 2% inoculation rate

▲ *S. thermophilus*   ●*L. bulgaricus*   ⬢ Mixed culture
Test organism is Chr. Hansen's (CH-1)

Adapted from Tamime (1977a)

TABLE 6.1. Selected characteristics of lactic acid bacteria associated with yoghurt

Column groups: "Growth" spans 10°C and 45°C; "Requirement for" spans Thiamine, Riboflavine, Pyridoxal, Folic Acid, Thymidine, Vit. B₁₂; "Carbohydrate utilisation" spans Aesculin through Xylose.

Micro-organisms	G+C mean %	Acid from glucose	Gas from glucose	Gas from gluconate	Aldolase	Lactic acid configuration	% acid in milk	NH_3 from arginine	Serological group	Growth 10°C	Growth 45°C	Thiamine	Riboflavine	Pyridoxal	Folic Acid	Thymidine	Vit. B_{12}	Aesculin	Amygdalin	Arabinose	Cellobiose	Fructose	Galactose	Lactose	Hippurate	Maltose	Mannitol	Mannose	Melezitose	Melibiose	Raffinose	Rhamnose	Ribose	Salicin	Starch	Sorbitol	Sucrose	Trehalose	Xylose
S. thermophilus		+	−	−	+	L(+)		−	X	−	+	+	−	−	−	−	−	−	−	V	−	+	+	+	−	−	−	−	−	−	V	−	−	−	+	−	+	−	V
L. bulgaricus	50.3	+	−	−	+	D(−)	1.7	−	E	−	+	−	+	−	−	−	−	−	−	−	−	V	V	+	−	−	−	V	−	−	−	−	−	−	−	−	−	−	−
L. lactis	50.2	+	−	−	+	D(−)	1.4–1.7	−	E	−	+	−	+	−	−	−	V	−	−	−	+	+	V	+	−	+	−	+	−	−	V	−	−	+	−	−	+	+	−
L. helveticus	39.3	+	−	−	+	DL	2.7	−	A	−	+	−	+	+	−	−	−	−	−	−	+	V	+	+	−	+	−	+	−	−	−	−	−	−	−	−	−	+	+
L. jugurti	39.0	+	−	−	+	DL	2.7	−	A	−	V	−	+	+	−	−	−	−	−	−	−	−	+	+	−	−	−	−	−	V	V	−	−	−	−	−	−	V	+
L. acidophilus	36.7	+	−	−	+	DL	0.8	−		−	+	−	+	−	+	−	−	+	+	−	+	+	+	+	−	+	−	+	−	V	V	−	−	+	−	−	+	+	−

+: positive reaction by 90% or more strains
−: negative reaction by 90% or more strains
V: Variable, slow or weak reaction
X: Ungrouped
G+C mean%: Mean % of guanine plus cytosine in DNA.
After: Bergey's Manual (1974); Hansen (1968); Rogosa and Hansen (1971); Ottogalli, Galli and Dellaglio (1979); Accolas et al. (1980).

Lolkema (1950b) suggested that during the spring months *S. thermophilus* required the following amino acids: leucine, lysine, cystine, aspartic acid, histidine and valine; during the autumn/winter months glycine, isoleucine, tyrosine, glutamic acid, methionine, as well as the six amino acids mentioned above, were essential.

Bautista, Dahiya and Speck (1966) also investigated the symbiosis theory, and supported the view that *L. bulgaricus* stimulates *S. thermophilus* by releasing glycine and histidine into the growth medium; they concluded that histidine rather than valine was the most important requirement. However, the stimulation by glycine and histidine, as reported by Bautista, Dahiya and Speck (*loc. cit.*), was very poor in comparison with the various amino acids observed by Pette and Lolkema (1950b). Accolas, Veaux and Auclair (1971) reported that the stimulation of *S. thermophilus* by a milk culture filtrate of *L. bulgaricus* was due to the presence of valine, leucine, isoleucine and histidine. Bracquart, Lorient and Alais (1978) and Barcquart and Lorient (1979) concluded that depleting the growth medium of valine, histidine, glutamic acid, tryptophane, leucine and isoleucine reduced the stimulation of *S. thermophilus* by 50%. Similar findings were reported by Higashio, Yoshioka and Kikuchi (1977a), where methionine was also included as a stimulatory amino acid; however, by far the most effective amino acid was valine (see also Shankar, 1977; Shankar and Davies, 1978; Hemme, Schmal and Auclair, 1981).

Galesloot, Hassing and Veringa (1968) investigated the opposite side of the symbiosis relationship between *S. thermophilus* and *L. bulgaricus*. They concluded that, under anaerobic conditions, the former organism produces a stimulatory factor for *L. bulgaricus* that is equal to or can be replaced by formic acid. Furthermore, the same workers looked at the effect of various heat treatments of milk, and found that in intensively heated milk, i.e. autoclaved and UHT, this stimulation was masked on account of a compound which could be replaced by the formic acid. However, after the normal heat treatment of milk used for yoghurt manufacture, e.g. 85–90°C, *L. bulgaricus* definitely needs the stimulatory factor produced by *S. thermophilus*. The normal presence of such a stimulatory factor in autoclaved milk (Auclair and Portman, 1957) appears to have been overlooked by both Pette and Lolkema (1950b) and Bautista, Dahiya and Speck (*loc. cit.*).

The production of formic acid by *S. thermophilus* was confirmed by Veringa, Galesloot and Davelaar (1968), and Bottazzi, Battistotti and Vescovo (1971) demonstrated that the presence of formic acid in milk increases the ratio of rods to cocci at concentrations between 30 and 50 γ/ml. This compares with the stimulation of *L. bulgaricus* by formate at 20–30 ppm as reported by Galesloot, Hassing and Veringa (*loc. cit.*) and Shankar (*loc. cit.*), or at 140 ppm (Accolas, Veaux and Auclair, *loc. cit.*). This variation in the level of formate required to promote activity could be attributed to the use of different strains of *L. bulgaricus*. Other stimulatory compounds, also produced by *S. thermophilus*, are pyruvic acid (Higashio, Yoshioka and Kikuchi, 1977b) and carbon dioxide (Driessen, Kingma and Stadhouders, 1982).

Other compounds which have been found to be stimulatory to yoghurt starter cultures are illustrated in Table 6.2. The addition of these compounds to the basic mix during the manufacture of yoghurt may present a legal problem. However, it is safe to assume that compounds which are milk-based can be used to fortify the basic mix, e.g. casein hydrolysate. The use of such compounds may be an advantage if yoghurt can be produced successfully using a single strain starter, i.e. *S. thermophilus* (Marshall and Mabbit, 1980; Marshall, Cole and Mabbitt, 1982).

It can be concluded from the above findings, therefore, that the release of stimulatory factors by yoghurt starter cultures takes place during the incubation period, and while *L. bulgaricus* provides the essential nutrients, i.e. amino acids for *S. thermophilus*, the latter produces a formic acid-like compound(s) which promote the growth of *L. bulgaricus*.

TABLE 6.2. *Compounds and factors other than individual amino acids* capable of promoting the growth of the yoghurt starter culture*

Organism	Treatment	Compound	References
S. thermophilus	Hydrolysis of casein by *Micrococcus caseolyticus*	Peptides containing lysine	Desmazeaud and Hermier (1972)
	Hydrolysis of glucagon by papain	Hepta- or pentapeptides containing histidine	Desmazeaud and Hermier (1973)
	Trypsin hydrolysed casein	Lower peptides and free non-aromatic amino acids	Hayashi, Irie and Morichi (1974)
	Addition	Tripeptides containing glutamic acid, histidine and methionine	Bracquart and Lorient (1979)
L. bulgaricus	Addition	Monosodium orthophosphate and sodium tripolyphosphate	Yu and Kim (1979)
	Addition	Purine, adenine, guanine, uracil and adenosine	Weinmann, Morris and Williams (1964)
	Tomato juice	Adenine and adenosine	Cogan, Gilliland and Speck (1968)
	Addition	Oxaloacetic and fumaric acid	Higashio, Yoshika and Kikuchi (1977b)
	Addition	Monosodium and disodium orthophosphate	Yu and Kim (1979)
Mixed cultures	Action of psychrotrophic bacteria	Liberation of nitrogenous compounds due to the breakdown of casein	Cousins and Marth (1977a, b)
	Addition of milk solids	General increase in nutrients and improved buffering capacity	Tramer (1973) Sellars and Babel (1978)
	Heating of milk	Activation of sulphydryl compounds, reduction in oxygen, lowering of pH, denaturation of whey proteins, partial hydrolysis of casein and destruction of natural inhibitors.	Refer to section on heat treatment of milk

* These amino acids are not the result of proteolysis caused by the yoghurt organisms (see text).

CHARACTERISTICS OF GROWTH

The metabolic activity of an organism is indicative, to some extent, of its growth rate, and one of the most popular tests for monitoring starter cultures is the development of acidity in the growth medium. Autoclaved, reconstituted skim milk (10–12 % TS) is mainly used, and the milk must be free from any inhibitory substances, e.g. antibiotics. The activity of a typical yoghurt starter culture and its isolated strains of *S. thermophilus* and *L. bulgaricus* is illustrated in Figs. 6.1 and 6.2, and there is a marked difference in the rate of acid development by the mixed starter as against the isolated single strains (see Fig. 6.2). It is also noticeable that the rate of acid development of *S. thermophilus* and *L. bulgaricus* increases with increase in incubation temperature, up to maxima of 40° and 45°C respectively; the former organism is initially more active than *L. bulgaricus* in relation to acid production. Although the activity of mixed strains is optimum at 45°C, it is recommended that, in order to maintain and/or achieve a ratio of 1:1 between *S. thermophilus* and *L. bulgaricus*, the organisms should be propagated together at 42°C using a 2 % inoculation rate (Kurmann, 1967; Tamime, 1977a).

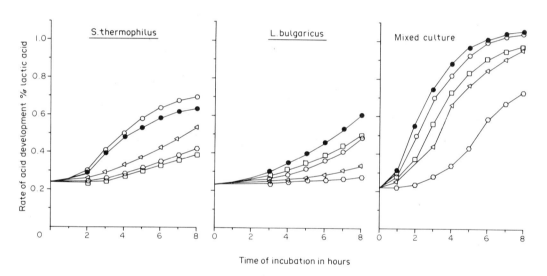

Fig. 6.2. The behaviour of single & mixed strain yoghurt cultures propagated at different temperatures in autoclaved skim milk (10 % TS) & 2 % inoculation rate

⬡ 30°C   △ 35°C   ○ 40°C   ● 45°C   □ 50°C; Test Organism is Chr. Hansen's (CH-1)

Adapted from Tamime (1977a)

EFFECT OF INHIBITORY AGENTS AND SUBSTANCES

The yoghurt organisms are very sensitive to a wide range of inhibitory substances, and these potential inhibitors can be classified into the following categories:

(a) compounds that are naturally present in milk;

(b)   (i) chemicals that gained access to milk due to antibiotic therapy of the dairy cow;
     (ii) cleaning and sanitising residues from farm and processing equipment;
    (iii) environmental pollution;
(c) bacteriophage attack.

A. Natural Inhibitors

There are various antimicrobial systems present in milk, and their major role is the protection of the suckling animal against infection and disease. These inhibitory systems have been recently reviewed by Reiter (1978), and their presence in milk can inhibit the growth of lactic acid bacteria. Auclair and Hirsch (1953) and Auclair and Berridge (1953) reported the inhibition of starter organisms by raw milk, and that pasteurisation and boiling of the milk improved culture activity. The inhibitory compounds, known as lactenins, are heat-sensitive, and are destroyed by heating the milk to 68–74°C (Auclair, 1954). Patel (1969) reported that *S. thermophilus* showed a growth inhibition in fresh raw buffaloes milk during the first $\frac{1}{2}$–2 hours of incubation, but a resumption of growth afterwards. He proposed that the loss of inhibitory action was due either to adaption of the organism to the lactenins, or to the destruction of the lactenins.

Another bactericidal component found naturally in milk is the peroxidase system, which consists of lactoperoxidase/thiocyanate/hydrogen peroxide [LP/SCN$^-$/H$_2$O$_2$ abbreviated as LP system]. Reiter (1978) reported that the sources of these compounds are:

—LP is synthesized in mammary gland;
—SCN$^-$ is derived from the rhodanese catalysed reaction with thiosulphate in the liver and kidney;
—H$_2$O$_2$ results from the metabolic activity of certain streptococci, or from the anaerobic growth of other bacteria.

In this system the inhibitory compound is the result of an oxidation reaction where the LP enzyme combines with H$_2$O$_2$ to oxidise SCN$^-$; however, the inhibition is reversible in the presence of some reducing compounds, e.g. cysteine and dithionite (Reiter, 1978). In general, most starter organisms are resistant to the LP system, but some lactic cultures can give rise to sensitive mutants (Auclair and Vassal, 1963). Alternatively, continual propagation of starter cultures in autoclaved milk can affect the susceptibility of the organisms to the LP system (Jago and Swinbourne, 1955). A preventive measure is the addition of peroxidase to autoclaved milk (Reiter, 1973), or the addition of reducing agents, e.g. cysteine and dithionite (Reiter, 1978). Incidentally, the LP system is inactivated by heating milk at 85°C for 16 seconds (Feagan, 1959a, b), so that the heat treatments of yoghurt milk (85°C for 30 minutes or 90–95°C for 5–10 minutes) and the bulk starter milk (93°C for $1\frac{1}{2}$–2 hours) are adequate enough to destroy the natural inhibitors (Storgards, 1969; Pearce and Brice, 1973).

Other inhibitory systems which may warrant some consideration are: *bacterial agglutinin* can cause agglutination of the starter organisms, thus affecting their metabolic activity and growth. *Leucocytes* in mastitis milk may cause inhibition of lactic starters through phagocytosis, and the heat treatment of such milk brings no significant improvement. Gajdusek and Sebela (1973) reported a 35% reduction in the activity of a yoghurt culture in milk containing large numbers of somatic cells; however, boiling of the milk for 2 minutes, or heating at 90°C for 20 minutes, inactivates the cells completely. *Late lactation* and *Spring milk* have some effect on the activity of yoghurt cultures; however, the reason for the bactericidal effect has not been elucidated yet. Certain types of *forage*, such as mouldy silage, turnips or vetch, may result in a milk containing inhibitory substances which can reduce the rate of acid production of the yoghurt starter culture, even after heating the milk at 90°C for 15 minutes (see review by Tamime and Deeth, 1980).

B. Chemical Inhibitors

There is a wide range of chemical compounds which can either inhibit the growth (microbiocidal) or reduce the activity (microbiostatic) of yoghurt starter cultures. These compounds may gain access to milk due to bad husbandry practice, negligence and/or environmental pollution. The sensitivity of the yoghurt organisms to these various compounds is summarised in Table 6.3.

TABLE 6.3. *Sensitivity of yoghurt starter cultures to various inhibitory compounds which could gain access to milk*

| Inhibitory substances | Inhibitory level | | |
	S. *thermophilus*	L. *bulgaricus*	Mixed culture
I. Antibiotics (per ml)			
Penicillin	0.004–0.010 I.U.	0.02–0.100 I.U.	0.01 I.U.
Streptomycin	0.380 I.U.	0.380 I.U.	1.00 I.U.
Streptomycin	12.5–21.0 μg	6.6 μg	
Tetracycline	0.130–0.500 μg	0.34–2.000 μg	1.00 I.U.
Chlortetracycline	0.060–1.000 μg	0.060–1.000 μg	0.10 I.U.
Oxytetracycline	0.400 I.U.	0.700 I.U.	0.40 I.U.
Bacitracin	0.040–0.120 I.U.	0.040–0.100 I.U.	0.04 I.U.
Erythromycin	0.300–1.300 mg	0.070–1.300 mg	0.10 I.U.
Chloramphenicol	0.800–13.000 mg	0.800–13.000 mg	0.50 I.U.
II. Disinfectant/Detergent (mg/litre)			
Chlorine compounds	100	100	50–> 2500
QAC	100–500	50–100	≥ 250
Ampholyte			≥ 1000
Iodophor	60	60	≥ 2000
Alkaline detergent			> 500–1000
III. Insecticides (ppm)			
Malathion			200
N-methylcarbamates			20
IV. Miscellaneous (ppm)			
Fatty acids	1000		
Ethylenedichloride ⎫ Methylsulphone ⎬	10–100		
Acetonitrile ⎫ Chloroform ⎬ Ether ⎭	10		

Adapted from Tamime and Deeth (1980).

1. Antibiotic residues

Antibiotics and/or other antimicrobial agents are used by man for the treatment of diseases, and one of the major diseases in the dairy cow, which can affect the quality and yield of milk, is mastitis. Today there are known to be about 1000 different types of antibiotic, and according to Barron (1976) the following antimicrobial compounds (penicillin, streptomycin, neomycin, chloramphenicol, tetracycline, sulphonamide, cloxacillin and ampicillin) are widely used in the United Kingdom for the treatment of mastitis. In view of the immense number of antimicrobial drugs used by veterinary medicine, an attempt has been made to classify only the most widely used antibiotics, and the overall characteristics of this group and their possible effect on yoghurt starter cultures is illustrated in Table 6.4. Furthermore, depending on the type of antibiotic used, the "mode of action" of these drugs on *S. thermophilus* and *L. bulgaricus* can be summarised as follows:

TABLE 6.4. *Classification and mode of action of some antibiotics*

Source or origin	Antibiotics produced	% of production	Possible function and mode of action on the yoghurt starter culture
I. Microbial			
Actinomycetales *Streptomyces* sp.	Streptomycin		* Protein synthesis inhibitors
	Tetracylines		** ,, ,, ,,
	Neomycin		* ,, ,, ,,
	Erythromycin	58	* ,, ,, ,,
	Chloramphenicol		** ,, ,, ,,
Nocardia sp.	Ristocetin		* Cell wall inhibitors
Micromonospora sp.	Gentamicin		* Protein synthesis inhibitor
Aspergillales *Penicillum notatum*	Penicillin Xanthocillin		* Cell wall inhibitors
Fusidium coccineum	Fusidic acid	18	Nucleic acid inhibitors
Aspergillus fumigatus	Fumagillin		
Bacillaceae *Bacillus licheniformis*	Bacitracin		* Cell wall inhibitors
Bacillus brevis	Gramicidins	9	* Alter cell membrane permeability
	Tyrocidin		* Disorganise cell membrane structure
Bacillus polymyxa	Polymyxin		,, ,, ,, ,,
II. Synthetic	Sulphonamide		Reaction or site inhibited is folate synthesis
	Penicillin	12	* Cell wall inhibitors
	Chloramphenicol		** Protein synthesis inhibitors
III. Plant Extracts	Alkaloids		
IV. Miscellaneous	Drugs extracted from algae, lichens and animals	3	

* Microbiocidal.
** Microbiostatic.

Adapted from Edwards (1980); Garrod, Lambert and O'Grady (1973).

—interference with the cell membrane structure and permeability;
—interference with cellular metabolism of proteins, carbohydrates and lipids;
—interference with energy yielding transformations in the cell;
—inhibition of various enzymes and phosphorylation systems;
—blocking the synthesis of DNA and RNA during cell division.

During the intramammary injection of antibiotics for the treatment of mastitis in the dairy cow, these antimicrobial compounds are retained in the udder tissues and gradually diffuse into the milk.

Thus, milk from treated cows must be withheld for 72 hours for two main reasons: firstly, residual antibiotics in milk are a potential public health hazard, and secondly, low levels can affect the behaviour and activity of the starter culture (see Table 6.3), resulting in a poor yoghurt and/or economic loss for the manufacturer. Hence, a number of governments have introduced a payment penalty scheme for milk containing >0.02 International Units (I.U.) of penicillin/ml; among the tests methods are the disc assay, the 2,3,5-triphenyl-tetrazolium chloride (TTC), bromocresol purple (BCP) or the Charm test. Some of these methods use *S. thermophilus* as the test organism because of its sensitivity to antibiotics (see Table 6.3), but unfortunately the available methods are prone to certain drawbacks:

—the sensitivity of *S. thermophilus* can vary in relation to the strain used [see Reinbold and Reddy (1974)];
—the above test methods relate only to the presence of penicillin, or, more precisely, the sensitivity of *S. thermophilus* to penicillin, but not other types of antibiotics. For example, Cogan (1972) observed that *L. bulgaricus* is more sensitive than *S. thermophilus* to streptomycin, and to cause a 50% inhibition of growth, 1.6–4.45 and 7.3–13.00 μg/ml of streptomycin were required respectively. Thus, a milk which passes the antibiotic test may contain enough streptomycin to inhibit the growth of *L. bulgaricus*.

The major effect of antibiotic residues in yoghurt milk is to cause a breakdown in the symbiotic relationship between *S. thermophilus* and *L. bulgaricus*, or a slow down in the rate of acid development, i.e. longer processing time, and this can, in time, lead to syneresis or wheying-off. To combat such problems, the following measures have been recommended:

(1) The use of milk for the manufacture of yoghurt that is *free* from antibiotics.
(2) The addition of penicillinase or penicillinase-producing organisms e.g. *Micrococcus* spp. to milk in order to inactivate residual penicillin contamination (Reiter, Vazquez and Newland, 1961; Vazquez and Reiter, 1962).
(3) Heat treatment of milk can reduce the potency of some antibiotics. Tramer (1964) reported an 8% inactivation of penicillin at 72°C for 15 seconds, or 20% at 87.7°C for 30 minutes, or 50% at commercial sterilisation temperatures; terramycin lost 2/3 of its potency at 85°C for 30 minutes; but streptomycin and chloramphenicol remained stable and unaffected.
(4) The use of antibiotic-resistant yoghurt strains (see Table 6.5); however, the quality of yoghurt produced by such strains was not reported. Thus, these developed cultures may have different characteristics, such as reduced rates of acid and flavour production, or the inability to ferment certain carbohydrates, and these changes could adversely affect the performance of a culture during commercial production.

TABLE 6.5. *Development of yoghurt starter cultures resistant to different antibiotics*

Antibiotics	Achieved resistance level/ml	References
Penicillin	3.0 I.U.	Hargrove *et al.* (1950)
Streptomycin	500 µg	
Chlortetracycline	70–120 µg	Solomon,
Chloramphenicol	40–50 µg	Scortescu and
Streptomycin	500 µg	Bilbile (1966)
Ampicillin	50 µg	Ferri *et al.* (1979)
Cephalexin	150 µg	
Chlortetracycline	≤50–150 µg	

2. Detergent and disinfectant residues

Detergents and disinfectants are widely used in the dairy industry for the cleaning and sanitising of dairy equipment on the farm and in the creamery. The general specification and classification of these preparations is discussed elsewhere, but basically, the detergent formulations contain alkali compounds, e.g. sodium hydroxide, while the sanitising agents are quaternary ammonium compounds (QAC) or iodine or chlorine-based compounds.

Inorganic acids are also used for cleaning and disinfecting purposes. Therefore, residues of these compounds in milk can be attributed to two main causes: firstly, negligence, bad management or a faulty cleaning-in-place (CIP) system; the latter is more likely to occur on the farm or in milk tankers. Secondly, it is the practice of some milk producers to add biocidal compounds to milk in order to improve its keeping quality. This latter approach is not recommended for public health reasons, and also the presence of such compounds in milk can adversely affect, or totally inhibit, the growth of starter cultures.

It can be observed from Table 6.3 that the susceptibility of *S. thermophilus* and *L. bulgaricus* to cleaning residues is increased in monocultures as compared with the mixed cultures, and this variation could be attributed to:

(a) differences or variations in the strains of bacteria being used by different researchers;
(b) variation between batches of the commercial detergents and disinfectants tested;
(c) variation in the test method used to measure the levels of inhibition;
(d) greater resistance as a result of the symbiotic growth activity.

Another possible source of detergent and/or sterilant residues is the glass bottle washer, for in some countries, glass bottles are still used for packaging stirred or set yoghurt. In the latter type of yoghurt, Nikolov (1975) concluded that if the milk contained above 2.5% of bottlewash liquid, consisting of 1% sodium hydroxide, the chlorine concentration, i.e. > 100 mg/litre, was high enough to inhibit the growth of *S. thermophilus* and *L. bulgaricus*.

3. Environmental Pollution

Incidents of insecticide residues in milk have been reported, and this occurrence could well be due to either post-milking contamination, or to feeding cattle with fodder that has been sprayed with an insecticide to combat some disease. Milk containing malathion (200 ppm) N-methylcarbamate (20 ppm) will inhibit the growth of the yoghurt organisms (see Table 6. However, Deane and Patten (1971) observed that 100 ppm of malathion or trichlophon in milk had little effect on the rate of lactic acid development by yoghurt cultures, but some variation in cell morphology did occur after several culture transfers. When viewed under a light microscope (using ordinary staining techniques) the recorded changes included a decrease or increase in cell size, and the formation of longer chains. In addition, Deane and Jenkins (1971) propagated *L. bulgaricus* alone in milk containing the same insecticides, and observed under the electron microscope, the following morphological changes: the rod cells were longer, wider or narrower, and showed a compact protoplasm and frequent flaking of the cell wall material; there were fewer cross-walls produced.

C. Bacteriophages

Bacteriophages (phages) are viruses which can attack and destroy the yoghurt organisms, and the resultant failure of lactic acid production leads to poor coagulation of the process milk. The occurrence of such viruses in mesophilic dairy starter cultures, e.g. cheese starters, was first reported by Whitehead and Cox (1935), and for the past few decades research work on the phages of mesophilic lactic acid bacteria has been intensified, primarily because of the economic importance of cheese in the dairy industry. However, interest in phages that can attack thermophilic lactic acid bacteria, i.e. the yoghurt cultures, has been aroused in recent years for the following reasons: firstly, world production figures of yoghurt have increased significantly, and product failure results in great economic loss to the industry; secondly, the manufacture of yoghurt is more centralised, and phage attack could become a major problem; thirdly, strains of *S. thermophilus* and *L. bulgaricus* are widely used in the manufacture of high-temperature scalded cheese, e.g., the Swiss varieties, and hence, phage problems could result in both a slow "make" and a low quality cheese.

These bacterial viruses consist basically of a polyhedral head and protruding tail, and according to Lawrence, Thomas and Terzaghi (1976) and Sandine (1979) the streptococcal phages consist of a double-stranded nucleic acid core (DNA) and a protective coat of protein. In view of the lack of observable features, a number of different characteristics have been used in an attempt to classify the phages of mesophilic starters, and these characteristics include: virulant or lysogenic behaviour, host range, morphology, serological reactions and nucleic acid homology, but no universally accepted system of classification has yet been devised (see Lawrence, Thomas and Terzaghi, *loc. cit.*). However, with little information available on the phages of thermophilic lactic starters, the reported or proposed systems of nomenclature of these phages are mainly based on morphological features and host relationships.

According to Pette and Kooy (1952) the sensitivity of *S. thermophilus* strains to phage attack can be described under one of three headings:

   (i) phage-insensitive;
  (ii) phage-tolerant, i.e. carriers of the particles;
 (iii) phage-sensitive, i.e. phages cause complete lysis of the cell.

Sarimo and Moksunen (1978) proposed a similar classification, but incorporated some morphological features as well. For example:

1st Group— Phages that attack all hosts and look similar to each other. The head structure is hexagonal (50–55 nm in diameter), the tail length ranges from 217 to 239 nm and tail width from 4 to 8 nm.

2nd Group— Phages that can only infect the "autolytic" strains, i.e. cells which disintegrate readily after the stationary phase.

3rd Group— Phages that can attack only the "homologous" host, i.e. phages which are named after the host strain where they were first isolated (Mullan, 1979). They have a hexagonal head 60 nm in diameter with a very short or absent tail. Incidentally, tailess phages have been reported by Soldal and Langsrud (1978).

The Russian workers Koroleva *et al.* (1978) divided phage particles from *S. thermophilus* into two groups based on morphological observations:

(a) Regular polyhedron head 40 nm in diameter, and tail 220 nm in length and 8 nm in width.
(b) The other phage sizes are: head 65 nm in diameter, tail 420 nm in length and 8 nm in width.

However, Accolas and Spillmann (1979a) observed that six out of seven *S. thermophilus* phages were similar, i.e. polyhedral, or possibly octahedral, the head was 49–53 nm in diameter, the tail length ranged from 200 to 224 nm (with the exception of one, i.e. 130 nm) and the tail width from 8 to 9 nm; the tail tip had a small plate covered with short prongs or a fibrous mass. The seventh type of phage had no specific tail-tip structure.

The distinctive features of *L. bulgaricus* phages are:

(i) shorter in overall length in comparison with *S. thermophilus* phages, e.g. 116–198 nm, with the exception of those phages studied by Peake and Stanley (1978), where the length varied from 205–215 nm;
(ii) the presence of a "collar" structure (Accolas and Spillman, 1979b);
(iii) The appearance of up to ten "cross-bar" structures intersecting the tail at intervals (Peake and Stanley, *loc. cit.*).

It can be concluded that research work on the phages of thermophilic lactic starters is still "in its infancy", but Table 6.6 does, nevertheless, review the morphology of those bacteriophages of the yoghurt organisms that have been reported in the literature up to the present time, and Fig. 6.3 shows some of the morphological characteristics of the different phages.

It is also relevant, concerning the viruses attacking *S. thermophilus* and *L. bulgaricus*, that:

(a) If milk is the origin of phage contamination, then heat treatment at 85°C for 20 minutes ensures their destruction (Stolk, 1955).
(b) The optimum temperature of phage proliferation is the same as the optimum growth temperature of the host, i.e. *S. thermophilus* phages at 39–40°C and *L. bulgaricus* phages at 42–43°C (Sozzi, Poulin and Maret, 1978).
(c) Chemical sterilisation of equipment using 0.1 % quaternary ammonium compounds, 70–90 % ethanol, 0.5–1.0 % potassium permanganate or 50–100 mg available chlorine/litre causes the destruction of *S. thermophilus* phages (Ciblis, 1966).
(d) Phages are species and/or strain specific, i.e. phages of mesophilic lactic starters do not attack thermophilic starter cultures, and furthermore, *S. thermophilus* phages do not attack *L. bulgaricus* strains.

TABLE 6.6. *Morphology of bacteriophages of yoghurt starter cultures*

Organism	Origin	Head structure	Size (nm)	Tail length × Diameter (nm)	Tail tip	Other relevant information
S. thermophilus	U.S.A.	–	90–95	270 × –	–	Central fibre 200 × 4 nm
	Germany	–	70	237 × –	–	One central fibre
	Switzerland	Octahedron	60	255 × 11.5	Basal plate is present—size 18 nm	
		Octahedron	60	255 × 12		
	France	Polyhedron	60	240 × 8	–	Presence of polytail > 1000 nm
		–	60	222 × 10.5	–	
	U.S.A.	–	60–65	236 × 10	Spherical	
		–	60–65	290 × 10	–	
	U.S.S.R.	Polyhedron	40	220 × 8	–	
		Polyhedron	65	420 × 8	–	
	Finland	Hexagonal	50–56	217–239 × 4.8	–	Very short tail
		Hexagonal	60		–	
	Switzerland & France	Polyhedral or Octahedron	50	213 × 8	+	Terminal tail structure is not included in the length of the tail. Tail tip structure resembled a small plate, i.e. fitted with short prongs or fibrous mass.
			50	130 × 8	+	
			49	209 × 9	+	
			52	200 × 9	+	
			50	224 × 9	+	
			50	200 × 9		
			53	208 × 9		
L. bulgaricus	U.S.A.	–	59.4	198 × 6.6	–	Sheath size of contracted tail 17.5 × 77
		–	50	175 × 5	–	
	U.K.	Hexagonal	56–62	205–215 × –	Basal plate	The tail is intersected at intervals by cross-bar structures and the number varies up to a total of ten.
	Switzerland & France	Polyhedral or Icosahedral or Octahedron	44	116 × 8	+	Terminal tail structure is not included in the length of the tail. Tail tip structure bear short prongs or cluster of short fibres.
			55	140 × 9	+	
			53	128 × 8	+	
			52*	160 × 8	+	
			52*	160 × 8		

(+) Present; (–) Not reported or not present; (*) Presence of a "Collar".

Adapted from Accolas and Spillmann (1979a, b); Peake and Stanley (1978); Sarimo and Moksunen (1978); Koroleva *et al.* (1978); Reinbold, Reddy and Hammond (1982).

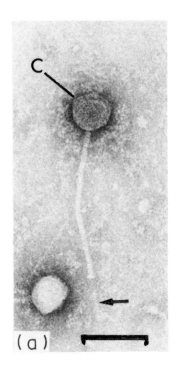

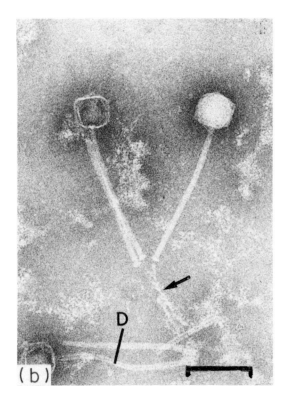

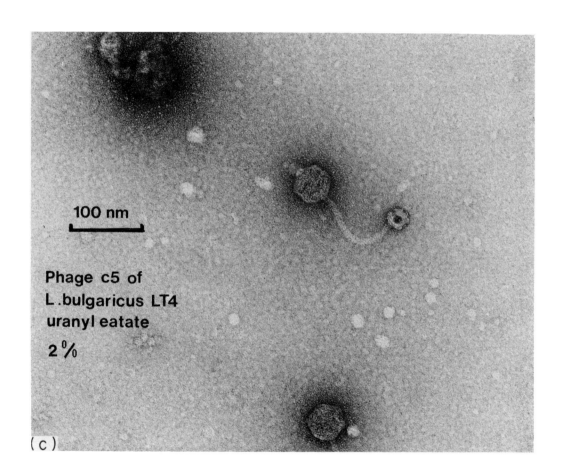

100 nm

Phage c5 of
L.bulgaricus LT4
uranyl eatate
2 %

(c)

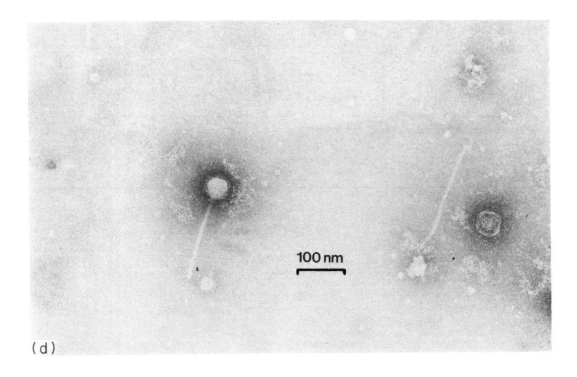

(d)

Fig. 6.3.   Morphology of bacteriophages of *S. thermophilus* and *L. bulgaricus*

(a) *Phage sc of S. thermophilus CNRZ 457*
Phage is stained with 2 % phosphotungstic acid (PTA) at pH 6.5. Bar = 100 nm. Note the isometric head (size # 50 nm) with its mottled appearance and (c) some capsomers being visible. The tail is fairly long (# 200 × 9 nm), non-contractile, flexible and regularly striated. The tip of the tail (→) fitted with a small plate and central fibre.

(b) *Phage st2 of S. thermophilus CNRZ 440*
Phage is stained with 2 % PTA at pH 6.5. Bar = 100 nm. Similar to phage sc. Note the full head (white) and empty ones (black). The small base plates (→) and fibres. (D) a ghost exhibits its axial duct.

(c) *Phage c5 of L. bulgaricus LT4*
Phage is stained with 2 % uranyl acetate (UA) at pH 6.5. Bar = 100 nm. Note the isometric head (50–55 nm), the non-contractile flexible and regularly striated tail (135–140 × 9–10 nm) and large basal plate (# 25 nm).

(d) *Phage y5 of L. bulgaricus Y5*
Phage is stained with 2 % UA at pH 6.5. Bar = 100 nm. Note the isometric head (50–55 nm) with large triangular "facets" (octahedron or icosahedron). A very small fibrous collar may be seen at head/tail junction. The tail is non-contractile, regularly striated (160 × 8 nm). The tail tip is described as "inflorescence like", and is possibly composed of short fibres which are delicate and labile, and hence not clearly visible.

After Accolas & Spillmann (1981)

Reprinted with permission of Laboratoire de Technologie Laitière, INRA, 78350 Jony-en-Josas, France, and Labor Für Milchwissenschaft, Eidgenössische Technische Hochschule Zürich, (ETH-Z), Eisgasse 8, CH-8004 Zürich, Switzerland.

It is evident, therefore, that one or more of the following precautionary measures should be practise in order to eliminate or control phage attack:

—use aseptic techniques for the propagation and production of starter cultures;

—ensure effective sterilisation of utensils and equipment;

—ensure proper heat treatment of the milk;

—restrict movement of plant personnel in starter handling room, and locate starter room far away from production area;

—check filtration of air into the starter room and production area;

—"fog" the atmosphere in the starter room with hypochlorite solution, or the use of laminar-flow cabinets for small-scale culture transfers;

—grow starter culture in phage inhibitory/resistant medium (PIM/PRM);

—use a daily rotation of phage unrelated strains (or phage-resistant strains) of *S. thermophilus* and *L. bulgaricus*;

—produce the bulk starter culture or even the retail product using a direct-to-vat system.

REFERENCES

ACCOLAS, J. P. and SPILLMANN, H. (1979a) *Journal of Applied Bacteriology,* **47,** 135.

ACCOLAS, J. P. and SPILLMANN, H. (1979b) *Journal of Applied Bacteriology,* **47,** 309.

ACCOLAS, J. P. and SPILLMANN, H. (1981) Personal communication.

ACCOLAS, J. P., VEAUX, M. and AUCLAIR, J. E. (1971) *Le Lait,* **51,** 249.

ACCOLAS, J. P., HEMME, D., DESMAZEAUD, J. J., VASSAL, L., BOUILLANNE, C. and VEAUX, M. (1980) *Le Lait,* **60,** 487.

AUCLAIR, J. E. (1954) *Journal of Dairy Research,* **21,** 323.

AUCLAIR, J. E. and BERRIDGE, N. J. (1953) *Journal of Dairy Research,* **20,** 370.

AUCLAIR, J. E. and HIRSCH, A. (1953) *Journal of Dairy Research,* **20,** 45.

AUCLAIR, J. E. and PORTMAN, A. (1957) *Nature,* **179,** 782.

AUCLAIR, J. E. and VASSAL, Y. (1960) *Journal of Dairy Research,* **30,** 345.

BAUTISTA, E. S., DAHIYA, R. S. and SPECK, M. L. (1966) *Journal of Dairy Research,* **33,** 299.

BERGEY'S MANUAL (1957) In *Bergey's Manual of Determinative Bacteriology,* 7th edition, Ed. by Breed, R. S., Murray, E. G. D. and Smith, N. R. Williams & Wilkins Co., Baltimore, U.S.A.

BERGEY'S MANUAL (1974) In *Bergey's Manual of Determinative Bacteriology,* 8th edition, Ed. by Buchanan, R. E. and Gibbons, N. E. Williams & Wilkins Co., Baltimore, U.S.A.

BOTTAZZI, V., BATTISTOTTI, B. and VESCOVO, M. (1971) *Milchwissenschaft,* **26,** 214.

BRACQUART, P. and LORIENT, D. (1979) *Milchwissenschaft,* **34,** 676.

BRACQUART, P., LORIENT, D. and ALAIS, C. (1978) *Milchwissenschaft,* **33,** 341.

CIBLIS, E. (1966) *XVIIth International Dairy Congress,* **C,** 395.

COGAN, T. M. (1972) *Applied Microbiology,* **23,** 960.

COGAN, T. M., GILLILAND, S. E. and SPECK, M. L. (1968) *Applied Microbiology,* **16,** 1215.

COUSINS, M. A. and MARTH, E. H. (1977a) *Journal of Food Protection,* **40,** 475.

COUSINS, M. A. and MARTH, E. H. (1977b) *Cultured Dairy Products Journal,* **12**(2), 15.

DEANE, D. D. and JENKINS, R. A. (1971) *Journal of Dairy Science,* **54,** 749.

DEANE, D. D. and PATTERN, M. M. van (1971) *Journal of Milk and Food Technology,* **34,** 16.

DESMAZEAUD, M. J. and HERMIER, J. H. (1972) *European Journal of Biochemistry,* **28,** 190.

DESMAZEAUD, M. J. and HERMIER, J. H. (1973) *Biochemie,* **55,** 679.

DRIESSEN, F. M., KINGMA, F. and STADHOUDERS, J. (1982) *Netherland Milk and Dairy Journal,* **36,** 135.

EDWARDS, D. I. (1980) In *Antimicrobial Drug Action,* Macmillan Press Ltd., London, U.K.

FEAGAN, J. T. (1959a) *The Australian Journal of Dairy Technology,* **14,** 110.

FEAGAN, J. T. (1959b) *The Australian Journal of Dairy Technology,* **14,** 117.

FERRI, R. F., FERNANDEZ, E. D., L'ANZA, C. G. and FERMANDEZ, E. A. (1979) *Dairy Science Abstracts,* **41,** 871.

GAJDUSEK, S. and SEBELA, F. (1973) *Dairy Science Abstracts,* **35,** 364.

GALESLOOT, Th. E., HASSING, F. and VERINGA, H. A. (1968) *Netherland Milk and Dairy Journal,* **22,** 50.

GARROD, L. P., LAMBERT, H. P. and O'GRADY, F. (1973) In *Antibiotic and Chemotherapy,* 4th edition, Churchill Livingstone, Edinburgh, U.K.

GAVIN, M. (1968) In *La Lyophilisation des Cultures de Yoghourt,* These No. 4227, l'Ecole Polytechnique Fédérale, Zurich, Switzerland.

GRIGOROFF, S. (1905) Cited by Gavin (1968).

HANSEN, P. A. (1968) In *Type Strains of Lactobacillus Species—A Report by the Taxonomic Subcommittee on Lactobacilli and Closely Related Organisms.* American Type Culture Collection, Maryland, U.S.A.

HARGROVE, R. E., WALTER, H. E., MALKAMES, Jr., J. P. and MASKELL, K. T. (1950) *Journal of Dairy Science*, **33**, 401.

HAYASHI, M., IRIE, R. and MORICHI, T. (1974) *Bulletin of the National Institute of Animal Industry*, **28**, 59.

HEMME, D. and NARDI, M. (1980) *Le Lait*, **60**, 375.

HEMME, D., SCHMAL, V. and AUCLAIR, J. E. (1981) *Journal of Dairy Research*, **48**, 139.

HEMME, D., WAHL, D. and NARDI, M. (1980) *Le Lait*, **60**, 111.

HIGASHIO, K., YOSHIOKA, Y. and KIKUCHI, T. (1977a) *Journal of Agricultural Chemical Society of Japan*, **51**, 203.

HIGASHIO, K., YOSHIOKA, Y. and KIKUCHI, T. (1977b) *Journal of Agricultural Chemical Society of Japan*, **51**, 209.

JAGO, G. R. and SWINBOURNE, M. F. (1956) *Journal of Dairy Research*, **26**, 123.

KOROLEVA, N. S., BANNIKOVA, L. A., MYTNIK, L. G. and BESPALOVA, I. A. (1978) *XXth International Dairy Congress*, **E**, 564.

KURMANN, J. (1967) *Lait Romand*, **43**(67), 508; (69), 523; (79), 599 and (83), 639.

LAWRENCE, R. C., THOMAS, T. D. and TERZAGHI, B. E. (1976) *Journal of Dairy Research*, **43**, 141.

LONDON, J. (1976) *Annual Reviews Microbiology*, **30**, 279.

LÜERSSEN, A. and KÜHN, M. (1908) Cited by Gavin (1968).

MARSHALL, V. M. E. and MABBITT, L. A. (1980) *Journal of the Society of Dairy Technology*, **33**, 129.

MARSHALL, V. M. E., COLE, W. M. and MABBITT, L. A. (1982) *Journal of Dairy Research*, **49**, 147.

METCHNIKOFF, E. (1910) In *The Prolongation of Life*, Revised Edition of (1907), Translated by Mitchell, C., Heineman Ltd., London, U.K.

MULLAN, W. M. A. (1979) *Dairy Industries International*, **44**(7), 11.

NIKOLOV, N. M. (1975) *Dairy Science Abstracts*, **37**, 341.

ORLA-JENSEN, S. (1931) In *Dairy Bacteriology*, 2nd Edition, Translated by Arup, P. S. J. & A. Churchill, London, U.K.

OTTOGALLI, G., GALLI, A. and DELLAGLIO (1979) *Journal of Dairy Research*, **46**, 127.

PATEL, J. D. (1969) *Journal of Food Science and Technology—Mysore*, **6**, 209.

PEAKE, S. E. and STANLEY, G. (1978) *Journal of Applied Bacteriology*, **44**, 321.

PEARCE, L. E. and BRYCE, S. A. (1973) *New Zealand Journal of Dairy Science and Technology*, **8**, 17.

PETTE, J. W. and KOOY, J. S. (1952) *Netherland Milk and Dairy Journal*, **6**, 233.

PETTE, J. W. and LOLKEMA, H. (1950a) *Netherland Milk and Dairy Journal*, **4**, 197.

PETTE, J. W. and LOLKEMA, H. (1950b) *Netherland Milk and Dairy Journal*, **4**, 209.

PETTE, J. W. and LOLKEMA, H. (1950c) *Netherland Milk and Dairy Journal*, **4**, 261.

REINBOLD, G. W. and REDDY, M. S. (1974) *Journal of Milk and Food Technology*, **37**, 517.

REINBOLD, G. W., REDDY, M. S. and HAMMOND, E. G. (1982) *Journal of Food Protection*, **45**, 119.

REITER, B. (1973) *Journal of the Society of Dairy Technology*, **26**, 3.

REITER, B. (1978) *Journal of Dairy Research*, **45**, 131.

REITER, B., VAZQUEZ, D. and NEWLAND, L. G. M. (1961) *Journal of Dairy Research*, **28**, 183.

RETTGER, L. F. and CHEPLIN, H. A. (1921) In *A Treatise on the Transformation of the Intestinal Flora with Special Reference to the Implantation of Bacillus acidophilus*, Yale University Press, U.S.A.

RETTGER, L. F., LEVY, M. N. and WEINSTEIN, L. (1935) In *Lactobacillus acidophilus and its Therapeutic Application*, Yale University Press, U.S.A.

ROGOSA, M. and HANSEN, P. A. (1971) *International Journal of Systematic Bacteriology*, **21**, 177.

SANDINE, W. E. (1979) In *Lactic Starter Cultures Technology*, Phizer Cheese Monographs Vol. VI, Chase, Phizer & Co. Inc., New York, U.S.A.

SARIMO, S. S. and MOKSUNEN, R. L. I. (1978) *XXth International Dairy Congress*, **E**, 565.

SHANKER, P. A. (1977) In *Inter-Relationship of S. thermophilus and L. bulgaricus in Yoghurt Cultures*, Ph.D. Thesis, University of Reading, U.K.

SHANKAR, P. A. and DAVIES, F. L. (1978) *XXth International Dairy Congress*, **E**, 467.

SIMONDS, J., HANSEN, P. A. and LAKSHMANAN, S. (1971) *Journal of Bacteriology*, **107**, 382.

SOLDAL, A. and LANGSRUD, T. (1978) *XXth International Dairy Congress*, **E**, 563.

SOLOMAN, E., SCORTESCU, G. and BILBILE, V. (1966) *Dairy Science Abstracts*, **28**, 423.

SOZZI, T., POULIN, J. M. and MARET, R. (1978) *Journal of Dairy Research*, **45**, 259.

STOLK, K. (1955) *Netherland Milk and Dairy Journal*, **9**, 37.

STORGARDS, T. (1964) In *Fermented Milks*, IDF Annual Bulletin, Part III, Brussels, Belgium.

TAMIME, A. Y. (1977a) In *Some Aspects of the Production of Yoghurt and Condensed Yoghurt*, Ph.D. Thesis, University of Reading, U.K.

TAMIME, A. Y. (1977b) *Dairy Industries International*, **42**(8), 7.

TAMIME, A. Y. and DEETH, H. C. (1980) *Journal of Food Protection*, **43**, 939.

TRAMER, J. (1973) *Journal of the Society of Dairy Technology*, **26**, 16.

VAZQUEZ, D. and REITER, B. (1962) *Dairy Industries*, **26**, 525.

VERINGA, H. A., GALESLOOT, Th. E. and DAVELAAR, H. S. (1968) *Netherland Milk and Dairy Journal*, **22**, 114.

WEINMANN, D. E., MORRIS, G. K. and WILLIAMS, W. L. (1964) *Journal of Bacteriology*, **84**, 263.

WHITEHEAD, H. R. and COX, G. A. (1935) *New Zealand Journal of Science and Technology*, **16**, 319.

YU, T. J. and KIM, I. H. (1979) *Korean Journal of Food Science and Technology*, **11**, 200.

CHAPTER 7

Biochemistry of Fermentation

Micro-organisms sustain their life cycles via a large number of interrelated/complex metabolic pathways covering both biosynthetic and energy-yielding functions. Each individual metabolic pathway consists of many reactions which, in turn, are regulated by different enzyme systems, and hence it is the level of enzyme synthesis and activity which maintains and controls the functions of the microbial cell (Stanier, Doudoroff and Adelberg, 1971). One regulatory (or feedback) mechanism is derived from low molecular weight compounds which result from the breakdown of nutrients (carbohydrates, proteins, lipids and other minor constituents) present in the growth medium. The composition of this medium is, therefore, important in relation to the build-up and division of the microbial cells, but in the case of yoghurt its effect on the metabolism and growth of *Streptococcus thermophilus* and *Lactobacillus bulgaricus* also influences the properties and characteristics of the product. For this reason, the biochemical reactions initiated by the yoghurt organisms are fundamental to the manufacture of a high quality product, and hence it is pertinent to consider them in some detail.

CARBOHYDRATE METABOLISM

A. Metabolic Pathways

The microbial cells derive their energy requirements via different systems; for example, the cytochrome system for terminal electron transport, the enzymes that operate the anaplerotic pathways, the tricarboxylic cycle, or by fermentation. The lactic acid bacteria, however, do not possess any of the former three systems, and energy can only be supplied by the fermentation of carbohydrates (Lawrence, Thomas and Terzaghi, 1976); lactose is the only sugar present in milk, and the yoghurt organisms utilise it for this purpose. The catabolism of lactose by *S. thermophilus* and *L. bulgaricus* takes place inside the cell, and hence the initial step is to transport the lactose molecule across the cell wall membrane.

In the homofermentative group N lactic streptococci, the transport of lactose across the cell membrane involves the phosphoenolpyruvate (PEP)-dependent: phosphotransferase (PTS) systems, and lactose is phosphosylated to glucosyl β-(1,4)-galactoside-6P (lactose-P) during its translocation. Inside the cell, lactose-P is hydrolysed to D-glucose and galactose-6P by the enzyme β-D-phosphogalactosidase (β-P gal). Glucose is metabolised to pyruvate via the Embden Meyerhof pathway (EMP), and lactate dehydrogenase converts the pyruvate to lactic acid; the initial steps involve the normal glycolytic sequence. The metabolism of galactose-6P is somewhat different

295

from glucose utilisation, in that firstly, it is converted to glyceraldehyde-3P via the D-tagatose-6P pathway, and secondly, the glyceraldehyde-3P is catabolised to pyruvate and lactic acid by the normal glycolysis cycle (Lawrence, Thomas and Terzaghi, *loc. cit.*; Law and Sharpe, 1978; Lawrence and Thomas, 1979). Whether such transport or metabolic pathways occur in the yoghurt organisms is not, apparently, yet known.

It is most likely that the transport of lactose across the cell membrane of *S. thermophilus* and *L. bulgaricus* is mediated by the action of the enzyme galactoside permease. These organisms possess the enzyme β-D-galactosidase (β-gal) which hydrolyses the lactose inside the cell to D-glucose and β-D-galactose. The former monosaccharide is metabolised, in both *S. thermophilus* and *L. bulgaricus*, to lactic acid as in group N lactic streptococci, but the catabolism of galactose by the yoghurt organisms is not well established. Evidence of galactose accumulation in yoghurt (Goodenough and Kleyn, 1976; O'Leary and Woychik, 1976a, b; Tamime, 1977a, b) indicates that the monosaccharide is not metabolised to any great extent, and permeates out through the cell membrane. However, a second enzyme, β-Pgal (also present in cheese starter cultures), has been reported in *L. bulgaricus* (Permi, Sandine and Elliker, 1972) and in *S. thermophilus* (Somkuti and Steinberg, 1978, 1979a; Farrow, 1980), and Table 7.1 indicates the relative activities of β-gal and β-Pgal in the yoghurt organisms; the former enzyme is normally more active. It is possible, however, that β-Pgal becomes more active under certain conditions, i.e. in synthetic media, where galactose is metabolised by some strains of *L. bulgaricus* (Snell, Kitay and Hoff-Jørgensen, 1948; see also Table 6.1) and in *S. thermophilus* (Reddy, Williams and Reinbold, 1973; Somkuti and Steinberg, 1979b; see also Table 7.2). In the presence of β-gal and β-Pgal enzymes in the yoghurt organisms, the intracellular hydrolysis of lactose yields D-glucose, β-D-galactose and/or galactose-6P. In view of the fact that some of yoghurt bacteria are capable of fermenting galactose, it is possible that the galactose-6P is catabolised to lactic acid via the same D-tagatose-6P pathway that is present in group N lactic streptococci. However, in commercial practice the production of lactic acid is more likely to occur via the glycolysis of glucose, and to a lesser degree via the D-tagatose-6P pathway of galactose utilisation, for it is possible that the latter metabolic pathway is suppressed in

TABLE 7.1. *Comparison of β-D galactosidase and β-D phosphogalactosidase activities in the yoghurt starter cultures*

Organism	Origin	β-gal	β-Pgal	References
L. bulgaricus*	ATCC 12278	2,363	158	Permi, Sandine and Elliker (*loc. cit.*)
L. bulgaricus**	B-6	5.82	–	
	B-56	5.27	–	
	y B-62	3.29	–	Toba *et al.* (1981)
S. thermophilus**	510	4.10	–	
S. thermophilus***	NCDO 573	236	38	Farrow (*loc. cit.*)
	NCDO 821	833	91	

ATCC (American Type Culture Collection—USA).
NCDO (National Collection of Dairy Organisms—UK).
Other cultures were obtained from National Institute of Animal Industry, Chiba, Japan.

  * Crude cell free extracts of lactobacilli.
    Expressed as μmol of *o*-nitrophenol liberated from *o*-nitrophenyl-β-D-galactopyranoside or *o*-nitrophenyl-β-D-galactopyranoside-6-phosphate per mg of enzyme protein/min under the assay conditionn used. These preliminary screening data were obtained at pH 7.0.
 ** Cell-free extracts of lactic acid bacteria.
    Expressed as μmol of *o*-nitrophenol liberated from *o*-nitrophenyl-β-D-galactopyranoside per mg of protein/min.
*** Units of enzyme $\times$ 10^3/mg dry cell weight and one unit of enzyme activity released 1 μmol ONP/min.

TABLE 7.2. *Adaptability and/or ability of* S. thermophilus *to ferment certain carbohydrates*

Number of strains tested	Group	Carbohydrate fermentation		
		lactose	glucose	galactose
12	A	+	+	+
18	B	+	+	−
1	C	+	−	−

(+) Positive reaction.
(−) Negative reaction.
Group B and C failure to utilise galactose suggests that strains are devoid of D-tagatose-6P pathway.

Adapted from Somkuti and Steinberg (1979b).

S. thermophilus and *L. bulgaricus* in the presence of a more readily fermentable sugar, i.e. glucose. The possible pathways of lactose utilisation by the yoghurt starter bacteria can, therefore, be integrated as illustrated in Fig. 7.1.

Some strains of lactic acid bacteria utilise the carbohydrates in the growth medium for the production of polysaccharide materials, and examples of such organisms are *Streptococcus mutans*, *Streptococcus bovis* and *Leuconostoc mesenteroides* which have the ability to produce

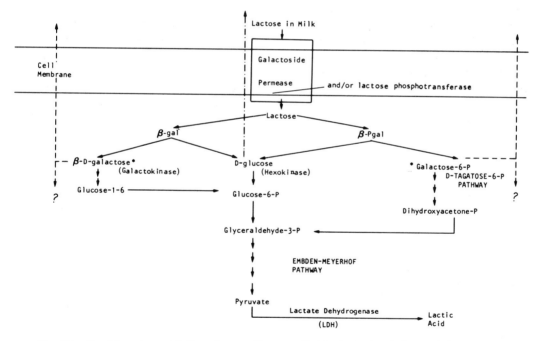

Fig. 7.1. Possible major metabolic pathways of lactose utilisation by *S. thermophilus* and *L. bulgaricus*

* Possible metabolic pathways of some *S. thermophilus* and *L. bulgaricus* strains that can utilise galactose.

– – – Release of galactose into milk by some strains of *S. thermophilus* and *L. bulgaricus* which are unable to utilise galactose.

–·–·– Release of glucose into milk by RR starter culture for the "slime" production (see text).

? Possible alternative metabolic pathway.

297

extracellular dextrans (Brooker, 1979). Sharpe, Garvie and Tilbury (1972) isolated a similar material, slime, from some heterofermentative *Lactobacillus* spp., and it was found to be glucan, probably dextran, consisting of α-1-6-glycosidic linkages. Incidentally, a "slime" material is also produced by some yoghurt starter cultures, e.g. the RR culture which was developed in The Netherlands to enhance the viscosity of yoghurt (Galesloot and Hassing, 1966; see also Tamime and Robinson, 1978; Luczynska *et al.*, 1978). The work of Tamime (1977a, b, 1978) suggested that the chemical composition of the polysaccharide material produced by starter culture RR was a glucan. Thus, the "slime" yielded only glucose after acid hydrolysis, and Fig. 7.2 confirms the similarity between "slime" produced by culture RR and a sample of β-glucan. However, it is not yet apparent how the biosynthesis of such polymers occurs in the *S. thermophilus* or *L. bulgaricus* strains of starter culture RR. However, as glucose is the only monosaccharide required for the

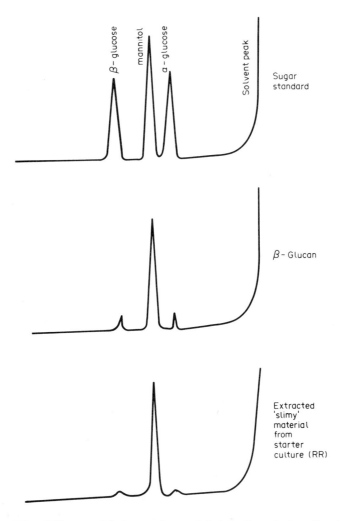

Fig. 7.2.   GLC traces of β-glucan and suspected glucan from starter culture (RR)

After Tamime (1977a)

298

synthesis of the polymer, it is possible that glucose permeates through the cell membrane into the milk, and in the presence of glycosyltransferase the polymer is formed. Alternatively, these organisms may indulge in some type of capsule formation whereby the polymer is synthesised, but whatever the mechanism, it is evident that the carbohydrate metabolism of culture RR is somewhat different from other yoghurt starter strains.

B. Production of Lactic Acid

The catabolism of lactose by *S. thermophilus* and *L. bulgaricus* results mainly in the production of lactic acid (see Fig. 7.1), and although the conversion process consists of many different biochemical reactions it can be simplified by the following equation:

$$\text{Lactose} \quad + \quad \text{Water} \longrightarrow \text{Lactic acid}$$
$$C_{12}H_{22}O_{11} \qquad\qquad H_2O \qquad\qquad 4C_3H_6O_3$$

Lactic acid is important during the manufacture of yoghurt for the following reasons: firstly, the lactic acid helps to destabilise the casein micelles by progressively converting the colloidal calcium/phosphate complex (in the micelle) to the soluble calcium/phosphate fraction which diffuses into the aqueous phase of the milk. This results in the micelles being gradually depleted of calcium, so leading to coagulation of casein at pH 4.6–4.7 and the formation of the yoghurt gel. Once this physical condition has been established, soluble calcium lactate is formed, and according to Dyatchenko (1971) the destabilisation reaction can be summarised as follows:

$$
\begin{array}{ll}
\text{Calcium—caseinate—} & + \quad \text{Lactic acid} \longrightarrow \text{Casein complex} \\
\text{phosphate complex} & \qquad\qquad\qquad\qquad\qquad + \\
& \qquad\qquad\qquad\qquad \text{Calcium lactate} \\
& \qquad\qquad\qquad\qquad\qquad + \\
& \qquad\qquad\qquad\qquad \text{Calcium phosphate}
\end{array}
$$

Secondly, the lactic acid gives yoghurt its distinctive and characteristic taste, i.e. sharp and acidic, and it can also enhance or contribute to the "nutty" and/or "aromatic" flavour of the product.

Lactic acid bacteria possess the enzyme lactate dehydrogenase (LDH) for the synthesis of lactate from pyruvic acid (see Fig. 7.1). Lactate is the latin word for acid, e.g. lactic acid, derived from milk. Different forms of lactic acid can be produced, e.g. L(+), D(−) or DL(±), and such isomers differ in the configuration of the second carbon atom, as follows:

$$
\begin{array}{cc}
\text{COOH} & \text{COOH} \\
| & | \\
\text{HO}-\text{C}-\text{H} & \text{H}-\text{C}-\text{OH} \\
| & | \\
\text{CH}_3 & \text{CH}_3 \\
\\
\text{L(+) Lactic acid} & \text{D(−) Lactic acid}
\end{array}
$$

In yoghurt starter cultures, *S. thermophilus* produces mainly L(+) lactic acid (Garvie, 1978; Hemme, Nardi and Wahl, 1981), and D(−) lactic acid is produced by *L. bulgaricus* (Gasser, 1970; Gasser and Gasser, 1971; see also review by Tamime and Deeth, 1980). The LDH enzyme is situated in the cytoplasm of the bacterial cell, and according to Garvie (1980) the activity of this enzyme is, in

299

the yoghurt organisms, dependent on nicotinamide adenine dinucleotide (NAD)/reduced nicotinamide adenine dinucleotide (NADH). The former coenzyme is regenerated from NADH during the conversion of pyruvic acid to lactic acid. However, some strains of *S. thermophilus* contain an LDH enzyme which is activated by fructose, 1,6-diphosphate (FDP) (Wolin, 1964; Garvie, 1980), and such enzymes show an absolute requirement for FDP at physiological pHs; the reaction is virtually non-reversible, and the enzyme reacts weakly with lactic acid and NAD.

During the manufacture of yoghurt, *S. thermophilus* grows faster than *L. bulgaricus* (see Fig. 6.1), and hence L(+) lactic acid is produced first followed by D(−) lactic acid. The percentage of each isomer present in yoghurt is an indication of the following:

(a) Yoghurt, which contains more than 70% of L(+) lactic acid has been inoculated with a starter culture which consists predominantly of *S. thermophilus* (Kunath and Kandler, 1980), or the fermentation has been carried out at a temperature below 40°C, or the product has been cooled at a "low" acidity, and the cooled yoghurt contains around 0.8% or less lactic acid.

(b) Yoghurt containing more D(−) lactic acid than L(+) lactic acid has been incubated at too high a temperature, i.e. 45°C or more, or for a long period whereby the product has become highly acidic, or has suffered from prolonged storage, or the starter inoculation rate was more than 3%, or the starter contained more rods than cocci.

Yoghurt usually contains 45–60% L(+) lactic acid and 40–55% D(−) lactic acid (Puhan, Banhegyi and Flüler, 1973; Puhan, Flüler and Banhegyi, 1973, 1974; Vanderpoorten and Renterghem, 1974; Kielwein and Daun, 1980; Aleksieva, Girginova and Kondratenko, 1981) and the ratio of L(+):D(−) lactic acid could be used to assess the quality of yoghurt. However, Puhan, Flüler and Banhegyi (1973, 1974) examined 269 samples of commercial yoghurt and found that the ratio of L(+):D(−) ranged from as little as 0.34 (very acidic) to 8.28 (i.e. L(+) lactic acid predominant). A ratio of 2 was suggested by Blumenthal and Helbling (1974) to be consistent with a "good yoghurt". However, such an approach could be more useful in situations where the quality of yoghurt (i.e. sweet-low in acid or sharp-high in acid) has to be manipulated to meet the demands of consumers in different markets, i.e. a sharp and acidic yoghurt must contain a low ratio of L(+): D(−) and *vice versa*.

C. Production of Flavour Compounds

Starter cultures are primarily responsible for the production of the flavour compounds which contribute to the aroma of yoghurt. These compounds may be divided into four main categories:

—non-volatile acids, e.g. lactic, pyruvic, oxalic or succinic;
—volatile acids, e.g. formic, acetic, propionic or butyric;
—carbonyl compounds, e.g. acetaldehyde, acetone, acetoin or diacetyl;
—miscellaneous compounds, e.g. certain amino acids and/or constituents formed by thermal degradation of protein, fat or lactose.

There is general agreement in the literature that the aroma and flavour of yoghurt are basically due to the production of lactic acid and carbonyl compounds. Pette and Lolkema (1950) were the first to investigate the flavour of yoghurt, and they concluded that the aroma was due to the presence of acetaldehyde and other unidentifiable compounds; however, they also observed that the level of acetaldehyde was much greater in mixed cultures due to the associative growth of the yoghurt organisms, although *L. bulgaricus* played the more important role. This observation has been confirmed by many workers, and a summary of these results can be seen in Table 7.3.

TABLE 7.3.   *The production of carbonyl compounds (ppm) by yoghurt starter cultures*

Organism	Acetaldehyde	Acetone	Acetoin	Diacetyl
S. thermophilus	1.0–8.3	0.2–5.2	1.5–7.0	0.1–13.0
L. bulgaricus	1.4–12.2	0.3–3.2	Trace–2.0	0.5–13.0
Mixed cultures	2.0–41.0	1.3–4.0	2.2–5.7	0.4–0.9

Adapted From Tamime and Deeth (*loc. cit.*).

Organoleptic assessments of yoghurt by Pette and Lolkema (*loc. cit.*) and Schulz and Hingst (1954) showed that yoghurt was rated "best or high" by a taste panel when the product contained a low level of acetaldehyde, and they suggested that other carbonyl compounds may be primarily responsible for the typical "yoghurt" flavour and/or aroma. Such a view was shared by Bottazzi and Dellaglio (1967) who observed that single strains of *S. thermophilus* produced equal quantities of acetaldehyde and diacetyl, and that a ratio of 1:1 of these compounds typifies the desired aroma of yoghurt. However, in another publication from the same laboratory, Bottazzi and Vescovo (1969) attributed a "fullness" of yoghurt flavour to a ratio of 2.8:1 of acetaldehyde to acetone, both of which were produced by single cultures of *S. thermophilus*; only a small amount of acetone was produced by *L. bulgaricus*. Incidentally, the same workers did not observe any diacetyl production by these particular test organisms, whereas Dutta, Kuila and Ranganathan (1973) obtained 13 ppm of diacetyl (the highest level reported in the literature) from single strains of *S. thermophilus* and *L. bulgaricus* (see also Baisya and Bose, 1975; Mutai, Aso and Shirota, 1972). The production of such high levels of diacetyl and acetoin by single cultures does not appear to correspond with the reported levels of these compounds in yoghurt (see Table 7.3). These discrepancies could be attributed to variations in the strains of streptococci and lactobacilli used, or to differences in the analytical methods employed to detect the level of these carbonyl compounds, and/or to alterations in the level of milk solids, type of milk, and degree of heat treatment used during the preparation of the basic mix.

It could be argued, of course, that the presence of these carbonyl compounds is not essential, for instance, in fruit and flavoured yoghurts, but a high level of acetaldehyde is desirable for the typical aroma of natural or plain yoghurt, and Suzuki *et al.* (1979) concluded that yoghurt, which contained only 7 ppm acetaldehyde, had not sufficient of the desirable "yoghurt" flavour. Furthermore, the same workers detected high levels of diacetyl in fermented milks only in the presence of *S. lactis* var. *diacetylactis*, a view supported by many authors (see Table 7.3 for level of diacetyl production by mixed yoghurt cultures).

Robinson, Tamime and Chubb (1977) and Tamime (1977a) assessed, both organoleptically and for the presence of carbonyl compounds, samples of natural yoghurt made using different strains of starter cultures (CH-1 (normal), Boll-3 (viscous) and RR (slimy)—the former two cultures were obtained from Chr. Hansen's Lab A/S, Denmark and culture (RR) from NIZO, The Netherlands). The judging panel consisted of Mediterranean and non-Mediterranean nationalities. The preference trend was for yoghurt made by culture (CH-1), i.e. sharp and acidic, followed by (Boll-3), and the least preferred, especially by the Mediterranean group, was yoghurt made by starter (RR).

The level of acetaldehyde in these yoghurts is illustrated in Table 7.4, and it can be observed that starter culture (CH-1) produced the highest level of acetaldehyde, followed by (Boll-3) and finally (RR). Hence, these results tend to confirm that the typical aroma and flavour of natural or plain yoghurt is directly associated with the presence of carbonyl compounds, mainly acetaldehyde, in the product.

TABLE 7.4. *Detectable levels of acetaldehyde in yoghurts produced with different starter cultures*

Starter culture used	Acetaldehyde	
	(ppm)	Mean differences
CH-1	37.5	± 2.3
Boll-3	27.6	± 1.3
RR	10.4	± 0.3

Colorimetric test method was used which was non-specific for acetaldehyde as it measured the total content of ketones and aldehyde constituents.

These figures were mean of 10 samples and the acidity ranged from pH 4.0–4.1 or 1.1–1.2% lactic.acid.

After: Tamime (1977a); Robinson, Tamime and Chubb (*loc. cit.*).

During the manufacture of yoghurt, the production of acetaldehyde becomes evident only at a certain level of acidification, i.e. pH 5.0, reaches a maximum at pH 4.2 and stabilises at pH 4.0. Fortification of the yoghurt milk with milk solids, and certain heat treatments of the basic mix, can significantly increase the acetaldehyde content of the yoghurt (Gorner, Palo and Bertan, 1968). However, losses of acetaldehyde from yoghurt, after storage for 24 hours, are dependent on the type of milk used for processing, i.e. yoghurt made from "full fat or whole milk" showed little change in acetaldehyde content, while in "skim milk" yoghurt the level decreased (Yu and Nakanishi, 1975a, b). Furthermore, the production of acetaldehyde in yoghurt made from milk of different species can vary. Thus, Gorner, Palo and Bertan (1971) observed that acetaldehyde levels, after 3 hours of incubation, were highest in yoghurt made from cow's milk, followed by goat's milk and finally ewe's milk; the GLC peak heights of acetaldehyde in these yoghurts were 400, 23 and 2 mm respectively. The same observation was reported by Abrahamsen, Svenson and Tufto (1978), where 17.1 ppm of acetaldehyde were present in yoghurt processed from cow's milk, as compared to 4.7–5.5 ppm in goat's milk after 3 hours of incubation. The behaviour of the yoghurt starter cultures in these different types of milk is not well established, but one of the reason(s) for the observed changes in metabolism may be that both ewe's and goat's milk contains a substance which blocks the formation of a precursor required by the starter organism for the production of acetaldehyde (see later).

Other compounds which could be associated, perhaps indirectly, with flavour enhancement, or act as precursors for the formation of the major aroma compounds in yoghurt, are:

(1) Volatile fatty acids, e.g. acetic, propionic, butyric, isovaleric, caproic, caprylic and capric acids (Turic, Rasic and Canic, 1969; Dumont and Adda, 1973).
(2) Amino acids, e.g. serine, glutamic acid, proline, valine, leucine, isoleucine and tyrosine (Groux, 1976).
(3) Products of thermal degradation of milk constituents, i.e. 80–90°C for 15–30 minutes (Viani and Horman, 1976).

(a) From fat
    (i) keto acids (acetone, butanone, hexanone).
    (ii) hydroxy acids (v-valerolactone, δ-caprolactone, δ-caprilactone).
    (iii) miscellaneous (2-heptanone, 2-nonanone, 2-undecanone, pentane).
(b) From lactose (furfural, furfurylalcohol, 5-methylfurfural, 2-pentylfurane).
(c) From fat and/or lactose (benzyl alcohol, benzyladehyde, methylbenzoate).
(d) From protein
    (i) methionine (dimethylsulphide).
    (ii) valine (isobutyraldehyde).
    (iii) phenylalanine (phenylacetaldehyde).
(4) n-pentaldehyde and 2-heptanone produced by *L. bulgaricus* (Yu and Nakanishi, 1975a, b; Gronx and Moinas, 1974).

As mentioned earlier, the formation of acetaldehyde and other "aromatic" compounds by *S. thermophilus* and *L. bulgaricus* in yoghurt takes place during the fermentation, and the final levels are dependent on the presence of specific enzymes which are able to catalyse the formation of carbonyl compounds from the different milk constituents. Recently, Lees and Jago (1978a, b) have reviewed in detail the role of lactic acid bacteria in terms of flavour production in cultured dairy products, and Table 7.5 summarises the possible metabolic pathways and reactions initiated by *S. thermophilus* and *L. bulgaricus* during the formation of these flavouring compounds in yoghurt. By far the most important milk ingredients required by the yoghurt starter cultures for producing acetaldehyde are: lactose (mainly the glucose fraction) and the amino acids threonine and methionine. The work of Lees and Jago (1976a, b) has confirmed the formation of acetaldehyde and ethanol from glucose by *S. thermophilus* and *L. bulgaricus*: the reaction is catalysed by the enzymes aldehyde dehydrogenase and alcohol dehydrogenase. The former enzyme was present in both of the yoghurt organisms, but the latter enzyme, i.e. alcohol dehydrogenase, was only present in three out of four strains of *S. thermophilus* (see Table 7.6). The synthesis of acetaldehyde by the enzyme aldehyde dehydrogenase involves the reduction of acetyl-CoA or acetate, and the alcohol dehydrogenase reduces acetaldehyde to ethanol (Lees and Jago, 1978a).

The enzyme which is mainly associated, in this context, with threonine metabolism is threonine aldolase, and both *S. thermophilus* and *L. bulgaricus* possess this enzyme (see Table 7.6). However,

TABLE 7.5. *Possible origin of flavour compounds produced by* S. thermophilus *and* L. bulgaricus *during the manufacture of yoghurt*

Milk constituent	Reaction involving acetaldehyde formation	References
Lactose	Via pyruvate during glycolytic cycle	Seneca, Henderson and Collins (1950)
	Via acetyl phosphate or pyruvate	Lees and Jago (1966)
	Direct decarboxylation of pyruvate	Kennan and Bills (1968)
Amino acid	Valine ⟶ acetaldehyde + (possibly) alanine	White, Handler and Smith (1959)
	Threonine ⟶ acetaldehyde + glycine	Lees and Jago (1966, 1976a,b, 1977, 1978a,b)
	Cleavage of threonine to glycine and acetaldehyde	Sandine and Elliker (1970)
	Conversion of methionine ⟶ threonine ⟶ acetaldehyde + glycine	Shankar (1977)
Nucleic acid	Thymidine ⟶ acetaldehyde + glyceraldehyde-3-phosphate	Lees and Jago (1977)

Refer to Figs. 7.3, 7.4 and 7.5 for more detailed information.

TABLE 7.6. *Specific activities of enzymes metabolising or synthesising acetaldehyde in the yoghurt starter cultures*

| Organism | | Aldehyde** dehydrogenase | Specific activities* | | |
			Threonine aldolase	Deoxyribo- aldolase	Alcohol dehydrogenase
S. thermophilus	CSIRO	0.15	0.30	0.00	0.0 (0.1)
	TWI	1.05	0.10	2.32	5.0 (0.0)
	ST7	0.17	0.26	0.00	0.7 (0.1)
	NIZO	0.04	0.33	0.00	19.0 (0.0)
L. bulgaricus	B1	0.28	1.07	0.00	0.0 (0.2)
	B2	0.53	0.69	0.00	0.2 (0.0)
	B3	0.10	0.62	0.00	0.0 (0.1)
	B4	0.26	0.70	0.00	0.0

* μmoles $\times 10^{-2}$ of product formed or substrate utilised/min/mg protein.
** The values shown have been based on per mg dry wt. of cells.
 Values in parentheses give the alcohol dehydrogenase activities with $NADPH_2$ as cofactor.

Adapted from Lees and Jago (1978b).

threonine aldolase is more active in the lactobacilli than in the streptococci (Lees and Jago, 1976a, b, 1977), and according to Lees and Jago (1978a) the breakdown reaction is as follows:

$$CH_3CHOHCHNH_3{}^+COO^- \xrightarrow{\qquad} CH_3CHO \ + \ CH_2NH_3{}^+COO^-$$

| Threonine | Pyridoxal phosphate | Acetaldehyde | Glycine |

Another amino acid, methionine, can also increase the level of acetaldehyde in a growth medium inoculated only with *S. thermophilus* (Shankar, 1977). He observed that by fortifying the growth medium with 100–400 μg/ml methionine the level of acetaldehyde after 20 hours of incubation had increased from 1 ppm in the control to 10 and 14 ppm respectively in the test media. The proposed conversion of methionine to acetaldehyde plus glycine is illustrated in Fig. 7.3 (see also Rodwell, 1975; Truffa-Bachi and Cohen, 1968).

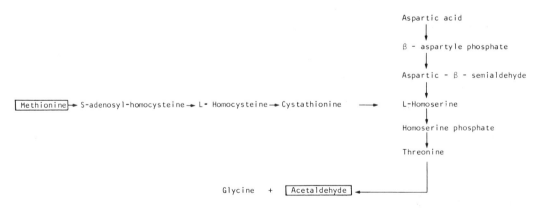

Fig. 7.3. The pathway for conversion of methionine to acetaldehyde by *S. thermophilus*

After: Shankar (*loc. cit.*).

Finally, Lees and Jago (1977) detected deoxyriboaldolase activity in one of four strains of *S. thermophilus* tested, but this enzyme was not active in *L. bulgaricus* (see Table 7.6). This enzyme, along with thymidine phosphorylase and deoxyribomutase, degrades DNA to 2-deoxyribose-5-phosphate, which is further broken down to acetaldehyde and glyceraldehyde; the possible pathway is illustrated in Fig. 7.4.

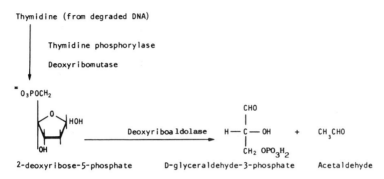

Fig. 7.4.   The formation of acetaldehyde from nucleic acid by deoxyriboaldolase present in *S. thermophilus*

Adapted from Lees and Jago (1977, 1978a).

It can be observed, therefore, that the production of acetaldehyde by *S. thermophilus* and *L. bulgaricus* may involve a number of different metabolic pathways, and Fig. 7.5 illustrates the possible routes by which acetaldehyde may be formed from carbohydrates, proteins and/or nucleic acids.

PROTEIN METABOLISM

Although yoghurt starter cultures are considered to be only weakly proteolytic, *S. thermophilus* and *L. bulgaricus* may, during the fermentation, cause a significant degree of proteolysis, and this activity may be important for the following reasons:

(a) The enzymatic hydrolysis of milk proteins results in the liberation of peptides of varying sizes and free amino acids, and these possible changes can affect the physical structure of yoghurt.
(b) As discussed elsewhere, the liberation of amino acids into the milk is essential to the growth of *S. thermophilus*.
(c) Although amino acids and peptides may not contribute directly towards the flavour of yoghurt, they do act as precursors for the multitude of reactions which produce flavour compounds (see Groux, *loc. cit.*; Viani and Horman, *loc. cit.*).

The range of products released by proteolysis is dependent on two main factors: firstly, the components of the milk protein fraction, and secondly, the types of proteolytic enzymes that the yoghurt organisms may possess.

305

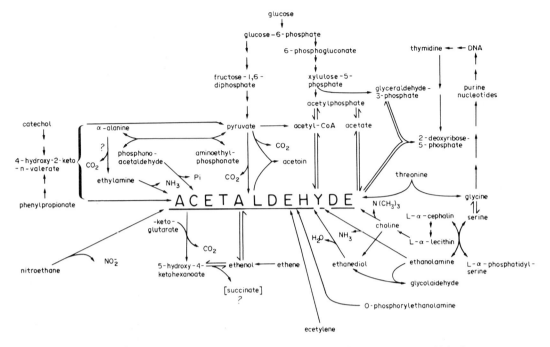

Fig. 7.5. Diagrammatic representation of the known reactions involving acetaldehyde

After Lees and Jago (1978a).

Reprinted with permission of *Journal of Dairy Science.*

1. Constituent compounds of the milk protein molecule

The protein fraction in milk is composed of casein, whey proteins and non-protein nitrogen, and although the protein molecule is highly complex, it is important, in the present context, to describe very briefly the structure of the protein molecule, and show where hydrolysis may occur.

The basic constituents of a protein molecule are compounds known as amino acids. These are about 19–20 different types of amino acids which have been identified in milk proteins, and their basic structure is as follows:

$$\begin{array}{ccc} NH_2 & & NH_3^{(+)} \\ | & & | \\ R-C-COOH & \text{``Zwitterion''} & R-C-COO^{(-)} \\ | & & | \\ H & & H \end{array}$$

Each amino acid may consist of one or more amino groups (NH_3^+) and one or more carboxyl groups (COO^-). All the amino acids show asymmetry about the α-carbon atom—where the amino group is next to the carboxyl group—with the exception of glycine where R = H. The nomenclature of the amino acids is similar to that of the carbohydrates, i.e. D and L indicate their configuration about the α-carbon atom. Some amino acids are cyclic, e.g. proline which is referred to as an "Imino Acid", but their structure is similar to α-amino acids.

These amino acids are the basic units of the protein molecule, and polypeptide chains are built up of sequences of amino acid residues; the structure of the chain is as follows:

$$\left[\begin{array}{ccc} N & CH & C \\ | & | & \| \\ H & R & O \end{array} \right]_n$$

The build-up of a polypeptide chain results in a loss of water from the amino acids, and the bonds between the adjacent units are known as peptide bonds, e.g. —NH.CO—. These polypeptide chains then link together due to presence of various forces, e.g. hydrogen bonds, covalent and non-covalent bonds, and this aggregation leads to the formation of the protein molecule.

2. Proteolytic enzymes

These enzymes, as the name suggests, are specific in their action, and their main function is to catalyse the hydrolytic cleavage of the peptide bonds which form the backbone of the protein molecule. The action of the proteolytic enzymes on the peptide bond may be represented as follows:

$$
\begin{array}{c}
R \\
| \\
\ldots\ -HN.CH.CO \\
\\
HO
\end{array}
\quad
\begin{array}{c}
\\
\\
HN.CH.CO \longrightarrow \ldots \\
\\
H
\end{array}
\quad
\begin{array}{c}
R \\
| \\
\ldots\cdot-HN.CH.COOH + \\
\end{array}
\quad
\begin{array}{c}
R_1 \\
| \\
H_2N.CH.CO \longrightarrow \ldots
\end{array}
$$

Enzymes acting on peptide bonds are known as peptide hydrolases, and up to the present time a large number of such enzymes have been identified. In the past the name given to an enzyme was derived from the substrate involved, but this approach has created such confusion in the field of enzymology, that the Nomenclature Committee of the International Union of Biochemistry was established to consider a classification of universal application to enzymes and coenzymes. The latest communication of this committee was published by Anon. (1979), and the appropriate classification of the peptide hydrolases is summarised in Table 7.7. It can be observed that the peptide hydrolases are divided into two main groups, i.e. the peptidases and the proteinases, and according to Anon. (1979) the scheme for classifying and numbering the enzymes is as follows:

—the first number after EC (enzyme classification) indicates to which of the six main classes the enzyme belongs;
—the second figure indicates the sub-class;
—the third figure gives the sub-sub-class;
—the fourth figure is the serial number of the enzyme in its sub-sub-class.

It is probable that this system will be widely adopted in due course, and hence in the present text the terms peptidases and proteinases are used in accordance with the new scheme.

TABLE 7.7. *Enzyme nomenclature of peptide hydrolases*

Enzyme	Classification and general characteristics
I. Peptidases EC. 3.4.11–3.4.17	A. α-Aminoacylpeptide hydrolases EC 3.4.11.1–3.4.11.14 (catalyse the hydrolysis of single amino acids from N-terminus of peptide chain)
These enzymes are also known as exopeptidases which specifically catalyse the hydrolysis of terminal α-amino or α-carboxyl groups of the peptide bonds.	B. Dipeptide hydrolases EC 3.4.13.3–3.4.13.12 (catalyse the hydrolysis of specific dipeptide substrates)
	C. Dipeptidylpeptide hydrolases EC 3.4.14.1–3.4.14.3 (catalyse the hydrolysis of dipeptide at N-terminus) Peptidyldipeptide hydrolases EC 3.4.15.1–3.4.15.2 (catalyse the hydrolysis of dipeptide at C-terminus)
	D. Serine carboxypeptidases EC 3.4.16.1–3.4.16.3 (catalyse the hydrolysis of single residue from C-terminus; opt. activity at acidic pH range) Metallo carboxypeptidases EC 3.4.17.1–3.4.17.8 (catalytic action same as above; opt. activity in the presence of divalent cations)
II. Proteinases EC 3.4.21–3.4.24	A. Serine proteinases EC 3.4.21.1–3.4.21.33 (histidine and serine are involved in the catalylic process)
These enzymes are also known as proteolytic enzymes, endopeptidases or peptidyl-peptide hydrolases, which catalyse the hydrolysis of the "internal" peptide linkages of protein.	B. Thiol proteinase EC 3.4.22.1–3.4.22.15 (sometime referred to as "SH-proteinase" which have a cystein in the active centre)
	C. Carboxyl-proteinases EC 3.4.23.1–3.4.23.14 (catalytic process yield a acidic residue; opt. activity < pH 5)
	D. Metalloproteinases EC 3.4.24.1–3.4.24.12 (requiring metal ions in the catalytic process)

Peptidylamino-acid hydrolases or acylamino-acid hydrolases, i.e. EC 3.4.12.1–3.4.12.13 have been transferred to EC 3.4.16, 3.4.17 and 3.4.22.

Adapted from Anon. (1979).

The hydrolysis of protein to yield amino acids can, therefore, be accomplished in two major stages:

1st Stage   2nd Stage

$$\text{Protein} \xrightarrow{\text{Proteinases}} \text{Polypeptides} \xrightarrow{\text{Peptidases}} \text{Amino Acids}$$

A. Peptide Hydrolases of the Yoghurt Organisms

The data, which was compiled by Tamime and Deeth (*loc. cit.*) on the proteolytic activity of *S. thermophilus* and *L. bulgaricus* indicate that both organisms possess different peptidases and proteinases. The former organism is considered to have more peptidase activity than *L. bulgaricus*, and only limited proteinase activity, while the ability of *L. bulgaricus* to hydrolyse casein confirms that proteinase activity is much higher in the lactobacilli. This pattern of peptide hydrolysis in the yoghurt organisms provides further evidence of the symbiotic relationship which exists between *S. thermophilus* and *L. bulgaricus*. Thus, the proteinase activity of *L. bulgaricus* hydrolyses the casein to yield polypeptides, which in turn are broken down by the peptidases of *S. thermophilus* with the liberation of amino acids.

The most comprehensive work on the peptidases and proteinases of the yoghurt organisms has been conducted in France at the Institut National de la Recherche Agronomique (INRA)/Jouy-en-Josas, and in the United Kingdom at the National Institute for Research in Dairying (NIRD)/Shinfield, nr. Reading. A summary of their results is presented in Table 7.8, and it can be observed that the classification and nomenclature of the peptidases of the yoghurt organisms is well established. However, the same is not true for the proteinases of these organisms, although Table 7.9 shows the pattern of casein catabolism by *S. thermophilus* and *L. bulgaricus* which is predominantly attributed to proteinase activity. With the limited data available on casein hydrolysis it is difficult to generalise, but the increased proteolytic activity of *L. bulgaricus* mutant strains (see Table 7.9) developed after exposure to gamma radiation, X-ray radiation, UV radiation or chemical mutagens, suggests that differences between ordinary strains may have resulted in the observed variations of casein hydrolysis (see also Dilanian, Markarian and Sarkisyan, *loc. cit.*; Krsev, 1976; Singh and Ranganathan, 1974a, b, 1977a, b, 1978, 1979; Singh, Ranganathan and Chander, 1978). Although mutant strains of *L. bulgaricus* with increased proteolytic activity were not specifically selected for the yoghurt industry, such activity is desired during the early maturation stages of some varieties of Swiss type cheese.

Assays of *S. thermophilus* and *L. bulgaricus* for peptide hydrolases reveal that such enzymms are either cell bound and/or are intracellular. However, Miller and Kandler (1967a) reported that *L. bulgaricus* possess an extracellular protease, an observation which was not confirmed by other workers.

Based on the data compiled by Tamime and Deeth (*loc. cit.*), the activity of the peptide hydrolases of the yoghurt organisms appears to be at a maximum under the following conditions:

(a) most intense activity is during the log phase;

(b) the rate of proteolysis decreases during storage, or after the stationary phase has been reached;

(c) the ratio of *S. thermophilus* and *L. bulgaricus* in the starter culture can affect the level of amino acids in yoghurt, and for example, 70 $\mu g \%$ is liberated at a ratio of 1:1, followed by 50 $\mu g \%$ at 1:2 and 41 $\mu g \%$ at 2:1. However, the acidity of these yoghurts was rather high, i.e. 1.9 % lactic acid for the 1:1 ratio, and it is possible that the high level of liberated amino acids in the product was associated with the proteolytic activity of *L. bulgaricus* which becomes the predominant organism in such an acidic environment (refer later for further discussion);

(d) in yoghurt (24 hours old) the spectrum of amino acids changes in relation to the ratio of cocci:rods, i.e. at a ratio of 1:1, tryrosine, phenylalanine and leucine formed 56 % of the amino acid pool, but at a ratio of 3:1 proline accounted for 71 % of the free amino acids;

TABLE 7.8. *Proteolytic enzymes of the yoghurt starter cultures*

Enzyme nomenclature	Substrate	S. thermophilus	L. bulgaricus	Other comments	References
I. Peptidases					
A. α-Aminoacylpeptide hydrolases					
1. Aminopeptidase EC 3.4.11.1	L-leucyle-L-Leucine	Present in all 7 strains tested.		Intracellular, active also on dipeptides and β-naphthyl-amides.	(4)
EC 3.4.11.1 or 3.4.11.2	Leucyl-p-nitroanilide		Activity 0.28–1.11 μg, present in all 6 strains tested.	A unit of enzyme activity produces 1 μmole p-nitroaniline/min.	(7 & 8)
EC 3.4.11.1 or 3.4.11.2	L-leucine-p-nitroanilide	Activity 14.5 at opt. pH 7.0 and at 42°C.	Activity 4.0 at opt. pH 6.0 and at 37°C.	Cell bound, 1 unit of activity = 1 nmole product released min^{-1} from 1 mg protein or 1 mg cell mass.	(10)
2. Arginine aminopeptidase EC 3.4.11.6	Arginine	Present in some strains, it is inactive on dipeptides.		Intracellular, it removes N-terminus from arginine.	(4)
3. Aeromonas proteolytica aminopeptidase EC 3.4.11.10		Opt. activity at pH 6.4 and at 35°C, MW 62,000 and it requires metal ion, e.g. Zn^{++}.		Removes N-terminus amino acids from L-leucyle-peptides, amides and β-naphthylamide.	(9)
B. Dipeptide hydrolases					
1. Prolyl dipeptidase EC 3.4.13.8		Present in all strains.		Active on numerous dipeptides.	(4)
2. Dipeptidase EC 3.4.13.11		Opt. activity at pH 7.5 and at 50°C, MW 50,000 and it requires metal ion.		Specific for hydrophobic dipeptides with apolar, bulky N-terminal amino acids.	(9)
EC 3.4.13.11	Glycine-tyrosine		Activity 18.5 μg, detected in some strains.	A unit of enzyme activity produces 1 μmole tyrosine/min.	(7 & 8)
C. Peptidyldipeptide hydrolase					
1. Dipeptidyl carboxypeptidase EC 3.4.15.1		Most active against di-, tripeptides with N-terminal leucine.		Removes leucine amino acid residue.	(1)
II. Proteinases					
A. Metalloproteinase EC 3.4.24.4	Glucagon and insuline-β-chain	Present in all strains tested, MW 39,000, and it requires metal ion e.g. Mn^{++}.	Not detected.	Intracellular, preferential cleavage by splitting α-NH_2 of hydrophobic amino acids e.g. tyrosineleucine and glycine-phenylalanine bonds.	(2, 3, 5, 6, 7 & 10)

(1) Bottazzi (1967); (2) Desmazeaud (1974); (3) Desmazeaud (1978); (4) Desmazeaud and Juge (1976); (5) Desmazeaud and Hermier (1968); (6) Desmazeaud and Zevaco (1976); (7) El-Soda, Desmazeaud and Bergère (1978a); (8) El-Soda, Desmazeaud and Bergère (1978b); (9) Rabier and Desmazeaud (1973); (10) Shankar and Davies (*loc. cit.*).

Adapted From Tamime and Deeth (*loc. cit.*) and Anon. (1979).

TABLE 7.9. *Proteinases activity of the yoghurt starter cultures*

Substrate	S. thermophilus	L. bulgaricus	Caseinolytic activity	References
Milk	Low activity.	Extracellular protease in cell free filtrate.	Activity against native > than isoelectric casein.	(10)
		Location of enzyme is intracellular.	No change in electrophoresis pattern.	(12)
	All strains tested caused increase in TCA soluble nitrogen.			(2)
	Opt. activity at pH 7 in sediment from lysozyme-treated cells.	Opt. activity at pH 7 in cell-bound and cell-free enzyme from lysozyme treated cells.		(8, 9)
	Activity in cell free extracts.			(13)
	12.3% hydrolysed after 14 days at 37°C.	Intracellular, activity at pH 7.0 and 20–37°C; opt. temperature at 37°C and pH 6–7.	β- > α-casein (Na-caseinate).	(7, 11, 16)
CASEIN and whey proteins		Strains tested produced a single proteinase, cell bound and cell soluble, opt. activity at pH 5.2–5.8 and at 45–50°C.	β- > α- and κ-casein (Tris-caseinate) and activity against bovine whey proteins was relatively low.	(14)
		Mutant strains (see text).	β- > α_s- and κ-casein (whole casein), α_s > β-and κ-casein (purified casein),	(1, 19)
			α_s-and κ- > β-casein.	(3, 6, 17, 18)
		Intracellular, activity monitored for sialic acid released.	κ- > α_s casein.	(11)
^{125}I casein	7 strains tested and activity ranged from 10:1.		κ- > α_s and β-casein; κ-and α_s- hydrolysed but not β-casein.	(3)
N,N-dimethyl β-casein	Cell bound, opt. activity 0.15 n moles min^{-1} cell mass at pH 7.5 and at 40°C, weak proteinase activity.	Cell bound, opt. activity 4.0 nmoles min^{-1} mg^{-1} cell mass at pH 6.0 and at 40°C.	β-and κ-casein are hydrolysed but not α_s, casein.	(4, 5)
			Lactobacilli proteinase hydrolysed β- > α_s- > whole casein > κ-casein > β-lactoglobulin > α-lactalbumin.	(15)

References: (1) Argyle, Mathison and Chandan (1976); (2) Carini and Resmini (1968); (3) Chebbi, Chander and Ranganathan (1974 & 1977); (4) Desmazeaud (1978); (5) Desmazeaud and Juge (*loc. cit.*); (6) Dilanyan *et al.* (1971); (7) D'yachenko and Shidlovskaya (1971); (8) Formisano, Percuoco and Percuoco (1972 & 1973); (9) Formisano, Percuoco *et al.* (1974); (10) Miller and Kandler (1967a & b); (11) Ohmiya and Sato (1968, 1969 & 1978); (12) Poznanski, Lenior and Mocquot (1965); (13) Rabier and Desmazeaud (*loc. cit.*); (14) Sato and Nakashima (1965); (15) Shankar and Davies (*loc. cit.*); (16) Shidlovskaya and D'yachenko (1968); (17) Singh and Ranganathan (1977a & b & 1979); (18) Dilanian, Markarian and Sarkisyan (1970); (19) Chandan, Argyle and Mathison (1982).
Adapted from Tamime and Deeth (*loc. cit.*).

(e) the hydrolysis of whey proteins in milk yields lower levels of non-protein nitrogen as the ratio of *L. bulgaricus* to *S. thermophilus* is decreased;

(f) free fatty acids, e.g. capric and, to a lesser degree, oleic, can reduce the proteolytic activity of the starter cultures, and can affect the texture of the coagulum;

(g) enhanced proteolytic activity in yoghurt is observed during the manufacture of lactose hydrolysed yoghurt, due perhaps, to protease residues present in the β-D-galactosidase preparations (Hemme *et al.*, 1979);

(h) milk which was precultured with psychrotrophic bacteria prior to the manufacture of yoghurt was found to support enhanced proteolytic activity; however, the product developed unacceptable flavours;

(i) bitterness in yoghurt is usually attributed to the production of bitter peptides by the proteolytic activity of *L. bulgaricus*; however, fermentation of the milk at 44°C yields yoghurt which is less likely to be bitter than yoghurt produced at 38°C.

B. Products of Proteolysis

The profile of nitrogenous compounds in yoghurt, as compared with milk changes due to the proteolytic activity of *S. thermophilus* and *L. bulgaricus*, both during the fermentation period and, to a lesser degree, during the cold storage of the product. Basically, the change amounts to an increase in the level of soluble nitrogenous compounds, which also includes the liberation of amino acids, and the release of peptides from the milk proteins.

1. Soluble nitrogenous compounds

The most comprehensive study in this field was conducted by Miller and Kandler (1967a, b) and a summary of their results is given in Table 7.10. These figures confirm that different strains of yoghurt organisms vary in their proteolytic activity, and further, that the amounts of dialysable nitrogen released by *L. bulgaricus* and *S. thermophilus* (490 and 302 mg/litre) are compliant with the view that the former organism is more proteolytic than *S. thermophilus*. The same trend can be observed in relation to the amounts of amino acid nitrogen, urea nitrogen and peptide nitrogen (see Table 7.10), but the especial capacity of *S. thermophilus* to increase the level of ammonia nitrogen in cultured milks is due to the ability of the lactic streptococci to split urea.

2. Liberation of amino acids

The spectrum of free amino acids in milk and yoghurt (see Table 7.11) is dependent on several variables such as follow.

(a) Type of milk. Milks from different species (cow's, sheep's and goat's) have different contents of amino acids, i.e. ≤ 10, 3.78 and 20.6 mg/100 ml respectively, and in addition, goat's milk has, relative to the others, much higher levels of alanine, glycine, glutamic acid, serine, and thereonine.

312

TABLE 7.10. *Soluble nitrogenous fractions from milk and milk cultured with L. bulgaricus and S. thermophilus*

		Dialysable N		Ammonia N		Amino acid N		Urea N		Peptide N	
		mg/l	%	mg/l	%	mg/l	%	mg/l	%	mg/l	%
Milk		249	4.7	30	0.6	20	0.4	62	1.2	137	2.6
L. bulgaricus	Av (6)	490	9.3	73	1.4	166	3.1	96	1.8	155	2.9
	Range	438–545	8.3–10.3	63–89	1.2–7.9	56–314	1–5.7	51–146	1–2.8	71–270	1.3–5.4
S. thermophilus	Av (5)	302	5.7	144	2.7	21	0.4	10	0.6	127	2.4
	Range	222–406	4.2–7.7	88–190	1.7–3.6	16–26	0.3–0.5	3–30	0.1–0.9	117–197	2.0–3.7

Data compiled from Miller and Kandler (1967a, b).

After Tamime and Deeth (*loc. cit.*).
Reprinted with permission of *Journal of Food Protection*.

TABLE 7.11. *Free amino acid content (mg/100 ml) of milk and yoghurt*

Amino acid	Cow's Milk	Cow's Yoghurt	Goat's Milk	Goat's Yoghurt	Sheep's Milk	Sheep's Yoghurt
Alanine	0.16–0.64	1.17–3.80	1.33	3.83	0.56	1.30
Anginine	0.16–0.96	0.70–1.39	0.40	0.67	0.26	0.85
Aspartic acid	0.23–0.52	0.70–1.20	0.22	1.37	0.18	1.75
Glycine	0.30–0.53	0.28–0.45	5.91	6.06	0.15	0.25
Glutamic acid	1.48–3.90	4.80–7.06	3.54	3.78	1.08	4.10
Histidine	0.11	0.80–1.70	0.45	1.28	0.10	0.50
Isoleucine	0.06–0.15	0.15–0.40	0.18	0.43	0.06	0.25
Leucine	0.06–0.26	0.70–1.82	0.21	1.25	0.23	0.45
Lysine	0.22–0.94	0.80–1.11	0.60	2.35	0.19	0.72
Methionine	0.05	0.08–0.20	0.10	0.35	0.05	0.15
Phenylalanine	0.05–0.13	0.17–0.61	0.11	0.35	0.08	0.15
Proline	0.12	5.40–7.05	0.65	4.35	0.11	4.30
Serine	0.08–1.35	1.50–2.90	3.05	3.51	0.20	2.00
Threonine	0.05–0.26	0.24–0.70	3.34	2.80	0.13	0.55
Tryptophan	Trace	0.2	No reported value		No reported value	
Tyrosine	0.06–0.14	0.18–0.61	0.30	0.60	0.16	0.24
Valine	0.10–0.25	0.90–1.86	0.30	0.50	0.24	0.90
Total	3.29–10.31	18.77–33.06	20.60	33.48	3.78	18.46

Data compiled from Tamime and Deeth (*loc. cit.*).

(b) Methods of manufacture. Slightly higher levels of amino acids are obtained when the fermentation is carried out at 42°C for 2–3 hours, rather than at 42°C for 1 hour followed by 5–6 hours at 30–32°C; the total amino acid contents of such yoghurts were 23.6 and 19.4 mg/100 ml (Rasic, Stojslavljevic and Curcic, 1971; Rasic *et al.*, 1971; Stohslavljevic, Rasic and Curcic, 1971).

(c) Ratio of rods to cocci. Due to the fact that *L. bulgaricus* is more proteolytic than *S. thermophilus*, the higher the ratio of rods to cocci in the starter culture, the higher the amino acid content is likely to be in the corresponding yoghurt. Nachev (1970) studied various strains of *L. bulgaricus*, and classified them into three groups based on fermentation of sugars and types of amino acid released. The 1st group (118 strains) was characterised by releasing the following amino acids—leucine, glutamic acid, asparagine and proline—and an absence in the medium of β-alanine, tryptophan and aminobutyric acid. The second group (six strains) differed in that no glutamic acid was released, while the third group (one strain) was noted for the presence of tryptophan.

(d) Conditions during storage. The temperature of storage of yoghurt can affect the level of free amino acids in the product, i.e. the higher the storage temperature, the greater the increase in free amino acids. Ottogali *et al.* (1974) stored full and low (1 %) fat natural yoghurts at 4° and 20°C for a duration of 60 days, and the increases in the level of amino acids in these yoghurts were (at 4°C) 2.36 and 1.00, and (at 20°C) 7.57 and 14.65 mg/100 ml respectively. However, the same workers observed no increase in the level of amino acids in lemon and orange flavoured yoghurts stored under the same conditions for the same period of time, a difference that was attributed to the presence of natural metabolic inhibitors in the fruit, or the effect of some bacteriocidal agent added to the fruit concentrate, or the high acidity of the fruit preparation.

(e) Level of lactic acid. The amino acid content of yoghurt is dependent on the titratable acidity of the product. According to Luca (1974), yoghurts which contained 1.9 and 1.72–1.73 % lactic acid

had total amino acid contents of 70 and 41–50 mg/100 g respectively. Incidentally, the figure of 70 mg/100 g of yoghurt is the highest level reported in the literature, and it could be argued that such acidic yoghurt could be the result of prolonged incubation, and hence the amino acid content reflects directly the extent of the metabolic activity of the starter culture.

The final amino acid content of yoghurt made from cow's milk may range from 18.7–33 mg/100 ml (see Table 7.11), and it is probable that the acidities of these yoghurts were 1.0–1.4 % lactic acid. It is important, of course, that the total amino acid content of yoghurt reflects a balance between proteolysis and assimilation by the bacteria. Some amino acids, such as glutamic acid, proline and, to a lesser degree, alanine and serine, are presumably not required by the yoghurt organisms, and thus accumulate in larger quantities in the product than the remaining amino acids which are utilised by *S. thermophilus* and *L. bulgaricus* during growth and/or fermentation.

3. Release of peptides

As mentioned earlier, some of the proteolytic enzymes which the yoghurt bacteria possess release peptides into the product. The only work carried out on this aspect of the fermentation has been reported from Bulgaria by Tanev and Zivkova (1977), and in this study they monitored the behaviour of the short-chain peptides in Bulgarian yoghurt during cold storage. The technique of peptide mapping, which included high-voltage electrophoresis and "finger-printing" by descending paper chromatography and differential staining of the peptides was neatly demonstrated on both milk and yoghurt stored at 4°C for 1, 2, 3 and 65 days. The size and composition of these short-chain peptides was not given, but Table 7.12 summarises the distribution of these peptides in yoghurt.

TABLE 7.12. *A study of short-chain peptides* in Bulgarian yoghurt*

Position and/or direction of short-chain peptides	Milk	Yoghurt (days old)			
		1	2	3	65
Cathode (−)	2, 30	–	1, 8	–	–
Zero	0, 0	0, 0	–	–	–
Anode (+)	1, 18	1, 12	2, 16	2, 16	1, 36
	8, 34	1, 27	3, 15	2, 77	2, 11
	10, 46	13, 27	6, 12	8, 31	6, 21
	15, 36		9, 12	9, 26	11, 12
	15, 42		11, 30	9, 44	21, 46
			15, 10	11, 10	22, 19
			15, 25	11, 31	22, 32
			15, 30	13, 54	25, 47
			20, 10	14, 35	
			20, 34	15, 10	
			26, 13	18, 10	
				18, 12	
Total	7	4	12	12	8

* First figure (mm) coordinates in electrophoresis direction.
 Second figure (mm) coordinates in chromatography direction.

Adapted from Taner and Zivkova (*loc. cit.*).

LIPID/FAT METABOLISM

Acyl-glycerols constitute 96–98% of the total milk lipids/fats, and the remaining fraction consists of phospholipids, sterols, fat-soluble vitamins (A, D, E and K), fatty acids, waxes and squalene. The lipids are found in the following phases of the milk: the fat globules, the membranes of the fat globules and the milk serum, and the proportions of these fractions can vary in relation to such factors as species of mammal, breed, stage of lactation and type of feed (Jenness and Patton, 1959; Kurtz, 1974). The acyl-glycerols present in milk are formed by the esterification of the alcohol radicals of the glycerol with one, two or three fatty acids residues to yield mono-, di- or triacyl-glycerides (triglycerides) respectively. Therefore, in broad terms the enzymatic hydrolysis of milk lipids takes place at the ester linkages yielding eventually free fatty acids and glycerol. The enzymes are known as lipases, and their mode of action may be specific to certain bonds on the glycerol molecules, i.e. similar to the action of the peptide hydrolases. A simplified sequence of lipids hydrolysis is as follows:

$$\text{Triglycerides} \xrightarrow{\text{Lipase}} \text{Di-} \xrightarrow{\text{Lipase}} \text{Mono-} \xrightarrow{\text{Lipase}} \text{Fatty acids} + \text{Glycerols}$$

The lipase enzymes in yoghurt may originate from the starter culture, or from microbial contaminants that survived the heat treatment of the milk. Incidentally, the lipases which occur naturally in milk are inactivated at ordinary pasteurisation temperatures (Deeth and Fitz-Gerald, 1976). Therefore, any reduction in the percentage of fat, or increase in the level of fatty acids (free or esterified), or increase in the content of volatile fatty acids in yoghurt can be attributed to lipid metabolism by micro-organisms, including *S. thermophilus* and *L. bulgaricus*. However, before evaluating the role of the different lipases reported to be present in the latter organisms, it is pertinent to look at some factors which can affect the degree of lipolysis.

1. Fat content of yoghurt

The fat content of yoghurt differs from one country to another according to the existing or proposed standards for the chemical composition of the product, or alternatively in relation to the types of yoghurt produced (see Table 10.4). From such data it can be seen that four broad categories of product exist:

(i) <1%,
(ii) >1 and <3%,
(iii) >3 and <4%,
(iv) >4.5%,

and the degree of lipolysis is likely to be greater in yoghurts of high fat content.

2. Homogenisation

The process is carried out on the basic mix, and it is widely practised in the yoghurt industry for two main reasons: firstly, to reduce the size of the fat globules, and thus prevent "creaming" or fat

316

separation in the milk during incubation, and secondly, to improve the viscosity and texture of yoghurt. However, the extent of lipolysis in homogenised milk is much greater than in unhomogenised milk, due, in large measure, to the destruction of the protective layer of the fat globule, i.e. the fat globule membrane (Mulder and Walstra, 1974).

Although the hydrolysis of fat by the yoghurt starter cultures occurs only to a limited degree, it may still be enough to contribute towards the flavour of the product. In fact, only Formisano et al. (loc. cit.) reported any appreciable loss of lipids—a decrease of 3.4% of fat in yoghurt stored for 21 days at 4°C, an observation not noted by other workers.

However several authors have detected lipase activity in S. thermophilus and L. bulgaricus, and a list of these enzymes is shown in Table 7.13; the nomenclature of the enzymes is based on the substrate being hydrolysed, rather than on the "systematic" approach suggested by Anon. (1979). Nevertheless, all these lipolytic enzymes in the yoghurt bacteria are reported to be located in the cytoplasm, since after cell disruption, very little activity is associated with the cell membrane (see also DeMoraes and Chandan, 1982).

TABLE 7.13. *Lipases reported to be present in yoghurt starter cultures*

Enzyme	Substrate	S. thermophilus	L. bulgaricus
Tributyrinase	Tributyrin	+ + +	+ +
Trioleinase	Soy milk and olive oil	+	
Glycerol ester hydrolase	Milk fat	+ +	
Esterases	Tween 40 and 60 and α-napthyl acetate or butyrate	+	+ + +
	Triacetin		(Trace)
Tricaproinase	Tricaproin		+

Due to different enzyme assay procedures employed, the lipase activity is expressed as high (+ + +), medium (+ +) or low (+).

Data compiled from: Angeles and Marth (1971), Formisano, Percuoco and Percuoco (1972, 1973), Formisano et al. (loc. cit.), Morichi, Sharpe and Reiter (1968), Otterholm, Ordal and Witter (1968), Umanskii et al. (1974).

A. Products of Lipolysis

1. Changes in the level of free and esterified fatty acids

The free and esterified fatty acids of yoghurts made from cow's, sheep's and goat's milk was studied by Rasic and Vucurivic (1973) and Rasic, Vucurovic and Obradovic (1973), and the changes which occurred are summarised in Table 7.14. From such data, it seems that the increase (or decrease) in the level of free fatty acids in the different types of yoghurt is inconsistent, and this variation probably reflects a difference in behaviour of S. thermophilus and L. bulgaricus in cow's, sheep's and goat's milk.

In another investigation from another laboratory (Formisano et al., loc. cit.), the reported change in the free fatty acids in yoghurt was somewhat simplified, in that there was a liberation of long-

TABLE 7.14.   *Changes in free fatty acid content of yoghurts made with fatty acids from different mammals*

Fatty acids	Cow	Sheep	Goat
Caproic	–	I	–
Caprylic	I	I	D
Capric	–	–	–
Lauric	I	I	D
Myristic	I	I	D
C-15	–	D	–
Palmitic	I	D	I
Palmitoleic	–	–	–
Stearic	D	D	–
Oleic	D	D	–
Linoleic	–	–	I

(I) Increase ⎰
(D) Decrease ⎱ by more than 1% as compared with milk

(–) Signifies no change

Adapted from Rasic and Vucurovic (1973), Rasic, Vucurovic and Obradovic (*loc. cit.*).

chain fatty acids into the product, and the final pattern did not change significantly during cold storage.

2. Changes in the level of volatile fatty acids

During the manufacture and storage of yoghurt, there is an appreciable increase in the total level of fatty acids in the product. Data on the release of fatty acids by single strains of *S. thermophilus* and *L. bulgaricus* and by mixed cultures have been reported by many investigators, and of the two organisms, the *Lactobacillus* produces more of these acids than *S. thermophilus*. The increase in the level of volatile fatty acids in yoghurt is dependent on several variables, such as the strains of starter bacteria, type of milk (i.e. cow's, buffalo's or goat's), duration and temperature of incubation, temperature of heat treatment of the milk and/or the age of yoghurt (Dutta *et al.*, 1971a, b; Dutta, Kuila and Ranganathan, *loc. cit.*; Singh, Khanna and Chander, 1980). However, a slight decrease in volatile fatty acids was observed in the presence of low concentrations of citric acids in milk (Dutta *et al.*, 1972).

More recently Yu and Nakanishsi (1975a, b, c) and Yu, Nakanishi and Suyama (1974) have reported in detail the level of certain fatty acids in whole and skim-milk cultured with yoghurt starter bacteria. Their data are shown in Table 7.15, and it can be observed that, after 24 hours of incubation at 37°C only a small degree of lipolysis has been exhibited by *S. thermophilus* and *L. bulgaricus*. It could be argued, however, that the origin of volatile fatty acids in fermented milks, and in particular in those based on skim milk, may not be the result of lipid metabolism by the yoghurt organisms, but may arise from the breakdown of other milk constituents, e.g. the amino acid pool, as suggested by Nakai and Elliot (1965); in the course of oxidative deamination and decarboxylation, the amino acid is split to its corresponding volatile fatty acid.

Moreover, Morichi, Sharpe and Reiter (*loc. cit.*) have pointed out that the presence of "true esterases" in lactic acid bacteria, e.g. *L. bulgaricus*, is difficult to verify, since some proteolytic enzymes and other factors in milk exhibit esterase activity. It is safe to assume, therefore, that the

TABLE 7.15. *Changes in volatile fatty acids in whole and skim milk fermented with* L. bulgaricus *and* S. thermophilus

Acids	Milk	Control	L. bulgaricus		S. thermophilus		Mixed	
			37°C/24 hr	37°C/72 hr	37°C/24 hr	37°C/72 hr	37°C/24 hr	37°C/72 hr
Total VFA (mg/100 g)	whole	3.20	6.05	6.26	4.90	4.19	6.88	7.55
	skim	2.97	5.89	6.32	4.88	3.79	6.80	7.20
C2	whole	0.21	0.55	1.26	0.51	0.45	0.57	0.48
	skim	0.20	1.95	1.36	0.45	0.37	0.12	0.20
C3	whole	trace	trace	trace	0.05	0.03	0.22	0.11
	skim	–	0.05	0.05	0.03	0.03	trace	trace
i-C4	whole	0.03	0.03	0.05	0.05	0.04	0.13	0.14
	skim	0.03	0.04	0.61	0.05	0.05	0.03	0.06
n-C4	whole	0.39	0.74	0.94	1.21	0.97	1.05	1.44
	skim	0.38	0.50	0.96	1.20	0.90	0.66	1.08
i-C5	whole	0.05	0.21	0.21	0.14	0.10	0.15	0.06
	skim	0.03	0.13	0.18	0.11	0.09	0.07	0.17
n-C5	whole	–	–	–	–	–	*	
	skim	–	trace	trace	–	–		
n-C6	whole	1.09	1.73	1.24	1.24	1.05	1.56	2.57
	skim	1.13	1.72	1.35	1.25	1.07	2.40	2.04
C8	whole	0.97	1.44	0.99	0.74	0.53	1.78	1.64
	skim	0.96	1.30	1.18	0.87	0.56	2.26	2.36
C10	whole	1.21	1.59	1.30	0.91	1.10	2.65	2.22
	skim	1.10	1.81	1.74	1.06	0.68	3.11	2.92

* Test was not determined.
Data compiled from Yu, Nakanishi and Suyama (*loc. cit.*), Yu and Nakanishi (1975a, b, c).

After Tamime and Deeth (*loc. cit.*).
Reprinted with permission of *Journal of Food Protection*.

detected esterase (lipase) activity of the yoghurt bacteria (see Table 7.13) is directly related to the action of proteolytic enzymes rather than lipases. Such a conclusion is in accord with the higher production of volatile fatty acids by *L. bulgaricus*, i.e. it is probably due to peptide hydrolases rather than lipases.

VITAMIN METABOLISM

Milk contains both fat- and water-soluble vitamins, and Table 9.2 indicates the levels of these vitamins in milk (full fat and skim), and in the corresponding yoghurts. The content of these vitamins changes during manufacture for the following reasons.

1. Decrease

(a) An excess of dissolved oxygen and/or a moderate heat treatment of milk can reduce significantly its vitamin content, and the most susceptible ones are vitamins C, B_6, B_{12} and folic acid (Hartman and Dryden, 1974).

(b) Excessive heat treatments of the milk, e.g. boiling for 5 minutes, cause even greater losses of the above vitamins; for example, vitamin B_{12} is reduced by 1.78 μg/litre (Rasic and Panic, 1963).

(c) The yoghurt starter bacteria utilise some of the vitamins present in milk during the fermentation period to meet their growth requirements. This factor contributes, to some extent, to a reduction of the nutritional properties of the product. However, the quantities consumed are dependent on the rate of inoculation, the strain of yoghurt starter and the conditions of fermentation (Shahani, Reddy and Joe, 1974).

(d) Some vitamins decrease during the storage of yoghurt at 4°C, i.e. vitamin B_{12} (Rasic and Panic, *loc. cit.*; Cerna, Pickova and Blattna, 1973), and Reddy, Shahani and Kulkarni (1976) observed, during the storage of yoghurt at 5°C for 16 days, losses of folic acid and vitamin B_{12} of 28.6 and 59.9% respectively. The same workers also observed a decrease in the biotin, niacin and pantothenic acid contents, and they attributed these losses to the combined effect of microbial catabolism during the incubation period, and chemical decomposition of these vitamins during cold storage. This latter aspect was confirmed in yoghurt made by the direct acidification method rather than by microbial fermentation.

2. Increase

Vitamins which increase during the actual manufacture of yoghurt are niacin and folic acid, because they are actively synthesised by the starter cultures. According to Reddy, Shahani and Kulkarni (*loc. cit.*), the increases in folic acid and niacin in yoghurt (made from whole milk fortified with 2% solids-not-fat and incubated for 3 hours at 42°C) amounts to 3.946 and 22 μg/100 g respectively (see also Table 7.16); losses in storage (see above) may exceed these gains in due course. Although there is a general agreement in the literature that vitamin B_{12} decreases during yoghurt production, Mittic, Otenhajmer and Obradovic (1974), Shahani, Reddy and Joe (*loc. cit.*) and Kilara and Shahani (1978) found that some species of *Lactobacillus* and strains of yoghurt starter culture synthesise vitamin B_{12}.

TABLE 7.16. *Effect of incubation temperature upon vitamin synthesis in yoghurt*

Vitamin (μg/100 g)	Pasteurised milk + 2% non-fat dry milk solids	Yoghurt (3 hours incubation) Incubation temperature °C			
		37	40	42	45
Folic acid	0.371	3.736	4.042	4.317	3.928
Niacin	120	126	130	142	136

After Reddy, Shahani and Kulkarni (*loc. cit.*).

In the view of the existing evidence (see also Deeth and Tamime, 1981) it is safe to conclude that *S. thermophilus* and *L. bulgaricus* synthesise niacin and folic acid and, to a lesser degree, vitamin B_6 during the production of yoghurt, and it is of some interest to consider the possible metabolic pathway(s) involved in the synthesis of these vitamins.

A. Biosynthesis of Folic Acid (Folacin)

The "folic acid group" (or "folates") is a generic name given to around ten different compounds which share a basic structural unit connected to "conjugates" of different numbers of glutamic acid residues. These folates are, therefore, made out of carbon, hydrogen, nitrogen and oxygen atoms, and their formulae range from $C_{15}H_{12}N_6O_4$ to $C_{49}H_{61}N_{13}O_{24}$. Thus, some or all of these compounds are active as folacin, and a typical structure of one such compound, i.e. pteroyl-glutamic acid [p-(2-amino-4-oxodihydropteridyl-6-)-methyl-aminobenzoyl-L-glutamic acid], which may be synthesised by the yoghurt bacteria is as follows:

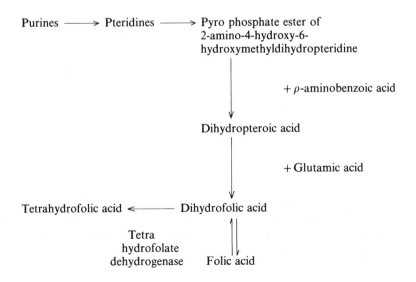

Folic acid
$C_{19}H_{19}N_7O_6$

Many organisms require folacin as a growth factor. It functions as a coenzyme in many different biochemical reactions, i.e. as an activator and carrier of carbon units during oxidation, and it participates in the metabolism of purines, pyrimidines and some amino acids (Hartman and Dryden, *loc. cit.*). However, the synthetic pathways of folic acid in *S. thermophillus* and *L. bulgaricus* are not well established, and Anon. (1970) suggested that the synthesis of this compound in animals, plants and micro-organisms probably involves the following biochemical reactions:

Purines ⟶ Pteridines ⟶ Pyro phosphate ester of
2-amino-4-hydroxy-6-
hydroxymethyldihydropteridine

$+ p$-aminobenzoic acid

Dihydropteroic acid

$+$ Glutamic acid

Tetrahydrofolic acid ⟵ Dihydrofolic acid

Tetra
hydrofolate
dehydrogenase   Folic acid

321

B. Biosynthesis of Niacin

Hartman and Dryden (*loc. cit.*) referred to niacin activity as being exhibited by nicotinic acid and nicotinamide. The former compound constitutes part of the structure of the two important coenzymes, i.e. NAD and nicotinamide adenine dinucleotide phosphate (NADP). These two coenzymes are composed of adenylic acid and nicotinamide ribotide linked through their phosphate groups (see Fig. 7.6); however, NADP contains an additional phosphate group (Stainer, Doudoroff and Adelberg, *loc. cit.*). As NAD and/or NADP are essential for many oxidative/reductive biochemical reactions, the niacin synthesised by *S. thermophilus* and *L. bulgaricus* may originate from the nicotinamide fraction arising during the formation of NAD and/or NADP. The biosynthesis of these nucleotides involves, basically, the following steps: firstly, the synthesis of a sugar moiety [possibly derived from the available milk sugar(s)], and secondly, the synthesis of the pyrimidine or purine base. Alternatively, after this formation of NAD and/or NADP, the nicotinamide fraction could be released as a result of the degradation of these nucleotides, but whether nicotinic acid could be derived from the released nicotinamide must be subject to further investigation.

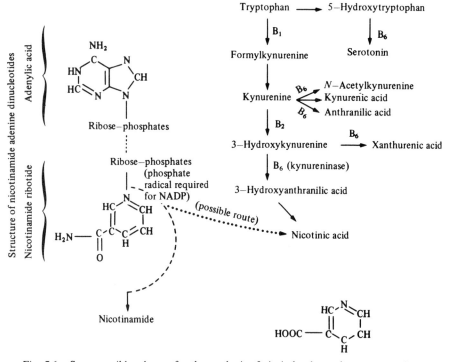

Fig. 7.6.   Some possible schemes for the synthesis of niacin by the yoghurt starter cultures

Adapted from Anon. (1970) and Stanier, Duodoroff & Adelberg (*loc. cit.*).

However, nicotinic acid is derived by a few bacteria from the metabolism or breakdown of tryptophan, a pathway which is dependent on the availability of certain vitamins, e.g. thiamine, riboflavin and vitamin B_6, to activate the required enzymes (Anon., 1970). As *S. thermophilus* and *L. bulgaricus* utilises these vitamins and tryptophan does not accumulate during yoghurt production, it is possible that these organisms use the vitamins for the synthesis of niacin. In view of the limited information in this field, Fig. 7.6 can do no more than illustrate some possible schemes for the synthesis of niacin by the yoghurt starter bacteria.

C. Biosynthesis of Vitamin B₆

The activity of vitamin B_6 is exhibited equally by the following compounds: pyridoxine, pyridoxal and pyridoxamine (Hartman and Dryden, *loc. cit.*). The basic structure of these compounds is similar in that it consists of a pyridine ring, but they differ in the respect of the radical components as follows:

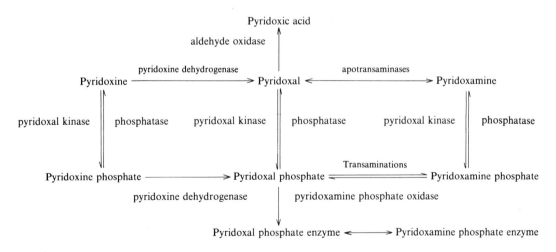

Pyridoxine $(C_8N_{11}NO_3)$ R = CH₂OH
Pyridoxal $(C_8H_9NO_3)$ R = CHO
Pyridoxamine $(C_8H_{12}N_2O_2)$ R = CH₂NH₂

According to Anon. (1970), no information is available on the biosynthesis of the pyridine ring in micro-organisms, plants or animals; however, the different forms of vitamin B_6 are interconvertible by micro-organisms in accordance with the scheme illustrated below.

In view of the limited knowledge of the synthesis of vitamin B_6 in general, it is difficult to suggest any possible metabolic pathway by which *S. thermophilus* and *L. bulgaricus* might synthesise this vitamin.

MISCELLANEOUS CHANGES

The biological activity of *S. thermophilus* and *L. bulgaricus* during the manufacture of yoghurt is highly complex, and further work is required to elucidate some of the metabolic pathways employed by these organisms. Nevertheless, numerous changes do occur in the milk, and some of the additional minor changes in the milk constituents are:

(i) a reduction in the level of citric acid;
(ii) the content of hippuric acid is lost altogether;
(iii) the levels of acetic and succinic acids are increased.

Another compound, which must not be neglected in milk and yoghurt, is uracyl-4-carboxylic acid, better known as orotic acid [or orotate anion (pKa = 2.4)]. This compound is metabolised by the yoghurt starter cultures, most probably by *L. bulgaricus*, and its content in milk is reduced by around 50 %, i.e. from 8.3 to 3.4–4.2 mg/100 ml, during the manufacture of yoghurt (Okonkwo and Kinsella, 1969a). However, orotic acid possesses some significant therapeutic properties, since it plays an important role in the biosynthesis of nucleic acids. Furthermore, according to Larson and Hegarty (1979), the level of orotic acid in cultured dairy products is dependent on the degree of fermentation, and the amount of soluble whey solids in the product (see also Okonkwo and Kinsella, 1969b).

Finally, the presence of other metabolites, for example β-D-galactosidase (Kilara and Shahani, 1976; Rao and Dutta, 1977, 1978), and various antitumor and antimicrobial agents (Reddy, Shahani and Banerjee, 1973; Pulsani, Rao and Sunki, 1979; Rao and Pulsani, 1981) must not be forgotten, for such agents might be of medical and therapeutic value to humans.

REFERENCES

ABRAHAMSEN, R. K., SVENSEN, A. and TUFTO, G. N. (1978) *XXth International Dairy Congress*, E, 828.
ALEKSIEVA, P., GIRGINOVA, T. and KONDRATENKO, M. (1981) *Dairy Science Abstracts*, **43**, 381.
ANGELES, A. G. and MARTH, E. H. (1971) *Journal of Milk and Food Technology*, **34**, 69.
ANON. (1970) In *Geigy—Scientific Tables*, 7th Edition, Ed. by Diem, K. and Lentner, C. Published by Geigy Pharmaceuticals, Ciba—Geigy Ltd., Basle, Switzerland.
ANON. (1979) In *Enzyme Nomenclature – The International Union of Biochemistry*, Academic Press Inc. (London) Ltd., London, U.K.
ARGYLE, P. J., MATHISON, G. E. and CHANDAN, R. C. (1976) *Journal of Applied Bacteriology*, **41**, 175.
BAISYA, R. K. and BOSE, A. N. (1975) *Indian Journal of Dairy Science*, **28**, 179.
BLUMENTHAL, A. and HELBLING, J. (1974) *Dairy Science Abstracts*, **36**, 331.
BOTTAZZI, V. (1967) *Dairy Science Abstracts*, **29**, 156.
BOTTAZZI, V. and DELLAGLIO, F. (1967) *Journal of Dairy Research*, **34**, 109.
BOTTAZZI, V. and VESCOVO, M. (1969) *Netherland Milk and Dairy Journal*, **23**, 71.
BROOKER, B. E. (1979) In *Microbial Polysaccharides and Polysaccharases*, Society of General Microbiology, Ed. by Berkeley, R. C. W., Gooday, C. W. and Ellwood, D. C. Academic Press Inc. (London) Ltd., London, U.K.
CARINI, S. and RISMINI, P. (1968) *Annali di Microbiologia ed Enzimologia*, **18**, 57.
CERNA, J., PICKOVA, J. and BLATTNA, J. (1973) *Dairy Science Abstracts*, **35**, 413.
CHANDAN, R. C., ARGYLE, P. J. and MATHISON, G. E. (1982) *Journal of Dairy Science*, **65**, 1408.
CHEBBI, N. B., CHANDER, H. and RANGANATHAN, B. (1974) *Journal General Applied Microbiology*, **20**, 149.
CHEBBI, N. B., CHANDER, H. and RANGANATHAN, B. (1977) *Acta Microbiologica Polonica*, **9**, 281.
DEETH, H. C. and FITZ-GERALD, C. H. (1976) *Australian Journal of Dairy Technology*, **31**, 53.
DEETH, H. C. and TAMIME, A. Y. (1981) *Journal of Food Protection*, **44**, 78.
DEMORAES, J. and CHANDAN, R. C. (1982) *Journal of Food Science*, **47**, 1579.

DESMAZEAUD, M. J. (1974) *Biochimie,* **56,** 1173.
DESMAZEAUD, M. J. (1978) *XXth International Dairy Congress,* **E,** 469.
DESMAZEAUD, M. J. and HERMIER, J. H. (1968) *Annales de Biologie Animale Biochimie et Biophysique,* **8,** 565.
DESMAZEAUD, M. J. and JUGE, M. (1976) *Le Lait,* **56,** 241.
DESMAZEAUD, M. J. and ZEVACO, C. (1976) *Annales de Biologie Animale Biochimie et Biophysique,* **16,** 851.
DILANIAN, Z., MARKARIAN, K. and SARKISYAN, R. (1970) *VIIIth International Dairy Congress,* **IE,** 122.
DILANYAN, Z. Kh., ARUTYUNYAN, R. K., MARKARYAN, K. V. and AKOPYAN, A. A. (1971) *Dairy Science Abstracts,* **33,** 222.
DUMONT, J. P. and ADDA, J. (1973) *Le Lait,* **53,** 12.
DUTTA, S. M., KUILA, R. K. and RANGANATHAN, B. (1973) *Milchwissenschaft,* **28,** 231.
DUTTA, S. M., KUILA, R. K., RANGANATHAN, B. and LAXMINARAYANA, H. (1971a) *Indian Journal of Diary Science,* **24,** 107.
DUTTA, S. M., KUILA, R. K., RANGANATHAN, B. and LAXMINARAYANA, H. (1971b) *Milchwissenschaft,* **26,** 158.
DUTTA, S. M., KUILA, R. K., SABHARWAL, V. B. and RANGANATHAN, B. (1972) *Journal of Food Science and Technology/India,* **9,** 207.
D'YACHENKO, P. F. and SCHIDLOVSKAYA, V. V. (1971) *Dairy Science Abstracts,* **33,** 56.
DYATCHENKO, P. (1971) In *Chemistry of Milk,* Ministry of Meat and Milk Industry, Tallinn, U.S.S.R.
EL-SODA, M. A., DESMAZEAUD, M. J. and BERGÈRE, J. L. (1978a) *XXth International Dairy Congress,* **E,** 475.
EL-SODA, M. A., DESMAZEAUD, M. J. and BERGÈRE, J. L. (1978b) *Journal of Dairy Research,* **45,** 445.
FARROW, J. A. E. (1980) *Journal of Applied Bacteriology,* **49,** 493.
FORMISANO, M., PERCUOCO, G. and PERCUOCO, S. (1972) *Dairy Science Abstracts.* **34,** 324.
FORMISANO, M., PERCUOCO, G. and PERCUOCO, S. (1973) *Dairy Science Abstracts,* **35,** 137.
FORMISANO, M., COPPOLA, S., PERCUOCO, G., PERCUOCO, S., ZOINA, A., GERMANO, S. and CAPRIGLIONE, I. (1974) *Annali de Microbiologia ed Enzimologia,* **24,** 281.
GALESLOOT, Th. E. and HASSING, F. (1966) *Dairy Science Abstracts,* **28,** 184.
GARVIE, E. I. (1978) *Journal of Dairy Research,* **45,** 515.
GARVIE, E. I. (1980) *Microbiological Reviews,* **44,** 106.
GASSER, F. (1970) *Journal of General Microbiology,* **62,** 223.
GASSER, F. and GASSER, C. (1971) *Journal of Bacteriology,* **106,** 113.
GOODENOUGH, E. R. and KLEYN, D. H. (1976) *Journal of Dairy Science,* **59,** 601.
GORNER, F., PALO, V. and BERTAN, M. (1968) *Milchwissenschaft,* **23,** 94.
GORNER, F., PALO, V. and BERTAN, M. (1971) *Dairy Science Abstracts,* **33,** 800.
GROUX, M. (1976) In *Nestlé Research News 1974/75,* Ed. by Boella, C. Nestlé Product Technical Assistance Co. Ltd., Lausanne, Switzerland.
GROUX, M. and MOINAS, M. (1974) *XIXth International Dairy Congress,* **IE,** 293.
HARTMAN, A. M. and DRYDEN, L. P. (1974) In *Fundamentals of Dairy Chemistry,* 2nd Edition, Ed. by Webb, B. H., Johnson, A. H. and Alford, J. A. AVI Publishing Co. Inc., Connecticut, U.S.A.
HEMME, D., NARDI, M. and WAHL, D. (1981) *Le Lait,* **61,** 1.
HEMME, D., VASSAL, L., FOYEN, H. and AUCLAIR, J. P. (1979) *Le Lait,* **59,** 597.
JENNESS, R. and PATTON, S. (1959) In *Principles of Dairy Chemistry,* Chapman & Hall Ltd., London, U.K.
KEENAN, T. W. and BILLS, D. D. (1968) *Journal of Dairy Science,* **51,** 1561.
KIELWEIN, G. and DAUN, U. (1980) *Dairy Science Abstracts,* **42,** 361.
KILARA, A. and SHAHANI, K. M. (1976) *Journal of Dairy Science,* **59,** 2031.
KILARA, A. and SHAHANI, K. M. (1978) *Journal of Dairy Science,* **61,** 1793.
KRSEV, L. (1976) *Dairy Science Abstracts,* **38,** 688.
KUNATH, P. von and KANDLER, O. (1980) *Milchwissenschaft,* **35,** 470.
KURTZ, F. E. (1974) In *Fundamentals of Dairy Chemistry,* 2nd Edition, Ed. by Webb, R. H., Johnson, A. H. and Alford, J. A. AVI Publishing Co. Inc., Connecticut, U.S.A.
LARSON, B. L. and HEGARTY, H. M. (1979) *Journal of Dairy Science,* **62,** 1641.
LAW, B. A. and SHARPE, M. E. (1978) In *Streptococci,* The Society for Applied Bacteriology – Symposium Series No. 7, Ed. by Skinner, F. A. and Quesnel, L. B. Academic Press Inc. (London) Ltd., London, U.K.
LAWRENCE, R. C. and THOMAS, T. D. (1979) In *Microbial Technology: Current State, Future Prospects,* 29th Symposium of the Society for General Microbiology, Ed. by Bull, A. T., Ellwood, D. C. and Ratledge, C. Cambridge University Press, London, U.K.
LAWRENCE, R. C., THOMAS, T. D. and TERZAGHI, B. E. (1976) *Journal of Dairy Research,* **43,** 141.
LEES, G. J. and JAGO, G. R. (1966) In *Proceedings of Australian Dairy Manufacture Research Seminar,* April 1966, Melbourne, Australia.
LEES, G. J. and JAGO, G. R. (1976a) *Journal of Dairy Research,* **43,** 63.
LEES, G. J. and JAGO, G. R. (1976b) *Journal of Dairy Research,* **43,** 75.
LEES, G. J. and JAGO, G. R. (1977) *Journal of Dairy Research,* **44,** 139.
LEES, G. J. and JAGO, G. R. (1978a) *Journal of Dairy Science,* **61,** 1205.
LEES, G. J. and JAGO, G. R. (1978b) *Journal of Dairy Science,* **61,** 1216.

LUCA, C. (1974) *Dairy Science Abstracts*, **36**, 633.

LUCZYNKA, A., BIJOK, F., WAJNERT, T., KAZIMIERCZAK, W., LIPINSKA, E., KOSIKOWSKA, M. and JAKUBCZYK, E. (1978) *XXth International Dairy Congress*, **E**, 836.

MILLER, I. and KANDLER, O. (1967a) *Milchwissenschaft*, **22**, 150.

MILLER, I. and KANDLER, O. (1967b) *Milchwissenschaft*, **22**, 608.

MITIC, S., OTENHAJMER, I. and OBRADOVIC, D. (1974) *Dairy Science Abstracts*, **36**, 656.

MORICHI, T., SHARPE, M. E. and REITER, B. (1968) *Journal of General Microbiology*, **53**, 405.

MULDER, H. and WALSTRA, P. (1974) In *The Milk Fat Globule—Emulsion Science as Applied to Milk Products and Comparable Foods*, Commonwealth Agricultural Bureaux, Farnham Royal, U.K.

MUTAI, M., ASO, K. and SHIROTA, M. (1972) In *Conversion and Manufacture of Foodstuffs by Microorganisms*, Yakult Institute, Saikon Publishing Co., Japan.

NACHEV, L. (1970) *Dairy Science Abstracts*, **32**, 181.

NAKAI, T. and ELLIOT, J. A. (1965) *Journal of Dairy Science*, **48**, 287.

OHMIYA, K. and SATO, Y. (1968) *Journal of Agricultural and Biological Chemistry*, **32**, 291.

OHMIYA, K. and SATO, Y. (1969) *Journal of Agricultural and Biological Chemistry*, **33**, 669.

OHMIYA, K. and SATO, Y. (1978) *Journal of Agricultural and Biological Chemistry*, **42**, 7.

OKONKWO, P. and KINSELLA, J. E. (1969a) *Journal of Dairy Science*, **52**, 1861.

OKONKWO, P. and KINSELLA, J. E. (1969b) *American Journal of Clinical Nutrition*, **22**, 532.

O'LEARY, V. S. and WOYCHIK, J. H. (1976a) *Journal of Applied and Environmental Microbiology*, **32**, 89.

O'LEARY, V. S. and WOYCHIK, J. H. (1976b) *Journal of Food Science*, **41**, 791.

OTTERHOLM, A., ORDAL, Z. J. and WITTER, L. D. (1968) *Applied Microbiology*, **16**, 524.

OTTOGALLI, G., RISMINI, R., RONDIMINI, G. and SARACCHI, S. (1974) *Dairy Science Abstracts*, **36**, 314.

PERMI, L., SANDINE, W. E. and ELLIKER, P. R. (1972) *Applied Microbiology*, **24**, 51.

PETTE, J. W. and LOLKEMA, J. (1950) *Netherland Milk and Dairy Journal*, **4**, 261.

POZNANSKI, S., LENOIR, J. and MOCQUOT, G. (1965) *Le Lait*, **43**, 3.

PUHAN, Z., BANHEGYI, M. and FLÜELER, O. (1973) *Schweizerische Milchwirtschaftliche Forschung*, **2**, 53.

PUHAN, Z., FLÜELER, O. and BANHEGYI, M. (1973) *Schweizerische Milchwirtschaftliche Forschung*, **2**, 53.

PUHAN, Z., FLÜELER, O. and BANHEGYI, M. (1974) *XIXth International Dairy Congress*, **IE**, 451.

PULUSANI, S. R., RAO, D. R. and SUNKI, G. R. (1979) *Journal of Food Science*, **44**, 575.

RABIER, D. and DESMAZEAUD, M. J. (1973) *Biochimie*, **55**, 389.

RAO, M. V. R. and DUTTA, S. M. (1977) *Journal of Applied and Environmental Microbiology*, **34**, 185.

RAO, M. V. R. and DUTTA, S. M. (1978) *XXth International Dairy Congress*, **E**, 495.

RAO, D. R. and PULUSANI, S. R. (1981) *Journal of Food Science*, **46**, 630.

RASIC, J. and PANIC, B. (1963) *Dairy Industries*, **28**, 35.

RASIC, J. and VUCUROVIC, N. (1973) *Milchwissenschaft*, **28**, 220.

RASIC, J., STOJSLAVLJEVIC, T. and CURCIC, R. (1971) *Milchwissenschaft*, **26**, 219.

RASIC, J., VUCUROVIC, N. and OBRADOVIC, B. (1973) *Milchwissenschaft*, **28**, 168.

RASIC, J., CURCIC, R., STOJSLAVLJEVIC, T. and OBRADOVIC, B. (1971) *Milchwissenschaft*, **26**, 496.

REDDY, G. V., SHAHANI, K. M. and BANERJEE, M. R. (1973) *Journal of the National Cancer Institute*, **50**, 815.

REDDY, K. P., SHAHANI, K. M. and KULKARNI, S. M. (1976) *Journal of Dairy Science*, **59**, 191.

REDDY, M. S., WILLIAMS, F. D. and REINBOLD, G. W. (1973) *Journal of Dairy Science*, **56**, 634.

ROBINSON, R. K., TAMIME, A. Y. and CHUBB, L. W. (1977) *The Milk Industry*, **79**, 4.

RODWELL, V. (1975) In *Review of Physiological Chemistry*, 15th Edition, Ed. by Harper, H. A. Lange Medical Publications, California, U.S.A.

SANDINE, W. E. and ELLIKER, P. R. (1970) *Journal of Agriculture and Food Chemistry*, **18**, 557.

SATO, Y. and NAKASHIMA, J. (1965) *Journal of Agricultural Chemical Society, Japan*, **39**, 292.

SCHULZ, M. E. and HINGST, G. (1954) *Milchwissenschaft*, **9**, 330.

SENECA, H., HENDERSON, E. and COLLINS, A. (1950) *American Practitioner for Digestive Treatement*, **1**, 1252.

SHAHANI, K. M., REDDY, G. V. and JOE, A. M. (1974) *XIXth International Dairy Congress*, **IE**, 569.

SHANKAR, P. A. (1977) In *Inter-relationship of S. thermophilus and L. bulgaricus in Yoghurt Cultures*, PhD Thesis, University of Reading, Berkshire, U.K.

SHANKAR, P. A. and DAVIES, F. L. (1978) *XXth International Dairy Congress*, **E**, 467.

SHARPE, M. E., GARVIE, E. I. and TILBURY, R. H. (1972) *Applied Microbiology*, **23**, 389.

SHIDLOVSKAYA, V. V. and D'YACHENKO, P. F. (1968) *Dairy Science Abstracts*, **30**, 271.

SINGH, J. and RANGANATHAN, B. (1974a) *XIXth International Dairy Congress*, **IE**, 385.

SINGH, J. and RANGANATHAN, B. (1974b) *Acta Microbiologica Polonica*, **6**, 15.

SINGH, J. and RANGANATHAN, B. (1977a) *Indian Journal of Dairy Science*, **30**, 70.

SINGH, J. and RANGANATHAN, B. (1977b) *Indian Journal of Experimental Biology*, **15**, 490.

SINGH, J. and RANGANATHAN, B. (1978) *Journal of Dairy Research*, **45**, 123.

SINGH, J. and RANGANATHAN, B. (1979) *Milchwissenschaft*, **34**, 288.

SINGH, J., KHANNA, A. and CHANDER, H. (1980) *Journal of Food Protection*, **43**, 399.

SINGH, J., RANGANATHAN, B. and CHANDER, H. (1978) *XXth International Dairy Congress*, **E**, 517.

SNELL, E. E., KITAY, E. and HOFF-JØRGENSEN, E. (1948) *Archives of Biochemistry*, **18,** 495.

SOMKUTI, G. A. and STEINBERG, D. H. (1978) *Journal of Dairy Science*, **61** (Suppl. 1), 118.

SOMKUTI, G. A. and STEINBERG, D. H. (1979a) *Journal of Applied Biochemistry*, **1,** 357.

SOMKUTI, G. A. and STEINBERG, D. H. (1979b) *Journal of Food Protection*, **42,** 881.

STANIER, R. Y., DOUDOROFF, M. and ADELBERG, E. A. (1971) In *General Microbiology*, 3rd Edition, The Macmillan Press Ltd., London, U.K.

STOJSLAVLJEVIC, T., RASIC, J. and CURCIC, R. (1971) *Milchwissenschaft*, **26,** 147.

SUZUKI, I., WATANABA, M., KITADA, T., KATO, S. and MORICHI, T. (1979) *Japanese Journal of Zootechnical Science*, **50,** 796.

TAMIME, A. Y. (1977a) In *Some Aspects of the Production of Yoghurt and Condensed Yoghurt*, PhD Thesis, University of Reading, Berkshire, U.K.

TAMIME, A. Y. (1977b) *Dairy Industries International*, **42**(8), 7.

TAMIME, A. Y. (1978) *Cultured Dairy Products Journal*, **13**(3), 16.

TAMIME, A. Y. and DEETH, H. C. (1980) *Journal of Food Protection*, **43,** 939.

TAMIME, A. Y. and ROBINSON, R. K. (1978) *Milchwissenschaft*, **33,** 209.

TANEV, G. and ZIVKOVA, A. (1977) *Milchwissenschaft*, **32,** 280.

TOBA, T., TOMITA, Y., ITOH, T. and ADACHI, S. (1981) *Journal of Dairy Science*, **64,** 185.

TRUFFA-BACHI, P. and COHEN, G. N. (1968) *Annual Review Biochemistry*, **37,** 79.

TURCIC, M., RASIC, J. and CANIC, V. (1969) *Milchwissenschaft*, **24,** 277.

UMANSKII, M. S., MATVEEVA, S. K., BOROVKOVA, A. and OSTROUMOV, L. A. (1974) *XIXth International Dairy Congress*, **IE,** 337.

VANDERPOORTEN, R. and RENTERGHEM, R. von (1974) *XIXth International Dairy Congress*, **IE,** 573.

VIANI, R. and HORMAN, I. (1976) In *Nestlé Research News 1974/75*, Ed. by Boella, C. Nestlé Products Technical Assistance Co. Ltd., Lausanne, Switzerland.

WHITE, A., HANDLER, P. and SMITH, E. L. (1959) In *Principles of Biochemistry*, 2nd Edition, McGraw Hill, New York, U.S.A.

WOLIN, M. J. (1964) *Science*, **146,** 775.

YU, J. H. and NAKANISHI, T. (1975a) *Japanese Journal of Dairy Science*, **24,** A27.

YU, J. H. and NAKANISHI, T. (1975b) *Japanese Journal of Dairy Science*, **24,** A79.

YU, J. H. and NAKANISHI, T. (1975c) *Japanese Journal of Dairy Science*, **24,** A117.

YU, J. H., NAKANISHI, T. and SUYAMA, K. (1974) *Japanese Journal of Dairy Science*, **23,** A195.

CHAPTER 8

The Preservation and Production of Starter Cultures

INTRODUCTION

The manufacture of yoghurt is now more centralised than in the past, and while successful production is directly related to the processing techniques employed, the correct selection, preservation, handling and propagation of the starter cultures helps to standardise and maintain uniformity in the quality of the end product.

Yoghurt cultures consist of two species, i.e. *S. thermophilus* and *L. bulgaricus*, and as these organisms are mainly grown and propagated together, they are referred to as *mixed strain* starter cultures. The culture organisms are preserved in small quantities known as *stock cultures*. When these cultures are reactivated for use in the dairy, a scale-up system of propagation is employed to supply to required volume. For example, if the daily production of yoghurt is 25,000 litres and rate of inoculation is 2%, then the amount of starter needed is 500 litres. Therefore, the various stages of propagation are:

$$\text{Stock} \xrightarrow[0.4\ \text{ml}]{2\%} \text{Mother} \xrightarrow[20\ \text{ml}]{2\%} \text{Feeder} \xrightarrow[10\ l]{2\%} \text{Bulk} \xrightarrow[500\ l]{2\%} \text{Processing vat}$$

The stock and mother cultures are propagated in the laboratory, while the feeder and bulk cultures are produced in the starter room of the dairy. The above various stages of culture propagation are illustrated in Fig. 8.1.

An active bulk starter culture must have the following characteristics:

—it must contain the maximum number of viable cells;
—it must be free from any contaminants, e.g. coliforms or yeasts and moulds;
—it must be active under processing conditions in the dairy, and hence maintenance of the intermediate and other cultures is extremely important.

These latter starter cultures are grown in sterile media, mainly milk, under aseptic conditions, and the activity of such cultures can be maintained by applying one or other of the following approaches (Foster, 1962): Firstly, reducing or controlling the metabolic activity of the organisms by ordinary refrigeration; this is for short-term storage of a starter culture where it can be kept

328

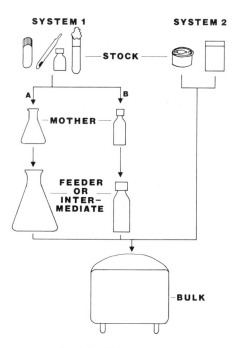

Fig. 8.1. Culture preparation

viable for up to a week. Secondly, concentration and separation of the organisms from their wastes, followed by resuspension in a sterile medium and finally preservation by drying or freezing (Tamime and Robinson, 1976; Tamime, 1981). The latter forms are used for extended storage of the starter bacteria, and such cultures may be obtained from stock collections available in dairy research establishments, colleges or culture bank organisations, or from commercial starter manufacturers.

Some of the methods of starter culture preservation involve concentration of the bacteria, as well as various techniques of drying and freezing, and hence, the viability of a preserved culture may be dependent on:

—the basic growth medium,
—the presence of cryoprotective agents,
—the rapid removal of metabolic compounds, e.g. lactic acid and carbonyl compounds,
—the nature of the suspending medium (if employed),
—conditions of freezing and/or drying,
—rate of thawing (deep frozen cultures),
—method of concentration.

The latter aspect, sometimes referred to as cell biomass concentration, is of great importance; the number of bacterial cells per unit weight or volume is measured by counting the number of colonies produced, after serial dilution, on an agar medium, and the results are recorded as colony-forming units (CFU)/ml or g.

The cell biomass can be concentrated by one of the following systems.

1. Mechanical means

The available equipment, e.g. Sharples separator, desludging separator, clarifiers, or bactofuge, may cause some physical damage to the bacterial cells, thus reducing the rate of survival during the preservation stage. Alternatively, ultracentrifuges (20,000 × g) can be used, and it is possible that these cause least physical damage to the cell.

2. Chemical neutralisation

The two different organisms in the yoghurt starter cultures can tolerate different levels of acidity in the growth medium, with *S. thermophilus* being more sensitive to lactic acid than *L. bulgaricus*. Thus while *L. bulgaricus* can survive beyond 2 % lactic acid, the former organism can tolerate up to 1.2–1.5 % lactic acid, and hence it is essential that the lactic acid is either removed or neutralised in order to protect the yoghurt organisms. Sodium or ammonium hydroxide are widely used, but the latter compound is usually recommended. The reaction between lactic acid and the neutralising compounds results in the formation of sodium or ammonium lactate. However, at a certain level lactate starts to inhibit the starter organisms also, and as a result the cell biomass concentration is limited to $<10^{10}$ CFU/ml.

3. Diffusion culture

This technique involves the use of selected semipermeable membranes to concentrate micro-organisms, and in principle this process consists of the following steps:

—growth of the starter culture in a restricted volume of medium;
—provision of a system that allows fresh growth nutrients to permeate "in" through the membrane;
—and the metabolic waste materials to diffuse "out".

This constant replenishment of the medium allows the concentration of bacterial cells to build up beyond normal levels, and using the diffusion culture technique with cheese starters Osborne (1977) and Osborne and Brown (1980) have reported achieving $>10^{11}$ CFU/ml. Although the waste metabolites diffuse out from the growth medium, some of the lactate is retained, and this does tend to limit the cell biomass concentration. No work has been reported with the yoghurt organisms, but it is possible that the principle of this technique could be applied to concentrate *S. thermophilus* and *L. bulgaricus*

METHODS OF PRESERVATION

A. Liquid Starter

Starter cultures can be preserved in a liquid form using one of two different growth media. The first type is reconstituted skim milk powder (10–12 % SNF) which is free from antibiotics. The milk is sterilised by autoclaving at 10–15 psi for 10–15 minutes, and a sample is incubated for a week at 30°C to check its sterility. After inoculation (1 or 2%), the milk is incubated at 30°C for 16–18 hours or at 42°C for 3–4 hours. At the end of the incubation period, the clotted culture must be cooled immediately, and it can then be stored for up to a week at ordinary refrigeration temperature, e.g. <10°C. Personal experience suggests that if the acidity of the cold culture is around 0.85% lactic acid, both the activity of the starter and the ratio of cocci to rod (1 : 1) is easily maintained. This type of starter culture is referred to in the industry as a *working stock culture*. Alternatively, cool, autoclaved milk may be inoculated with a starter culture, and then stored under refrigeration for incubation whenever it is required. It is worthwhile pointing out that successive subculturing is labour-intensive, expensive and can induce mutant strains; furthermore, trained personnel are required to perform such duties in the laboratory. A maximum limit of 15–20 subcultures is recommended for the yoghurt starter bacteria to safeguard the proper ratio between cocci and the rods, and to reduce the effect of mutation.

A slightly extended preservation of liquid cultures can be achieved using litmus milk (reconstituted skim milk powder 10–12% SNF; 2% litmus solution (5%); 0.3% yeast extract; 1% dextrose/lactose; enough calcium carbonate to cover the bottom of the test tube; 0.25% and 1% of panmede and lecithin respectively adjusted to pH 7). The growth medium is autoclaved at 10 psi for 10 minutes and incubated for a week to check sterility (Shankar, 1975). The inoculated medium is incubated for a short period of time (42°C for 12 hours), and stored under ordinary refrigeration; it is only necessary to reactivate the culture once every 3 months. This type of preserved liquid culture is known as a *reserve stock culture*.

B. Dried Starters

An alternative method for the preservation of yoghurt starter cultures is drying. The different drying methods used are:

—vacuum drying,
—spray drying,
—freeze drying or lyophilisation,
—freeze drying of concentrated cultures to give concentrated freeze-dried cultures (CFDC).

The main objectives behind these developments are: firstly, to reduce the work load which is involved in maintaining liquid cultures; secondly, to improve the shelf-life of the preserved cultures, and thirdly, to facilitate the dispatch of cultures by post without any appreciable loss in their activity.

According to Tofte-Jespersen (1974a, b, 1976), the drying process prior to 1950 was carried out under vacuum, and the results were not encouraging, i.e. the preserved dried cultures contained only 1–2% viable bacteria and to regain maximum activity several subculturings were required. In essence, this method of preservation consisted of taking an active liquid starter culture, adding lactose and calcium carbonate to neutralise the excess acid, followed by partial concentration of the mixture, i.e. removal of whey. The concentrated starters, which were by then in a granular form, were dried under vacuum.

Due to the poor results achieved by vacuum drying, alternative methods have been sought, and one of these methods is spray drying which was first used in Holland for the preservation of cheese starter cultures. Although the results proved promising, this technique has not been developed commercially. However, work in the United States (Porubcan and Sellars, 1975a) showed that the addition of certain compounds, e.g. ascorbic acid and monosodium glutamate, helped to protect the bacterial cells during the drying process. Furthermore, Porubcan and Sellars (1975a) recommended that starter cultures must be propagated in a buffered medium. The objectives of buffering are primarily to increase the number of viable organisms/volume of sample, and secondly to neutralise certain metabolites, mainly lactic acid, which, beyond a certain level, can inhibit bacterial growth. Cultures preserved by this process retained their activity after storage for 6 months at 21°C.

Another spray-dried yoghurt culture was developed in Sweden (Anderson, 1975a, b—Swedish Patent (1974) No. 369 460) for which the following advantages were claimed:

  (i) drying at high temperatures 75–80°C without causing any bacterial damage;
  (ii) maintaining different ratios of *S. thermophilus* : *L. bulgaricus* in the preserved culture. For example, a ratio of 40 : 60 in a dried culture can be used for the production of a sharp flavoured yoghurt (due to high level of *L. bulgaricus*), while for a milder flavoured yoghurt a ratio of 60 : 40 can be used.

The Swedish method of spray drying can be summarised as follows:

  —propagate the starter culture in sterilised concentrated skim milk (18–24 % TS);
  —fortify the growth medium with lysine, cystine and cyanocobalamime;
  —dry at a temperature of 75–80°C.

Although this development claimed many advantages, the system is not widely used.

Freeze-dried or lyophilised yoghurt cultures are produced when the starter culture is dried in the frozen state. This method of starter preservation enjoys widespread popularity and aims at increasing the reliability of preserved cultures, i.e. the dried cultures should provide a high number of viable organisms and the maximum percentage survival during storage, as compared with vacuum or spray-dried starter cultures.

In the lyophilised cultures, the survival rate is high and only a small quantity is needed to inoculate the mother culture. The number of viable bacteria/unit of addition is of the same order of magnitude as in the liquid starter culture (Tofte-Jespensen, 1974b, 1976). It can be observed, however, that freezing and drying can damage the preserved organisms and, in particular, the bacterial cell membrane. As mentioned elsewhere, this damage can be minimised by the addition of certain cryogenic agents to the cell suspension, and according to Morichi (1972 and 1974) the protective solutes are of a hydrogen bonding and/or ionizing group in nature. Hence, these compounds stabilise the cell membrane, and so prevent, to a certain degree, cellular injury during preservation procedures. The effect of such solutes on the survival of the yoghurt organisms is illustrated in Table 8.1. It can be concluded from the work of Morichi (1972) that the survival of *L. bulgaricus* was enhanced by L-glutamic acid, L-arginine and acetyl glycine, and that of *S. thermophilus* by the above-mentioned compounds, DL-pyrrolidone carboxylic acid and DL-malic acid; furthermore, *L. bulgaricus* is more vulnerable to cellular damage than *S. thermophilus* (see Table 8.1).

In view of the relative susceptibility of the yoghurt organisms to the freeze-drying process, many different protective compounds have been studied, and a review of the results is given in Table 8.2.

332

TABLE 8.1. *Effect of cryogenic agents* on the survival rate of freeze-dried yoghurt bacteria (Figures as percentages of original numbers)*

Micro-organisms	L-Glutamic acid	L-Arginine	L-Lysine	DL-Threonine	DL-Pyrrolidone-carboxylic acid	Acetyl glycine	DL-Malic acid
S. thermophilus	35–40	21–40	6–7	7–11	24–48	29–44	52–59
L. bulgaricus	16–21	20–35	1–10	6–10	9–11	7–23	6–15

The range of survival (%) is due to different strains tested.
* Suspending medium (0.06 M and pH 7).

Adapted from Morichi (1972).

Milk solids are widely accepted as a very good cryogenic agent for the preservation of starter cultures, and the use of levels up to 20–25% TS has been reported (see Table 8.2); however, 16% TS in the growth medium is a realistic level, and a typical procedure for the preservation of a mixed strain yoghurt starter culture is illustrated in Fig. 8.2.

The scientific data mentioned above provide an abundance of technical information with reference to *S. thermophilus* and *L. bulgaricus* and the optimum conditions required for high survival rates during freeze-drying, and a summary of the recommendations is presented in Table 8.3.

Lyophilised cultures tend to have a long lag phase, and require to be subcultured at least twice to obtain an active liquid culture. Hence, for the production of bulk starter, "System 1" is used (see Fig. 8.1), for otherwise large quantities of dried culture are needed for direct inoculation of the bulk starter, and a long incubation period is required. Such an approach is not advisable for two main reasons: firstly, the bulk starter may not be active when used for the manufacture of yoghurt, and secondly, from an economic point of view, it can be a very costly approach. More recently, concentrated freeze-dried cultures (CFDC) have appeared on the market, and it is feasible to use such cultures for direct inoculation of a bulk starter (see Fig. 8.1, System 2); or alternatively, for direct-to-vat inoculation of milk for the small-scale manufacture of yoghurt. In both cases, although the production time may be extended by 2–3 hours, considerable savings can be achieved by eliminating the need for trained personnel to handle the starter cultures.

C. Frozen Starters

The final physical form in which the yoghurt starter cultures can be preserved is frozen, and such cultures are available as two different types:

—deep or sub-zero freezing (−30 to −40°C),
—ultra low temperature freezing (−196°C) in liquid nitrogen.

TABLE 8.2. *A selection of different cryogenic compounds employed during the production of freeze-dried yoghurt starter cultures*

Method of preparation	Reference
Skim milk + 3 % lactose Horse serum + 8 % glucose Naylor and Smith (1946) reducing medium	Briggs *et al.* (1955)
Skim milk + 1 % peptonised milk + 10 % saccharose Concentrated milk (20–25 % TS) Starter + milk + rennet Biomass in whey + skim milk + 10 % saccharose + 1–2 % Na-glutamate	Gavin (1968)
Suspend washed cells in skim milk (10 % TS) + 0.5 % ascorbic acid + 0.5 % thiourea + 0.5 % ammonium chloride	Sinha, Nambudripad and Dudani (1970) Sinha, Dudani and Ranganathan (1974)
Grow culture in concentrated milk (19.36 % TS)	Nikolova (1974)
Propagate starter in skim milk (16 % TS) ↓ Mix 30 % with 10 % sucrose + 5 % gelatin + 2 % Na-glutamate ↙ ↘ + 5 % Na-citrate + 5 % Na-acetate (for streptococci) (for lactobacilli)	Lagoda and Bannikova (1974, 1975)
Propagate starter culture in skim milk (11 % TS) + 0.1 % Tween 80 ↓ Suspend biomass in 6 % malt extract	Speckman (1975)
Propagate starter in milk based medium (pH adjusted to 0.6–6.5) + additives (L-ascorbic acid, mono-Na-glutamate, aspartate compound + Cryoprotective agent (inositol, sorbitol, mannito, glucose, sucrose, corn syrup, DMSO, starches, PVP, maltose, mono or disaccharides).	Porubcan and Sellars (1975b)
Grow lactobacilli in MRS broth + 10 % (w/v) cryogenic agent (casitone, lactose, malt extract, milk solids, mono-Na-glutamate, Myvacet, whey powder, or peptonised milk) Grow streptococci in all purpose Tween + 10 % (w/v) cryogenic agent (casitone, dimethyl sulphoxide, glycerol, lactose, malt extract, milk solids, mono-Na- glutamate, pectin, peptonised milk, whey powder).	Kilara, Shahani and Das (1976)
Propagate lactic acid bacteria (LAB) in low lactose medium fortified with soya and casein protein (0.13–0.26 % w/v). The mixture is continuously buffered and freeze- drying commences at a certain cell biomass concentration.	Hup and Stadhouders (1977)
Mix starter culture + 10 % sugar solution, or 5–10 % peptone solution or polymer 1500	Nikolova (1978)
Cultures grown in reconstituted skim milk powder (10 % TS), buffered to pH 6.9 or neutralized with marble ↙ ↘ + yeast extract and + yeast extract, vitamin E Tween 80 and (for streptococci) sheeps serum (for lactobacilli)	Naghmoush *et al.* (1978)
Grow culture in skim milk + 1.5 % Na-glutamate and 8 % sucrose	Ozlap and Ozlap (1979)

Adapted from Tamime (*loc. cit.*).

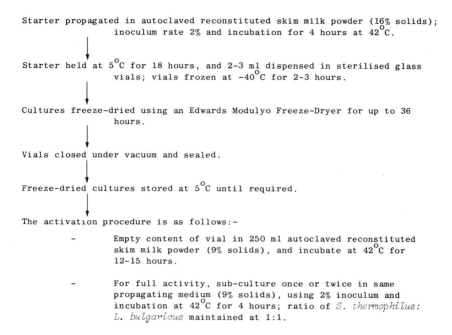

```
Starter propagated in autoclaved reconstituted skim milk powder (16% solids);
              inoculum rate 2% and incubation for 4 hours at 42°C.

Starter held at 5°C for 18 hours, and 2-3 ml dispensed in sterilised glass
              vials; vials frozen at -40°C for 2-3 hours.

Cultures freeze-dried using an Edwards Modulyo Freeze-Dryer for up to 36
              hours.

Vials closed under vacuum and sealed.

Freeze-dried cultures stored at 5°C until required.

The activation procedure is as follows:-

        -     Empty content of vial in 250 ml autoclaved reconstituted
              skim milk powder (9% solids), and incubate at 42°C for
              12-15 hours.

        -     For full activity, sub-culture once or twice in same
              propagating medium (9% solids), using 2% inoculum and
              incubation at 42°C for 4 hours; ratio of S. thermophilus:
              L. bulgaricus maintained at 1:1.
```

Fig. 8.2. A typical procedure for the preservation and utilisation of freeze-dried yoghurt starters

After Tamime and Robinson (*loc. cit.*).

Reprinted with permission of Dairy Industries International.

1. Deep or sub-zero freezing

Sterile liquid milk freshly inoculated with an active starter culture is deep frozen at -30 to $-40°C$ for the preservation of a mother or feeder culture. Such frozen cultures can retain their activity for several months when stored at $-40°C$ and this method of culture preservation became popular in the dairy industry because deep frozen cultures produced in centralised laboratories could be dispatched to a dairy in dry-ice whenever required. These cultures are mainly packed in plastic containers, and a typical example is the Astell-type plastic bottle. The reactivation procedure for the deep frozen cultures is as follows:

—remove starter from freezer, i.e. at $-40°C$;
—thaw the starter very quickly in water bath at $20°C$;
—incubate at $42°C$ until the desired acidity is reached;
—cool and store overnight in the refrigerator;
—subculture for the propagation of feeder or bulk starter (see Fig. 8.1, System 1).

An alternative type of deep frozen culture involves freezing an active liquid starter at $-40°C$. The process consists of propagating the culture in a continuously neutralised growth medium in

TABLE 8.3. *A summary of recommendations for the preservation and handling of yoghurt starter cultures by the freeze-drying method*

Stage of processing	Recommendations
I. Growth medium	Milk fortified with yeast extract and hydrolysed protein. Neutralise growth medium to pH range 5–6. Propagate organisms at optimum incubation temperature to maintain ratio between cocci and rods.
II. Cell biomass and suspending medium	Provide a culture of $>10^{10}$ colony-forming unit (CFU)/ml (refer to text for various methods). Neutralise suspending medium to a pH range 5–6. Remove carbonyl compounds from suspending medium and fortify it with non-reducing sugars, amino acids and/or semicarbazide; the carbonyl compounds can react with amino groups in the bacterial cells and can accelerate their death. Harvest *S. thermophilus* towards the latter part of exponential phase and *L. bulgaricus* in the early stages of stationery phase. Suspend *S. thermophilus* in skim milk + sodium malate and *L. bulgaricus* in skim milk + a solution of lactose and arginine hydrochloride.
III. Drying, packaging and storage	Freeze cultures at $-20°$ to $-30°C$ and dry at a temperature between $-10°$ to $30°C$. Dry cultures to less than 3% moisture. Vacuum package the dried cultures. The presence of oxygen can damage bacterial cells. Hence, recommended packaging materials are glass vials and laminated aluminium foil sachets. For long-term storage, keep dried cultures at $5–10°C$ or $-20°C$.
IV. Reactivation	Follow instructions of starter culture manufacture. Propagate dried cultures once or twice in autoclaved reconstituted skim milk powder (10–12% TS) free from any inhibitory agent to obtain an active mother culture. Rehydrate at temperature of $20–25°C$ to prevent leakage of cellular ribonucleotides from damaged cells of *L. bulgaricus*.
V. Miscellaneous	Provide sterile conditions during various stages of preparation and reactivation processes. *S. thermophilus* preserves well, while *L. bulgaricus* is more sensitive to freezing and drying.

order to optimise the bacterial cell number/ml. The bacterial mass is then separated using a Sharples separator, and the cells are resuspended in a sterile growth medium and/or protective agent prior to packaging and freezing. As mentioned earlier, the preserved cultures must be stored at $-30°$ to $-40°C$, and be dispatched to dairies in insulated boxes filled with dry-ice.

The activity of deep frozen starter cultures tends to deteriorate after a certain time in storage due to several factors:

(i) freezing can cause cell damage, in particular to *L. bulgaricus*. However, Imai and Kato (1975) reported that an "improved" medium for frozen cultures held at $-30°C$ contains 10% skim milk, 5% sucrose, fresh cream and 0.9% sodium chloride or 1% gelatin. The same workers also observed that the presence of sodium acetate caused the starters to become sensitive to injury. Other cryogenic compounds recommended for the preservation of concentrated cultures by freezing at $-30°C$ are: sodium citrates, glycerol or sodium β-glycerophosphate (Tamime, *loc. cit.*).

(ii) The use of mechanical separators for the concentration of the bacterial cells may cause some injury, so that the starter becomes sensitive to freezing.

(iii) The destruction of bacterial cells during freezing is mainly due to an increased concentration of electrolytes and other solutes both inside the cell and in the suspending medium, rather than to mechanical damage as the result of ice crystal formation (Keogh, 1969). The former situation results in the denaturation of protein components and enzymes of the bacterial cell, while the concentration of electrolytes outside the cell results in the dehydration of the protoplasm due to the diffusion of water through the cell wall membrane.

2. Ultra-low temperature freezing

Ultra-low temperature freezing at $-196°C$ in liquid nitrogen is by far the most successful method of preserving starter cultures, and the reviews by Gilliland and Speck (1974) and Hurst (1977) illustrate the extent of research work which has been carried out in this field. The advantages of this technique of starter preservation have been summarised by Keogh (*loc. cit.*) as follows:

(i) at such low temperatures the water molecules do not form large size crystals;
(ii) the biochemical processes inside the cell cease to function, so that in biological terms, the bacterial cell is at a "standstill".

As a result Keogh (*loc. cit.*) reported that the lactic streptococci (i.e. cheese starter cultures) require no protective agent in the suspending medium when preserved at $-196°C$. However, *L. bulgaricus* is still found to be susceptible to freezing damage, and the recommended cryogenic agents which can improve the survival rate, stability and resuscitation after storage are: Tween 80 and sodium oleate (Smittle, Gilliland and Speck, 1972; Smittle *et al.*, 1974). Bulgarian workers reported that good results were obtained when yoghurt starter cultures were frozen at 0.36% lactic acid (Tamime and Robinson, *loc. cit.*).

In order to maintain the activity of the preserved starter at ultra-low temperatures, the cultures are neutralised, concentrated, packaged and finally frozen, and Fig. 8.3 illustrates the various stages in the production of such cultures. Normally the concentrated starter is packed in an aluminium can of 70 ml capacity, i.e. the recommended volume to inoculate 1000 litres (225 gal) of milk. The cans are fitted with a pull-ring-type closure, which is convenient for easy opening. However, for smaller quantities, e.g. 5 ml, the culture can be packed in a screw-capped polypropylene ampule which resists cracking in liquid nitrogen. Another type of packaging material which may be used is the laminated carton. While the aluminium can and the polypropylene ampule are stored in liquid nitrogen, the laminated carton is stored in a special container in an atmosphere of nitrogen vapour. Incidentally, the latter type of packaging material is used to pack "pelleted" concentrated cheese starter cultures (see Fig. 8.4).

These developments in liquid nitrogen freezing of the yoghurt starter cultures are primarily aimed at the preservation of the feeder/intermediate culture for the preparation of the bulk starter (see Fig. 8.1, System 2). However, the ultimate objective is to employ such cultures for direct-to-vat inoculation of milk for the production of yoghurt, for although their use can lead to a prolonged manufacturing time (longer lag phase – see later), the advantages can be summarised as follows:

—convenience,
—culture reliability,

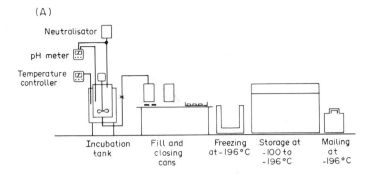

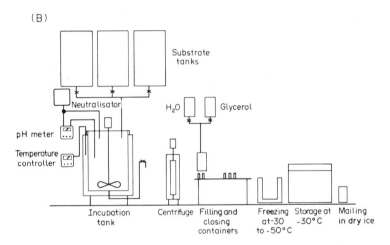

Fig. 8.3. The principle stages involved in the production of ultra-low temperature and deep frozen yoghurt starter cultures

(A) The process for the production of Redi-set cultures.
(B) The process for the production of DVS cultures (see also Porubcan and Sellars, 1979).

Reproduced by courtesy of Chr. Hansen's Lab. A/S, Copenhagen, Denmark

—improved daily performance,
—improved strain balance,
—greater flexibility,
—better control of bacteriophages,
—improvement in quality of product.

However, in practice, certain drawbacks may possibly be encountered, such as:

(i) too great a dependence of the dairy on the starter manufacturer;

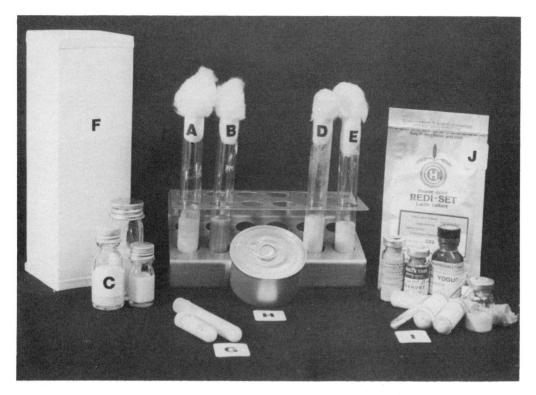

Fig. 8.4. The preservation of yoghurt starter cultures by different methods

(A) Liquid (incubate and store under refrigeration)
(B) Litmus milk (partially incubated followed by refrigeration)
(C, D, & E) Frozen at −30°C (inoculate, incubate and then freeze, or inoculate and freeze)
(F) Concentrated low-temperature frozen cultures (cheese starter in granular form)
(G) Frozen in liquid nitrogen (polyproplyene ampule)
(H) Frozen in liquid nitrogen (pull ring can)
(I) Freeze-dried
(J) Concentrated freeze dried

(ii) non-availability of liquid nitrogen facilities; however, at present, special containers are supplied by the starter manufacturer to customers for the transportation and storage of cultures in liquid nitrogen;

(iii) apportioning of responsibility in case of starter failure;

(iv) a natural reluctance within the dairy industry to introduce a new technology in place of one that is well established as satisfactory;

(v) the longer time required for manufacture of yoghurt.

It can be observed from the preceding account that yoghurt starter cultures are available in a number of forms (see Fig. 8.4), and depending on the method of preservation, the viable cell/ml or g can vary slightly; Table 8.4 illustrates some typical differences between the available types of commercially produced yoghurt cultures.

TABLE 8.4. *The viable cell count of some yoghurt starter cultures from Chr. Hansen's Laboratory Ltd.; the liquid culture provides a base-line for comparison*

Type of culture or method of preservation	Total viable cell count
Liquid (fresh or active)	$3-5 \times 10^8$/ml
Freeze-dried (Dri-Vac)	$2-3 \times 10^9$/g
Concentrated freeze-dried	$4-6 \times 10^{10}$/g
Ultra-low temperature freezing (Redi-Set)	2×10^9/ml

After Cowan (1981).

PRODUCTION OF THE STARTER CULTURE

One of the main criteria of "success" during the preparation of the starter is the production of an "active" culture, i.e. a starter which consists of very large number of viable cells, so that when it is added to milk the fermentation process is initiated as quickly as possible. During the growth of the yoghurt organisms the cells divide and increase in number up to a certain level, and then start to die. This behaviour gives rise to the characteristic "growth curve" illustrated in Fig. 8.5, and it can be seen that the rate of cell division is divided into four different sections:

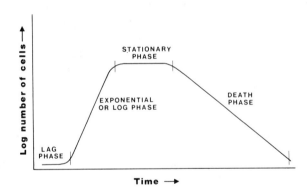

Fig. 8.5. The growth curve characteristics of a population of viable unicellular microorganisms

(i) Lag phase. This is the phase which follows immediately after inoculation of the milk. The delayed bacterial activity could be due to adjustment or adaption of the organism in a new medium.

(ii) Log phase. During this phase the cells display maximum activity, i.e. shortest generation time, so long as optimum conditions (nutrients and temperature) are available.

(iii) Stationery phase. At a certain point, the cell viable number remains constant due to a

lack of nutrients and an accumulation of waste metabolites, e.g. lactic acid in milk; i.e. death of old cells and production of new cells is in balance.

(iv) Death phase. The number of viable cells starts to diminish, mainly due to unfavourable growth conditions.

It is safe to assume that there is a direct relationship between the activity of the starter and its "age", and an active culture falls somewhere on the growth curve between the upper middle region of the log phase and the beginning of the stationary phase (see Fig. 8.5). Therefore, the most active type of starter is the liquid culture, which is characterised by having a short lag period followed by a rapid rate of acid development; on average the inoculation rate may vary between 2–3%, and the starter may contain in excess of 10^8 viable organisms/ml. By contrast, the direct-to-vat starters, e.g. concentrated freeze-dried or the ultra-low-temperature frozen cultures, tend to show a slightly longer lag phase as compared with the liquid culture, and this may be due to:

(a) Although the cell concentration is in the region of 10^9–10^{12} CFU/ml, the inoculation rate is relatively small (see Table 8.4). For example, the liquid nitrogen frozen cultures are employed, after melting at 20°C in hypochlorite solution, at a rate of 70 ml/1000 litres of milk, or the CFDC at a rate of 5 g/500–1000 litres. The use of higher inoculation rates is not recommended for two main reasons: firstly, it increases cost of production, and secondly, it leads to excessive metabolic activity by the starter which can lead to difficulties in controlling the fermentation process, and the yoghurt can be of an inferior quality, i.e. bitter. In addition, the larger the inoculum of the starter culture (including liquid cultures), the greater the tendency for whey syneresis to occur in yoghurt.

(b) The longer lag phase needed by these cultures is an indication that their metabolism, at the time of inoculation, is at a very low level, and hence more time is required for the essential adaptation. Incidentally the quality of the milk must be very good, because the presence of any inhibitory agents (e.g. antibiotics or detergents residues) can ultimately reduce the activity of the starter culture.

The longer lag phase period required by direct-to-vat starter cultures may increase the yoghurt processing time by around 2 hours as compared with the use of a liquid starter, and longer production time may not be attractive to large creameries; in this latter situation, these types of starter culture can be utilised for direct-to-vat bulk starter production.

PRODUCTION SYSTEMS FOR STARTER CULTURES

As illustrated earlier in Fig. 8.1, there are two main methods for the production of bulk starters. The first method (System 1) is a simple scale-up system of starter propagation (stock ⟶ mother ⟶ feeder or intermediate ⟶ bulk); however, the second method (System 2) is direct-to-vat inoculation of the bulk starter. In either system the aim is to produce a pure active culture free from contaminants, mainly bacteriophages, and the different methods which have been devised may be divided into three main categories: firstly, the use of simple microbiological techniques, secondly, the employment of mechanically protected equipment and tanks, and thirdly, the propagation of starter in phage resistant/inhibitory medium (PRM/PIM).

341

A. Simple Microbiological Techniques

In this system the equipment/materials used are basically laboratory utensils and a starter tank, and may consist of the following items:

—glass test tubes, McCartney bottles, 250 ml flasks (for propagation of mother culture);
—2–5 litre flasks (for production of feeder culture);
—graduated and Pasteur pipettes.

Reconstituted skim milk powder (10–12 % TS) is used as the growth medium, and the glassware containing the milk is plugged with non-absorbent cotton wool. The whole is sterilised in an autoclave at 121°C for 10 minutes for small volumes (i.e. up to 250 ml), or for 15 minutes for larger quantities (i.e. 2–3 litres). However, the milk for the feeder culture is normally only steamed for 1 hour. It is recommended that a sample of sterilised milk for the mother cultures should be incubated at 30° or 50°C for 2 days prior to use in order to check its sterility. Pipettes are sterilised in an oven at 160°C for a minimum of 2 hours.

The reactivation and subculturing procedures must be carried out under extremely hygienic conditions. For example, the freeze-drying ampoule is wiped with alcohol before breaking the glass, or alternatively, if a liquid stock culture is used, the lip of the test tube or McCartney bottle must be "flamed" over a bunsen burner when the cotton wool or the screw cap is removed, and again immediately before replacing it. It is also recommended that the starter working area and atmosphere should be clean, i.e. the air must be filtered, and if possible, the whole starter laboratory should be under positive pressure; unfiltered air does not enter the room whenever the door is opened. Alternatively, subculturing can be carried out in a laminar-flow hood or cabinet to reduce the possibility of airborne contamination.

The production of a bulk starter using this system requires a simple design of tank, i.e. batch pasteuriser/starter incubator. The tank is not pressurised, and at subculturing the lid is opened and the starter is poured into the milk. An example of such a tank is the Silkeborg/Pasilac type C31a or Alfa-Laval starter vat ER (see Fig. 8.6).

Very small quantities e.g. 45 litres, of bulk starter can be produced in an ordinary milk churn or similar stainless steel container. A water bath or thermostatically controlled cabinet may be used as a combined pasteuriser, cooler and incubator for the production of limited volumes of bulk starter.

It is worthwhile mentioning at this stage that this method is used also for the production of the feeder starter used for inoculating the mechanically protected Jones tank (refer below for further information).

B. Mechanically Protected Systems

Two aspects of starter production in mechanically protected systems are important: firstly, the growth medium is heat treated and cooled to incubation temperature in a completely enclosed vat, and secondly, the inoculation of the starter takes place through a barrier which prevents the entry of air. Since 1950 there has been a great improvement in starter culture equipment, mainly due to the centralisation of fermented dairy products manufacture, and hence the demand for large quantities of bulk starter. As a result, different types of mechanically protected systems have been developed, and the following are, perhaps, the most important.

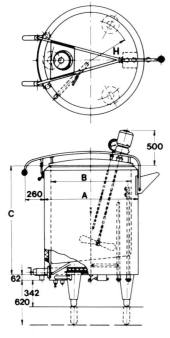

Litres	A	B	C	H
320	896	750	955	320
500	996	850	1108	370
1000	1356	1210	1118	550

Measurements in mm.

Dimensions

Dimensions in mm, sizes in litres.

Size	A	B	C	D	E	F
250	915	790	1500	1780	580	2030
400	1036	888	1590	1870	665	2230

Fig. 8.6.   Schematic illustrations of two 'simple' design starter tanks

Pasilac/Silkeborg	Alfa-Laval
(c31a)	(ER)

Reproduced by courtesy of Pasilac/Silkeborg Ltd., Preston, UK and Alfa-Laval A/B, Lund, Sweden

1. The Lewis system

The development of this technique is well documented by Lewis (1956) and Cox and Lewis (1972), and it involves the use of two-way hypodermic needles to carry out the transfer of stock to mother culture, mother culture to feeder culture and feeder culture to bulk starter; all inoculations take place through a barrier of chlorinated water. In order to facilitate easy transfer of the cultures during each stage of propagation, re-usable, collapsible polythene bottles are used (115 and 850 ml capacity) for the mother and the feeder cultures respectively. The polythene bottles are fitted with Astell rubber seals and a screw cap. These bottles are filled with the growth medium (10–12% reconstituted skim milk free from antibiotics), sealed and capped; the contents are thus isolated from aerial contamination throughout the sterilisation, inoculation and incubation stages. At the intermediate transfers, the annular space of the Astell rubber seal is flooded with 100–200 mg/litre

343

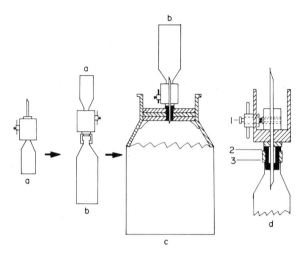

Fig. 8.7. Schematic illustration of the Lewis system for starter cultures transfers

(a) Mother Culture
(b) Feeder/Intermediate Culture
(c) Bulk Culture
(d) Detail of Needle Assembly
    (1) Tap
    (2) Astell Seal
    (3) Hypochlorite Solution
After Tamime (*loc. cit.*).

Reprinted with permission of Applied Science Publishers Ltd.

hypochlorite solution, and finally the bottle containing the established culture is squeezed to discharge the inoculum. The overall technique is illustrated schematically in Figs. 8.7 and 8.8.

For the Lewis system, the milk is heated in a tightly sealed vessel, and for safety reasons the tank is fitted with a pressure relief valve. During the heating stage some air may escape, but when the milk is cooled, no air enters the tank. The stainless steel pressure vessel is totally submerged within an insulated water tank, which provides maximum protection from aerial contamination as well as maintaining a constant temperature during incubation. The agitator shaft is fitted with a double mechanical seal, and water under pressure is fed to the seal housing to ensure efficient protection against contamination, cooling and lubrication. The transfer of the feeder culture to the bulk tank is carried out through a sterile barrier, i.e. water containing sodium hypochlorite solution. The specification of the Lewis tank, which is manufactured by Wincanton Engineering Ltd., UK, is illustrated in Fig. 8.9.

Ordinary milk churns, e.g. 22.7 or 45.5 litre capacity, fitted with special reflex lids can also be used for the Lewis system of starter propagation; the necessary equipment can be seen in Fig. 8.10.

2. Alfa-Laval system

This system is described in detail by Anon. (1975), and in principle it is somewhat similar to the Lewis method except that: firstly, the tank is of a different design, and is fitted with a special filter

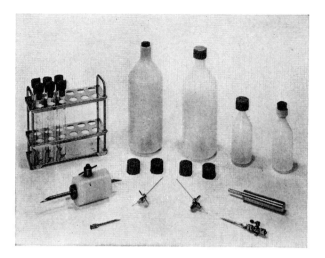

Fig. 8.8. Astell equipment for starter culture propagation

Reproduced by Courtesy of Astell Hearson Group, London, UK.

consisting of hydrophobic paper with pre-filters on each side. The whole filter unit is enclosed in a protective casing. During the heat treatment of the milk, the air diffuses out through the filter from the tank, and vice versa during the cooling stages. It is critical that the filter sterilises the air to reduce the effect of airborne contamination. Secondly, in the Lewis system, starter transfer from one container to another relies entirely on squeezing the collapsible polythene bottle to eject the culture, while the Alfa-Laval method uses sterilised air (see Fig. 8.11).

Glass bottles are used for the propagation of the mother culture, and stainless steel cannisters for the feeder stage. The bottles are sealed with rubber stoppers and a metal screw cap with an annular space. During culture transfer two disposable sterile syringes are used. The first syringe, which is short, is connected to the air supply, and it is fitted with an aseptic filter to sterilise the air. The second syringe is long enough to reach the bottom of the glass bottle (see Fig. 8.12) and is connected to the feeder container. Thus, when the air supply is switched on, it is sterilised through the filter and enters the bottle via the short needle. This results in a build-up of pressure in the head space of the bottle, and this forces the culture through the long needle in to the feeder cannister.

The feeder container has two fittings, one for compressed air, and the other in the form of a bore made of stainless steel pipe which connects to the bulk starter tank during culture transfer (refer to Fig. 8.13). These fitments are equipped with special valves with quick release couplings. Incidentally, there are specially designed units known as "Viscubators" (Fig. 8.14) for the propagation of the mother and feeder/intermediate cultures under specified conditions. These units are thermostatically controlled for the heat treatment of the starter milk, cooling the milk to the incubation temperature, maintaining the temperature during the fermentation, and finally cooling the culture to $<10°C$ until it is required. A schematic illustration of culture transfer from the feeder container to the bulk starter tank can be seen in Fig. 8.15, and a smilar system of bulk starter production is manufactured by Diessel GmbH & Co. in West Germany (see Rasic and Kurmann, 1978).

345

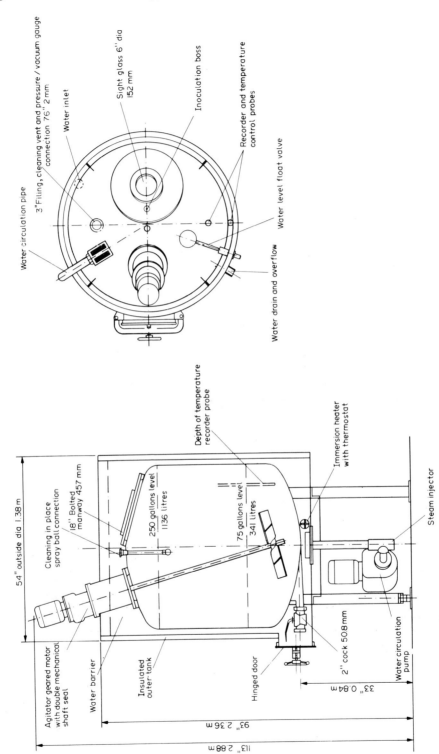

Fig. 8.9. A schematic illustration of the Wincanton Engineering bulk starter tank for the propagation of starter cultures using the Lewis system

Reproduced by courtesy of Wincanton Engineering Co. Ltd., Sherborne, UK.

Fig. 8.10.

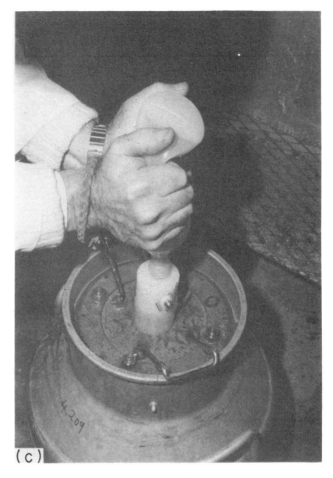

Fig. 8.10. The use of milk churns for the production of small quantities of starter culture using the Lewis system

(a) Milk churn with special lids
(b) The lid assembly
(c) Inoculation

3. The Terlet-Zutphen system

These starter culture vessels are manufactured in Holland. The vessels are hermatically sealed, i.e. no ingress or exit of air, and the capacities range from 5 to 50 litres for the mother and feeder cultures. Heating is provided by means of steam injection into the insulated water jacket of the vessel, and the temperature is controlled by an automatic controller unit. After sterilisation of the milk, the steam is replaced by chilled water to cool the milk to 40–45°C. The starter culture is inoculated through a special grafting plug or membrane using a sterile hypodermic syringe. During the incubation period, the temperature is maintained at 40–45°C, and at the desired acidity the active culture is cooled to <10°C. A dial thermometer is always provided to check the temperature of the culture, and in some instances the unit is fitted with a pH meter plus a recorder

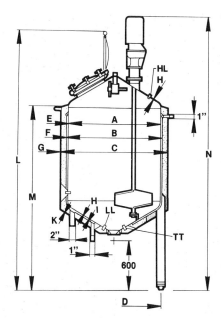

Fig. 8.11. Schematic illustration of an Alfa-Laval aseptic starter tank

HL   High level pH electrode
LL   Low   ,,   ,,   ,,
TT   Resistant thermometer

Reproduced by courtesy of Alfa-Laval A/B, Lund, Sweden

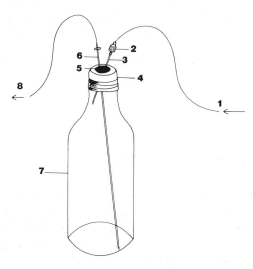

Fig. 8.12. Schematic illustration of the Alfa-Laval mother culture system

(1) Inlet of air supply   (5) Rubber seal
(2) Filter   (6) Long syringe
(3) Short syringe   (7) Glass bottle
(4) Metal screw cap with an annular ring   (8) Culture outlet to feeder container

349

to monitor the changes in acidity. Incidentally, the grafting plug is also used during the subsequent stages of culture transfer, and sterile air helps to transport the active culture from the mother apparatus to the feeder vessel and finally on to bulk starter tank. This technique is similar in principle to the Alfa-Laval system described above (see Fig. 8.16).

Terlet-Zutphen manufacture two different types of bulk starter tank, i.e. the "Tank model" and the "Hinged cover model". Both types of starter tank have a bottom-driven paddle fitted with a special inner cylinder through which is circulated hot or chilled water; this increases the surface area of the tank in contact with the milk, and so raises the efficiency of heat transfer. The starter tanks are also fitted with a baffle-plate which improves the mixing of the milk and/or active culture during the heating and cooling stages. The manway cover of these tanks is hermetically sealed, and a water seal can also be provided as an optional precautionary measure.

The build-up of pressure in the bulk starter tank during the heat treatment of the milk is reduced by a specially designed air filtration and sterilisation unit (see Fig. 8.17). In principle, the pre-filter

(a)

Fig. 8.13

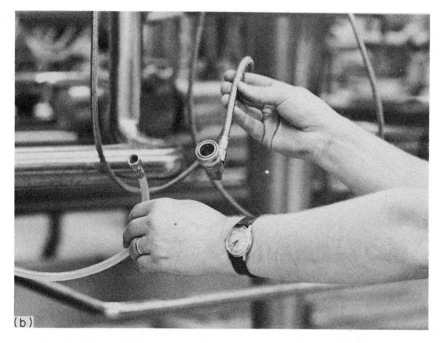

Fig. 8.13. Pipes, valve connections and fittings of the feeder intermediate culture container

(a) Temperature dial.
   Right hand pipe is for air supply.
   Left hand plastic pipe is for culture outlet.
(b) Special valve fittments with quick release coupling.
   Pipes-description as in (A).

Reproduced by courtesy of Alfa-Laval A/B, Lund, Sweden.

collects the dust from the air, the fan generates a slight positive pressure in the head space of the tank, and a special filter catches any airborne phage particles. The function of the fan is to ensure that a positive air pressure is always maintained, and the pressure is automatically controlled through the operation of pneumatic valves which regulate the flow of air. Such units are installed with all types of bulk starter tanks. All tanks are also fitted with same grafting membrane for culture transfer, and identical temperature and/or pH control units.

4. The Jones system

The Jones tank is not a pressurised starter culture vessel, since air in the head space of the tank is forced out during heat treatment of the milk, and enters again during the cooling stages. However, a slight positive pressure inside the tank can be achieved by incorporating a fan unit in the air filtration/sterilisation system. The design of this tank includes the following features which act as a mechanical barrier to infection: first, the manway cover, the inoculation port and the drive-shaft of the agitator system (top-driven type) are specially designed to fit into separate moats which can be flooded with hypochlorite solution; such barriers are referred to as water seals. Second, the

351

Fig. 8.14. Equipment for the propagation of mother and feeder starter cultures

On site view of an Alfa-Laval Aseptic Viscubator beside a yoghurt production line, (note the bulk starter tanks, incubation tanks, plate cooler and buffer tanks).

Reproduced by courtesy of Alfa-Laval, A/B, Lund, Sweden

filtration and sterilisation of the air can be achieved using either a bacteriological filter, or alternatively, a combination of non-absorbent cotton wool and heat. In the latter system, a set of concentric pipes is arranged around the relevant openings, and the space between the pipes, i.e. the air passage, is packed with cotton wool; steam is passed through the inner pipe. In practice, the heat from the steam sterilises the air, and the cotton wool merely filters any dust or other airborne particles from the air.

It is important that the filtration unit is activated at all times during the heat treatment of the milk, the incubation period and the cooling of the active culture, thus ensuring that the air entering the tank is always sterile. Incidentally, if air accidentally enters the bulk starter tank through one of the water seals, the hypochlorite concentration is high enough to sterilise it.

352

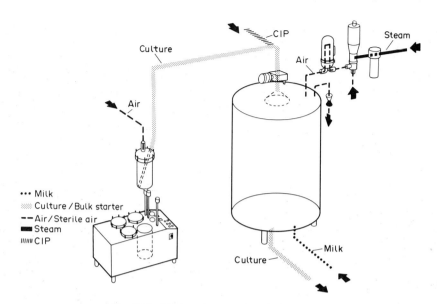

Fig. 8.15. Alfa-Laval starter preparation system

Reproduced by courtesy of Alfa-Laval A/B, Lund, Sweden

The inoculation port, which is also fitted with a water seal, is situated on the top of the tank and the procedure of culture transfer is as follows:

(a) place a "ring of flame" or other source of heat, e.g. steam, around the inoculation port;
(b) remove the cover;
(c) pour in the feeder culture;
(d) replace the port cover;
(e) remove "ring of flame".

The provision of a sterile point of entry for the inoculum is due, therefore, to the combined effect of heat, and a slight positive pressure in the head space of the tank. This ensures that the flow of air is always in the upward direction, i.e. from inside the tank to the atmosphere, and this minimises the possibility of airborne contamination.

The development of this system has been well documented by Whitehead (1956) and Robertson (1966a, b), and one of the earlier design specifications of the Jones starter tank is shown in Fig. 8.18. The Jones tank is manufactured in the United Kingdom by Burnett & Rolf Ltd., and in recent years the major developments that have taken place in the design of this type of starter tank are: firstly, the top-driven agitator has been replaced by a bottom-driven mechanism which reduces the number of water seals on top of the tank, and secondly, there has been a modification of the inoculation port. This new system of culture transfer was developed by the manufacturer primarily to meet the specifications for a starter vessel required for the production of cheese bulk starter cultures, and in particular, the transfer of the feeder culture to the bulk stage is carried out via a compartment flooded with hypochlorite solution; in the earlier models of the Jones tank (see Fig. 8.19 "A"), the cover of the inoculation port had to be removed during culture transfer.

In brief, the new system of culture transfer is as follows:

(a) The feeder culture is prepared in the traditional way, but the container is fitted with an Astell seal (for the transfer of mother culture to feeder) and an elastomeric diaphram which seals the end of a 20-cm long stainless steel pipe.

(b) During bulk starter inoculation, the feeder container is upturned and forced onto a sharp cannular which is submerged in hypochlorite solution (see Fig. 8.19 "A").

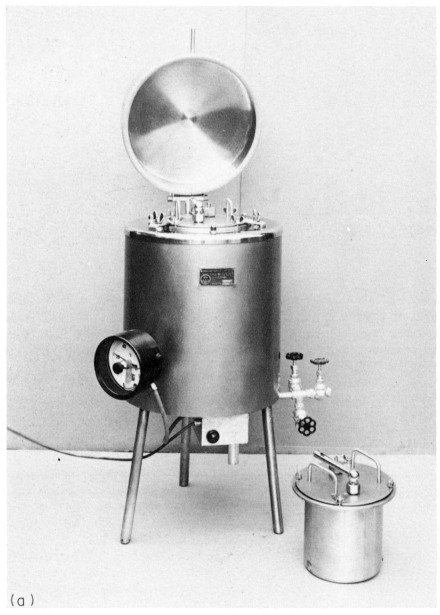

(a)

Fig. 8.16

Fig. 8.16

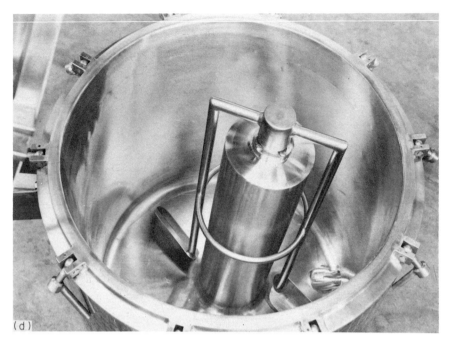

Fig. 8.16.   Starter culture vessels manufactured by Terlet-Zutphen/Holland

(a) Mother culture apparatus (b) Top view of mother culture vessel (c) Feeder/intermediate culture vessel (d) Type of paddle used in bulk starter vessel fitted with inner cylinder (see text) (e) Bulk starter culture tank and the air filtration assembly

Reproduced by courtesy of Van den Bergh & Partners Ltd., Windsor, UK and N.V. Machinefabriek Terlet, Zutphen, Holland.

356

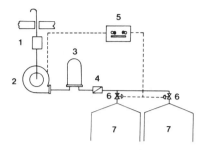

Fig. 8.17. Terlet-Zutphen air filtration and sterilisation unit

(1) Pre-filter
(2) Fan
(3) Bacteriological filter
(4) Non-return valve
(5) Switch panel
(6) Pneumatic valves
(7) Bulk starter culture tanks

Reproduced by courtesy of Van den Bergh & Partners Ltd., Windsor, UK and N.V. Machinefabriek Terlet, Zutphen, Holland.

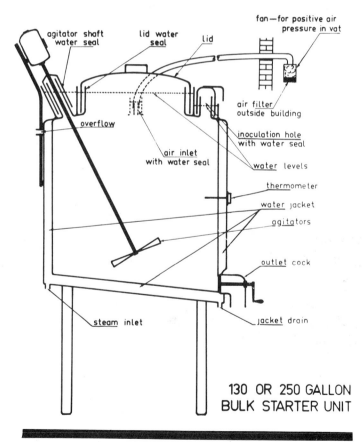

Fig. 8.18. Schematic drawing of the Jones type bulk starter tank

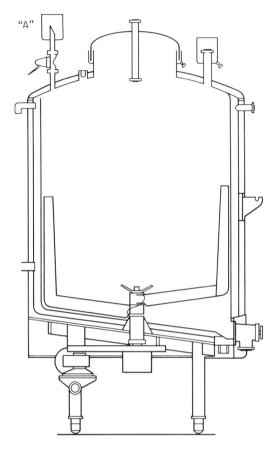

Fig. 8.19. Schematic drawing of the (Burnett & Rolfe Ltd.) Jones tank fitted with a modified inoculation port

Reproduced by courtesy of Burnett & Rolfe Ltd., Rochester, UK.

(c) The moment the diaphram is ruptured, the valve in the tank inlet is opened, and the active cultures flows into the tank.

(d) Finally, the valve is closed and the feeder container is removed, during this process, neither the inoculation spout nor the active culture are exposed to the atmosphere, so eliminating altogether aerial contamination during culture transfer.

Incidently, a similar culture tank is manufactured in the Republic of Ireland by Golden Vale Engineering (GVE). The broad specifications of this tank are: (see Fig. 8.20)

(a) the manway, inoculation spout and agitator-shaft are top mounted and liquid sealed;
(b) capacities range from 300 to 2000 gallons;
(c) the outlet valve has an internal seal;
(d) an air filtration/sterilisation unit is employed.

Another bulk starter tank was described in detail by Tofte-Jespersen (1979). In some aspects this tank is similar to the Jones system, but one distinctive feature of this tank is the air

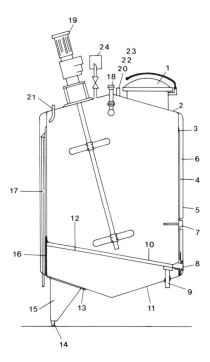

Fig. 8.20.   Specifications of the starter culture tank manufactured by Golden Vale Engineering

(1) Manway cover	(13) Patch plate
(2) Conical top	(14) Adjustable ball feet
(3) Inner body	(15) Conical legs
(4) Dimple jacket	(16) Skirt
(5) Outer body	(17) Dimple jacket outlet
(6) Insulation	(18) Detergent inlet
(7) Thermometer	(19) Agitator unit
(8) Outlet pipe with flange	(20) Sterile air connection
(9) Dimple jacket outlet	(21) Inlet connection
(10) Inner bottom	(22) Vent connection
(11) Conical end	(23) Inoculation fitting
(12) Dimple bottom	(24) Inoculation spout

Reproduced by courtesy of Golden Vale Engineering Ltd., Charleville, Republic of Ireland.

filtration/sterilisation unit which aims to clean the air of dust and bacteriophage particles (see Fig. 8.21). A positive pressure is also maintained in the head space of the tank, so that air-borne contamination is prevented during culture transfer, inspite of the open inoculation spout.

5. Silkeborg/Pasilac system

This type of tank is manufactured by Silkeborg/Pasilac Ltd. in Denmark. The tank is not designed as a pressure vessel, i.e. air inside the tank escapes during the heating of the milk and

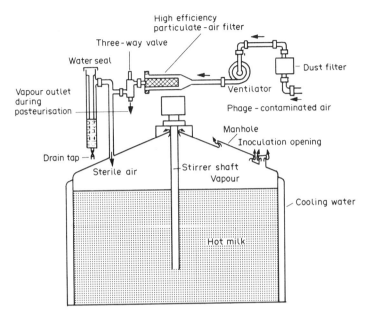

Fig. 8.21. Bulk starter tank incorporating a special air filtration unit

After Stadhouders, Bangma and Driessen (1976).
Reprinted with permission of Nordeuropaeisk Mejeri-Tidsskrift.

returns during cooling, and hence all air entering the vessel must be filtered and sterilised. It may be argued, therefore, that the tank is similar to the Jones system, i.e. top mounted agitator and manway cover (with water seal), a system of air filtration, and the provision of a slight positive pressure in the head space of the tank, but one major difference is the method of inoculation. The Silkeborg/Pasilac tank is fitted with a special flexible membrane and, during culture transfer, it is necessary to use a sterile hypodermic needle; a technique which is similar to the Lewis method. An illustration of such a tank is shown in Fig. 8.22.

6. Miscellaneous systems

It can be observed from the preceding section that a wide variety of mechanically protected tanks are available on the market for the production of phage-free bulk starter cultures. However, some leading manufacturers of dairy equipment fabricate starter vessels which cannot be categorised as "mechanically protected" tanks. An example of such a tank (Fig. 8.23) is manufactured by Damrow DEC in the United States, and the manway cover has to be opened during culture transfer. It could be argued, therefore, that this system of bulk starter production could lead to aerial contamination, but the importance of such incidents can be minimised by using concentrated starters for direct inoculation of the bulk starter milk, and, possibly, by using PRM/PIM (see following section). Hence, the production of an active culture in open tanks depends on the maintenance of high standards of hygiene.

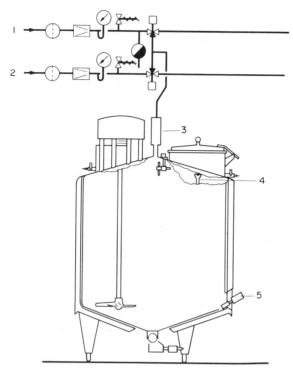

Fig. 8.22. Schematic drawing of the aseptic Silkeborg/Pasilac tank incorporating a positive pressure air system

(1) Steam
(2) Air
(3) Filter
(4) Rubber membrane for injecting culture inoculum
(5) Thermometer and pH probe

Reproduced by courtesy of Pasilac/Silkeborg Ltd., Preston, UK.

C. PRM/PIM

The basic ingredients of PRM/PIM are: milk solids, sugar, stimulatory compounds (yeast extracts, pancreas extract and/or hydrolysed cereal solids), phosphate-citrate buffer, and chelating compounds (ammonium or sodium phosphates). The latter compounds are essential to bind the free calcium (Ca^{++}) and magnesium (Mg^{++}) ions in the growth medium, and in particular Ca^{++} which is required by bacteriophages during their proliferation and replication. Such growth media have been formulated mainly for cheese starter cultures, and to a very limited degree for *S. thermophilus* and *L. bulgaricus*, and furthermore, the data compiled by Tamime (1981) on PRM/PIM indicate that, except under certain conditions, they are not very effective. At the present time, therefore, PRM/PIM are not widely employed in the yoghurt industry, and it is safe to conclude that, although such an approach may result in success with the mesophilic lactic starter cultures, its application for the production of phage-free, yoghurt bulk starter cultures is an unlikely development.

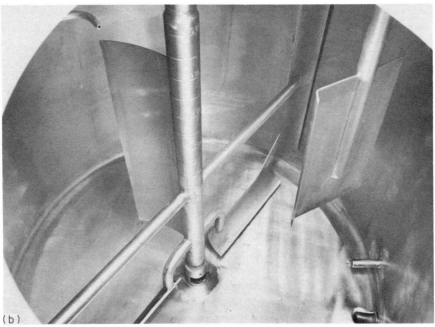

Fig. 8.23

CONCLUSIONS

In the past few decades there have been many developments in the field of starter culture technology, i.e. preservation, maintenance and production. The ultimate objectives of this work were to secure the availability of different strains of yoghurt starter cultures for the dairy industry, to ensure the purity and activity of these culture(s), and to devise appropriate systems for their use in the production of bulk starters in a creamery. The mechanically protected starter tanks were developed primarily for the cheese industry in order to control the proliferation of phage during the production of bulk starter cultures, but in view of the fact that *S. thermophilus* and *L. bulgaricus* are also vulnerable to bacteriophage attack (see Chapter 6), the same precautionery methods have been adopted in the yoghurt industry.

At present there is a growing tendency for yoghurt producers to use concentrated (frozen or CFDC) cultures for the production of bulk starters, and with some of the mechanically protected systems, these cultures pose problems during culture transfer. For example, in case of frozen cultures packaged in cans (pull-ring type), the transfer of the thawed culture from the can to the starter tanks is carried out using a sterile hypodermic syringe, and hence it could be difficult to employ these cultures in conjunction with the Burnett and Rolf or GVE tanks (see Figs. 8.19 and 8.20); similar difficulties arise with the pelletted concentrated frozen cultures, where thawing prior to inoculation is not recommended, and with CFDC, particularly when using the Lewis system. However, these difficulties will be readily overcome as starter culture technology progresses, and the production of bulk starters within a creamery will no longer be the hazardous operation that it was a few years ago.

REFERENCES

ANDERSON, L. (1975a) *Dairy Science Abstracts*, **37**, 310 (Swedish Patent (1974) No. 369 470).
ANDERSON, L. (1975b) U.S. Patent 3 876 808.
ANON. (1975) In *Culture Preparation*, Alfa-Laval Technical Bulletin, No. TB 60738E, Alfa-Laval A/B, Lund, Sweden.
BRIGGS, M., TULL, G., NEWLAND, L. G. M. and BRIGGS, C. A. E. (1955) *Journal of General Microbiology*, **12**, 503.
COWAN, B. C. (1981) Personal communication.
COX, W. A. and LEWIS, J. E. (1972) In *Safety in Microbiology*, Society for Applied Bacteriology—Technical Series No. 6, Ed. by Shapton, D. A. and Board, R. G. Academic Press Inc., (London) Ltd., London, U.K.
FOSTER, E. M. (1962) *Journal of Dairy Science*, **45**, 1290.
GAVIN, M. (1968) In *La Lyophilisation de Cultures de Yoghurt*, Thesis No. 4227, Ecole Polytechnique Federal, Zurich, Switzerland.
GILLILAND, S. E. and SPECK, M. L. (1974) *Journal of Milk and Food Technology*, **37**, 107.
HUP, G. and STADHOUDERS, J. J. (1977) U.S. Patent No. 4 053 642.
HURST, A. (1977) *Canadian Journal of Microbiology*, **23**, 936.
IMAI, M. and KATO, M. (1975) *Journal of Agricultural Chemical Society Japan*, **49**, 93.
KEOGH, B. P. (1969) In *Symposium of Dairy Fermentation Technology*, Ed. by Linklater, P. M. University of New South Wales, Australia.

Fig. 8.23. Bulk starter culture tank manufactured by Damrow DEC

(a) Side view
(b) Inside view of the tank showing the scraper/agitator and baffle

Reproduced by courtesy of DEC International, Kolding, Denmark.

KILARA, A., SHAHAMI, K. M. and DAS, N. K. (1976) *Cultured Dairy Products Journal,* **11,** 8.

LAGODA, I. V. and BANNIKOVA, L. A. (1974) *Dairy Science Abstracts,* **36,** 59.

LAGODA, I. V. and BANNIKOVA, L. A. (1975) *Dairy Science Abstracts,* **37,** 778.

LEWIS, J. E. (1956) *Journal of the Society of Dairy Technology,* **9,** 123.

MORICHI, T. (1972) In *Mechanism and Prevention of Cellular Injury in Lactic Acid Bacteria Subjected to Freezing and Drying,* IDF Scientific Conference 56th Annual Session—Japan, IDF, Brusells, Belgium.

MORICHI, T. (1974) *Japan Agricultural Research Quarterly,* **8,** 171.

NAGMOUSH, M. R., GIRGIS, E. S., GUIRGUIS, A. H. and FAHMI, A. H. (1978) *Egyptian Journal of Dairy Science,* **6,** 39.

NAYLOR, H. B. and SMITH, P. A. (1946) *Journal of Bacteriology,* **52,** 565.

NIKOLOVA, N. (1974) *Dairy Science Abstracts,* **36,** 596.

NIKOLOVA, N. (1978) *XXth International Dairy Congress,* **E,** 584.

OSBORNE, R. J. W. (1977) *Journal of the Society of Dairy Technology,* **30,** 40.

OSBORNE, R. J. W. and BROWN, J. V. (1980) *Journal of Dairy Research,* **47,** 141.

OZLAP, E. and OZLAP, G. (1979) *Dairy Science Abstracts,* **41,** 871.

PORUBCAN, R. S. and SELLARS, R. L. (1975a) *Journal of Dairy Science,* **58,** 787.

PORUBCAN, R. S. and SELLARS, R. L. (1975b) U.S. Patent No. 3 897 307.

PORUBCAN, R. S. and SELLARS, R. L. (1979) In *Microbial Technology,* Volume 1, 2nd Edition, Ed. by Peppler, H. J. and Perlman, D. Academic Press Inc., New York, U.S.A.

RASIC, J. L. and KURMANN, J. A. (1978) In *Yoghurt Scientific Grounds, Technology, Manufacture and Preparations,* Technical Dairy Publishing House, Copenhagen, Denmark.

ROBERTSON, P. S. (1966a) *Dairy Industries,* **31,** 805.

ROBERTSON, P. S. (1966b) *XVIIth International Dairy Congress,* **D,** 439.

SHANKAR, P. A. (1975) Personal communication.

SINHA, R. N., NAMBUDRIPAD, V. K. N. and DUDANI, A. T. (1970) *XVIIIth International Dairy Congress,* **IE,** 128.

SINHA, R. N., DUDANI, A. T. and RANGANATHAN, B. (1974) *Journal of Food Science,* **39,** 641.

SMITTLE, R. B., GILLILAND, S. E. and SPECK, M. C. (1972) *Applied Microbiology,* **24,** 551.

SMITTLE, R. B., GILLILAND, S. E., SPECK, M. L. and WALTER, W. M. Jr. (1974) *Applied Microbiology,* **27,** 738.

SPECKMAN, C. A. (1975) *Dissertation Abstracts International* B, **35,** 3474.

STADHOUDERS, J. J., BANGMA, A. and DRIESSEN, F. M. (1976) *Nordeuropaeisk Mejeri-tidsskrift,* **42,** 190.

TAMIME, A. Y. (1981) In *Dairy Microbiology,* Vol. II, Ed. by Robinson, R. K. Applied Science Publishers Ltd., London, U.K.

TAMIME, A. Y. and ROBINSON, R. K. (1976) *Dairy Industries International,* **41,** 408.

TOFTE-JESPERSEN, N. J. (1974a) *South African Journal of Dairy Technology,* **6,** 63.

TOFTE-JESPERSEN, N. J. (1974b) In *A New View of International Cheese Production,* published by Chr. Hansen's Lab. A/S, Copenhagen, Denmark.

TOFTE-JESPERSEN, N. J. (1976) *Dairy and Ice Cream Field,* **159,** 58A.

TOFTE-JESPERSEN, N. J. (1979) *Journal of the Society of Dairy Technology,* **32,** 190.

WHITEHEAD, H. R. (1956) *Dairy Engineering,* **73,** 159.

CHAPTER 9

The Nutritional Value of Yoghurt

The chemical composition of a foodstuff provides a useful indication of its potential nutritional value, and the data shown in Table 9.1 indicate the main components of some typical natural and fruit yoghurts. If these figures are accepted at face value, then it is evident that yoghurt could prove an important introduction to any diet. At the same time, it must be accepted that numerical values reveal only part of the story, and even if the almost mystical properties ascribed to yoghurt are ignored for the moment, there are some aspects of the behaviour of yoghurt in the human body that are not revealed by chemical analysis (Robinson, 1977).

It is of some interest, therefore, to look at the constituents of yoghurt in a little more detail, and, in particular, to assess the likely nutritional importance of the materials concerned (see also the reviews by Deeth and Tamime, 1981, and Alm, 1982).

CARBOHYDRATES

A. "Available" Carbohydrates

The expression "available carbohydrates" is intended to cover all those carbon compounds that can be assimilated by the human body, and hence can act as a source of energy for metabolism. In the case of natural yoghurt, a number of mono- and disaccharides are present in trace amounts, but lactose remains the dominant sugar; even after fermentation, the yoghurt may contain some 4–5 % lactose (Tamime, 1977). The reason for this residue is that the process milk is often fortified to 14–16 % TS, i.e. up to around 7 % lactose, so that the lactose content of the end-product is little different from normal milk. What is different, however, is the effect that these apparently identical levels of lactose can have on people who are so-called "lactose-intolerant", and the nature of this reaction is of considerable medical interest.

1. Lactose-intolerance

Most children possess, at birth, the ability to secrete the enzyme lactase, so that the lactose in mother's milk is readily broken down into glucose and galactose. These monosaccharides, and

365

especially glucose, are readily metabolised, but as the energy demands of the child increase, so other foods become more important. In many communities this change means that milk plays an increasingly unimportant role in the diet, and as lactose intake falls, so the secretion of lactase declines. A point is then reached quite early in development when lactose can barely be assimilated at all, and the free lactose produces a range of unpleasant symptoms, such as abdominal bloating, cramp and diarrhoea. This reaction to the ingestion of milk is usually referred to as "primary lactose intolerance", and Garza and Scrimshaw (1976) have described a clinical test for confirming this form of deficiency. Thus, similar reactions can be observed with patients suffering from a congenital absence of lactase, or if the walls of the intestine become severely disfigured as a consequence of malnutrition, but in the present context it is the widespread primary intolerance that is most relevant.

Thus, the occurrence of this primary reaction is observed extremely rarely among Europeans who consume milk or processed milk products throughout their lives, but is a common phenomenon in communities where supplies of liquid milk are scarce or erratic. Yet curiously enough, these latter groups may well rely on the production of various types of yoghurt to provide an outlet for any milk which is available, and the failure of lactose in yoghurt (as against lactose in liquid milk) to provoke an intolerance reaction is something of a curiosity.

The most obvious explanation is that micro-organisms in the yoghurt continue to metabolise the lactose even after ingestion, so that the residual lactose content reaching the small intestine is too low to cause an adverse reaction (Gallagher, Molleson and Caldwell, 1974). Certainly some lactic organisms would be tolerant of the acidity of the human stomach, e.g. *Lactobacillus acidophilus*, and the presence of such bacteria in at least some starter cultures is a reasonable surmise. Even some strains of *L. bulgaricus* are tolerant of the low pH encountered, and so it is feasible to suggest that some breakdown of lactose does continue in the stomach, and even into the intestine. Similarly, enzymes secreted previously may continue to act after ingestion, and some evidence to this effect has been found by Goodenough and Kleyn (1976).

One further effect that may be relevant in this context is that yoghurt is already coagulated prior to entering the stomach, while liquid milk is clotted by the acid/enzymes in the body (Davis and Latto, 1957). This difference could mean that the yoghurt coagulum remains partially intact after ingestion, and hence that the diffusion of lactose towards the walls of the intestine is slowed down (Khan, Macrae and Robinson, 1979). This inhibition could be just sufficient to allow the lactase within the yoghurt to break down enough of the lactose to prevent an adverse reaction, but, as yet, objective data are not forthcoming. Nevertheless, the views of Bahrs (1971) and Kretchmer (1972) confirm the overall hypothesis that yoghurt is a perfectly acceptable foodstuff for groups prone to lactose-intolerance.

This degree of acceptability means that yoghurt can provide a useful source of energy in a diet, for while natural yoghurt contains around 6.4 g of carbohydrate/100 g, fruit yoghurts may contain up to 18–20 g of sucrose and other available carbohydrates. If each gram of sugar provides around 4 calories of usable energy, then the contribution of yoghurt towards combating a dietary deficit of energy can be appreciated.

B. Unavailable Carbohydrates

Although natural yoghurt is based entirely on milk, stirred, fruit yoghurts usually have stabilisers incorporated to reduce whey separation during distribution. The usage of these stabilisers has been considered in detail elsewhere, but it is worth noting that many of them are complex carbohydrates. Thus, guar gum, locust-bean gum, as well as the carrageenans and cellulose derivatives, are long-chain polysaccharides composed of regular arrangements of monosaccharide units, and it is significant, in the present context, that the molecules cannot be attacked by digestive enzymes in the human body.

It is for this reason that these hydrocolloidal materials are often referred to as unavailable carbohydrates (Robinson and Khan, 1978), and as such they may contribute to human nutrition by way of:

(a) providing a "bulking agent" for the contents of the intestine, so stimulating intestinal peristalsis and avoiding some of the risks of colonic malfunction;

(b) absorbing some of the potentially toxic chemicals that may be formed in the large intestine as the result of bacterial action;

(c) acting to further delay the diffusion of sugars to the intestinal wall, a function that could help both lactose-intolerant patients, and those prone to post-prandial hyperglycaemia. Thus, the surge in insulin production that is required, after each meal, in order to stabilise the level of glucose in the blood places an undesirable strain on the hormonal system of even normal subjects, and for mild or incipient diabetics the sudden demand poses particular problems. If the inclusion of unavailable carbohydrates in the meal reduces the rate of entry of glucose into the blood, then the stimulus for insulin production will also decline, and this trend towards homeostasis can be regarded as biologically attractive.

The level of stabiliser incorporation is, of course, rather low (> 0.5 %), but even so, it is an aspect of yoghurt consumption in industrialised countries that should not pass unnoticed. It may also be relevant that some of the available stabilisers are reported to depress blood cholesterol levels (Jenkins et al., 1975), an action also attributed to yoghurt itself (Mann and Spoerry, 1974; Mann, 1977; Hepner et al., 1979). The exact reason for this hypocholesterolemic effect of natural yoghurt is not clear (Richardson, 1978), but the fact that yoghurt is more active in this respect than unfermented milk implies that some enzyme system or metabolite of bacterial origin may well be involved.

PROTEIN

The proteins in milk are of excellent quality biologically, and both the caseins and whey proteins (lactalbumins and lactoglobulins) are well endowed with essential amino-acids. An indication of levels encountered is shown in Table 7.11, and it is clear that milk is a most valuable dietary component. The fact that the protein content of yoghurt is often elevated by concentration, or addition of skim milk solids, means that it is an even more attractive source of protein than liquid milk. The relevance of this point is highlighted by the number of protein-enriched yoghurts that are available in industrialised countries, and consumption of around 200–250 ml of yoghurt/day can easily provide an individual with the minimum daily requirement of animal protein (15 g) (Altschul, 1965).

Obviously, such data are impressive in their own right, but two further points about the proteins in yoghurt should be borne in mind.

In the first place, it is important that the proteins in yoghurt are totally digestible, a feature enhanced by the fact that some degree of initial proteolysis is caused by the starter organisms themselves. The extent of this breakdown will depend on the strains of bacteria being employed, but, in general, at least some release of amino-acids and peptides can be expected during incubation and storage (Breslaw and Kleyn, 1973).

The other pertinent characteristic is that the milk proteins in yoghurt are already coagulated prior to ingestion, and in addition to the possible effect discussed earlier, the "soft clot" formed in the stomach may have other benefits. Thus, the contrast between the ingestion of yoghurt and liquid milk has some parallel with the comparative behaviour of warm milk and cold milk, for which the caseins in cold milk form a "hard clot" in the presence of acid in the stomach, the modified caseins (see p. 54) in warm milk coagulate more gently (Jay, 1975). The advantage of this latter type of coagulum is alleged to be:

(a) the softer structure does not give rise to any feeling of discomfort; and
(b) the more "open" nature of the casein aggregates allows the proteolytic enzymes of the alimentary canal freer access during digestion.

It is, of course, impossible to quantify, or even assess with any degree of objectivity, effects of the type mentioned above, but belief in their existence is sufficiently widespread as to give some credence to the general hypothesis. What is beyond dispute, however, is that yoghurt is an excellent source of protein, and that this fact alone justifies its inclusion in a diet.

LIPIDS

Although much of the yoghurt sold in industrialised countries is produced from skim milk, traditional materials have always contained some 3–4% milk fat. The influence of these lipid materials on the consistency and "mouth-feel" of yoghurt has been discussed elsewhere, but it should not be forgotten that lipids are an integral part of a "balanced diet".

Thus, humans have a double requirement for lipids, in that they possess:

(a) storage fat—composed of saturated fatty acids, and serving as a source of energy or as a protection for vital organs;
(b) structural fat—which, with proteins, forms many of the essential membranes in animal cells, particularly in areas like the brain.

It is essential, therefore, that the human diet provides an adequate source of fats, a point that is of especial relevance for children. Thus, fats are a most valuable source of energy, with each gram providing around 9 calories. When this figure is viewed in relation to the fact that malnutrition in children is often associated with a lack of calories to metabolise available protein, then the potential relevance of this "compact" source of energy is evident. It is also important that yoghurt is widely accepted by children as a foodstuff, and hence developing countries, in particular, would be well advised to look closely at the merits of yoghurt for school-feeding programmes.

In addition to this basic advantage from consuming full-fat yoghurt, it must also be stressed that milk fat contains an extremely wide range of fatty acids. Most of these are present in the form of various glycerides, but over 400 individual fatty acids have been identified in cow's milk (Patton and Jensen, 1975). Obviously, it is quite impossible to assign a physiological role to all but a handful of these acids, but the fact that they are present in a normal mammalian secretion merely confirms that "ignorance of function" should not be equated with "no function".

There is, of course, every incentive for a manufacturer to remove the fat from the process milk and sell it as cream, but it is clear that, both organoleptically and nutritionally, the interests of the consumer may be better served by leaving a reasonable level in the end-product. Such a proposal would not find universal acceptance, for some authorities would be concerned at the additional intake of saturated fatty acids that would be involved. However, the evidence linking fats of dairy origin with coronary and similar problems is, to say the least, tenuous, and hence yoghurt manufacturers should be encouraged to base their judgements concerning fat content on the broader concept of quality. Whether such an aim is feasible in light of the vociferous "anti-cholesterol" lobby remains to be seen, and certainly in some countries like the United States challenging consumer groups could spell financial ruin.

The tragedy of this situation is that it is once again the consumer who loses out, and once again for no reason capable of objective assessment. The totally irrelevant demand for "nutritional labelling" of yoghurt and other foods falls into the same category, because it is more than evident that the nutritional value of yoghurt cannot be summarised by a few figures stamped on the side of a retail carton. In effect, therefore, the consumer will be "paying" for a quite useless set of data, in that:

(a) the information implies that the designated nutrients will be absorbed into the human body, whereas, in fact, chemical analyses should never be equated with nutrient availability;

(b) in the case of yoghurt, any serious consideration of its nutritional value must include the question of whether the product possesses special therapeutic properties, and clearly no label could honestly convey to a consumer that yoghurt may be more than a mere carton of chemical compounds.

VITAMINS AND MINERALS

The increase in SNF in yoghurt as compared with liquid milk carries with it the implication that the level of inorganic ions/unit weight is also going to be higher, and this view is confirmed by the data in Table 9.1. In most cases the figures speak for themselves, but the position of calcium is,

TABLE 9.1. *Some typical values of the major constituents of milk and yoghurt*

Constituent (units/100 g)	Milk Whole	Milk Skim	Yoghurt Full fat	Yoghurt Low fat	Yoghurt Fruit
Calories	67.5	36	72	64	98
Protein (g)	3.5	3.3	3.9	4.5	5.0
Fat (g)	4.25	0.13	3.4	1.6	1.25
Carbohydrate (g)	4.75	5.1	4.9	6.5	18.6
Calcium (mg)	119	121	145	150	176
Phosphorus (mg)	94	95	114	118	153
Sodium (mg)	50	52	47	51	–
Potassium (mg)	152	145	186	192	254

The total milk solids content of the yoghurts is broadly similar, hence the increase in the SNF in the low fat variety. The nutrient levels in the fruit yoghurt will vary with the type of fruit.

Adapted from Deeth and Tamime (*loc. cit.*).

perhaps, rather special. Thus, not only can yoghurt act as a source of calcium for sufferers of lactose intolerance, but also calcium supplied by yoghurt may be better absorbed and utilised than calcium made available in other forms (Dupuis, 1964).

The relative availability of vitamins in yoghurt is much more difficult to assess, because, unlike minerals, many vitamins are sensitive to the conditions of processing. Thus, the method of fortification, e.g. addition of milk powder or membrane processing, the heat treatment of the mix, the strains of starter bacteria and the conditions of fermentation can all alter the absolute and/or relative concentrations of the more important vitamins. For this reason, the figures quoted in Table 9.2 should be regarded merely as a guide to the vitamins available in yoghurt, and hence as an indication that, although regarded by many as a "convenience food", it is certainly not a trivial item in terms of potential nutritional value.

TABLE 9.2. *Some typical vitamin contents of milk and yoghurt*

Vitamin	Milk		Yoghurt	
(Units/100 g)	Whole	Skim	Full fat	Low fat
Vitamin A (IU)	148	–	140	70
Thiamin (B_1) (μg)	37	40	30	42
Riboflavin (B_2) (μg)	160	180	190	200
Pyridoxine (B_6) (μg)	46	42	46	
Cyanocobalamine (B_{12}) (μg)	0.39	0.4	–	0.23
Vitamin C (mg)	1.5	1.0	–	0.7
Vitamin D (IU)	1.2			
Vitamin E (IU)	0.13	–	–	Trace
Folic Acid (μg)	0.25	–	–	4.1
Nicotinic Acid (μg)	480	–	–	125
Pantothenic Acid (μg)	371	370	–	381
Biotin (μg)	3.4	1.6	1.2	2.6
Choline (mg)	12.1	4.8	–	0.6

Adapted from Deeth and Tamime (*loc. cit.*).

YOGHURT AND HEALTH

Although yoghurt and similar foods have long occupied a place in the diets of peoples from the Middle East and Central Europe, the Western world adopted a totally casual attitude to the product until rumours of its health-giving properties became rife. In particular, the views of Metchnikoff (1910) linking longevity among the hill tribes of Bulgaria and their consumption of yoghurt caused a considerable flurry of interest.

In essence, it was suggested that one aspect of approaching senility in humans involved an undesirable passage of noxious compounds from the intestine to the blood stream, and that these chemicals arose from the action of putrefactive bacteria in the lower ileum and colon. If the activity of these bacteria could be suppressed, then, so it was argued, the adverse effects of their metabolic products would no longer be manifest, and the individual might anticipate a longer and healthier life. Such an hypothesis sounded perfectly reasonable, and the role of yoghurt in curtailing the putrefactive bacterial action was readily explained as follows:

(a) the lactic acid bacteria in yoghurt are tolerant of a low pH, whereas most bacteria show optimum growth and metabolism around neutrality. Therefore, as the acidic yoghurt passed along the intestine, the lactic acid in the food, and, perhaps, that still being secreted by the bacteria, would kill the undesirable microflora;

(b) it was further suggested that this effect of the yoghurt was enhanced by the ability of *L. bulgaricus* to become established in the intestine, and to gradually dominate the resident microflora. This latter change ensured the continued absence of the putrefactive organisms even during periods of reduced yoghurt availability, and hence the "vitality" of the consumer would be maintained.

Over the years these ideas have been the subject of intense discussion and investigation, and an objective appraisal of their merits is still of some interest.

A. Effect of Acidity

There is no doubt that bacteria in the large intestine produce a range of phenolic compounds, such as sketol and indole, which could damage living tissue. Whether they could have any discernible effect on the intestinal wall, or even be absorbed, will depend on their concentration, the ability of other gut contents, e.g. hydrocolloids, to absorb them, and their residence time, but, nevertheless, there is definite concern over their possible involvement in the initiation of cancer in the lower intestine (Aries *et al.*, 1969). Any process that tended to suppress their production could, therefore, be advantageous, and the action of lactic acid in suppressing the putrefactive bacteria could be one such process.

Whether, in fact, any of the acid in yoghurt can survive the neutralising effect of the bile components is open to debate, but the prospect remains that yoghurt could change, albeit slightly, the pH gradient within the intestine. If this change does occur, then there could well be a basis of truth in Metchnikoff's proposal, and certainly the traditional products of Bulgaria would have been extremely acidic.

B. Effect of the Bacteria

It is well known that *Streptococcus thermophilus* is intolerant of acidity, and hence it is most unlikely that this species would survive passage through the stomach. However, *L. bulgaricus* is able to resist acidity to a much greater degree, and it is quite feasible that, at least, a percentage of the bacteria in yoghurt will reach the intestine in a viable state (Acott and Labuza, 1972). The reaction of these same bacteria to the bile salts, including sodium taurocholate and glycolate, is a different matter, for *in vitro* studies have indicated that *L. bulgaricus* is inhibited by their presence (Lembke, 1964). Before accepting this evidence, however, it is important to note that:

(i) the behaviour of micro-organisms in a "test-tube" may well be different from their activity in the human body;

(ii) certain strains of *L. bulgaricus* have been implanted in the intestines of laboratory rats, and it is possible that other strains could survive and compete in the human intestine (Mabbit, 1977).

Evidence in support of the idea that the habitual consumption of yoghurt could lead to modification of the intestinal flora in man is, therefore, somewhat conflicting, and yet the contrary evidence does not detract from the original thesis. Thus, it should not be forgotten that the natural yoghurt being consumed by the hill tribes in Eastern Europe was a very different product from that found today in the local supermarket.

In particular, the microflora would have been extremely variable, for while modern yoghurt is fermented almost exclusively by *S. thermophilus* and *L. bulgaricus*, the traditional product would have contained a mixture of various lactic acid bacteria such as *L. acidophilus*, *L. jugurtii*, *L. helveticus* and *Bifidobacterium bifidum*; the possible association of *L. acidophilus* and *B. bifidum* is of especial interest.

Thus, both these organisms are known to be capable of establishment in the human intestine, and hence the suppression of putrefactive bacteria becomes a definite possibility (Gotti, 1977). This influence might be enhanced with some strains of lactic acid bacteria by the secretion of antimicrobial agents (Shahani, Vakil and Kilara, 1976). Thus, Pulusani, Rao and Sunki (1979) observed the production of bacteriostatic agents in skim-milk cultures of both *S. thermophilus*, and *L. bulgaricus*, and showed that extracts were active against *Pseudomonas* spp. and *Escherichia coli*, as well as salmonellae. Other authors, such as Rubin (1977) and Spillman, Puhan and Banhegyi (1978), feel that lactic acid is the only anti-microbial agent of any importance, but the overall consensus of opinion still tends to the view that yoghurt does possess antibacterial properties that are not solely dependent on low pH.

Whatever the final outcome of the various controversies surrounding the influence of yoghurt on the health of human beings, there can be little doubt that its overall nutritional value makes it a most desirable addition to any diet. If the consumer appeal of both natural and fruit yoghurts is also placed on record, together with its excellent performance in respect of public health, then it is evident why yoghurt is among the most popular of fermented dairy products.

REFERENCES

ACCOTT, K. M. and LABUZA, T. P. (1972) *Food Product Development*, **6**, 50.
ALM, L. (1982) In *The Effect of Fermentation on Nutrients in Milk and Some Properties of Fermented Milk Products*, Huddinge University Hospital, F69, S-141 86 Huddinge, Sweden.
ALTSCHUL, A. M. (1965) In *Proteins: Their Chemistry and Politics*, Basic Books, New York, U.S.A.
ARIES, V., CROWTHER, J. S., DRASER, B. S., HILL, M. J. and WILLIAMS, R. E. O. (1969) *Gut*, **10**, 334.
BAHRS, W. (1971) *Milchwissenschaft*, **26**, 71.
BRESLAW, E. S. and KLEYN, D. H. (1973) *Journal of Food Science*, **40**, 18.
DAVIS, J. G. and LATTO, D. (1957) *Lancet*, **272**, 274.
DEETH, H. C. and TAMIME, A. Y. (1981) *Journal of Food Protection*, **44**, 78.
DUPUIS, Y. (1964) In *Fermented Milks*, IDF Bulletin, Part III, Brussels, Belgium.
GALLAGHER, C. R., MOLLESON, A. G. and CALDWELL, J. H. (1974) *Journal of American Dietetics Association*, **65**, 418.
GARZA, C. and SCRIMSHAW, N. S. (1976) *American Journal of Clinical Nutrition*, **29**, 192.
GOODENOUGH, E. R. and KLEYN, D. H. (1976) *Journal of Dairy Science*, **59**, 601.
GOTTI, M. (1977) *Industria del Latte*, **13**, 51.
HEPNER, G., FRIED, G., ST. JOER, S., FUSETTI, L. and MORIN, R. (1977) *American Journal of Clinical Nutrition*, **32**, 19.
JAY, J. L. (1975) *International Flavours and Food Additives*, **6**(5), 279.
JENKINS, D. J. A., LEEDS, A. R., NEWTON, C. and CUMMINGS, J. H. (1975) *Lancet*, **1**, 1116.
KHAN, P., MACRAE, R. and ROBINSON, R. K. (1979) *Laboratory Practice*, **28**, 260.
KRETCHMER, N. (1972) *Scientific American*, **227**, 71.
LEMBKE, A. (1963) *Milchwissenschaft*, **18**, 215.
MABBIT, L. A. (1977) *Journal of the Society of Dairy Technology*, **30**, 220.
MANN, G. V. (1977) *Atherosclerosis*, **26**, 335.
MANN, G. V. and SPOERRY, A. (1974) *American Journal of Clinical Nutrition*, **27**, 464.

METCHNIKOFF, E. (1910) In *Prolongation of Life*, Revised edition of 1907, Translated by Mitchell, C. Heinemann, London, U.K.

PATTON, S. and JENSEN, R. O. (1974) *Progress in the Chemistry of Fats and Other Lipids*, **14**, 163.

PULSANI, S. R., RAO, D. R. and SUNKI, G. R. (1979) *Journal of Food Science*, **44**, 575.

RICHARDSON, T. (1978) *Journal of Food Protection*, **41**, 226.

ROBINSON, R. K. (1977) *Nutrition Bulletin*, **4**, 191.

ROBINSON, R. K. and KHAN, P. (1978) *Plant Foods for Man*, **2**, 113.

RUBIN, H. E. (1977) *Dissertation Abstracts International*, B, **37**, 4894.

SHAHANI, K. M., VAKIL, J. R. and KILARA, A. (1976) *Cultured Dairy Products Journal*, **11**(4), 14.

SPILLMAN, H., PUHAN, Z. and BANHEGYI, M. (1978) *Milchwissenschaft*, **33**, 148.

TAMIME, A. Y. (1977) *Dairy Industries International*, **42**(8), 7.

CHAPTER 10

Quality Control in Yoghurt Manufacture

The quality of a product can be defined against a wide range of criteria, including, for example, chemical, physical, microbiological and nutritional characteristics, or simply in relation to its overall appeal to potential consumers. As a result, quality has to be judged by a range of tests of varying degrees of objectivity, and yet all of them can be useful in ensuring that a product is:

(a) safe for human consumption, and conforms to any regulations laid down by Public Health Authorities;
(b) capable of achieving a specified shelf-life without spoilage;
(c) of as high an organoleptic standard as can be achieved within existing constraints of manufacture.

The examination of these points implies, naturally enough, a critical laboratory assessment of the retail product, but it is essential to bear in mind that the end-product can only be as sound as the raw materials from which it is made, and in hygienic terms as "clean" as the plant in which it was manufactured. This breadth of involvement means that quality control must be regarded as an all-embracing concept, and, furthermore, one that demands constant attention. Thus, enthusiasm in response to a crisis is of little value in maintaining standards, and the successful companies are those that rate quality appraisal a high priority. Even small firms with minimal facilities can achieve a great deal by maintaining records of simple features like incubation times, product acidity and so on, and even though the services of a consultant may be required for more specialised examinations, the value of routine monitoring should never be underestimated.

It is also important that no two plants are ever identical, and hence the personnel responsible for routine examinations must exercise their discretion as to which tests are both desirable and feasible in a given situation. An excellent account of the principles and practice of microbiological quality control in the dairy industry has been published recently by Lück (1981), and anyone likely to be concerned with the hygienic aspects of production would be well advised to consult this work. Thus, many of the ideas discussed by Lück are relevant in the present context, and although quality control is a broad concept, hygiene is inevitably a dominant feature.

Nevertheless, there are some special characteristics of yoghurt that set it apart from other dairy products, and hence it is necessary to consider how the standard procedures of quality control apply specifically in this case.

374

MONITORING OF PROCESS PLANT

The acidity of yoghurt means that spoilage is often associated with yeasts and moulds, and the latter in particular often have their origin in the microbial flora of the air. It is important, therefore, that the ventilation and, if applicable, air filtration plant should be considered as possible sources of contamination. Packaging materials stored adjacent to the filling line can also cause problems, as incidently can the unnecessary movement of personnel, and these aspects of plant operation deserve constant attention. If the problem of airborne contamination becomes really serious, then one of the air sampling methods described by the USPHS (1959) could be employed to isolate the source(s) of the invading propagules.

However, although yeasts and moulds of atmospheric origin can be important, especially at certain times of the year (Gregory, 1961), it is the contact surfaces of the plant that usually pose the greatest threat to product security. This stricture applies particularly to plants involved in the production of pasteurised yoghurt, for in this situation the expected shelf-life will run to several weeks. In small factories, strict attention to hygiene and visual inspections may be all that can be achieved, but with large plants, regular monitoring of tanks, pipelines and other equipment is essential to ensure the maintenance of hygienic conditions.

For large items of equipment, one technique of almost universal application is the "Swab Method" (BSI, 1968), in which a damp swab of cotton gauze (or some approved alternative) is rubbed over a designated area of the contact surface. The swab is then agitated in a known volume of a physiologically neutral solution, and once the micro-organisms are deemed to have been removed from the swab, samples of the solution, diluted if necessary, are examined by the plate count method. Milk agar is a most useful medium for dairy equipment, and after incubation at 30°C for 72 hours, a colony count is obtained which can readily be transformed into a figure for colony-forming units (CFU/) 100 cm² of equipment surface.

The regular examination of selected or critical components of the production system can provide a useful indication of any decline in standards of cleaning, and the "Rinse Method" (BSI, 1968) can provide similar information for small items or containers. The performance to tests of this type on successive occasions (same operator and same conditions) is somewhat variable, and hence variations from the "norm" for a given plant are more important than the values themselves. Nevertheless, some suggested "standards" have been cited by Harrigan and McCance (1976), and these figures can serve as a guide:

Colony-forming units per 100 cm²	Conclusion
500 (coliforms— < 10)	Satisfactory
500–2,500	Dubious
2,500 (coliforms— > 100)	Unsatisfactory

Different plants will, naturally enough, achieve different levels of cleanliness even under "ideal" conditions, and the manufacturer of yoghurt is perhaps fortunate that the product is fairly resistant to spoilage, at least of bacterial origin. Its reaction to yeasts and moulds is quite different, however, and if yeasts become the dominant contaminant, then numerous problems can be expected during retailing.

As an alternative to these procedures, an agar contact method may be employed in which either the sterile surface of a small, prefilled plate, or the exposed surface of an agar sausage (Cate, 1965), is placed in contact with the test surface. If the surface is not too heavily contaminated, then dividual, or clumps of, micro-organisms adhere to the agar surface, and, after incubation, give se to colonies that may be counted. The results can again be related to a known area of plant surface, and as with data obtained in other ways, can provide an indication of the efficacy of the cleaning procedures.

It is clear, therefore, that examinations of the type outlined above are valuable as a means of both monitoring performance and eliminating potential hazards, and the testing of raw materials has much the same function.

EXAMINATION OF RAW MATERIALS

A. Liquid Milk

The basic ingredient of most yoghurt is whole milk or skim milk, and hence the quality of the incoming milk is an important consideration. The methods of extracting representative samples will vary with the size of factory concerned, but it is essential that the portion examined truly reflects the quality of the bulk (IDF, 1969a).

The extent of any examination will depend on the scale of the operation, but may well include, as a minimum, some of the tests indicated in Table 10.1. In some countries a standard plate count is preferred to the dye-reduction test, but unless the additional labour and expense can be justified as a long-term commitment, then the simplicity of the metabolic test could have much to recommend it.

B. Milk Powder

Although the process milk can be concentrated by evaporation or ultrafiltration, raising the total solids of the mix through the incorporation of a milk-based powder is still widely practised. In some places, skim milk or full-cream milk powder may be the only feasible raw material, but whatever the precise role of the powder, an examination of each consignment to ensure its adherence to agreed specifications can avoid problems at a later stage. Standard methods for monitoring the solubility of a milk powder and the production of sediments are well established, and the moisture and fat contents of a powder can likewise be recorded by agreed procedures.

Each consignment must also be tested for antibiotics, and a microbiological examination covering the groups of organisms suggested by Davis (1981) should be routine. Some proposed specifications are indicated in Table 10.2, and with good manufacturing practice there is no reason to suppose that these standards cannot be attained. The yoghurt manufacturer is fortunate, however, in that the process milk does receive a severe heat-treatment, e.g. 85°C for 30 minutes or equivalent, and hence some latitude in respect of the microbiological quality of the milk powder can be tolerated. The same margin of freedom applies to the stabilisers or other ingredients added prior to heating, but materials incorporated into the finished yoghurt, e.g. fruit and flavouring/colouring agents, need to be monitored with particular care. Fruit, in particular, can prove a troublesome source of yeasts or moulds, and in any yoghurt that contains sucrose, fungal infections can rapidly lead to spoilage and consumer rejection. The importance of this aspect can be judged from the standards proposed for some typical fruits (see Table 10.3), and any additional

TABLE 10.1. *Some of the tests that might be applied to raw, whole milk or skim milk to be used in the production of yoghurt*

Examination	Reason	Method	Source of Information
(i) Total solids content	to allow for accurate concentration/fortification of the process milks	Hydrometer	BSI (1959)
(ii) Fat content	if full-cream yoghurt is being made	Gerber Method Foss Milkotester	BSI (1955), Foss Electric (UK) Ltd., York (Anon., 1980a)
(iii) Antibiotics	to prevent inhibition of the starter culture	Intertest Method Disc Assay Technique	Intervet Laboratories Ltd., Cambridge. (Anon., 1980b) Oxoid Ltd., London (Anon., 1980c)
(iv) Dye-reduction Test	although the process milk is heat-treated, the use of milk of low bacteriological quality should be avoided (see below)	Resazurin Test	BSI (1968)
(v) Taints	chemical taints in the milk can arise if cows eat unusual crops, e.g. garlic; proteolytic or lipolytic enzymes, often of microbial origin, can produce off-flavours	Odour Test	

TABLE 10.2. *Some suggested specifications for milk powders to be employed in the production of yoghurt*

Microbiological Standards	Satisfactory	Doubtful	Unsatisfactory	Physical/Chemical standards
(All figures as colony forming units/g.)				*Acidity*—The acidity of reconstituted skim milk powder (9% TS) should not exceed 0.15% lactic acid.
				Solubility—The sediment in a solubility Index Tube (ADMI, 1971) produced by 10 g of skim milk powder should not exceed 0.5 ml.
Spray-dried powder				*Scorched particles*—Employing the apparatus specified in BSI (1973), the filter disc should conform to Disc B of the ADMI photographic standards.
Viable count	< 10,000	10,000–100,000	> 1000,000	
Coliforms	< 10	10–100	> 100	
Yeasts	< 10	10–100	> 100	*Moisture content*—The moisture content of skim milk powder should not exceed 3.5%.
Moulds	< 10	10–100	> 100	
Staphylococci (coagulase-positive)	< 10	10–100	> 100	*Fat content*—The fat content of skim milk powder should not exceed 1.25%.
Roller-dried powder				*Inhibitory substances*—Employing the Intertest or other appropriate method, the powder should be screened to ensure that it does not contain more than 0.02 IU/g of inhibitory substances.
Viable count	< 1000	1000–10,000	> 10,000	

After Davis (1981).

TABLE 10.3. *Some typical microbiological specifications that can be applied to (i) fruits and (ii) ingredients including chocolate employed in the manufacture of yoghurt.*

Organisms	Count (colony-forming units/g)
(i) Moulds	< 10
Yeasts	< 1
Total count	< 1000
Coliforms	negative
(ii) Moulds	< 10
Yeasts	< 10
Total count	< 2000
Coliforms	negative

After Spinks (1981).

natural or artificial flavours should achieve at least the same specifications. Sucrose can also, on occasions, act as a source of yeasts and moulds, and although rarely a source of infection, its presence should not be forgotton if spoilage problems should arise. Success or otherwise in this area can be judged in relation to the microbiological standards proposed for the end-product (see Table 10.8), and "failure" at this latter point can often be traced to faulty ingredients. A further, and sometimes unexpected, source of contamination can be the bulk starter, and an additional function of quality control centres on the provision of a viable, clean culture.

C. Starter Culture

The type of starters available have been discussed earlier, but the most popular material for inoculation of the production vessels is still a liquid culture containing *Streptococcus thermophilus* and *Lactobacillus bulgaricus* in the ratio of 1 : 1. In practice, this requirement is taken to mean one short chain of streptococci: one short chain of lactobacilli, and checking this balance by direct microscopic examination is a useful means of ascertaining the likely suitability of a culture. If the count is made quantitative as well, i.e. with a Breed Smear technique, then the value of the approach can be improved still further. If the number of bacteria is too high to be counted directly, then a 10^{-1} dilution in quarter-strength Ringer's solution can be made prior to preparation of the slides (Robinson and Tamime, 1976). If the sample is agitated for 30 seconds before the 0.01 ml aliquot is removed, then the areas of the slide (1 cm^2) will contain a countable number of bacteria. Staining with Newman's stain, or after defatting, with methylene blue (Cooper and Broomfield, 1974) or Gram's stain (Davis, Ashton and McCaskill, 1971) is a useful aid to differentiation, and for routine purposes the number of fields to be examined can be reduced from the figure required in theory (Wang, 1941; Wilson, 1935) to give an accurate count. Thus, Tamime (1977) found that if ten fields were counted, on a five by five cross-pattern to overcome uneven spreading, then a reasonable estimate of the cell count/ml of a starter culture could be obtained. The only adjustment required was in relation to the expected ratio, because the chains of streptococci tend to breakdown into small units of two or three cells. If each one of these units is recorded as "1", then the ratio of streptococci: lactobacilli rises to around 2.7 : 1, and this ratio has been found to be stable for cultures incubated at 42°C.

379

An alternative technique for obtaining information on the ratio between the two organisms, either within a starter or in the retail product, is the plate count. Obviously viable counts are more time-consuming than microscopic counts, but they do offer the advantage of recording only viable colony-forming units, and for the most part these units can be equated with individual cells. The fact that dilution and plating will have broken most of the chains necessitates a modification of the expected ratio, and figures of 5–10 streptococci : 1 lactobacilli may well become the accepted "norm"; the chains of streptococci counted as "1" in the "clump count" tend to be longer than the chains of lactobacilli. The normal procedure for such an examination will involve the use of a differentiating medium capable of providing a visual separation of the colonies on the basis of colour or colony morphology; it is also possible to employ two media, each one being selective for only one organism.

A selection of such media is shown in Table 10.4, and the final choice will probably reflect the preference of the individual operator. Thus, while a single differentiating medium may be preferred for visual counts, the introduction of automatic colony counters may necessitate a

TABLE 10.4. *Some of the media which can be employed to enumerate the desired bacteria in yoghurt or starter cultures*

Culture or	Micro-organism	
agar medium	*S. thermophilus*	*L. bulgaricus*
TGV	Smooth	Irregular, or hairy or rough
TGV + Na-acetate	No growth	Growth
LAB	Smooth	Irregular, or hairy or rough
LAB + penicillin	No growth	Growth
TYLB	Growth	Growth
TYLB + penicillin	No growth	Growth
Lee's agar	Yellow colonies	White colonies
L-S	Round colonies, red with clear zone (<0.5 mm)	Irregular, red colonies with opaque zone (>1.0 mm)
Lactic agar (low pH)	No growth	Growth
Trypticase soy agar	Growth	No growth
Micro-assay	Growth	No growth
Trypsin digest agar	No growth	Growth
Eugon	No growth	Growth
Streptosel agar	Growth	No growth
HYA	High mass 1–3 mm	2–10 mm
Special agar	Round oval colonies (0.1–0.2 mm), white with red centre	Irregular, uniformly red colonies (1 mm) surrounded with cloudy zone
RCA	No growth at pH 5.5	Growth
PCAM	Growth well after 24 hr at 37°C and pH 7.0	Sparse growth
M 17 + β-glycerophosphate	Growth at pH 6.8	No growth
ST	Growth at pH 6.8	No growth
LB	No growth	Growth
TPPY-Eriochrome agar	Oval colonies (1–3 mm), convex, opaque, white violet and often with a darker centre	Transparent and diffuse colonies (4–6 mm), unidentified shape with an irregular edge

After: Robinson and Tamime (*loc. cit.*), Anon. (1980c), Eloy and Lacrosse (1980), Johns, Gordon and Shapton (1978), Shankar and Davies (1977), Driessen, Ubbels and Stadhouders (1977), Bracquart (1981).

change to the use of selective media, i.e. only one species will grow. However, even with electronic aids, the time and labour involved can only be justified for special purposes, and hence for routine examinations of starter cultures, simple activity tests may be more than adequate.

1. Activity tests

The essential characteristic of a good starter for yoghurt is that it shall produce the desired level of lactic acid within a given time, and a simple test for this characteristic involves:

 (i) making a 1:10 dilution of the starter with 9 ml of Ringers solution ($\frac{3}{4}$ strength);
 (ii) placing 10 ml of process milk into a test-tube, and adding 1 ml of diluted starter;
 (iii) incubating the inoculated milk for 4 hours at 42°C.

At the end of this time, the acidity of the milk should be around 0.85–0.95 % lactic acid, and any cultures that fail to achieve these figures should be regarded with suspicion. This concern stems from the fact that, with the system of daily starter propagation, the balance between the organisms can change over a number of transfers. During manufacture, this swing may be manifest in a number of undesirable ways, and an early warning of impending problems, gained through the activity test, can be helpful.

A useful, if not so informative, variant of this approach is the Resazurin Test. Thus, if 1 ml of culture is added to a test-tube containing 9 ml of process milk and 1 ml of Resazurin solution, then reduction of the dye should take place inside 45 minutes at 37°C. This test is not, perhaps, as satisfactory as the production of acid, but as a quick guide to viability it can be useful, particularly if performed, as it should be, on a routine basis, so that it is variations in performance that are recorded rather than values in isolation.

2. Absence of contamination

The presence of gas bubbles in a starter culture or an "unclean" smell are a clear indication of gross contamination, and a useful confirmatory test is that catalase reaction. Thus, the starter organisms are catalase-negative, so that if 5 ml of a culture are added to 1 ml of hydrogen peroxide (10 vol), the formation of gas bubbles indicates a considerable infection by non-starter bacteria.

If the starter is being propagated on a daily basis, then a routine examination for coliforms may be worthwhile, for although the high acidity should restrict their survival, slow acid development can allow sufficient build-up to give "taints" or "off-flavours" to the retail product. The straightforward test for "acid plus gas" in single strength MacConkey Broth is usually adequate for this purpose, and if three tubes of broth are inoculated at three consecutive dilutions of the starter, e.g. down to 10^{-2}, an indication of numbers of presumed coliforms can be obtained; absent in 1 ml of starter should be regarded as the acceptable standard.

Although an examination for coliforms can be helpful, if only as an indicator of poor hygiene, the presence of yeasts or moulds at > 10/ml of starter is likely to lead to spoilage during the shelf-life of the retail product. Contamination of this magnitude can be readily monitored using Malt Extract Agar acidified with lactic acid, and a 10^{-1} dilution of the starter is convenient for incorporation into pour plates (1 ml/petri dish). Particular attention should be paid to any signs of infection by species capable of utilising lactose, e.g. the yeasts *Kluyveromyces fragilis* or *K. lactis*, and their presence must be regarded as a stimulus for immediate action; namely the propagation of a fresh mother-culture.

The routine examination of bulk starters is essential where culture maintenance is on an "in-plant" basis, and if the necessary laboratory facilities are not available, then consideration should be given to the use of freeze-dried or deep frozen cultures for direct inoculation of the bulk starter milk. Thus, the cultures available from commercial manufacturers have an excellent record in respect of freedom from contamination and overall performance, and hence the yoghurt manufacturer can normally be excused the rigours of a detailed starter examination.

QUALITY APPRAISAL OF RETAIL PRODUCTS

However advisable it may be to monitor standards of plant hygiene, or to insist that raw materials meet agreed specifications, it is the end-product that must pass the final test—is it acceptable to the consumer? In some countries the imposition of standards aims to encourage the maintenance of quality, but for the most part, the nature of the product in terms of consistency and/or related features ensures that the proposed standards are met with little difficulty. Nevertheless, analysis of the end-product is an essential feature of quality control, because problems in manufacture are almost certain to manifest themselves as "faults" in the product, and hence examinations at this stage:

(i) protect the consumer from the purchase of poor quality product, or in the extreme cases, product that might constitute a health hazard;

(ii) protect the manufacturer from the inconvenience and expense of a barrage of "return" goods;

(iii) assist in the smooth operation of a plant by identifying variations in product quality at an early stage, so that any necessary corrective actions can be taken before the onset of serious problems.

The appraisal of product quality has become, therefore, a vital function of factory operation, and the gamut of examinations that may be performed can be considered under the following headings:

(a) analysis of chemical composition;
(b) assessment of physical characteristics;
(c) microbiological analysis;
(d) assessment of organoliptic characteristics;

and a routine examination of these features should enable the quality control manager to spot deviations from the "norm" well ahead of the stage when production schedules might be placed in jeopardy.

A. Analysis of Chemical Composition

Many countries have legal standards, or at least provisional regulations, covering the composition of yoghurt, and a selection of the existing proposals is given in Table 10.5. The

TABLE 10.5. *Some existing or proposed standards for the chemical composition of yoghurt in terms of milk fat and minimum solids-not-fat (SNF)*

Country of origin	Types of yoghurt based on % fat				% SNF
	Balkan	Normal	Medium	Low	
Argentina	–	2.8	0.5	0.5	–
Australia	–	3.0	1.5–0.5	0.5	–
Denmark	–	3.8	1.8–1.5	0.3	–
FAO/WHO	–	3.0	3.0–0.5	0.5	8.2
Finland	–	2.5	–	–	–
France	–	3.0	–	1.0	–
Israel	–	3.0	1.5	0.5–0.2	–
Italy	–	3.0	–	1.0	–
Kenya	–	2.25	1.25	–	8.5
Lebanon	–	3.0	–	–	8.2
Netherlands	4.5	3.2	–	0.3	–
New Zealand	–	3.25	2.0	0.5	8.5
Switzerland	–	3.0	2.5–1.5	0.5	–
Sweden	–	3.0	–	0.5	–
South Africa	–	3.3	2.5–1.5	0.5–0.1	8.3–8.6
UK	–	3.5	2.0–1.0	0.3	8.5
USA	–	3.8–3.0	2.8–2.0	1.0–0.5	8.25–8.30
West Germany	10.0	3.5	1.8–1.5	0.5	–

Adapted from: Robinson and Tamime (*loc. cit.*); Anon. (1977).

requirement over "SNF" is, in reality, more decorative than essential, because the quality of a normal yoghurt with an SNF below the stipulated minimum could leave much to be desired. An overall measurement of total solids could, however, be of value as a check that concentration or fortification has been carried out correctly, and a modification of the standard gravimetric method for milk has been proposed (Pearson, 1976) as suitable for yoghurt. The sample is neutralised before drying with 0.1 N strontium hydroxide, and 0.0048 g/ml of alkali is deducted from the dry weight of the sample. Davis and McLachlan (1974) suggest the use of vacuum-drying with sodium hydroxide as the reagent, but either technique provides a convenient method of monitoring total solids. The remaining component, namely fat, is of interest not only in relation to proposed legal standards, but also because most yoghurts are designated as low, medium or full fat, and hence it is important that the description should not be misleading.

The gravimetric methods of determining fat in yoghurt (e.g. the Rose Gottlieb Method) are regarded as the most accurate (Davis, 1970), but for routine purposes the normal Gerber method, but using 11.3 g of yoghurt in a milk butyrometer, is totally appropriate. All these examinations should be performed on the natural yoghurt prior to the addition of fruit, and monitoring the acidity is also more straightforward in the absence of additives.

The production of lactic acid beyond the point of coagulation is monitored principally in relation to consumer preference, and hence the selected end-point will vary not only from country to country, but also with the type of yoghurt. Thus, in The Netherlands, for example, Bulgarian yoghurt may have an acidity of up to 1.48 % lactic acid, while other types are usually sold with a maximum of 1.17 % lactic acid (Netherland Standards, 1967). The IDF (1969b) have suggested a minimum of 0.7 g lactic acid per 100 g of retail product, and hence the measurement of acidity is an important feature of production.

Although the relationship between titratable acidity and pH is not straightforward in a highly buffered system like yoghurt (Lück, Kriel and Mostert, 1973), the direct electrometric determination of pH is extremely convenient. Thus, once a correlation has been established between pH and the desired characteristics of a particular type of yoghurt, then routine monitoring during manufacture can become a normal practice. However, to maintain a close check on the acidity of the retail product, it is usually desirable to test representative samples of the cooled yoghurt for titratable acidity.

The measurement is a composite one including the "natural" acidity of the milk and the "developed" acidity arising from bacterial activity, but as the natural acidity should not vary a great deal (assuming that the milk is standardised for total solids), titratable acidity is a reasonable indication of the performance of the starter culture. The problems of measuring acidity by direct titration have been discussed by Jeness, Shipe and Sherbon (1974), and for the analysis of yoghurt, the approach is based on the technique employed for liquid milk. Thus, the normal method involves transferring a known volume of weight of natural yoghurt to an evaporating basin, and then neutralising the acidity with caustic soda. A detailed summary of some of the suggested methods is shown in Table 10.6, and it is noticeable that the expression of results differs from country to country. In practice, these national preferences are not important, but for comparative purposes a chart, such as shown in Appendix I, can always be constructed.

The subjective nature of the end-points is more relevant, because it implies that some variation between operators has to be accepted, and hence a comparison of results from different laboratories may not always be possible. It means also that, in any given laboratory, the measurement of titratable acidity should be carried out under standardised conditions, i.e. a specific location in the laboratory with a non-variable light source, and that the actual titration should be performed by the same person. If these restrictions can be met, then titratable acidity becomes a most useful measurement, because not only can the figures be linked fairly accurately with consumer preferences, but through the component for developed acidity, changes in performance of the starter bacteria are rapidly manifest.

The monitoring of other components, particularly non-dairy ingredients, is probably not important as a routine, but the introduction of regulations, such as those indicated in Table 10.7, could require extra analyses. Thus, the addition of a starch containing fruit pureé to a yoghurt base already incorporating a starch stabiliser could raise the total above the suggested 1 % level, and preservative levels would need to be similarly monitored, at least on an occasional basis. The timing and extent of such analyses will differ from company to company, and standard texts, such as Pearson (loc. cit.) or the AOAC (1970), should be consulted concerning appropriate methods and their application.

B. Assessment of Physical Characteristics

Yoghurt is normally retailed in one of three physical states, namely set yoghurt, stirred yoghurt and fluid or drinking yoghurt, and each type has quite distinctive characteristics. The typical gel structure of a set type, for example, could never really be mistaken for the semi-fluid form of the stirred variety, but the low viscosity of some "stirred" brands leaves the consumer with little option but to drink them. This degeneration of product image is obviously regrettable, and although the release of an occasional "poor" batch is inevitable, the question of "desirable viscosity" is always somewhat vexing. In practice, each manufacturer will probably adopt an agreed "in-house" standard for viscosity (or consistency in the case of set yoghurt), and then operate to this specification, so that the routine assessment of these physical features becomes a normal part of quality control.

TABLE 10.6. *A selection of methods for determining the titratable acidity of milk and other dairy products*

Country and method	British standards	Danish standards	Dornic method	Netherlands standards	Soxhlet-Henkel method	*Tamime and Robinson (unpublished)	Thorner method	United States AOAC
Sample	10 ml	25 ml	10 ml	10 ml	50 ml	10 gm	10 ml	20 ml or 20 gm
Dilution	—	—	—	—	—	—	2:1	2:1
Phenolphthalein	1 ml 0.5% in 50% alcohol	13 drops, 5% in alcohol	1 drop, 1% in alcohol or 2 drops, 2% in alcohol	0.5 ml, 2% in 70% alcohol	2 ml, 2% in alcohol	1 drop, 0.5% in 50% alcohol	5 drops, 5% in alcohol	2 ml, 1% in alcohol
Alkali	0.1 N NaOH or N/9 NaOH	N/10 NaOH	N/9 NaOH	N/10 NaOH	N/4 NaOH	N/9 NaOH	N/10 NaOH	0.1 N NaOH
End point	Pink matching rosanaline standard	Constant red pale colour	Light rose	Pink matching fuchsin standard	Light rose	Light rose to persistent pink colour		First persistent pink
Expression of results	g lactic acid/100 ml or % lactic acid	Danish = ml of N/10 NaOH times 4/100 ml	D = tenths of a ml N/9 NaOH/10 ml	N = tenths of a ml of 0.1N NaOH/ml	SH = ml N/4 NaOH/100 ml	g lactic acid /100 g l or % lactic acid	T = ml N/10 NaOH/ml	% lactic acid or ml 0.1 N NaOH/100 g

Adapted from Robinson and Tamime (*loc. cit.*).

TABLE 10.7. *Some proposed or existing regulations concerning the introduction of non-dairy ingredients into yoghurt*

Country	Stabiliser level	Fruit	Preservatives
Denmark	Nil	10–15%	Nil
France	–	Up to 30%*	–
Italy	–	Up to 30%*	In fruit
United Kingdom	Starch ⎫ Pectin ⎬ 1% Geltain ⎭	Up to 30%*	Sulphur dioxide (60 ppm) or Benzoic acid (120 ppm) or Methyl-4-hydroxybenzoate (120 ppm) or Ethyl-4-hydroxybenzoate (120 ppm) or Propyl-4-hydroxybenzoate (120 ppm) or Sorbic acid (300 ppm)
	Alginates ⎫ Agar ⎬ Edible gums ⎬ 0.5% Celluloses ⎭		

* Colours/flavours as applicable regulations.

After Robinson (1976), Foods & Drugs Act (1975).

1. Stirred and fluid yoghurt

The range of methods that are available to measure the viscosity of fluid and semi-fluid products has been discussed by Sherman (1970), and the choice of method is really a matter of operator preference. Thus, in the present context, interest centres on making an objective comparison between samples, or between a sample and an "expected result" representing product of acceptable quality, and a number of simple techniques can be employed for this purpose.

At one end of the scale some producers rely on extremely simple techniques, such as:

(i) scoop a sample of yoghurt onto the back of a spoon, and then gently incline the spoon downwards—the rate at which the yoghurt drips from the spoon is a reflection of its viscosity; the same technique will also reveal any irregularities in the coagulum;

(ii) insert a plastic teaspoon into a typical retail carton of yoghurt—if the spoon remains upright, the product has an acceptable viscosity;

and although these approaches are subjective in the extreme, they do offer a guide as to the quality of the end-product.

It is more usual, however, to rely on more reproducible techniques, and a number of these are available. Thus Davis (1970) described the use of a rotating cylinder which could be tilted until the yoghurt began to pour, and the angle necessary to initiate "flow" could be taken as a measure of product viscosity. The time taken for a standard metal sphere to descend a certain distance through a prescribed volume of yoghurt has also provided a convenient method of comparison (Ashton, 1963), and a diagram of the apparatus employed by Pette and Lolkeme (1951) is shown in Fig. 10.1. The flow rate of yoghurt through funnels of prescribed orifice size provides another alternative, and in the "simple" Posthumus funnel shown in Fig. 10.1, the time taken for the yoghurt "surface" to pass between the starting "points" and the centrally located "needle" is a measure of the viscosity of the product (Posthumus, 1954). A similar approach has been employed in Holland (Galesloot, 1958) and also in South Africa (Ginslov, 1970), while in Sweden the Swedish Dairies Association played a major role in the development of the apparatus shown in Fig. 10.2 (Storgards, 1964). The time taken for a yoghurt sample of known volume of flow down

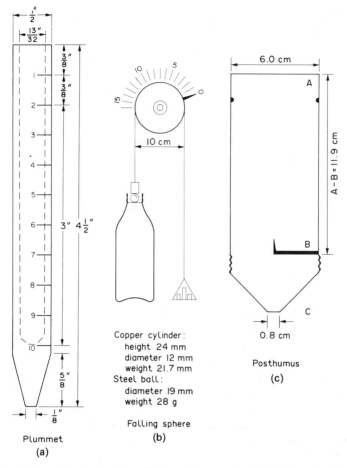

Copper cylinder:
  height 24 mm
  diameter 12 mm
  weight 21.7 mm
Steel ball:
  diameter 19 mm
  weight 28 g

Falling sphere
(b)

Plummet
(a)

Posthumus
(c)

Fig. 10.1. A selection of devices that have been used to assess the physical characteristics of yoghurt

a) The 'Plummet' devised by Hilker (1947) for measuring the body of cultured cream, and which has also been suggested for yoghurt.

b) Diagram of a falling-sphere apparatus used to estimate the firmness of yoghurt. The steel sphere is slightly heavier than the 'weights', and hence sinks into the yoghurt; the distance recorded on the dial is a measure of the strength of the coagulum (Pette & Lolkeme, *loc. cit.*).

c) Posthumus Funnel (Posthumus, *loc. cit.*)

an inclined plane, with or without weirs, has also been advocated, as has the "Plummet" (see Fig. 10.1), but perhaps the most universally accepted approach is that employing a rotational viscometer (see Fig. 10.3), or the Torsion Wire apparatus.

The ease of operation makes the rotational viscometer, such as the Brookfield Synchro-Lectric, a popular choice, and once the type of spindle and its speed of rotation have been established for a given product, then comparison between successive batches presents few problems. This simplicity means that it is reasonable to stimulate that a stirred yoghurt should have a viscosity that falls within certain preset limits, and the physical nature of a fluid yoghurt could be similarly described. The handling of batches that fall outside these categories is a matter for company policy, but clearly, monitoring this aspect of product quality can be undertaken on a routine basis.

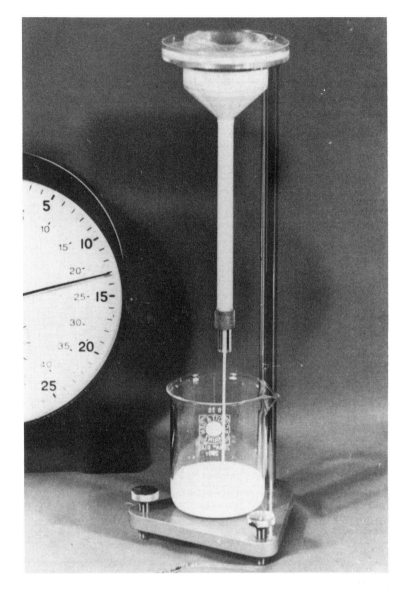

Fig. 10.2. One of the so called "funnel systems" for measuring the consistency of stirred yoghurt

This Viscometer is set-up as shown, and with the outlet blocked, is filled up (Swedish Funnel System) to the 'brim' with the yoghurt. The time is then recorded for the liquid level to reach the mark at the discharging hole. An orifice size of 3 mm. is recommended for stirred yoghurt.

Reproduced by courtesy of Enolacto Ltd., London, UK.

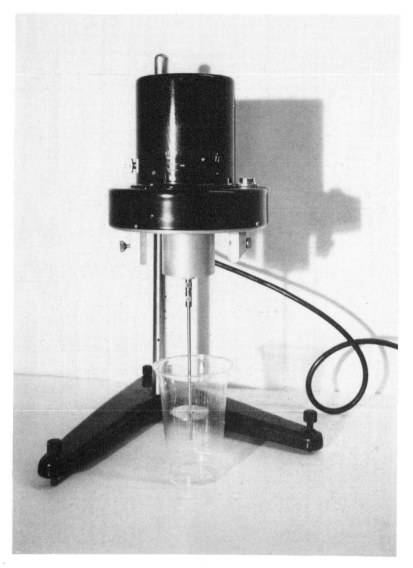

Fig. 10.3.   A rotational viscometer that would be suitable for comparing the viscosity of different samples of stirred-yoghurt

The spindle is lowered to a prescribed distance into the yoghurt, and then rotated at an appropriate speed. The 'drag' experienced by the spindle is recorded, and the figure can be converted into a measure of viscosity in centipoises.

2. Set yoghurt

The essential gel structure of set yoghurt means that assessment of the product must be approached in a somewhat different manner, for any technique that destroys the delicate coagulum is of little value.

389

The falling sphere technique can be adapted (Pette and Lolkema, *loc. cit.*), but the most appropriate technique makes use of a conventional penetrometer (see Fig. 10.4). The only special requirement is the spindle and cone, and in trials described by Robinson and Tamime (*loc. cit.*), a perspex cone, 2.5 cm in diameter and with an apical angle of 100°, was used to examine the consistency of set yoghurt in retail pots of 135–140 g capacity. The cone, after being located centrally over the pot, covered around 50 % of the exposed surface of the yoghurt, and hence the

Fig. 10.4. A standard penetrometer of the type that can be employed to measure the consistency of set yoghurt

The timer is shown on the right, together with a selection of 'cones' (see text).

risk of "edge effects" from the carton was minimised. The weight of the spindle was chosen in relation to the product, e.g. a light spindle (13.4 g) for examination at 42°C immediately after incubation, and a heavier spindle (47.4 g) for assessment of the firm coagulum found in yoghurt held subsequently at 7°C for 24 hours. These changes in spindle weight were necessary to discriminate, at a given temperature, between samples of different gel strengths, but the fact that comparisons were possible at 42°C made it possible to predict the consistency of the retail product prior to final cooling.

The technique is, therefore, both reliable and versatile, and hence standardising the rheological properties of set yoghurt becomes a straightforward exercise. Other physical features or faults, for example "lumpiness", usually become apparent during sensory analysis, and hence these problems will be discussed later.

C. Microbiological Analysis

The microbiological examination of he finished product may include checks on the survival of the starter organisms, as well as for the presence of undesirable spoilage or pathogenic organisms.

Interest in the former examination stems from the fact that low population levels of *S. thermophilus* and *L. bulgaricus* may be association with:

(i) long incubation times;
(ii) poor flavour development;

while excessively high levels can result in:

(i) too rapid or excessive acidification;
(ii) syneresis;
(iii) imbalance of flavour components;
(iv) spoilage from continued acid production during storage.

In addition, it has been suggested that "yoghurt should contain abundant and viable organisms" (FAO/WHO, 1972), and whatever the value of this precise form of words, there is a general feeling that yoghurt should contain live bacteria unless specifically designated as "pasteurised" or "heat-treated". The methods available for examining the starter flora of yoghurt have been discussed elsewhere (see Starter Cultures), and an indication of the results that might be anticipated is shown in Table 10.8. The wide variations are a reflection of both between batch and between "brand" differences, but the "standard" suggested by Davis and McLachlan (*loc. cit.*) for a "good quality" yoghurt should be readily attainable. Obviously, it would be unreasonable to propose that counts below this level are a cause for concern, but at the same time it is probably true that if flavour and acid development are satisfactory, then figures of 10×10^{-6} per species will be inevitable consequence, and hence results of this order are a fair indication that the organoleptic properties of the yoghurt will be satisfactory. Any serious deficiencies in this respect will probably have been reflected in starter performance during incubation, but a tendency towards high counts may only raise problems later, particularly if the refrigerated retail net-work is sub-standard; for the most part, consumer complaints on the basis of "excessively sour" yoghurt will be minimal.

TABLE 10.8. *Some proposed standard methods for examining the microbiological quality control of yoghurt*

Country	Colony count	Yeast and mould	Coliform	Psychrotrophic
United Kingdom	Nutrient agar 30°C for 72 hr	Malt agar or salt dextrose agar 25–30°C up to 5 days	MacConkey broth 30°C for 72 hr Presumptive coliform streak on violet red bile agar 30°C for 24 hr	
United States	Standard method agar or lactic agar of Elliker, Anderson and Hannesson (1956)	Acidified potato glucose agar-if count is low inoculate 10 ml in 3 plates evenly and then count total colonies on 3 plates	Violet red bile agar or deoxycholate lactose agar or brilliant green lactose bile broth	Standard method agar 7°C for 10 days
IDF	Culture medium free from carbohydrates. Incubate twice (a) 30°C for 48 hr (b) 20°C for 48 hr	Agar medium containing yeast extract and glucose + oxytetracycline 25°C for 96 hr	Brilliant green lactose bile broth 30°C for 48 hr	—
Czechoslovakia		Malt agar	Meat peptone agar + lactose and bromthymol blue	
West Germany		Wort agar (Koch's plate method)	—	—

After: Robinson and Tamime (*loc. cit.*) (see also **APHA**, 1978; Australian Standards, 1978; **BSI**, 1970).

Reproduced with permission of *Journal of the Society of Dairy Technology.*

An examination of yoghurt for contaminant organisms is, as indicated earlier, concerned with:

(a) protection of the consumer from any potentially pathogenic species;
(b) assurance that the material will not undergo microbial spoilage during its anticipated shelf-life.

and these issues are of vital importance to any company. Thus, apart from the moral obligation that a company has to its customers, the financial losses that can accrue from the release of suspect products are motivation enough to give quality control a high priority.

As far as pathogens are concerned, yoghurt with an acidity of around 1 % lactic acid is a fairly inhospitable medium and really troublesome pathogens like *Salmonella* spp. will be incapable of growth (Hobbs, 1972). Coliforms will also be inactivated by the low pH, and, in addition, some species may be susceptible to antibiotics released by the starter organisms (see Chapter 9). Whether *Staphylococcus* spp., and in particular coagulase-positive strains, can survive in acidic media is a matter of some dispute, but to date there have been no records of staphylococcal food poisoning being associated with the consumption of yoghurt in the United Kingdom (Gilbert and Wieneke, 1973). For this reason, an examination for staphylococci is not normally required for yoghurt (see Table 10.9), and even the test for coliforms is probably of more value as an indicator of plant hygiene than as a warning that the product may constitute a health risk.

TABLE 10.9. *An indication of the numbers of starter bacteria (CFU/ml) that have been isolated from retail cartons of yoghurt and some suggested "standards" relating to both contaminants and "desirable organisms"*

		Yoghurt	
Organism	Natural	Strawberry	Blackcurrant
S. thermophilus $\times 10^6$/ml	10–820	35–1100	80–1850
		54–250	
L. bulgaricus $\times 10^6$/ml	11–680	5–360	5–400
		<1–150	

Suggested *advisory* standards:

	Satisfactory	Doubtful	Unsatisfactory
S. thermophilus $\times 10^6$/ml	> 100	100–10	< 10
L. bulgaricus $\times 10^6$/ml	> 100	100–10	< 10
Coliforms/ml	< 1	1–10	> 10
Yeasts/ml	< 10	10–100	> 100
Moulds	< 1	1–10	> 10

After: Davis, Ashton and McCaskill (*loc. cit.*), Robinson (1976).

More significant from the producer's standpoint is the examination for yeasts and moulds, for these organisms are capable of spoiling yoghurt well within an anticipated sell-by date. Thus, many fungi are little affected by low pH, and with ample sucrose and/or lactose available as energy sources, unacceptable deterioration can be rapid. Yeasts, whether lactose-utilisers like *K. fragilis* and *K. lactis* or more cosmopolitan species, such as *Saccharomyces cerevisiae*, are a major concern, and to avoid in-carton fermentation (often manifest by a "doming" of the lid of the carton), Davis, Ashton and McCaskill (*loc. cit.*) have suggested that yoghurt, at the point of sale, should contain less than 100 viable yeast cells/ml; above 1000 cells/ml would imply a serious risk of deterioration. Moulds tend, on the whole, to develop more slowly than the yeasts, and hence should rarely be visible in retail products. Nevertheless, genera such as *Mucor, Rhizopus, Aspergillus, Penicillium* or *Alternaria* can product unsightly superficial growths of mycelium if cartons remain undisturbed for any length of time. For this reason, a mould count of up to ten colony-forming units/ml of retail product has been rated as "doubtful quality" by Davis, Ashton and McCaskill (*loc. cit.*).

At one time, fruit was the major source of fungal contamination, but now that the majority of ingredients will be heat treated prior to use, infections from this course should have been eliminated. Airborne spores or yeast cells can prove more difficult to control, particularly during certain months of the year, and unless a serious lapse in plant hygiene is suspected, high yeast or mould counts usually indicate contaminants in the atmosphere. The unexpected variety of yeast species isolated from yoghurt by Tilbury *et al.* (1974) and Suriyarachchi and Fleet (1981) can probably be explained by this type of chance contamination, and regular monitoring of the air in the processing area, and of representative samples of the end-product, employing acidified malt agar can provide a warning of impending problems; if spreading colonies are anticipated, a medium containing Rose Bengal can be substituted (Anon., 1980c).

Overall, therefore, it is clear that well-made yoghurt should not present a manufacturer with many complaints as far as microbiological quality is concerned, and although some authorities (see Table 10.9) suggest that a total viable count and an examination for coliforms is desirable, it is probable that many laboratories confine their attention to yeasts and moulds. This seemingly perfunctory approach is fair indication that yoghurt is generally recognised as a "safe" product (Rothwell, 1979), and that consumer complaints, should they arise, are more likely to centre on the organoleptic properties of the retail product.

D. Assessment of Organoleptic Characteristics

The ultimate judge of any product is, in a free society, the consumer, and although brand awareness only accounts for some 20 % of "decisions of purchase" (Kroger and Fram, 1975), deliberate avoidance of a brand as the result of dissatisfaction is another situation completely. To some extent, the chemical and physical analyses suggested earlier, e.g. titratable acidity and viscosity, will provide a reasonable indication that the normal "in-house" standards have been achieved, but the use of some form of taste panel to perform a final check is usual practice. The composition of such panels can range from "one man and a plastic teaspoon" through to a full panel of trained tasters selected and organised along the lines proposed by Amerine, Pangbourne and Roessler (1965). Obviously no one would dispute the skill of the "individual" (Harper, 1962), but the more objective and quantifiable the acquired data can be made, the easier the task of maintaining standards over a long period of time.

This latter approach is, of course, more time-consuming, and might involve:

(i) convening a panel of about five judges (with alternatives) on the basis of their knowledge of the product, and their willingness to participate on a regular basis;
(ii) obtaining agreement among the judges on the characteristics of a good quality yoghurt, and what is meant by the terminology that may be applied to certain faults or defects;
(iii) the derivation of a scheme of assessment that might be employed as part of the routine quality control procedures.

The ultimate selection of a scheme will rest with the panel concerned, but Figs. 10.5 to 10.9 show some of the schemes that have been proposed and/or employed in various countries. The inclusion

Yoghurt evaluation

Date:-
Taster:-
Code No:-

    a. Appearance & Colour   . . . .
       Defects. . . . .
    b. Body & Texture   . . . .
       Defects. . . . .
    c. Flavours   . . . .
       Defects. . . . .

                  Overall score   . . . .

Judge the three characteristics on the 1–5 scale.
    5 Excellent
    4 Very good
    3 Good
    2 Fair
    1 Poor

The overall score is obtained by multiplying the flavour score by 2 and then adding the score to the rest.
An excellent yoghurt gives an overall score of 20.
Possible defects:

    Appearance & Colour:-   Extraneous matter, lack of uniformity, unnatural colour, surface discolouration, wheying-off, fat separation, gassiness.

    Body & Texture:-   Too thin, gelatinous, chalky, lumpy or granular, slimy.

    Flavour:-   Excess acid, excess sugar, excess stabiliser, excess milk powder, yeasty, unclean.

Fig. 10.5.   One of the schemes proposed for the quality appraisal of yoghurt

After Pearce & Heap (1974).

of microbiological data in the Austrian scheme (see Fig. 10.7) is perhaps debatable, but beyond that, the over-riding factors must be operational simplicity and the ability of the procedure to discriminate between samples.

A few practice runs will quickly establish the preferences of a particular panel, and it should then be possible to accept, perhaps with modification, one of the available schemes. It is worth noting, however, that the description of defects can be a valuable part of the exercise, because the quality controller may then be in a position to indicate why the particular batch of yoghurt has scored poorly in certain respects. Thus, as shown in Table 10.10, some degree of association between a "recognised faults" and "likely causes" does exist, and hence an accurate description from a taste panel can speed the implementation of remedial action.

In some instances defects are not readily identifiable as to cause, and the apparently seasonal occurrence of "granulation" in yoghurt is a case in point (Robinson, 1981). Thus, although there is evidence linking poor process control with the formation of small, protein-rich "lumps" in yoghurt—a fault especially noticeable in fruit yoghurts—there have been reports that the defect is most prominent during the spring and autumn months (Cooper, Kipling and Gordon, 1974). Whether this periodicity is linked with seasonal changes in milk composition has not been established, nor is it clear why some manufacturers observe the problem but others do not. Nevertheless, if the quality control records are accurately maintained, then it is possible that a

A. "Karl Ruher Scheme" The Nine Point Scheme

Score	Judgement	Quality	Range	Class	Quality Assessment Overall Classification
9	Excellent	—		(Upper	
8	V. Good	V. Good	I	(Medium	Free of objections
7	Good	Good		(Lower	
6	Satisfactory	Satisfactory		(Upper	
5	Mediocre	Average	II	(Medium	Still acceptable
4	Sufficient	Sufficient		(Lower	in commerce
3	Imperfect	Bad		(Upper	
2	Bad	Bad	III	(Medium	Unsaleable
1	V. Bad	Bad		(Lower	

B. The Five Point Scheme

The five point scheme is as follows:-

Characteristics	Maximum Points	Multiplying Factor	Total Points	% of Points
Flavour	5	5	25	50
Appearance	5	2	10	20
Consistency	5	2	10	20
Smell or Odour (aroma)	5	1	5	10
			50	100

Points	Description of Properties
5	Very good, ideal.
4	Good.
3	Satisfactory, little mistakes.
2	Not very satisfactory, distinct mistakes
1	Not satisfactory
0	Bad, tainted.

Fig. 10.6. One of the schemes proposed for the quality appraisal of yoghurt

After: Bergel (1971 a&b)

pattern of occurrence will emerge, and with it, perhaps, some proposals for preventing, or at least minimising the impact of, this deleterious change.

CONCLUSIONS

If the essential requirements for manufacturing a high-quality yoghurt were to be tabulated, then the list might look rather like this:

—milk of good quality and adequate SNF;
—correct heat treatment;
—an active, well-balanced and contaminant-free starter culture;

Characters Assessed	Score
Appearance and Consistency	5
Aroma	3
Flavour	8
Microbiological Examination	4
	20 Total

Expected Characters

Appearance and Consistency:-
  jelly-like coagulum, porcelain-like surface,
  no wheying-off, coagulum cuts to give a
  clean surface.
Aroma: not too sour, aromatic.
Flavour: typical pleasant yoghurt taste, mild to slight acidic.

Microbiological Results

Presence of coliforms/Yeasts and Moulds in the volumes indicated.

Points/test	0.1 ml	0.01 ml
2	− ve	− ve
1	+ ve	− ve
0	+ ve	+ ve

Range of Score	Excellent	Good	Fair	Poor
Appearance and Consistency	5	4	3	2–0
Aroma	3	2	1	0
Flavour	8	7	6–5	4–0
Micro.	4	2	1	0

Class	Total Points	Flavour	Microbiological
1st	16 & above	7 & above	3 & above
2nd	10	5	1
3rd	Less than 10	Less than 5.	Less than 1

Fig. 10.7. A scheme for the appraisal of natural set yoghurt

After: Fütschik (1963).

—a clean and well-maintained plant;
—correct inoculation rate;
—correct incubation times and temperatures;
—an avoidance of rough handling of the coagulum, particularly during cooling;
—the use of high-quality fruit or other ingredients;
—correct storage of retail product preferably below 5°C;

and what is important about this list is that all these areas must, for effective operation, be monitored by quality control. The actual degree of surveillance will vary in the light of experience in a particular plant, but the principle must be the same, namely that the quality controller should have an accurate picture of the entire operation, for without this, the smooth running of the plant and the quality of the end-product will be at risk. Some ideas concerning the performance of this function have been set down in this chapter, but it is important that, except where legal requirements dictate otherwise, quality control staff should be prepared to adjust or adapt techniques to suit their own situation.

The scheme has been approved by the American Dairy Science Association.

	Source
Flavour	40
Body & Texture	30
Appearance & Colour	20
Package	5
	95 Total

Defects to be noted

Flavour:- Acid, bitter, coarse, fermented/fruity, lacks freshness, metallic, rancid and unclean.

Body and Texture:- Rubbery, stringy, grainy and weak/soft.

Appearance:- and Colour:- Free whey, lacks uniformity, slimy, surface discoloured, and unnatural colour.

Range of Score:-	*Excellent*	*Good*	*Fair*	*Poor*	*Acceptable for retail*
Flavour	40	38–39	36–37	<35	31–40
Body and Texture	30	28–29	26–27	<25	25–30
Appearance & Colour	20	18–19	16–17	<16	15–20

Fig. 10.8.   One of the schemes proposed for the quality appraisal of yoghurt

After: Angevine (1975).

The scheme has been approved by the American Dairy
Science Association

The Cultured Milk Score Card

Item	Perfect Score
Flavour	45
Body & Texture	30
Acidity	10
Appearance	10
Container & Closure	5
Total	100

Flavour defects:- Bitter, cheesey, coarse, flat, undeveloped, high acid, metallic, yeasty, miscellaneous.

Body & Texture defects: Curdy, gassy, lumpy, ropy, thin body, wheyed-off.

Acidity defects:- High, low.

Fig. 10.9.   One of the schemes proposed for the quality appraisal of yoghurt

After: Nelson & Trout (1964).

A microbiologist may, for example, have a strong preference for a particular medium, and because such changes may be harbingers of a more serious problem it is important that they are detected early. Similarly, values for titratable acidity vary from operator to operator, so that again the establishment of a routine must have priority. If this necessity for continuity is appreciated, together with the fact that fermentation is fundamentally a biological process rather than a series of inanimate chemical reactions, then quality control of yoghurt manufacture should become a straightforward commitment.

TABLE 10.10. *Some common defects of yoghurt? and an indication of some possible causes and remedies*

Defect	Possible causes	Remedy
Syneresis	Low SNF or fat content. High mineral content in milk. Unsufficient heat treatment/ homogenisation of milk. Too high incubation temperature. Low acidity, e.g. pH 4.8. Adventitious enzymes capable of coagulating protein. Disturbance of coagulum prior to cooling. Unspecified.	Adjust formulation. Blend with milk of low mineral content. Adjust process conditions. Reduce temperature to 42°C. Ensure pH 4.4. Eliminate source. Adequate cooling. Addition of stabiliser. Change culture to "viscous" type.
Low viscosity	Low total solids. Insufficient heat treatment/ homogenisation of milk. Too low incubation temperature. Too low inoculation rate. Prolonged agitation. Unspecified.	Adjust formulation. Adjust process conditions. Raise temperature to 42°C (or increase time). Raise inoculum to around 2% v/v. Improve mechanical handling system. Addition of stabiliser. Change culture to 'viscous' type.
Bubbles in coagulum	Poor storage conditions. Contamination with yeasts. Contamination with coliforms. Excessive aeration of mix.	Check temperature of refrigerated rooms. Eliminate source of infection. Poor plant hygiene or contaminated starter culture. Control agitation.
Granular coagulum	Poor mixing of milk powder. Agitation prior to cooling. Too high incubation temperature. Too low inoculation rate. Unspecified.	Adjust process conditions. Adequate cooling. Reduce temperature to 42°C. Raise inoculum to around 2% v/v. Change culture to 'viscous' type.
Flavour problems	Insipid. Unclean. Bitter. Sour. Malty/Yeasty. Rancid.	Lower inoculation rate to 2%. Extend incubation time. Raise inoculation rate to 2%. Reduce incubation time. Check for contamination with coliforms. Lower inoculation rate to 2%. Change starter culture. Lower inoculation rate to 2%. Check temperature to storage. Suspect contamination by yeasts. Check quality of raw milk.

REFERENCES

ADMI (1971) In *Standards for Grades of Dry Milks,* American Dry milk Institute Inc., Illinois, U.S.A.

AMERINE, M., PANGBOURNE, R. M. and ROESSLER, E. B. (1965) In *Principles of Sensory Evaluation of Foods,* Academic Press Inc. (London) Ltd., London, U.K.

ANGEVINE, N. (1975) Personal communication.

ANON. (1977) *KS 05–34 Specifications for Yoghurts,* Part 1 and 2, Kenyan Bureau of Standards, Nairobi, Kenya.
ANON. (1980a) In *The Milko-Tester,* A/S N. Foss Electric, Hillerod, Denmark.
ANON. (1980b) In *A New Era in Antibiotics Testing,* Intervest Laboratories Ltd., Cambridge, U.K.
ANON. (1980c) In *The Oxoid Manual,* 4th Edition, Oxoid Ltd., Basingstoke, U.K.
AOAC (1970) In *Association of Official Analytical Chemists,* 11th Edition, Ed. by Horwitz, N., Chicilo, P. and Reynolds, H. Benjamin Franklin Station, Washington, U.S.A.
APHA (1978) In *Standard Methods for the Examination of Dairy Products,* 14 Edition, Ed. by Marth, E. H. American Public Health Association, Washington, U.S.A.
ASHTON, T. R. (1963) *Journal of the Society of Dairy Technology,* **16,** 68.
Australian Standards (1978) In *AS 1095.2.11—Methods for the Examination of Dairy Products,* Standards Association of Australia, Sydney, Australia.
BERGEL, C. (1971a) *Deutsche Milchwirtschaft,* **22**(26), VIII.
BERGEL, C. (1971b) *Deutsche Milchwirtschaft,* **22**(40), V.
BRACQUART, P. (1981) *Journal of Applied Bacteriology,* **51,** 303.
BSI (1955) In *BS-696 Gerber Method for the Determination of Fat in Milk and Milk Products,* British Standards Institution, London, U.K.
BSI (1959) In *BS-734 Density Hydrometers for Use in Milk, Ibid.*
BSI (1968) In *BS-4285 Methods of Microbiological Examinations for Dairy Purposes, Ibid.*
BSI (1970) In *BS-4285 (Sup. No. 1) Methods of Microbiological Examinations of Milk Products, Ibid.*
BSI (1973) In *BS-4938 Method for the Rapid Determination of Sediment in Milk by Filtration, Ibid.*
CATE, L. TEN (1965) *Journal Applied Bacteriology,* **28,** 221.
COOPER, P. J. and BROOMFIELD, A. R. (1974) *XIXth International Dairy Congress,* **IE,** 447.
COOPER, P. J., KIPLING, N. and GORDON, J. E. (1974) *XIXth International Dairy Congress,* **IE,** 733.
DAVIS, J. G. (1970) *Dairy Industries,* **35,** 139.
DAVIS, J. G. (1981) In *Dairy Microbiology,* Vol. II, Ed. by Robinson, R. K. Applied Science Publishers, London, U.K.
DAVIS, J. G. and McLACHLAN, T. (1974) *Dairy Industries,* **39,** 139.
DAVIS, J. G., ASHTON, T. R. and McCASKILL, M. (1971) *Dairy Industries,* **36,** 569.
DRIESSEN, F. M., UBBELS, J. and STADHOUDERS, J. (1977) *Journal of Biotechnology and Bioengineering,* **19,** 821.
ELLIKER, P. R., ANDERSON, A. W. and HANNESSON, G. (1956) *Journal of Dairy Science,* **39,** 1611.
ELOY, C. and LACROSSE, R. (1980) *Dairy Science Abstracts,* **42,** 691.
FAO/WHO (1972) In *Joint FAO/WHO Food Standards Program,* Cx 5/70, 15th Session, Rome, Italy.
Food & Drugs Act (1979) In *Composition & Labelling—The Preservatives in Food Regulations 1979 No. 752,* Statutory Instruments, Ministry of Agriculture, Fisheries & Food, London, U.K.
FÜTSCHIK, J. (1963) *Osterreichische Milchwirtschaft,* **18,** 132.
GALESLOOT, Th. E. (1958) *Netherland Milk & Dairy Journal,* **12,** 130.
GILBERT, R. J. and WIENEKE, A. A. (1973) In *The Microbiological Safety of Food,* Ed. by Hobbs, B. C. and Chistian, J. H. B. Academic Press Inc. (London) Ltd., London, U.K.
GINSLOV, B. O. (1970) *South African Journal of Dairy Technology,* **2,** 79.
GREGORY, P. H. (1961) In *The Microbiology of the Atmosphere,* Leonard Hill, London, U.K.
HARPER, R. (1962) *New Scientist,* **11,** 396.
HARRIGAN, W. F. and McCANCE, M. E. (1976) In *Laboratory Methods in Food and Dairy Microbiology,* 2nd Edition, Academic Press Inc. (London) Ltd., London, U.K.
HILKER, V. (1947) *Journal of Dairy Science,* **30,** 161.
HOBBS, B. C. (1972) *Journal of the Society of Dairy Technology,* **25,** 47.
IDF (1969a) In *Standard Methods for Sampling Milk and Milk Products,* IDF/50, Brussels, Belgium.
IDF (1969b) In *Compositional Standards for Fermented Milks,* IDF/47, *Ibid.*
JENESS, R., SHIPE, W. F. and SERBON, J. W. (1947) In *Fundamentals of Dairy Chemistry,* 2nd Edition, Ed. by Webb, B. H., Johnson, R. H. and Alford,   AVI Publishing Co. Inc., Connecticut, U.S.A.
JOHNS, F. E., GORDON, J. F. and SHAPTON, N. (1978) *Journal of the Society of Dairy Technology,* **31,** 209.
KROGER, M. and FRAM, S. R. (1975) *Journal of Food Technology,* **29,** 52.
LÜCK, H. (1981) In *Dairy Microbiology,* Vol. II, Ed. by Robinson, R. K. Applied Science Publishers, London, U.K.
LÜCK, H., KRIEL, J. B. and MOSTERT, J. F. (1973) *South African Journal of Dairy Technology,* **5,** 129.
NELSON, J. A. and TROUT, G. M. (1964) In *Judging Dairy Products,* 4th Edition, Olson Publishing Co., Milwaukee, U.S.A.
Netherland Standards (1967) *Digest of Health Legislation—WHO,* **18,** 755.
PEARCE, L. E. and HEAP, H. A. (1974) *Town Milk—Journal of the New Zealand Milk Board,* **22,** 18.
PEARSON, D. (1976) In *The Chemical Analysis of Foods,* 7th Edition, Churchill Livingstone, London, U.K.
PETTE, J. W. and LOLKEMA, H. (1951) *Netherland Milk & Dairy Journal,* **5,** 27.
POSTHUMUS, G. (1954) *Official Orgaan FNZ,* **46,** 55.
ROBINSON, R. K. (1976) *Dairy Industries International,* **41,** 449.
ROBINSON, R. K. (1981) *Dairy Industries International,* **46**(3), 31.
ROBINSON, R. K. and TAMIME, A. Y. (1976) *Journal of the Society of Dairy Technology,* **29,** 148.
ROTHWELL, J. (1979) *Health and Hygiene,* **3,** 1.

400

SHANKAR, P. A. and DAVIES, F. L. (1977) *Journal of the Society of Dairy Technology,* **30**, 28.

SHERMAN, P. (1970) In *Industrial Rheology,* Academic Press Inc. (London) Ltd., London, U.K.

SPINKS, J. (1981) Personal communication.

STORGARDS, T. (1964) In *Fermented Milks,* IDF Annual Publication—Part III, Brussels, Belgium.

SURIYARACHCHI, V. R. and FLEET, G. H. (1981) *Journal of Applied and Environmental Microbiology,* **42**, 574.

TAMIME, A. Y. (1977) In *Some Aspects of the Production of Yoghurt and Condensed Yoghurt,* PhD Thesis, University of Reading, Berkshire, U.K.

TILBURY, R. H., DAVIS, J. G., FRENCH, S. and EMRIE, F. K. E. (1974) In *Proceedings of the 4th International Symposium on Yeasts,* 8–12 July, Vienna, Austria, Vol. I, p. F8.

USPHS (1959) In *Public Health Monograph No. 60,* U.S. Public Health Service, Washington, U.S.A.

WANG, S. H. (1941) *Journal of Bacteriology,* **42**, 297.

WILSON, G. S. (1935) In *Bacteriological Grading of Milk,* Series No. 206, HMSO, London, U.K.

APPENDIX I

Different Ways in Which Titratable Acidity is Expressed and Their Relative Values to % Lactic Acid

% Lactic acid	Soxhlet-Henkel (°SH)	Thorner (°T)	Dornic (°D)
0.0000	0	0.0	0.00
0.0225	1	2.5	2.25
0.0450	2	5.0	4.50
0.0675	3	7.5	6.75
0.0900	4	10.0	9.00
0.1125	5	12.5	11.25
0.1350	6	15.0	13.50
0.1575	7	17.5	15.75
0.1800	8	20.0	18.00
0.2025	9	22.5	20.25
0.2250	10	25.0	22.50
0.2475	11	27.5	24.75
0.2700	12	30.0	27.00
0.2925	13	32.5	29.25
0.3150	14	35.0	31.50
0.3375	15	37.5	33.75
0.3600	16	40.0	36.00
0.3825	17	42.5	38.25
0.4050	18	45.0	40.50
0.4275	19	47.5	42.75
0.4500	20	50.0	45.00
0.4725	21	52.5	47.25
0.4950	22	55.0	49.50
0.5175	23	57.5	51.75
0.5400	24	60.0	54.00

Appendix I (*Contd.*)

% Lactic acid	Soxhlet-Henkel (°SH)	Thorner (°T)	Dornic (°D)
0.5625	25	62.5	56.25
0.5850	26	65.0	58.50
0.6075	27	67.5	60.75
0.6300	28	70.0	63.00
0.6525	29	72.5	65.25
0.6750	30	75.0	67.50
0.6975	31	77.5	69.75
0.7200	32	80.0	72.00
0.7425	33	82.5	74.25
0.7650	34	85.0	76.50
0.7875	35	87.5	78.79
0.8100	36	90.0	81.00
0.8325	37	92.5	83.25
0.8550	38	95.0	85.50
0.8775	39	97.5	87.75
0.9000	40	100.0	90.00
0.9225	41	102.5	92.25
0.9450	42	105.0	94.50
0.9675	43	107.5	96.75
0.9900	44	110.0	99.00
1.0125	45	112.5	101.25
1.0350	46	115.0	103.50
1.0575	47	117.5	105.75
1.0800	48	120.0	108.00
1.1025	49	122.5	110.25
1.1250	50	125.0	112.50
1.1475	51	127.5	114.75
1.1700	52	130.0	117.00
1.1925	53	132.5	119.25
1.2150	54	135.0	121.50
1.2375	55	137.5	123.75
1.2600	56	140.0	126.00
1.2825	57	142.5	128.25
1.3050	58	145.0	130.50
1.3275	59	147.5	132.75
1.3500	60	150.0	135.00
1.3725	61	152.5	137.25
1.3950	62	155.0	139.50
1.4175	63	157.5	141.75
1.4400	64	160.0	144.00
1.4625	65	162.5	146.25

Appendix I (*Contd.*)

% Lactic acid	Soxhlet-Henkel (°SH)	Thorner (°T)	Dornic (°D)
1.4850	66	165.0	148.50
1.5070	67	167.5	150.75
1.5300	68	170.0	153.00
1.5525	69	172.5	155.25
1.5750	70	175.0	157.50
1.5975	71	177.5	159.75
1.6200	72	180.0	162.00
1.6425	73	182.5	164.25
1.6650	74	185.0	166.50
1.6875	75	187.5	168.75
1.7100	76	190.0	171.00
1.7325	77	192.5	173.25
1.7550	78	195.0	175.50
1.7775	79	197.5	177.75
1.8000	80	200.0	180.00
1.8225	81	202.5	182.25
1.8450	82	205.0	184.50
1.8675	83	207.5	186.75
1.8900	84	210.0	189.00
1.9125	85	212.5	191.25
1.9350	86	215.0	193.50
1.9575	87	217.5	195.75
1.9800	88	220.0	198.00
2.0025	89	222.5	200.25
2.0250	90	225.0	202.50
2.0475	91	227.5	204.75
2.0700	92	230.0	207.00
2.0925	93	232.5	209.25
2.1150	94	235.0	211.50
2.1375	95	237.5	213.75
2.1600	96	240.0	216.00
2.1825	97	242.5	218.25
2.2050	98	245.0	220.50
2.2275	99	247.5	222.75
2.2500	100	250.0	225.00

APPENDIX II
Temperature Conversion*

Centigrade/Celsius $°C = 5/9 (F-32)$ $= 0.555 (F-32)$ °C		Fahrenheit $°F = (9/5 \times C) + 32$ $= (1.8 \times C) + 32$ °F	Centigrade/Celsius $°C = 5/9 (F-32)$ $= 0.55 (F-32)$ °C		Fahrenheit $°F = (9/5 \times C) + 32$ $= (1.8 \times C) + 32$ °F
−31.7	−25	−13.0	−15.0	5	41.0
−31.1	−24	−11.2	−14.4	6	42.8
−30.6	−23	−9.4	−13.9	7	44.6
−30.0	−22	−7.6	−13.3	8	46.4
−29.4	−21	−5.8	−12.8	9	48.2
−28.9	−20	−4.0	−12.2	10	50.0
−28.3	−19	−2.2	−11.7	11	51.8
−27.8	−18	−0.4	−11.1	12	53.6
−27.2	−17	1.4	−10.6	13	55.4
−26.7	−16	3.2	−10.0	14	57.2
−26.1	−15	5.0	−9.4	15	59.0
−25.6	−14	6.8	−8.9	16	60.8
−25.0	−13	8.6	−8.3	17	62.6
−24.4	−12	10.4	−7.8	18	64.4
−23.9	−11	12.2	−7.2	19	66.2
−23.4	−10	14.0	−6.7	20	68.0
−22.8	−9	15.8	−6.1	21	69.8
−22.2	−8	17.6	−5.6	22	71.6
−21.7	−7	19.4	−5.0	23	73.4
−21.1	−6	21.2	−4.4	24	75.2
−20.6	−5	23.0	−3.9	25	77.0
−20.0	−4	24.8	−3.3	26	78.8
−19.4	−3	26.6	−2.8	27	80.6
−18.9	−2	28.4	−2.2	28	82.4
−18.3	−1	30.2	−1.7	29	84.2
−17.8	0	32.0	−1.1	30	86.0
−17.2	1	33.8	−0.6	31	87.8
−16.7	2	35.6	0	32	89.6
−16.1	3	37.4	0.6	33	91.4
−15.6	4	39.2	1.1	34	93.2

Appendix II (*Contd.*)

°C		°F	°C		°F
1.7	35	95.0	25.6	78	172.4
2.2	36	96.8	26.1	79	174.2
2.8	37	98.6	26.7	80	176.0
3.3	38	100.4	27.2	81	177.8
3.9	39	102.2	27.8	82	179.6
4.4	40	104.0	28.4	83	181.4
5.0	41	105.8	28.9	84	183.2
5.6	42	107.6	29.4	85	185.0
6.1	43	109.4	30.0	86	186.8
6.7	44	111.2	30.6	87	188.6
7.2	45	113.0	31.1	88	190.4
7.8	46	114.8	31.7	89	192.2
8.3	47	116.6	32.2	90	194.4
8.9	48	118.4	32.8	91	195.8
9.4	49	120.2	33.3	92	197.6
10.0	50	122.0	33.9	93	199.4
10.6	51	123.8	34.4	94	201.2
11.1	52	125.6	35.0	95	203.0
11.7	53	127.4	35.6	96	204.8
12.2	54	129.2	36.1	97	206.6
12.8	55	131.0	36.7	98	208.4
13.3	56	132.8	37.2	99	210.2
13.9	57	134.6	37.8	100	212.0
14.4	58	136.4	38.3	101	213.8
15.0	59	138.2	38.9	102	215.6
15.6	60	140.0	39.4	103	217.4
16.1	61	141.8	40.0	104	219.2
16.7	62	143.6	40.6	105	221.0
17.2	63	145.5	41.1	106	222.8
17.8	64	147.2	41.7	107	224.6
18.3	65	149.0	42.2	108	226.4
18.9	66	150.8	42.8	109	228.2
19.4	67	152.6	43.3	110	230.0
20.0	68	154.4	43.9	111	231.8
20.6	69	156.2	44.4	112	233.6
21.1	70	158.0	45.0	113	235.4
21.7	71	159.8	45.6	114	237.2
22.2	72	161.6	46.1	115	239.0
22.8	73	163.4	46.7	116	240.8
23.3	74	165.2	47.2	117	242.6
23.9	75	167.0	47.8	118	244.4
24.4	76	168.8	48.3	119	246.2
25.0	77	170.6	48.9	120	248.0

Appendix II (*Contd.*)

°C		°F	°C		°F
49.4	121	249.8	73.3	164	327.2
50.0	122	251.6	73.9	165	329.0
50.6	123	253.4	74.4	166	330.8
51.1	124	255.2	75.0	167	332.6
51.7	125	257.0	75.6	168	334.4
52.2	126	258.8	76.1	169	336.2
52.8	127	260.6	76.7	170	338.2
53.3	128	262.4	77.2	171	339.8
53.9	129	264.2	77.8	172	341.6
54.4	130	266.0	78.3	173	343.4
55.0	131	267.8	78.9	174	345.2
55.6	132	269.6	79.4	175	347.0
56.1	133	271.4	80.0	176	348.8
56.7	134	273.2	80.6	177	350.6
57.2	135	275.0	81.1	178	352.4
57.8	136	276.8	81.7	179	354.2
58.3	137	278.6	82.2	180	356.0
58.9	138	280.4	82.8	181	357.8
59.4	139	282.2	83.3	182	359.6
60.0	140	284.0	83.9	183	361.4
60.6	141	285.8	84.4	184	363.2
61.1	142	287.6	85.0	185	365.0
61.7	143	289.4	85.6	186	366.8
62.2	144	291.4	86.1	187	368.6
62.8	145	293.0	86.7	188	370.4
63.3	146	294.8	87.2	189	372.2
63.9	147	296.6	87.8	190	374.0
64.4	148	298.4	88.3	191	375.8
65.0	149	300.2	88.9	192	377.6
65.6	150	302.0	89.4	193	379.4
66.1	151	303.8	90.0	194	381.8
66.7	152	305.6	90.6	195	383.6
67.2	153	307.4	91.1	196	384.6
67.8	154	309.2	91.7	197	386.6
68.3	155	311.0	92.2	198	388.4
68.9	156	311.8	92.8	199	390.2
69.4	157	314.6	93.3	200	392.0
70.0	158	316.4	93.9	201	393.8
70.6	159	318.2	94.4	202	395.6
71.1	160	320.0	95.0	203	397.4
71.7	161	321.8	95.6	204	399.2
72.2	162	323.6	96.1	205	401.0
72.8	163	325.4	96.7	206	402.8

Appendix II (*Contd.*)

°C		°F	°C		°F
97.2	207	404.6	121.1	250	482.0
97.8	208	406.4	121.7	251	483.8
98.3	209	408.2	122.2	252	485.6
98.9	210	410.0	122.8	253	487.4
99.4	211	411.8	123.3	254	489.2
100.0	212	413.6	123.9	255	491.0
100.6	213	415.4	124.4	256	492.8
101.1	214	417.2	125.0	257	494.6
101.7	215	419.0	125.6	258	496.4
102.2	216	420.8	126.1	259	498.2
102.8	217	422.6	126.7	260	500.0
103.3	218	424.4	127.2	261	501.8
103.9	219	426.2	127.8	262	503.6
104.4	220	428.0	128.3	263	505.4
105.0	221	429.8	128.9	264	507.2
105.6	222	431.6	129.4	265	509.0
106.1	223	433.4	130.0	266	510.8
106.7	224	435.2	130.6	267	512.6
107.2	225	437.0	131.1	268	514.4
107.8	226	438.8	131.7	269	516.2
108.3	227	440.6	132.2	270	518.0
108.9	228	442.4	132.8	271	519.8
109.4	229	444.2	133.3	272	521.6
110.0	230	446.0	133.9	273	523.4
110.6	231	447.8	134.4	274	525.2
111.1	232	449.6	135.0	275	527.0
111.7	233	451.4	135.6	276	528.8
112.2	234	453.2	136.1	277	530.6
112.8	235	455.0	136.7	278	532.4
113.3	236	456.8	137.2	279	534.2
113.9	237	458.6	137.8	280	536.0
114.4	238	460.4	138.3	281	537.8
115.0	239	462.2	138.9	282	539.6
115.6	240	464.0	139.4	283	541.4
116.1	241	465.8	140.0	284	543.2
116.7	242	467.6	140.6	285	545.0
117.2	243	469.4	141.1	286	546.8
117.8	244	471.2	141.7	287	548.6
118.3	245	473.0	142.2	288	550.4
118.9	246	474.8	142.8	289	552.2
119.4	247	476.6	143.3	290	554.0
120.0	248	478.4	143.9	291	555.8
120.6	249	480.2	144.4	292	557.6

Appendix I (*Contd.*)

°C		°F	°C		°F
145.0	293	559.4	147.2	297	566.6
145.6	294	561.2	147.8	298	568.4
146.1	295	563.0	148.3	299	570.2
146.7	296	564.8	148.9	300	572.0

* Find the known temperature to be converted in the "boxed" column, then read the conversion to the left for °C and/or right for °F.

Example: Convert the following known temperature, i.e. 50

    10.0   50   122.0

$\therefore$ 50°C = 122.0°F

or 50°F = 10.0°C

APPENDIX III

Volume Units

	Metric (SI)			*Imperial (Imp) and US*
	Litre	=	1000	Gallon
	Hecto-	=	100	Yard
(Prefixes)	Deca-	=	10	Food
	Deci-	=	0.1	Inch
	Centi-	=	0.01	Pint
	Milli-	=	0.001	Fluid ounce
	Micro-	=	0.000,001	Drams

	To Convert Volume	*Multiply By*
Millilitres to	gallons (Imp)	0.00022
	gallons (US)	0.00026
	fluid ounces (IMP)	0.03520
	fluid ounces (US)	0.03380
Cubic centimetres to cubic inches		0.06100
Cubic metres to	cubic inches	61.0×10^{-3}
	cubic feet	35.3000
	gallons (Imp)	220.0000
	gallons (US)	264.1700
Litres to	cubic feet	0.03500
	cubic inches	61.03000
	fluid ounces (Imp)	35.19600
	fluid ounces (US)	33.81400
	gallons (Imp)	0.21990
	gallons (US)	0.26420
	pints (Imp)	1.75980
	pints (US)	2.11340
	quarts (Imp)	0.87990
	quarts (US)	1.05670
Fluid ounces (US) to	cubic inches	1.80500
	gallons (US)	0.00780
	litres	0.02950
	millilitres	29.57000
	fluid ounces (Imp)	1.04100

Appendix III (*Contd.*)

Fluid ounces (Imp) to	gallons (Imp)	0.00630
	millilitres	28.41000
	fluid ounces (US)	0.96000
Pints (Imp) to	litres	0.56800
	pints (US)	0.83270
Pints (US) to	litres	0.47320
	pints (Imp)	1.20090
Quarts (Imp) to litres		1.13650
Quarts (US) to litres		0.94600
Cubic feet to	cubic inches	1728.0000
	gallons (Imp)	6.4810
	gallons (US)	7.4810
	litres	28.3200
Cubic inches to	cubic centilitres	16.3870
	cubic feet	0.00058
	gallons (Imp)	0.0036
	gallons (US)	0.0043
	litres	0.0164
	fluid ounces (US)	0.5540
Fluid drams to fluid ounces (US)		0.1250
Fluid ounces to drams (US)		8.0000
Fluid ounces (Imp) to litres		0.0208
Fluid ounces (US) to litres		0.0296
Gallons (Imp) to	cubic feet	0.1600
	cubic inches	277.3000
	litres	4.5460
	gallons (US)	1.2009
	millilitres	4546.0000
	cubic metres	0.0046
	ounces (Imp)	160.0000
Gallons (US) to	cubic feet	0.1337
	cubic inches	231.0000
	litres	3.7853
	gallons (Imp)	0.8327
	millilitres	3785.0000
	cubic metres	0.0038
	fluid ounces (US)	128.0000

APPENDIX IV

Weight/Mass Units

Metric (SI)	Imperial
Tonnes	Ton
Kilograms	Pound
Grams	Ounce
	Grains

	To Convert Weight	Multiply by
Gram to	grain	15.4300
	ounce	0.0353
	pound	0.0022
Kilogram to	ounce	35.2700
	pound	2.2040
Ounce to	gram	28.3500
	grain	437.0000
	pound	0.0625
Pound to	gram	453.6000
	grain	7000.0000
	kilogram	0.4500
	ounce	16.0000
Grain to	ounce	0.0023
	pound	0.00014
	gram	0.0648

	To Convert Weight per Volume	Multiply by
Gram/litre to	grain/gallon (Imp)	70.1140
	grain/gallon (US)	58.4000
	grain/ounce (US)	0.4600
	pound/gallon (US)	0.0083
Gram/millilitre to	pounds/gallon (US)	8.3450

Appendix IV (*Contd.*)

Pound/cubic foot to	{ gram/cubic centimetre { pound/gallon (US)	0.0160 0.1337
Pound/gallon (US) to	{ gram/millilitre { pound/cubic foot { gram/litre	0.1198 7.8410 119.9470

APPENDIX V
Miscellaneous Units

To Convert to SI units	Multiply by
1. *Velocity*	
cm/s	1.0000×10^{-2} m/s
m/h	2.7778×10^{-4} m/s
ft/s	3.0480×10^{-1} m/s
ft/h	3.4667×10^{-5} m/s
mile/h	4.4704×10^{-1} m/s
2. *Volumetric flow*	
cm³/s	1.0000×10^{-6} m³/s
m³/h	2.7778×10^{-4} m³/s
ft³/s	2.8317×10^{-2} m³/s
cm³/min	1.6667×10^{-8} m³/s
l/min	1.6667×10^{-5} m³/s
ft³/min	4.7195×10^{-4} m³/s
ft³/h	7.8658×10^{-6} m³/s
gal (Imp)/min	7.5766×10^{-5} m³/s
gal (Imp)/h	1.2628×10^{-6} m³/s
gal (US)/min	6.3089×10^{-5} m³/s
gal (US)/h	1.0515×10^{-6} m³/s
3. *Viscosity*	
A. Dynamic	
g/cm s	1.000×10^{-1} kg/m s
kg/m h	2.7778×10^{-4} kg/m s
lb/ft s	1.4882 kg/m s
lb/ft h	4.1338×10^{-4} kg/m s
B. Kinematic	
cm²/s	1.0000×10^{-4} m²/s
m²/h	2.7778×10^{-4} m²/s
ft²/s	9.2903×10^{-2} m²/s
ft²/h	2.5806×10^{-5} m²/s
4. *Density*	
g/cm³ °C	1.0000×10^{3} kg/m³
lb/ft³ °F	1.6018×10 kg/m³
lb/gal (Imp)	9.9779×10 kg/m³
lb/gal (US)	1.1983×10^{2} kg/m³

APPENDIX VI

Work/Energy and Other Related Units

Different units are used to measure energy, and to convert to SI units the following multiplication factors are used:

	Quantity	SI Factor
1. Energy		
	cal	4.1868 J
	kcal	4.1868×10^3 J
	Btu	1.0551×10^3 J
	Horse power (hp)/h (metric)	2.6477×10^6 J
	hp/h (Imp)	2.6845×10^6 J
	kW/h	3.6000×10^6 J
	ft lb f	1.3558 J
	Therm	1.0551×10^8 J
	Thermic	4.1855×10^6 J
2. Calorific Value (volumetric)		
	cal/cm^3	4.1868×10^6 J/m^3
	$kcal/m^3$	4.1868×10^3 J/m^3
	Btu/ft^3	3.7260×10^4 J/m^3
	$Therm/ft^3$	3.7260×10^9 J/m^3
3. Coefficient of Expansion (volumetric)		
	$g/cm^3\,°C$	1.0000×10^3 $kg/m^3\,°C$
	$lb/ft^3\,°F$	$28.8330 \times$ $kg/m^3\,°C$
4. Heat Flux		
	$cal/s\,cm^2$	4.1868×10^4 W/m^2
	$kcal/h\,m^2$	1.1630 W/m^2
	$Btu/h\,ft^2$	3.1546 W/m^2

Appendix VI (*Contd.*)

---

5. *Heat Release Rate*

   A. *Mass*

cal/s g	4.1868×10^3 W/kg
kcal/h kg	1.1630 W/kg
Btu/h lb	6.4612×10^{-1} W/kg

   B. *Volumetric*

cal/s cm^3	4.1868×10^6 W/m^3
kcal/h m^3	1.1630 W/m^3
Btu/h ft^3	1.0350×10 W/m^3

6. *Heat Transfer Coefficient*

cal/s cm^2 $^\circ$C	4.1868×10^4 W/m^2 $^\circ$C
kcal/h m^2 $^\circ$C	1.1630 W/m^2 $^\circ$C
Btu/h ft^2 $^\circ$F	5.6704 W/m^2 $^\circ$C

7. *Power*

cal/s	4.1868 W
kcal/h	1.1630 W
Btu/s	1.0551×10^3 W
Btu/h	2.9308×10^{-1} W
hp (metric)	7.3548×10^2 W
hp (Imp)	7.4570×10^2 W
ft lb f/s	1.3558 W

8. *Specific Enthalpy*

cal/g	4.1868×10^3 J/kg
Btu/lb	2.3260×10^3 J/kg

9. *Specific Heat*

cal/g $^\circ$C	4.1868×10^3 J/kg $^\circ$K
Btu/lb $^\circ$F	2.3260×10^3 J/kg $^\circ$K

10. *Thermal Conductivity*

cal/s cm^2 ($^\circ$C/cm)	4.1868×10^2 W/m^2	
kcal/h m^2 ($^\circ$C/m)	1.1630 W/m^2	($^\circ$C/m)
Btu/h ft^2 ($^\circ$F/ft)	1.7308 W/m^2	
Btu/h ft^2 ($^\circ$F/in)	1.4423×10^{-1} W/m^2	

APPENDIX VII

Force and Pressure Units

To convert force and pressure units to SI units, the following multiplication factors are used:

	Quantity	Factor
A. Force		
	dyn	1.0000×10^{-5} N
	kg force	9.8067 N
	lb force	4.4482 N
	ton force	9.9640×10^3 N
B. Pressure		
	dyn/cm²	1.0000×10^{-1} N/m²
	kg f/m²	9.8067 N/m²
	standard atmosphere	1.0133×10^5 N/m²
	atmosphere or kg f/cm²	9.8067×10^4 N/m²
	bar	1.0000×10^5 N/m²
	lb f/ft²	4.7880×10 N/m²
	lb f/in²	6.8948×10^3 N/m²
	mm mercury (Hg)	1.3333×10^2 N/m²
	inch Hg	3.3866×10^3 N/m²

APPENDIX VIII

Length and Area Units

Metric (SI)	Imperial
Kilometre (km)	Mile (mi)
Metre (m)	Yard (yd)
Centimetre (cm)	Foot (ft)
Millimetre (mm)	Inch (in)

$$1 \text{ metre} = 100 \text{ cm} = 1000 \text{ mm}$$
$$1 \text{ kilometre} = 1000 \text{ m}$$

$$1 \text{ metre} = 39.4 \text{ in} = 3.28 \text{ ft} = 1.09 \text{ yd} = 0.621 \times 10^{-3} \text{ mile}$$
$$1 \text{ yard} = 3 \text{ ft} = 36 \text{ in}$$
$$1 \text{ mile} = 1760 \text{ yd}$$

To Convert Length	Multiply by
Inches to centimetres	2.5400
Feet to metres	0.3048
Yards to metres	0.9144
Miles to metres	1,609.0000
Centimetres to inches	0.3940
Metres to feet	3.2810
Metres to yards	1.0936
Kilometres to miles	0.6213

To Convert Area	Multiply by
Square inches to square centimetres	6.4520
Square feet to square metres	0.0929
Square yards to square metres	0.8360
Square centimetres to square inches	0.1550
Square metres to square feet	10.7640
Square metres to square yards	1.1970

APPENDIX IX

Pearsons Square Method, Algebraic Method

PEARSONS SQUARE METHOD

If the raw materials used for the manufacture of yoghurt are: skim milk (9% solids-not-fat and 91% water), skim milk powder (97% solids-not-fat and 3% water) and cream (50% fat), calculate the quantities of the above raw materials required to produce a 500-litre batch of yoghurt with 16% total solids and 1.5% fat in the final product. Calculate first the quantities of skim milk and skim milk powder required to give the desired level of solids-not-fat (14.5%).

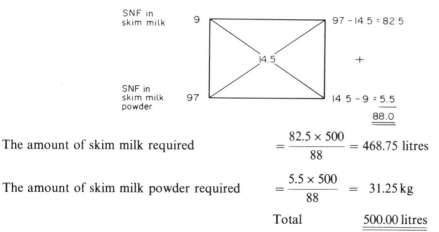

The amount of skim milk required $= \dfrac{82.5 \times 500}{88} = 468.75$ litres

The amount of skim milk powder required $= \dfrac{5.5 \times 500}{88} = 31.25$ kg

Total 500.00 litres

Since the above mix contains only small quantities of fat, e.g. 0.1%, the balance of the required fat comes from the cream as follows:

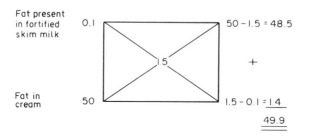

The amount of fortified skim milk required $= \dfrac{48.5 \times 500}{49.9} = 485.97$ litres

The amount of cream required $= \dfrac{1.4 \times 500}{49.9} = 14.03$ litres

$$\text{Total} \qquad \underline{\underline{500.00}} \text{ litres}$$

Although the above calculation does not take into consideration the amount of solids-not-fat present in the cream (4.5%) and the starter culture inoculum (12%), the accuracy is sufficient for most practical purposes. However, as an additional check, the final composition of the yoghurt can be calculated as follows:

Product	Weight in litres	Weight of fat supplied (kg)	Weight of solids-not-fat supplied
Skim milk	485.97	$\dfrac{0.1 \times 485.97}{100} = 0.49$	$\dfrac{9 \times 485.97}{100} = 43.74$
Skim milk powder	31.25	–	$\dfrac{97 \times 31.25}{100} = 30.31$
Cream	14.03	$\dfrac{50 \times 14.03}{100} = 7.02$	$\dfrac{4.5 \times 14.03}{100} = 0.63$
Starter culture at 3% rate of inoculation	15.00	–	$\dfrac{12 \times 15}{100} = 1.8$
Total	546.25	7.51	76.48

$\therefore$ the % of fat in yoghurt $= \dfrac{100 \times 7.51}{546.25} = 1.37$

The % of solids-not-fat in yoghurt $= \dfrac{76.48 \times 100}{546.25} = 14.00$

Hence, the difference in the composition is 0.13% fat and 0.5% solids-not-fat, and such small margin of error is due to the fact that the cream (SNF) and the starter inoculum (SNF) are not considered. If such small % of fat and SNF is compensated for, then the prepared mix will have the desired level of fat and SNF.

THE ALGEBRAIC METHOD

This method of calculation takes into consideration all the raw materials used for the manufacture of yoghurt, in order to obtain exactly the quantities required for a balanced mix; an approach which is similar to that used in the ice-cream industry (Hyde and Rothwell, 1973). For example, if the aim is to prepare a mix for yoghurt production which has the following chemical composition (1.5% fat and 14.5% SNF), and the dairy materials used are whole milk, skim milk, skim milk powder and a liquid starter culture, the composition of the raw materials can be taken as:

X = kg of whole milk (3.5% fat, 8.5% SNF and 88.0% water);
Y = kg of skim milk (0.1% fat, 9.0% SNF and 90.0% water);
Z = kg of skim milk powder (97% SNF and 3% water).

If the inoculation rate of the starter culture (12% SNF and 88% water) is 3%, then in a batch of 100 units, 3 kg of culture would be used containing (0.36 kg SNF and 2.64 kg of water).

For convenience, the liquid ingredients could be measured in litres, and the procedure of calculation is as follows:

The source of fat is whole milk (3.5%) and skim milk (0.1%), and the level in the mix is 1.5%.

$$\frac{3.5X}{100} + \frac{0.1Y}{100} = 1.5 \tag{1}$$

The source of SNF is whole milk (8.5%), skim milk (9%) and skim milk powder (97%), and the level in the mix is 14.5%; however, the amount of SNF (0.36 kg) which originates from the starter culture must be deducted, i.e.

$$\frac{8.5X}{100} + \frac{9Y}{100} + \frac{97Z}{100} = 14.5 - 0.36 = 14.14 \tag{2}$$

The source of water is whole milk (88.0%), skim milk (90.9%), skim milk powder (3.0%) and the weight of the water from the starter culture; therefore, the formula becomes:

The amount of water present in the mix is equal to:

$100 - ($wt. of fat $+$ wt. of SNF $+$ wt. of water from the starter culture$)$
$100 - (1.5 + 14.5 + 2.64) = 81.36$

$$\frac{88X}{100} + \frac{90.9Y}{100} + \frac{3Z}{100} = 81.36 \tag{3}$$

Multiply equations (1), (2) and (3) by their denominator, i.e. 100,

$$3.5X + 0.1Y = 150 \tag{4}$$

$$8.5X + 9Y + 97Z = 1414 \tag{5}$$

$$88X + 90.0Y + 3Z = 8136 \tag{6}$$

Calculate the value of X from equation (4)

$$X = \frac{150 - 0.1Y}{3.5} \tag{7}$$

Substitute the value of X (7) in equation (5) and (6)

$$8.5\frac{(150 - 0.1Y)}{3.5} + 9Y + 97Z = 1414 \tag{8}$$

$$88\frac{(150 - 0.1Y)}{3.5} + 90.9Y + 3Z = 8136 \tag{9}$$

Multiply equation (8) by its denominator, i.e. 3.5

$8.5(150-0.1Y)+31.5Y+339.5Z=4949$

$1275-0.85Y+31.5Y+339.5Z=4949$

$31.5Y-0.85Y+339.5Z=4949-1275$

$30.65Y+339.5Z=3674$ (10)

Multiply equation (9) by its denominator, i.e. 3.5

$88(150-0.1Y)+318.15Y+10.5Z=28\,476$

$13,200-8.8Y+318.15Y+10.5Z=28\,476$

$318.15Y-8.8Y+10.5Z=28\,476-13\,200$

$309.35Y+10.5Z=15\,276$ (11)

Divide the value (Z) in equation (10) by the value (Z) in (11) in order to calculate the multiplication factor by which the value (Y) can be calculated

$$\frac{339.5Z}{10.5Z}=32.33333$$

Multiply equation (11) by the factor 32.33

$10\,001.29Y+339.47Z=493\,873.08$ (12)

Subtract equation (10) from (12)

$10\,001.29Y+339.47Z=493\,873.08$

$30.65Y+339.5Z=3674$

$9970.64Y+zero\phantom{.5Z}=490\,199.08$

(The value of Z is approximately equal)

$$\therefore Y=\frac{490\,199.08}{9970.64}$$

$= 49.16\,\text{kg}$ or litres of skim milk required

Substitute the value of Y in equation (10) to calculate the value of Z

$49.16(30.65)+339.5Z=3674$

$1506.75+339.5Z=3674$

$339.5Z=3674-1506.75=2167.25$

$$\therefore Z=\frac{2167.25}{339.5}$$

$= 6.38\,\text{kg}$ of skim milk powder required

Substitute the value of Y in equation (7) to calculate the value of X

$$X = \frac{150 - 0.1(49.16)}{3.5}$$

$$= \frac{150 - 4.916}{3.5}$$

$$= \frac{145.08}{3.5}$$

$= 41.45$ kg or litres of whole milk required

Therefore add the weights of the raw materials required:

whole milk	41.45
skim milk	49.16
skim milk powder	6.38
starter culture	3.00
Total	99.99

The above total should amount exactly to 100, but the slight discrepancy is due to various approximations made in the above calculations; however, a second check from the above weights of raw materials can be made to confirm the chemical composition of the final yoghurt:

Product	Weight in kg	Weight of fat supplied	Weight of SNF supplied
Whole milk	41.45	$\frac{3.5 \times 41.45}{100} = 1.45$	$\frac{8.5 \times 41.45}{100} = 3.52$
Skim milk	49.16	$\frac{0.1 \times 49.16}{100} = 0.05$	$\frac{9 \times 49.16}{100} = 4.42$
Skim milk powder	6.38	***	$\frac{97 \times 6.38}{100} = 6.19$
Starter culture	3.00	***	$\frac{3 \times 12}{100} = 0.36$
	99.99	1.50	14.48

The above example could be applied to calculate exactly the weight of any dairy raw material which could be used for the manufacture of yoghurt (see Table 2.6), and since the quantity or unit of a 100 is used, it can be easily converted to a much larger volume of production.

REFERENCE

HYDE, K. A. and ROTHWELL, J. (1973) In *Ice Cream,* Churchill Livingstone Ltd., London, UK

Index